D1482275

THE TRUTH OF CHRISTMAS
Beyond the Myths
The Gospels of the Infancy of Christ

RENE LAURENTIN

Translated from the French by
Michael J. Wrenn
and associates

ST. BEDE'S PUBLICATIONS
Petersham, Massachusetts

Originally published in France under the title
Les Evangiles de L'Enfance du Christ
Vérité de Noël au-delà des mythes

PRINTED IN THE UNITED STATES OF AMERICA

5 4 3 2 1

Nihil Obstat: Fr. Marie Lamy de la Chapelle
Abbé of Notre-Dame de Tournai

Imprimatur: J. Thomas, del. ep.
Tournai

December 10, 1982

The *Nihil obstat* and *Imprimatur* are official declarations that a book or pamphlet is free of doctrinal and moral error. No implication is contained therein that those granting the *Nihil obstat* and *Imprimatur* agree with the content, opinions or statements expressed.

Cover design by M. Elizabeth Kloss, OSB
Cover photo: THE HOLY FAMILY UNDER A TREE, Ludolph Buesinck, 1599/1602-1669, German, after Abraham Bloemaert, chiaroscuro woodcut, used by permission of the Worcester Art Museum, Worcester, Massachusetts.

LIBRARY OF CONGRESS CATALOGING IN PUBLICATION DATA

Laurentin, René.
The truth of Christmas beyond the myths.

Translation of: Les évangiles de l'enfance du Christ.
Bibliography: p.
Includes index.
1. Bible. N.T. Luke I-II—Criticism, interpretation, etc. 2. Bible. N.T. Matthew I-II—Criticism, interpretation, etc. 3. Jesus Christ—Nativity. I. Title.
BS2595.2.L2813 1986 226'.206 85-1402
ISBN 0-932506-34-8

CONTENTS

TRANSLATOR'S PREFACE

I first had the good fortune and privilege of meeting the gracious priest and scholar, Father René Laurentin, in Paris in May of 1981. I was anxious to meet him since I had read with a great deal of interest his article "Exégèses réductrices des Evangiles de l'infance" ("Reductionistic Exegeses of the Infancy Gospels") in the 1979 edition of the theological journal, *Marianum*. What he had written on this occasion reflected similar cautions being expressed by a number of Catholic and non-Catholic spcialists in the United States and elsewhere.

Actually, in October, 1980, a group of eighty Evangelical Protestant and Roman Catholic scholars and pastoral leaders convened in Ann Arbor, Michigan, for a colloquy on the challenges which contemporary society presents to Christians of all traditions. One of the papers delivered at the colloquy was entitled *Modern Approaches to Scriptural Authority*. The speaker elaborated a number of counter-productive tendencies in scriptural scholarship on this side of the Atlantic which were akin to those which had been examined by Laurentin in his 1979 article and continue to be by an increasing number of other North American and European scholars since then.

These tendencies, which are frequently based on faulty philosophical presuppositions incapable of taking proper account of the reality of the supernatural and divine revelation, are currently viewed by the scholars who take exception to them as serving to undermine the Church's pastoral and educational efforts in the area of homiletics and catechetics.

In the conclusion of his work, *Jesus and His Mother* (the French original of which was published in 1974 and which has just appeared in English), one of the most renowned and respected Scripture scholars, Father André Feuillet, S.S., made the following appeal:

> But what imposes itself as an absolutely necessary preliminary is

> a radical purification of the exegetical methods that have led to this tragic and lamentable result: the total historical devaluation of the Infancy Narratives of St. Matthew and St. Luke. There is in our day a strange tendency which abuses comparisons with the Old Testament in order to depreciate the history of salvation, especially Gospel history. The fact that such or such a detail of the childhood of Jesus, of the baptism, of the Transfiguration, of a miracle of Jesus, of the dialogue with the Samaritan woman, etc., reminds us of certain Old Testament narratives does not authorize us to conclude scientifically to a mere theological construction elaborated from traditional motifs. Such a method opens the door to all sorts of fantasies and to negations that carry the most serious consequences. It is high time we began reversing the process.[1]

Feuillet wisely observes in the same work that if the great pioneers of modern exegesis (Lagrange, Allo, de Grandmaison, Huby, Prat, Lebreton) were living today, they would be "aghast" at the facility and levity with which some modern Catholic exegetes, claiming to continue their work, treat the Gospel narratives of the fourth Gospel and almost everything in the Infancy narratives of St. Matthew and St. Luke as nothing more than theological contructions, doctrinal edifices of the evangelists or the community. Feuillet observes:

> Such a position, which prides itself on being objective and scientific, in reality is neither, for it disregards completely the intention, so clearly expressed both by St. Luke and by St. John, to provide as foundation for Christian faith reliable facts and real interventions of God in history, and not fabrications of their mind and imagination.[2]

What Father Feuillet called for back in 1974, at least with respect to the Infancy narratives, I respecfully submit history will show to have been realized in *The Truth of Christmas Beyond the Myths: The Gospels of the Infancy of Christ* of Father Laurentin.

This work appeared in its French original in 1982 and was awarded First Prize for Religious Literature by the French Academy only a few months after its publication.

Joseph Cardinal Ratzinger, Prefect of the Sacred Congregation for the Doctrine of the Faith and President of the Pontifical Biblical

Commission, chose to write a Preface for the third French edition in 1983.

Translations of this work into German, Italian, Spanish and Portuguese are currently underway.

This translator wishes to express gratitude to his colleagues in this effort, all of whom assisted him in translating various sections of the work: Father John Paddack, Archdiocese of New York; Father Gerald E. Murray, Archdiocese of New York; Father Paul Margand, Diocese of Lincoln, Nebraska; Doctor Matthew O'Connell, Doctor William Marshner, Christendom College, Doctor Vincent Branick of the Marian Library of the University of Dayton.

My gratitude also to St. Bede's Publications, Petersham, Massachusetts for accepting the translation for publication, and finally to Father René Laurentin himself whose civility and patient, non-polemic, scholarly character and priestly style are an honor to the Church which he so selflessly serves and a credit to the Republic of France, which has seen fit, on two occasions, to bestow upon him Her highest decorations for his scholarly and patriotic contributions to that Nation.

Reverend Michael J. Wrenn
Director,
Archdiocesan Catechetical Institute
St. Joseph's Seminary
Dunwoodie
Yonkers, New York
December 8, 1985

[1] André Feuillet, *Jesus and His Mother*, transl. by Leonard Maluf, St. Bede's Publications, Still River, Massachusetts, 1984, p. 265.

[2] *Ibid.*, p. 169.

PREFACE

Since the Enlightenment, the narratives concerning the infancy and Resurrection of Christ, which form the beginning and end of the Gospels, have come to the forefront of historical criticism. This is not surprising, for they go far beyond the bounds of ordinary historical probability: they confront us with the immanent action of God in the world, which touches even our bodily reality. The continuity of tradition underwent a great shock in the Catholic church at the time of Vatican II; this brought out in all their fullness the questions posed by historical criticism, so far as to affect Catholic theology itself and the very preaching of the Gospel.

It became apparent then that traditional apologetics had been too simplistic in its opposition to the application of the methods of literary criticism to the delicate fabric of the infancy Gospels. This naive realism became untenable in the light of newly-acquired knowledge about these texts. Thus, over the past several years, we have witnessed an almost total capitulation in the face of the thought patterns which arose out of the Enlightenment. The infancy Gospels came to be considered as *theologoumena*, behind which one should not seek historical reality, since they are only imaged expressions of the Christology of the Evangelists. For the Christian, the mystery was thus reduced to myth which, no matter how beautiful it may be, cannot replace the reality sacrificed in the process.

René Laurentin, who in 1965 gave us an exceptional book about the first two chapters of Luke, has now turned his full attention to the two infancy Gospels, in Matthew and Luke, with the sound scholarship, perceptiveness, and deep spiritual penetration which characterize his work. He has also employed all the tools of modern criticism to advantage. He replaced a realism which was naive and superficial with a new, informed realism which focuses on the specific relation between the event and its literary expression, and which discovers, in that very correlation, the richness of the real occurrence. He shows how the varied symbolism of the texts opens itself to a truth whose richness penetrates deeper than the surface level. He also shows how the particular experience of each evangelist led him to interpret the events with a depth which a simple narrative could never attain.

With this book, the infancy Gospels are restored to us with a new life. It was worth taking them through the fire of criticism in order to reach a depth of perception which apologetics alone could never establish. Laurentin instructs us anew in Christian meditation, by teaching us to read the texts with the evangelists themselves. This book, which fulfills the best potentials of modern theology, stirs in me a feeling of profound gratitude; it deserves widespread recognition. May it find many attentive readers who learn from it and discover anew the richness and realism of the Christian faith.

Cardinal Joseph Ratzinger
Prefect of the Sacred
Congregation for the
Doctrine of Faith and
President of the Pontifical
Biblical Commission

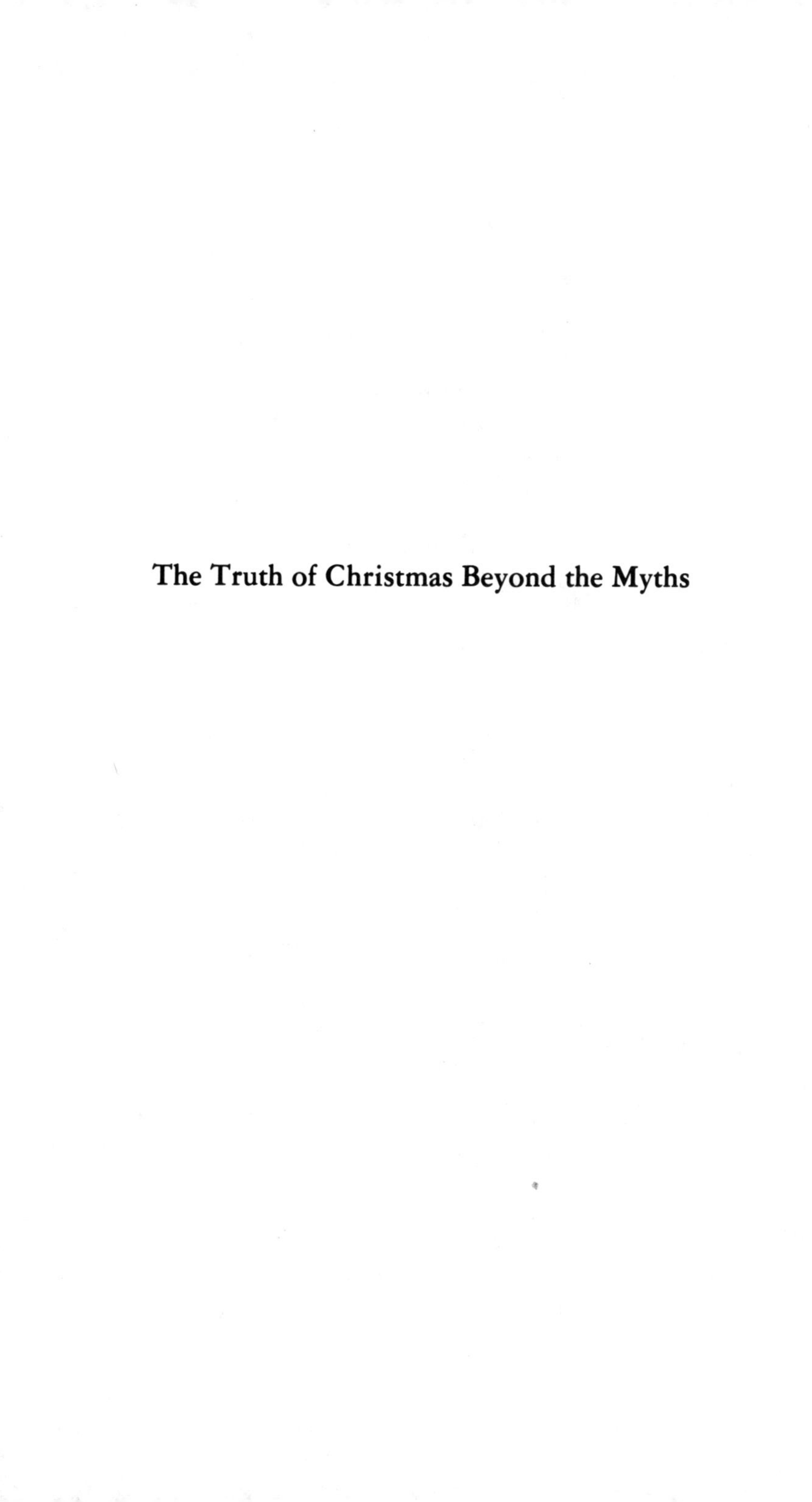

The Truth of Christmas Beyond the Myths

ABBREVIATIONS

Bib	*Biblica*
BibKir	*Bibel und Kirche*
BibT	*Bible Translator*
BibZ	*Biblesche Zeitschrift*
CBQ	*Catholic Biblical Quarterly*
CSCO	*Corpus Scriptorum Christianorum Orientalium*
DBS (or DBSup)	*Dictionaire de la Bible Supplement*
DS	*Dictionaire Spiritualité*
EB	*Estudios Biblicos*
JBL	*Journal of Biblical Literature*
JewQ	*Jewish Quarterly Review*
JSS	*Journal of Semitic Studies*
JTS	*Journal of Theological Studies*
LXX	Septuagint
Mar	*Marianum*
NovTest	*Novum Testamentum*
NRT	*Nouvelle Revue Théologique*
NT	New Testament
NTS	*New Testament Studies*
OT	Old Testament
RechScRel	*Recherches de Sciences Religieuses*
RevBen	*Revue Benedictine*
RHLR	*Revue d'Histoire et de Litterature Religieuse*
RQ	*Revue de Qumran*
RSPT	*Revue des Sciences Philosophiques et Théologiques*
Sources	Collection *Sources Chrétiennes*, Editions du Cerf
TDNT	*Theological Dictionary of the New Testament* (Kittel)
Th	*Theology*
ThS	*Theologische Studien und Kritiken*
ThZ	*Theologische Zeitschrift*
TOB	*Traduction oecuménique de la Bible*
TUU	*Text und Untersuchungen zur Gieschichte der Altkirchliche Literature*
ZKT	*Zietschrift für Neutestamentliche Wissenschaft*

INTRODUCTION

The infancy Gospels occupy an important place in Christianity. Christmas remains the most popular feast in the liturgical calendar, a popularity it owes to the infancy Gospels.

An Unavoidable Question

Matthew 1-2 and Luke 1-2 present a new factor in relation to the primitive evangelization (the kerygma) which began "at the baptism of John" (Acts 1:22; cf. 2:17, 36; 10:37-43); they look back in time from this event in order to respond to the unavoidable questions about the origin of Jesus Christ. Where did he come from?

There was no model for answering that question. The most obvious, for the mentality of that time, was that Christ had "descended from heaven." This formula is a common theme of John the Evangelist.[1] But historical reality would not support this explanation. If we look into this claim even superficially, no matter how appropriate it may have seemed to the culture of the times, reality offers us a different view. That the Messiah was born without much of a stir at Nazareth, the Gospel of his public life was not able to keep secret. How are we to explain this apparent disgrace? And since the messianic title bestowed on Jesus by the crowds was "Son of David,"[2] what are we to make of the very strong local tradition that Jesus was not the son of Joseph? Does he thereby lose the label required of the Messiah?

There was no model for answering these questions either. Luke and Matthew had to open up a path in uncharted territory. They each did this without consulting the other, based on information that was more than ninety-five percent different. They resolved the difficulties according to the diversity of their respective sources and theological perspectives: Matthew, the Jew, and Luke, the converted pagan. Their success and their agreement, despite differences, are surprising, given the circumstances. The Gospel as a whole is a permanent best-seller whose impact is ever relevant; this fact is particularly true of the infancy Gospels.

The Underestimated Gospels

However, scientific attempts to study the Bible, which have proliferated since the last century, have not dealt kindly with these popular Gospels. When the Church at first resisted the application of secular methods to the sacred text, the rationalist pioneers of scientific exegesis acted with the superiority of the all-knowing professor.[3] They criticized or corrected the infancy Gospels as if they were student essays, and, accusing them of inconsistencies, contradictions, and inaccuracies, they treated them as myths or fictions, contrary to the very clear statement of Luke 1:1-4. The assurance of superior knowledge was combined with the intoxication of handling new tools to discern a substratum hidden under the surface.

This assurance, however, suffered from the limitations inherent in each method of investigation. Philosophical presuppositions, rationalist, idealist, positivist, even psychoanalytic often guided the analyses. The infancy Gospels have been especially criticized and dismembered. Working from the perspective of Kant and Hegel, and anxious to reduce myth to reason, Strauss (1835) saw here *theologoumena*, theological fiction expressing in the form of a narrative an a priori theological idea.

The belated conversion of Catholics to scientific methodologies has often been accompanied by a conversion to the ideologies behind them. The slogan of *theologoumena* has enjoyed great popularity, without a reappraisal of its arguments or presuppositions. The infancy Gospels were reduced to the status of fable in the minds of certain people. Some priests, hastily "initiated" into these so-called scientific explanations, dared no longer to preach the Christmas Gospel, "knowing" that it was a myth.

Faced with these developments, apologetics has often reacted too naively in considering the texts to be the material equivalent of the event. In defending, with just cause, the reference of the narrative to a real event, it has not known how to assess the mysterious transposition which always exists between an event and the language which describes it, the truth of which can be found only in the order of intention.

We are therefore faced with two forms of naiveté: a prescientific one which is enlightening, when it is prayerful, but pathetic when it is no longer supported by tradition, and the opposite naiveté of false learning, which reduces these admirable Gospels to the mediocrity of the interpreter. It is thus important to take up the scientific tools of exegesis in the service, not to the detriment, of the text. A century and a half of critical labor has not been lost; the gains are considerable. But it is necessary to eliminate the blunders and pretences which have often masked authentic discoveries. Discernment is an immense, a Herculean, task. How many learned stupidities, without foundation or future, have been repeated over and over again by articles and other publications whose ideologies distort the objective focus of the Gospel!

The Motive Behind this Book

The author should explain here why he is returning once more to the infancy Gospels after his two previous books entitled *Structure et théologie de Luc 1-2* (1956) and *Jésus au temple: Luc 2:41-52* (1966). In part it is because a new wave of historical criticism has recently called into question some gains which were the fruit of a broad ecumenical agreement. It is important to confirm the progress thus achieved. But above all, the author's two books cited above dealt with Luke without treating Matthew 1-2, or the surprising convergence of these two totally different Gospels, or their historicity. In addition, fifteen years of study have brought some new facts, conclusions, and methods which it is important to put to use, notably the study of semiotics, which developed in the 1960s. Finally, it is important to grasp the convergence of these various approaches.

Method

To gather together all the insights which can throw light on the infancy Gospels, we will proceed in three stages. First we will analyze Luke 1-2. Then we will analyze Matthew 1-2, employing for both Gospels each of the scientific methods: textual criticism, literary criticism, and semiotics. This examination may seem heavy and labored, but it is called for by the requirements of scientific exactness, for each method is specific, and attains its goal only in its own field. You cannot put together conclusions like the pieces of a puzzle. To overcome the impression of an overly disjointed analysis, however, we have brought together the principal conclusions into an analysis of the Gospel's narrative program. This might bring us under some criticism by semioticians, but it seemed indispensable to us in order not to lose the non-specialist reader. This approach will not prevent us from evaluating, at the end of the book, whether all these conclusions converge or not.

The successive study of Luke 1-2 and then of Matthew 1-2, since these Gospels are so different, leads to one key question: Are they in agreement?

After the purely exegetical stage (the analysis of texts), an entirely different question will be posed: that of historicity. This is no longer a matter of explaining the text by its sources or by its internal structure, but rather of attempting to grasp its reference to the events, to the reality which was the infancy of Jesus Christ. This question is dependent upon entirely different methods. It leads to consideration of the *meaning* of the account; for reference (to the real event) is inseparable from the meaning (or the symbolism) of the text.

These successive examinations will show, from multiple but converging angles, the coherence, the richness, the brilliant quality of the infancy Gospels.

One final question remains: What is the distinctive, unparalleled quality of Christmas which has made it the most popular of all feasts and an inexhaustible source for spiritual renewal? Is it not simply that Christmas is the kernel of the Christian experience? It is important to recognize this. Understanding it is analogous to the process whereby a pianist discovers a musical score by actually playing it. In conclusion, we will attempt to recapture, from within, the experience of the two evangelists: Matthew, persecuted preacher of a church in silence; Luke, the evangelist of the Holy Spirit, who was predisposed by the experience of Pentecost to preserve the witness of Mary who "kept all these things, pondering them in her heart" (2:19, 51).

Part I
Luke 1-2

Luke 1-2 is a surprisingly rich Gospel. The more one delves into it, the more one is overwhelmed and surprised at the liberty with which criticism has attempted to pull it to pieces. Fortunately, unlike a monument or an organism, a text survives the violence to which it is subjected. It survives the autopsies and ends up intact after dissection. Interpretations come and go but the Gospel remains, bearer of a witness which goes beyond it.

The successive critical methods, to the extent to which they have been seriously and objectively applied, have demonstrated the coherence of this infancy Gospel. It is truly the work of Luke. You can recognize in it his style and his vocabulary, diversified by his sources, which he respects even while engaged in rewriting them.

We will confine ourselves to the conclusions resulting from each of the methods: first, textual criticism; then literary criticism, applied to the composition, the genesis, the sources, and the literary genres of the text. Finally, the semiotic study, to be carried out on new ground.

Let us anticipate a possible misunderstanding: this author's work, written in 1956, was called *Structure et théologie de Luc 1-2*. The word *structure*, which was intended to provide interest and a new approach to the work, did not yet have the sense of *structuralism*, inasmuch as that theory had not yet been fully developed. Thus the book dealt only with the *literary* structures of the Gospel: its symmetries, refrains, landmarks, and coherent references to the OT. It did not consider the structures which semiotics deciphers today on the level of meaning.

I
TEXTUAL CRITICISM

Scientific Reconstruction of the Text

Textual criticism arose at the time when the Roman Church acknowledged only one official text: the Vulgate, according to the typical edition. The importance of establishing the original Greek text of the NT, from the manuscript variants, was seen to be absolutely essential. For a long time this process was designated as *reconstruction criticism*, a methodical study of the variants revealed by manuscripts and citations. This discipline took hold in the eighteenth century with Griesbach, who codified its principal rules: the preference for the shortest, for the most difficult reading, for the one which explains many others. The critical edition of the NT was produced, however, only in the nineteenth century (Tischendorf, 1869-1872; B. F. Westcott and F. J. A. Hort, 1881; Nestle, 1898) and the critical edition of the OT (M. A. Goshen-Gottstein) is still in its very first fascicles, being published by the Hebrew University of Jerusalem.

The collation of manuscripts in the form of critical apparatus demonstrated the remarkable stability of the biblical text. Nevertheless, taste for novelty, together with methodological prejudices, created mishaps along the way, and emphasized out of all proportion some aberrant, if not imaginary, variants.

As far as Luke 1-2 is concerned, two points have been the object of controversy: the attribution of the Magnificat to Mary and, consequently, the integrity of the account of the annunciation.

1. THE MAGNIFICAT ATTRIBUTED TO ELIZABETH (Lk 1:46)

How should the phrase which introduces the Magnificat be read?

Mary said (the common reading), or
Elizabeth said?

External Criticism

The extremely rare variant "Elizabeth" first appeared in the eighth critical edition of the NT of Tischendorf.[1] It is attested by only three Latin manuscripts:

a = Vercellensis (fourth-fifth century)
b = Veronensis (fifth century)
1* = Rhedigerianus (eighth century, corrected into "Mary").[2]

This variant is confined to a limited part of the Latin world, where Tertullian (ca. 150-222) was already a witness to the reading Mary.[3] The variant finds no support in any Greek manuscript, not even in the *Codex Bezae*, which is so rich in unusual variants, nor in the Syrian or Coptic manuscripts.

The antiquity of the manuscript witnesses which attest to the reading Mary, starting as they do from the second and third centuries, removes every foundation from the artificial hypothesis that Marian fervor could have caused the transfer from Elizabeth to Mary. Such an argument could not refer to a time prior to the fifth or sixth century in the East and later in the West. It is anachronistic.

External criticism thus excludes the reading Elizabeth, and "no one dares to hold that it is original," said Lagrange (1922, 44). No present day edition adopts this reading.

The supporters of Elizabeth generally fell back upon the hypothesis put forward by A. Durand (1893, 74-77). The variant would be explained by a primitive reading, "and she said" (*kai eipen*), without specification.[4] Some would have specified Mary; others Elizabeth. This hypothesis is supported by the classic principle of preferring a source-reading which takes into account various derived readings. But this preference has foundation *only* if the explanatory reading is attested by some manuscripts. Since this is not the case here, the hypothesis is artificial and contrived.[5] It is better to look for the explanation of the isolated reading *in* some accident.[6]

If the attribution of the Magnificat to Elizabeth caused so much ink to flow, it is because of its novelty, and the attraction of all controversial positions involving the Virgin. Passions are the key to explaining the excessive proliferation of such a non-productive controversy.

Internal Criticism

Lacking any serious foundation on the level of external criticism, the Elizabeth hypothesis looked for a justification in internal criticism. It is bad methodology to change a text for reasons of logic when there is no manuscript tradition. Nevertheless, the endurance of the controversy invites us to examine the arguments, beginning with the better ones.

The case of Elizabeth, elderly and sterile, is analogous to that of Hannah, whose thanksgiving canticle for the unhoped-for birth of Samuel (1 Sm 2:1-10) inspired the Magnificat.

But, if Elizabeth was the one who sang the NT canticle, she would have most certainly kept the reference to sterility (1 Sm 2:5). This is exactly what she does refer to, *not* in the Magnificat, but in the thanksgiving which concludes the first annunciation in 1:25:

> Elizabeth said, "Thus the Lord has done to me in the days when he looked on me, *to take away my reproach* among men."

This brief canticle of Elizabeth rules out the idea that the second, the Magnificat, be also attributed to her. There would then be not only two canticles (1:42-45 and 1:46-55), but three (with 1:25). Some strong reasons are needed for thus overemphasizing Elizabeth and reducing Mary to silence.

It has been said that the mention of the *tapeinōsis* (low estate, poverty) should be applied to Elizabeth, not to the Virgin Mary. This is to forget, however, that the context contrasts Mary, situated in the low (*katebē*, 2:51) and scorned place which is Nazareth (1:26), with Elizabeth, situated in the "mountains" of Judea (1:39; 2:4) near Jerusalem to which one goes up (2:42), and who belongs to the upper echelons of the priestly caste (1:5). From the simple semiotic point of view (this point has been analyzed according to the semiotic method of A. Gueuret), to speak of low estate or humility (1:48; cf. 1:52) is to refer back to her who lives in the low place and cannot pride herself on possessing any illustrious lineage: to the young village girl, Mary, and not to the wife of the priest, who is herself of the priestly line (1:5).

The subsequent text manifests the poverty, not of Elizabeth, but of Mary: without lodging for the birth of her child and reduced to the offerings of the poor at the presentation (2:24; cf. Lv 12:8). Finally, virginity (1:27) was not a title of honor in the cultural context of the OT. It had a negative connotation. Thus the daughter of Jephthah, doomed to ritual murder, asked her father for a respite to "mourn her virginity," the unfinished state of a woman without a child, before her father consigns her to immolation (Jgs 11:37).[7] The totally novel meaning of "not knowing man" (1:34) was not at all honored.

It has also been said that it would seem abnormal to repeat the name of Mary after the Magnificat (1:56) to signify her departure after a three month stay, if she had already been named at the start of the canticle. But between 1:46 and 1:56 there are ten verses which require the recalling of the subject for the sake of clarity. For example, the angels named at the start of the very short Gloria canticle (only one verse, 2:14), are mentioned again in the following verse, which signifies their departure. Exactly the same schema is given for the departure of Mary after her canticle, and thus demolishes this third argument.[8]

Finally, Mary plays the principal role in this sequence, and the evidence that this canticle in its textual location is to be attributed to her has so embarrassed those who favor the reading of Elizabeth, that some of them have transferred the Magnificat to 1:25 (where she is already reciting a short canticle) or to 1:41. Such a gratuitous hypothesis only shows the desperate nature of the position.[9] The same can be said for the hypothesis of Sahlin who attributes the Magnificat to Zechariah and the Benedictus to the prophetess Anna.[10]

According to Harnack, the *kai* would indicate that the same person, Elizabeth, continues to speak. If Mary began to speak, he says, it would have been necessary to put *de*. This argument is refuted by 1:18, 19, 30; 2:10, 49 where *kai* introduces a new speaker.[11]

It has been claimed that if Mary had pronounced this canticle, it would have been necessary to mention the inspiration of the Holy Spirit, as in the case of Zechariah in 1:67. Only Elizabeth, "filled with the Holy Spirit," was given the ability to prophesy. But this is to forget that Mary was the first to be mentioned in connection with the Holy Spirit, in the broader context of 1:35, "The Holy Spirit will come upon you" (cf. Lagrange, p. 45). This first manifestation of the Spirit, which

Luke expresses in the same terms as that of Pentecost (Acts 1:8) is presented as the point of departure (or even the *source*) of the ones which follow. Elizabeth attributes Mary's greeting to the pouring out of the Holy Spirit (1:43) with whom both she and her son are filled (1:42 and 1:15).

It has been observed that in 1:46 the verb *megalynei*, the first word of the Magnificat, is suited to Elizabeth, whom God has *magnified*, according to 1:58. But the verb *megalynō* is applied in two opposite senses: in the Magnificat (1:46) it is the singer who magnifies the Lord, but in 1:58, it is the Lord who magnifies Elizabeth. The reappearance of the word with such a different reference-point destroys the argument. It is superfluous to add that the idea of greatness, implied in the verb *megalynei* would be suitable also to Mary, who is glorified by the context, and whose Son will be great without any reservation (*megas*, 1:32).

The arguments of internal criticism are thus weak, and for the most part nonexistent. In examining them, we can see how many actually argue in favor of Mary. The arguments for attributing the Magnificat to Mary are of exceptional weight.

She plays the principal role in this sequence; she appears at once as the one loved and preferred by God (1:28); the Spirit, who has spoken through the prophets, "comes upon" her first (1:35); her coming produces the event of the visitation; it is she who is praised by Elizabeth; the last word comes from her in a thanksgiving hymn.

The function of the Magnificat is to be a response of Mary, glorified by Elizabeth, in this scene of encounter and communication. To reduce this dialogue to a monologue would be a misinterpretation, destructive of the very movement of the text, in which Mary, glorified by her cousin, who is filled with the Spirit, accepts this glory only so as to refer it to God alone.

As far as Elizabeth is concerned, her thanksgiving would be superfluous here, because she has already expressed it in her brief canticle in 1:25.[12] This thanksgiving is now superseded; the coming of "the mother of the Lord" (1:43) determines another stage. That which now touches Elizabeth is no longer the end of her humiliation; it is the stirring of her child under the movement of the Spirit which fills her, indeed, fills both her and him (1:15; 1:41), at the coming of Mary, bearer of the "Lord" (1:43).

Other arguments follow along the same line:

The two canticles are attributed to the recipients of the two annunciations, Zechariah and Mary. This argument, which R. E. Brown judges "the best," is strengthened by the Zechariah-Mary parallelism which structures chapter 1. The sequences concerning Mary end with her canticle, just as do the sequences devoted to Zechariah. Luke could even have been motivated to place the Magnificat after the visitation for the sake of a better parallelism, since the Benedictus does not come until the end of the account.[13] The Magnificat closes very well the extraordinarily laudatory sequence devoted to Mary.

Several characteristics connect the canticle with Mary:

—She comments on and confirms the *makaria* (blessed are you) addressed to her by Elizabeth (1:42, 45) when she prophesies, *"All generations will call me blessed" (makariousin me).*

—She thanks God, who has glorified her. She returns to the Almighty the lofty praise which Elizabeth addressed to her, taking up Elizabeth's themes and several of her words in the same order.[14]

—The messenger of the annunciation praises Mary according to the grace of God who has looked upon her (1:28, 30). Now it is for this very thing (God's looking upon her) that the singer herself makes thanksgiving (1:48).[15] The context distinguishes her clearly from Elizabeth, who is praised solely for the faithful carrying out of the Law (1:5-6).

—She gives herself the title of servant (*doulē*) at the conclusion of the annunciation (1:38) as she does at the beginning of the Magnificat (1:48).

The following parallels are equally favorable to Mary:

—The power of God, 1:49, echoes 1:37: "Nothing is impossible with God." This in itself is reminiscent of Genesis 18:14, the word of Yahweh to Abraham concerning the birth of Isaac. (Cf. a further reference to Abraham in 1:55.) The same root, *dyna*, in *ouk adynatesei*, indicates no lack of power on the part of God (cf. *dynamis* in 1:35).

—The fear of God (1:50) finds a response on the part of Mary in 1:29 (the same verb, *phobeō*).

By way of confirmation, and reading more deeply into the text, we can see that she who gives thanks *for herself*, in the first part of the canticle (1:47-49) and for all the people in the second part (1:49-56), can be clearly identified with Mary, Daughter of Zion, personification of all the people, according to what is implicit in the message of Gabriel (see below, pp. 52, 53, 59-60).

We will not take up the argument which R. E. Brown holds to be "the most convincing," that Luke may have belatedly introduced the Magnificat precisely to reassert the important value of Mary by concocting the *theologoumenon* of 1:28-56 (1977, 335-336, 349). This is merely the application of his hypothesis on the late origin of the Magnificat that Luke would have borrowed from the poor Jewish-Christian circles (*anawim*). That the honor accorded to Mary may be a fiction, and that the origin of the Magnificat may be unknown to her are hypotheses stemming from presuppositions which unreasonably and fruitlessly take away from the value of the text.

Brown has at least clearly perceived that Luke assigns more value to Mary than to Elizabeth. This evaluation should be recognized, as should his acknowledgment that there are "better arguments" for Mary than for Elizabeth. That is the least that could be said. Neither external nor internal criticism leads to the slightest probability for attributing the Magnificat to Elizabeth. Textual criticism shows the rare, late, and unsupported version to be aberrant. Not one edition of the NT has retained it.

How are we to explain the very rare reading, Elizabeth? It could be due to a material accident. But if this accident or something like it could have been transmitted in the small circle located around Origen (or Jerome?), attested by certain manuscripts of Irenaeus and Nicetas and by the three Latin manuscripts enumerated above (see nn. 1-6, above), it must be because of the resemblance of the Magnificat to its prototype: the canticle of the elderly and barren Hannah in 1 Samuel 2:10. The circumstances suggested the attribution of this canticle to Elizabeth, who was also an elderly and barren woman. This remains the best argument of those who held the critical thesis.

Semiotics

Does semiotics contribute any new reasons for holding that Elizabeth spoke the Magnificat? A. Gueuret put forward this hypothesis in a talk given at the Ecole des Hautes Etudes, and published shortly thereafter.[16] She restricts herself to saying that Elizabeth, like Mary, would be "semiotically suited to pronounce this canticle," an ambiguity which obscures the clarity of her analyses of this point.

To the historical-critical arguments already examined, this essay adds the following considerations or options:

A. Gueuret holds the annunciation to be an insertion into the Elizabeth cycle (1:24-57). But the annunciation is the key element, Christ's starting point. The first announcement only brings out the inner meaning of this fundamental scene, as we shall see more precisely later (see sequential divisions, pp. 14-25, 134).

As the author of the Magnificat, Elizabeth would be in a superior position to Mary, as "embracing the Spirit with which she is *filled*" (1:41), while the Spirit would merely come upon Mary, who would thus be embraced by him (1:35). This verbal contrast should not make us forget that, for Luke, the presence of God *upon* Mary implies his presence in her (see p. 150), nor that Elizabeth boldly attributes the outpouring of the Holy Spirit which fills her to the voice of Mary, the recipient of the first Pentecost (1:35).

Another argument which the article of 1977 considered to be decisive is that Zechariah and Elizabeth are situated in a "hierarchical class" while Joseph and Mary appear "as one couple among many," in the "common condition of their social situation" (p. 9). But we shall see that the contrast between the hierarchical situation of Zechariah-Elizabeth and the low estate of Mary (1:48) is structured in this way precisely to make the point that the superiorities of the Law are reversed by the grace of God (cf. 1:51-53), who favors the poor, among whom are Mary and Christ himself. This contrast between the Law and grace is so essential to the structuring of the text that it would seem to be the most illuminating feature of Luke 1-2 (see below, p. 228).

In short, semiotics would not furnish any argument for the Elizabeth thesis unless it chooses to study Luke 1-2 on the level of the substratum of fables, which has been the testing ground of this discipline. Let us add that Agnes Gueuret's thesis was more perceptive in seeing, in certain respects, the superiority of Christ over John the Baptist and of Mary over the parents of John,[17] and that her study contains observations which have value as arguments.[18]

2. MARY "BETROTHED" IN LUKE 2:5

Working within the mode of textual criticism I would like to examine an interesting point concerning the status of Mary in Luke and Matthew. That Mary should be described as "betrothed"[19] in 1:27 seems obvious enough, although in the Jewish world the word would be too weak to mean an agreement to marry, with juridical value; i.e. the sealing of the marriage contract, or the first stage, before actual cohabitation, the last stage. But that the same word should be used in 2:5, at the hour of giving birth, is surprising when compared with Matthew 1:24-25. There are, therefore, some variants among the manuscripts.

—*Emnēsteumenē* is attested by all the Greek manuscripts and almost all the versions.

—*Gunaiki autou*, his wife, is attested by X and Syriac Sinaitic.

—*(M)emnēsteumenē autō gunaiki*, the wife betrothed to him (a very rare reading).

The second reading seems to have been introduced to harmonize Luke with Matthew. It has been supported by those who consider Luke 2 as independent from Luke 1, ignoring the virginity of Mary.

The third reading is a clumsy conflation of the first two.

The first reading demands recognition in all respects. It is the most ancient, the best attested, the only one represented by the Greek manuscripts.

It is also the *lectio difficilior*, for it is paradoxical to call Mary betrothed at the birth of Jesus. It is too simple a correction to say "his wife." Nowhere does Luke call Mary the wife of Joseph, even though he mentions, at several points, "the parents" (2:27, 41) and "the father and mother of Jesus" (2:33; cf. 48).[20]

3. THE VIRGINAL CONCEPTION (Lk 1:34-37)

Is it necessary to speak here of the thesis of J. Hillman (1891), taken up by Harnack and R. Bultmann, which denies the authenticity of verses 1:34-37 in Luke on the virginal conception, and tries to prove that they were interpolated?

External criticism supplied no arguments on behalf of this notion. One cannot consider as an "argument" the fact that the Codex b Veronensis of the *Vetus latina* replaces 1:34 with 1:38 "Behold the handmaid of the Lord" (*contingat mihi secundum verbum tuum*). This must be a simple accident of the copyist. Only S. Spitta (1906, 286-289), followed by H. J. Vogels (1950/51, 256-260), and a few others tried to see here the primitive reading. But R. Bultmann himself indicated that one could not rely on such an argument.

We are dealing here then less with a debate within textual criticism than with an attempt at internal criticism, at the level of the proto-history of the text—one of the dangerous techniques of the historical-critical method.

Lacking a proper exegetical argument, since the notion is founded solely on a priori presuppositions, those who would suppress the virginal conception could not agree on the extent of the interpolation. At the minimum it should consist of 1:34b, but some would include Luke 1:34a, 35, 36, 37, or even 38.[21]

These amputations would alter the well-constructed symmetry of the annunciations to Zechariah and Mary, which implies in both cases a symmetry question-objection. It is to avoid this difficulty that the latest supporters of this thesis have reduced the suppression to 1:34b.

These eliminations destroy the coherence of the text. Luke 1:35 becomes hard to explain, and the sign of the miraculous conception of Elizabeth, given in 1:36 as a pledge of the power of God (1:37), loses its *raison d'être*. From the semiotic point of view we shall see how essential 1:34b and the following verses are to the narrative account. In short, one cannot touch this harmonious text without falling into incoherence.

The fundamental error of these amputations was to seek to revise a perfectly attested text, without any foundation in external criticism. Endeavors like these, outmoded today, compel us to measure the importance of presuppositions in exegesis.

In short, textual criticism has served only to establish and clarify the authenticity of Luke 1-2.

II
LITERARY CRITICISM

Literary criticism uses diverse methods. We shall not get into the details of lexical and grammatical study, which are at the foundation of all the rest, but we will present an appraisal of the methods which have delved most deeply into the misunderstood meaning of the text: its composition, dynamic, genesis, and sources, and, finally, the identification of its literary genre. We will draw further conclusions wherever that is possible.

A. COMPOSITION

PARALLELISM AND ITS CONTRASTS

The most apparent characteristic of the literary structure is the parallel between John the Baptist and Jesus. For each of them, the narrative of their infancy is developed in four stages:

	John	*Jesus*
Annunciation	1:5,25	1:26-38
Birth	1:57-58	2:1-20
Circumcision	1:59-79	2:21
Growth	1:80	2:40-52

Quantitatively, we find a curious balancing of emphasis in the way the material is presented. There are twenty verses concerning the birth of Jesus, and two concerning the birth of John. Conversely, the rite of circumcision in the case of Jesus is given only one verse, while this same event in John's case is recorded in twenty-one verses.

Qualitatively, these parallels are the manifestation of a gradation and contrast between John the precursor and Jesus the Messiah. This is what underlies the later texts of the Gospel (3:15-16; 7:18-33; 16:16; and Acts 1:5, 22). This concern was prompted by the fact that John the Baptist was the object of a cult independent of that of Christ, which

Paul encountered in his missions, as we know from Acts 18:25 and 19:3-4.

a. The Two Annunciations

The two annunciations manifest the most precise parallelism, in the following stages:

Stages	*John*	*Jesus*
Presentation of the characters	1:5-7	1:26-27
Appearance of Gabriel	1:8-11	1:26, 28
Fear of the interlocutor	1:12	1:29
"Do not be afraid"	1:13	1:30
Announcement of the birth	1:13-14	1:31
Greatness and mission of the child	1:15-17	1:32-33
Question—objection	1:18	1:34
Response of the angel	1:19-20	1:35-37
Conclusion	1:21-25	1:38

Even in this first section of the John-Jesus parallel, where the symmetry is at its greatest, dissymmetries and contrasts are not lacking, and they are essential to the meaning of the account. The disproportion is striking from the first lines.

Luke 1:5-10	*Luke 1:26*
In the days of Herod,	In the sixth month the angel Gabriel was sent
king of Judea, there was a priest named Zechariah, of the division of Abijah; and he had a wife of the daughters of Aaron,	to a city of Galilee . . . , to a virgin betrothed to a man named Joseph, of the house of David;
and her name was Elizabeth. And they were both righteous before God, walking in all the commandments and ordinances of the Lord blameless. But they had no child, because Elizabeth was barren, and both were advanced in years.	the virgin's name was Mary.

Now while he was serving as the priest before God when his division was on duty, according to the custom of the priesthood, it fell to him by lot to enter the temple of the Lord and burn incense. And the whole multitude of the people were praying outside at the hour of incense.

Two couples are presented: Zechariah-Elizabeth, elderly persons; Mary and Joseph, given in marriage, which indicates youthfulness.

The first couple seems to have the upper hand in value, quantitatively and qualitatively. What is at first striking is the lengthy praise the evangelist makes of their conduct, without giving a parallel concerning Joseph and Mary.

The same advantage exists on the level of situations and functions. Zechariah finds himself in that high place which is the capital, in the one sanctuary; Mary, in a despised province and village (Jn 1:46; 7:41, 52). Zechariah is chosen by lot (that is to say, chosen by God himself: cf. Acts 1:24 and 25), to exercise the highest mediating function between God and the people at prayer. He is shown in all his glory, in contrast with the humble villagers Mary and Joseph.

The same advantage on the sociological level: Zechariah is of pure priestly race, as is his wife (1:5). Mary, on the contrary, is not distinguished by any lineage, a striking contrast, for of the four characters presented here at the beginning, she is the only "orphan": Joseph is highly distinguished as a descendant of King David.

And yet Mary, the orphan, is set in a relief which disrupts the initial parallelism. She is named first, before Joseph, against the normal precedence, which is respected in regard to Zechariah and Elizabeth. She is mentioned twice in this same verse (27). In our synopsis of the two annunciations, she finds herself, the first time, in parallel with Zechariah, the supreme character (a priest, a virgin), and the second time with Elizabeth his wife. (Joseph is only perfunctorily mentioned between these two references to Mary.) This prepares for what follows, where she is going to be in parallel with Zechariah, the addressee of the annunciation; the masculine precedence is reversed.

The two couples have one point in common: both are childless. This is a source of frustration for the first couple, characterized as a sterility without hope. But in the case of the young couple, this situation could appear as a "not yet," meaning only that such an event has not yet occurred, if the insistent repetition of the word "virgin" were not already preparing for something else.

But the most evident contrast is that which breaks the parallelism from the first words of the account: the angel does not appear to Zechariah until the end of the six verses (1:11). To Mary, he appears immediately, before Mary herself has been presented, and his first words form part of the presentation:

The Appearance of the Angel

Luke 1:11	*Luke 1:26-28*
And there	In the sixth month
appeared to him	was sent
an angel of the Lord	the angel Gabriel
standing on the right side	
of the altar of incense	from God . . . ;
	He came to her [Mary];

The priest goes up to meet the angel. But it is the angel who comes down to Mary: "The lesser goes to the greater," comments A. Gueuret in her semiotic thesis. This contrast begins to suggest a paradoxical reversal of values in favor of the poor, along with a decentralization of the sacred which is evinced in John 4:24: The eschatological cult, which is no longer at Jerusalem or on Mount Gerazim, but in all places where there are those who worship in spirit and in truth. The annunciation to Zechariah takes place in the Temple, the dwelling place of God (cf. 1:9; 2:49); the annunciation to Mary, in a marginal and disparaged province.

For Zechariah, it is a vision. For Mary, the hearing alone is specified. This introduces a laudatory apostrophe by the angel, without parallel in the annunciation to Zechariah:

[The angel. . .] said to her
—Rejoice,
Object-of-the-favor-of-God
The Lord is with you.

This original salutation is composed of two elements:
1. An absolute invitation to joy, without motivation, as in the eschatological announcements of the prophets.
2. A name which God gives from on high to Mary, as happens in the Bible to those who receive a mission (e.g. Jgs 6:12). This name signifies the gratuitous benevolence of God (*charis*, 1:30, the root of the word *keCHARItōmenē*, 1:28).

If Luke has not balanced praise of Mary with that of Zechariah and Elizabeth, it is because the praise comes from on high, from God himself; whence the initial disproportion, disturbing for those who try to heighten the parallelism.

Whereas the parents of John the Baptist have been praised for their practice of *the Law*, Mary is praised by virtue of grace alone. The word *charis*, characteristic of the last two evangelists, and used frequently only in Luke and Paul, appears twice in the annunciation to Mary:
1. *KeCHARItōmenē*, the name which is given to her, (1:28),
2. *Heures Charin*, you have found grace, this last verse being a commentary on the first (1:30).

Zechariah's advantage according to the Law is at once reversed by the divine message, which proclaims the advantage of Mary according to grace and of Mary alone, since Joseph is not included in the praise, in contrast with Zechariah and Elizabeth, "the two" (*amphoteroi* repeated in 1:6, 7) being closely linked on the same level; while Luke begins in 1:26 to dissociate the second couple, Mary-Joseph, he insists on the unity of the first. The symmetric parallelism is maintained in the following passages.

The "Trouble" or Fear

Luke 1:12	*Luke 1:29*
And Zechariah was troubled when he saw him	But she was greatly troubled at this saying,

Kecharitōmenē: The Name Given Mary: Object-of-the-Favor-of-God (Lk 1:28)

Usage

The verb *charitoō* appears only once in the OT, Sir 18:17: "Indeed, does not a word surpass a good gift: Both are to be found in a *kecharitōmenos* man."

Here is the word in its minimal sense. Certain authors have translated it as "gracious" or "graced," in order to render by an alliteration this word derived from *charis*, grace; "gracious man," says Fitzmyer, (*Luke 1-9*, 1981, p. 345), the RSV and the NEB. But the TOB version and Osty prefer *charitable,* another alliteration from the root *charis,* which corresponds better with the meaning of the word.

One finds this word in the Apocryphal writings: *Acts of Philip* (4th-5th centuries), 48: "Philip said to him: 'You are *kecharitōmenos* in the peace of Christ, because there is no duplicity in your soul.' " (*Acta Apostolorum Apocrypha*, ed. M. Bonnet, Darmstadt, 1959, II-II, p. 21).

The Martyrdom of Matthew, a gnostic work of the 3rd-4th century, "Grace" (*charis*) to you and peace, o *kecharitōmenon* child (1, id., II-I, p. 218, where there is without doubt influence of the vocabulary of Luke).

Meaning

Charis means favor, disinterested benevolence, coming from God. *Kecharitōmenē* does not therefore mean "full of grace" as it is translated in the Vulgate. That would be, in Greek, *plērēs charitos* (used for Christ in Jn 1:14, but also for Stephen in Acts 6:8; cf. 7:55).

Does this mean that *kecharitōmenē* means only the extrinsic favor of God? From two points of view it means much more:

1. Theologically, it is a matter of the favor of God the creator, who makes good those whom he considers with love.

2. Philologically, verbs in *oō* signify a transformation of the subject:

   leukoō, to whiten
   argyroō, to make silvery
   chrysoō, to gild
   kakoō, to damage
   douloō, to enslave
   typhloō, to blind
   (and a few others of which Father de la Potterie sent me an instructive list).

Charitoō, thus does not just mean to look upon with favor, but to transform by this favor or grace. St. John Chrysostom, who knew his own language, understood this well. He writes, in his commentary on Eph 1:6, that the apostle "does not say *echarisato*" (from *charizomai*, twenty times in the NT, twelve times in the OT) as if we were merely considered with grace, i.e., gratuitously, "but *echaritōsen*" (from *charitoō*), that is to say, transformed by grace. "He has not only freed us (*apēllaxen*) from our sins, but made us worthy of love (*eperastous*)." (*On the Epistle to the Ephesians*, c. 1, Hom. 1, no. 3, PG 62, col. 13).

Import

One should not reduce this word to a lesser sense in 1:28, for the following reasons:
—the tense of the verb: perfect passive (and the probably Hebrew substratum) gives a strong sense: "You who were and remain the object of the grace of God," as Osty paraphrases;
—it is a *new name* given to Mary, as to Gideon (Jgs 6:12). Fitzmyer (1981, 345) recognizes this value of the word. This conclusion ought to be situated in a culture where the *name* had a sovereign importance, an ontological sense;
—this name is given to Mary in the name of God himself by the angel, his messenger. This is confirmed by the subsequent context: *the Lord is with you*;
—it establishes an eschatological context, in reference to Zep 3. The name given to Mary is at the height of this fulfillment of salvation history;
—this name prefaces the vocation given to Mary to be the mother of the Messiah, Son of God: another new aspect to which the context gives all its importance;
—the word "grace" (and the root *chari*) have an important structural value in Luke 1-2: we will note further on the inclusion constituted by 1:28 and 30 (which comments on it: *you have found grace*), and the two verses which refer *charis* (grace) to Christ: 2:40 and 52 (the last verses of the infancy Gospel). At the level of the semiotic square, we shall see that this word in Luke has a value analogous to that which it has in Paul and that the theme of Law opposed to grace (attested elsewhere in Luke) explains the very structure of Luke 1-2 (see below, p. 228).

On the *chaire* (rejoice), see below, Part I, ch. 2, n. 73).

<table>
<tr><td>and fear fell upon him.</td><td>and considered in her mind
what sort of greeting
this might be.</td></tr>
</table>

Zechariah was troubled by the vision; Mary, by the hearing, an invitation to messianic joy and an unheard-of praise. (The trouble of Zechariah and of Mary is expressed by the same verb *etarachtē*, but strengthened for Mary by the nuance of a superlative which is given by the prefix *di: dietarachtē*).

The rest is a contrast in favor of the young Galilean maiden. The priest is passive under the shock: "Fear fell *upon him.*" As for Mary, she acts, she reflects. The word *dielogizeto* derives from the same root as dialogue and dialectic. Here, as elsewhere, the Gospel of Luke goes against the stereotypes according to which women are characterized by passivity and men by activity. Matthew applies these stereotypes, but Luke takes these formulas and twists them to get an opposite meaning.

The parallelism is accentuated in the next verse:

Beyond the Fear

Luke 1:13	*Luke 1:30*
But the angel said to him "Do not be afraid, Zechariah, for your prayer is heard."	And the angel said to her, "Do not be afraid, Mary, for you have found favor with God."

The formula *do not be afraid* is a stereotyped clause to quell the shock before a manifestation of God.[1] But this symmetry leads into another contrast, in the same line: concerning Zechariah, his "prayer is heard." Here we learn of his desire. For Mary, no desire, no request is manifested. To her, all is freely given, all is grace. This is the meaning of the name which has been given to her.

Then comes the message:

Annunciation of a Birth

Luke 1:13-17	*Luke 1:30-33*
Your wife Elizabeth	Behold you will conceive in

will bear you a son, and you shall call his name John.	your womb and bear a son, and you shall call his name Jesus.
And you will have joy and gladness, and many will rejoice at his birth;	
for he will be great before the Lord, and	He will be great,
he shall drink no wine nor strong drink,	
and he will be filled	and he will be called the *Son of the Most High*
with the Holy Spirit,	and the Lord God will give to him, the throne of
even from his mother's womb; And he will turn many of the sons of Israel to the Lord their God, and he will go before him in the spirit and power of Elijah *to turn* *the hearts of the fathers* *to their children* (Mal 3:23) and the disobedient to the wisdom of the just, to make ready for the Lord a people prepared.	his father David and he will reign over the house of Jacob forever and of his kingdom there will be no end.

Here again, the verbal symmetry is only the framework of a contrast which grows step by step. An abundance of words concerning John the Baptist, a more intense brevity concerning Jesus.

It is announced to Zechariah that his wife will bear *Him* a son, because it is the man who counts. It is to him alone that the annunciation is made, it is to him that the posterity will belong. On the other side, Mary, the woman, is the sole focus. Joseph, although named as the man of the couple (1:27), remains outside this perspective. Exact parallelism with Zechariah would have called for the formula "you will bear Joseph a son." There is nothing of this sort here.

Zechariah, the father, is invited to give his son the name John (which he will be prevented from doing in 1:59, 61). But it is Mary, the mother, and not Joseph (again excluded on this ground, against Mt 1:21 and 25), who will give Jesus his name.[2]

Where the two children are described as *great* (1:15 and 32, a new coincidence of parallelisms), the adjective is qualified in two different ways: it is attributed to John the Baptist in a relative way, "great *before God*." It is attributed to Jesus in an absolute way, "he will be great."[3]

The two names have meanings which mark a gradation: John means *Yahweh gives mercy,* Jesus, *Yahweh is Savior.*

The contrast is amplified in the prophetic announcements about the two children. John is characterized first by asceticism, Jesus by the transcendence of Son of God. John, by his labors as a prophet of conversion and as precursor; Jesus by his reign without end.

The symmetry, broken by the very different missions of the two infants, the servant and the divine king, is re-established by the parallel questions of Zechariah and of Mary:

Questions-Objections

Luke 1:18	*Luke 1:34*
How shall I know this? For I am an old man, and my wife is advanced in years.	How will this be? For I do not know man [here again, no mention of the spouse]

These are the two objections:

1. Zechariah's old age no longer permits him to father a child.
2. The choice which Mary has made, "not to know man" (in the biblical, sexual sense of the word), is opposed to God's design.

Zechariah's question, formulated in terms of *knowing* might lead one to think of a doubt, while Mary holds to asking *how*, and ponders the way of reconciling the irreconcilable. But her objection (it is indeed an objection)[4] is bolder to the extent that she opposes not an established fact, but her human will to the divine will.

She specifies her ambiguous position of "virgin" (twice in 1:27), betrothed in marriage to a man, by saying: "I do not know man," which signifies on her part an unusual intention.

Seeing the strict parallelism of the two objections, the contrast of the two responses is surprising: Zechariah is reproached for his incredulity. He is punished, stricken with dumbness.

Mary, on the contrary, receives a favorable response which is the focal point of the message. The angel reveals to her that this Son of the Most High (1:32) will come from God alone, and specifies the theophanic character of his coming (which we will analyze further on). Her paradoxical intention falls in line with that of God.

Response of the Angel

Luke 1:19-20	*Luke 1:35*
And the angel answered him, "I am Gabriel who stand in the presence of God; and I was sent to speak to you and to bring to you this good news.	And the angel said to her,
And behold, you will be silent and unable to speak until the day that these things come to pass,	"The Holy Spirit will come upon you, and the power of the Most High will overshadow you; therefore the child to be born will be called holy, Son of God" (cf. Lk 1:45: Blessed
because you did not believe my words, which will be fulfilled (*plērōthēsontai*) in their time."	is she who believed that there would be a fulfillment [*teleiōsis*] of what was spoken to her from the Lord).

The strict parallelism of the two introductions, "In response, the angel said to him/her," puts in relief a striking contrast: Zechariah is punished, Mary is exalted. Why? It seems that this is due not so much to any significant differences in their objections—these differences are really slight—as to the *right to speak*, which is recognized in Mary's case, but not in the priest's case.[5] Further, Zechariah, who asked for a sign[6] receives none other than his punishment, and Mary, who did not ask for one, receives a sign.

> Behold, your kinswoman Elizabeth in her old age has also conceived a son; and this is the sixth month with her who was called barren (Lk 1:36) for "nothing is impossible with God" (Gn 18:14; see p. 8).

For Zechariah the dialogue is ended. For Mary, it progresses further. The parallel in increasing contrast is completed in an ironic, if not comic, break. The priest, officiating in his glory, is no longer able to speak. He is reduced to gestures of powerlessness on which the text is quite insistent, not without pleonasm, while Mary speaks and concludes with an admirable response of faith:

Conclusion

Luke 1:22	*Luke 1:38*
When he came out, He could not speak to them,	Then Mary said:
and they perceived that he had seen a vision in the temple and he made signs to them and he remained dumb.	"I am the handmaid of the Lord; let it be to me according to your word."

One further contrast: Zechariah leaves the angel, but the angel leaves Mary; here again we find the initial contrast.

Disjunction

Luke 1:23	*Luke 1:38*
When his time of service was ended, he went home.	The angel departed from her.

The annunciation to Zechariah is immediately followed by its realization.

> After these days, his wife Elizabeth conceived, and for five months she hid herself, saying, "Thus the Lord has done to me in the days when he looked on me, to take away my reproach among men" (1:24-25).

Here is a last contrast, rather disconcerting for those who tend to exaggerate the parallelism of the two annunciations. Nothing is said about the *realization* for Mary. This realization, prophesied for the future in 1:35 as a major theophany, is actually excluded from the narrative. Nowhere is it specified that she "conceived," as it is said of Elizabeth. The fact is manifested solely by its consequences, in the events which follow.

The discreet and hidden thanksgiving of Elizabeth will be balanced off by the episode of the visitation, which will overflow with lyricism in the joy and thanksgiving of Elizabeth and even more so in that of Mary, whose very coming initiates this new stage.

In short, the parallelism of the two annunciation narratives, manifested by some key words, is limited to the structure. It is never strictly material, and it serves above all to bring out, by means of contrasts, the glory of Jesus and of his mother. The account dissociates the couple Joseph-Mary, in order to manifest the union of Mary with God alone, all throughout the text (1:28, 30-32, and 35 where the two "you's" stress this union with God).

The parallelism is toned down even more in the following passages where the accounts of the birth, circumcision, and growing-up of the two children accentuate the contrast, in favor of Jesus. Let us briefly go over these further parallels.

b. The Two Births

The birth of John is a joyous event, but his father, still under the blow of punishment, is, as it were, absent. The account is limited to two verses: 1:57-58.

The birth of Jesus is narrated on a more extensive scale (2:1-10). Joseph appears again, but only as a witness to the Davidic line (2:4-5). This second birth is manifested by a theophany: the glory of God himself surrounds the shepherds (2:9); the divine attributes of the child Jesus are revealed to them (2:11); they recognize him (2:15-16) and announce the Good News (2:18; cf. 2:10).

c. The Two Circumcisions

On the other hand, in the case of John the Baptist (1:59-79) who comes under the Law (cf. 1:5-8; 7:28; and above all 15:16; see below,

p. 140), the circumcision is the object of an extended narrative (1:59-79). Reduced to one verse for Christ (2:21), it is limited to fulfilling the giving of the name of Jesus, prescribed in the annunciation.

d. The Public Manifestation of Jesus (Lk 2:22-52)

Properly speaking, there is no public manifestation of John the Baptist. The question of the people, "What then will this child be?" and the canticle of Zechariah (1:68-79) belong to the sequence concerning the circumcision, after which he withdraws into the desert (1:80). He will be hidden there until his manifestation (*anadeixis*, 1:80) as an adult (Lk 3).

Jesus, on the other hand, is publicly manifested forty days after his birth and again at age twelve, in eschatological theophanies (2:21-52) whose conclusive significance for the infancy Gospels we will explore further on. At this point Mary moves into the background. From this moment all glory is referred to Christ.

e. The Refrains of Growth and Development

The John-Jesus parallelism, thrown into the shade by the unilateral development of the theophanies, is skillfully taken up again at the conclusion by the refrains of growth.[7] But here again, the amplification and weight are on the side of Jesus, for whom the refrain is repeated, with distinctive formulas in which the words wisdom and grace stand out.

John (Lk 1:80)	*Jesus (Lk 2:40)*	*Jesus (Lk 2:52)*
The child grew (*ēuxanen*) and became strong in spirit (cf. Jgs. 13:24) and he was in the wilderness till the day of his manifestation to Israel (Lk 3:1-18)	The child grew and became strong, filled with wisdom; and the *grace* of God was upon him.	And Jesus increased (*proekopten*) in wisdom and in stature and in *grace* (*charis*) with God and man.

This section may have been inspired by some biblical models:

Isaac: "The child *grew*, and was weaned" (Gn 21:8).
Ishmael: "He *grew up* and lived in the *wilderness*" (Gn 21:20 like John the Baptist in Lk 1:80).
Samson: "The boy *grew*, and the Lord blessed him. And the *Spirit* of the Lord began to stir him in the camp of Dan" (Jgs 13:24-25).
Samuel: "The boy Samuel *grew* in the presence of the Lord" (1 Sm 2:21) and "The boy Samuel continued *to grow*, both in stature and in grace with the Lord and with men" (1 Sm 2:26).
David in 2 Sm 5:10: "David became greater and greater, for the Lord, the God of hosts, was with him" (this last text concerns the growth of royalty, but the formulas are parallel to Lk 2:40).

The word *to grow* appears in all these refrains, with reference to God in these last instances, and in Luke 1-2 it has a stronger meaning and appears with some new words: *wisdom* and *grace* are brought in to characterize the (unique) growth of Jesus.

Between John and Jesus, the variants at first glance appear to be minimal:

1. The word *ēuxanen* which means the growth of John in 1:80, is taken up for Jesus in 2:40, but replaced by *proekopten* (he advanced or developed) in 2:52.
2. John the Baptist is characterized by the *spirit* of the prophets (in line with 1:15 and 1:41) and Jesus by *wisdom* (2:40 and 52) in its fullness (*plēroumenos*: 2:40).
3. John the Baptist is situated in the *wilderness* (like Ishmael), and Jesus "advanced before God and *before men*" (a striking contrast between the isolation of John the Baptist and Jesus' growing up in the midst of humanity).
4. Finally, and above all, Jesus is characterized by grace (*charis*): it is upon him (2:40) and in him (2:52), correlative expressions of transcendence and of immanence. The infancy of Jesus ends with this word *charis*, with which the annunciation to Mary (1:28-30) had begun. Jesus is the prototype of *charis* (which Paul set against the Law), but this *charis* is anticipated in her who gives him birth in faith. The recurrent use of this word *grace* at the beginning (1:28 and 30) and at the end (2:40 and 52) constitutes a sort of inclusion which increases the importance of the word.

The Format

Exegetes have wavered between two types of format:
—Bipartite: the infancies of John and of Jesus unfold along the same stages: annunciations, births, circumcisions, manifestations, growth.
—Tripartite: if one makes into a third part (outside the diptych) the concluding pieces that are without parallel, the visitation after the two annunciations (1:39-56), and the double scene in the Temple (2:22-51).[8]

This breakdown matters little. Luke never thought of it. His format is not prefabricated. It is, indeed, not an external framework; rather, it unfolds from the inside. If it is truly under-girded by the John-Jesus parallelism, this is done in the hope of establishing a contrast, in which the first highlights the second, and the second relativized the first. It matters little that the irreducible freedom of development so conceived pains those with geometric minds. This plan responds in depth to a problem that Luke encountered on his travels (Acts 18:25 and 19:3-4): those communities which recognized the baptism of John and did not know that of Christ and the Holy Spirit. Jesus, Son of God, being the center of all, gives rise to more ample developments. The last two episodes, which have no point of reference in the life of John the Baptist, have value as the conclusion of the infancy Gospel (2:22-52). This amplification polarized by Jesus follows the very movement of Luke's plan.

B. ANTECEDENTS AND PREHISTORY OF THE TEXT

The historical-critical method has engaged in considerable efforts aimed at reconstructing the genesis of Luke 1-2: antecedents, components, and modifications of the definitive test which has come down to us.

A first series of hypotheses assumed one source from which Luke and Matthew drew their differing episodes.

For A. Resch (1897),[9] it was an infancy Gospel, written in Hebrew and entitled *Tōlēdōth Iēshūa' (Genesis of Jesus* = Mt. 1:1). Luke and Matthew supposedly shared its multiple episodes. The Prologue of John and the *Apology* of Justin (second century) would also have used it. This hypothesis was the catalyst for a minutely detailed inventory of biblical parallels of Matthew 1-2 and of Luke 1-2, and also for some remarkable points of contact of the latter with the Prologue of John. It is still profitable to consult Resch in this respect. But the hypothesis is artificial. Among its implausabilities the most inexplicable would be that, drawing from one text, Matthew and Luke have not retained any common *episode*; they have shared the *fact* of the birth at Bethlehem, but in totally different contexts: wise men and shepherds, house and manger. Though the hypothesis of this Hebrew account has gained no followers, the idea of a common source dominated the debate in the following years. Two different approaches were taken in line with this model.

According to L. Conrady (1900),[10] Matthew 1-2 and Luke 1-2 derived from the *Protoevangelion of James*. The evangelists would have shared the sequences, eliminating the docetic and mythological aspects, and adapting it to their purpose: apologetic in Matthew, filled with biblical citations; artistic and lyric in Luke, his canticles being a prime example. This is a rather flimsy proposal, since the precedence of the *Protoevangelion* is not a defensible proposition.

For R. Reitzenstein (1901),[11] an Egyptian fragment from the sixth century in which the conception of Mary is explained by the Word of God would seem to be the source of Matthew 1-2 and Luke 1-2. This is another fictitious hypothesis, which accords an entirely imaginary antiquity and influence to a late fragment which is itself apparently derived from Luke.

Other hypotheses arose from the prestigious model which explained the formation of texts by the progressive amalgamation of earlier texts.

D. Volter[12] created the hypothesis of a Baptist Source which recounted the origin of the precursor (1:5-80). His birth would seem to have been announced to the father (1:13-20), then to the mother (1:26-38), later transferred to Mary.[13] The annunciation to Mary would then originally have been the annunciation to Elizabeth, who would have sung the Magnificat; the visitation being the addition of a later revision.

This hypothesis dominated the debate for a long time. Developed by

Erdmann (1932),[14] then by Dornseiff (1936),[15] it has been pushed to its most outlandish conclusion by S. Geyser (1956),[16] for whom the Baptist Source recounts the Bar-Mitzvah examinations of the precursor in the wilderness of Judah, before Essene masters. According to this schema, Luke would have transferred this episode to Jesus to minimize the importance of the Baptist and the Essenes (2:41-52).

P. Winter,[17] an expert in Jewish culture and the author of numerous articles on Luke (1953-1958), worked out the following reconstruction: according to him, the Baptist Source, the work of a disciple of John (inspired by Jgs 13 and, more immediately by Pseudo-Philo, *Liber Antiquitatum Biblicarum*) was adapted and completed by a Jewish-Christian close to James. He introduced Mary into the Baptist Source (in correcting and amplifying 1:26-36), and composed the account of the visitation (1:39-46a and 56); he also created a history of the birth of Jesus, parallel to that of John the Baptist (2:4-21), basing it on Micah 5, and used another source ("temple-source") containing the presentation and the finding in the Temple (2:22-52); some Maccabaean war psalms were taken up and used by Luke as canticles.[18]

These studies contain some observations which are of interest, but they are of unequal value,[19] and provide no sort of proof.

The myth of a Baptist-Source was imposed with such force that several authors up to very recently have found in it *the* source from which everything else derived, the accounts relative to Christ being nothing more than an adaptation of primitive accounts attributedto the Baptist. For W. Resenhoeft,[20] Luke 1-2 seems to be derived from an account of the origins of John the Baptist, considered to be the Messiah. It would have comprised the annunciations to Zechariah, then to Elizabeth (which Luke then transformed into the annunciation to Mary), the canticles of Elizabeth (the Magnificat) and of Zechariah, the birth of John the Baptist which Luke transformed into the birth of Jesus, the annunciation to the shepherds, the presentation in the Temple, and the encounter of the baby John with Simeon and Anna. In short, according to Resenhoeft, 1:26-56 and 2:1-8 were originally accounts concerning John the Baptist which Luke transferred to Jesus. All this in two neatly worked out pages!

Short of these daring attempts, which have never convinced anyone, a number of authors think that what concerns John the Baptist represents a document stemming from his followers. But there are considerable divergences on the extent of this source, its nature, its historicity, its origin: certain authors would postulate a family milieu. Others, with Benoit,[21] have expressed the most telling reservations about the existence of such a source.[22] According to these authors, the work was simply composed by Luke, using various documents.

The proposals for identifying a source for the canticles[23] (which are such a prominent feature of Luke 1-2) or for the scenes in the Temple have been even less successful in establishing acceptable conclusions. Even less helpful have been the attempts which have been made to combine a variety of sources.[24] C. A. Briggs[25] thought that he could distinguish at the source of Luke 1-2, seven poems, several of which he asserted were transformed into narrative accounts; K. L. Schmidt thought that he could discover here seven separate accounts or narrative traditions joined together by Luke,[26] while H. Schürmann[27] perceived five accounts and three hymns, from diverse sources, in addition to the Baptist narrative.

In 1945, H. Sahlin[28] attempted to reconstruct a Hebrew proto-Luke 1-2, eliminating whatever appeared to him to be more evolved, notably the scene of the finding in the Temple, which does not lend itself well to a retroversion into Hebrew. He has the Magnificat (1:46-56) sung by Zechariah in 1:68, and the Benedictus by the prophetess Anna in 2:38. The virginity of Mary is not mentioned and the theology would therefore be of an adoptionist type. The ambition of reconstructing a primitive text by means of pure internal criticism and suppression of the apparent singularities of Luke 1-2 proved to be Utopian. But the retroversion of the infancy Gospel into Hebrew, and the comparative observations to which such a transposition gives rise are often enlightening. They bring to light the possibility that Luke 1-2 (the style and theology of which differ in some manner from the rest of Luke) derives from a Jewish-Christian source, written or oral, certain characteristics of which Sahlin brings out. In the end, he deserves credit for taking up the indications of a semitic substratum of Luke 1-2.

In 1953, P. Gächter[29] attempted the most daring and painstaking reconstruction, prompted by a concern to determine the historicity of the text. Mary's account, the principal witness of the infancy (2:19 and 51), was, according to his theory, transmitted by two routes: the infancy of John, by a friend of Elizabeth, who received her information from Mary, at the time of the visitation; the infancy of Jesus, by another woman, and then by a Jewish priest of the clan of Abijah (1:5), writing at the beginning of the ministry of John the Baptist; another priest then collated these elements with the hymns in a Hebraic redaction. A few additions were then made by another hand, in 1:17 and 75, and around the year 40, a pedantic and narrow-minded translator created a literary version, weighted down with useless and incoherent glosses (in 1:5, 26, 27, 33, 35, 37, 65; 2:5, 8, 39). Finally, according to Gächter, Luke incorporated this work into his Gospel, with minor chronological additions in 1:5 and 2:1-2. As interesting and penetrating as the many observations of Gächter may be, the reconstruction belongs in the realm of science-fiction. The author boldly reconstructs the events: Mary, betrothed in October, 9 B.C., went to Bethlehem immediately after her marriage with Joseph, five months before the birth of Jesus, which Gächter located in March, 7 B.C.

The great lesson of this recapitulation is that the genetic reconstructions have not made much progress, other than by way of elimination. However alluring the hypotheses, and however fruitful the observations which they spark, no important acquisition has obtained acceptance in this line. These reconstructions, which are incompatible with one another, seem to ignore each other like so many tapestries woven according to the most diverse grids. They have not made much progress due to a lack of verifiability. Scientific work is, by definition, controllable and perfectible. These hypotheses reflect more presuppositions than objective conclusions. One can reconstruct a text to the extent that one possesses the earlier texts, used or integrated within the text at hand. That is not the case here, and that is why the hypotheses make no progress and get bogged down. The text resists these contradictory dismantlings.

What *can* be retained along the lines of this genetic analysis is the probability of an archaic Jewish-Christian source (written or oral). Archaisms and semitisms characterize Luke 1-2 and Acts 1-2. The proof seems established today (by the statistical study of S. C. Farris, on the basis of criteria established by Raymond Martin) that Luke 1-2 presents the indications of a translation to the same extent as the LXX (see the special note, p. 163, and the Bibliography).

These two chapters reflect a Jewish-Christian community, without doubt that of Jerusalem, which includes "Mary" and "the brothers of Jesus" (Acts 1:14). One finds in the Gospel of the infancy of Christ as in the Gospel of the infancy of the Church these same Hebraic[30] and familial characters. It is in such a community that family memories could have been gathered together, preserved, and meditated upon in pure Christian light, while we remain unable to describe the genesis of the sources, or to sort out the role played by oral tradition and the eventual elements of redaction.

In the exploration of the prehistory of the text, one objective path of research has made progress: the identification of the *sources* of Luke 1-2, for he consistently uses prophetic texts. This is the best key for grasping both the meaning of the texts and the manner in which revelation occurred as the awareness of the transcendence of Jesus, Messiah and Son of God.

C. LUKE 1-2, LUKE AND PAUL

1. Luke 1-2 and Luke

Attempts at a genetic reconstruction of Luke 1-2 have proved disappointing. But one method of examination has proved most illuminating: a study of the infancy Gospel in the context of the rest of Luke.

The Lucan authenticity of Luke 1-2 has long been a matter of controversy. As early as the second century the gnostic Marcion contested it, and some scholars have sought to deduce from his opposition that he possessed a primitive text of the third Gospel which contained no infancy narrative. St. Ephrem was credited with a similar view, since the Armenian version of his commentary on the *Diatessaron* ends with the gloss: "Luke began with the baptism of John." But the *Diatessaron*, compiled by Tatian in the middle of the second century, used these first chapters, and Ephrem includes them in his commentary. His cryptic gloss means only that Luke locates the beginning of the ministry of Jesus after his baptism, and that, in Ephrem's view, only the miracles accomplished after that event are worthy of faith, thus excluding those recounted by the Apocrypha of the infancy.[31] But other Christian authors of the second century were well aware of the infancy Gospels: Justin (*Apology* 34; *Dialogues* 78 and 80), St. Irenaeus (*Adv. Haereses* 3, 10, 1, 4-5) and the Muratorian fragment.

We will give only a rough sketch of the debate which was set in motion at the end of the last century by the historical-critical propensity to cut up the texts into mosaics of archaic sources. The striking (but well integrated) contrast between the refined Hellenism of the prologue (1:1-4) and the semitic structure of the infancy narrative which begins at 1:5 was exploited by many. J. Hillman (1891), P. Corssen (1899), F. Conybeare (1900), and H. Usener (1903)[32] among others maintained that Luke 1-2 was a later interpolation in Luke.

A. Harnack refuted this hypothesis and maintained the unity of Luke. The more developed lexicographical and stylistic analyses of Gresham Machen (1922) scientifically confirmed this.[33]

H. Conzelmann nevertheless reopened the debate (1954). Utilizing the systematic approach of *Redaktiongeschichte* and striving to remain in line with Lucan theology, he saw an absolute heterogeneity between the theological structure of the Gospel of Luke (as far as it had been defined) and that of Luke 1-2, which would seem to represent a collection of legends and disparate traditions.[34]

The refutations have been numerous and effective on the following bases:

1. The *vocabulary* of Luke 1-2 is that of Luke; this was shown statistically by R. Morgenthaler:[35] In 2:1-20, chosen as a test-piece, one finds twenty-five of the sixty most frequent words in Luke, of which nineteen are also among the most frequent words in Acts. In Luke 1-2, forty-six of the sixty-two most frequent words of the third Gospel appear, of which many are typically Lucan. Among the sixteen which do not appear in the Gospel, three appear in Acts. Of seventy-one favorite words of the author of Acts, twenty-four appear in Luke 1-2, for four of which he has a marked preference (*eis, kata, pneuma, charis*[36]). These words have a particular frequency in Luke 1-2 and Luke 24, which could indicate the same Jewish-Christian source.

Binary and Ternary Repetitions in Lk 1-2

Luke used such repetitions to mark insistence or emphasis.

1. *Binary Occurrences*

—*hiereus* in 1:5 and *hierateuein* in 1:8

—*ephēmeria* (division) in 1:5 and 8

—*thymiasai* in 1:9 and *thymiama* in 1:10

—*dikaioi* and *dikaiōma* in 1:6

—*ōphthē* (was seen) in 1:11 and *idōn* (seeing) in 1:12

—*hestōs* ("standing at the right of the altar" in 1:11) and *parestēkōs* (standing before God in 1:19)

—The angel (of the Lord) in 1:11 and 13

—*chara* and *charēsontai*, meaning joy in 1:14; to which is added, in the same verse, *agalliasis*

—*epistrepsei* in 1:16 and *epistrepsai* in 1:17 (very redundant)

—Spirit and *dynamis* of Elijah in 1:17; Spirit and *dynamis* of the Most High in 1:35

—*laos* (people) in 1:10 and 17

—*probebēkotes* in 1:7 and *probebēkuia* in 1:18 for Zechariah and Elizabeth

—*mē dynamenos* (powerlessness) in 1:20 and *ouk edynato* in 1:22

—*eskirtēsen* (leapt, referring to John in his mother's womb) in 1:41 and 1:44

—"In the Temple" with *eis* in 1:9 and *en* in 1:22

—"When the days were accomplished" in 2:21-22; cf. 1:25, 57 and 2:6

At times the duality tends toward a trilogy:

—The "six months" of Elizabeth (1:26, 36) are prepared for by the "five months" of 1:25. Mary is called "Virgin" twice in 1:27, but made known equivalently as Virgin in 1:34. Jesus is twice called Son of God in 1:32 and 35, with a further mention of this in other terms in 2:49: "I must be in my Father's house."

2. *Ternary Occurrences*

—Threefold revolution of the Magnificat, of knowledge, power and resources (1:51, 52, 53)

—Three mentions of the Law in 2:22, 23, 24 (with two later detached mentions in 2:27 and 39, therefore 3 + 2)

—Three mentions of the Holy Spirit in 2:25, 26, and 27

—Three mentions of Jerusalem at the Presentation (2:22, 25, and 38)

—Three mentions of Jerusalem at the time of the finding in the Temple (2:41, 43, and 45)

—Three mentions of the Temple (*hieron*) in 2:27, 37, 46

N.B. One could mention the (dual) return of the verb *to call* in 1:32 and 35; then 2:21 and 23 (John-Jesus), with compound elements: synthesis (visitation, 1:39-56) and developments (2:22-52) which manifest the transcendence of Jesus.

2. The turns of phrase and *style* are also typically Lucan. According to the observations of P. Winter, N. Turner, and D. E. Haenchen (properly evaluated by J. de Freitas Ferreira[37]), it is the same *koine* Greek, with Hebraisizing formulas, which is also found in the rest of Luke's work. One also finds, in Luke 1-2 the characteristic Lucan tendency to use doublets of words, phrases and sections.[38]

The plan of Luke 1-2 is binary (John-Jesus), with compound elements: synthesis (the visitation, 1:39-56) and developments (2:22-52) which manifest the transcendence of Jesus.

3. The *theology* of Luke 1-2 has Lucan characteristics.[39] Indeed Oliver finds in Luke 1-2 a trilogy characteristic of Luke

—"Prophet of the Most High" (1:76)

—"Son of the Most High" (1:32)

—"Power of the Most High" (1:35)

which characterizes respectively John the Baptist, Jesus, and the Holy Spirit.[40]

The theme of the Holy Spirit has the same importance and the same character in Luke 1-2, in Luke, and in Acts.[41]

Luke 1-2 introduces the themes of salvation history which are developed in the rest of the Gospel and in Acts. The origin of Christ is attributed to the Holy Spirit (1:35) as is the origin of the Church (Acts 1-2).[42]

If Conzelmann had looked more closely at these points of contact and this continuity of style and thinking, it would have helped him to rethink his linear theology of time and of the center of time according to Luke. L. Legrand observes that the debate over the unity of Luke 1-2 and Luke is one of the very few which have led to a genuine consensus.[43]

The points of contact between Luke 1-2 and Luke are striking. Some of these points have been given special attention in this book.

—The John-Jesus relationship, which is the foundation of the structure of Luke 1-2, is found again not only at the beginning (3:1-22) but in the body of the Gospel (7:18-35; 16:16; cf. 5:33; 11:1).[44]

—The *Son of God* theology is the same in all the theophanies which often recur in the Gospel of Luke, always with similar themes and expressions—which we will examine below. The account of the trans-

figuration in Luke is closer to 1:35 than to that of the other evangelists, due to the mention of *glory* (9:32; cf. 2 Pt 1:17).
—The infancy (Luke 2) and the passion (Luke 23-24) take up a number of similar expressions and terms.[45]

It seems logical to conclude from these interwoven threads that the unity of Luke 1-2 and Luke is a sound proposition. But we are left with the following problem: Luke is clearly distinguished by his style and vocabulary; does this point to authorship, or did he adapt his material with the help of a translator, (or was he adaptor-translator himself)? Analogous cases in the history of literature invite prudence, and we would incline towards the second alternative, since it is not possible to delimit the role proper to Luke in relation to a written or oral source. The *translation* factor appears, in any case, undeniable, following the work of S. C. Farris (see the Bibliography).

2. Luke 1-2 and Paul

The connections between Luke and Paul have been somewhat systematically questioned. It is true that Luke does not reproduce the Pauline epistles, which undoubtedly he did not read. It is also true that the Jewish culture of Paul and the Hellenistic culture of Luke were very different. All in all, Paul was a thinker: he had a tightly structured theology, while the theology of Luke is a wide-open, transparent, historical vista, the view of a painter. In spite of these divergences one senses, nevertheless, a common experience from which flow certain similar structures, at times surprisingly analogous, and sometimes even including identical terminology.

We think (despite the numerous recent disputes on the "we" passages of Acts) that Luke was a companion of Paul; yet he was not a shadow or a doublet, but a complementary figure. His conciliatory gentleness, his straightforwardness with the Gentiles, his affable humanity might have greatly served the fiery apostle, whose harshness often gave rise to strong reactions. Paul's doctrine seems to us to have been transmitted to Luke in a profound way, and not simply as a well-learned lesson. Similarities in terminology do not abound, but they are significant in the infancy Gospel.

This is surprising, since Paul was not in the least interested in the infancy of Christ, and only touched on the Incarnation in an episodic and uneasy manner, as we shall see.[46] The whole of Luke 1-2 can be summed up in this formula of Paul in Galatians 4:4:

"Born of a woman" (1:25-38 and 2:5-16).
"Born under the law" (2:22-24, and more broadly 2:22-49).

Luke 1:35, the pinnacle of the Christology of Luke, manifests remarkable similarities of vocabulary and structure with Romans 1:3 (studied by L. Legrand).[47]

Romans 1:3-5	*Luke 1:31-35*
The gospel concerning his *Son*, who was	He will be called the *Son* of the Most High
descended from David according to the flesh	You will conceive in your womb and bear a son. The Lord God will give to him the throne of his father David.
designated. . . according to the *Spirit*	The Holy *Spirit* will come upon you. Therefore the child to be born will be called Holy, the
Son of God	*Son of God.*
in *power*	The *power* of the Most High will overshadow you
By his resurrection from the dead	[from the conception above, 1:32]
	You shall call his name
Jesus Christ our Lord	Jesus (1:32).
Through whom we have received *grace*. . .	You have found grace (*charin*, 1:28-30).

This is one of the rare passages where Paul considers the Incarnation of Christ, Son of God, and it undoubtedly takes the form of an ancient Christian profession of faith, in which Jesus is first called Son of God, then descended from David, with reference to the Holy Spirit and to the power of God as in 1:35.

Need we say that Luke, after Paul, belatedly transposes the schema of divine filiation from the Resurrection to the conception of Christ? Nothing gives us the right to say that the formulas of Luke are later than those of Paul, for Luke assumes here a Jewish-Christian heritage, which is possibly and even probably earlier. One ought to bring together, rather than oppose and contrast, what Luke and Paul have taken up from the earliest tradition of the Church.

It is fitting to bring together the *horistentos* of Paul: Jesus "*designated* Son of God in power according to the Spirit," and the double formula, important for Luke, which occurs in 1:32 and 35 (and again, more profoundly, in 2:21 and 22, which we will examine later):

> [He] will be called Son of the Most High (1:32).
> He will be called Holy, Son of God (1:35, after mention of the *Spirit*, coming upon him 1:35a).

In both cases, it is God who calls from on high (Luke) or constitutes (Rom 1:3). This word had a far deeper meaning in the first century. To be called, as we have seen, meant both "to be" and "to be recognized, manifested."

Paul and Luke used analogous formulas to express an extremely new mystery before which Paul remained ill-at-ease. Here as elsewhere Paul appealed to the vocabulary of the Christian communities: professions of faith and hymns.

If Paul was making reference here to the Davidic sonship of Christ, a concept much cherished by the primitive tradition, it is surprising to see that in Gal 4:4 he does not say, "Christ born from man" (a son of David) which would have been natural, but "born of woman," which surprisingly ties in with the perspective of Lk 1:32-35.

In both texts (Rom 1:3-4 and Lk 1:32-35), the word of God is revelatory of divine sonship. The manifestation and guarantee of this sonship are attributed in the same manner to the Holy Spirit and to the power of the Most High. This double sign is linked with equal validity to the Incarnation or to the Resurrection according to the respective theologies: it belongs to the logic of Paul to speak only of the *dynamis* and of the Spirit from the time of the glorification which is the focal point of his initial experience and of his theology; likewise, it belongs to the internal logic of Luke, historian of the origins, to carry out this same discernment from the very point of departure.

The differences which we can identify here are more in the nature of contrasts than of opposites. In both texts we find the same awareness of divine sonship; and in both, the same archaic vocabulary is used to express two very different events, which represented for each author the moment of grace *par excellence*: for Luke, the annunciation to the Virgin Mary; for Paul, his experience on the road to Damascus.

Contrary to what some scholars would have us believe, there is no prefabricated schema here of the divinization of Christ, a structure which was supposedly first applied to the Resurrection, then transferred to the baptism of John, and then back to the conception of Jesus, and even further back to a time of pre-existence. Certainly the gradual awareness had been progressive and difficult. But it did not follow a simple schema constructed by an impressive and well-polished ideology.

Legrand studied other analogies (less striking and less structured) between Luke 1 and Romans 10. He also discerns the affinities between Luke and Paul.[48]

A. Contri[49] is struck by other affinities of vocabulary (more superficial) between the Magnificat and the christological hymn of Philippians 2:6-11:

> [Christ Jesus] who, though he was in the form of God, did not count equality with God a thing to be grasped, but emptied himself, taking the form of a servant, being born in the likeness of men. And being found in human form he humbled himself and became obedient unto death, even death on a cross. Therefore God has highly exalted him and bestowed on him the name which is above every name, that at the name of Jesus every knee should bow, in heaven and on earth and under the earth, and every tongue confess that Jesus Christ is Lord, to the glory of God the Father.

Working from the theory that they may have depended on common sources, Contri has discovered some analogies, not only in the theocentrism of the two passages (Lk 1:47, 52, and Phil 2:11), but in the contrasts of lifting up and bringing down (Lk 1:51-53; Phil 2:8-9), of humility (Lk 1:48, and Phil 2:8, the same root *tapein*) and of glorification, of poverty, and of wealth (contrasting Lk 1:53 and 2 Cor 8:9). Mary and Christ are described as servants (Lk 1:48 and Phil 2:7) in line with the Servant poems. Finally, there are the striking confessions of the name of God (Lk 1:4 and Phil 2:8), and the glorification by all generations (Lk 1:48) and all tongues (Phil 2:11).[50]

I was surprised to find in Luke 1-2 the inspiration, impulse, and indeed the very vocabulary of the beginning of Ephesians (1:3-14). They seem to share the following elements:

1. A common theology:
—blessed by God (*eulogētos o Theos*): Ephesians 1:3; Luke 1:64, 68;
—reference to the Father: Ephesians 1:3; Luke 2:4;
—the sonship of Christ: Ephesians 1:3; Luke 2:11;
—the role of the Spirit: Ephesians 1:14; Luke 1:35, 41, 65.

2. A common cosmology:
—the world: Ephesians 1:4; Luke 2:1. The terminology is different, but there is the same concern for universality;
—the conjunction of heaven and earth: Ephesians 1:10; Luke 2:14.

3. A common view of salvation:
—redemption: *lytrosis* in Luke 1:68 and 2:38; *apolytrosis* in Ephesians 1:7 and 14;
—the remission of sins;[51]
—salvation *in* Jesus Christ (*sōtēria*): Ephesians 1:13; Luke 1:69, 71, 77.

4. The same gifts:
—grace: Ephesians 1:6-7; Luke 1:28, 30 and 2:40 and 52;
—glory: Ephesians 1:6, 12-14; Luke 2:19, 32;
—wisdom and understanding: Ephesians 1:9; Luke 2:52. They share the word *sophia*, but Ephesians 1:9 gives *phronēsis* for understanding while Luke 2:47 uses *sunēsis*;
—*eudokia*: Ephesians 1:5, 9; Luke 2:14;
—faith: Ephesians 1:13; Luke 1:45;
—the good news of the gospel (*euaggelizō*): Ephesians 1:13; Luke 2:10;
—making Christ known (*gnōrizō*): Ephesians 1:9; Luke 2:15.

Certainly, the development of Paul has its own dimensions, which go beyond Luke 1-2: our adoption in Christ; *agapē*; recapitulation in Christ (Eph 1:10); but we find in both texts the same thanksgiving, the same fulfillment in Christ which Paul expresses by the word *plērōma* (Eph 1:10) and Luke by the repeated refrains of fulfillment which culminate in 2:21-22, as we have seen. I would not say that there is any evidence of influence of Ephesians 1 on Luke 1-2, despite the abundance of apparent points of contact. Yet, it is surprising to encounter such an accumulation of similar terms[52] with such convergence of different themes and subjects.

The faith of Luke and the faith of Paul are similarly structured from within, along the same axis on which the movement of the Spirit, grace and the thanksgiving which is its overflowing consequence are identified. The resemblance is due to an inspiration, the same in both, which seized upon the very same key-words to translate a unique, inexplicable relationship to God, with a twofold reference, a) to the roots of the Incarnation and to the eschatology which begins to be fulfilled, and b) to the gift of God and to his praise.[53] The affinities of Luke, and more especially of Luke 1-2, with Paul are hard to deny.

D. THE SOURCES

The identification of the source-text of Luke 1-2 will help us to delve into one of the main thrusts of the genesis of the text. It throws light on the meaning and underlying significance of the text, since it was in reference to the OT that Christian reflection on Christ was then being conducted.

The use of OT texts is a common practice in the NT. According to Luke, Christ himself recommended this method, and gave examples of it (Lk 24:7, 26-27, 32, 46-47; Acts 1:20; 2:17-21, 25-35). This method of rereading of the Scriptures and making them relevant to new events was not original to the NT. At the time of the exile, the traditions concerning the Exodus had inspired the prophetic texts on the liberation of the exiles from Babylon, in Deutero-Isaiah (Is 40:2; 43:16-21, and so on).

This method is called *midrash*. Let us be clear about its meaning, for this word has often been misunderstood and incorrectly defined.

Midrash is not, strictly speaking, a particular literary genre. It is a search (the literal meaning of the root *darash*): seeking to explain the present life-experience in the light of the Word of God. It is a way of making Scripture relevant to life, and life to Scripture. Such was the exegesis of the NT and in particular of the infancy Gospels. A confrontation of the Bible with life constantly sparks off new light.

A twofold error has cast confusion or uncertainty on this method of interpretation, especially as concerns Luke 1-2.

Some have unfortunately and wrongly defined midrash on the basis of later decadent forms, as if they were the typical forms. This pitfall has been quite judiciously denounced by R. Le Deaut, a master in matters of Jewish exegesis.[54]

Others have defined midrash as pure fable-writing, an arbitrary setting of the Scriptures according to one's imagination. This degrading definition, coming from rationalistic exegesis (analogous to the irreparable debasement which the word *myth* has suffered in the same cultural milieu), has become outdated for a long time now, as a result of the works of A. Robert and R. Bloch.[55] R. Le Deaut has confirmed this: midrash is not a literary genre, it defines a mode of exegesis.

However, the major eschatological event which was the life of Christ revolutionized midrash, observes C. Perrot.[56] He shows how the meditation of the Christian community, centered on Christ, "turns the midrash upon itself" (1967, 516). At Qumran, the biblical text was already being adapted to the present life of the people. But the Gospel goes even further and begins more radically from the life of Christ, seeing in it the fulfillment of Scripture. Whereas Scripture was the measure of the event, Christ has become the measure of Scripture.

Midrashic exegesis, which proceeds by way of symbolic and suggestive comparisons, is a constant process of religious meditation. It has been carried on spontaneously under other designations, or without designation, in the whole tradition of the Church, up until our own days. I heard the parents of a devout family say, after the dramatic loss of a child, "God had given him to us, God has taken him back from us, blessed be his Holy Name." This application of the prayer of Job (1:21) to their own particular circumstances of mourning was a midrash, although these simple people did not know its name. The base communities of Latin America do midrash in commenting on and praying, in their new situation, the Magnificat, the canticle of liberation of the poor.[57] Charismatics quickly come to recognize the charisms of Mary as a model of their own experience.

This definition of *midrash* as a way of making the event relevant to Scripture and Scripture to the event is particularly appropriate for Luke 1-2, the fruit of a long meditation on the Scriptures. It is undoubtedly not by chance that Luke characterizes this confrontation as a meditation and refers it to the *rhēmata* (Hebrew: *debarim*), a word which means both *words* and *events*.

The principal Scripture passages which Luke 1-2 employs are: 2 Samuel 7:14; Micah 5:2ff., Malachi 3 and Daniel 9.[58] These are now unanimously agreed upon,[59] but it is important to continue to assess these identifications, to specify the meaning of those which are accepted (Dn 9; Mal 3, for example), and to confirm those which are still a matter for debate[60] (Zep 3; Ex 40:35, and 1 Sm 6 being the most important).

There are clear rules by which one can recognize the use of this midrashic mode: first, the twofold coincidence of *terms* and *meanings*; second (and this is a criterion which has been frequently misunderstood), the coherence and convergence of the source-texts. Those who have accused Luke of error or negligence have not understood that this coherence does not take place at the level of literalness or materiality, but at the level of a daring concretization which is made in order to penetrate the disconcerting newness of Christ. Thus in Luke 1-2 we find a convergence in Jesus of the messianic prophecies and the theophanic prophecies, those which announced the eschatological coming of the Lord himself: as he came, in the time of Moses, to take possession of the Ark of the Covenant to exercise his theocratic reign in the midst of the people, so it was hoped since the exile and the disappearance of the Ark of the Covenant that he would come anew to his people.[61]

The reflection/confrontation of which Luke speaks in 2:19, grasps the meaning not only of the words (*sensus verborum*), but also of the events (*sensus rerum*). The ambiguity of the word *rhēmata* is thus full of meaning. (This word is found frequently in Luke 1-2; P. Bossuyt and

J. Radermakers translate this as "words-events.") The task of making the texts relevant in the newness of Christ does not limit itself to delineating a strictly literal sense, but broadens into what is at times called a fuller sense (*sensus plenior*).

Whenever in Luke Jesus is identified with the Messiah, Mary is identified with the *Gebirah*, mother of the king, a very important character according to the background of Jewish culture.[62] To the extent to which the coming of Jesus is identified with the eschatological coming of *God himself* to his people, Mary is identified with the eschatological Daughter of Zion and with the Ark of the Covenant, where the prophets located this new presence. This identification has been more precisely concretized in Luke 1.

Let us examine these two kinds of prophecies. First of all, Luke makes use of some major messianic prophecies and makes them pertinent to the narratives.

1. MESSIANIC PROPHECIES

2 Samuel 7

This is the prophecy of Nathan to David: he will have an heir who will secure his reign forever. To this son, God himself will be a father.

2 Samuel 7:12-16	*Luke 1:31-33*
I will raise up[63]	
your offspring after you,	
who shall come forth from	And behold, you will conceive
your body,	in your womb and bear a son,
and I will establish . . .	[and you shall call his
his kingdom.	name Jesus].
I will be his father, and	He will be great, and will be
he shall be my son.	called the *Son* of the
	Most High and the Lord God
	will give him
Your throne shall be	the throne of his father
established forever.	David.
Your *house* and your	He will reign
kingdom shall be made	

sure *forever*	*forever* over the
before me.	*house* of Jacob
	and of his *kingdom*
	there shall be no end.

The similarity of meaning and the literal contacts leave no doubt. The use of this Samuel text achieves an identification between Jesus and the royal heir promised to David.

The citation by Luke makes the text relevant to Christ: "He will be great" is applied to him directly, not to the descendants, taken globally or abstractly. And above all, *divine sonship* goes before *Davidic sonship* in Luke. It is set forth in unprecedented relief. It is no longer only a matter of the paternal sentiments of God, but of the title Son of God given to the Messiah. The realization of the prophecy in the person of Jesus is thus clear and strong.

Isaiah 7:14

One might wonder if Luke had another source in mind at this juncture: Isaiah 7:14 (which is an echo of the prophecy in 2 Sm 7) and the texts in Isaiah which unfold this prophecy. The literal contacts are less precise in Luke 1:26-33 than in Matthew 1:23 (where Is 7:14 is quoted); nevertheless they warrant our attention.

Isaiah 7:14	*Luke 1:26-35*
	The angel Gabriel was sent...
Behold a *virgin* (LXX)	to a *virgin*...
shall *conceive*	—Behold you *will conceive*
	in your womb (cf. Is 12:6)
and *bear a son*	and *you shall have a son*
and *shall call his name*	and *you shall call his name*
God-with-us.	Jesus.

Isaiah 9:6-7	*Luke 1:32-33*
	He will be great and will
A *son* is given to us...	be called *Son* of the

	Most High;
upon the *throne of David,*	the Lord God will give to him the *throne of David* his father, and he will
and over his kingdom forever,	reign forever (cf. Dn 7:24, 27) and of his kingdom there will
Peace with no *end.*	be no *end.*

Isaiah 11:2	*Luke 1:35*
The *Spirit* of the Lord shall rest *upon* him	The Holy *Spirit* will come *upon* you

Isaiah 12:6	*Luke 1:35*
For great in your midst is the *Holy One* of Israel.	The child to be born will be called *Holy* the Son of God.

Isaiah took up the formulas of 2 Samuel 7:12-16, and clarified them on a number of points, the same ones which Luke takes up again: the kingdom without end, the role of the Holy Spirit in this messianic event, the divine names given to the Messiah ("Wonderful Counselor, Mighty God," according to Is 9:6) and accentuation of the mother of the Messiah.[64]

Daniel 7 and 9

It is evident that Luke 1-2 depends on Daniel 7 and 9. The name Gabriel alone would suffice to guarantee this link, as the only two OT texts where this name figures are Daniel 8:16 and 9:21. The appearance of the messenger of this prophecy signifies the presence of the Messiah. Indeed, the return of the angel Gabriel and the fulfillment of his prophecy in announcing the immediate coming of the Messiah motivates the entire dynamic of Luke 1-2.

We shall examine later the most surprising parallel which Luke uses with reference to Daniel (9:24), one of the principal messianic prophecies of the OT: that of the seventy weeks. Luke tallies this with "the time" of the infancy narrative. (See below, pp. 64-66, 120-121.)

But the parallel between Luke 1-2 and Daniel 7-9 is illustrated by many coincidences, which I examined in detail in *Structure et théologie de Luc 1-2*[65]:

—In Luke 1:10-11, as in Daniel 9:20-21, Gabriel appears at the hour of the evening "oblation."

—In Luke 1:12, as in Daniel 10:7, the appearance of Gabriel gives rise to "fear."

—In Luke 1:13, as in Daniel 10:12, Gabriel says: "Do not be afraid."

—In Luke 1:13, as in Daniel 9:20, the seer prayed in distress and is now answered.

—In Luke 1:19, as in Daniel 9:20-21 and 10:11, Gabriel, who stands before God, is sent to speak in the name of God.

—In Luke 1:20 and 22, as in Daniel 10:15, the seer remains "dumb."

—In Luke 1:22, Luke uses the word "vision" (*optasia*), a word used six times in Daniel 9-10, according to the version of Theodotion. Use of this word is rare in the NT, appearing only four times, three of which are in Luke (here in 1:22; 24:23, and in Acts 26:19).

—In Luke 1:28, as in Daniel 9:23, the seer is described as favored by God: in Daniel, as the object of his mercy; in Luke, as the object of his favor or grace.

—In Luke 1:29-30, there is a recurrence of fear and of the injunction "Do not be afraid," as in Daniel 10:11 and 12, cf. verse 7.

—In Luke 1:35, Christ is described as "Holy" *par excellence.* He is consecrated in fulfillment of the Law in Luke 2:23, a probable echo of the anointing of the Holy of holies according to Daniel 9:24. Luke 1:35 seems to imply the sense of a royal and divine anointing.[66]

Other parallels are evident, concerning Mary:

—In Luke 1:29, as in Daniel 8:15, she reflects and tries to understand, like Daniel.

—In Luke 2:50, as in Daniel 8:27, she is silent and remains without understanding.

—In Luke 2:51, as in Daniel 7:28, she keeps these things in her heart.

2. A PROPHECY BOTH MESSIANIC AND THEOPHANIC

Micah 4-5

Luke's account of the birth of Jesus makes use of the prophecy of Micah 4-5. This prophecy, which is in the tradition and ambience of 2 Samuel 7:14 and Isaiah 7:14, is cited more explicitly in Matthew 2:5. But its implicit citation in Luke is established by the abundance of common terms and themes.

Micah 5:2-3	*Luke 2:4, 6-7*
	Joseph also went up from Galilee to Judea to the city of David which is
But you, O *Bethlehem* Ephrathah [who are little to be among the clans of Judah], from you shall come forth for me one who is to be ruler in Israel, [whose origin is from of old, from ancient days.]	called *Bethlehem*
Therefore he shall give them up until the time when she who is in travail has brought forth.	While they were there, the time came for her to be delivered. And she *gave birth* to her first-born son.

Further examination reveals many points of contact: pastures and flocks (Mi 5:4; Lk 2:8), the glory of the Lord (Mi 5:4; Lk 2:9) in reference to the shepherds; the Messiah is identified with peace in Micah 5:4 as in Luke 2:14.

We detailed the terminological contacts in the Hebrew and Greek in *Structure* (1956).[67] The shared meanings are more important than the shared words. The use of Micah as a source-text is an effort to authenticate the dynastic nature of the birth of Jesus in Bethlehem, David's place of origin (1 Sm 16:1), which Luke twice calls "the city of David," contrary to the usage which reserved this name for Jerusalem (2 Sm 5:7, 9; 6:10, 12). The mention of the shepherds recalls David's role as a shepherd (1 Sm 16:11; 17:34-35). Luke 2:9 shares with the LXX version of Micah 5:4 reference to the *glory* of the Lord. To these instances of source-texts from messianic prophecies one could add the numerous, but more tenuous, points of contact adduced by Winter[68] between Micah 4 and Luke 2.

The idea common to Micah 4 and Luke 2:7-8 is the manifestation of the Messiah-king (a tradition represented by the Jerusalem Targum on Gn 35:19). The setting and the image are the same: the poor country setting of Bethlehem, and the shepherds where King David was once a shepherd, the manifestation of the Messiah at the end of time (Mi 5:2 hearkens to "a return to the days of old," to the origins). But in Micah 4 (unlike Mi 5) it is not the kingship of a human Messiah, *but that of Yahweh himself* which is being considered (Mi 4:6-7):

> Those who were dispersed. . . I will make them a remnant. . . a strong nation. . . and *Yahweh will reign* over them, on the mountain of Sion, from now on and forever (Mi 4:7).

This text is seen as a basis for giving a transcendent meaning to the title *Kyrios* (Lord) given to Jesus in Luke 2:11.

We thus find in Micah 4-5 the astonishing identification between the two aspects of the eschatological reign announced by the prophets: that of the *Messiah*, and that of *Yahweh himself*. This convergence is sketched out in the OT (see above, ftnt. 61); Luke formalizes it in the birth of Jesus Christ. This daring identification is reinforced by that of the mother of the Messiah (Mi 5:2-3) with the Daughter of Zion (Mi 4:10).[69]

In drawing these parallels and making these identifications, Luke is merely carrying on the tradition of midrashic reflection and exegesis of the NT, in which the divine titles are applied to Jesus.[70]

Malachi 2-3

The first theophanic prophecy to which Luke refers, Malachi 2-3, appears in the announcement to Zechariah (1:16-17) and in his concluding canticle (1:76), which takes up again in a very literal way Malachi 2:6, 7 and 3:1, 4:5-6.[71]

Malachi 2-3 evokes a messenger who is identified with Elijah (Mal

4:5; Lk 1:17). This prophet (Mal 4:5; Lk 1:76) who comes to convert (Mal 4:5; Lk 1:16-17) is precursor of Yahweh himself:

Malachi 3:1	*Luke 1:17, 76*
Behold, I send my *messenger* to prepare the way before me, and the *Lord* whom you seek will suddenly come to his Temple; the messenger of the covenant in whom you delight.	 . . . and he will go before him in the spirit and power of Elijah. . . . the prophet of the Most High for you will go before the *Lord* to prepare his ways.

The Lord in Luke 1-2 (1:43; 2:11) is Christ himself, recognized as such by Elizabeth, and proclaimed by the angels from his birth: "A savior who is Christ the Lord."[72] It is the ways of the Gospels which John prepares (3:3-5, 15-18; 7:24-28).

Zephaniah 3:16-17

The annunciation to Mary uses and concretizes Zephaniah 3:14-17, which is one of a series of three eschatological announcements made to the Daughter of Zion, personification of Israel: (Zep 3:14; Zec 9:9; cf Lam 4:22). She is invited to rejoice because *the Lord is coming to her.* Zephaniah, who presents a maximum of parallels with Luke 1:28-33, must be considered its source (already established in *Structure*, 1956, p. 64-71).

Zephaniah 3:14-17	*Luke 1:28-33*
Sing aloud, O daughter of Zion; shout, O Israel!	
Rejoice, O daughter of Jerusalem.	*Rejoice*, full of grace,
The king of Israel, *the Lord is with* *you*. . .	 *The Lord is with* *you*!
Do not fear, O Zion. . .	*Do not fear,* Mary. . .
The Lord, your God, is	And behold

in your midst a
warrior

who *saves*...
The King of Israel,
the Lord is with you.

you will conceive
in your womb
and bear a son, and
you shall call him
Lord, *Savior*
And he will reign
(cf. Zep 3:15b)

The messianic "rejoice" of Zephaniah 3:14 is taken up in Luke 1:28. Given the Hebrew substratum and the archaic character of the text, it is clear, as the Greek Fathers understood, that this *chaire* is not the everyday greeting of the Greeks. When it was a question of the ordinary salutation, the Hebrew *shalom*, the evangelists did not hesitate to use "peace," and not "rejoice." This salutation is followed by a new title, full of grace, given to Mary in Luke 1:28, and what follows makes even clearer the unparalleled and transcendent eschatological nature of the event.[73]

The prophecy announces that Yahweh himself is coming to reside in Zion, as King and as Savior, to which the name of Jesus (in the Hebrew Yahweh-Savior) literally corresponds (1:31).

All these bold traits of Zephaniah 3 are concretized in two aspects in Luke 1:

1. The coming of *the holy God* into the Daughter of Zion, his people, is the coming of the *Son of God* (1:31-35) who deserves the transcendent name of *holy*. But he is also identified with the son of David; as such he will be conceived and will be born (1:31). Only a purely symbolic identification could serve to introduce this unheard-of revelation, which later theology would have so much trouble formulating in an abstract fashion, as an "incarnation" or humanization of the Son of God.

2. In Luke 1:28-35 the Daughter of Zion, who was destined to receive within herself the Lord of glory, is personified in Mary, Mother of the Messiah-Son of God, whose exceptional conception will be noted in 1:35 as the eschatological manifestation of the shekinah (presence of God).[74]

Exodus 40:35

The identification of the Holy One born of Mary with the God who dwelt in the Ark of the Covenant, is made explicit in 1:35. Mary is here also identified with the Ark of the Covenant.

Exodus 40:34-35	*Luke 1:35*
The cloud overshadowed the meeting tent and the glory of the Lord filled the tabernacle	The power of the Most High will overshadow you; therefore the child to be born will be called holy, the Son of God (Nm 9:18-22, 2 Chr 5:7; 6:2).

Exodus 40:35 is not a prediction. But Luke gives it the value of a typological announcement, according to the usage of Jewish tradition which is attentive to the meaning of the *events* as much as of the *words*. The Ark of the Covenant (which by then had disappeared) is the symbol of the eschatological presence of the Messiah.

In Exodus 40:35, as in Luke 1:35, this presence is described according to a twofold spatial schema:

—*Presence above,* like the cloud, sign of the transcendence of God, covering with his shadow the place of his presence. The use by Luke 1:35 of the technical term *episkiasei* (Hebrew: *shākan*, whence comes *shekinah*: the specific term for this first aspect) is significant.

—*Presence within,*[75] as that of the glory in the Ark of the Covenant. This presence, which the book of Exodus represented as a radiant light, becomes here that of a mysterious transcendent personage, of whom 1:35 speaks in the neuter (*to gennōmenon*, as elsewhere in Mt 1:20—*to gennēthen*), in deference to the inexpressible: "that which will be born." Jesus is given two titles by means of which his identification with God is indicated: *Son of God* and *holy*, which is the proper name of God in the OT.[76] *Holy* and *glory* (Ex 40:35) are here equivalent: glory is the manifestation of the *Holy One* of Israel.[77]

We will find this same schema, presence above, presence within (which will later be called shekinah),[78] and attributes of glory and power in the later Gospel theophanies:

—Baptism (3:22), where the Holy Spirit comes upon Jesus as in 1:35.
—Transfiguration, which reproduces the exact schema of Exodus 40:35 and Luke 1:35:

> A cloud came and *overshadowed (epeskiazen)* them, and a voice came out of the cloud saying: This is my Son, my "Chosen One" (9:35).

Luke uses the word *glory* in his version of the Transfiguration, as in Exodus 40:35, unlike the two other synoptics:

> Peter and those who were with him . . . kept awake, and they saw his *glory* (9:32)

We find the same expression in the recalling of the Transfiguration in 2 Peter 1:17:

> He received honor and *glory* from God the Father and the voice was borne to him by the majestic *Glory*, "This is my beloved Son, with whom I am well pleased."

The solemn self-confession of Jesus to the high priest follows the same scheme:

> From now on the Son of Man shall be seated at the right hand of the *power* of God (22:69).

Matthew and Mark add "and coming on the *clouds of heaven*" (clarification of shekinah) and in Luke 22:70 the question comes "Are you the Son of God then?"—the same terms as in 1:35. The constancy with which Luke expresses these key terms guarantees the meaning of 1:35 for us. The judgment text (22:69-70), like the annunciation, joins together divine sonship and human sonship. The text in its use of "*power*" (*dynamis*) in these two places is not expressive of an effect of the power of God, but a way of pointing out the transcendence of the Son of God.

We will find the same identification, more developed, but expressed through the same images and the same concepts in John 1:14:

> And the Word became flesh and dwelt among us (*eskēnōsen*), full of grace and truth, and we have beheld his *glory*.

The same elements are consistently articulated:
—*Glory*, identified with Christ, the transcendent Son of the Father. John moves on from signs and symbols to the direct expression of the Incarnation.
—The *Ark of the Covenant (skēnē*, clearly signified by the word *eskēnōsen*) is identified with the Word made flesh by John; with Mary the Daughter of Zion by Luke, because it is to her that it was said: "The power of the Most High will overshadow *you*."

The astonishing way in which the figure of Mary is accentuated indicates that she is the first dwelling place of the Son of God. This corporeal unity allows for a kind of "communication of idioms" between mother and son during pregnancy, for Elizabeth as for Mary (1:35-44): what is said of the mother, Luke transfers to the son and vice versa. It is John the Baptist who is filled with the Holy Spirit, according to the announcement to Zechariah in 1:15, but it is Elizabeth alone who is said to be filled with the Holy Spirit in 1:41. What follows shows this communication or transference, since "the babe leaped for joy" (1:44), a sign that the grace of the mother extends to the son and vice versa. It is obviously not a question of ontological but of symbolic identification.

2 Samuel 6:1-11

The narrative of the visitation adds clarity to 1:35. It is woven with allusions to the transfer of the Ark of the Covenant to Jerusalem by King David. The Ark, established by Moses, according to Exodus 40:35, entered Canaan with Joshua (Jos 3:6; 8:33). It had stayed a long time in Shiloh, north of Bethel, where a temple had been built (Jos 18:1; 1 Sm 1-3); taken as a spoil of war by the Philistines (1 Sm 4), it was recaptured by David (2 Sm 5:6). Chapter 6 recounts its recovery and the ascent to Jerusalem. The topographical and terminological contacts between the two narratives are numerous from the first verse:

2 Samuel 6:2	*Luke 1:39*
	In those days
David *arose*	Mary *arose*
and *went*...	and *went*...into the

from Baale—*Judah* to bring up from there the Ark of God.	hill country to a city of *Judah*.

Mary, like David, sets out on her journey. The same mountainous region of Judah must be climbed. However, in this first verse, it is David who travels, and not yet the Ark of the Covenant. But he comes to bring it up to Jerusalem. Luke associates the ascent of the Ark with the journey of Mary carrying Jesus, David's heir, in the same hill country (1:32). We already have here a coherent set of contacts: meaning, terms, and topography.

David is afraid (like Mary in 1:30) and this fear inspires these words which Elizabeth takes up:

2 Samuel 6:9	*Luke 1:43*
How can the Ark of the Lord come to me! [enter my house][79]	And why is this granted me, that the mother of my Lord should come to me?

Luke omits the episode of Uzzah, but picks up the themes and expressions which characterize the climb: joy, chants, and dance:

—In 2 Samuel 6:12 we find the joy of the people in Jerusalem and of David (*en euphrosunē*); in Luke 1:44, the joy of Elizabeth and of John the Baptist (*en agalliasei*).

—The dance of David (2 Sm 6:14, 16, 21b) and that of John the Baptist (Lk 1:41-44): the leap of joy in the womb of his mother is described in these two verses by the expression *eskirtēsen* (from*skirtaō*). The verb means to jump, to leap, to dance; and, indeed, it is *skirtaō* which Symmachus uses to translate 2 Samuel 6:16.[80]

The cries of the people accompanying the Ark are described, as is the cry of Elizabeth, by the word *kraugē* (2 Sm 6:15 and Lk 1:42): the word *phōnē* describes the voice of the people in 2 Samuel 6:15 and also that of Mary in 1:44. As for the word *anephōnēsen*, which expresses the cry of Elizabeth in 1:42, it is used exclusively in the OT for *liturgical* acclamations (1 Chr 16:4, 5, 42), and more especially for the acclamations accompanying the transfer of the Ark of the Covenant (1 Chr 15:28; 2 Chr 5:13: this word not being found elsewhere in the LXX).

The Ark goes up to Jerusalem (the very direction Mary takes). It is led to the *house* of Obededom (2 Sm 6:10) and Mary enters the *house* of Zechariah (Lk 1:40).

Samuel 6:11	*Luke 1:56*
The Ark of the Lord	Mary
remained	remained
in the house of Obededom	with her [Elizabeth]
three months.	about *three months.*

Yahweh blesses Obededom and his entire house,[81] in which the Ark is left (2 Sam 6:11-12). He also blesses the house of Zechariah: Elizabeth and her babe who leaped with joy (1:41, 44-45; cf. 1:15).

In both cases the scene has the character of a theophany. Such exact and converging analogies of terms and meanings can hardly be accidental. The identification is typological as in the preceding parallel: the mother of the Lord is the new "Ark of the Lord," and her Son is the Lord (1:43) residing in this living dwelling place.

Several other texts display how Luke 1-2 identifies Jesus at the same time with the awaited Messiah and with God himself. Correlatively we see the identification of Mary with the mother of the Messiah (the object of several prophecies: Is 17:14; Mi 1-5) and with the eschatological Daughter of Zion (Zep 3).[82] Other more limited instances attest to the development of a similar reflection, sometimes more especially significant as it remains implicit or elliptical. The dynamic of this faith in search of formulas is revealing.

Judith 13:18-19 and Luke 1:42

Luke 1:42 takes up Judith 13:18-19, substituting *Jesus* for *Lord God.*

Judith 13:18-19	*Luke 1:42*
Blessed are you...	Blessed are you
among all women	among women

and blessed	and blessed
(*eulogemenos*)	(*eulogemenos*)
is the *Lord God.*	is the *fruit of your womb.*

The titles given to Jesus (identified as Lord in 1:43 and 2:11) are so utilized as to impress on us his transcendence. Certain prophets of the OT were already moving in this direction: e.g. Isaiah 11 and Daniel 7:13 for whom the Son of Man comes on the clouds of heaven. Thus Jesus is described as great, without restriction (in contrast to John the Baptist, 1:15 and 32), a quality the Bible seems to reserve for God.[83] The suggestive ambiguity of 1:17 and 76 on the role of John the Baptist as precursor tends toward identifying the child Jesus with God: he (John) will go before him (God, 1:17); you (John) will go before the Lord to prepare his ways (1:76). In the same way, Isaiah 8:14 refers to Yahweh as the "rock of stumbling"; the prophecy of Simeon transfers the imagery to Jesus (2:34).

The application to Christ of texts concerning Yahweh is not restricted to Luke. It is common throughout the NT to express the divinity of Christ in this way. It is especially notable in the case of Paul, who does not give the title of God to Christ, except in two much-disputed passages. He reserves to the Father the title of God, and refers to Christ as Lord, while applying to him biblical texts relevant to Yahweh. It is by these identifications that he conveys his implicit divinity. It is in this setting that the title Lord, used twice to refer to Christ in Luke 1-2, takes on its transcendent import.

Significance of a Textual Convergence

The biblical parallels attest in a coherent and convergent way to the identification of the Messiah with the God who comes to his people, and of God, the theocratic king, with the promised Messiah. This identification was prepared by the texts in which the Messiah took on divine proportions (Is 9; Dn 7; Ps. 2, etc.), and by those in which God seemed to have come himself to reign among human beings and become human in their midst.[84] The revelation of God-made-man is the convergence of these two concepts.

Luke 1-2 extends this convergence. It avoids breaking the divine unity by suggesting the mediatory distinction between God and the Son of God. It is very careful not to identify the *divine sonship* with the virginal conception. This conception with a human father appears as the sign, not merely of a transcendent action of God, but also of the divine identity of the one who is born. The Holy Spirit and the power of God in 1:35 appear less as the cause of this new birth than as guarantor of the divine identity of the Son of God, signified by the sign of the shekinah. The identification (given by pure grace) of the child with the glory of God which resided in the Ark of the Covenant prepares us to understand the astonishing title of *glory*, formally given to Christ by Simeon in 2:32-34.[85] What is truly gripping is the paradoxical transformation of the glory by its identification with this silent child: the Messiah-Lord, recognized, although hidden, by his identification with the poor.

The admirable quality of this revelation by means of symbolism is that it conserves the humble quality of the infancy of Christ. Thus it is that in Luke 1-2, the glories of this world (then so prestigious) no longer count, and are revolutionized by the canticle of Mary (1:51-53). The very destiny of the child Jesus sets in motion this fundamental line of the Gospel. The Son of God comes as a poor one for the poor.

The study of the allusions and biblical reworkings in Luke 1-2 thus brings us to an essential awareness of that key moment in the history of salvation.

E. THE DYNAMIC OF LUKE 1-2

What is most significant and most misunderstood in Luke 1-2 is the dynamic of these two chapters: the impetus which underlies the John-Jesus diptych. This dynamic is heavily structured with surprising gradations which the semiotic study of the narrative structure will reveal. It is strongly linked to the gift of the Spirit as we will see (cf. 1:15, 35, 47, 67; 2:25-27).[86]

1. Impetus and Progression

The narrative is woven with futures: announcements and canticles.[87] We are in eschatology. The text refers, step by step, to the fulfillment of the prophecies and predictions of the OT and extends them by means of others which announce, in a veiled and rich manner, the Passion and Resurrection. The novelty of these "fulfillments" takes us from wonderment (1:21, 63; 2:18, 33) to amazement (2:47, 48).

The narrative is in constant movement, in journeys, some of which are "in haste" (1:39 and 2:16). After the prelude to the announcement in the Temple under the sign of the Law, which ends ambiguously with the chastisement of Zechariah, the priest, and the silence of the old couple (1:20, 23, 24), we witness the irresistible ascent from Nazareth to Jerusalem. The narrative takes us first to the hill country of Judah (the visitation and the birth of Jesus), to the Temple of Jerusalem (the presentation and the finding in the Temple).

This impetus is linked to the hope of the poor of Yahweh: those oppressed (1:51-53), at the mercy of their enemies (1:71 and 74), who "await the consolation of Israel" (2:25) and "the redemption of Jerusalem" (2:38).

It is characterized by the joy which is one of the leitmotifs of Luke 1-2:

> And you will have joy (*chara*) and gladness (*agalliasis*) and many will rejoice (*charēsontai*) at his birth (1:14).
> Rejoice! [the first word of the announcement to Mary, 1:28 *chaire*].
> The babe in my womb leaped for joy (*agalliasis*, 1:44).
> My spirit rejoices (*ēgalliasen*) in God my Savior (1:47).
> I bring you good news (*euaggelizomai*) of a *great joy* (*chara megalē*) which will come to all the people (2:10).[88]

This joy reaches its peak in the thanksgiving expressed in the canticles.

In Luke we find the proto-Pentecost of the newly-born Christ which prefigures that of the infant Church in Acts 2. The Spirit, who first of all comes upon Mary and points out the divine identity of the One within her who is the Holy One and the Son of God, returns symmetrically three times upon the priestly family of John the Baptist, Elizabeth, and Zechariah (1:15, 41, 67), and upon Simeon who greets Christ in the Temple (2:25, 26, 27).

This dynamic concludes with the two Temple episodes which continue to puzzle exegetes, particularly the first one. It is important to unravel this enigmatic point where all the main threads of Luke 1-2 meet. An exploration at the level of literary methods will be indispensable as a preparation for the semiotic stage of this study. Let us, therefore, see how the Presentation and the Finding in the Temple are the conclusion and the climax of the dynamic of Luke 1-2.

2. The Presentation: Eschatological Fulfillment

It is clear that the presentation in Luke 1-2 is a point of arrival: Jesus of Nazareth goes up to Jerusalem and the Temple. But the converging lines which determine the significance of this event are complex. The clearest is that the episode begins under the Law (mentioned three times in 2:22-24), and ends in the Spirit (also mentioned three times in 2:25-27); the prophetic consequences of this unfold in 2:28-38, and conclude with the Law in 2:39.

In order to find our way through the enigmas of this episode, we must study each of the main threads which make up this eschatological schema:

1. Fulfillment of the prophecies.
2. Fulfillment of the oracles of Gabriel.
3. Fulfillment of the Law.
4. Fulfillment of the Spirit.

1. FULFILLMENT OF THE PROPHECIES

Among the prophecies that Luke 1-2 takes up (discussed in the preceding section), Malachi 3:1-24 and Daniel 9 undergird the entire dynamic and are fulfilled in the presentation.[89] Luke 1-2 follows closely the main thread of Malachi 3. Let us recall the movement which goes from the precursor to the Lord coming into his Temple.

John the Baptist

Malachi 3:1-3	*Luke 1-2*
Behold, I send my messenger to prepare the way before me.	[The sending of John the Baptist the precursor, 1:15-17] He will go before him (1:16), You will go before the Lord (1:76).

Jesus in the Temple

And the Lord whom you *seek* will come into his *temple*,	When the parents brought in the child Jesus to the *temple* (2:27) Jesus the *Lord* (1:43; 2:11), *sought* him (2:44, 45)
But who can endure the *day* of his coming? He will *purify* the sons of Levi.	When the *day* came for *their purification* they brought him up to Jerusalem to present him to the Lord.

The schema is clear: in Malachi as in Luke, we pass from the messenger (John the Baptist) to the Lord, whose manifestation is the entry into the Temple. We shall see how Luke echoes—in a subtle but not ambiguous way—this eschatological purification.

Daniel 9:24

Even more startling is the parallel to Daniel 7-9 in Luke 1-2. This prophecy was located in the Temple and concerned the Temple, and it is the entrance of Jesus into the Temple (2:27) which is its fulfillment (cf. the repetition of the verb *to fulfill* in 2:21 and 22).

We have seen how the double announcement of Gabriel, the angel of messianic prophecy of the seventy weeks, was woven with allusions to this prophecy. These reminiscences come to fruition when Jesus enters the Temple: it is there that the initial announcement to Zechariah took place. It is there that Luke understands their fulfillment, the last links being the following:

Daniel 9:24	*Luke 1-2*
Seventy weeks	[The seventy weeks detailed by Luke below]:
are decreed concerning your people and your holy city,	They brought him up to Jerusalem (2:22) on the day
to atone for iniquity,	of *their* purification
to seal both vision	[no *vision* in 2:22-29]
and *prophet* and	[The *prophecy* of Simeon, sealed by his death, 2:26, 29].
	Jesus-Messiah
to *anoint*	[*anointed*, 1:32-35],
a most *holy* place.	"called *Holy*" (2:23).

The most astonishing concretization of Luke 1-2 is that of the seventy weeks. It might seem very subtle. But the successive time references of the infancy are structured with a coherent insistence which could not be ascribed to chance.

The principal moments of this chronology are brought out in a refrain which reappears four times in its most complete form:

> And at the end of these *days* (*hōs eplēsthēsan ai hēmerai*, 1:23; 2:5, 21, cf. 1:57).

The word *day* is used with unusual frequency: twenty times in Luke 1-2, partly because of this refrain. The verb *pimplēmi*, often weakened and softened by translators, tends to mean the eschatological fulfillment of the seventy weeks.

The refrain marks, first of all, the point of departure in the sanctuary where Zechariah is celebrating: when his *days* of Temple service were fulfilled (1:23), with the double echo: "Until the *day* that these things come to pass" (1:20) and "After these *days*, Elizabeth conceived" (1:24).

This is followed by the insistent mention of the six months between the conception of Elizabeth and that of Mary: "in the *sixth month*"

(1:26, the first words of the annunciation narrative); "Elizabeth, your cousin, is in her *sixth month*" (1:36, cf. the introductory mention of the five months Elizabeth was in seclusion, 1:25). The fulfillment refrain reappears nine months later for the birth of Jesus. "And while they were there, the *time* came for her to be delivered" (2:6).

Finally the refrain returns twice more, in two successive verses, to mark the stages of the seventy weeks (emphatic repetition). "When the eight *days* were *fulfilled* for his circumcision" (2:21) and "When the *days* were *fulfilled* for their purification" (2:22).

These 8 + 33 days, prescribed by Leviticus 12, were well known as the usual ritual, the 8th day being the first of the 33. The total, including the 9 months of the pregnancy[90] and the 40 days thus emphasized by Luke give:

6 x 30 = 180: from the announcement in the Temple to the annunciation
9 x 30 = 270: from the annunciation to Christmas
+40: from Christmas to the presentation
Total: 490 = 70 x 7 = 70 weeks.

The point of departure of the "days," to which Luke insistently returns, is identical in Daniel 9:21-24; it is the same Gabriel (Dn 9:21; Lk 1:19) who appears, at the same hour of oblation (Dn 9:21; Lk 1:19), in a prayer situation (Dn 9:21; Lk 1:13), to speak of the 70 weeks with the same eschatological and messianic meaning.

The point of arrival is topographically the same: Jerusalem (Dn 9:7, 12, 16, 25) and the Temple (Dn 9:27; cf. 9:24). They are explicitly named in Luke 2 only when Jesus enters the Temple (2:22 and 27).

But what could such a parallel mean? It is a matter of transposition or concretization, according to the midrashic interpretation prevalent at the time.

The 70 weeks are not applied to the same point. The meaning in Daniel 9:24 is in some way obscure and remains subject to discussion. What seems clear here is this:

7 weeks: from the return from exile to the reconstruction of the Temple

62 weeks: from the reconstruction to the death of Onias (the high priest, therefore anointed = messiah in Hebrew)
½ week of persecution
½ week until the end
70 weeks total.

Luke locates the 70 weeks in the time which separates Zechariah's announcement and Jesus' entrance into the Temple in Jerusalem, the same place which Luke is careful to name explicitly only when Jesus gets there.

Moreover, he seems to transfer to the Christ Messiah (hence anointed and designated as Holy and, in a sense, suggesting transcendence) the anointing of the "Holy of Holies" which Daniel 9:28 attributes to the Temple. We should not be surprised by this transposition. Daniel himself gave an example of it. He took as his point of departure the 70 years of Jeremiah (25:11-12; 29:10) which he used explicitly. But Jeremiah placed the fall of Babylon and the deliverance of Israel *after the fall of Jerusalem*, at the end of a symbolic period of 70 years (namely 10 weeks of years, the Sabbath cycle). Daniel uses this number as a symbolic light on the present crisis, in the direction of the messianic solution: the arrival of the Son of man and purification of the Temple, and, consequently, of the people. He transforms the 70 years of Jeremiah into 70 weeks of years. Luke (or his source) in his turn transposed it according to the symbolic process of midrashic meditation, by which Luke 1-2 defines the movement of his Gospel.

Where the other evangelists use Daniel 9 (a prophecy which holds a prominent place in the NT), they also transform its literal meaning. The computation of Luke and his theology are clearer and more explicit than Daniel's: the prophet characterizes the coming of the Messiah by a mysterious number of 70 weeks, about which there is still much dispute and great haziness. But 70 weeks was precisely the time separating the first announcement of Gabriel to Zechariah in the Temple (1:10-11) from the coming of Jesus to that same Temple. That place was very dear to the primitive Judeo-Christian community in Jerusalem, "continually in the temple" (Acts 2:46; cf. Lk 24:53); still more so when the persecutions forced them to leave the Temple.

Luke's "methodology" may seem strange to us today, but it fit in perfectly with the cultural milieu of his time. Such a computation is not unique in the NT. At the beginning of his Gospel, John 1-2, so closely related to Luke 1-2,[91] also calculates the days of the first week of Christ's ministry (Jn 1:29, 35, 43; 2:1) to characterize the miracle of Cana as Pentecost according to the analysis of A. Serra (1977, 182-215). Mention of the third day (Jn 2:1) belongs to the symbolism of Pentecost which was at that time the feast of the Covenant. Significantly, Luke adopts the same schema in Acts 10:9, 23, 24, 40, 44 to indicate that the baptism of Cornelius the centurion was a pentecost. The identity of these formulas is amazing, in spite of some subtleties in their application.

John 1:29-2:12	*Acts 10:8-38*
1:29: The next day (*tē epaurion*)	10:9: The next day (*tē epaurion*)
1:35: The next day	10:23: The next day
1:43: The next day	10:24: The next day
2:1: on the third day	10:40: The third day
2:12:They stayed for a few days (*ou pollas hēmeras*)	10:48: Peter stays for a few days (*hēmeras tinas*)[92]

Luke attaches a particular importance to the prophecy of Daniel 9.[93] He shows an attraction for the number seven[94] particularly to qualify duration. In the infancy narrative he mentions the seven years of widowhood of Anna and her eighty-four years (7 x 12, the number of nations multiplied by the number of Israel, the number twelve returning for the twelve years of Jesus in 2:41).

We should not forget the symbolic value attributed to numbers in that civilization: its *gematry*. In our times, their exclusively quantitative and mechanical valuation has weakened the symbolic dimension.

In short, Luke transposes this prophecy of Daniel, as do Matthew 1-2 and the other authors of the NT. He applies the 70 weeks to the time from the inaugural oracle of Gabriel in the Temple to the coming of Jesus into that same Temple (not without a tendency to identify Christ and the Temple, as Jn 2:21 does explicitly). What is important for him is the *fulfillment* of this prophecy, noted in the refrain

(2:21-22), shown by the first conjunction of Christ the Lord (2:11) with the Temple, a relation which will be made clear in the final episode of Luke 1-2: the finding.

2. FULFILLMENT OF THE ANNUNCIATION TO MARY 1:32-35

In Luke 1:32 and 35, the annunciation of Gabriel to Mary attributed two names to Christ: first of all, the human name, "You will call him. . . *Jesus*" (1:31), then his divine name, "He will be called *Holy one, Son of God.*" The context (referring to Ex 40:35) gives these two names a transcendent reference. The presentation is "the fulfillment" (cf. 2:21-22 and 39) of this twofold prediction announced by the angel Gabriel, messenger of God.

The Human Name of Jesus

Luke 1:31	*Luke 2:21*
You shall *call* (*kaleseis*)	He was *called* [*eklēthē*, the same verb as *kaleō*]
his *name Jesus*	*Jesus* [Savior], the *name* given [literally: called *klēthen*, repetition of the verb *kaleō*] by the angel before he was
You will *conceive* (*sullēmpsē*) *in* your *womb* (*en gastri*).	*conceived* (*sullēmphethēnai*) *in* the *womb* (*en koilia*).

The points of contact in terminology and themes between the annunciation and the fulfillment are very marked:
—The attribution of the name of *Jesus*, with the redundant usage of the verb *kaleō* (2:21).
—Reference to the *angel* who prescribed it.
—The redundant "conceived in the womb" in 1:31 is the same as in 2:21. We say redundant, because *syllambanō* by itself was sufficient to convey the notion of conception, as it does with Elizabeth (1:24 and

36). The addition *en koilia* (2:21) seems to serve as a means of bringing the prophecy of Zephaniah 3:15 to bear on the present event, as was already done in the annunciation message: "You will conceive in your womb" (*en gastri*: 1:31). This otiose and surprising expression echoes literally and materially the *beqirbek* of Zephaniah 3:15. In using it Luke tempers it somewhat by using the more obvious, elegant, and specific Greek word to mean the maternal womb: *en koilia* (see above, ftnt. 74).

In 2:23 the same verb *kaleō* returns to attribute the name *Holy* to Christ, also foretold by the angel, but fulfilled (manifested) in the Temple, through the agency of the Law. One should not forget the context of the shekinah which gives its importance to the name *Holy* in 1:35.

Luke 1:35	*Luke 2:23*
The angel said to her:	They brought him . . . to present him to the Lord (as it is written in the Law of the Lord, "Every male that opens the womb
[He] will be called *Holy* (*hagion klēthēsetai*)	shall be called *holy*" (*hagion klēthēsetai*, Ex 13:1) for the Lord.

This comparison will seem more tenuous because it is limited to two words: "called holy." Luke transposes the expression in Exodus 13:1 "he will be *consecrated*" to "he will be *called holy*."

> Consecrate (sanctify) to me all the first-born;[95] whatever is the first to open the womb among the people of Israel both of man and of beast, is mine (Ex 13:1).

The translation in 2:23 evidently attempts to conform the OT text to the words of Gabriel in 1:35 in order to attribute to Christ a divine name.

In the progression of 2:21-24, on the "eighth day" Christ receives the name of Jesus (that is *Savior*, cf. 2:11), prescribed by the angel, and the transcendent name *Holy*, specific designation of God in the OT.[96]

This double name comes, not only from the oracle of Gabriel, but from a previous fulfillment contained in the oracle of the angels at the birth of Jesus (2:11):

> For to you is born this day a *Savior* [= translation of the human name of Jesus], who is Christ the *Lord* [the latter title has a transcendent significance in this context].

According to Luke, these two oracles find their fulfillment in the two rites: that of circumcision (2:21), where the child receives his name, and that of presentation in the Temple, at the end of the seventy week period, where the Law of the Lord attests typologically that this child is the Lord of the Temple he enters. It is the Temple that is defined by his coming rather than he by the Temple.

3. FULFILLMENT OF THE LAW

Luke considers the attribution to Christ of the two names announced from above as fulfillment of the Law. The word "law" is repeated in each of the three verses: 2:22, 23, 24:

> And when the time came for their purification according to *the law of Moses*, they brought him up to Jerusalem to present him to the Lord (as it is written in the *law of the Lord* [Ex 13:1], "Every male that opens the womb shall be called holy to the Lord") and to offer a sacrifice according to what is said in the *law of the Lord* (Lv 12:1-8), "a pair of turtledoves, or two young pigeons" (2:2-24).

This text seems to be legalistic in the extreme. It not only names the Law three times, but it cites it twice. These are the only two explicit citations from the OT found in Luke 1-2 (Exodus 13:1, and Leviticus 12:8) from which he takes the words beginning with verse 21. It would, therefore, seem that Luke is going to relate materially the "fulfillment" of the prescribed rites for the mother and the first-born. But here the narrative deviates, because it describes something different from the ritual fulfillment of the Law. It is so disconcerting that most exegetes see an inaccuracy or blunder at this point. In fact, the text does seem to accumulate anomalies. The first sentence seems absurd.

"When the time came for *their* purification," Luke begins. To whom is this plural referring: *their* (dropped in many translations, but inescapable in the original Greek)? According to the Law of Moses, to which this verse refers, the purification concerns the *mother only*:

> She shall be unclean seven days; as at the time of her menstruation, she shall be unclean. And *on the eighth day* the flesh of his foreskin shall be *circumcised*. Then she shall continue for thirty-three days in the blood of her purifying; she shall not touch any hallowed thing, nor come into the sanctuary, until the days of her purifying are completed. . . And when the days of *purifying* are completed, whether for a son or for a daughter, she shall bring to the priest at the door of the tent of meeting a lamb a year old for a burnt offering, and a young pigeon or a turtledove for a *sin offering* and make atonement for her; then she shall be clean from the flow of her blood. This is the law for her who bears a child, either male or female. And if she cannot afford a lamb, then she shall take *two turtledoves* or *two young pigeons*, one for a burnt offering and the other for a *sin offering*; and the priest shall make atonement for her, and she shall be clean (Lv 12:2-8).

Luke avoided association of the Virgin with this purification and sacrificial offering. He turns the rite away from the mother, by applying it to a plural subject; neither Mary nor the purification are mentioned subsequently: the Law seems to be referred to only in relation to the presentation (2:22) and consecration of the child (2:23; cf. 2:27).

To avoid this strange plural (their purification), the *Codex Bezae* (prolific in unusual variants) reads the possessive in the singular. The exegetes, puzzled by the same difficulty, have attempted to adopt this reading. Unfortunately for this hypothesis the manuscript reading has this possessive, not in the feminine, but in the masculine: *autou*.

Could it be the purification of *Jesus* then? This solution would be most alien to the Jewish Law, to the NT and to the Christology of Luke himself. Lagrange inclines to this reading, by virtue of the fact that Jesus appears to be the sole subject of the ceremony described in 2:22-24. Luke does use a rather ambiguous word (*katharismos*). But purification of a new-born child had no foundation in the Law, and would not fit the context, as Jesus is presented in a purely sacred sense beginning with 1:35.[97] The obvious grammatical hypothesis, working from the context, would be to connect this plural possessive to the parents of Jesus, because it was obviously they who "brought him up to Jerusalem to present him to the Lord" (2:22). But this solution does not fit any biblical context. Purification refers to the blood of the mother. The father has nothing to do with it. Joseph could not be involved in it under any circumstance.

This first anomaly is related to others which we will have to examine in order to discover to whom the expression "*their* purification" refers.

The second anomaly is that the parents, whose role is important since they take the child to Jerusalem, are not explicitly named. Joseph's name disappears after 2:16 and Mary's after 2:19. The generic expression "parents" will only reappear much later, at 2:27. Following the last mention of Mary in 2:19, the shepherds become the grammatical subject of verse 20. But they seem to have left the scene in verse 21. The act of circumcising could at any rate not be attributed to them. Luke omits here mention of any human subject. He expresses the circumcision in the passive, without referring it to anyone (in marked contrast to 1:59-62 where parents and neighbors are in turn actively present for the circumcision and naming of John the Baptist). Mary, however, should have been named in 2:21, since it is to her alone that Gabriel had said "*You* shall call his name Jesus" (1:31). It is surprising that Luke does not take up this reference, since he takes up all the others very literally: "[The child] was called Jesus, the name given by the angel before he was conceived in the womb" (2:21). Mary's role is completely hidden.

The third anomaly: Mary remains hidden in the following verse (2:22), the one in which the purification is mentioned, which should, according to the terms of "the Law" (Lv 12:3 and 8), concern her alone. This hiddenness is the counterpart of the curious transfer which would attribute the purification to a plural subject.

There is more: the sacrifice of purification should be offered "for the sin" of the mother, according to the Law as cited in 2:24, an offering of "two turtledoves or two young pigeons." But Mary is completely absent from the context, as is also reference to sin. This sacrifice does not seem to concern her person, but rather Jesus presented in the

Temple, the sole object of the previous context, 2:22b and 23.

The unsuspecting reader would think that this sacrifice was being offered for the child on the occasion of the *presentation*, which quickly came to take the place of any notion of a purification (2:22b), and then came to represent the consecration of Jesus as the Holy One (2:23).[98]

The candid reader does indeed unwittingly agree with Luke's thought. The evangelist transferred the purification sacrifice to the child, turning the sacrifice of "two turtledoves or two young pigeons" to another intention, the rite of the Nazirite's consecration to God, according to Numbers 6:10: "On the eighth day he shall bring two turtledoves or two young pigeons to the priest." After having followed Leviticus 12 closely (the purification text which prescribed this sacrifice for the sin of the mother), Luke (and undoubtedly his source before him) relates the offering of the two turtledoves or pigeons to the consecration of Jesus called *Holy* (2:23) in a typological and transcendent sense which goes beyond the letter of the Law.[99]

At least one point is clear: the presentation of Jesus seems to absorb all the rest. But since it is said with such solemnity that this rite is meant to fulfill the Law of the Lord, one would expect to find a strict and literal application of it. However, on this issue, the anomalies continue.

The presentation rite of the first-born, which is given a great deal of emphasis, "to present him to the Lord, as it is written in the Law of the Lord" (2:22), is, actually, foreign to the Law. It has been assumed that this may have been a pious custom for which a singular example could be adduced: the presentation of Samuel in the Temple of Shiloh (1 Sm 1:19-28). Burrows tended to think that Luke 2 was patterned after this narrative, likening Jesus to Samuel. But Samuel, once presented in the Temple, scarcely weaned, is left there to stay, while Jesus returns to Nazareth (2:39 and 51). The analogy is, therefore, remote and contrasting.

Luke, who created for Jesus this unknown rite of the presentation, is silent on the well-known rite of the ransom of the first-born (Nm 18:15; cf Ex 13:13; 34:20; Lv 27:11-12, 27). It is, however, about this rite that the insistent mention of the Law reminds us, and it could be understood in the sense of the consecration implied in 2:23. But according to the Law, this ransom of the first-born did not take place on the fortieth day (that of the purification of the mother, indicated in 2:22) but "in the month of the birth."

Finally, this rite included ransoming the first-born for "five silver shekels," according to Numbers 18:16.

So, why place the rite pertaining to the child on the day assigned to the purification of the mother? Why is there no mention of the five silver shekels? And why refer to the child the oblation which the Law prescribed for the mother?

Luke is so well aware of what he is doing that before concluding he will not forget to tell us about ransom or *redemption* (*lutrōsis*). But it is the redemption of Jerusalem (2:38, analogous to the redemption of the people in 1:68). This transference invites the consideration that he transfers correlatively the purification of 2:22 to Jerusalem, named for the first time in this same verse. The recurrence of Jerusalem in the first and last verse of this scene (2:22 and 38) confirms the importance of this word and of the transposition in which the meaning of this narrative lies. These transfers of meaning may surprise a modern mind. The constant process of typology was familiar in the Judeo-Christian milieu of the time.

We can marvel that 2:24 uses a commonplace ritual prescription, pertaining to every first-born male, to signify the transcendent name *Holy* attributed to Jesus by Gabriel's oracle (1:35). Is not this singular qualification of Christ too far removed from this ordinary rite?

Such transpositions of meaning are common throughout the NT. Let us take an example related to 2:23, which also deals with sacrificial *ritual typology*, an example no less bold, but more familiar to all: John 19:36. The evangelist recalls the familiar action of soldiers proceeding to the breaking of the shin-bones of the crucified, to speed up their death (because they could survive longer if, held up by their legs, they continue to breathe). Having come to Jesus, he writes, "They did not break his legs" (Jn 19:33). And he solemnly comments, "For these things took place that the Scripture might be fulfilled,[100] 'Not a bone of him shall be broken' " (Jn 19:36).

The Law cited prescribed that Jewish families not break the bones...of the paschal lamb. Literally that does not concern either

Roman soldiers or Jesus. But for the evangelist, the meaning of the text is not only literal (the meaning of the words), it is typological (the meaning of the realities). It is Jesus who gives full meaning, in retrospect, to the Law and to the prophets.[101] The soldiers did not break his bones, because Jesus was "already dead" (Jn 19:33). John recognizes in this the fulfillment of the Law relative to the ritual paschal victim. This parallel then identifies Jesus the Redeemer with the paschal lamb. Such a procedure depends on midrashic concretizations. Christ is the eschatological fulfillment of Scripture and of history. He gives them a new dimension and importance.

According to the same method of concretization, the fact that the first-born are considered *holy* (according to Ex 13:1) takes on a special typological value. For Luke 2:7, he is "*the first-born*" *par excellence,* according to the theology of the NT.[102]

So Christ the Lord, entering the Temple as "light of the nations and glory of Israel" (2:32), gives the Law its transcendent fulfillment. According to this same typology, the *redemption* of the first-born, devoid of meaning if applied to this Redeemer and Savior, is transferred to Jerusalem in 2:38; the *purification* (2:22), which does not pertain to the Virgin, is equally transferred to the people. Luke sees here the fulfillment of the prophecy of Malachi 3 concerning the eschatological entrance of the Lord into his Temple: "He will purify the sons of Levi." But Luke is not content with the sons of Levi. The context refers to the purification of all the people. This exegesis is not new. It had been considered by Lagrange,[103] who dismissed it, saying that if Luke was referring to the Jews he would have mentioned them explicitly as John 2:6 does, when dealing with a similar theological intent in relation to the water jars at Cana.

The identification of the Jews as those to whom the purification in 2:22 applies, must, however, be maintained for the following reasons:

—The determining qualification ("for the purification *of the Jews*") found in John 2:6 is omitted in other cases. Matthew 4:23 speaks of "*their* synagogues," meaning "the synagogues of the Jews," while the immediate context does not mention them. The case is not an isolated one. Yet in Matthew 4:23 the context in the preceding scene is misleading, since it speaks first of the boat, then of the father of the sons of Zebedee, then of Galilee (cf. Mk 1:39 and Lk 4:44, who specifies "the synagogues of Judea"). "Their synagogues" is found in varying degrees of ambiguity in Matthew 9:35; 10:17; 13:54, while this possessive is not to be found in the two other synoptics.

—The purification of the people and of the Temple is postulated by both OT texts that lie behind Luke 1-2: Daniel 9:24 and Malachi 3. The theme of the purification is consistent with Malachi 3.[104] We find it again under several forms in John 1-2, which has many similarities with Luke 1-2, undoubtedly because these chapters come from the same Judeo-Christian and Johannine tradition. Thus we find "the purification of the Jews" in the Cana scene (Jn 2:6 and Lk 2:22), and also at the time of the cleansing of the Temple, which has the same purpose (Jn 2:14-21).

—In the verse where he speaks of "their purification," Luke names the city of Jerusalem under the form of *Hierosolyma*, a name which refers to the profane city, while *Hierousalem*, the cultic sacred name, which refers to the holy city, is used subsequently: five times in Luke 2:25, 38, 41, 43, and 45, where the reference is no longer to this purification but to the coming of the Lord.[105]

—The purification of Jerusalem, suggested in the first verse of the presentation narrative (2:22), matches the "redemption of Jerusalem" in the last verse, thus forming an inclusion. The transfer and the meaning complement one another.

4. FULFILLMENTS OF THE SPIRIT

From the Law to the Prophets

The typological fulfillment of the Law (with its concretizations and transfers) is followed by the fulfillment realized by the Spirit. The shift is magnificent and follows a familiar formula in Luke (after the Law, the Spirit, or more precisely stated, after the Law, the prophets) precisely at a point where it is a matter of showing that the Law and the prophets foretold the passion of Christ.[106] This prophetic fulfillment according to the Spirit first takes the form of a double prediction by Simeon (2:29-32; 34-35), then of an evangelization similar to that of the shepherds (2:10, 18, 20) on the part of the prophetess Anna.

First Prophecy: Light and Glory

The first prediction of Simeon, the canticle Nunc Dimittis (2:29-32), presents a very marked eschatological feature underscored by the return of the word "seeing" in reference to three terms:

—seeing death (2:26);
—seeing the Lord's anointed (2:26);
—seeing salvation (2:30).

The equivalence between "seeing Christ" and "seeing death" echoes the OT conviction: one cannot see God and live.

> You cannot see my face; for man shall not see me and live . . . while my glory passes by . . . , I will cover you with my hand and you shall see my back (Ex 33:20, 22,23).

As Moses saw the *glory* of God, from behind, so Simeon sees this glory (2:32) in the humility of the childhood assumed by Christ the Lord (cf. 2:11). He is going to see death because he saw the *glory of God* (2:32), his salvation (2:30). Such is the underlying symbolism. And so Simeon asks the Lord to liberate him (literally "to unbind" him) from life. He can see death since he saw this Christ who is salvation, light, and glory. Those are the three titles he gives him in the Nunc Dimittis:

> Lord, now lettest thou thy servant depart in peace, according to thy word; for mine eyes have seen thy *salvation* (*sōtērion*) which thou hast prepared in the presence of all peoples, a *light for revelation* to the Gentiles, and for *glory* to thy people Israel (2:29-32).

These three titles are a commentary on the three names given to him in the preceding text.

1. *Salvation* carries the same meaning as the human name of Jesus (2:21), that is *Savior* (cf. 2:11; 1:47, 69, an etymological allusion) but in an abstract form which has superlative and absolute value: your salvation.

The following two titles (2:32) are rather a commentary on the transcendent name *Holy*, proclaimed in 1:35 and 2:23 (*hagion klēthēsetai*).

2. *Light* is a title of God,[107] and an attribute of the divine. In Deutero-Isaiah, from which the canticle of Simeon takes its inspiration, God says: "A law will go forth from me, and my justice for a light to the peoples" (Is 51:4). It is to the mysterious Servant that he says, "I have given you as a covenant to the people, a light to the nations" (Is 42:6), an expression that Simeon applied to Jesus. In this verse there seems to be an identification of Jesus with the Servant. The context in Isaiah does not of itself imply a transcendent meaning. What does give rise to it (as a later development) is the reference here to Malachi 3:1, which leads to a consideration of Christ as Lord, as he makes his eschatological entrance into the Temple.

3. *Glory* of your people Israel (2:32) poses a similar problem. "Glory" points more specifically to God himself, and that is the case in 2:9 but Deutero-Isaiah (46:13; 49:3 and 44:23), the source of the canticle of Simeon, should invite caution. However, is not celebrating the eschatological glory of Israel tantamount to celebrating the actual glory of God, shining in his people, as well as in the figure of the Ark of the Covenant, according to the prophecy of Isaiah? It is to God alone that the word "glory," presented so absolutely, appropriately belongs. But here too the expression is ambiguous, and the ambiguity is only lifted by the convergences in the context.

The canticle thus recognizes the twofold designation of Christ, the one according to his human name, which signifies salvation, the other according to his divine name, which identifies him as Lord, and *Holy*.

Second Prophecy: The Shadow of the Passion

The surprise of the father and the mother underscores the importance of this revelation: its theophanic character. It exceeds the humble situation of the tiny child (*to paidion* in 2:27f.).

Mary, upon whom the Spirit first descended (1:35), and who prophesied in 1:46-55, returns to the condition of ordinary and obscure faith and now it is Simeon, in the role of a prophet, who recognizes and celebrates the Christ. We are still in the dynamic of the future, but now we are progressing in a new direction.

The luminous prophecy which identifies Jesus with the glory of God (2:32) gives way to a sorrowful prophecy addressed to Mary alone, who will be involved in this human sorrow.

> Behold, this child is set for the fall and rising of many in Israel, and for a sign that is spoken against (and a sword will pierce through your own soul also), that thoughts out of many hearts may be revealed (2:34-35).

Exegetes in general acknowledge that this is one of the most difficult passages of the the third Gospel. True prophecies always remain mysterious and hidden. Two main interpretations divide the exegetes.

For P. Benoit, the sword of sorrow symbolizes the effects of the division of the people (already mentioned in the first verse), with Mary understood as the Daughter of Zion, the personification of the people Israel. This interpretation would draw on Ezekiel 14:17: "A sword will go through the land."

Feuillet, without completely dismissing this interpretation, objects that the sorrow of the Daughter of Zion "cannot be the after-effect of the divine judgment which will strike the chosen people," but that it is referred to the sorrow of Christ himself, who is at the center of the scene and with whom it is more clearly associated. The reference of 2:35 would be to Zechariah 12:10 as taken up by John in 19:37, "They shall look on him whom they have pierced."

Benoit objects that this refers to the piercing of Christ and not Mary. We must answer, with Feuillet, that both must be identified and that John 19:25-27, 34 and Luke 2:35 refer to a common tradition of the Judeo-Christian community of Jerusalem in which John and Mary lived (cf. Acts 1:14), and that the piercing of Christ morally affected his mother.

We shall return to the linking (the program) in this prophecy in the semiotic section (below, pp. 193-207).

Following the dynamic of Luke 1-2, let us underscore the contrast between the euphoric expressions of the first prophecy (light, glory) and the dysphoric expressions of this one: downfall, contradiction, piercing (*dieleusetai* in Lk 2:35; cf. Ez 14:17) by a sword. This is not to put the two main interpretations in opposition because the accent is on the division of the people (first and last stich); but the center of this composition in chiastic form (second and third stichs) refers, in a parallel fashion, to the contradiction of Christ, to the passion, which concerns his mother also, but refers primarily to himself.[108]

A decisive exegetical argument suggests that we retain this identification of Simeon's sword and the passion. The evangelist (who will not speak again of Mary during the passion[109]) expresses the very deep sorrow that she feels in the scene which follows the presentation, when for three days she searches for Jesus in Jerusalem at the time of the Passover. In 2:48, she expresses her anxiety by a very emotionally charged word, the verb *odynaomai*, which Luke will take up again to describe the tortures of the rich man in hell (16:24). The use of this strong word, seemingly surprising when used in the instance of a child momentarily lost and happily found, becomes easier to understand if we study the scene of the finding of Jesus in the Temple as a prefiguration of the passion.

In conclusion, the presentation in the Temple concerns the dynamic of Luke 1-2 for the following reasons:

It is the fulfillment of the oracle of Gabriel: Jesus is qualified by the double name announced by the angel, the human name, *Jesus* (1:35; 2:23) and the divine attribute, holy. It is the fulfillment of eschatology —the coming of the Lord to his Temple, according to Malachi 3, together with the purification of the Temple and the people. It is the time of an eschatological pentecost of which Simeon, moved by the Spirit (2:23-25), and Anna, designated as "prophetess," are the type and the sign.[110] Simeon and Anna recognize his transcendent titles which Simeon proclaims, and the future of his mission, under the mysterious sign of contradiction and the sword (2:34-35).

3. The Finding: Typological Prefiguration of the Passion

The episode of the finding (2:41-52) emphasizes the double theme of glory and of the cross.

At the end of the Jerusalem pilgrimage, the child Jesus, twelve years of age, remains in the city, unknown to his parents. They search for him for three days, with great anguish (2:48); at last they find him in the Temple. To the question of Mary, his mother, "Why have you treated us so?" Jesus, the child, answers in a majestic tone of voice,

"How is it that you sought me? Did you not know that I must be in my Father's house?" (in the Temple, 2:49).

It would seem, therefore, that he is going to stay there and let his parents return to Nazareth alone. However, he "went down" with them and would be obedient to them (2:51). Luke relates the episode using the themes and vocabulary which he will use again in chapters 23 and 24 on the passion and Resurrection. This statement of Jesus has a triple function and a triple meaning:

—It expresses consciousness of being Son of the heavenly Father—not of Joseph.

—It implies a reference to the passion (as we shall presently see).

—It expresses the necessity of a return to the Father, which is the end and purpose of his life (in progress since the preceding episode). Here the dynamic of Luke 1-2 looks ahead to the more distant future.

This is not the place to prepare a detailed exegesis of the finding, to which we have already dedicated a book (*Jésus au Temple*) and whose remarkable development we will analyze further in the semiotic section. Here let us examine the importance of this episode for the dynamic of Luke. We will do it in summary fashion, by explaining Luke's enigmatic sentence in 2:50 concerning the impact of that first word on the parents of Jesus: "They did not understand."

What the Parents "Did Not Understand" (2:50)

What is it that Jesus' parents did not understand? Could it have been the fact that Jesus calls himself "Son of God"? No, because Mary, who asks the question, had received an explicit revelation concerning this, according to 1:32 and 35. It would be senseless to suppose a contradiction of this proportion in an author as coherent as Luke. [111]

Nor is it a question of giving a psychological response. The stylized literary genre of the Gospels does not permit this. In it a few objective and meaningful traits are given, not the endless rambling of emotions, as in a novel. The psychologist is doomed to stray more or less from the objectivity of the text.

The narrative presents an enigma which the parents did not instantly understand; it offers data for its solution only in the long run, thus leaving room for the meditation of the reader as for that of Mary herself (2:51).

The initial superficial evidence is that Jesus' parents did not understand why he "did that" to them. They should not have searched for him, he says. They should have understood that he had to be "in his Father's house." On this level, the answer is easy. If the narrative stopped there, it could be explained by saying that Jesus confirms here the message of the annunciation: he is the Son of the Most High (1:32), "Son of God" (1:35). Joseph is not his biological father. He recalls the mystery of his origin and remains aloof (1:28-37).

Some authors stop there, underscoring the performance of Jesus at age twelve, the age of bar mitzvah.[112] Though the setting appears to be negative (his parents are not informed, 2:43, the separation is painful to them, 2:48), here Jesus manifests his intelligence (2:46), his future quality as a teacher (*didaskalos*), and his consciousness of his divine sonship and his mission.

But this divine sonship is something Mary had understood from the beginning, according to 1:32-38. So what is it she did not understand? The text reveals three correlative areas of incomprehension.

a. Ambiguity concerning Jesus' father (Joseph or God?)

This is contained in the words of 2:47-48. In her question, Mary mentions the father of Jesus. It concerns the adoptive earthly father, Joseph, who is with her: "*Your father* and I have been looking for you."

Jesus answers by taking up this word and referring it to another father: "Did you not know that I must be in *My* Father's house?"[113]

This transposition of the same word with the same possessive adjective, by the same son, creates a perfectly misleading ambiguity. Familiarity with the text smooths over the difficulties for us. The Gospels are full of word-transfers which are not "plays on words."[114] They have the specific function of a symbol, that of raising the mind from the material to the spiritual plane, from the visible sign to the invisible and profound reality. That cannot happen without paradox or ambiguity.

Sometimes Jesus takes his cue from daily life. When the apostles become worried that they are short of bread for the meal (Mt 16:6, 11, 12), he summons them saying, "Beware of the leaven of the Pharisees and Sadducees." He chooses this word, suggested by their hunger, as the starting point, to teach about the deviations which threaten the clerics and doctors of yesterday and of today.

To the sons of Zebedee, who request the first two places in his kingdom, on his right and on his left, he asks, "Can you drink the cup?" They answer, not comprehending, "We can," because they are thinking of the royal cup of an enthronement banquet. But Jesus is speaking about the cup of his passion (Mk 10:35-44; Mt 20:20-23).

This stylistic device is particularly common in the fourth Gospel. In John 2:19 (a Temple scene, related to 2:41-52), Jesus says, "Destroy this temple. . . " But he is speaking of his body, which will be destroyed by the passion (Jn 2:21). The transfer of meaning is the same as in Luke 2:48-50, although with different modalities. The listeners "will understand" only after the Resurrection (cf. 2:50).

There are three similar transpositions of meaning in Jesus' dialogue with the Samaritan woman at Jacob's well, in the Gospel of John:

—The living water which he proposes (4:10-13) is not the water from the well (4:12) but from the Holy Spirit (4:14; 7:38-39).

—The food which he has (4:32) is not the material food that the disciples "bought in town" (4:8) nor that which others could have brought him: "My food is to do the will of my Father" (4:32).

—The ambiguity continues on the level of nourishment (4:35-37). Jesus invites his disciples to look at the fields already "white for the harvest" (4:35), but he is speaking of the spiritual harvest of the kingdom.

The same paradox comes to play, in the form of misunderstanding, all throughout the discourse on the bread of life. After the multiplication of the loaves of bread, Jesus speaks to the crowds of another bread. It is himself. He is the "bread which came down from heaven" (6:41, 51, 58). They reject what seems to them a double absurdity. He did not come down from heaven, he is the son of Joseph (6:42); and how would they be able to eat his flesh (6:52)? This misunderstanding is the key to the whole dialogue. It is also the constant key in the parables, that the spiritual teaching goes counter to all likelihood. For example, the master of the house praises the steward who robs him (Lk 16:8). Returning at night, the master puts on his apron and serves the servants who were on watch to serve him (Lk 12:37). He gives the harvesters of the last hour as much as those of the first, and he pays them first (Mt 20:1-16).

This misleading procedure appears especially when Jesus speaks about his family. They warn him that "his mother and his brothers" are looking for him. He looks around at his disciples seated around him and says, "My mother and my brethren are those who hear the word of God and do it" (Mt 12:50; cf. Lk 8:21). He transfers the family titles to his disciples.

It is in this perspective that one should understand Christ's words condemning family relationships:

> If anyone comes to me and does not hate his own father and mother, he cannot be my disciple (Lk 14:26).
>
> For I have come to set a man against his father, and a daughter against her mother (Mt 10:35).
>
> I have not come to bring peace, but a sword (Mt 10:34; cf. Lk 12:51).
>
> (This sword makes us think of Simeon's prophecy, concerning the maternal anguish of Mary on Jesus' behalf, in 2:35.)

These themes shed light on the family episode of the finding which shows at the same time both the break (2:43-50) and the complementary duty, "Honor your father and your mother" (18:20; 2:51). The way in which Jesus refers us from the earthly father to the heavenly Father is only the first of the misunderstandings of the Gospel, always with the same function: testing and pedagogy. That is the most immediate reason for the parents' misunderstanding. Two other reasons are implied in the text when it is read in depth, but they go in other directions.

b. Apparent contradiction concerning the place where Jesus "must" be

The second area of incomprehension is the echo of the first on the topographical level. The misunderstanding does not concern just the father, but the place. Jesus justifies his action by saying, "I had to be in my Father's house."

Since it concerns his heavenly Father, it is, therefore, in the Temple that he must live, not in the house at Nazareth. One would think Jesus was going to stay in the Temple, like Samuel (1 Sm 2), or perhaps like Mary, as she is portrayed in the fabulous tales of the *Protoevangelion of James*; presented in the Holy of Holies, raised there by the ministry of angels.

But contrary to this indication, Jesus returns to Nazareth (2:51). This apparently contradictory return shows that the momentary gesture of Jesus has not an immediate meaning, but a *prophetic* one. His word concerns the future. His meaning could only be understood in time.

We should not be surprised at this contradiction. We find it again in the dialogue of Jesus with his brothers (the entire clan of blood relatives from Nazareth) in John 7. They admire his works (7:3), but do not believe in him (7:5). They invite him to go to Jerusalem to manifest himself to the world (7:3-4). Jesus clearly answers, "Go to the feast yourselves: I am not going up to this feast. . . ."

> But after his brethren had gone up to the feast, then he also went up, not publicly but in private (Jn 7:10).

His action contradicts his word and the contradiction seems radical. It is only apparent. Jesus does not go up as his brothers requested, in order that one may "see his works," that he may "manifest himself to the world" (7:3-4), and probably begin a political career. He goes up in a different way, not "to manifest himself" but "in private" (7:10).

In both texts there is a family break on the occasion of a festival (Lk 2:41; Jn 7:2, 8, 10) with a topographical contradiction between the word of Jesus and his action, but in the reverse order. In John 7, the issue is going up to Jerusalem for the festival; in Luke 2:48-50, it is going down to Nazareth after the festival; in John 7, he goes up in private, in Luke 2:46-48, he manifests himself openly to the admiration of the listeners, and goes down in submission to his parents. We are dealing therefore with analogies of structure and not of influence.

This second area of contradictions, rooted in the topography, no longer concerns the being of Jesus, his mysterious reference to the Father, but his actions and his mission.

c. Mysterious prefiguration of the passion and of the return to the Father

But there is a third area of incomprehension relative to a far distant future. The action of Jesus announces the return to the Father to be accomplished by his death (23:46). It is precisely this that Mary could not understand *ante factum* according to 2:50.

The "finding" narrative is woven with key words and themes which Luke will later use to describe the passion:

—It is the same place, highly symbolic: Jerusalem, named in 2:41, 43, and 45 (a significant trilogy), then in 23:7, 28; 24:13, 18, 33, 47, and 52.

—It is an ascent, signified by the verb *anabainō* (2:42 and 18:31) with the announcement of the passion (2:49; 18:32-34), and incomprehension (2:50; 10:34).

—It is the same time: Passover. This word, rare in the NT, does not appear between 2:41 and the six times it is used in chapter 22: 1, 7, 8, 11, 13, and 15. It is at the very time of the *feast*(2:41; 22:1).

The "must" (*dei*) which governs the response of the child Jesus, is the leitmotif through which he will announce or will explain his passion, assumed as the will of the Father.[115]

> The son of man must suffer many things, and be rejected by the elders. . . and be killed, and on the third day be raised (9:22).
> I must go on my way; for it cannot be that a prophet should perish away from Jerusalem (13:33).
> But first [the Son of Man] must suffer many things and be rejected by this generation (17:25).
> This scripture must be fulfilled in me: "And he was reckoned with transgressors" (22:37).
> The Son of man must be delivered into the hands of sinful men, and be crucified, and on the third day rise (24:7).
> Was it not necessary that the Christ should suffer these things and enter into his glory? (24:26).
> Everything written about me in the law of Moses and in the prophets and the psalms must be fulfilled. . .: It is written that the Christ should suffer and on the third day rise from the dead (24:44, 46).

In short, "must", in the mouth of Christ, signifies his passion in reference to the Scripture which announced it.

Jesus disappears for "three days" (2:46), which prefigure the "three days" of his death. The formula has symbolic value in the Gospel.[116]

The sorrow of the passion is represented by the prophetic sword of Simeon (2:35), and its first realization, by the anguish which Mary expresses in her use of the climactic word *odunōmenoi* (2:48).

The search of the parents parallels the search of the holy women at the tomb and, likewise, the respective reproaches are similar: Jesus answers his mother, "How is it that you sought me?" (2:49) and the angel answers the holy women, "Why do you seek the living among the dead?" (24:5).

The first word of the child Jesus and the last that he pronounces before his death express the same idea, the return to the Father:

> I had to be in my Father's house (2:49).
> Father, into your hands I commend my spirit (23:46).

These allusions to the passion had begun with the nativity narrative, according to the detailed analysis of Serra.[117] They were made explicit with the prophecy of the sword (2:34-35), as we saw.

The announcement of the passion, like the prophetic announcement of the child Jesus, provokes incomprehension. We find an echo of 2:50 after the second announcement of the passion.

> "The Son of man is to be delivered into the hands of men." But they did not understand this saying, and it was concealed from them, that they should not perceive it (9:44-45).

Likewise, after the third announcement:

> "We are going up to Jerusalem and everything that is written of the Son of man by the prophets will be accomplished. For he will be delivered to the Gentiles, and will be mocked and shamefully treated and spit upon; they will scourge him and kill him, and on the third day he will rise." But they understood none of these things; this saying was hid from them, and they did not grasp what was said (Lk 18:31-34; cf. Lk 24:25 and Mk 10:38, parallel Mt 20:22,24).

This parallel shows that the incomprehension does not have to be taken in a negative sense in Luke. It underscores, not the culpability of those who do not understand, but the difficulty of understanding: an advice that is directed to the readers. The evangelist explicitly states at times that the apostles still do not understand (Mt 15:16-17; 16:11-12); and John says positively that the disciples understand only later the hidden prediction of the passion made by Jesus under the symbol of the Temple (as in 2:49): "He spoke of the temple of his body" (Jn 2:21).

For Mary, the long-range understanding is indicated by means of the refrain which follows immediately after 2:50: "And his mother kept all these things (*rhēmata*) in her heart" (2:51).[118]

This positive refrain (an echo of 2:19) indicates that Mary's meditation in search of understanding continued up to the mature understanding yielded by the Gospel of Luke. It is an invitation to the reader so that he or she too may come to understand a difficult and long hidden mystery.

In short, the narrative of the finding prefigures the passion and the definitive return of Christ to the Father. These converging traits bear this out.

The two arrivals of Jesus to the Temple, which conclude the infancy Gospel, fulfill at the same time the eschatological prophecies of Malachi 3 and Daniel 9:24, the oracles of Gabriel (1:32-35) and the typology of the Law. However, these two scenes are not only a culmination, they prefigure the future of Christ not only in respect to his ministry, outlined by the scene in the Temple where Jesus appears already as teacher, but mainly the prophecy (2:34-35) and the typology (2:40-49) of his death and of his return to the Father. The dynamic of Luke 1-2 is not due only to the liveliness of the style of the narrative and the themes as analyzed at the beginning. Over and above these, it has a deep theological import.

We will observe that it does not draw to a close with the discreet glorification of the Temple, but rather with Jesus paradoxically going down to Nazareth to lead an obedient life (2:51), a hidden life from which he will not emerge until the age of thirty (3:23).

Conclusion

The dynamic of Luke 1-2, is manifested on the surface by a number of literary marks: oracular and prophetic predictions, aorists pointing to an already-realized future in the lyricism of the canticles, travels oriented toward Jerusalem, haste, joy, thanksgivings. This dynamic is, when we read it in depth, the messianic and eschatological thrust of these two chapters. What is happening there is, therefore, the fulfillment of the Law and of the prophets (cf. 2:22-28, *typological* fulfillment in the case of the Law, and *complete* fulfillment by way of unforeseen realization in the case of the prophets). This transition to the new order, characterized by the coming of a Messiah identified with God, is the occasion for a series of transfers which renew the literal sense of some OT texts:

—The purification of Mary (2:22), who does not need to be purified, is transferred to Jerusalem.

—The redemption of Jesus, who does not need to be redeemed, is transferred to Jerusalem.

—The sacrifice of the purification becomes the sacrifice of consecration, by a transfer from Leviticus 12 to Numbers 6:10.

To the realization of the OT types and prophecies are added new predictions which force us beyond the infancy to the future of Christ and salvation, including his passion (2:35, 41-49) and his return to the Father (2:49). This dynamic is, therefore, a theology of history, the fulfillment of which is given with Christ the Lord. From the time of his hidden childhood and even from his very origin, what Scripture announced finds its true meaning and reality. But it is not a static fulfillment. The infancy of Jesus, where the awaited reality is realized, prefigures and begins the final advent of salvation.

F. LITERARY GENRE

The identification of literary genre is one of the most important tasks of criticism because it enhances the evaluation of the text in terms of content, significance, and historicity. Such an identification has not been made for Luke 1-2.

Status Questionis

Formgeschichte (the study of the history of genre), launched by Dibelius (1919) and Bultmann (1922), seems to have particularly overlooked the infancy narratives of Luke 1-2 and Matthew 1-2. This systematic method, which consists in the dissection of the pericopes of Jesus' public life, faltered over the infancy narratives, so different are they from the rest of the Gospel. There one finds no miracles, no parables, no discourses. It was, therefore, a text which would not yield to this systematic method.

After H. Gressmann (1914),[119] Bultmann and Dibelius hastily catalogued Luke 1-2 and Matthew 1-2 in the category of "legend," which Bultmann defined as "elements of tradition which are not miracle stories in the proper sense of the term, and which are not historical, but rather religious and edifying."[120]

We see here the emergence of one of the presuppositions which have so severely hampered the attempts made towards developing a scientific exegesis: the postulate according to which what is "religious," edifying, of the order of faith, is unreal and must be explained in terms of fiction. This method, which may indeed be necessary in the case of certain pathological visionaries, has been applied to Christ whose Incarnation has renewed religious phenomena in the direction of faith, and restored the supernatural to the realm of lived experience.

At the opposite pole, P. Gächter, a staunch defender of historicity, dauntlessly explained Luke 1-2 as the result of many traditions, gathered successively from several sources.[121] This orientation may be correct, but Gächter's construction is artificial and contrived.

Attempts have been made to locate these narratives in relation to the known forms: Munoz Iglesias[122] has shown that the narratives find their models in the biblical forms, with no direct relationship to non-biblical literature. It is a "popular" story, according to Cerfaux,[123] an "infancy legend" according to A. G. Wright and others.[124]

But these vague formulas do not clearly indicate of themselves if we are dealing with historical narratives (like the earlier life of Paul in Acts 22:3 and 26), mythological ones (like the infancy of Hercules), or philosophical ones (like the infancy of Demosthenes and Alexander in *The Parallel Lives* by Plutarch).

To speak of midrash[125] is to remain equally vague, for midrash is not a literary genre, but a mode of exegesis. It is a shame that midrash has been misunderstood and wrongly defined in this way, because this method is typical of biblical and Christian thinking, that is, the definition of events in the light of Scripture and, as we have seen, the re-definition of Scripture in the light of Christ. Midrash is in fact turned around by the coming of Christ, inasmuch as in him Scripture is unexpectedly fulfilled and also yields a new and hidden meaning,[126] the meaning of words as well as their symbolic reality. Christ *is* the rock in the desert (1 Cor 10:4), the manna, the bread of life (Jn 6), the paschal lamb (Jn 19:36), the Temple (Jn 2:19), and the cornerstone (1 Pt 2:6). Mary *becomes* the Ark of the Covenant (Lk 1:35 and Ex 40:35; Lk 1:39-56 and 2 Sm 6) and the eschatological Daughter of Zion (Lk 1:28-32 and Zep 3).

The presuppositions of historical rationalism, stemming from Hegel, defined the literary genre of the infancy Gospels as *theologoumenon*, an expression of the idea which people had about Christ in fictitious narrative form. This schema was applied particularly to the virginal conception, which was excluded a priori by philosophical presuppositions.[127] Along these lines, F. Kattenbusch[128] considered the infancy Gospels as a Christian *haggādāh*, a staging of the Pauline doctrine in the form of infancy narratives. To treat the text in this way is to ignore the historical homogeneity of the infancy narratives with what follows (formally stressed in 1:1-4) and the very way the first Christian generation became aware of the mystery of the Incarnation, not by means of ideology like the Gnostics, but by an essentially realistic reference to Christ in the context of community. We must not confuse the living tension between Scripture and the events with an ideological construction, according to which the events were merely spun out of Scripture. In the chapter on historicity we will see why the infancy Gospels exclude this hypothesis (Part III, pp. 309ff.).

Legrand showed the apocalyptic character of Luke 1.[129] This observation is correct, but I do not think he means by that a literary genre properly so-called, because an apocalypse (revelation of the mystery) is a many-faceted mode of expression, and Legrand clearly shows how Luke strips the classical apocalyptic genre of all vivid elements (cosmic or otherwise),[130] which could give the appearance of being its essential element, and creates a new apocalyptic, characterized by its moderation.

If we want to evaluate the literary genre of Luke 1-2 accurately, we have to go beyond the labels. According to the established principles of

Formgeschichte, we must begin with the literary genre of each individual pericope in order ultimately to evaluate the whole.

The first assertion is that the pericopes in Luke 1-2, more than any others in the Gospel, belong to a wide variety of literary genres, and this has helped to lead people astray.

Three Announcements

The infancy Gospel of Luke begins with two announcements: one to Zechariah (1:5-25) and the other to Mary (1:26-38), followed in chapter 2 by the announcement to the shepherds (2:8-20).

Numerous studies[131] have been devoted to explaining these announcements (particularly the first two), often classifying them as replicas of a prefabricated model. Announcements concerning births are numerous in the Bible: Gn 16:11-12 (Agar), 17-19-21 (Abraham); Ex 3-4 (Moses); Jgs 13:3-7 (Samson); Is 7:14-17; and in the haggadic traditions of Jewish literature, preeminently the *Biblical Antiquities* by psuedo-Philo (ed. *Sources Chrétiennes,* v. 229, well examined by C. Perrot in *RechScRel,* 1967, pp. 481-518). In addition we must mention the *Protoevangelion of James*, a more neglected text which contains numerous announcements directed to the future parents of Mary, Anna (4:1) and Joachim (4:2), then to Zechariah (8:3), Mary (11:1-3), Joseph (14:2), and Salome (20:3-4). The comparative studies of these announcements have often tended to see in them a determining model for the annunciation of Mary, which would therefore not be the expression of an event, but a mere literary product. These attempts relied heavily on the single issue of the similarities, but led all objective minds to grasp the originality of the annunciation. The analogies are relatively striking with the announcement to Zechariah, but the return of the stereotyped formulas has no explanatory value. It is less a pre-established model than a very free framework in which the analogies can be explained in part by the event which is being expressed. The comparison of the announcement to Zechariah with the announcement to Mary showed, step by step, that the very obvious parallelisms of formulas are very limited, and essentially form the basis for contrast. For Mary, in fact, it is no longer a question of the birth of a prophet, or even a precursor, but the birth, under a new and unprecedented condition, of a Messiah with transcendent characteristics.

Furthermore, from the simple point of view of literary forms, the announcement to Mary is less a narrative about *birth* than about *calling*. While the evident analogies with the births of Ishmael, Isaac, Moses, and even Samson remain valid, an even clearer analogy can be made with the announcement to Gideon. Like Gideon, Mary begins by receiving a name which explains God's choice and her mission. He is addressed as "valiant warrior" (Jgs 6:12) and Mary as object *par excellence* of God's favor (*kecharitōmenē*, Lk 1:28). In both cases the motive is the salvation of the people. The expression repeated in Judges 7:14 and 15, defines the very meaning of the name prescribed for Jesus, which means Savior (1:31; cf. 1:47 and 2:11). In short, this second announcement combines the two aspects, birth and vocation, an unprecedented literary pairing.

The differences are obvious between the announcement to Zechariah and the announcement to Mary; the contrast is no less obvious with Gideon. This judge is himself the "savior" of the situation. But it is not Mary who is the savior, it is Jesus, her son. The name given her does not precisely define a mission as it does for Gideon. It is a name of gratuitous love, not of function. Would we say however that Mary receives here the function of mother of the Messiah? This function had a considerable importance in the milieu of the OT (1 Kgs 14:21; 15:2, 10; 22:42, cf. 53; 2 Kgs 9:6; 12:1; 14:2; 15:2, 23; 18:2; 22:1, 23:31, 36; 24:18). The King's mother bore the prestigious title of *Gebirah* (a name of power). She had an official place at the court and undoubtedly a crown. She received honors of the first order. While Bathsheba prostrated herself before David her husband, Solomon, her son, prostrated himself before her (1 Kgs 1:16, 31 and 2:19). But Luke does not mention any of these glorious attributes associated with the court and its pomp with reference to Mary.

If the annunciation came to be presented as a stereotype, it was by selecting retrospectively from this original text antecedent texts by virtue of their similarity to it, while candidly stating in return that the annunciation is the most complete form of the type or model under consideration. This is merely a consequence of the method utilized, which collated the analogies in reference to the annunciation, thus reducing it to these multiple references. The Synoptic recapitulations have a number of false windows. The elements, the arrangement, and, particularly, the meaning are very different. We must not hastily establish as norms the often commonplace formulas which recur in nativity narratives. They depend upon a cultural framework or backdrop, not an arrangement of content. Even more misunderstanding has derived from the fact that scholars have usually neglected to compare the two announcements in Luke 1 with the announcement to the shepherds in 2:9-14, which is also quite different and original.

These studies have not dwelt on the comparison with the infancy of Samuel (1 Sm 1-2) which has held E. Burrows' attention.[132] He sought there the key to Luke 1-2; and while there are many suggestive points of contact between the two narratives, the importance lies in the contrasts which can be observed between them.

There has been too much emphasis on the model of the birth narratives, while narratives dealing with calling have been rather neglected, notably those concerning the prophets (Is 6:1-13; Jer 1:4-10; Ez 1:2-3; cf. Hos 1:1 and Zech 1:1-2). They reveal less concrete analogies, but not less light as to the substance.

More recent works have insisted on the model of the calling announcement; the closest model to the announcement to Mary is undoubtedly the announcement of Nathan to David (2 Sm 7:14). The basic, common point concerns the birth of the Messiah, but in Luke's re-working of this text we find a profound metamorphosis of the twofold sonship which was prophetically outlined in the announcement to David: human sonship is no longer a matter of a father or of a normal genealogy, but the case of a virgin, conceiving by God alone, in total break with genealogy (1:30-32). As to the sonship of the Messiah with respect to God, which in the case of David is on the purely moral level, it becomes an identification of the Messiah with God.

We are dealing then with a special, out-of-the-ordinary, historical-prophetic narrative, in which God, the master of history, reveals and proposes the fulfillment of the most essential promises of the OT, an unexpected fulfillment at the level of the new reality which is Christ. This is an essential feature of the literary genre of the annunciation.

But the annunciation also has an apocalyptic character, as Legrand has amply demonstrated. It contains some of the original traits of the apocalyptic tradition, a tradition which was in direct line with prophetic discourse. But here we have a new form of apocalypse, discreet, without flare or fantastic imagery of any kind. It has an eschatological character, as the comparison with Zephaniah 3 demonstrated, but it is a new eschatology which surpasses received patterns and turns them upside down.

The annunciation also provides a fulfillment to the literary genre of the sealing of a covenant between God and human beings, as A. Serra[133] has shown: by her *fiat*, in 1:38, Mary plays a similar role to the people of God in their assent to the Covenant at Sinai: "All the words which the Lord has spoken, we will do" (Ex 24:3 and 7). (She will repeat these same words more literally in the other covenant narrative at the first miracle of Jesus in Cana of Galilee, "Do whatever he tells you" [Jn 2:5].) By virtue of this we come to a fourth model which is even more fundamental. But what is proposed to Mary, the birth of a child, would not be welcomed by a betrothed person. On the contrary, she manifests her resolve not to know man. It is without knowing man, through God's power, that she gives human birth to the Son of God, whose name means Savior because he will reconcile God and human beings.

The three instances of sealing a covenant which we have just mentioned, namely Moses at Sinai (Ex 24), the annunciation (Lk 1:35), and Cana (Jn 2), all have a *theophanic* character. God shows his glory in each of them. This last trait, like the others, assumes in the annunciation a new form, one of unprecedented fullness, although extremely discreet (as also at Cana). The child's conception is signified with reference to the presence of God in the Ark of the Covenant. But the glorious coming of the Holy One, of the Son of God, into Mary, is announced in the future (1:35) and, out of reverence for the ineffable character of the event, its realization will in no way be described.

The properly theocratic character of the annunciation differentiates it from the announcement to Zechariah. The announcement to Mary is the first of a series of theophanies which manifest the divinity of Christ throughout Luke's Gospel, and key words reappear in each of them and some other texts (e.g. Rom 1:3):

Announcement to Mary (1:35): The *Holy Spirit* will come upon you, and the *power* (*dynamis*) of the Most High will *overshadow* (*episkiasen*) you; therefore, the child to be born will be called *Holy*, the *Son of God* (literal echo of the theophany of Ex 40:35: the Glory of Yahweh taking possession of the ark).

Baptism (3:21-22): The *heaven* was opened and the Holy *Spirit* descended *upon him* in bodily form, as a dove, and a voice came from heaven: "You are *my* beloved *Son*, with you I am well pleased."

Transfiguration (9:29-35): The appearance of his countenance was altered, and his raiment became dazzling white. . . . They saw his glory. . . . Peter said to Jesus: "Let us make three booths" (allusion to the booth of the Ark of the Covenant). As he said this, a *cloud* came and *overshadowed* (*episkiazen*) them. And a voice came out of the *cloud* saying: "This is my *Son*, my chosen."[134].

Confession of Christ Before the High Priest (22:69-70): But from now on the Son of Man shall be seated at the right hand of the *power* of God (Mt 26:64 adds "and will come"); on the *clouds* of *heaven* (Dn 7:13 LXX; Mt 24:30; 26:64, "*with* the clouds of heaven," according to the Aramaic and "Theodotion" text; Mk 14:62). And they all said: Are you the *Son of God* then? And he said to them: *You say that I am.*

Resurrection (Rom 1:3-4): *Descended from David according to the flesh and designated Son of God in power.* According to *the spirit of holiness* by his resurrection from the dead, Jesus Christ our Lord.

The key elements of these theophanies are:

—The sign of the cloud as presence over characterized by the verb *episkiasei*, which refers to the shekinah; God being present over as *Holy Spirit*[135] and *power.*
—Glory (identified with Christ in Lk 9:32 and Jn 1:14; cf. Lk 2:32, alluded to by Lk 1:35 in reference to Ex 40:35).
—The title Son of God (and Holy: 1:35) given to Christ.

All these connected elements are not always explicit, but are more or less understood implicitly.[136] We are dealing with a collection of signs and of key words which express the divine identity of Christ, with notes of glory, power, and holiness. They are neither stereotypes nor labels, but rather a variety of means used by some Christians to give expression to what we call today the divinity of Christ or the Incarnation. No concept of it was given in advance: the expression had to be invented. It began with the application to Christ of some titles, some transcendent properties, some biblical texts which until that time had been applied solely to God. The evangelists did this first of all in the initial narrative and the final narrative, the baptism of Christ and his Resurrection, in which Paul affirmed very early the divinity of Christ the Lord (Rom 1:4; cf. Acts 13:33). Intuitively knowing, in faith, that this transcendence of Christ was something unique, they expressed it, in an analogous way, by interpreting other major episodes of his life: his conception (1:35), his transfiguration (9:29-35), his appearance before the High Priest (22:69-70), and his preexistence (Jn 1:1-2; 8:24, 28, 58; 13:19), proclaimed by ancient Christian hymns (Phil 2:6-11; Col 1:13-20; Heb 1:1-4 and, very early, by 1 Cor 8:6). The Christians of the first generation were not in possession of those conceptual instruments which came to suffer so many vicissitudes at the time of the councils; rather, they expressed their faith by signs and references, for the most part symbolic and vivid. The authors of the NT turn to them, each in his own way; hence, the diversity of formulas and their arrangements.

Luke 1-2 is a witness to a stage of that ancient Judeo-Christian reflection which seems to have made its mark on the level of style more than of thought. These two chapters are marked by a series of more or less explicit theophanies, the annunciation to Mary being just the first. There are four others:

—At the visitation, Mary is identified with the Ark of the Covenant by comparison with 2 Samuel 6.
—At the nativity, glory surrounds the shepherds in the framework of another covenant schema celebrated by the Gloria in 2:14.
—At the presentation, Jesus, recognized as "light" and "glory", comes as Lord into his Temple.
—Finally, in the last scene, that of the finding, he declares himself Son of God (as before the tribunal of elders in 22:70). Both scenes refer to the passion and the return to the Father.

In short, the announcement to Mary transcends the announcement to Zechariah as a calling and covenant scene and by its eschatological, apocalyptic and theophanic characters.

The three announcements of Luke 1-2 are quite different. The announcement to Zechariah (1:11-20) is the one which remains truest to the birth narratives of the OT. It concerns the birth of a singular prophet (the last one, the counterpart to Elijah, who was the first one) the precursor of the Messiah (1:17).

The announcement to Mary (1:26-38) upsets the pattern of famous announcements (births as well as vocations) since it concerns the Messiah, Son of God, identified with God himself, and that implies for the mother: bond, vocation, and participation. She is personally involved in the forming of the covenant destined for all.

The announcement to the shepherds (2:8-15) concerns a birth, not in the future, but one already realized. It is not directed to parents awaiting a child, but to the people as beneficiary of the Messiah. It is the collective dimension of the covenant which becomes manifest. That implies for them—the shepherds (*poimenes*, a term which refers also to the church officials)—a call to evangelization (2:10), which they are going to realize (2:18; cf. 2:20). Should one say that Mary exercises the same role when she leaves "with haste" (1:39) for Elizabeth's home? The impetus is expressed by the same formula (1:39 and 2:16), but the function is different: Mary does not spread the news, she radiates it, and her Son radiates it in her in that singular, undifferentiated mother-child condition which is the most curious characteristic of the visitation narrative. She shares in his glory.

The final original feature is that the announcement to the shepherds begins with a visible theophany (conforming to the most classic type of apocalypse), and yet in contrast with this brilliant glory, the manifestation of Christ the Lord is nothing but humility. The sign given to recognize him is not a new radiation of glory, it is the common manger where the child is laid.

The literary genre of the announcements of Luke 1-2 is not then a prefabricated model, which would explain the content of the texts. These are clearly different from the models to which many scholars would reduce them. Their value lies, not in their fidelity to the literary norm, but in the contrasts which they present to it. The three announcements, very different from each other, turn out to be original forms, particularly the last two, in which Jesus is the object. The newness of Christ transforms the cultural frameworks, and explodes the pre-existing models.

The Visitation (1:39-46)

What was the biblical model for the visitation? Exegetes have searched in vain. This scene is undoubtedly a travel narrative. Luke relied on this analogy in carefully basing his narrative on the liturgical journey of the Ark of the Covenant up to Jerusalem (see above, p. 56). But it is an irregular journey in all its characteristics and its effects.

We could search for the model also in OT encounters. But the human encounters which emerge are reunions and reconciliations. The encounter between Mary and Elizabeth is totally spontaneous. In it, the two announcements of Luke 1 converge and flow as one: it is the key-stone of their construction, says Legrand (1981, 218). There, as in 1:28-30, all is grace (*charis*).

Furthermore, it is not a question here of a simple human encounter; it is the Son of God, already identified by the shekinah, and recognized as Lord by Elizabeth, who manifests himself through Mary's visit. From this point of view, the visitation would seem to be the counterpart of God's visitations, as with Abraham, according to Genesis 18. The Holy Spirit provokes the encounter and the sharing (1:15, 35, 41) of the mothers and their two infants who, though still hidden and represented by their mothers, are already active. The transcendent coming of Christ the Lord is the source of blessings (1:41-55).

Like the annunciation, the visitation is an original bringing together of themes which find novel fulfillment: journey, meeting, benevolent manifestation of God; it is already a "protopentecost" (Lk 1:41 and Acts 2:4) demonstrated by an outpouring of prophetic charisms and thanksgiving. Here again, there was no prefabricated model. The unprecedented compactness of this successful conjunction of themes is truly amazing.

Two Births

The biblical birth narratives unfold according to so many patterns that they have discouraged any attempt to identify them by a stereotype. The births of John and of Jesus do not present significant analogies (1:57-58 and 2:1-20). They are more radically differentiated than the announcements. The birth of Jesus, in line with the annunciation, offers us the feature of a new liturgy of heaven and of earth celebrated in song by the Gloria of the angels (2:14). It is a cosmic expansion at a time when the Temple, the traditional ceremonial focus, is going to disappear. That indicates a new covenant, here openly eschatological. We can also discern a contrasted theophany: first the brilliant manifestation of God himself surrounding the shepherds (2:9), then the discovery of Christ the Lord in humble surroundings. We will come back to this contrast, which helps to signify the union of heaven and earth, of God and the human beings whom he loves.

Two Circumcisions

The very rare biblical narratives of circumcisions (Gn 17:26-27; Jos 5:2-8; 14:10; 1 Mc 1:60; 2:46; cf. Acts 7:8; 16:3; 21:21) have equally discouraged all attempts to search for a literary model. The two circumcisions of Luke 1-2 could not be less alike (1:59-79 and 2:21). They have in common only the mention of the rite with its date (the eighth day, 1:59 and 2:21; cf. Gn 17:12; 21:4; Lv 12:3; Acts 7:8) and the naming. In contrast to the structure of the birth narratives, here the account concerning Christ is brief. This imbalance occurs because the narrative characterizes Jesus by his *being* and John the Baptist by his *mission* and his future action. John's circumcision is the first vivid manifestation of the meaning of his name *Yehôhānān* (Yahweh has mercy).[137]

This mercy manifests itself vividly with the father, Zechariah, who, freed from his punishment, is filled with the Holy Spirit, which is protopentecost, after those of Mary (1:35) and Elizabeth (1:41; cf. 1:15), and before Simeon's (2:25-27). His prophecy, the Benedictus, sprinkled with allusion to the name of John, announces the role of the precursor. The new, and common element is that the two circumcision narratives aim to bring out the two significant names assigned from above to John and Jesus.

The Presentation

The presentation of Jesus in the Temple is not a standard biblical scene. It was not at all customary to recount the presentation of a hero. The only precedent is in chapter 1 of 1 Samuel,[138] and Samuel's presentation is quite different. It is not tied to a prescription of the Law. The timing is different: in 1 Samuel 1:22-24 it takes place after Samuel is weaned, while in Luke it takes place forty days after Jesus' birth. Samuel "remains there forever" (1 Sam 1:22) while Jesus returns to Nazareth (2:39). The significance of the act is quite different, for the presentation of Jesus, according to Luke, has an apocalyptic and theophanic character. He who bears the divine names of *Holy, Lord, Son of God*, visits the Temple as a poor child, but he is recognized by the witnesses as the salvation (*sōtērion*, 2:30), the glory (*doxa*, 2:32), and the redemption (*lytrōsis*, 2:38) of Israel. The newness shines forth everywhere, and always in the same direction. Across the anecdotal diversity, the great themes converge.

The Finding

Although *Formgeschichte* has shown little interest in the infancy Gospels as a whole,[139] foreign as they are to its standard grids (except to put them all together under the literary genre of "legends," i.e., imaginary and mythological stories), it has been quite interested in the episode of the finding, because of its analogies with the scenes of Jesus' public life. This school would identify it as an initial but imaginary biographical feature. Bultmann puts the episode in the genre of the "legendary," in the sense of an "edifying story."[140] Dibelius[141] sees here a typical case of a *Personallegende* intended to edify by showing the holiness of the hero: the child Jesus, by prolonging his stay in the Temple, would surpass his parents in piety. His intelligence (2:47) and wisdom (2:40 and 52) would also stand in contrast to his parents' incomprehension.[142] That is an artificial classification. The episode does not highlight the piety of Jesus at all. Not a word is said about his praying, and the story of his eluding his parents does not have the character of a good example for children. It is, rather, a paradoxical scene, which acquires its meaning in the same way as the preceding scenes, as a prophecy, an apocalypse, a theophany.

B. Van Iersel (1960, 161-173) makes a better use of the schemas of *Formgeschichte*, when he puts the pericope in the literary genre which Dibelius calls a "paradigm" and Bultmann calls an "apophthegm"—i.e., "narratives having as their function the framing of a memorable maxim of Jesus" (for example, Mk 10:13-16). The genre is characterized by a sparing and concise development, enclosed between symmetrical formulas. This last point is verified here:

They *went up*, as was the custom (2:42).
He *came down* with them and went to Nazareth (2:51).

This scene framed between an ascent and a descent is the first (theophanic) self-confession of Christ, Son of God, in the divine place which is the Temple. It is the prophetic prefiguration of his passion. Here again, any reduction to stereotypes proves futile.[143] Comparison with the biblical stories of children lost and found again (Joseph in Gn 37-46) sheds no light on the literary genre here. And the ending of the pericope is presented in a context so original, so bewildering, so contrasting, that a number of exegetes have seen here an inconsistency or awkwardness (see above, pp. 80-89).

The confluences observed in the preceding scenes converge here again on a new dimension: the future of the Christ, in its most radical originality, i.e., the passion and return to the Father, who is the source of the salvation of all human beings.

Growth and Development

It is the words about Jesus' growth and development which find the most convincing model in biblical antecedents. The Jerusalem Bible's translation of 1 Samuel 2:26 might lead one to think that a perfect stereotype is at work:

1 Samuel 2:26	*Luke 2:52*
Meanwhile the boy Samuel	And Jesus
went on growing	increased
	in wisdom
in stature	and in stature
and in favor	and in favor
with Yahweh	with God
and with men.	and men.

But the Hebrew does not use the word *stature* nor the word *favor*. In the Jerusalem Bible, the translation of 1 Samuel 2:26 has been discreetly filled out under the influence of Luke 2:52. It is a sort of modern *midrash* that up-dates Samuel in reference to Christ. Here is the literal translation of the refrain which recurs in 1 Samuel 2:21 and 2:26:

> The boy Samuel grew up in the presence of Yahweh (2:21).
> And the child Samuel went on *growing* and was *good* with God and with men (2:26).

We have seen how Luke modulates this refrain differently for John the Baptist and for Jesus.[144] The mention of *sophia* (wisdom) and *charis* (grace or favor) is proper to Christ in the two refrains which concern him (2:40 and 52). The word *sophia* thus frames the final sequence, which has links with wisdom literature, as we argued in detail in *Jésus au temple*.[145] The return of the word *charis* brings us back to the first words of the annunciation (1:28 and 30).

The Canticles

The canticles, a literary genre almost absent from the NT (unless we assimilate to that genre the prayers of Christ himself and the Pauline fragments of primitive Christian hymns), fit the well-known model of biblical psalms and canticles; at every step they employ customary expressions, long-since identified by scholars from Plummer[146] to Brown, who adds some Qumran parallels.[147] These reworkings illustrate the traditional character of prayer in those days, and its trait of *anamnēsis*. The canticles are organically joined to the context of the narratives.

The first two, i.e., the Magnificat and the Benedictus, are akin to traditional thanksgiving canticles. But they also have a prophetic character: they predict the future of Mary (cf. the use of the future tense in 1:45) and that of John the Baptist (the future tense is used again in 1:76). In addition, there are etymological allusions to the names of the two children, prefigurations of their missions of salvation and mercy.[148]

The Magnificat corresponds to a specific biblical model: the canticle of Hannah (1 Sm 2:1-10). It is situated in this tradition, but has been reworked in such a way as to give it a profound new meaning. Need one see in it an echo of the "martial language of Qumran"?[149] In any case, it has a salvation-historical content which goes far beyond the canticle of Hannah. It is more solidly structured. Mary's personal thanksgiving expands to become that of the whole people, before moving back into the personal with the mention of Abraham (1:55), who is the prototype of incipient faith, as Mary is the prototype of eschatological faith. The singer presents herself, not as a woman released from barrenness, but as the Daughter of Zion, freely showered with graces by God.

The first part of the Benedictus (1:68-75) carries an act of thanksgiving comparable to the Magnificat, but the second part (1:76-79) is a prophetic thanksgiving for the birth of the hero, John the Baptist. Unlike Mary in the Magnificat, Zechariah does not have here a role as prototype and representative. He effaces himself behind the "we" of the people of Israel, who are the ones offering thanks in this case.

The three other canticles are short, and each is marked by a powerful originality.

First comes *Elizabeth's thanksgiving*: "Thus has the Lord done for me, in the days when he looked upon me, to take away my reproach among men" (Lk 1:25). These words conclude the preceding scene. Elizabeth still hides in the shadow of shame, from which God is in the process of freeing her.

The *Gloria*, shorter yet, has an unusual density. It is a heavenly canticle: the canticle of the angels. The strong manner in which it brings together the heavens and the earth, God glorified, and humans, the object of his love (2:14), signifies a new and reciprocal covenant, in which our ascending praise encounters God's all-encompassing love. This covenant is realized in the Savior and Lord (2:11). In this regard, the canticle expresses what is essential to the scene, and it transcends the formal comparisons which exegetes have been able to discover in it.

Its brevity should not surprise us; we have the model of Psalm 116 as a thanksgiving psalm consisting of two short verses. The celestial liturgy is continued by an earthly liturgy, amazingly stripped down: the visit of the shepherds resembles the visitation of Mary; but she was carrying and bringing the Christ, while they go to him. Their visit leads not to a new canticle but to the praise and proclamation of the Good News (2:18, 20).

The *Canticle of Simeon* is the thanksgiving of a man who, from now on, can look death in the face (2:26, 29) since he has seen the Christ (2:26) and caught a glimpse of "the glory" (2:32). But it is also a theophanic glorification of that child who presented himself at the Temple with the offering of the poor. The locale of this new liturgy (that of Simeon) is the temple of stone, the place of God's presence. But its true locus is God's new presence in the Messiah-Savior, whom the prophet takes into his arms (2:28). While the first two canticles (the Magnificat and Benedictus) celebrated the new event through the archaic expressions of pre-existing songs, this canticle has recourse to the formulas of Deutero-Isaiah, which it uses to express the eschatological manifestation of divine glory, with its universalist consequences (2:32).

Predictions

The Magnificat (1:48b) and the Benedictus (1:76-78) include predictions. So does the Nunc Dimittis in its last verse (2:32). There follows a formal prediction of the darker aspects of Christ's future (2:34-35). To this are added announcements concerning John (1:14-17) and Jesus (1:31-33, 35), the future precursor and the future Messiah: two oracles, plus the future projections implied by the prophecy of Elizabeth (1:42-45) and by the words of hope spoken by the prophetess Anna (2:38). These unparalleled predictions, marked for the most part by the use of the future tense, concern the future of the Christ Son of God, as does the first prophetic saying of Christ himself, at the time of the finding in the Temple (2:49).

Conclusions

The conclusions of this analysis are contrasting, but each is valid in itself. The infancy Gospel of Luke 1-2 is composed of a mosaic of astonishingly varied literary genres: narratives recounting births, circumcision, visitation, presentation, finding, refrains of growth, lyrical pieces, and predictions and prophecies.

Yet, it is neither heterogeneous nor composite. Its eschatological dynamic assures the convergence and unity of everything it subsumes: literary models, updated biblical texts, axioms of salvation history.

This unity within diversity can best be explained if we recognize that we are dealing with the fruit of a long meditation, as is indicated in 2:19 and 2:51 (cf. 1:66). This meditation, enlivened by the indwelling Christ, renews the standard literary genres. This is why the present unity is polyvalent without being disparate. The coming of Christ the Savior is at once humble narrative and eschatological fulfillment, new birth, new creation, new covenant, new theophany. But all of these are perfectly unified. The components revealed by analysis are like the colors of a rainbow within the simplicity of sunlight. The intensity of meditation has recaptured pluralism and integrated it again, from within.

Since we are dealing, in fact, with the human origin of Jesus, we are certainly dealing with infancy stories of a biographical character; or rather, we are dealing with the comparison of two infancies—that of John the Baptist, which is destined to shed light on that of Christ, who is of another order, both as Messiah and as Son of God: a terminus of eschatological expectation and not simply a precursor (1:17 and 76). The meditation of which Luke 1-2 is the product has discovered, selected, and stylized the significant elements in this comparison. The contemplative density underlying it was so strong that it has transfigured or transformed each of the literary genres used to express this new manner in which God makes himself present to humans.

The new presence of the Lord, begun in Mary (1:35) and marked by rare signs of glory (2:9), is distinguished by prophetic testimonies and eschatological happenings, even before the Messiah, the Son of God, manifests himself to the world through the preaching of the Gospel.

This infancy is thus transcendent, apocalyptic, eschatological, theophanic. But this transcendence is without glory for him who is still only an infant (*brephos*) and a small child (*paidion*, a neuter word) like other infants (e.g. John the Baptist in 1:41, 44, 59, 66, 76, 80). This apocalypse is discreet and without fanfare. This scarcely obvious eschatology is affirmed in absolute assurance of the future (notably expressed by the Magnificat, where everything seems already fulfilled:

1:51-54, 78; 2:14, 32). This theophany does not alter the mute and humble condition of the child Jesus. Yet, already, the infancy Gospel describes his very being with unsurpassable force and light. Nowhere in the Gospels are the titles and texts which are usually reserved for Yahweh himself so freely and fully applied to Christ as they are here. Nowhere else are these titles stated in so varied, so rich, and so profound a manner—transcendent titles united with concrete terms that characterize his human nature: Son of the Most High (1:32), Son of God (1:35), Holy One *par excellence* (1:35 and 2:23; cf. 4:34 and Jn 6:40), Savior and Lord (2:11), light and glory (2:32). It is remarkable that Christ's being should be exalted with such power while his childhood remains devoid of marvels.[150]

These are the same titles which the ancient *Gloria in excelsis Deo* uses to confess the divinity of Christ:

> You alone are Holy (1:35; 2:23).
> You alone are Lord (1:43; 2:11).
> You alone are the Most High (cf. 1:32; 2:14) Jesus Christ (2:11), with the Holy Spirit (1:35) in the glory of God the Father (cf. 1:35; 2:9, 32, 49).

This literary genre is a transitional stage between the OT, woven as it is with biblical allusions and formulas, and the mature manifestation of the Messiah (Lk 3-24). The infancy story prefigures the Gospel in that it is based on the relation of John to Jesus, which relation will also inaugurate the manifestation of the Christ (Lk 3). The canticles also show this transitionality by their OT character, stocked with prophecies and yet with a very new assurance of God's triumph, as in the Magnificat (1:51-53). This transition from the Old to the New Testament is perceptible in the progression of Luke 1-2: from the first particularly archaic verses (1:5-25), to the first utterance of the son of God, saying in a word what is essential to the Gospel—his being and his future, polarized by his return to the Father (2:49)—as he will do once more before the Sanhedrin, at the end of Luke's Gospel (22:66-70).

In short, maintaining the humility of the initial obscurity and poverty of the Messiah, this infancy narrative is not a fabrication but an *anamnēsis*, a discernment of what he was from the beginning. It enables the reader to grasp his nature through "signs" that are tenuous and disconcerting (2:12, 34).

Let us not be surprised if we are overwhelmed at the richness of this Gospel. It cannot be contained in a neat framework, for it exploded the conventional frameworks to explain the newness of Christ through its most unusual features: the silence, the weakness, the poverty itself. Transcendence appears in modest form. The tension between human realism and the divine dimension is profound, and this tension is ingeniously portrayed by the midrashic updating of the Scriptures to express the most radical paradox of God's love coming among humans: his identification with the poor. The annunciation to Zechariah is a prelude whose character is deliberately kept old-testamental in tone. The point of departure for the revelation of Christ is the annunciation to Mary, which proceeds to develop its consequences. All the essentials are indeed given at a stroke with this announcement (especially 1:35). That is why one cannot designate the literary genre here with a ready-made label. This genre comes out of a deep meditation, carried on in a Judeo-Christian community whose secret we shall have to try to penetrate, if we are to complete our exegetical task.

The Titles of Jesus in Luke 1-2

Names signifying humanity and humility

—the begotten one (*to gennōmenon*, a neuter expression: 1:35)
—baby (*brephos*, a neuter noun: 2:12, 16)
—small child (*paidion*, another neuter noun: 2:17, 27, 40)
—child, servant (*pais*: 2:43, cf. 1:54, 69: Israel and David)

Messianic titles

—Christ (2:11, 26)
—King (1:32-33: He shall reign)
—Peace (if Lk 2:14 is an echo of Mi 5:4, he himself will *be* "Peace")

Divine Titles

Here we are dealing with names attributed principally and specifically to God, though some of them may be extended by participation (such as "Holy") or may admit a weaker interpretation. For example, "Savior" and "Lord" could be used of the patriarchs or biblical heroes. But the context of Luke 1-2 leads us in a convergent manner towards the stronger sense of the words.

—Great without restrictive modifiers (see Laurentin, *Structure*, p. 36, n. 3).

—Savior (2:11), which the Bible applies almost exclusively to God (see below, Part III, ch. IV, n. 31) and "God my Savior," which seems to be an etymological allusion to Jesus-Savior (1:47).

—Salvation (an abstract term which has the force of a superlative) under two forms: *sōtēria* (Lk 1:69) which certainly refers to the Christ, heir of David (1:71 and 77); cf. "Horn of Salvation" in 1:69 (divine title); and *sōtērion*, where Simeon identifies Jesus-Savior with Salvation (Lk 2:30).

—Lord (1:43, and 2:11)

—Holy (1:35, 2:23), a word used in the Gospel as a profession of faith: Jn 6:69; cf. Mk 1:24; Lk 4:34; Acts 2:27; 3:14; 13:35—these are texts which the *Concordance of Maredsous* classifies under the rubric *holy*: substantive, divine name. Cf. also 1 Pt 1:15, 1 Jn 2:20; Rev 3:7 and 16:5. (Cf. above, Part I, ch. 2, n. 76).

—light (2:32)
—glory (2:32)
—Son of the Most High (1:32)

—Son of God (1:35), in a much stronger context than the preceding; cf. 2:49, where Jesus himself expresses his relation as Son to the Father (below, pp. 145-147).

These titles acquire their full force if we place them in the context of their dynamic and their convergence. They are situated in a *movement of identification of Jesus with the Lord*, a movement which cuts short any confusion by designating him as a distinct person: Son of God. This title takes on new meaning in Luke 1-2, going beyond the lesser senses which can be found in the Bible or at Qumran (see further: the excurses, pp. 145-147).

III
SEMIOTIC STUDY

A. WHAT IS SEMIOTICS?

Having completed an examination of Luke 1-2 under the microscope of classical exegesis, we now move on to a different method of study: semiotics. This is a new field, and it is still in the stage of proving its worth, yet it seems to offer surprising resources for further progress in understanding the Gospels.[1]

Semiotics (also called *semiology*, from the Greek *sēmeion*, sign) has as its object the study of how signs produce (or induce) a meaning. It starts with the observation that meaning depends upon the structured organization of signs—whence the name "structuralism," by which this method is known to the public. It only came into being in the 1960s.

It is an offspring of linguistics, in the line of development opened by Ferdinand de Saussure (d. 1913), who tried to explain how elementary sounds (phonemes) are organized to produce a meaningful *language* by a structured interplay of differences and contrasts. Many applications were soon discovered and multiplied in ethnology (Lévi-Strauss), anthropology, psychoanalysis (Lacan), history, music, and cinema (C. Metz). Currently, semiotics is on the cutting-edge of exegetical research.

The application of structural semiotics, no longer to linguistics but to the analysis of texts and their meaning, was born in the wake of the Russian morphologists. V. Propp had discovered that folk tales display a small number of personage-types according to some simple models. He analyzed them in his *Morphologie du conte* (1928). The word morphology was not taken in a linguistic sense but in a botanical one, with a view to classifying these folkloric figures. A. J. Greimas reduced this inventory to a structured and coherent model, which has since shown itself to be workable. This is the semiotics, founded upon organic and controllable bases, to which we refer in the present work.

Both the word and the project have antecedents. They go back to the Stoics who founded the logical theory of the syllogism in the third century B.C. The semiotic square is found in Apuleius (mid-second century, *Opera*, Leipzig, 1832, 2, 165).The project was taken in various further directions in the seventeenth century by Leibniz; in the nineteenth by G. Boole (axiomatics) and Sanders Pierce (or C. W. Morris), who tried to elaborate a general theory of the sign so as to allow for a unification of the sciences. But these were just evanescent, philosophical speculations. The semiotic project succeeded, paradoxically, on the basis of linguistic technique (Saussure), when semiotics became a *procedure* instead of a *theory*—a procedure that works on material and objective indices by explaining the genesis of meaning from significative base-elements (called *sememes*) which produce it. What matters is not these elements themselves but their relations and correlations: their organization.

What does this mean? We can ask ourselves how the marks which a designer or caricaturist puts on paper allow us to recognize a person, a landscape, a scene. In a nutshell, it is the effect of well-ordered contrasts between blacks and whites. Their coherent arrangement can be examined. Today there exists a semiotic of the plastic arts; it is moving forward according to the methodological principle which has led to success in the modern sciences: explaining the complex by the combination of simple elements; the higher by the lower; meaning, by the organization of elementary signs.

Structural semiotics, then, is the application of a general method to the particular field of the study of texts. It has taken its place among the human sciences by virtue of the fact that it studies texts not by intuition but by a methodical exploration of the elements whose combination and succession produce meaning. Thanks to the objectivity of these criteria, and thanks even to their limitations, semiotics provides the possibility of going forward in a controllable and verifiable manner—the distinguishing trait of a scientific method.

The semiotic study of a text, such as we are about to make of Luke 1-2, goes through the following stages or procedures:

1. The first approach consists in discerning the differences and

contrasts that betray meaning in different registers: diverse grammatical data, diverse times, places, and modalities. These preliminary observations are still pre-semiotic and are not ordinarily reproduced in published studies. But it seemed useful to us to include these preliminary approaches here, as a kind of access-ramp to this difficult method, which often seems closed to the non-initiate.[2]

2. Next, sequential division (also called extraction) draws lines according to changes in time, place, and *actant*, between the sequences, sub-sequences, and segments of the narrative.

3. The first properly semiotic stage is the identification of the narrative program, which governs the coherent transformations of the story. The program is realized by a subject in quest of an object, and it progresses by conjunctions and disjunctions. We may take as an example La Fontaine's fable, "The Crow and the Fox": "Mr. Crow perched on a tree had a piece of cheese in his beak." The crow's "program" is inscribed within these opening words. It is to eat the cheese, which he already has "in his beak" (conjunction). The counter-program of the fox is to make him drop it (disjunction). He succeeds at his objective by flattery, and draws a lesson from this performance.

4. The program is achieved within the framework of a structured model. Greimas has given this a remarkably simple and workable form. He reduces the personage-types of the Russian morphologists to six categories, grouped into three pairs:

—subject and object, embodying volition;

—addresser and addressee, embodying communication (the addresser is the one who sets the terms of agreement for the performance to be achieved, putting the value on it; the addressees are those who benefit from it);

—helpers and opponents, embodying action, wherein those who *advance* or *hinder* the subject's performance intervene.

In fairy tales (which serve as a source for the development of this model), the *subject* or hero is often a Prince Charming, but he can also be a valiant little tailor who will become a prince by proving himself through the accomplishment of some exploit. The *object* is often the princess whom he will marry. The addresser is the king and father who proposes a test, such as slaying a dragon who is laying waste the region. The subject-hero must accomplish the exploit (the main qualifying and glorifying test) planned by the king-addresser for the benefit of certain addressees, who are often his people, hard pressed by calamities. Along the way, the hero will find *helpers* and *opponents*, who are not necessarily people, but may be anthropomorphized animals or objects. The hero and his adversary are themselves the addressers of their respective and conflicting programs, and they are also the addressees—which illustrates the diversity of possible combinations among the poles of this well-constructed grid.

In brief, the six categories of actants are patterned according to the following schema, helpers and opponents being simply modalities of the subject:

Addresser → Object → Addressee
↑
(helpers) — Subject — (opponents)

5. A final stage tries to unlock the deep structures of signification, using the form of the semiotic square. It is a question of grasping, beneath the changing surface of the story, the fundamental category which explains its coherence, its homogeneity (the parallels within the story), and the interplay of narrative paths. In Greimas' model, the explanatory category takes the form of Apuleius' square, which is defined by four correlative elements

A and B (the upper horizontal side of the square) are in the relation of *contrariety*, the diagonals (AA* and BB*) give the relation of *contradiction*, and the two verticles (AB* and BA*) give that of *correlation*.

Here is one example given by Greimas:

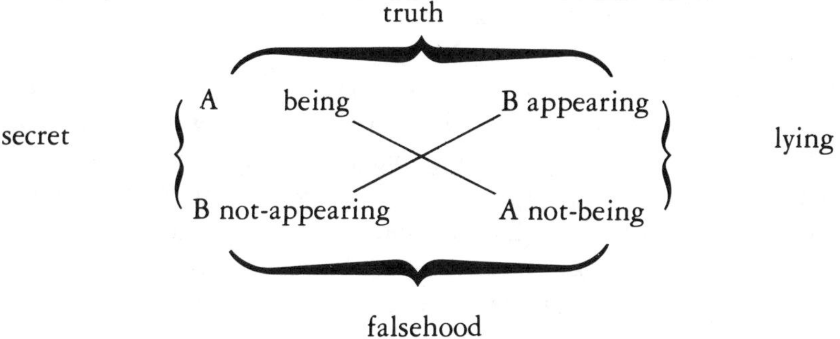

By way of example, this schema yields a good account of the biblical story of Susanna and the old men (Dn 13): Susanna is bathing in the *secret* of her garden (not-appearing). The old men come upon her unawares (she *appears* to their eyes in her captivating *being*). They wish to take advantage of her, in secret: this vice (*not-being*) would lie under the protective shadow of *not-appearing*. Upon her refusal, they attribute to her the very vice she has resisted: they say that they surprised her with a lover (*lying*). They disguise their vice under their respectability (*appearing*). Daniel, the true judge and representative of God, confounds their lie by showing the contradiction of their illusory *appearing*. He reduces them to their falsity (*not-being and not-appearing*) and restores Susanna to her truth, i.e. the conformity of her pure *being* with her *appearing*. Her reputation is rehabilitated, her life saved.

It will be necessary for us to beware, therefore, of the following temptations.

First, the temptation to seclude ourselves in the semiotic method, under the illusion that it is the *total* explanation of any text. It really explains only one aspect—namely, meaning—insofar as that can be produced by the interplay of differences within discourse. But the real meaning of a text far exceeds the "produced meaning."

As a consequence, we will avoid reducing the texts to the scope of the instrument. It sometimes happens that semiotics uses texts the better to forge its tool, while the tool should really be used to the benefit of the text. It is more important to shed some light on the text than to formalize procedures. This is not to neglect the tool, but merely to take care that it is put to good use.

Remarkable as the grids of semiotics may be, and however fruitful their use, one must weigh their relative nature, for they constitute working hypotheses, perfectible and revisable. Indeed, one of the strengths of semiotics is that it tries to verify and revise its grids. Thus Blanché enlarged the original semiotic square into a hexagon so as to represent not only the contrasts of a text but also the *graduality* and the continuities. In a case where a text puts into question one of the grids of semiotics, it is important to avoid reducing the text to the grid; one should rather gauge to what extent it outstrips it, either in order to revise the tool or to ascertain its limitations.

In this book we will try to avoid jargon, not out of contempt, for technical language is useful in semiotics as in every other scientific discipline. It ensures an intellectual rigor and coherence, but it is often forbidding and confusing for non-specialists. Sometimes it dissociates the words it uses from their customary meaning. For example, the term *manipulation* is used within this discipline to mean the action of the one who "causes the doing" ("determines the subject to act"). But in everyday language, *manipulation* has a pejorative meaning. To apply it to God, to make him the great manipulator, would be to caricature unendurably that transcendence which Luke 1-2 respects so admirably. Besides, technicality of language is often avoidable. For the benefit of our readers, we have avoided it as much as possible. We hope that the specialists will forgive us.

This book will avoid systematization. As with any scientific discipline, semiotics tends to enclose itself in its own system, to defend its autonomy, its specificity, its coherence, and its efficaciousness. This is useful for the constitution of a new science, but any effort to systematize risks reducing or excluding a part of reality to which the scientific spirit must remain completely open, lest it decay.

Finally, this book will avoid erecting this remarkable method into a philosophical system. Any method tends to set itself up as a philosophy, by the extrapolation of its own perspective. The philosophy which too often underlies the historical-critical method is very damaging to faith. The same risk presents itself in working with semiotics. Thus certain theoreticians have gone so far as to say that it is not human beings who make language, but language that makes human beings.

This adage has been used to reinforce the primacy of objectivity over explanatory refuge in subjectivity (e.g., the intention of the author), and this has been beneficial for semiotic practice, but it is clear that we will not be able to eliminate either the author[3] or the event. Semiotic analysis objectively gives an account of the meaning "produced" by structured relations of elementary components (sememes).

This word *produced* is methodologically stimulating, but it calls for caution. I should prefer to say *induced* meaning, with a keen awareness that every meaning worthy of the name implies a going beyond: the end achieved goes beyond the concept; intentionality goes beyond the symbol, just as sight goes beyond the lens of the glasses. The objective procedures of semiotics tend to put aside this "beyond," to attribute it to intepretation or subjective reechoing. This exclusion advantageously prohibits uncontrollable extrapolations and incoherencies, but it oversteps its limits whenever it denies that which lies beyond its limits. The gaze of the semiotician must remain open in order to go further, by refining his tool, by recognizing, whenever necessary, the irreducible originality of the text and of the new signification which it communicates.

In Luke 1-2, this originality is a reference to transcendence itself, communicated in the humility of the manger.

Having taken account of these limitations of semiotics, of this openness which it must retain, and of the proper tasks of exegesis, the analysis which follows adopts these options:

—To use semiotics as an instrument and not as an end.

—To avoid, as much as possible, difficult terms which would render this book unreadable or forbidding to the uninitiated reader and, more generally, to avoid whatever would shroud the text.

In short, accepting entirely the specificity, the precision, and the objectivity of the semiotic method, we will avoid sacrificing to it the text, which is the object of our inquiry. We will try to use the instrument for the benefit of the text itself. We will seek less to formalize the procedures than to refine them in order to penetrate the meaning of the text. This is not contempt for the tool, but economy of means. Too many of the methods studied in the preceding pages have sacrificed the Bible to their particular totalitarianism; a repetition of these mistakes would be a disservice both to the Bible and to this remarkable and promising method.

B. GUIDEPOSTS OF MEANING

1. Some Coordinates on the Grid

Semiotic analysis is not grammatical analysis. But certain grammatical elements have a semiotic value. We take them up insofar as they frame or condition meaning.

In this complex network, we stress two significant data:

a. Tenses of verbs

The aorists are the thread of the *narrative* (in the past). The futures appear in *prophetic announcements* (1:13-17, 32, 35). In the canticles which have prophetic value, we find a subtle proportioning:
—The present expresses thanksgiving: "My soul magnifies the Lord" (1:46).
—The future characterizes the prophecies:

> All generations will call me blessed (1:48b).
> And you, child, will be called the prophet of the Most High, for you will go before the Lord (1:76).
> A sword will pierce through your own soul (2:35).

—The aorists of the Magnificat (1:51-55) no longer mean a *past*, as in the narrative, but God's victorious *present* which will be realized invincibly in the future of his people, "forever" (1:55). This grammatical tense expresses (with, as it were, unwavering faith) the infallibility of God's design, notwithstanding the contrast it may present to the present situation (a fact which has often disconcerted exegetes):

> He put down the mighty from their thrones and exalted those of low degree; he filled the hungry with good things and the rich he has sent empty away (1:52-53).

What God has promised is assured in God, in a supratemporal manner, independent of past or present vicissitudes. The aorist here takes on a prophetic futurist meaning, a value that is particularly acute in a time when Israel is under foreign occupation. To sing "he has cast down the mighty from their thrones," was a seditious cry in the time of Herod's reign (1:52). Herod was a cruel tyrant, whose heir and namesake, Herod Antipas, will later in the Gospel be one of the actors at the trial of Jesus (23:6-12). The Magnificat is provocative.

J. Dupont,[4] the author of this analysis, adds that, "The aorists of verses 48-49 refer to what has happened at the moment of the Annunciation (1:28-35)." This event and its consequences (the revolution proclaimed in the Magnificat in 1:51-53) are the fulfillment of the promise made to the fathers.

b. The subject of active verbs

In Matthew 1-2, the subject of the active verbs is generally Joseph, while Mary is exclusively passive: Joseph takes and she is taken (six times in Matthew 1-2). In Luke 1, the opposite schema is at work. Joseph is passive (excluded from the accomplishment of the program), and Mary is active. Joseph takes an active role again only at the beginning of the next chapter (2:4-5), as a David-descendant, in order to qualify Jesus (who is not his biological son) as son of David by bringing about the conjunction of his birth with the "city of David," the king whose messianic heir he is. Joseph then disappears to yield place to Mary, the sole subject of the childbirth. After this, he is included only conjointly with her, in the parental activities related to the presentation and the finding narrative (2:22, 41-49). But Mary alone speaks (2:48) and internalizes the event (2:19, 51). She alone becomes linked to the tragic and contradictory destiny of the Messiah (2:35).

In the same way, in 1:24-62, Elizabeth is in an active positon, while her husband, active as a priest in 1:8-19, is reduced to muteness and powerlessness (1:20-62). This will lead to curious and significant particularities of expression, which we have yet to study.

2. Chronology

The chronological data in Luke 1-2 are very abundant. We find the words:

—*hour* twice: 1:10; 2:38, where the hour of Jesus' arrival at the Temple marks the synchrony of two meetings, functionally complementary, of Christ with Simeon and with Anna;

—*day* twenty times: a record frequency, as this word is the measure of the chronology in Luke 1-2;[5]

—*month* four times: 1:24, 26, 36, 56;

—*year* four times: 2:36 (the seven years of Anna's marriage), 2:37 (her eighty-four years, a multiple of 7 x 12); 2:41 (each year), 2:42 (the twelve years of Jesus);

—*genea*, age or generation, in 1:48 and 50, "from age to age";

—*aiōn*, century or major duration, three times in lyrical contexts: 1:33, 55 (the end of the Magnificat), 70 (in the Benedictus);

—*time* (*chronos*) once: 1:57 (the equivalent of day which the refrain of fulfillment reserves for Jesus' steps towards Jerusalem).

This abundance of terms contrasts with Matthew 1-2, where all these words are lacking (except *day*, once in 2:1).[6] The duration of time plays an important role in this narrative of the beginning of Christ's life: it has a consistent importance, with a recurrence of meaningful parallels, the key word being the word *day*, which occurs more often than all the other six words put together (twenty as against sixteen).

Time in Luke is not an indefinite flow; it realizes a *fulfillment*, underscored by the recurrence of the verb *pimplēmi*[7] tied to the word *day* in the refrain "after the days were fulfilled." This refrain occurs:

—in 1:23, at the point of departure;

—in 2:6, for the birth of Jesus (contrary to the birth of John the Baptist where the days, *hemerai*, are not differentiated, but merely generalized as *chronos*, time);

—finally, in 2:21-22, where the refrain is repeated to introduce the two ceremonies which mark fulfillment in the calculation of ritual time: circumcision on the "eighth day," and purification/presentation on the fortieth day.

Repetition of the refrain unifies the two measures: the biological and the liturgical.

1. The biological times are:
—the first six months of Elizabeth's pregnancy, mentioned with insistence (1:24, 26, 36, 56) to gauge the length of time between the annunciation to Zechariah and the annunciation to Mary (1:26 and 36);
—the nine months between Mary's conception (1:31) and the birth of Jesus, signified by the return of the refrain in 2:6. In total, 6 months + 9 months = 450 days.

2. The time of the Law (the schedule of rites):
—Zechariah's offering in the Temple (1:9, where he lingers: 1:21);
—the feast of the Passover (2:22, 41-42), celebrated by Jesus' parents according to the custom, is allotted three days (2:46), which evokes the triduum of Christ's death;
—but, above all, there is the *liturgical time* prescribed for the performance of the circumcision (1:59; 2:21) and the purification (2:22, 40 days). This is represented by the ceremony of the presentation: 40 + 450 = 490 days, or 70 weeks.

The semiotic analysis confirms and specifies what we have established on the literary level.[8]

What dominates Luke's calculations of duration is the time of the addresser, i.e., God, the author of the Law, who has foreseen and foretold through the prophets the manifestation of the Christ. "It was necessary" is one of the prophetic refrains throughout Luke's Gospel, from 2:49 to 24:26 and 44.

The time of God contrasts with that of Caesar (this world's addresser, who imposes his authority from without, blindly, while God orients things from within, stimulating human liberty by his Spirit, showering it with his love and revelations (e.g., 1:28-35).

What is important to Luke is this interior duration, inspired, accomplished, and fulfilled by God himself. Prophetic aorists and futures characterize this time of God, who causes the eschaton and the new creation to emerge.

3. Topology:
The Spatial Framework of the Story

A story unfolds in a space. The topology of Luke 1-2 is very rich both quantitatively and qualitatively. Changes of place assume a considerable prominence in the progression and meaning of the narrative. Let us try to grasp them objectively, according to their various aspects and structures.

1. *Geographical space* is the most obvious:
Everything begins in Jerusalem, without the city's being named explicitly, but it is evident that we are in the unique sanctuary of the capital (1:9), where Zechariah is going to officiate in the Temple ritual. It is a solemn place for the story's point of departure.

An important spatial shift places the second sequence at Nazareth in Galilee. It is there that the Christ is announced and conceived.

It is important to establish that this symbolism of place (typology) is based on the contrast between the holy city, Jerusalem, to which one goes *up* (2:4, 42) and a lowly peasant town, Nazareth in Galilee, to which one goes *down* (2:51). Both Nazareth and Galilee are the object of popular scorn (Jn 1:46 and 7:41, 52). Yet it is at Nazareth that the important event happens which commands the totality of chapter 2 and indeed of Luke's Gospel. Thereafter, four journeys of Jesus and his mother are recorded as *ascents* (1:39; 2:4, 22 and 42) and the culmination of the infancy narrative is realized in the Temple in Jerusalem, where it began. This schema can be applied also to the Gospel of Luke as a whole, which ends with the scene of the disciples returning joyously to Jerusalem, "and were continually in the temple blessing God" (24:53).

But we must not stop our analysis here, for Luke ends the infancy narrative on a paradoxical note, with Jesus' *descent* to Nazareth, to live in humble obedience (2:51). Was this done to explain Jesus' hiddenness until his baptism? Or was it perhaps done to signify the fact that Jerusalem as the center of worship is superseded by the new Temple— as in Stephen's famous speech against the Temple "made with human hands" (Acts 7:48)?

2. More than geographical space, there is *sacred space*—a space defined in terms of God and his manifestations:
The first place that Luke designates is not Jerusalem (which is left implicit, as we have seen) but the sanctuary (*naos*). The priest enters there (1:9), while the multitude of the people remain outside, though

in union with him through prayer (1:10). It is the place of the angel who "stands in the presence of God" (1:19). Jesus' first public manifestations take place in the Temple (at the presentation and at the finding).

Between these Temple episodes, which act as a kind of frame (1:9 and 2:27, 37, 46, 49), the annunciation occurs at Nazareth. Must we then see Nazareth, a marginal place, as a profane place in opposition to the Temple, the sacred place and the goal of the ascending journey? As regards the current language of the time, I think the answer must be yes. That language characterized these two places as the low one and the high one, speaking of ascent (1:39; 2:4, 42) and descent (2:51)—idioms which have an analogous parallel in the contrast between the humility of Mary and the sacerdotal splendor of Zechariah.

Nonetheless, Nazareth is the place of the initial, fundamental, and major manifestation of God. It is there, we have seen, that (according to Luke) a theophany is realized, described in terms analogous to God's own act of taking possession of the Ark of the Covenant.

Semiotically, while the place of the apparition to Zechariah was the sanctuary, that of the apparition to Mary is Mary herself, not her house, which is not named. Mary is "substituted for the sanctuary," notes Gueuret rightly (*op. cit.*, 180), and this observation confirms the literary criteria according to which she appears as the new Ark of the Covenant, the new sanctuary of Yahweh.

Following Gueuret, we can be still more specific. For Zechariah, the place where qualities are acquired is the sanctuary. In the case of Mary, she herself becomes the sacred dwelling place of God, and this new dwelling place is situated utopically (in the etymological sense of the word, without a named place, in Galilee). But Zechariah departs disqualified from the sacred space of the Temple, while Mary departs, qualified, from the humble and despised place where God comes to her and upon her.

It is the beginning of the evangelical revolution: the Good News announced to the poor, the first recipients of the Kingdom (1:51-53 and 6:20). It is as Daughter of Zion, representative of the people, that Mary receives and conceives him who is called *Holy par excellence*

(1:35) and Son of God (1:32, 35). It is through her that the sacralization will extend to John the Baptist and his mother, filled with the Holy Spirit when Mary comes to greet them in their "house" at the visitation (1:40).[9]

The sacralization of space is more complex at the time of the nativity (2:1-20). Here the glory of God appears visibly in the form of a light in the night. It surrounds the shepherds in the countryside (2:9), but not the Messiah, lying in his crib deprived of all radiance. The manifestation of God's glory comes, then, only to invest the shepherds, these poor ones, as the first witnesses to the "Good News" of "Christ the Lord" (2:10-11). It is he, from then on, who is the sacred place, while Mary stays in the background in the role of a meditative witness.

Indeed, it is Jesus who sacralizes the Temple at his presentation. When Simeon "takes him in his arms," this gesture ("somatic," i.e., corporeal, in semiotic emphasis) connects and identifies the initial presence of Christ in Mary with his presence in the Temple, which is less important as a building than as a place of those who worship in spirit and in truth. This symbolism outlines the transition from architectural temple to temple-of-living-stones, about which 1 Peter 2:4-7 will speak. It is in accord with the Johannine tradition (underlying Luke 1-2) whereby the body of Christ is the new Temple (Jn 2:21).

The topological significance of Luke 1-2 is thus not so much the irresistible ascent of Christ, from a secular place to the holy place of the Temple, as it is the overthrowing of the standard categories of sacred and profane by the very person of the Son of God. Henceforth, the sacred is where he is. The categories of high and lowly, of center and periphery (Jerusalem and Nazareth) are surpassed. This relativization of geographic sacrality is full of consequences throughout the narrative.[10] What we see breaking through here is that decentralization which is explicitly asserted in the related theology of John 4:21-23:

> But the hour is coming and now is, when the true worshipers will worship the Father in spirit and truth.

In short, from Nazareth to Jerusalem, and back to Nazareth, space plays a structural role and inculcates the sense of a new relation with

God. The concept of sacred space must be redefined in light of the new manifestation of God.

3. *Divine space* is signified in terms of altitude, in imagery referring to the Lord and the Messiah:
God is called the Most High (*hypsistos*) three times in Luke 1-2 (1:32, 35, and 76). It is significant that this designation is found only ten times in the whole NT,[11] seven of which are in Luke-Acts. This insistence—which is reinforced by Luke 2:14, "Glory to God in the highest" (*en hypsistois*) and by Luke 1:78, where the Messiah-star rises from on high (*ex hypsous*, cf. 1:52: *hypsoō* for the raising of the poor)—manifests the importance accorded to the category "high," to characterize the Messiah (1:78) and his coming (1:32, 35, 76) with a reference to heaven (cf. 2:14). This insistence tends to express (in a manner still symbolic and implicit) the pre-existence of the Son of God, who comes from on high, as Wisdom does in Sirach 24:3.

Luke 2:14 links the loftiness of God with the lowliness of men on earth:

> Glory to God in the highest (*en hypsistois*) and on earth, peace among men with whom he is pleased.

This is the only passage in Luke 1-2 where heaven is mentioned: the angels "return" there (2:15) at the end of the announcement (2:13), and the heavens are not mentioned again until they are opened at the baptism of Jesus (3:21-22). It is peculiar that heaven, a common word in the NT (it appears 283 times), appears in the infancy narrative only at this point, where the God-to-man relation is constantly being described. This is because the infancy Gospel capitalizes on an existential relation, whose aspects must be evaluated in order to grasp the spiritualization of space according to Luke 1-2.

The localization of God "on high" is attested by the formulas in which the Holy Spirit comes *upon* Mary (1:35), *upon* Simeon (2:25), or *upon* Jesus (2:40; the preposition *epi* in all three cases).

The same elevation is signified by the prefix *ep* in:
—*ep-eiden* for Elizabeth: God looks on her from on high (1:25);
—*ep-eblepsen* for Mary in 1:48: the same meaning.

This code thus places value on what is high, but discreetly, and without circumscribing God in any way. The loftiness of God does not lower humans at all, but elevates them and comes to meet them, disregarding all apparent spatial distance. God is not tied to space. He looks on Elizabeth's "shame" so as to "take it away" (1:25), and on the lowliness (humility and poverty) of his servant Mary, so as to exalt her in her very poverty (1:48). He exalts the poor (1:52) of whom she is the prototype.

This presence *upon* is equivalently (and analogously) signified as presence *within*, for Mary as for John, Elizabeth, Simeon, and Jesus himself. The Vulgate was so imbued with this meaning that, where the Greek says the Holy Spirit was *upon* (*epi*) Simeon, it translates this *in* him (*in eo*).

The presence of God is also expressed by the preposition "with" (*meta*) which signifies conjunction, communion: for Mary in 1:28, "The Lord is *with* you;" for John the Baptist in 1:66, "The hand of the Lord was *with* him."

One must also read the preposition "before" (*enōpion*, five times) in this perspective:

—John the Baptist is great *before* God (1:15);

—he goes *before* him (in fact, before the Messiah-Lord, 1:17 and 76);

—Gabriel stands *before* God, and, on the part of an angel, this connotes the higher place which is heaven (1:19);

—the people aspire to serve in justice *before* God (1:75).

The loftiness of God *expresses* symbolically his invisible transcendence but does not prevent him from being close to the earth whose Creator he is. He manifests his presence there. He does great things there (1:49, 58) for Mary and for Elizabeth (cf. 1:25). He gives (1:32), he satisfies (1:53), he helps (1:54) and visits his people (1:68-78) without having to descend or condescend.

The loftiness of God is thus not at all material, overwhelming; it does not weigh down upon humans. It awakens dynamism and liberty in them. The space of God is not so much engulfing as inspiring and stimulating, as the frequent reference to the Holy Spirit also indicates.

A brief inventory of other less structured aspects of space will lead us to the same conclusion.

4. *Domestic space* has a secondary place in Luke:

The word "house" occurs twice to designate Zechariah's residence (1:23, 40), and once Mary's (1:56), which seems to be still distinct from Joseph's (a point which Mt 1:18 confirms historically). But the narrative will not situate Jesus in any house, in contrast to Matthew 2:11. He is born without lodging,[12] in the manger, and the multiple references to Nazareth do not make explicit mention of any house, even where the context could easily have led to naming one (2:51); similarly, in Luke 1:26, Luke says only that the angel entered unto Mary (*pros autēn*), without reference to any residence or building. Jesus is not placed in any earthly dwelling except the Temple, "in his Father's house" (2:49), and in this respect the Temple itself is only a symbol. This is why Jesus leaves it after having said that it was necessary for him to remain "in his Father's house." He refers, by this prophetic gesture, to the heavenly dwelling of the "Most High." Here we are confronted anew with divine space: it is identified with the "place" of Jesus, who is "the glory of the people" and of the Temple.

The fact that Jesus has, according to Luke 1-2, no other dwelling than Mary during her pregnancy (1:32-56), and the Temple (2:22-49), leads us to examine another topological dimension.

5. *Corporeal space* has an important place in this qualitative topographical structure:

It is first of all the space of pregnancy for the two mothers, expressed by two sayings:

—*en gastri* (in your inner parts) with reference to Mary: "You will conceive in your womb" (1:31). This generic expression seems to echo the *beqirbēk* (in your midst) of Zephaniah 3:15;

—*en koilia* (in your womb) is more frequent: 1:15, 41, 42, 44 (for Elizabeth) and 2:21 (for Mary).

This somatic perspective is continued by means of the three refrains on the growth of the two children, John the Baptist (1:80) and Jesus (2:40-52), a growth in size (*hēlikia*, as is specified in 2:52).

In the symbolic language of the Bible, there is a continuity between the body and psyche. Luke also mentions the heart of Mary, the place where she keeps the word-events of the Lord (2:19 and 51), and her psyche (her life), which a sword will pierce (2:35).

Corporeal images are employed, moreover, to signify the living relation of God to souls:

—the bowels (*splagchna*) of his mercy (1:78; lit., RSV translates this "his tender mercy");
—the might of his arm (1:51);
—his hand, which is with John the Baptist (1:66);
—his gaze (1:25, 48).

There is thus a symbolic continuity between the body and the spirit, which leads us to the following theme.

6. *Interior (spiritual) space* corresponds to the influence of the Spirit:
Three persons are filled with the Holy Spirit, i.e., with the dynamic presence of God:
—John (1:15),
—Elizabeth (1:41),
—Zechariah (1:67).

Equivalently, Simeon receives an inner prompting (2:26) and a motion from the Spirit urging him toward the Temple (2:27). But the Holy Spirit had already been situated "upon him" (2:25), as previously "upon Mary" (1:35)—indeed in a more transcendent sense for her, since in this verse it is a matter of a manifestation of the shekinah upon Jesus (cf. 2:40) and upon her. This position of transcendence (*upon*) does not exclude immanence (*within*) but rather implies it.

This multiform presence of the Holy Spirit does not replace the spirit of the persons who benefit from it. He awakens their liberty, their very dynamism:
—John the Baptist is "filled with the Spirit" (1:15) to walk before God "in the spirit and power of Elijah" (1:17), in imitation of this prophet. Further on, he "grows and is strengthened in spirit" (1:80).
—Mary's prophetic "spirit," as she herself says (1:47), "rejoices in God her Savior."

7. *Relation to God* serves to unify the threefold space—domestic, corporeal, and spiritual—which we have just analyzed, and it does so thanks to the distinctive traits of the divine space.

First it is conjoined to and communicative with human space; these multiple conjunctions are expressed under all sorts of symbols, signs, and mediations which resolve into a fruitful interiority—without the text's ever speaking of ascent or descent between heaven and earth.

It also respects human space. Apocalyptic manifestations thereby become manifestations in humility, and this is true even for the Messiah-Lord himself. The single visible manifestation of glory (2:9) vanishes and becomes interiorized in the Lord Jesus lying in the manger, somewhat as the thunderbolt, storm, and earthquake served only to announce the "gentle stillness" which was for Elijah the very presence of God. Luke's perspective is not without precedent in the prophets.

Likewise, Simeon knows that one cannot see God and live (Ex 33:20). He "sees death" (2:26) "in peace" (2:29), since he has "seen the Christ of the Lord" and his "glory" (2:32); yet he sees this only in the form of the small child whom he takes into his arms (2:28). This makes one think of Moses, who saw God only "from behind" (Ex 33:23). These same experiences lie behind John 1:14, "The Word was made flesh. . . and we have beheld his glory." This same idea is even more vividly expressed in 1 John 1:1: "That which we have seen with our eyes, which we have looked upon and touched with our hands, concerning the word of life." John sees this glory even in the passion. Luke 1-2 is already caught up in this line of thought, albeit less explicitly. Theophanic space, that of God's manifestation among men, is realized in the humility of Jesus among the poor.

Finally, the Most High overthrows human evaluations as to what is "high" and "low." Nazareth is preferred to Jerusalem for the first and essential manifestation, which later times will call the Incarnation: the conjunction of the Holy One, the Son of God, with Mary (1:35). Mary, who is situated not only in lowly Nazareth but among the poor, according to her own words (1:48), identifies herself with the poor whom God exalts (1:52). God's revolution alters the coordinates of human space. It "puts down the mighty from their thrones and exalts the humble" (1:52). Although God is situated on high, his revolution does not create a hierarchy in space but leads to integral communion and communication between God and human beings.

It is no less true that the God of mercy (*eleos*, a term quite frequent in Luke 1-2) and of power is the source from whom all things come and towards whom all things re-ascend through service (1:74; 2:37; cf. 1:17) and praise (2:20; cf. 1:17, 45f., 68-79).[13]

Space, finely modulated according to aspects ranging from geography to divinity, from the corporeal to the inner world, is, with time, one of the privileged frameworks in which are inscribed the new relations between God and humans, according to Luke 1-2.

C. MODES

The narrative programs (the progression of narratives) are based primarily on the use of the modes which Greimas identified, which he described according to the following table:

Modes	potential	concretized	realized
exostatic (transitive)	obligation	power	action
endostatic (immanent)	volition	knowledge	being

The six modes are grouped with reference to two coordinates:
—The vertical coordinate extends from the exterior to the interior; the upper level articulates those modes which connect various subjects, the lower level, those which concern a single subject.
—The horizontal coordinate goes from the determination ('desiring to' or 'having to') through the means ('knowing' or 'being able to') to the realization ('being' or 'doing').

More concretely, the scope of these categories accounts for all possible narrative programs in an infinite number of combinations:
—I ought to, but I don't want to: dramas of dispute;
—I want to, but I can't: dramas of impotence;
—I want to, but I don't know how: dramas of ignorance.

In each case, one mode is modified by the negative of another (in the first instance, obligation is modified by negative volition, etc.). 'Doing' can also be modified by 'doing'; for example, 'to cause to do' is manipulation, 'to cause to be done' is creation.

These categories illumine a vast field for analysis. To show their application to the infancy narratives, let us take one example. The account of the finding in the Temple (2:40-52) unfolds within the mode of 'knowing'—Jesus remains in Jerusalem without his parents' knowledge (2:43). They do not know where he is and so they search for him. He, on the other hand, manifests his wisdom before the wise men (2:47). He manifests his divine knowledge, his consciousness of being the Son of God, called to return "home" via the passion and the three days in the tomb (a prophetic knowledge). This knowledge surpasses the parents who "do not understand" (2:50). But Mary progresses in knowledge through her meditation (2:51).

One of the constant themes of these narratives is that knowledge and power reside with God. In Luke, they inspire the dynamic and creative actions of people. In Matthew, on the other hand, the knowledge and intentions and power of God direct events from on high, and these progress in obedience to his will.

For the most part, we have retained the modes which semiotics has outlined, as well as some others which seemed significant for various reasons, though they have no organic place in the dictionaries of semiotics: coordinates of grammar, possession, action.

We will encounter, in passing, other modes, such as 'light,' so important as a symbol of revelation in the Christmas night, and other 'signs' which can be connected with the category of knowledge.

The conjunctions and disjunctions of the action do not call for a separate examination, since they form the fabric of the narrative in all of its aspects. They concern topography, chronology, knowledge, and power, and to examine them here would only lead to repetition. The predominant feature of Luke 1-2 is the conjunction with God, and through God with others, in the sharing of the Gospel.

D. SEQUENTIAL DIVISION

How should one divide the sequences of Luke 1-2? Published studies hold varying positions:

The Lyons group (CADIR) relies on the dyptichs, without proposing a division in the strict sense:

1. Two annunciations
2. Two nativities
3. Two circumcisions
4. Two childhoods
5. Two canticles (Zechariah and Mary)
6. Two visitations (Mary to Elizabeth and the shepherds to Bethlehem)
7. Two presentations of Jesus at the Temple.

We shall keep in mind the importance attached to dyptichs from the semiotic point of view.

M. Rosaz (Paris group) retains the seven classic sequences, on which there is a wide consensus from the literary point of view, and divides them each into numerous *lexia* (fifty-eight in all) according to changes of actants or other changes.

A. Gueuret works methodically to base her division on the following semiotic criteria:

1. Change of time, place, actant: the principal criterion.
2. Parallels (isotopies—see appendix for exact definition): for instance, Zechariah's functions as a priest frame the second subsequence (1:8-23).
3. Refrains: growth of the children (1:80 for John the Baptist; 2:40 and 52 for Jesus) and remembrance (1:66, 2:19 and 51); but she does not take up the refrain of the days being accomplished (1:23, 57; 2:6, 21-22) which underscores the time-flow (see above, ftnt. 7).
4. Finally, the *egeneto* which recurs fifteen times in Luke 1-2, indicating the important moments of the narrative.[14]

Following these criteria, she reduces the sequences to three:

1. 1:5-80, "which deal principally with the child of the first couple, John";
2. 2:1-40, the birth and presentation of Jesus in the Temple;
3. 2:41-52, the finding in the Temple, these two latter sequences deal with "the child of the second couple, Jesus."

One might be surprised that the presentation should be joined to the nativity, despite the changes in time, place, and actants; one might also be surprised at the disproportionate lengths of the sequences, the first being nearly double the length of the other two combined. But Agnes Gueuret subdivides the main sequence of chapter 1 into four *sub-sequences*:

1. The introduction of the parents of John the Baptist (1:5-7);
2. The annunciation to Zechariah (1:8-23);
3. The Elizabeth cycle (1:24-58);
4. The circumcision of John the Baptist (1:59-79; 1:80 is not mentioned).

One might inquire into the choices which govern this hierarchy of sequences and sub-sequences:

—Doesn't detaching the introduction of John the Baptist's parents into a first sub-sequence obscure the strongly asserted parallelism between the two annunciations, which both begin with the introduction of a couple, of whom only one member receives the announcement? Semiotics cannot afford to ignore this kind of formal evidence, the source of isotopies.

—Inversely, why associate the Elizabeth cycle with only one sub-sequence? In the course of this cycle, important changes occur in time, place, and actants. First, Elizabeth conceives in the house of Zechariah (1:24) near Jerusalem, then comes the annunciation to Mary in Galilee (1:26-38), then her visit to Elizabeth (same house, 1:40), and the birth of John. Gueuret's grouping gives this third sub-sequence a disproportionate length: thirty-three verses, compared to three for the first. Gueuret tempers the disproportion by distinguishing (on the basis of greater or lesser reinforcements in the presentation of the text) four segments in the Elizabeth cycle:

a. her conceiving (1:24-25);
b. the annunciation to Mary (1:26-38);
c. the visitation (1:39-56);
d. the birth of John the Baptist (1:56-58).

To be sure, this grouping has the advantage of gathering the nine months of Elizabeth's pregnancy into a single sub-sequence, including the double mention of the sixth month (1:26 and 36); and perhaps this is why Bossuyt and Radermakers have adopted it.[15] But the text is not centered upon Elizabeth. Its meaning is altered by recentering it that way.

The difficulties in adopting this sequential division are not only those indicated on the level of literary analysis. From the semiotic point of view, there are the following objections:

1. This plan does not highlight (in fact it obscures) the *parallelism* between the two annunciations, although it is strongly asserted and emphasized by numerous isotopies (some thirty common words). These analogous parallels, which symmetrically mark out the two sequences, are an important generator of contrasted progression and meaning.

2. The change in time, place, and actants which marks the beginning of the annunciation, a simple segment in the proposed division, is more distinct than that between the second and third sequences of the same outline. More important still, the annunciation seems to us to mark the true starting point for the Gospel of Jesus Christ, which will dominate all of chapter 2. Doesn't making it a mere segment of a sub-sequence obscure its importance, its newness, and its being the very wellspring of Luke's progression in 1-2?

3. It seems difficult to reduce the annunciation to an event[16] in the midst of a sequence devoted to Elizabeth. The announcement to Zechariah and Elizabeth's conception function significantly to enhance the value of the annunciation to Mary, which unites both actions (with all the negative features removed) and which has as its object the Messiah, the Son of God. This contrast manifests, step by step, the superiority of Christ, as well as that of his mother over Zechariah, in respect to grace and law, faith and incredulity. It reverses the sociological hierarchy in which a priest of the Temple would take precedence over a young woman of the provinces. This is an essential source of meaning.

We may ask ourselves if this misleading option in an otherwise excellent analysis may not be explained in part by the dependence of semiological grammar on the semiology of tales: i.e., on an initial model, which the Gospel invites us to transcend.[17] But this option is taken for another reason also, one which can be traced back through the historical-critical exegesis of the past hundred years and more. The interruption in the narrative of the birth of John the Baptist by the annunciation to Mary and by the visitation (1:26-56) has been considered an interpolation into a primitive Baptist source, which would be homogeneous without it.[18] According to this perspective, the proposed sequential division would do justice to a primitive and archaic state of the material in Luke 1. But even aside from the fact that this hypothetical Baptist source is much debated, the point remains that the actual and definitive text of Luke—the sole text available for semiotic analysis—only uses the John the Baptist narrative to throw emphasis upon the Christ and his ontological qualification (as Gueuret's analysis elsewhere demonstrates very well).

Let us not overestimate the importance of sequential division. It is somewhat relative. If objective criteria point out, in varying degrees, junctures and transitions, the articulations of the narrative are nonetheless supple and diverse; the organic arrangement into large sequences, sub-sequences, and segments is dependent, in large measure, upon disputable options. The structuring is interior, and every schematization is in part artificial, because imposed from without.

If one were to persist in emphasizing the middle position of the annunciation and the visitation, that is, in between the two sequences of which Elizabeth is the principal subject (1:5-25 and 1:57-80), it would then be necessary to take the two sequences (especially the annunciation), not as a marginal element or as parenthetical, but as the high-point of the narrative and the starting point of its whole dynamic;[19] the annunciation and the visitation introduce Christ who is the heart of the narrative. They show his first manifestation of radiance, and they bring out that grace (*charis*) with which the crucial part of the narrative begins and ends (1:28, 30; 2:52). In line with this hypothesis it would be necessary to consider the composition of chapter 1 as a sort of chiasm, a frequent schema in the Bible, easily visualized through the formula BAAB, that is, an inversion like "prince charming, charming prince."[20]

Without denying the merits of a solution constructed around the Elizabeth cycle, it seems that this construction, with its hierarchy of sequences, sub-sequences, and disproportionate segments, is not the best means of accounting for the narrative. According to the semiotic criteria (which here confirm the literary criteria), the parallelism of the two annunciations, clearly defined by changes in actants, locations, and times, should be taken as basic. We therefore propose the following option:[21]

1. The announcement to Zechariah of the birth of John the Baptist (1:5-25);

2. The announcement to Mary of the birth of Jesus (1:26-38);

3. The visitation, the keystone of the two preceding sequences (1:39-56; cf. L. Legrand);

4. The birth and circumcision of John the Baptist (1:57-80);

5. The birth of Jesus (2:1-20);

6. The circumcision and presentation of Jesus in the Temple (2:21-40);

7. The second manifestation at the Temple and conclusion (2:41-52).

We propose this plan, not in a systematizing spirit, nor as a scheme which Luke supposedly followed, but as the alignment which best accounts for the inner organization of his text.

This plan reflects, as faithfully as possible, the empirical data furnished by a text that resists perfect symmetry. The plan takes its point of departure in the parallelism of the annunciations (sequence 1-2), then of the nativities (sequence 4-5), each of the two parallel narratives leading to a sequence whose object is the manifestation of Christ. The visitation (sequence 3) effects an admirable convergence of the two annunciations and a harmonious transition between the two sequences ending (1:5-25) and beginning (1:57-80) with Elizabeth. The three final sequences (5-7) set aside John the Baptist, hidden in the desert (1:80), to highlight the double manifestation of the Christ child (2:21-52).

The slight dissymmetries, though baffling to a geometrical mind, have their justification.[22] In short, here as elsewhere, objective fidelity to the text leads one to recognize its irreducible originality. Sequential division objectively shows some well-founded connections but has neither explanatory power nor reductive force. The narrative presents itself as a living being whose parts one cannot divide without destroying its life, as in a dissection. A text keeps its living character, even though writing freezes it in a definitive materiality; one may approach it, circumscribe it, make sense of it, but one can never explain it fully.

E. NARRATIVE PROGRAM FOR LUKE 1-2

We are now ready to begin the first properly semiotic stage of our work, the analysis of narrative programs.

By *narrative program* we mean the coherent sequence of transformations which determine the progress of the story.

We speak of *narrative programs* in the plural because each sequence has its own program, the progression and articulation of which it is important to grasp.

Unlike Matthew 2, the programs of Luke 1-2 are not conflictual (except for the argument between Elizabeth and her neighbors, 1:59-61, and the opposition between God's people and their enemies, 1:51-52, 71; 2:34-35). Luke has a tendency to gloss over conflicts. Progression occurs through the transcending of man's program by the revelation and the gift of God himself, who revolutionizes and transfigures everything.

1. Announcement to Zechariah (Lk 1:5-25)

Introduction of Characters (Lk 1:5-7)

The narrative program of the first sequence is set by the introduction of the two characters. Zechariah and Elizabeth, as a couple, have in common their pure priestly lineage (1:5) and, especially, their fidelity in "walking in all the commandments and ordinances of the Lord blameless." Their program is thus the exemplary practice of the Law of God, which characterizes both of them. Luke, the enunciator, intends to emphasize this, since none of his other characters are given such a long introduction.

But this eulogy gives way to a declaration that is scandalously out of line with the OT promises of reward for virtue: "But they had no child, because Elizabeth was barren, and both were advanced in years" (1:7). Many English translations thus turn the initial *kai* (and) into a more explicit *but* or *however*, and with good reason, because there is an adversative contrast here: their fidelity should have merited blessing and posterity. Their sterility is irreversible because they are "both advanced in years." The beginning states a contradiction which succeeding segments will resolve.

The Announcement (Lk 1:8-23)

A new narrative program is set in motion as we continue:

> And it happened (*egeneto*) while he was serving as priest before God when his division was on duty, according to the custom of the priesthood, it fell to him by lot to enter the temple of the Lord and burn incense. And the whole multitude of the people were praying outside at the hour of incense (1:8-10).

The repetition of analogous terms (*hierateuein*, and *hierateias, thumiasai* and *thumiamatos*; cf. *ephēmerias* in 1:8 as in 1:5) characterizes the new program; it is priestly and liturgical, and thus remains in line with the previous program "according to the custom" of the Law, to which Zechariah is faithful. He is chosen by lot to offer incense (1:9), and the drawing of lots is considered a providential means of being chosen by the Lord himself (cf. Acts 1:22-26). God as addresser begins to emerge here. Zechariah thus penetrates the sanctuary as the sole subject of the liturgical program, in a setting that is sacred, secret, exceptional, and glorifying. His wife disappears. She does not have access to the sanctuary. The priest who is "inside" (prefix *eis* of *eiselthōn*, 1:9, and the preposition *eis*) is contrasted with the people who are "outside" (*exō*), but also "in prayer," united to that invisible liturgy.

Zechariah's program does not lead to the completion of the rite. It is diverted by a supernatural event:

> There appeared to him an angel of the Lord standing on the right side of the altar of incense (1:11).

The new program emerges here, unexpectedly, no longer earthly but heavenly: God's program is presented by the angel of the Lord in a visual apparition (*ōphthē*),[23] and it is "upon seeing (*idōn*) him" that Zechariah "was troubled and fear fell upon him" (1:12).

In response to his (already speechless) dismay, the angel speaks. After the classic invitation "do not fear," the first words of the narrative program put an end to the paradoxical sterility of this exemplary couple (her "reproach" Elizabeth will say later in 1:25):

> Your prayer is heard, and your wife Elizabeth will bear you a son, and you shall call his name John (1:13).

The previous context was insufficient to acquaint us with the prayer and the desire of Zechariah. We discover it here. The angel addresses him alone. Although his wife is mentioned, the posterity is referred to him alone, "Your wife will bear *you*. . . ." To him alone, by virtue of his paternal authority, is the name-giving prescribed. These nuances should be noted, not only by contrast with Mary, the single subject of her annunciation (which contains no reference to Joseph), but also in reference to Elizabeth, who will soon assume prominence, while Zechariah will find himself excluded. For the moment, the exclusion of the father is not on the horizon. The announcement is altogether euphoric for him, and it extends to the people as a whole, with no special reference to Elizabeth:

> You will have joy and gladness, and many will rejoice at his birth (1:14).

Here the horizon broadens. We are no longer in the semiotic of tales, where the object-infant comes to fulfill the parents' desire. The birth of this infant puts an end to the frustration of the parents. The people, mentioned as petitioners in verse 10, are immediately established as receivers of the predestined child.

The angel explains this broadening of perspectives; his message is the narrative program of John the Baptist's career, as it will come to pass at the very beginning of the Gospel (Luke 3).

As the future hero is described, the first conjunctions and disjunctions occur. The future hero is characterized first of all by his value in the sight of God himself (conjunction with reference to heaven):

> He will be great before the Lord [who confers greatness](1:15).

The other side of the coin is his asceticism (disjunction with reference to earth):

> He shall drink no wine nor strong drink (1:15).[24]

Abstinence from food and drink is the other side of a privileged conjunction with God; these two traits will mark John's entire career (1:66, 80; 3:2-18):

> He will be filled with the Holy Spirit, even from his mother's womb (1:15).

This verse sets the narrative program of the visitation, when this performance will be realized (1:41 and 44).

The angel next programs John the Baptist's ministerial functions, to convert, to prophesy, and to be a forerunner:

> And he WILL TURN many of the sons of Israel to the LORD their God, and he will go BEFORE *him* in the spirit and power of ELIJAH TO TURN [second use of the verb *epistrephein*] THE HEARTS OF THE FATHERS TO THE CHILDREN, and the disobedient to the wisdom of the just, to make ready for the Lord a people prepared (Lk 1:16-17; [the words in capitals are borrowed from Mal 3:1, 24]).

—*Convert-maker* is the dominant theme. It opens and closes the discourse with a pleonastic insistence: the double use of *epistrephein*, the double final application of that conversion to father-child relationships and then to those between unbelievers and the just. (It will be observed that the fathers are on the side of the unbelievers, and the children on the side of the just.) The other two traits appear in the center of the discourse:

—*Precursor*: "He will walk before him." "Him," according to the immediate context, refers to God. But in the larger context of the Gospel, this reference is to Christ. We have already pointed out this dynamic ambiguity.

—*Prophet*: This title, which Zechariah makes explicit in the Benedictus, is already signified by the symbolic identification with Elijah.

Malachi 3 was the reference-source for these three titles or traits. But whereas in Malachi 3 priority was given to the role of precursor, in Luke 1:16-17 it is the function of convert-maker which integrates the other two traits. The last words bring this out very clearly: John's mission is "to prepare for the Lord a people prepared" for the eschatological times.

Here Zechariah objects, "How shall I know this (*gnōsomai*)? For I am an old man, and my wife is advanced in years" (1:18). In spite of his desire and his fidelity, Zechariah does not enter into God's will (*volition*, one of the six modes which we described above). His objection (of sterility) appears to be well-founded, more so than that of Abraham before the pledge of the Promised Land: "How am I to know that I shall possess it" (Gn 15:8)? But whereas Abraham obtained a sign of covenant, the angel reproaches Zechariah for his lack of faith and gives him no sign other than a chastisement.

Before pronouncing this sanction the angel, with great dignity, reveals his name and station as a representative of God:

> I am Gabriel, who stand in the presence of God; and I was sent to speak to you, and to bring you this good news (*euaggelisasthai*). And behold, you will be silent and unable to speak until the day that these things come to pass, because you did not believe my words, which will be fulfilled in their time (1:19-20).

The mention of time announces the end of the chastisement; it will cease with the accomplishment of the program itself, namely, with giving John the Baptist his prescribed name (1:64). Once again, what is stated here is the subsequent narrative program.

"The people" wonder at Zechariah's delay (what is inside escapes those outside), but when he comes out, he cannot speak or announce the Good News received.

The people (the perceptible addressees) guess that the priest has had a vision (interpretative 'knowing'). The following stage emphasizes how powerless Zechariah is; he wishes to speak but cannot. There is great emphasis placed on the chastisement, as there was in its pronouncement, "He made signs to them and remained dumb" (1:22).

Elizabeth's Conception (Lk 1:24-25)

Here begins the third sub-sequence which starts, like the previous one, with the key word *egeneto* (it happened). We encounter here, for the first time, the formula-refrain which periodically marks the accounting of the seventy weeks between this starting point and the entry of Jesus into the Temple:

> And it happened (*egeneto*) when his time of service was ended, he went to his home (1:23).

There is a break here both in time and in space. Zechariah leaves the sanctuary for his house, mentioned here for the first time.[25] He leaves after the days provided for his liturgical service, but it seems understood that his muteness did not permit him to accomplish the rites of prayer.

In any case, from this verse on he disappears totally (until 1:62, except for insignificant mentions at 1:40 and 59, in which he is not an actant). His wife Elizabeth, who had fallen out of the action after his entry into the Temple, reappears in the house and becomes the single subject of this last sub-sequence (1:24-25). The act of conception is reported with reference to her alone, without Zechariah's role being in any way indicated. She acknowledges in faith God's gracious gift.

She give thanks for this "reproach" being removed by God the addresser,[26] yet she still hides herself:

> After these days his wife Elizabeth conceived, and for five months she hid herself, saying, "Thus the Lord has done to me in the days when he looked on me, to take away my reproach among men (1:24-25)."

The scene ends as it began, before God (1:6, 8, 14); here, explicitly under his gaze (*epeiden*), i.e., a gaze from on high, whose efficacy has been made manifest.

Formalization

In short, Zechariah and Elizabeth are an exemplary pair (1:5-6), deprived of a child (disjunction, 1:7), although their piety should have merited them this benediction. They learn that their prayers are "heard" by means of an oracle of God to the priest Zechariah, in the Temple, the house of God (1:8-18). But this happy announcement ends in a chastisement (1:19-22), which is astonishing in itself, in that questions similar to Zechariah's had been allowed by God in the past, in the case of Abraham (Gn 15:8 using the same terms; cf. 17:17). The scene thus ends on the twofold silence of Zechariah, who is mute, and of Elizabeth, who hides herself (1:24-25), thanking God in secret. The shadow in which she conceals herself has this function, to throw into high relief the episode which follows: the annunciation of the Messiah, the Son of God, a light that is subtle rather than brilliant.

2. *The Annunciation to Mary (Lk 1:26-38)*

Introduction of Characters

The annunciation sequence begins with a total change of time,[27] of place and of actants:

> In the sixth month the angel Gabriel was sent from God to a city of Galilee named Nazareth, to a virgin betrothed to a man whose name was Joseph, of the house of David; and the virgin's name was Mary (1:26-27).

Again a couple is presented, but this time the whole incident is seen in reference to the apparition of an angel, which opens the sequence; everything begins with the impact of the Lord.

On the other hand, it is the woman who is named first here, not the man, as the receiver of God's project. Joseph is not named except in reference to her, inasmuch as she "is promised in marriage to him."[28]

Joseph is described as a descendant of David, a function which will not play a part until later on (2:3-4), to mark Jesus' connection to the line of David. Mary's ancestry is not described, unlike that of Elizabeth: it is unimportant, irrelevant to the narrative. Mary counts as the Lord's companion in dialogue, through the angel who mediates his transcendence. Her importance is emphasized not only by the priority which she is given in the account, but also by the fact that she is twice mentioned, and above all twice designated as virgin (1:27). This pleonasm deliberately sets the program for the pararadox which becomes explicit in 1:34—there is no conjunction between Mary and Joseph, her betrothed. The contrast is all the more striking in that the beneficiary of the first announcement was Zechariah, a man without his wife.

The Annunciation

Upon entering toward her, he said, "Rejoice, object-of-the-favor-of-God (*kecharitōmenē*); the Lord is with you" (1:28). (Luke does not say that the angel appears; he enters, and what follows avoids the specification "into her home," which would have emphasized a cohabitation which is not yet in effect. The word *pros* [toward] is purely directional.)

Mary's qualification is not a dynastic qualification, a human heritage, like that of Joseph. It is instead pure grace, and is made explicit by the angel's second utterance, "You have found grace (*charis*) before God" (1:30).

This appellation manifests what Agnes Gueuret calls "the figurative role of parents in regard to their children." The relation of Zechariah to the people prefigures that of John the Baptist, the future prophet (1:10, 16-17); that of Mary prefigures the Christ, who will be characterized at the end in terms of grace (2:40 and 52).

> But she was greatly troubled at the saying, and considered in her mind what sort of greeting this might be (1:29).

Mary's fear is not passive, as Zechariah's was, upon whom it "fell" (1:12). Her uneasiness, more vivid due to a more profound occurrence (prefix *di*), is deliberate and active; by a dialogical or dialectic process (forcefully signified by the verb *dielogizeto*), she questions the meaning of the vision.

The first verse could appear merely to announce the program of a young couple called to have children. In that case, however, Joseph would have been designated, like Zechariah, to receive the announcement. But it is to the Virgin alone (in the singular) that the angel says:

> Do not be afraid, Mary, for you have found favor with God. And behold, you will conceive in your womb and bear a son, and you shall call his name Jesus (1:30-31).

She alone is qualified to give this name which was commanded from on high (1:31b). This transfer of the paternal function, in contrast to Zechariah,[29] reinforces the semiotic exclusion of Joseph, although the narrative does not yet give any reason for it.

Jesus is next described with titles which surpass those given for John the Baptist. His titles define him less in terms of *doing*—we noted how John the Baptist was defined as one who was to *act*: to convert, to prophesy, to be a forerunner—than of *being*.[30]

> He will be great, and will be called the Son of the Most High; and the Lord God will give to him the throne of his father David, and he

Jesus, Son of God in Luke 1:32, 35, and 2:49
Range of Meaning

What does the title "Son of the Most High" (Lk 1:32), "Son of God" (Lk 1:35) signify, especially when Jesus uses the concept of divine sonship in order to act with freedom in relation to his adoptive father (Lk 2:49)? The expression "son of God" is not a new title created for Christ.

Extra-biblical Instances

The title was used in the surrounding civilizations:

The pharaohs were called "sons of god," born of the Sun god (C. J. Gadd, *Ideas of the Divine Rule in the Ancient East*, London, 1948, pp. 48-50; H. Frankfort, *Kingship and the Gods*, Chicago University, 1948, pp. 299-301).

In the Hellenistic and Roman world, the expressions "son of God" and "divine son" were applied to rulers (A. Deissman, *Biblical Studies*, Edinburgh, Clark, 1909, pp. 166-167) and to famous men (Plato, Pythagoras, Apollonius of Tyana) or miracle-workers (G. P. Wetter, *Der Sohn Gottes*, Göttingen, Vandenboeck, 1916; W. Grundmann, *Die Gotteskindschaft*, Weimar, 1934; M. Hengel, *The Son of God*, Philadelphia, Fortress, 1976). Among the Greeks and the Romans, the word "god" did not have the same meaning that it had for Jewish or Christian monotheism. In a polytheistic environment the expression signified "divine favor" or "divine adoption."

Old Testament

The expression has a wide application in the OT:

—for angels (Gn 6:2; Jb 1:6, 2:1; Ps 29:1; Dn 3:25)

—for Israel, as a collective singular (Ex 4:22: "My first born son is Israel"; Dt 14:1; Hos 11:1; Is 1:2; Wis 18:13). Soon, however, the term was reserved to the just (Wis 2:18) or the future people (already in Hos 2:1).

"Son of God" is sometimes applied to individuals (Sir 4:10). But if the Israelites at times invoked God as father (Sir 23:1, 4; 51:10; cf. Ps 89:26), no one called himself his son. Except at 2:18 and 5:5, Wisdom uses this title only for the Israelites of the past (Wis 9:7; 12:19, 21; 16:10, 26; 18:4).

—for the Davidic kings, for the promised Messiah (2 Sm 7:14; 1 Ch 17:13)

—for angels or earthly judges, according to the famous Psalm 82:6, which Christ cites as an argument *ad hominem* to his adversaries, "You are gods, sons of the Most High" (cf. Jn 10:34).

—for the faithful (Sir 4:10: "Be like a father to orphans . . . you will then be like a son of the Most High. He will love you more than does your mother"; and Wis 2:18. The meaning here, however, is symbolic and often characterized in the sense of 2 Sm 7:14: "I will be to him a father").

When applied to Jesus, the title Son of God (as an extension of this Davidic prophecy which had begun to have a concrete meaning in the OT) takes on a new significance, manifested clearly in what some call the "Johannine thunderbolt" in the synoptics: Luke 10:22 and Matthew 11:25-27.

Qumran

4Q174 Flor, fragment 1-2, 1:11 (*Discoveries in the Judean Desert*, Oxford, 5, pp. 53-55). The Son of God is identifed with the "offspring of David" (cf. Jer 23:5), citing 2 Samuel 7:14. This citation of the prophecy of Nathan adds nothing to the biblical text, but applies it more forcefully to the offspring of David "who will arise with the Interpreter of the Law."

4Q243, now being edited (cited by J. T. Milik, *The Books of Henoch*, Oxford, 1976; J. Fitzmyer, NTS 20, 1974, pp. 382-407 and *Wandering Aramean*, Missoula, 1979, pp. 90-94; Hengel, *The Son of God*, 1976, pp. 44-45) can be transcribed as follows (following Fitzmyer):

[He] shall be great upon the earth...
[They] shall make [peace] and all shall serve.
[He shall be called the son of] the [G]reat [God], and by his name shall he be named.
He shall be hailed [as] the Son of God,
and they shall call him Son of the Most High.
As comets (flash) to the right, so shall be their kingdom.
(For some) year[s] they shall rule upon the earth and shall trample everything (underfoot)...

This text (which has as yet neither been reproduced photographically nor officially published) remains enigmatic. Fitzmyer conjectures that it could treat of the son of a sovereign.

This text has been put forward because of the threefold contact with Luke 1:32 and 35; the personage is qualified as "great," "son of the Most High," and "son of God." What should we conclude?

The text confirms that the expressions "son of God" and "Son of the Most High" were used in Judaism at the time of Christ. Nothing allows us to give a transcendent value to the Qumran texts, given the present state of research.

The text of Luke 1-2 has a completely different value: Jesus is qualified there as "great" without either the restriction or the relativization which we find in Q246 (see Laurentin, *Structure*, p.36, n. 3.).

—Luke speaks of the divine filiation prior to human filiation (Davidic, Lk 1:32a and b).

—The title "Son of God" is joined not only to that of "great," but also to that of "holy."

The two titles of the Messiah "begotten" in Mary are qualified in Luke 1:35 by the shadow of the presence of God, with reference to Exodus 40:35 (shekinah). The mysterious "begotten Holy and Son of God" is the equivalent of what was the "glory of the Lord" in the Ark of the Covenant.

—The function of the intervention of the Holy Spirit for the virginal conception (according to the redaction of the text) is less to bring about this generation than to guarantee the divine sonship of him who was in no way born of man (Lk 1:34). This is different from the other characters mentioned above who have a human, natural filiation and who are then more or less adopted by God.

> will reign over the house of Jacob forever; and of his kingdom there will be no end (1:32-33).

The tone and vocabulary of this characterization of Jesus point to transcendence. The use of the term *Most High* (*hypsistos*) to designate God accents the fact that this child comes from above. (This idea is confirmed by the repetition of the same word at the high point of the message, 1:35.) Only afterwards is he referred to "David his father." The final words, "and of his kingdom there will be no end," confirm superiority over any human reign. In short, the Messiah is described with an unheard-of accumulation of transcendent terms, actualizing and reinforcing the prophecy of Nathan (2 Sm 7:14), taken up again in 1:31-33.

The Objection (Lk 1:34)

Like Zechariah, Mary expresses an objection, but in a very different way:

> How can this be, since I do not know man? (1:34).

The virgin, espoused to a man, objects that she does not know man. This disjunction is the opposite of the initial conjunction. It is the hinge of the narrative.

She expresses a present state, like the expression, I do not drink or I do not smoke; she is thus expressing an intention. The narrative does not explain the motive, nor the circumstances of this singular intention,[31] nor does the text explain how the marriage took place, nor if and how Joseph shared this intention, nor even how Jesus could be called son of David without being son of Joseph, the only connection to the "house" or family (1:27; 2:4). Unlike Matthew, Luke says nothing about these things. He is content to overcome the biological gap by a symbolic geographical connection in 2:4 and 11.

In contrast with Zechariah, the objection of Mary is accepted and honored:

> And the angel said to her, "The Holy Spirit will come upon you, and the power of the Most High will overshadow (*episkiasei soi*) you; therefore the child to be born will be called holy, the Son of God" (1:35).

The Response (Lk 1:35-37)

The response assures Mary that man will have no role in this birth which comes from God alone. The disjunction with man was required for this exclusive conjunction with God. The Son of God (1:32-34) can only become son of Mary (1:31) by a transcendent process. The manner in which Luke 1:35 signifies this divine conjunction between the Son, the mother, and God is remarkable.

Luke distances himself from every concept of theogamy. Like Matthew, he employs the verb *gennaō* (to beget) in the passive voice, thus avoiding any statement that it is God who begets. The subject remains hidden, ineffable. The divine action is signified by the words "spirit" (feminine in Hebrew, neuter in Greek) and "power" (feminine in Greek). Transcendence is accented because God is above (in the heights, as signified by the rare term Most High, 1:35), indicated by the combined use of the preposition *epi* and the prefix *ep-* (twice in 1:35a: *epeleusetai, episkiazein*). What is situated in Mary is not the action of God, but the one conceived who is holy, Son of God.

Another significantly unusual feature is that God is called *spirit*, with the qualification *holy*, indicating thus a spiritual, not a biological action. The power is not explicitly related to a bodily effect, but to the shekinah, thus to the transcendence of the presence of God.

The expression "the Holy Spirit will come upon you" is found again (substantially) in Luke at the baptism of Christ (3:22). There the text states, "The Holy Spirit descended upon him." However, at 1:35 Luke avoids saying that the Holy Spirit "descended." He thus distances himself again from any concept of a theogamy. He applies for Mary the formula by which Christ announces Pentecost to the apostles, "But you shall receive power when the Holy Spirit comes upon you" (Acts 1:8).

Mary does not disappear in this theophany. The twofold mention of God is referred most specifically to her: "The Holy Spirit will come upon you, and the power of the Most High will overshadow you."

We might be surprised by these expressions since the action of God concerns above all the Son of God coming into Mary, as appears in 1:35b. What is important is that the action of God is indicated less as an effective force (despite the word *dynamis*) than as a presence, according to the pattern by which the Bible signifies the presence of God *upon* and *in*[32] the Ark of the Covenant. The conception by Mary seems to change in 1:35, which places the Son of God in the position of Yahweh taking possession of the Ark. We hear no more of the words "you" and "your." "That which is begotten" (in her) is qualified objectively by two divine titles: "holy" and "Son of God."

The association of these two terms, in a context which recalls the manifestation of God immanent in the Ark of the Covenant, gives to this term an import completely different from that in the fragment of Qumran called *Text of Son of God*.[33]

The verb *klēthēsetai* (he will be called)[34] does not relativize but rather brings out, even emphasizes, this title. In this cultural environment, the *name* is the *being*; to say "Jesus is *called Lord*" is to say "he *is Lord*" (1 Cor 8:6; Acts 10:36). This way of speaking indicates at once that he *is* and that he is *absolutely recognized* as such. This is expressed with emphasis in Philippians 2:9, where Christ is designated by the divine name which God revealed to Moses and which the Jews did not pronounce:

> Therefore God has highly exalted him and bestowed on him the [divine] name which is above every name, that at the name of Jesus every knee should bow, in heaven and on earth and under the earth [universal lordship], and every tongue confess that Jesus Christ is *Lord* [equivalent of the Tetragrammaton YHWH, which the Hebrews never pronounced] to the glory of God the Father.

In short, the virginal conception is not a replication of the theogamic models. It does not explicitly refer to a formalized biological action of God. Rather, the virginal conception appears as a transcendent sign of the eschatological coming of God. The way in which the text omits reference to the corporal realization, which we discover very concretely by its effects in the episode of the visitation, is very remarkable. In a narrative as filled with meaning as this, an omission often highlights the essential idea.

Recalling our lengthy discussion (in the section on literary analysis), it may seem unnecessary to make a further semiotic analysis of 1:35 in relation to Exodus 40:35. But semiotics must go beyond literary analysis. It should recognize the integral meaning, as it is inscribed in the text, with its possible novel implications. Semiotics is an objective discipline called to rise to the measure of the text. If it has forged its first tools by formalizing the "conjunction" of a mother with a child who is qualified as a "possessed good," it must likewise recognize the conjunction of God with humans, including the new form of this conjunction which is Christ, the Son of God. This new reality, essential to the NT, caused great difficulties for the first Christian authors in their efforts to formulate it.[35] Even the deepest and strongest symbolic expression "the Word became flesh" (Jn 1:14) is not adequate. It circumvents the humanity of Jesus. It would be more exact to say "the Word became *man*." Luke 1 expresses this mystery better in less metaphysical language by the insistent identification of the son of Mary and the Son of God, by transferring to Christ attributes or texts belonging to God.

In short, the narrative program, which could seem merely to be the birth of a child announced to a young couple, undergoes here a profound transformation in order to express a new reality which is so far expressed only in the future tense. Since this new reality is inexpressible, its very realization will not be formally expressed, like the Resurrection, the realization of which is not described by any of the evangelists. The human conception of the Son of God will be manifested only by its effects, starting with the visitation, where the presence of the Son of God fills John the Baptist and his mother with the Spirit. The figurative language of the Ark of the Covenant was used to express this new reality. What is new with respect to these OT figures is that this symbolic model of the conjunction between God and his people appears in human form. The presence of God in the wooden ark (Ex 40:35) becomes that of Jesus in the womb of the virgin, the eschatological Daughter of Zion (1:35) and the new Ark of the Covenant.[36]

At 1:35, the high point of the scene, Mary receives a son (the Son of God) whom she had in no way requested. At 1:36 she receives in addition a sign which likewise she did not request, in contrast to Zechariah. This drama extends the contrast between Law and grace. The sign given to Mary is the conception of John the Baptist. It forms a link with the preceding scene:

> And behold, your kinswoman Elizabeth in her old age has also conceived a son; and this is the sixth month with her who was called barren. For with God nothing will be impossible (1:36-37).

The final words emphasize that the incredible miracle arises from the very *power* of God, the "addresser." We can note the occurrence of the root *dyna* in: the power (*dynamis*) of the Most High (1:35); *nothing* will be impossible (*adynatēsai*) for God[37] (1:37); see 1:49, *ho dynatos*, he who is powerful, who overturns the powerful ones (*dynastas*) from their thrones.

The Consent (Lk 1:38)

Mary concludes the scene with an act of faith. After having been graciously defined by God himself (1:28, 30, 35), she defines herself in return. She accepts, by her spiritual consent, the bodily conjunction with God announced for the future in 1:35:

> Behold, I am the handmaid of the Lord; let it be to me according to your word.

Reversal

Semiotic analysis confirms the contrast examined above from the literary point of view. Zechariah was presented in a position superior to that of Mary, according to the following oppositions:
—Jerusalem/Nazareth
—above/below
—man/woman
—priest/young girl from a Galilean village
—husband called to be a father/virgin in fact and intent (cf. Jgs 11:37-38), not even desiring a child (1:34).

These sociological advantages, however, are reversed in favor of Mary:
—Zechariah is qualified according to the Law; Mary according to grace.
—He is in passive confusion before the angel (1:12); she, in dynamic reflexion (1:29).
—His question is censured; Mary's is admitted and rewarded (1:19-20, 36-37).

—He is chastised, disqualified; she, qualified (1:35, 38).
—He becomes mute and powerless; she a participant. God accomplishes his work *without* Zechariah (1:20) and realizes it *with* Mary (1:38 and 45).

Formalization

Let us summarize the annunciation in semiotic terms. The narration begins by a triple shift: spatial, temporal, actorial. A new couple is presented who appear to be subject (as in the preceding sequence) but here the word *amphoteroi* (that is, "both," as used in 1:6 and 7) does not occur. The man, Joseph, son of David, is on a secondary level and disappears. Mary, who has no qualifying title, is the unique addressee of the message and of the double mission (the biological and the ritual: to give birth and to name the child). By the grace of God alone (1:28 and 30), she conceives a child (conjunction), which goes contrary to her intention not to know man (1:34). But here is much more than an infant. The narrative removes any biological basis (1:34-35) for his title as son of David (1:27 and 32b). It gives him the title of Son of God, the Holy One *par excellence*. The Son of God (1:32 and 35) has become the son of Mary (1:31) by a process which is announced and explained (1:35), but not described. There is an omission of the act of conception—announced (1:31) but not described. Mary, characterized in reference to the grace of God (1:28 and 30), further establishes herself by a question in a pre-established harmony with the design of God (1:34) and by perfect adherence (1:38), in contrast to the incredulity (and the muteness) of Zechariah. The qualifying trial leads to the principal trial, the conception of the Son of God, the realization of which will not be recounted but will be manifested by its consequences in the visitation (1:39-56).

The disjunction of Mary in relation to man (1:27 and 34) correlates with her conjunction with God alone, who comes upon her and in her (transcendent and immanent, 1:35). The high point of the narrative is the identification of the Son of God, of God himself, with the son of Mary. We have here the convergence of the coming of the Messiah and the theocratic coming of God announced for the last days (above, p. 63). The Messiah is defined as Son of God (1:32a) before being defined as Messiah (1:32b-33). He is defined on the level of *being* and not of action. The consequences of this definition (qualification) will be worked out in the infancy Gospel and in the Gospel as a whole. The semiotic analysis should proceed up to these observations according to the richness of the text in order neither to minimize nor caricature the annunciation. This is not the story of a young couple to whom a child is born, namely, the Messiah. It is the story of the virgin, the Daughter of Zion, the personification of the people, who receives the Son of God as her son, functioning less as queen than as "handmaid" (1:38). Using semiotics in the service of this text, we give both the text and semiotic analysis their due.

3. The Visitation (Lk 1:39-56)

Journey and the Meeting (Lk 1:39-40)

After the departure of the angel (1:38b), Mary takes the initiative to visit her cousin. It is a journey "program":

> In those days Mary arose and went with haste into the hill country, to a city of Judah, and she entered the house of Zechariah and greeted Elizabeth (1:39-40).

In order to bring out this program, Luke accumulates terms which indicate dynamism, point to Mary, and accent the journey. The word *anastasa* (arising, in order to *go*) is the most common term used to designate the Resurrection. It is a thrust toward what is above (prefix *ana-*), accented by the mention of "mountains" (*oreinē*) which is an appreciable enhancement of the mere hills of Judea. This "seme" is oriented toward Jerusalem, according to the topographical dynamic of Luke 1-2 (above, p. 122). The visitation is the first stage of this ascent, which starts with Nazareth, and proceeds to Jerusalem.

The angel did not command this journey. He simply informed Mary by way of a sign of the happy pregnancy of her elderly cousin. She departs, therefore, not by his order (a "mandating"), but by a personal inspiration—to share, not to verify, as the rest of the narrative shows. Her haste arises from the Holy Spirit, who plays the role of motivator during the entire Gospel (and in Acts).

Mary acts freely, and grace characterizes her actions, as early as 1:28

and 30 (where there appears again the root *char-*). The first ascent of Christ toward Jerusalem establishes the communication between the two mothers, the only visible characters, and between their children, still hidden within them.

The program of this meeting begins with the usual pattern of a greeting upon arrival:

> And she. . . greeted (*ēspasato*) Elizabeth (1:40).

The root signifies greeting and also embracing. The fact that the salutation[38] is qualified with insistence as a voice striking the ears (1:44) may not cancel the implication of the customary bodily embrace.

This salutation, normally used to indicate the end of a journey, becomes the point of departure for a new program, indicated by the word *egeneto*. The Holy Spirit, *having come upon* Mary (1:35), now *fills* Elizabeth (1:41). It is with the salutation of Mary that this divine gift is emphatically associated (1:41 and 44):

> And when Elizabeth heard the greeting of Mary, the babe leaped in her womb; and Elizabeth was filled with the Holy Spirit (1:41).

This formulation is surprising. What is signified here is the fulfillment of the narrative program presented in the annunciation to Zechariah which concerned *John the Baptist*: "He will be filled with the Holy Spirit even from his mother's womb" (1:15). We have already noted the Lucan characteristic which we see at work here: the "communication of idioms" between mother and child. Here the text simply says, "Elizabeth was filled with the Holy Spirit." For the same reason, the blessing of Mary (in the next verse) is mentioned before the blessing of the fruit of her womb (1:42) [who, however, is qualified as *Lord* (1:45)] and Elizabeth verbally refers her praise to the mother of the Lord, a praise which in the end concerns the Lord himself. In this scene a twofold identification of mother and child occurs.

The Prophecy of Elizabeth (Lk 1:42-45)

> And she exclaimed with a loud cry, "Blessed are you among women, and blessed is the fruit of your womb! And why is this granted me,

> that the mother of my Lord should come to me? For behold, when the voice of your greeting came to my ears, the babe in my womb leaped for joy" (1:42-44).

The prophecy of Elizabeth extends the message of the annunciation. Mary continues to be in the forefront (always as a sign). It is the mother of the Lord who is addressed, and it is to her voice that the text emphatically attributes the grace of the visitation (1:41 and 44).

This interpretation removes all ambiguity about the realization of what had been announced in 1:15. It is not only Elizabeth, but also John the Baptist who is filled with the Holy Spirit. The diffusion of the Spirit is without restriction. The visit of Mary carrying the Son of God (cf. *theophoros*) is the sign of this diffusion. Elizabeth recognizes the qualification which the mother of the Lord acquired by her consent in faith (1:38) in literal contrast with Zechariah (1:20):

> Blessed is she who believed that there would be a fulfillment of what was spoken to her from the Lord (1:45).

The last words, "from the Lord," are important. God as addresser is in no way forgotten nor diminished in this praise. It is from him that everything comes. It is to him that all goes, beyond praise and thanksgiving. He is the source of the meeting and the conjunctions or identifications multiplied by the narrative. It is his program which is accomplished beyond human vicissitudes.

The physical meeting (in journey) inspired by the Holy Spirit terminates in a meeting with God, a conjunction involving the two infants as well as the two mothers.

The Prophecy of Mary (Lk 1:46-55)

Mary speaks in her turn (1:46). She, however, does not return praise to Elizabeth. Her praise is addressed only to God. Theocentrism triumphs. Mary magnifies God (1:46).

This personal thanksgiving of Mary, Daughter of Zion, heir of the promises and of the new covenant now beginning, extends to all the people, of whom the singer is the personification. God looked upon Mary and magnified her because of her very humility; this divine act extends to all the poor:

> He has scattered the proud in the imagination of their hearts (*dianoia kardias autōn*), he has put down the mighty from their thrones, and exalted those of low degree; he has filled the hungry with good things and the rich he has sent empty away (1:51-53).

The dispersal concerns first of all the proud whom God confounds, not by violent action, but by "the imagination of their hearts," since pride is a false type of *knowing* which leads to self-destruction.

On the register of *power* and of *having*, the action seems to be attributed to God, who casts down and lifts up, filling the hungry, and apparently emptying the *hands* of the rich (this mention of hands manifests the high-handedness of possessions, in contrast to the bodily emptiness of those who are hungry).

The two final verses offer thanksgiving in the name of Israel, the servant of God, promoted in its entirety, by means of God's revolution, to the condition of the poor, the beloved of God.

In short, the Magnificat celebrates the benefits of God the addresser, first of all to Mary in the present, in the past, and even in the future ("All generations will call me blessed", *makariousin me*). Here Mary echoes Elizabeth, who called her *makaria*, blessed. The thanksgiving extends to the people of God for a present day virtually realized. Such is the future significance of the aorist, which the present situation would not seem to call for. Mary recapitulates the benefits of God in all their historical amplitude since the time of Abraham (1:55), who stands in a position which corresponds to hers. She personifies the eschatological goal (the new convenant signified by the annunciation) as he personified the initial and founding covenant.

The conjunction of God and humanity extends thus from the two women who prophesy, to the whole people, without yet opening up to the universalism which will be expressed later in the canticles of Zechariah (1:79) and Simeon (2:32).

The Return (Lk 1:56)

What is the significance of the short verse which closes the visitation scene immediately after the Magnificat?

> Mary remained with her about three months, and returned to her home (1:56).

Did Mary depart before or after the birth? Luke's style invites us to think that she remained until after the birth of John. Luke usually disposes of the principal character at the end of the sequence which concerns that character. Thus he describes John the Baptist's early life and his departure to the desert (1:80; see 1:66), before narrating the birth of Jesus (2:1-7). Thus he also paradoxically reports the imprisonment of John (3:20) before the baptism of Jesus (3:21-22). The three months of Mary's stay thus extend to and, we would argue, include the birth of John. The three months also have the function of introducing the birth of John the Baptist, signified in the following verse, "when the time came for Elizabeth to be delivered."

Formalization

Let us recapitulate the transformation of the narrative.

Mary's journey constitutes a spatial shift, in chronological continuity with the preceding scene. Its object is Mary's meeting with Elizabeth, who had been described to her as a sign in 1:36. There is then a continuity of actants.

In the framework of the unity of persons which characterizes pregnancy in Luke 1, Mary is presented as the subject operative of the transformation in Elizabeth and her child (a double subject of a state of being). It is clear, however, that beyond this sign, the radiance can be attributed to the Son of the Lord God, who is in her (1:43), and to the Holy Spirit, who "fills" John the Baptist (1:15) and his mother (1:41) conjointly. Mary and her son are recognized in the Spirit. Elizabeth and her son are changed by the Spirit (1:15 and 41).

How is the change signified?

—For John the Baptist, by the "dance" within the womb (1:41 and 44) which his mother characterizes as expressing joy (1:44) and which the announcement of 1:15 characterizes as a pouring in of the Holy Spirit.

—For Elizabeth, by a transition from silence, by which she marks the end of her shame (1:25), with the twofold effect: she is filled with the Holy Spirit (1:41) and expresses her joy with a great cry (1:42). She too expresses herself charismatically in 1:42-45. This analogy accents the identification between mother and son. The formula "filled with the Holy Spirit," apparently applied to John the Baptist alone in 1:15

and to the mother alone in 1:42, applies conjointly to one and the other, according to the isotopy of the two verses.

Elizabeth, qualified as a prophet by the gift of the Spirit, recognizes the glory of Mary and of her son as Lord (1:43), as well as the radiance that proceeds from this glory, in short, the eschatological gift of God, analogous to that which Luke expresses at Pentecost (Acts 2).

Mary, qualified by the gift of the Holy Spirit as early as 1:35 and recognized as such by Elizabeth, prophesies in her turn. She extends her personal thanksgiving as a poor woman (1:48) to all the people of the poor (occurrence of the root *tapein-*, 1:48 and 52). In short, in this scene as in the preceding, the newness shines forth from an apparently ordinary program. The voyage through the mountains ends in a divine communication which causes Elizabeth to pass from the rule of the Law (1:6) to the rule of the Spirit (1:41, the gift of grace according to the isotopic parallels of Luke 1-2). The prophetic charism of Elizabeth prefigures that of John. The charism of Mary and her very poverty prefigure Christ and his proclamation, "Blessed are you poor" (6:20). The glorifying test of the two mothers prefigures the future of the two sons.

All this is orchestrated by the reworking of 2 Samuel 6, thus likening Mary's journey to the transfer of the Ark of the Covenant and its temporary stay in a welcoming house on the way to Jerusalem. The thanksgiving which Elizabeth directs to Mary (a sign and a figure of grace), Mary refers to God alone, the ultimate point of reference from whom all comes, in strong contrast with her poverty and that of the poor whom God satisfies and fulfills (1:48, 51-53).

The departure of Mary (spatial shift) is mentioned by anticipation. The number three months, an allusion to 2 Samuel 6:11, seems to insinuate a symmetry between the first six months of Elizabeth, mentioned with insistence in 1:24, 26, 36, and the six months which remain for Mary.

4. The Birth and Circumcision of John the Baptist

Having completed the "Mary" sequence, Luke now turns his attention to John the Baptist, who occupies the end of the chapter: his birth (1:57-58), circumcision (1:59-79), and early life (1:80).

These stages have been programed for the future by the annunciation to Zechariah. The first one, "he will be filled with the Holy Spirit even from his mother's womb" (1:15), was accomplished at the visitation (1:41). The three others, likewise announced, will also be accomplished:

1. The birth: "Your wife Elizabeth will bear you a son" (1:13) is realized in 1:57-58.

2. The circumcision: "You shall call his name John" (1:13) is realized in 1:59-79.

3. The development: "He will be great before the Lord" (1:15) is realized in 1:80.

The Birth (Lk 1:56-57)

Elizabeth is the sole subject of this sequence. Zechariah, mute, remains excluded from the narrative. There is no change of place or duration, since 1:56 already situates us at the end of the three months. "The time for her to give birth" is fulfilled.

> Now the time came for Elizabeth to be delivered and she begot (*egenesen*) a son (1:57).

The last words are unusual. Luke says that Elizabeth *begot* (*egennsen*). This word is not normally used for a woman. Matthew 1-2 reserves it for fathers: it is they who "beget" (forty times throughout the genealogy in Mt 1:2-16), while women conceive and give birth or are indicated as the *origin* of the child by the particle *ek* (from), used also for the Holy Spirit. Although the virginal conception excluded a human father, Luke does not refer the act of begetting to Mary, in order not to obscure the fact that Christ had no other father but God (a precaution of vocabulary common throughout the NT). He repeats thus that Mary gave birth (*eteken*), twice in the same sentence (similar in other respects to the sentence describing Elizabeth as begetting):

Elizabeth (Lk 1:57)	*Mary (Lk 2:6-7)*
Now the time was come for Elizabeth, and she gave birth to a son.	And the time came for her to be delivered. And she gave birth to her first-born son.

"She begot" was so disturbingly irregular that the Vulgate translated it as *peperit* (in place of *genuit*). In the announcement to Zechariah, the verb "to beget" is used of Elizabeth with reference to the father: "Your wife will beget for you." But because of his objection and his lack of faith, Zechariah is excluded from the narrative until his rehabilitation (1:62), so that Elizabeth replaces him here and in the following verses. This is one of the main points of the narrative.[39]

The parents of John the Baptist seem at first to be acting as a subject in the "dual" (*amphoteroi*, 1:6 and 7), although sterility was attributed only to Elizabeth (1:7). The paternal subject, Zechariah, is then the single addressee of the annunciation (1:8-23). Elizabeth, eliminated by topographical change, seems forgotten. Zechariah, however, as unbelieving, punished, powerless (1:19-23), disappears after 1:24. Elizabeth becomes the sole subject (1:24-25). She is characterized by the charism of prophecy in 1:41-45. The thanksgiving concerns only her and her son in this episode of the visitation, as well as later in that of the birth:

> And her neighbors and kinsfolk heard that the Lord had shown great mercy to her, and they rejoiced with her [1:58, which parallels 1:14].

This restriction of the narrative to the single subject, Elizabeth, is all the more striking since the angel said to Zechariah: "Elizabeth will bear *you* a son. . . . And *you* will have joy and gladness" (1:13, 14). Zechariah, in the glory of the Temple was the single subject, and the joy of Elizabeth was only implied in that of the multitude: "Many will rejoice at his birth." The joy promised the father (1:14) is transferred here to the mother (1:41-44 and 58). The joy of the "many" announced by the angel is realized by the neighbors and relatives who rejoice "with her" (1:58). Paradoxically Zechariah still remains outside the narrative.

The motive for this joy is the "mercy" shown to Elizabeth. The word *eleos* (mercy) often translates a Hebrew *Hen* or *Haninah* in the LXX, and corresponds etymologically to the name of John: *Yohanan* (Yahweh has shown mercy). This word occurs almost exclusively in this section treating of John the Baptist. If as it seems to us, Luke 1-2 depends here on a Hebrew source, then we have clear etymological allusions to the names of the two infants, Jesus and John, according to a usage frequent in the Bible for the birth of heroes.[40]

Circumcision (Lk 1:59-66)

The following sequence, the most developed one, begins with the word *egeneto*, which stresses its importance with a temporal shift marking the date.

> On the eighth day they came to circumcise the child; and they would have named him Zechariah after his father (1:59).

The absence of Zechariah is noted because it was he whom the angel commanded, "You shall call his name John" (1:13). Zechariah continues to be excluded, and those who come to circumcise supply for his powerlessness. They wish to call him "Zechariah after his father." The decision is based on common usage, as appears in their objection in 1:61. Their program is based on customary action. They wish to attribute to the future prophet the name of the mute father, but it is a new thing which God has programed (1:13). Elizabeth proposes the name prescribed by the angel. "Not so; he shall be called John" (1:60). She who has "begotten" continues to take precedence over Zechariah as subject (of begetting, of joy, and here of an official ritual act). The narration does not formally specify the source of her knowledge which seems attributable to the Holy Spirit (1:41).

The neighbors persist in their anti-program by expressing the objection from usage and custom:

> None of your kindred is called by this name (1:61).

As in the preceding scenes, the normal program regulated by customary usage is here modified from above according to the prescription of the angel. The neighbors do not understand. They defend the custom. They appeal to the forgotten father who suddenly reappears (to confirm the new and not the old).

They made signs to him (*eneneuon*), inquiring "what he would have him called" (1:62). This communication without words supposes Zechariah to be *deaf* as well as *mute*. His lack of power, his exclusion is

Etymological Allusions to the Names of Personages in Luke 1-2

The Hebrew substratum of Luke 1-2 is the source for many allusions to the characters of the narrative. (I developed this idea in the article, "Traces d'allusions étymologiques en Luc 1-2" in *Biblica* 37, 1956, pp. 435-436; 38, 1957, pp. 1-23.) This series of indices converges with others which the article evaluated in a *status quaestionis* (pp. 453-456). But research into this topic has progressed a good deal since S. C. Farris, following the method of R. A. Martin (see bibliography), proved that Luke 1-2 statistically presents the characteristics of a text translated from a Semitic source, probably Hebrew—characteristics it shares with the Septuagint translation.

Let us recall here only how the etymological allusions to the names of the characters in Luke 1-2 are presented and the convergences which present them in diverse degrees.

John and Jesus

The name *Yeshûa'*, a contraction of *Yehôshûa'*, signifies *Yahweh is Savior*. In receiving this name from the angel, Jesus receives it from God himself. The root of the name occurs constantly in the passages which concern Jesus:

—"My spirit rejoices in *God* my *Savior*," sings Mary in the Magnificat (Lk 1:47). These words relate at once to God who saves and to *Jesus the Savior*, who is the starting point of this thanksgiving. (We could translate, *In Deo* JESU *meo*, like the Vulgate in Hab 3:13).

—God raised up (in Jesus) a force of SALVATION (Lk 1:69)

—A SALVATION which will liberate us from our enemies (Lk 1:71)

—John the Baptist will give to the people a knowledge of SALVATION [which will be concretely a knowledge of Jesus] (Lk 1:77)

—The oracle of the angles proclaims him SAVIOR and Christ-Lord (Lk 2:11)

—For Simeon, "to see the Christ" - to see Jesus (2:27, 2:30) - to see SALVATION. The abstract word *salvation* has the sense of a superlative in comparison with the concrete word, *Savior*. The Hebrew substratum is necessarily the very root of the name of Jesus Savior.

John likewise receives his name by an oracle of the angel. This Hebrew name *Yôḥānān*, a contraction of *Yehôḥānān*, signifies "*Yahweh has been* favorable, merciful, has shown pity."

The translation back into Hebrew uncovers the root of his name in numerous verses:

—Do not be afraid, Zechariah, for your prayer has been heard (Lk 1:13). In the Septuagint *deēsis* corresponds most frequently to *teḥinnāh* or *taḥănûn*, a hypothesis proposed several times since J. Hillmann, Loisy, etc. ("Traces," p. 441).

—Remembering his goodness (*eleos*, Lk 1:54)

—At the birth of John the Baptist the neighbors learned that God has filled his mother with his goodness (Lk 1:58; mercy, *eleos*, which often corresponds to the root *ḥnn*).

—In the Benedictus, which especially concerns John the Baptist, "God has shown mercy (*eleos*) to our fathers" (Lk 1:72).

—The salvation given by his "tender mercy" (*eleos*, cf. 1:50, his mercy is from age to age; Lk 1:78).

The substratum *ḥnn* is certain in Lk 1:72, since in the Septuagint this expression corresponds generally to the root *ḥānan*, but the word *eleos* alone only rarely translates this root. More frequently it translates *ḥesed*, which makes the other allusions more problematic.

The following arguments lend weight to this convergence:

1. The play on words concerning the names of predestined children are frequent in the Bible, beginning with Genesis 4:1; 4:25; 5:29. Many references can be found in "Traces," pp. 433-442.

2. The words which correspond to the Hebrew roots of the names of Jesus and John occur especially in the infancy Gospel and exclusively in the passages which concern John and Jesus:

—*eleos*, five times against one for the rest of the Gospel (Lk 10:37). The word does not occur in Acts. This word is not Lucan, and to show mercy (*poiēsai eleos*) appears only in Lk 1:72 and 10:37.

—*sōtēr* in Lk 1:47 and 2:11

—*sōtērion* in Lk 2:30

—*sōtēria* in Lk 1:69, 71, 77, always in a christological context. These are the only uses of these words in the third Gospel with the exception of 3:6 and 19:9.

—*sōtēria* occurs five times in Acts, where it implies etymological allusions: "in the name of Jesus" the cripple was healed, because "there is no salvation (*sōtēria*) in any other, and no other name has been given to men for them to be SAVED" (Acts 4:9-12). The redundant occurrence of the words "name," "Jesus," "salvation" (twice each) shows their importance in the translation back into Hebrew.

—The two uses of *sōtēr* (Savior in Acts 5:31 and 13:23), "Jesus-Savior," seem to imply also an etymological allusion based on the Semitic substratum.

—*sōtērion* is used only four times in the NT. Outside of Ephesians 6:17, it is found only in Lk 2:30 and 3:6 (with the same expression "to see salvation") and Acts 28:28. Each time, the reference is to Jesus.

3. More precisely, in the infancy Gospel the roots of the two names recur uniquely:

—in the *oracles* (1:13; 2:11)

—in the *canticles* concerning the two children: the Magnificat (at the visitation), 1:47 for Jesus and 1:54 for John; Benedictus, 1:69, 71, 77 for Jesus and 1:72, 78 for John; and the Nunc Dimittis, for Jesus alone in 2:30.

—finally, in the narrative of the birth of John, at the moment when his name is about to be given to him (Lk 1:59-62).

Zechariah and Elizabeth

The allusions to these names were studied in "Traces" (1957, 1-4, cf. 13). *Zkr*, the root of the name of Zechariah (Yahweh remembered), is found in Lk 1:54 and 72; *sb'*, the root of the name of Elizabeth (Yahweh has sworn) appears in 1:55 and 73.

A striking observation—the root of the three names of John the Baptist, Zechariah, and Elizabeth recur in two canticles: in the Magnificat (1:54-55), "In remembrance (*mnēsthēnai* = *zkr*, the root of the name of Zechariah) of his *mercy* (*eleous* = *hnn*, the root of the name of John) as he *spoke* (*elalēsen*) to our fathers" (to speak has the value of promise and oath which normally recalls *sb'* in the Hebrew substratum); and in the Benedictus (1:72-73) "To perform mercy (*eleos* = *hnn* = John) promised to our fathers and to remember (*mnēsthēnai* = *zkr* = Zechariah) his holy covenant, the oath (*horkon* = *sb'* = the root of the name of Elizabeth) which he swore (*ōmosen* = same root *sb'* = Elizabeth) to our father Abraham."

Here the root of the word "oath," softened by the Greek text of the Magnificat (1:55) is repeated according to the redundant mode of the Hebrew language. The substratum is thus more evident (for John and Elizabeth) in 1:73 than in 1:54-55.

Gabriel and Mary

See R. Laurentin, "Traces," (*Biblica*, 1956, pp. 447-448 and 1957, pp. 4-13).

These allusions confirm the interesting hypothesis, according to R. Kugelmann, which sees also the root *rûm*, meaning "elevated," in the theme of the first part of the Magnificat concerned with Mary.

in some way augmented by this note.[41] The increased intensification of his weakness makes the contrast all the more striking, and now it reaches its apex. The mute father responds by writing on a tablet:

> His name is John (1:63)!

He does not speak in the future tense as Elizabeth did, but in the present. His word is the equivalent of a realization. It has for him a qualifying and glorifying value, and also a healing value. It realizes the end of the program formulated by the angel, "You will be silent. . . *until the day* that these things come to pass. . . which will be fulfilled in their time" (1:20). Speech is given back immediately to Zechariah and he uses it only to bless God (1:64), a praise which will be enlarged later in his own canticle (1:68-79). All returns to God, who is not only the "sender" but also the author of the program (subject of doing, 1:25 and 28). In Luke 1-2 all comes from God by grace and returns to him in the form of thanksgiving.

This thanksgiving (an exercise of faith) extends not only to the neighbors and relatives, as in 1:58, and to the actants of the circumcision (1:59), but to *all*, with a pleonasm of terms signifying a totality. The birth of John the Baptist is not a domestic event. It is given for the good of all the people (addressees) as programed in 1:14:

> And fear came (*egeneto*) on all (*pantas*) their neighbors. And all these events (*rhēmata*) were talked about through all (*holè*) the hill country of Judea; and *all* who heard them laid them up in their hearts, saying, "What then will this child be?" For the hand of the Lord was with him (1:65-66).

The faith of the people, informed of the news, is first of all characterized by *fear*. This word, which frequently occurs in the theophanies of the OT and in Luke (1:12, 30; 2:9; 5:26; 7:16; 8:25, 35, 37; 9:34), manifests the awe of human beings before the gift of God which surpasses them. It signals their acclimatization to the transcendence of the divine gift. This fear is positive. It yields to a twofold diffusion. Not only is there mention of the events (*rhēmata*), but they are placed in the memory (1:66), in the heart, the place where the words and events of God can ripen, with an interrogation turned toward a future not yet unveiled: What then will this child be?

This question is qualified in a positive way, as a hope, by the explanatory clause of Luke (author-enunciator): "For the hand of the Lord was with him." The positive element here is the conjunction with God. The bodily figure of the hand (see 1:71 and 74) signifies his powerful presence. The natural consequence of these words, and the first response to the question posed, appears in 1:80, the concluding refrain of the chapter.

The Prophecy of Zechariah (the Benedictus: Lk 1:67-79)

Before this natural conclusion, however, the Benedictus is inserted here (1:68-79). We might be surprised (and think of it as a later addition) since it has already been said that Zechariah blessed God (1:64). Furthermore, the earlier statement uses the verb *eulogōn* which is also the first word of the Benedictus, *eulogētos:*

> And his father Zechariah was filled with the Holy Spirit, and prophesied, saying, "Blessed be the Lord God of Israel, for he has visited and redeemed his people" (1:67-68).

The theme of the Benedictus is analogous to that of the Magnificat, a thanksgiving to God for the fulfillment of salvation. The parallels are numerous. As in the Magnificat, the formulas of the psalms and biblical canticles are used in the Benedictus, but in three novel ways:[42]

1. The dismal situation of Israel, which is passed over in silence in the Magnificat, is made explicit in the Benedictus: enemies (twice mentioned), hatred (1:71), darkness and the shadow of death (1:79).

2. Zechariah does not exalt the wonders which God has done for *him* (as Mary does), but only for the people as collective addressees who say "we," and have their full importance here (1:68 and 77). Although a priest, Zechariah is not semiotically the personification of the people, as was the case with Mary, the Daughter of Zion, or Simeon and Anna, as we will see further on.

3. The Magnificat makes only imperceptible allusions (by way of etymology) to the infants, Jesus and John. The Benedictus clearly alludes to their missions.

Further, Jesus is implicitly mentioned in many ways by references to the prophetic program of Gabriel (1:30-35):

—The double mention of *salvation* is a new etymological allusion to the name of Jesus (1:69 and 71).
—"Raised up"[43] in the *house of David* corresponds to 1:30-33, where Jesus is announced as the royal heir promised to David (see 2:3-5).
—The mention of the *prophets* refers to the messianic predictions used in 1:32-35, especially 2 Samuel 7:14.

However, the allusion to the infant Messiah remains in the shadows, without either anachronism or retrospective specification.

This first part appears as an echo of the Magnificat, with numerous isotopic parallels: it ends likewise with a promise made to Abraham.

4. In the Benedictus, the people (addressees) come to the forefront. Liberated and engaged in the service of God (1:74), they seem to take on the role of addresser. Constantly they say "we" (1:71), with the corresponding possessive pronoun "our" enemies (1:71), "our" fathers (1:72), "our" father Abraham (1:73), "our" days (1:75). This "we" is not only Zechariah and the people in whose name he speaks (functioning again in this as a representative), but also the readers, whom Luke (the enunciator) invites to participate in this praise:[44]

> [He] has raised up a horn of salvation[45] for us in the house of his servant David, as he spoke by the mouth of his holy prophets from of old, *salvation* from our enemies, and from the hand of all who hate us to perform the mercy promised to our fathers, and to remember his holy covenant, the oath which he swore to our father Abraham, to grant us that we, being delivered from the hand of our enemies, might serve him without fear, in holiness and righteousness before him all the days of our life (1:69-75).

The second part of the canticle celebrates John the Baptist, as is fitting for Zechariah his father. He addresses him in the second person, speaking of a future which as an old man he will never see:

> And you, child, will be called the prophet of the Most High; for you will go before the Lord to prepare his ways (Mal 3:1 and 23) to give knowledge of salvation to his people in the forgiveness of their sins, through the tender mercy of our God, when the day shall dawn upon us from on high to give light to those who sit in darkness and in the shadow of death, to guide our feet into the way of peace (1:76-79).

The beginning refers to the programmation of Gabriel in 1:17. We find again the two functions of John, prophet and precursor, with the same ambiguity (precursor of God, according to the terms of the discourse, precursor of Christ, according to the context). We no longer find, however, the function of one who calls to conversion, maintained with pleonastic insistence in 1:16-17. This function is transformed in terms of *knowledge*.

The knowledge involved here is first of all that of salvation, whence comes the "remission of sins." The ambiguity between the visitation of God and that of the Messiah (1:68-69) continues under the symbolic image of a star which rises from on high to give light to those who are in darkness and the shadow of death. Here we have a probable allusion to the messianic prophecy of Balaam in Numbers 24:17, "A star shall come forth out of Jacob, and a scepter shall rise out of Israel." In the symbolism of that time, a star belonged to the divine realm rather than the human realm.[46]

This reference to light announces the Nunc Dimittis, where the symbol of light, which appeared previously in Isaiah, has a significance for the whole world. At this point in the narrative the "growth" refrain occurs, which would perhaps seem to have fitted more naturally with 1:66, before the Benedictus:

> And the child grew and became strong in spirit, and he was in the wilderness till the day of his manifestation to Israel (1:80).

In contrast to Jesus, who grows up in the house of Nazareth "before God and man" (2:52), the early life of John the Baptist is situated outside of his "home," which is mentioned, nonetheless, with insistence (1:23 and 40); his early life is spent in the desert. Contrary to the tendency of narrative grammar to define this episode by the relationship of the parents to the child-object, the aged parents, who are turned toward God, disappear after the circumcision. The child seems to grow up in the desert, at a distance, away from them and from the people, whose great joy he appeared at first to be (1:14).

Formalization

The birth of John the Baptist realizes the oracle of the annunciation to Zechariah (1:13-17). By giving his son the unusual name (1:61) which had been prescribed (1:13), Zechariah recovers his speech in accordance with the prescription of the angel. John the Baptist provokes pondering and questioning (1:66) which extend to "all of Judea" (1:65). He grows in the desert (1:80) "before the Lord," (1:15) alone "till the day of his manifestation to Israel" (1:80), also announced by the angel (1:15-17). This manifestation will be the object of Luke 3. The play of conjunctions and disjunctions appears thus as the accomplishment of the oracle of Gabriel, developing toward the inaugural role of John the Baptist. The response of the addressees is a mixture of questioning and thanksgiving (1:64 and 1:67-79). The progression is minor (i.e., not fully developed) since John the Baptist is only the precursor. This is balanced by the anecdotal vivacity of the narrative (1:57-66). The real fulfillment begins in chapter 2, which is dedicated exclusively to Christ.

The Narrative Program of Luke 1

At the end of this first chapter, we can consider the ensemble of narrative programs relating to the early history of John the Baptist. The coherence and unity of this section is illustrated by the recurrence of the formula "filled with the Holy Spirit" (1:15, 41, 67).

The key moments of the chapter are indicated by this formula which is applied successively to John the Baptist (1:15), Elizabeth (1:41), and Zechariah (1:67). The final verse situates the growth of the child John in the desert where his mission will later be fulfilled. Luke 1:80 thus programs the beginning of the Gospel (Luke 3).

We have here a triple pentecost, since Luke characterizes that event by the same formula, "They were all filled with the Holy Spirit" (Acts 2:4 and 4:31). The family of John the Baptist, exemplary according to the Law, received by anticipation the gift of the Spirit. This is implied in a significant movement.

Thus Zechariah and Elizabeth are presented under the sign of the Law, qualified by the observance of the commandments (1:6) and the rites (1:8-9), yet sterile and unfruitful (1:18). Within this figurative framework of the old order, the newness of the spirit bursts forth—with difficulty and not without testing, in the case of Zechariah.

The transformation of the narrative thus leads us from the Law, symbolized by this elder couple, to the Spirit, from the old covenant to the inner covenant of Pentecost, anticipated by the three members of this family of pure priestly lineage. Let us remember this conclusion, because it contains one of the elements whose full meaning will appear when we establish (on a deeper level) the semiotic square of Luke 1-2.

We need to situate this important stepping stone within the total context of chapter 1, because this pentecost of John the Baptist, Elizabeth, and Zechariah proceeds from the fundamental focus of this program: the coming of the Messiah, the Son of God. It is by him, by his mother who carries him and "greets" Elizabeth (1:40, 41, 44), that John the Baptist and Elizabeth are "filled with the Holy Spirit," that they are transferred from the old to the new covenant (1:41, 44).

How is this done? Mary is the first to receive the Holy Spirit, in terms parallel to those of Pentecost: "The Holy Spirit will come upon you" (1:35; Acts 1:8). Elizabeth attributed this double outpouring on herself and her son to the greeting of Mary (1:44). It is clear, however, that the voice of Mary (her greeting) was only a sign and a signal of it.

The child conceived through the power of the Spirit as the new presence of God in the new Ark (Mary) is the source of the proto-pentecost of his precursor.

The transition from the Law to the Spirit, which characterizes the infancy of John the Baptist, is thus achieved by Christ. This proto-pentecost is one stage on the road which will transform Israel into the "Church"[47] and lead from the Law to grace—a transition signified by the insistence on the word "grace" at the beginning of the annunciation (1:28 and 30). The disclosure of the Christ-Lord (1:32-35 and 43), still ambiguous in this first chapter, provides the narrative program of chapter 2. Jesus will be designated there by his major titles (2:11, 23, 29, 32) and will reveal himself publicly for the first time, revealing his consciousness not only of his divine sonship (2:49), but also of his mission which, in the last analysis, is defined by his return to the Father (2:49). Semiotics confirms and deepens the dynamic of Luke 1-2.

5. The Birth of Christ the Lord (Lk 2:1-20)

The Christmas sequence is clearly marked by the triple change of time (six months), of place (Bethlehem), and of actants (Joseph, Mary, and Jesus become the focus of the narrative).[48]

Within this sequence, the topographic and actantial changes mark four sub-sequences in the progressive continuity of time. They began with and are punctuated by the use of *egeneto* (2:6 and 15; see 2:13). The four sub-sequences concern:

1. The census, where Joseph is the sole actant of the transfer from Nazareth to Bethlehem (2:1-5).

2. The birth of Jesus (2:6-7), where Mary (previously in the orbit of Joseph, 2:5) becomes the only actant or subject (at the birth).

3. The annunciation to the shepherds (2:8-14), new subjects, the only beneficiaries of the triple celestial manifestation: the angel of the Lord, the glory of the Lord, then the heavenly host.

4. The visit of the shepherds to the manger (2:15-20) and the triple repercussion of their conjunction with Christ: the spreading of the good news (2:17), the meditation of Mary (2:19), the thanksgiving of the shepherds (2:20)—so that this scene, like the visitation, ends with praise.

The Census (Lk 2:1-5)

Like the preceding sequences, the narrative of the birth of Jesus begins with an earthly program, which will open up on the unexpected breakthrough of a celestial program where God is manifested.

The earthly program is that of the supreme power, Caesar Augustus, the one responsible for the Roman order. This power arises before we see how the actants of Luke will be concerned:

> In those days a decree went out from Caesar Augustus that all the world (*pasan tēn oikoumenēn*) should be enrolled (2:1).

The role of Caesar Augustus is not merely that of a chronological reference point, like Herod (1:5) or Tiberius Caesar in 3:1. He has the role of a universal addresser, as is evidenced by the repetition of the Greek word *pas* (all) in 2:1 and 3. He intends to make a census of the whole of the "inhabited world" (*oikoumenē*). Every power closes in upon itself, unaware of what takes place outside its control. The emperor, the universal addresser, thus encompasses the Messiah and his parents. The following details then localize the census by mention of the regional authority and at the same time bring out the universal and migratory character of the measure:

> This was the first enrollment, when Quirinius was governor of Syria.[49] And all went to be enrolled, each to his own city. And Joseph also went up from Galilee, from the city of Nazareth, to Judea, to the city of David, which is called Bethlehem, because he was of the house and lineage of David.

We turn from the supreme and universal level, characterized by the word *all*, to the individual case of Joseph. This person, who has been shown in a passive role until now, finds an active role for the first time. He accomplishes this enforced journey, which the first Greek word of the phrase *anabē*, characterizes as an ascent. The narrative does not dramatize the exodus of the Holy Family (as later tradition did) nor its poverty (which, however, is expressed in terms of deprivation and even rejection, 2:7). The journey to Bethlehem is presented as a particular application of the general principle that "all went to be enrolled, each to his own city." Joseph is situated in his role as son of David (mentioned in 1:27 "of the house of David," repeated in 1:69 and 2:4).

We have here the hinge of the narrative. This point appears in an even more deliberate manner since Bethlehem is characterized by the possessive adjective "his city" in apparent contradiction with 1:27 and especially 2:39, where Nazareth is given as the city of the parents of Jesus, "their own city." The text specifies with a certain pleonasm that this city functions as the place of origin (*oikos*, house) and of lineage (*patria*, 2:4).

We do not yet see where the narrative is going nor how Christ will be concerned, since the paternity of Joseph was (seemingly) excluded in 1:33-35.

Verse 5 progresses toward the theme. It informs us that it is not Joseph alone who goes to be enrolled. He goes up to Bethlehem:

to be enrolled with Mary, his betrothed, who was with child (2:5).

Joseph is in conjunction with Mary, herself in conjunction with the Messiah in her pregnancy. The census then concerns two persons and soon three, since the child will be born at Bethlehem. We see thus how the program posed in the annunciation of the angel to Mary is accomplished: "The Lord God will give to him the throne of his father David" (1:32).

This oracle is an echo of the messianic prophecy of Nathan (2 Sm 7:12-17). In a remarkable progression, Luke 2:4-14 does not use this prophecy again, but rather moves to Micah 5:1-5, which prophesies a Messiah arising out of Bethlehem (see above, p. 46). This oracle of God, the supreme addresser, bursts forth in contrast with the program of the legislator, Caesar Augustus, presented in 2:1. The irony of the narrative is that the census to which Jesus passively submits ("to be enrolled," 2:5) codifies his royal and sovereign status as Messiah. This Davidic qualification in the town of Bethlehem (the city of David) is confirmed by the heavenly oracle which declares him to be the Messiah-Lord (2:11), the king, of whose kingdom "there will be no end" (1:33). God the addresser (author of the prophecies and oracles) uses the blind power of Augustus (the great manipulator of populations) to authenticate the Messiah-King as a descendant of the founder of the dynasty (semiotically, a qualifying test for the Messiah-King).

Luke has, at this stage, not explained how Jesus, who was not the son of Joseph, could merit this title of son of David. He bases this qualification simply on the topographical conjunction. Indeed, to emphasize the disjunction apparent in Jesus not being the son of Joseph, Luke continues to refer to Mary as Joseph's "betrothed" (*emnēsteumenē*). Although this is a suitable word in 1:27, where we are introduced to the characters, it is astonishing to find this word at the time of Jesus' birth (and of the official cohabitation according to Mt 1:18-25). The function of this unusual usage is to remind us (in the wake of 1:34) that Mary did not "know man," and that Jesus is not the son of Joseph. It also makes the point that Mary made this journey, not as a daughter of David, but with Joseph, the head of the family, heir of the royal lineage, but subject to the decree of Caesar Augustus. She accompanies Joseph because of her marriage to him, which creates a juridical bond.

Luke thus quietly passes over the official conclusion of the marriage and the cohabitation (Mt 1:20-25).

The Birth (Lk 2:6-7)

In the birth narrative, Joseph is absent. The function of subject devolves on Mary alone. The birth is described with a striking sobriety in comparison to the haggadic narrations of the birth of Moses or the poetic developments of Virgil on the birth of his messiah in the fourth Eclogue. This central sub-sequence begins again with an emphatic *egeneto*:

> And while they were there, the time came for her to be delivered. And she gave birth to her first-born son and wrapped him in swaddling cloths, and laid him in a manger, because there was no place for them in the inn (2:6-7).

The whole activity is attributed to Mary alone. She gives birth, she wraps and places the baby in the manger without any suggestion of difficulty, pain, or obstetric help. (Less than a century later, the *Protoevangelion of James*, 19-20, added midwives to this scene because they were useful for providing testimony about her virginity.) But in Luke's Gospel, Mary is the subject of the action in this earthly program.

Since Luke makes frequent reference to Micah 4-5 to identify Mary with the mother of the Messiah and the Daughter of Zion, it is surprising that he narrates the birth of Jesus without the least reference to Micah 4:9-10:

> Pangs have seized you like a woman in travail. Writhe and groan, O daughter of Zion, like a woman in travail; for now you shall go forth from the city and dwell in the open country. . . . There you shall be rescued.

Like his source, Micah 5:2, Luke repeats the word "to give birth" twice, but he eliminates all pain. He describes Mary as serene and free in her movements, a suggestion which has influenced the Christian tradition of a birth without pain.[50]

He situates the birth in the city of David (a phrase repeated with

The Manger and the Swaddling Clothes

The Manger (phatnē)

H. J. Cadbury (*JBL* 45, 1926, pp. 317-319; 53, 1933, pp. 61-62) translated *phatnē* by "stall" or "feeding-place." But the fact that Jesus was laid (*aneklinen*) in the manger clearly indicates, according to current meaning, the only one indicated in the majority of dictionaries, a manger in the form of a crib. This meaning is retained by J. Fitzmyer (*Luke 1-9*, 1981, p. 408).

Luke is the only evangelist to use the word *phatnē*, manger. He uses it four times: three times in the episode of Christmas, where the manger is the sign given to the shepherds (2:7, 12, 16), and again at 13:15, "Does not each of you on the Sabbath untie his ox or his ass from the manger. . . ?"

In what sense is the manger a sign? Some have tried to explain it in reference to the lament of Isaiah 1:3:

> The *ox* knows its owner, and the *ass* its master's *crib*;
> but Israel does not know, my people does not understand.

The fervor of the shepherds, who would be able to recognize the manger would contrast with Israel's desertion according to Isaiah.

The Swaddling Clothes

The verb to wrap (*sparganoō*, twice in the Septuagint: Jb 38:9 and Ez 16:4) derives from the substantives, swaddling clothes (*sparganon*, the Hebrew root *ḥtl*). It is not used in the NT except in Luke in this birth narrative (2:7 and 12). Being wrapped in swaddling clothes is part of the sign of the manger in the annunciation to the shepherds (2:12) but is not mentioned again explicitly in 2:16 (the verse about the verification of the sign). The wrapping in swaddling clothes connotes the material care of the mother in 2:7 (see Ez 16:4, where the absence of swaddling clothes is a sign of abandonment). This detail seems to become (in 2:12) a sign of powerlessness and weakness (see Wis 7:4). According to the analysis of A. Serra (*Sapienza*, 1982, p. 206), this seems to be part of a play on allusions to the death of Christ.

Luke 2:7	*Luke 23:53*
She wrapped him	And he wrapped (it)
in swaddling clothes	in a linen shroud
and laid him in the manger	and laid him in a tomb

(2:12)	
lying (*keimenon*) in the manger	laid (*keimenos*, see 24:12; the linens placed: *keimena*, a variant in many mss. for 24:12)
(2:16)	*(24:12)*
They went with haste (*speusantes*),	Peter. . . ran (*edramen*) see 24:3,
and found. . . the babe. . .	[the women] did not find the body.

The medical theories of the ancients saw a parallel between pregnancy and death. (C. Vogel, "L'environnement culturel du défunt durant la période paléo-chrétienne." *Eph Liturgicae*, Rome, Subsidia 1, 1975, pp. 381-413.) Later iconography stressed the connection by giving the manger the appearance of a tomb and a sepulchre.

insistence in 2:3, 4, and 11), not in the fields, mentioned in the following verse with the shepherds. The theme of exile does not fit with Luke 2, since this narrative insists on the repatriation of the Messiah in the *Patria* (2:4). Yet Joseph's Davidic link is not stressed at this point.

At his birth Jesus is not qualified as a baby (*brephos*, which we find in 2:12 and 16), but first of all as a "first-born" (2:7), a word which is rare but of great importance in the NT.[51] It connotes the idea of a new creation. The use of the definite article, *ton hyion prōtotokon*, which article Luke 2:4 and 11 omitted in designating the city of David, emphasizes the importance that Luke gives to this title. The word sometimes indicates "only son" (*monogenēs*, in the *Psalms of Solomon* 13:8; 18:4; 4 Es 6:58). It was part of the current vocabulary, and does not alter the humble nature of the description. Yet it was suitable for the royal heir and the son of God; it functions especially to prepare the scene of the consecration of the first born (2:23).

The child was "laid in a manger," because there was no place (*ou topos*) for them in the inn. The Messiah was born in an *ou-topia*, in the etymological sense of the word which signifies a "non-place" (see the discussion of *katalyma* in the special note on page 180). He was born in the Davidic and royal city, as was fitting. And yet his poverty, which is placed in full relief in the Gospel of Luke, begins with his birth. The spatial and cultural disjunctions are as striking as the identifications that are already being made: on the one hand, Jesus is identified with the son of God; on the other, he is identified with the poor.

The Annunciation to the Shepherds (Lk 2:8-14)

The following sequence begins with the presence of new actants, in a new place, although nearby:

> And in that region [*chōra* connotes fields and the countryside], there were shepherds out in the field, keeping watch over their flock by night (2:8).

Like the word *chōra*, the word *agraulountes*, which means "to camp overnight in the open fields," situates the shepherds in the countryside in opposition to Jesus, who is situated in the city of David (2:4 and 11). The shepherds are in the night,[52] in opposition, not to the daytime (*hēmera*, used with a purely chronological value in 2:1 and 6), but rather to the light which bursts forth in this nocturnal setting (2:9). This atmosphere of vigil fits the eschatological parables, "An angel of the Lord appeared to them and the glory of the Lord shone around them" (*perielampsen*, 2:9). (The contrast between night and light has contributed to fixing the feast of Christmas at the time of the winter solstice, and to celebrating it with a night vigil and a midnight Mass. This poetic impact has thus inspired the tradition and also harmonizes very well with semiotics correctly understood.)

The important point, however, lies elsewhere. God the addresser has not yet been named in this second chapter. He appears suddenly, in 2:9. This is a new theophany, more explicit than the preceding one. The word *glory* appears for the first time in Luke 1-2. It indicates, in terms of light, the direct manifestation of God on the earth. Here this manifestation is not announced for the future, as in 1:35, but described. The glory of God is not only implied, as in 1:35 by the use of Exodus 40:35, but explicitly named. At Christmas, the presence of God is no longer enveloped in the womb of Mary, but enveloping. It envelops the shepherds.

This new theophany is the only one indicated as a visible and sensible event in Luke 1-2. All the others are abstract or implicit. Jesus, hidden in his mother's womb (1:35, 41-45) is still hidden in the manger (2:7, 12, 16). He remains poor and without splendor in the two childhood theophanies in the Temple (2:27-32 and 49). But the theophany which announces the Christmas scene is analogous to that of the transfiguration (9:29 and 32) in its radiance and manifestation of glory.

The most significant observation is that the glory of God does not transfigure the Christ-child. Rather it is the shepherds who are enveloped and transfigured. This shining sign brings them to the humility of the manger. From the second century on, this paradoxical conjunction appears so displaced that the *Protoevangelion of James* transferred the glory of the shepherds to Christ himself and shows Christ born in a stream of light:

Precarious Lodgings, The Cave and the Traditions of Christmas

What are the connections between Luke 1-2 and the "Christmas creches," those icons of the feast which have been popular since the time of Francis of Assisi? Let us distinguish what comes from the Gospel and what comes from later though very old traditions:

There was no place for them in the kataluma (Lk 2:7)

This text coincides in a striking way with the text of the prologue of John, "He came to his own home and his own people received him not" (Jn 1:11).

What is this *kataluma*? The interpreters alternate between two solutions:

1. The *caravansary*, where people on a journey camped; and the *khan*, where everyone had access to a roof under which he could sleep or tie his animal (Lagrange, *Luc*, 1927, p. 72), as in Jer 41:17, where Yohanan and his people stopped at the *khan* of Kimham, near Bethlehem.

2. A hospice on a journey; the "upper room" of the Last Supper (Lk 22:11) is also called a *kataluma*.

The last example and several others indicate that the word had a rather broad meaning as a place of reception. A number of translators prudently rely on this vague sense, used by the Septuagint:

logis (dwelling); A. Loisy (1924, p. 113)
lodging; R. E. Brown (1977, p. 392 and 401)
lodge; J. Fitzmeyer (1981, p. 391).

The translation "inn" is found in several authors (cf. J. Schmid, (1965, p. 88; *albergo*). Where he refers to a paying inn, Luke uses the word *pandocheion* (Lk 10:34). The wicked inn-keeper is a creation of medieval folklore.

What is clear is that there "was no place for them" in a normal lodging. The mention of the manger makes us think of a stable. The reason which could account for their being displaced might have been Mary's condition, on the point of giving birth. Her delivery would be a disturbance to others. "Because they could not find their place in the hospice," translates E. Delebecque (1976, pp. 1-13), and he comments: "The function of the causal preposition is to explain the reason the birth took place in a manger."

The cave of Bethlehem

According to the second translation, "there was no place for them in the visitors' room," we can conclude that for lack of a common room which constituted the house itself (see Mt 2:11), the Holy Family found a discreet place for the birth in an accompanying room—a stable, as the word manger suggests.

If we remember that they did not find a place in the caravansary (or *khan*), we can think of some precarious shelter—the famous cave of Bethlehem. It was attested from the middle of the second century by the *Protoevangelion of James* (17-18, *New Testament Apocrypha,* Hennecke-Schneemelcher, Philadelphia, vol. I, p. 383):

—"Where shall I take you and hide your shame?" [asked Joseph]. And he found a cave and brought her into it, and left her in the care of his sons, and went out to seek for a Hebrew midwife in the region of Bethlehem.

In the same way Justin (*Dialogue* 78,5) attests, "As Joseph did not have any place in the town to lodge (*katalusai*), it was in a cave (*spēlaiō*), near the village, that he lodged."

In very different ways the two authors relate the same tradition:

—in the *Protoevangelion,* Joseph finds a cave before even arriving at the village.

—in Justin (more conformable to Lk 2:7), it is from a lack of a place in the village that he finds this refuge.

—Origen (3rd century) tells us that this cave was venerated in his time. "If anyone wants further proof to convince him that Jesus was born in Bethlehem besides the prophecy of Micah and the story recorded in the gospels by Jesus' disciples, he may observe that, in agreement with the story in the gospel about his birth, the cave at Bethlehem is shown where he was born and the manger in the cave where he was wrapped in swaddling-clothes. What is shown there is famous in these parts even among people alien to the faith" (*Contra Celsum,* 1:50-51, tr. H. Chadwick, Cambridge University Press, p. 47).

—St. Epiphanius (*Haer.* 51,9) read Lk 2:7, "And Mary laid him in the cave" (*spēlaiō* in place of *phatnē*, manger).

Some have tried to explain this cave as a simple projection (*theologoumenon*) of Is 33:16, where the just "will dwell on the heights, his place of defense will be the fortresses of rocks." But this fortress, this eagle's nest, was not the model for the modest refuge of the newborn Jesus. Caves used as shelter at Bethlehem could have given rise to the tadition, others have said, and one could discuss the differences between Justin and the *Protoevangelion.* In any case it was not in accordance with the *Protoevangelion* that the place has been determined, since this cave is situated beyond Bethlehem, rather than on the way to it, for persons coming from the north. Finally, it is only in a rather artificial way that others still tried to explain the veneration of this cave by the cult of Mithras, or by Adonisiac antecedents (A. Barrois, in *DBS*, 1, 970-971. See J. M. Lagrange, *Luc*, 1927, p. 72, and H. Vincent and F. M. Abel, *Bethléem, le sanctuaire de la Nativité*, Paris, 1914).

The cave is thus a respectable tradition which inclines toward the hypothesis of the caravansary as the place from which the Holy Family would have been rejected. The vagueness of Luke could reflect his habitual concern to soften difficult concepts.

The ass and the ox

No animals appear at the crib in Luke's narrative. Tradition must be held responsible for this embellishment. Brown admits this dependence on Luke (*The Birth*, p. 419). But the foundation appears slight. In Luke there is the single word "crib" or "manger." For the later tradition which speaks of the ass and the ox, there are three words. A reminiscence would thus seem more probable. Origen (254) (*Homily* 13, PG 13, 1382), followed by Jerome (*The Praise of Paula*, PL 22, p. 884), inclines in this direction. But Pseudo-Matthew (Tischendorf, p. 80) points to Ha 3:2, LXX. The ass and the ox of the crib were already painted in the catacombs (G. A. Wellen, *Eine ikonographische abhandlung Uber das gottes mutterbild in Bruhchristlicher zeit*, Utrecht—Antwerp: Spectrum, 1961, pp. 49-55; and G. Jaszai, "Krippe" in *Lexicon der Christliche Ikonographie*, Freiburg: Herder, 1970, 657-658. See p. 6 of the present volume, Iconography of the fourth century).

The ass was already attested in the middle of the second century by the *Protoevangelion of James*, 17:3, but as used for riding.

> And a dark cloud covered the cave. . . and the midwife said. . . "My eyes have seen marvelous things today. Salvation is born of Israel." And immediately the cloud began to withdraw from the cave and a great light appeared in the cave such that eyes could not bear it. And little by little this light receded until there *appeared* a little child (*Protoevangelion* 19:2).

In like manner, many nativity scenes today make the manger of Jesus a source of light. However, this sort of mythology is foreign to Luke.

This visible theophany, transfiguring the shepherds, is unique in its kind, and is followed by the message to the shepherds:

> And they were filled with fear. And the angel said to them, "Be not afraid; for behold, I bring you good news (*euaggelizomai*) of a great joy which will come to all the people; for to you is born this day in the city of David, a Savior who is Christ the Lord" (2:9-11).

This is an annunciation. It develops according to a schema analogous to the first two (to Zechariah and to Mary, 1:5-38):
—manifestation of the angel (1:11, 26; 2:9-10);
—fear and reassuring words, "do not fear" (1:12-13, 30; 2:9-10);
—the announcement of the wondrous child (in the future tense in 1:13, 17, 31-33; in the present, in 2:11, "to you is born this day") with the titles which qualify him;
—a sign given (1:20, 36-37; 2:12);
—praise analogous to that of the visitation (1:41-56; 2:13-14);
—separation, with the departure of the angels in the last two announcements (1:38; 2:15).
However, an annunciation is by no means a prefabricated schema. That of the birth of Jesus is very different. It is situated in a universalist framework, "the census of all the world," and the manifestation of the celestial armies in their "multitude" (2:13). The joy announced (2:10) no longer concerns the future (1:14) but the present ("this day," 2:11).

What is addressed to the shepherds is a *Good News*, destined for proclamation, which they will fulfill in 2:17-18. For the first time we see the verb *to evangelize*, so dear to Luke, who uses it ten times in his Gospel, contrasted with one instance in all the others (Mt 11:4-5), and fifteen times in Acts. The joy announced is not only for the shepherds (for you, *hymin*), it is for "all the people" (2:10; see 1:14).[53]

The child is designated by three new titles, no longer ontological titles only, such as were given at the annunciation (Son of the Most High, 1:32; Son of God, Holy, 1:35), but functional titles which relate him precisely to the people.

—Savior, the meaning of the name Jesus (1:31) is made explicit here but was intended from the beginning by the numerous etymological allusions to this name (2:11,47,69,71,77; 2:11; cf. 2:30; see the special note "Christ the Lord," pp. 185-187).

—Christ (Hebrew: Messiah), that is, "anointed," appears here for the first time in the Gospel of Luke (see 2:26). It was probably implied in 1:32-33. It is explained in reference to the "city of David" (2:4 and 11), and qualifies the Messiah.

—Lord appeared in a still ambiguous manner in the prophecy of Elizabeth (1:43). Here the title "Lord" is proclaimed in a direct and forceful way, as in the baptismal professions of faith confessing that Jesus is Lord.[54] This third title borders on the ontological level.

This title contrasts in an astonishing way with the poverty of the correlative sign given to the shepherds. The sign[55] is found in the very contrast presented in this scene. The glory of God (2:9) is revealed in earthly poverty. The passive baby bound, lying, hidden, is himself the Savior-Christ-Lord (2:11). It is in these signs of hiddenness and humility there that we must know how to discern the glory which appeared only for an instant, like a signal in the night, to the shepherds.

This sign is orchestrated from heaven with an amplitude which corresponds to the universal census of Augustus. "The multitude of the heavenly host" addresses its praise to God, an event which makes us think of the Magnificat (1:50-53).

> And suddenly there was with the angel a multitude of the heavenly host praising God and saying, "Glory to God in the highest, and on earth peace[56] to men with whom he is pleased!"[57]

The canticle expresses, briefly but in very rich language, the wondrous exchange between heaven and earth, God and man (with one-

Christ the Lord (2:11)

Christ the Lord or the Christ of the Lord?

The title *Christos Kyrios* (Anointed Lord) without an article is unique in the NT. Some rare translations soften this abrupt formula into "Christ, the anointed of the Lord" (*Christos Kyriou*), the more commonplace expression, found in Lk 2:26.

According to P. Winter, *Christos Kyrios* is an erroneous reading. The context, however, invites us rather to think that in 2:26 the expression *Christos Kyrios* is called for by the structural parallelism and the theophanic continuity between the nativity and the presentation. Acts 2:36, where Luke likewise places *Christos* and *Kyrios* in apposition in the first discourse of Peter after Pentecost, is an argument in favor of this.

The expression *Christos Kyrios* was not without antecedents. It is found in the Septuagint, translating Lam 4:20 where "the Anointed of the Lord" seems to be Hezekiah and becomes "Christ the Lord" in the translation. We find this title again in the *Psalms of Solomon* 17:36, though certain scholars would argue that this too is a mis-translation. This is not certain. In any case, the Greek expression existed before Jesus, but in a rather undetermined sense against which Lk 2:11 stands in sharp contrast.

Lord, the most common designation of God

Lord (Greek: *kyrios*, Hebrew: *ădôn*, Aramaic: mārā') Master, he who has power to dispose of someone or something, is sometimes a common appellation (forty times in the Bible) applicable especially to kings (1 Sm 16:16; 24:8 and 10) or an employer (Mt 25:21, 23). But most often it is a proper name of God (more than 1,000 times in the Bible). It is this word which the Jews pronounced each time they had to read the tetragrammaton YHWH, which they did not say aloud out of respect for God's transcendence. There is reason, then, to presume the strict sense of the title in 2:11, and even in 1:43, although this is less clear at first sight.

Jesus himself made it clear that this title of Lord applied to him in his question to the Pharisees about Ps 110:1, "If David calls the Messiah Lord, how can he be his son?" (Mt 22:43, compared with Lk 1:43 and 2:11). By giving him this title "Lord," the early Church confessed the divinity of Christ, manifested by his Resurrection (Acts 2:34). This is the meaning of the primitive Aramaic invocation, *Marana'tha*, O Lord, come (1 Cor 16:22; Rv 22:20).

The fundamental Christian confession of faith was "Jesus is Lord" (Rom 10:9; 1 Cor 12:3; 16:23; Col 2:6; Rv 22:20f.). This affirmation of faith was only secondarily a protest against the pretention of the emperors (1 Cor 8:5-6; Rv 17:14; 19:16, "the Lord of Lords"). Correlatively the NT attributes to Christ the Lord the titles, functions, and properties of Yahweh himself: reigning (Acts 2:33), judging (10:42), "Lord of all" (10:36), and "the name which is above every name. . . Jesus Christ is Lord" (Phil 2:9-11).

What are the implications of this title in Lk 2:11?

According to Lagrange (1927, p. 75), "The absence of the article before *kyrios* can be understood in the same way as in the case before *Christos*. There is only one Lord and one Christ.

"*Kyrios*" was the epithet of the pagan gods or of the divinized emperors, as placed, however, *before* the name, e.g. the lord Serapis. In Lk 2:11 the title is placed afterwards, apparently to indicate that Christ is the only Lord.

Luke 2:11 is an oracle, proclaimed from on high by the messengers of God. This solemn formula recognizes and reveals the designation of Christ as Lord. The oracle intends to affirm the same thing as the professions of the Christian faith: the absolute lordship of Jesus Christ. We have already discussed how the other titles given to Christ emphasized his transcendence (see special note, p. 109).

Luke uses the same apposition of *Christ* to *Lord* in Acts 2:36 (its only other occurrence in the NT), that "the whole house of Israel may know with certitude that God has made him both *Lord* and *Christ*, this Jesus whom you crucified." Here as in 2:11 the glorious proclamation of Jesus as Lord is expressed in the context of his humiliation. Here it is the cross; in Lk 2:12, the manger, where the infant-Lord (*brephos* 2:12 and 16) was laid. We can conclude with A. George, "The title of Lord should be taken in its strongest meaning, *messianic* and *divine*, in 1:43 as in 2:11" ("La Royauté," *Sc. Eccl.* 14, 1962, p. 64; see also I. de la Potterie, *Mélanges B. Rigaux*, 1970, pp. 119-121).

Is this a theologoumenon?

This conclusion poses a problem. Is not the attribution of the title *Christ-Lord* to Jesus from his infancy a *theologoumenon*? Has not Luke simply projected retrospectively ("retrojected" as Fitzmyer says in *Luke 1-9*, 1981, p. 410) the post-resurrectional profession of faith onto the infancy of Christ in the framework of a fictitious narrative? This is the current explanation. It is a necessary conclusion of the methodological postulates received in a school which attempts to explain all texts by the surrounding environment and to try to reduce them to it. Prior to Pentecost, the expression "Jesus is Lord" would have been unthinkable, they say. This current methodology is so strongly rooted that J. Daniélou, who has elsewhere shown great courage in defending other aspects of historicity, holds to this explanation (1967, pp. 67-73).

At the risk of being labelled as a fundamentalist, the exegete is invited by objectivity itself to entertain another hypothesis. At Lourdes, Bernadette heard the strange formula, "I am the Immaculate Conception," which she did not understand, and which at first was denounced as a theological error (R. Laurentin, *Lourdes, Histoire authentique* 6, 1964, pp. 95-106). Is it not possible that at Christmas there was a similar revelation of Christ to a group of poor shepherds, and that the title "Christ the Lord" stems from this revelation? Such a phenomenon would be well within the tradition of the prophets. This revelation presents no anachronistic elements; the words are not new. "Christ Lord" is attested by certain ancient translations of the OT (cf. Lam 4:20). The framework of faith makes this hypothesis at least as objective as the idea of "the creative community" reflecting back and inventing a *theologoumenon* to explain this concept and title.

sided reference to the love of God for us). This is the conjunction between addresser and addressees.

The Visit and the Evangelization (Lk 2:15-20)

The celestial sequence ends with an actantial shift. The departure of the angels brings us back to earth. In the strictest earthly humility, with all lights extinguished, the shepherds will recognize the sign:

> [And it happened] (*kai egeneto*) when the angels went away from them into heaven, the shepherds said to one another, "Let us go over to Bethlehem and see this thing that has happened, which the Lord made known to us" (2:15).

The watchful shepherds did not receive an order to go to the manger. They themselves decided to go there. Nor was it a matter of some doubt to be resolved. Their departure is spontaneous, like that of Mary at the visitation (1:39).

> And they went with haste, and found Mary and Joseph, and the babe lying in a manger (2:16).

Through Mary and Joseph the shepherds discover the infant hidden in the manger. The sign received by hearing becomes an observable fact and, despite the paradoxical humility of what the shepherds discover, their faith is not disappointed. They divulge their faith and share it:

> And when they saw it they made known the saying (*rhēma*) which had been told them concerning this child; and all who heard it wondered at what the shepherds told them (2:17-18).

Their role is that of spreading the Good News (of the Gospel, 2:10) which they received. The humble word of the shepherds relays the angel's prophecy, with a sense of wonder.

Mary, who was the subject-operator of the birth (2:5-7), does not participate in this function of communication. Her part is completely interior and contemplative.[58] "But Mary kept all these things, pondering them in her heart" (2:19).

This function of interior memory extends that of the inhabitants of Judea, who already "laid up in their hearts" the events of the birth of

John the Baptist (1:66). Their memory, however, was characterized by a questioning, "What then will this child be?" Mary's action is characterized by its breadth, indicated by the word *panta* (all), and by an active confrontation. The verb *syntēreo* (to preserve, to observe, to examine) has a more analytic, a more contemplative nuance, and also a more active nuance than that of the verb "to lay up," employed in 1:66. Above all, the meditation of Mary is expressed by the word *symballousa*.[59] This verb, from which we derive the word *symbol*, characterizes the confrontation out of which meaning arises (the very same relationships by which semiotics attempts to grasp the production of meaning). In the cultural milieu in which Mary is situated in the context of Luke 1-2, the confrontation is that of the words-events, so well characterized by the double meaning of the word *rhēmata* (in Hebrew, *dabar*).

The last verse (2:20) refers back to the shepherds. It expresses their thanksgiving by the same word, *ainountes*, which characterizes the praise expressed by the angels in Luke 2:13. These men become evangelists:

> And the shepherds returned, glorifying and praising God for all they had heard and seen, as it had been told them (2:20).

Formalization

We must now formalize Luke 2:1-20. All begins with the conjunction of Jesus, the King-Messiah, with the city of King David. It is in this predestined place that the birth is realized. In the language of semiotics, we have a disjunction of Jesus from Mary, his mother, a conjunction with poverty, of which the manger is the earthly sign, a disjunction from the human habitat where he was not received (2:7), a conjunction with the animal habitat which suggests the Incarnation of the Lord. The symbolism approaches that which John boldly expresses by saying "The Word became *flesh*."

Here, in the night, appear the shepherds, symbols of watchfulness and poverty, the first addressees and messengers of the Good News. They are conjoined with the night. God realizes their conjunction with his own light, the glory (2:9). It is God himself who envelops them. The supreme addresser (hidden in the preceding scene, where he is suggested simply as the one in control of Caesar Augustus) appears directly to these poor ones. They are conscious of God, while Caesar was unconscious of him, and believed himself to be God, "Augustus" (2:1), according to the name which he assumed.

From the angel, the shepherds receive the word which reveals to them the new presence of God on earth, that of the Savior-Christ-Lord, of whom poverty is the sign. Here is deciphered the meaning of the name Jesus = Savior. The title of Christ (Messiah) is given to him for the first time (2:11) in the city of David with the divine title *Lord.* The message is followed by a celebration which involves "a multitude of the heavenly host" (the universe above after the universe below). Their praise celebrates the conjunction of heaven and earth. The descending movement and the ascending movement express a reciprocity, a cycle of communion. After this the angels withdraw, the heavens are closed, and only the earth remains.

The shepherds go spontaneously toward the earthly sign of poverty which was indicated to them. There this conjunction with the Messiah occurs: the conjunction heaven-earth, God-men, King-shepherds, is henceforth accomplished in him. The full meaning of the symbolism is revealed here. What follows is diffusion, the earthly consequence: the shepherds make the Messiah known, the Good News of the humble conjunction between heaven and earth extends to other addressees. The shepherds extend the evangelization (2:18) and the praise (2:20) of the angels, while Mary, anomalously mentioned between these two functions of the shepherds, contemplates at length the events which will form the basis of the infancy Gospel.[60]

In short, the movement goes from the earthly realm (the census, birth in precarious conditions) to the heavenly, to express the conjunction earth-heaven in the Savior-Christ-Lord who is also the baby laid in the manger. He realizes the conjunction of God with humanity at the level of the poor.

The play of communications (conjunction-disjunction), their organization, their dynamic, should not lead us to overlook the powerful new meaning transmitted in this humble and simple manner. The work of semiotics is to lead to the creative repose of the seventh day: contemplation.

Should the Circumcision (Lk 2:21) be Associated with Christmas or with the Presentation?

Two answers have been given to this question:
—With Christmas, since it occurred before Jesus was brought to Jerusalem (2:25), therefore at Bethlehem. The TOB (p. 198) and R. E. Brown (p. 394) adopt this solution for this historical reason.
—With the Presentation, according to A. Gueuret, P. Bossuyt (*Luc*, 1981, vol. 1, p. 15), and J. Fitzmyer (*Luke 1-9*, 1981, p. 418).

Many editions, however, do not come to a conclusion and make of this short verse a distinct paragraph, detached from the two sequences on either side of it (Nestlé, Lagrange, Osty, Pirot, *The Jerusalem Bible*).

The answer is indubitable: the circumcision is one with the Presentation, as A. Gueuret was able to see in a penetrating way, although the absence of a "topographical shift" (a change of place) between 2:19 and 20 argues semiotically for the other solution. The literary and semiotic division of the text differs from the direction suggested by the topographical and historical division for the following reasons:

1. Luke 2:21 and 22 begin with the refrain which is so important in Luke 1-2 "when the days were fulfilled" (generally eliminated by translations).

2. The two verses depend literally on Lv 12, which suggests the two ceremonies: the circumcision on the eighth day (Lk 2:21) and purification thirty-three days later (2:22); forty days in all. The formula "the days fulfilled" is repeated in Lv 12:4 and 6, and in Lk 2:21-22 (although following a different order). The repetition of the refrain in Lk 2:21-22 stresses not only the unity of the two verses but also their reference to Lv 12.

	Leviticus 12 (The Law)		*Luke 2:21-22*
6	When the *days* are *fulfilled*	21	and when were *fulfilled*
3	On the eighth day		eight days for him to be
	the flesh of his foreskin		
	shall be circumcised...		*circumcised*...
4	for thirty-three days she...		
	will touch nothing...		
	until the *days* of her *purification* are *fulfilled*...she	22	And when the *days* of their *purification* were *fulfilled*

6 shall bring to the priest. . . a
lamb for a burnt *offering*. . .
8 if she cannot afford a lamb,
then she shall take two
turtledoves or two
young pigeons

to present him to the Lord
24 and to offer a *sacrifice*
according to the Law
of the Lord,
a pair of *turtledoves* or
two *young pigeons*. . .

We have presented the text in such a way as to highlight the structural analogies. If one makes a comparison of the whole, the most striking observation is that Luke omits the redundant formulas concerning the impurity of the mother (12:2, 5), her *sin* (12:6), her blood (12:2, 4, 5, 7), her purification (12:4, 5, 6, 7), and the *atonement* (12:7, 8) which they required.

3. The same "hiddenness" of the subjects pertains. (This argument and the one that follows are the work of A. Gueuret).

4. The same function is apparent: to give to Christ the twofold names Jesus (Savior) and Holy.

6. The Presentation in the Temple

We have explored in great detail, from the literary point of view, the two episodes in the Temple which form the conclusion of Luke 1-2 (2:21-52; see above, pp. 62-89). The task remains of articulating the narrative program of these two episodes in order to clarify, from the semiotic point of view, the conclusions already established in the exegetical part of this book. We must look especially at the main lines of the structure and the coherence of this ending.

STRUCTURE

Sequential Division[61]

The semiotic divisions are well marked by the actantial changes of this pericope (changes of actants and of place: the Temple, Bethlehem, and Nazareth).

1. The program of the Law dominates verses 21-24: circumcision (2:21) and presentation (2:22-24) where the human characters are hidden (concerning the connection of 2:21 to this sequence, see the special note on the preceding pages).

2. The program of the Holy Spirit dominates the following verses (2:25-38):
—the motion of the Holy Spirit upon Simeon (2:25-27);
—Simeon's (somatic) conjunction with the Messiah in the Temple (2:28);
—his glorious prophecy concerning the Messiah, linked to his own death (2:29-32);
—his sorrowful prophecy related to the future death of the Messiah (2:33-35);
—the praise and evangelization of the prophetess Anna (2:36-38);

3. Conclusion:
—fulfillment (2:39a which echoes the first two words in 2:21 and 2:22);
—the return to Nazareth (2:39b);
—the growth of Jesus (2:40).

The Ordinary Program and the Theophanic Program

Like each of the preceding sequences, the presentation begins by spelling out an ordinary program: Jesus' first journey to Jerusalem, made to fulfill the ritual obligations of the Law. However, once again a new narrative program arises, one that causes astonishment (2:33), a transcendent, divine program, which determines another accomplishment to be fulfilled on the eschatological and theophanic level.

This is manifested by the idiosyncracies of this text, which have long puzzled exegetes.

God, "Subject of Doing"

The first unusual feature of the text is that God the addresser plays a major role here. He is the only one named, the only subject of "doing." The other actants are totally eclipsed.[62] This singularity helps to clarify numerous anomalies of the narrative which we outlined above.

First we must examine the disappearance of the human actants. Luke does not specify who performs Jesus' circumcision (2:21). He says only that Jesus "was circumcised" and "was called" by the name Jesus. The passive does not reveal any particular subject. This concealment is all the more unexpected, given the programmation of Gabriel (1:31), which was formally addressed to Mary alone, "You shall call his name Jesus." It would have been expected that this role would be recalled. But neither Mary nor any other person is named in this verse:

> And at the end of eight days when he was circumcised, he was called (*eklēthē*) Jesus, the name given (*klēthen*) by the angel before he was conceived in the womb [*the* womb and not *her* womb] (2:21).

It is striking to see to what degree Mary is eclipsed in this verse. Again, in 2:22 also, Luke does not say who carries Jesus to Jerusalem.

> And when the time came for their purification according to the law of Moses, they brought him up to Jerusalem to present him to the Lord (2:22).

Joseph disappeared from the narrative after verse 7; Mary, after verse 19; the shepherds, after verse 20. The laws of grammar would lead us to connect the action in verses 21-22 with the last-named subject (the shepherds), but the context clearly rules that out. Verse 27 states that those who brought him to the Temple were the parents of the child Jesus. But until that moment, well after the spatial shift (the arrival at Jerusalem), nothing is said of them.

In the literary study of the text, we proposed that this concealment of subject is done in order to avoid any idea of a purification of Mary and to make the point that the purification is transferred to the inhabitants of Jerusalem, the city named for the first time in verse 22.

A semiotic study will confirm this conclusion, but first of all it accounts for this obscuring of the parents. It is the reverse side of a positive phenomenon: this scene is theophanic, and God alone is the subject:

> And when the time came for their purification according to the law of Moses, they brought him up to Jerusalem to present him to the *Lord*, (as it is written in the law of the *Lord*, "Every male that opens the womb [= first-born, 2:7] shall be called holy to the *Lord*"), and to offer a sacrifice according to what is said in the law of the *Lord*, "a pair of turtledoves or two young pigeons" (2:22-24).

The Lord is named four times in these three verses. No human character is mentioned, neither the parents, nor the priests, who would be the expected actants in the scene.

Moses is the only person mentioned. He is named in the first verse (2:22a) in the expression "the law of Moses." This exception is only apparent, since Moses is not an actant in the rite. He is named simply as a substitute for the Lord, as his addresser in the communication of the Law to the chosen people. After the following verse, the expression used consistently is "the law of the Lord" (2:23, 24, 39).

Why this exception in 2:22a? It is because we are dealing with a negative operation, the purification. It is referred only to Moses, not to the Lord, who appears for the presentation, the manifestation and qualification of Jesus.

No doubt it is for the same reason that Luke here names Jerusalem by its profane name (*Hierosolyma*), since the scene deals, as we will see, with the purification and the redemption of this city, over which already hovers the shadow of the death of Christ (2:34). After this,

Luke will use only the wondrous and sacred name of *Hierousalēm* (2:25, 38, 41, 43, 45).

The positive side of this concealment of the human characters is that the Lord, engaged in an implicit manner as the subject of "doing" from 2:21-22 on, now enters explicitly into the scene as the only subject of verses 23-24. This entrance manifested that he was already the subject-addresser of the verbs used in the passive voice in 2:21.

He takes this place in the foreground in order to qualify Jesus with the double name prescribed from above:

1. His human name, *Jesus*, required at the annunciation;
2. His divine name, *Holy*, which will be typologically manifested by the actualization of the "law of the Lord."

It is this program, accented by the occurrence of the verb *kaleō* (to call, to name), which connects the circumcision (2:21) to the presentation (see special note, pp. 191-192).

THE PROGRAMMATION OF THE LAW: THE DOUBLE NAME OF JESUS

The Programmation of the Annunciation and Its Realization in Luke 2:21-23

In the cultural framework of the Bible, the concept of a name had considerable importance: the revelation of a name communicated the essence of a person. Thus the revelation of God's name to Moses communicated God himself, and the attribution in the NT to Jesus of the name "Lord" is a central expression of faith.[63]

For this reason, the angel Gabriel announced to Mary the double name of the Messiah, his name as man: Jesus, and his divine name as Son of God: Holy (1:31, 35). These words were pronounced in the future tense before Mary's consent (1:38), before she "conceived in the womb" (1:31 and 2:21).

The sequence 2:21-23 manifests the conjunction of Jesus with his two names in fulfillment of this program.

The Programmation of Christmas: Jesus, the First-Born (Lk 2:7)

Luke programed the ritual in 2:7 where he insists, with the use of the article, on this quality of "first-born," which belongs to Jesus for many reasons,[64] "[Mary]. . . gave birth to her first-born son."

Modification of the Text of the Law by Typological Application

Through the transfers of meaning which occur throughout Luke, the twofold name given to Jesus modifies the sense of an OT text in order to give added significance to the event: the Law surpassed and extended by the spirit. We have seen how Luke conforms the text of the Law to the programmation of the spirit. For example, where he transforms the text of Exodus 13:1, "Consecrate to me all the first-born" into a qualifying attribution of the divine name holy: "Every male that opens the womb shall be called holy" (*hagion klēthēsetai* replacing *hagiason me*). The same formula is then used by Gabriel "He will be called holy." In Luke's *sensus plenior* the Lord is more important than *the Law*; the significance more than the literal meaning.

Typological Transfers

This typological concretization brings to mind the other transfers of meaning which we analyzed from the literary point of view. Semiotic analysis brings out the meaning even more clearly:

1. The *purification* of the mother is not related to the mother of Jesus (who is carefully eliminated from the context), but transferred to the people, of whom Jerusalem is the symbol, and who appear for the first time in this verse, "their purification" (2:22).

2. The *redemption* of the first-born is not related to Christ, who is the Redeemer, but transferred to Jerusalem. The sequence concerning the Temple ends with the theme of the redemption (*lytrōsis*) of Jerusalem (2:38).[65] The purification (2:22) and the redemption (2:38) of Jerusalem form an inclusive whole which indicates the meaning of the scene, in the wake of Malachi 1-3 and Daniel 9:2 which underlie Luke 1-2.

These two transfers lead to a third:

3. The offering of the doves (2:24) which the Law prescribes (Lv 12:4-8) as a sacrifice for the purification of the mother (2:22), seems to be transferred to Jesus (2:24). It appears as a sacrifice of praise and of purity on the occasion of his presentation, indicated in the preceding verse, in such a way that Luke seems to pass without warning from the oblation of the "two turtledoves or pigeons" prescribed by Leviticus 12 to the offering of the same birds prescribed in Numbers 6:10 among

the rituals of holiness of the *nazirs* consecrated to God. For this reason the text says nothing about the redemption of the "first-born" for five shekels of silver (Nm 18:16) practiced on this occasion, but refers only to the offering of the two doves.

All these transfers are oriented in reference to God as addresser, the only explicit subject in Luke 2:22-24, with whom Jesus is identified by the name "holy" (2:23).

This double attribution of the human name of Jesus (Savior) and of a transcendent name progresses step by step all through Luke 1-2 according to the following progression:

Progression of Luke 1-2	Human name Jesus = Savior	Transcendent divine names: Lord, Holy, Glory
Lk 1:31	You shall call his name *Jesus*	
1:35		The begotten will be called Holy, Son of God
cf. 1:32		Son of the Most High
Visitation		
1:43		Lord
1:47	Savior	(God my Savior)
The Birth		
2:11	Savior	Lord
Presentation	He was called *Jesus*	
2:21		
2:23		Called holy
2:29	*sōtērion* (salvation)	
(2:32)		Light of the nations (glory)

The Conjunction-Identification of Jesus with Jerusalem and the Temple

These concretizations and transfers take place by the conjunction with Jerusalem and the Temple, named for the first time, let us remember, when Jesus entered there (2:22 and 27).

This conjunction implies a double reference:

—to God whose place is the *Temple* (2:49);

—to Israel, whose holy city is *Jerusalem*, a symbol of the people of God.

The presence of Christ the Lord fills the Temple. The Bible characterizes this presence as glory, and Jesus receives this title of glory in the prophecy of Simeon (2:32), in reference to Deutero-Isaiah who announced the eschatological manifestation of the glory of God in the Temple.

Jesus is identified with God and at the same time with the Temple, his dwelling. (We are on the road which Jn 2:13-22 will further explicate by saying that the body of Christ is the new temple.[66])

Jesus is likewise identified with the people he has come to purify, to console, and to redeem. These roles are manifested by the trilogy which identifies Jesus in diverse degrees as the purification of Jerusalem (2:22), the consolation of Israel (2:25), the liberation of Jerusalem (2:38).

Jerusalem (2:22, 25, 38) is a representation of Israel, as these isotopic parallels make clear. This is also confirmed by the textual variant of 2:38, where numerous manuscripts replace Jerusalem with Israel but give an identical meaning.[67]

Simeon and Anna: or, Prototypes of the People of Hope

This conjunction takes place by means of two characters who are the archetype of the consolation (2:25) and the redemption (or liberation) of Israel (2:38). In other words, they are the prototype of the hope of the poor of Yahweh, with whom the prophets identified the people of the promises.

Simeon takes the child in his arms, a somatic conjunction which implies an identification of the Son of God become a child with the people for whom he is salvation. Anna, the prophetess, a type of fasting, prayer, of ritual worship, identified with the Temple, which she *never leaves* (2:37-38).

These two characters appear successively, Simeon in 2:25-35 and Anna in 2:36-38. They appear under the sign of the *Holy Spirit*. Their "pentecost" takes the place of the Law under the sign of which both the infancy Gospel (1:5-6) and the sequences of the Temple (1:22-24) began. Simeon and Anna are the new prophets of the spirit. This pentecost of chapter 2 extends the pentecosts of chapter 1:15, 41, and 67.

THE PROGRAM OF THE HOLY SPIRIT (Lk 1:25-38)

The programmation of the Holy Spirit which began in 2:25 manifests that which was signified by the oracle of the angels in 2:11.

Prophetic Recognition of the Divine and Human Name

Simeon recognizes the significant titles of Jesus. First, the human name of "Jesus" (1:31), that is, Savior, explained by the oracle of the angels in 2:11, conferred in 2:21. Simeon expresses this in an abstract form:

My eyes have seen your salvation (*sōtērion*),

the abstraction having a superlative value.

Following this, the divine name of Christ is brought out, and he is designated as holy and son of God in 1:35, the meaning of which is elucidated by the title "Lord" in the oracle of Christmas (2:11). Simeon expresses this in symbolic terms, the implication of which we discussed above in reference to Isaiah 42:6 and 49:6: light of the nations (Is 51:4) and glory of Israel (cf. Is 17:3; Ez 8:4, 43:2; Mi 1:15).

The coming of Jesus into the Temple thus realizes what was promised by the prophets, the manifestation of God himself in the Temple. The meaning involves the identification of Jesus with the glory, i.e., with God, and his conjunction both with the people of Israel and with the nations which he will transfigure by his light.

Simeon addresses this prophecy of glory to God alone. Its novelty is punctuated by the wonder of the parents (2:33). It surpasses human understanding. Simeon then utters a second prophecy which he addresses to Mary alone.

Sorrowful Prophecy: the Contradiction and the Sword

After the glory of the people, the suffering comes from the same people. The contrast with the tone of the preceding prophecy is striking:

> Behold, this child is set for the fall and rising [or resurrection] of many in Israel and for a sign of contradiction [*sēmeion antilegomenon*] (and a sword will pierce through your own soul also), that thoughts out of many hearts may be revealed (2:34-35).

The programmation of this prophecy is by no means easy to grasp, perhaps due to the simple fact that it has the ambiguous nature characteristic of true prophecy.[68]

The first stich announces the contrasting effect of the mission of the Messiah among the people. He is predicted to be the "glory of Israel" (2:32). He is now established for the fall of some and the rising of others. There will be a division in Israel. (We note the occurrence of this last word in 2:32 and 34 as a clear reference to Christ's relationship to the people.)

The second stich evokes the same division in terms of opposition (prefix *anti-*) to the Messiah himself; a sign of contradiction. The image of the sword specifies the violent, dramatic character of this opposition. The sword alludes to the death of the Messiah, not without connection with the death of Simeon (alluded to twice, with the word "death" in 2:26 and "depart" in 2:29). The death of Simeon is under the sign of peace (2:29), but the Messiah's death is characterized by suffering and violence. The atmosphere is eschatological.

This death will be apocalyptic (*apocalyphthōsin*), i.e., revealing the arguments of the heart. This final trait seems to characterize the contrasting responses to the evangelical message of Jesus Christ after the Resurrection. "I have not come to bring peace, but a sword," says Jesus paradoxically (Mt 10:34; see Lk 12:51, "division").

This prophecy of sorrow for Mary programs a first realization which will take place in the following episode, where Mary expresses her sorrow with great intensity (2:48).

The Stumbling Stone and the Sword in Luke 2:34-35
What is the Substratum? What is the Meaning?

1. The Stumbling Stone and the Cornerstone (2:34-35)

"Behold, this child is set for the fall and rising (*anastasis*) of many in Israel, and for a sign that is spoken against."

—*Anastasis* also signifies resurrection.

—*Keimai* means to be established, placed, laid down in a very broad sense, but which especially fits a rock, "That which is placed on the tomb of Lazarus" (Jn 11:38). The *keitai* echoes *keimenon* (placed) of Luke 2:12 and 16, to describe Jesus, placed, laid in the crib, the other "sign" given in Luke 2. The image of the stone seems to underlie this dialectic of fall and rising (which is synthesized by the expression, "Sign that is spoken against") for the following reasons.

The symbol of the stone is applied to Christ throughout the NT with this twofold contradictory value: the stumbling stone (*lithos proskommatos*, Rom 9:32-33, an echo of Is 8:14; see 28:16 and 1 Pt 2:4), on which one stumbles, contrasted with the cornerstone (*akrogōniaion*) on which something is built up, constructed (1 Pt 2:6-9; cf. 1 Cor 3:11).

This twofold meaning is a part of the underlying structure of two texts of the OT:

—Isaiah 8:14, in which Winter sees the source of Luke 2:35, which is closer to the Hebrew than is the Septuagint. Here it is Yahweh himself who is the stone of stumbling and of building. Yahweh Sabaoth—it is he whom one must worship; it is he whom one must fear; it is he who makes one tremble. He is the sanctuary (edification) and the stumbling block, the rock which causes the two houses of Israel to fall (Is 8:14). All the accent is on the fall, but rising could be connected to the image of the sanctuary, i.e., of a building.

—Psalm 118:22 (no doubt a combination of Is 8:14 and 28:16) prepared the way to the thought that the stone of scandal, the object of contradiction, would become "the cornerstone" (Is 28:16) at the base or the summit of the construction. "The stone which the builders rejected has become the cornerstone" (Ps 118:22, used in Mt 21:42; Acts 4:11; Eph 2:20).

We find this twofold meaning in the NT:

Cephas is given several nuances:

—foundation (by the faith which confesses Christ: "On this rock I will build my Church," Mt 16:18), then

—scandal (*skandalon*, Mt 16:18 and 23),

—1 Peter 2:6-8 unites the two contradictory images by attesting, successively, Jesus Christ as "cornerstone" (*lithon akrogōniaion*), according to Isaiah 28:16

and "cornerstone" (*kephalēn gōnias*) according to Psalm 118:22, but also as the "stumbling stone" (*lithos proskommatos*), Is 8:14, on which one stumbles. The identification of the sanctuary with God becomes here the identification of the sanctuary (formed of living stones) with Christ.

The expression "sign of contradiction" (*semeion antilegomen*, lit. "sign that is spoken against") synthesizes the contrast of falling and rising which designates the adhesions and oppositions, the conjunctions and disjunctions with Christ, due to faith or lack of faith. One can see emerging here the image according to which he is the new sanctuary, according to Isaiah 8:14 (see John 2:21).

These oppositions arise from the interior thoughts or disputes of hearts (2:35b). The *dialogismoi* (often used pejoratively) signify mixed thoughts, in which sin often dwells. Is it their vehement outburst that is signified by the violent image of the sword?

2. The Piercing Sword (*romphaia*, 2:35)

This word is addressed to Mary; "And a sword will pierce through your own life also" (Lk 2:35).

The *romphaia* (studied by P. Benoit in *CBQ* 25, 1963, p. 251) is a two-edged sword or pick axe, originating in Thrace, which tends to be confused with the *machaira*, a curved, two-edged sword which the Septuagint employs frequently to translate *ḥereb*. In the metaphorical sense, the *romphaia* could be:
—the tongue: Ps 57:4; 59:8; 64:3,
—transgression: Sir 21:3,
—punishment: Wis 5:20; Ez 5:1-17; and especially Ez 14:17, the text closest to Luke because it unites the words *romphaia* and *dierchesthai*,
—judgment, in the sense of the Word of God which is "sharper than any two-edged sword" (Heb 4:12), penetrating all the way "to the division of soul (*psychē*, as for Mary in 2:35) and spirit" (see Eph 6:16; Rev 1:7). It is this which led Origen and a number of the Fathers following him to say that the "guilty thoughts (*dialogismoi*) of many hearts" were also hers. Not without a certain tendency to misogyny, he reasoned a fortiori: if the apostles fled before the passion, would not Mary, a weak woman, also have doubted. This false path was abandoned in the fifth century. Cyril of Alexandria, who returned three times to this theme, seems to testify to a key moment in this correction (Caro). (For a further discussion of the sword announced to Mary, see above, pp. 78-80).

This does not exclude the fact that Mary, the Daughter of Zion, according to Luke 1 (see pp. 52-53, 58) suffered from the arguments or disputes (*dialogismoi*) of her people against Christ.

Anna the Prophetess (Lk 2:36-38)

Like Simeon, Anna is a prototype, representing the "small remnant" of the poor of Israel, who hope for the "liberation of Jerusalem."

On the semantic level, Gueuret showed clearly that Jerusalem appears here in "metonymy for the saved people," in conjunction with the values represented by the protagonist Jesus:

> What this social place, constructed by the narrative, signifies is the new Jerusalem. . . whence comes Jesus as present in the here and now of society.[69]

The two representatives alluded to by Luke are clearly differentiated and contrasted.[70] While Simeon is designated by his name as simply "a man," Anna is presented in a detailed way as a daughter of Phanuel of the tribe of Asher. These two names seem to have been retained for their symbolic value. Phanuel (face of God) suggests the story of Jacob-Israel, who saw God face to face at the ford of the Jabbok River (Gn 32:30) yet did not lose his life, which can be related to Simeon, who sees the Messiah and "death" (2:26), "glory" (2:32), and "sword" (2:35). The name Asher signifies "fortunate" according to the play on the words of his mother Leah at his birth (Gn 30:13, perhaps used in Lk 1:42 and 48). It is the name of one of her last sons, a detail that fits the situation where the latter days are being ushered in.

This idea is accented by the old age of Anna, which Luke brings out emphatically. Simeon has always been presented as an old man because he spoke of his death, but his age is in no way specified. For Anna, on the contrary, Luke gives two figures: the seven years of her married life and the eighty-four years of her age.[71]

While Simeon *comes* to the Temple because of a contract (in the semiotic sense of the word, according to Gueuret, p. 136, in reference to 2:27) and an announcement (2:27), Anna never leaves the Temple. It is not specified if she recognized the child through the oracle of Simeon or as a prophetess.

She is not mentioned as having a physical conjunction with the child as Simeon did. While Simeon prophesies, without being called a prophet, she is called "prophetess" without her prophecy being specified.

Finally, Simeon has the function of recognizing the Messiah as Savior, light, and glory before God and his parents. Anna, on the other hand, like the evangelizing shepherds (2:18-20) has the function of spreading the Good News to all those waiting for the redemption of Jerusalem (2:38).[72]

Anna is associated with Simeon in the recognition of the Messiah in a divine and transcendent sense, as is implied by the ambiguity of the final verse which certain translations eliminate:

> She gave thanks to God, and talked about the child to all who looked forward to the deliverance of Jerusalem (2:38, NAB tr.).

However, the word "child" is not found in 2:38. Luke says, "She gave thanks to God, and spoke of him." According to the normal grammatical connection, it is of God that she speaks. However, according to the context, correctly understood in the TOB translation, it is effectively the child Jesus who appears to be the object of her discourse. This ambiguous identification manifests, among other things, a revelation in progress.

THE FULFILLMENT AND THE DEPARTURE

Luke 2:39 closes the scene with a spatial shift:

> And when they had performed everything according to the law of the Lord, they returned into Galilee, to their own city, Nazareth.

Fulfillment, which was the initial theme of 2:21-22, concludes the entire pericope (by using another verb, however, no longer *pimplēmi* but *teleō*). This semitic inclusion manifests the importance of the idea.

This fulfillment in Jerusalem, however, is followed by the return of the parents to "their city." There follows the refrain of "growth," which could seem to close the infancy narrative, just as 1:80 completed that of John the Baptist. But the visit of the Christ-Savior to the Temple will be reiterated with the manifestation of new values.

FORMALIZATION[73]

Convergences of a Fivefold Programmation

The directing threads woven in Luke 2:21-39 are blessed together harmoniously:

—The programmation of the annunciation by the oracle of Gabriel (the human name and the divine name of Christ in 1:31-32 and 35).
—The programmation of Christmas, where Jesus is designated as first-born (2:7) and, as such, privileged by the Law (2:23).
—The programmation of the biblical prophets: the coming of the Lord into his Temple, after the models of Malachi 3 and Daniel 9:24.
—The programmation of the Law (2:23) which the eschatological coming of the Christ-Lord fulfills in a typological manner.
—The programmation of the Holy Spirit, which confirms prophetically the typological testimony of the Law.

All is summarized in a triple conjunction which defines the mediating condition of Christ, which was so strongly manifested at Christmas (2:9-14).

1. The conjunction of the infant Christ with the names given through the angel: the human name, Jesus (Savior) and the divine name, Holy.

2. The conjunction of Jesus with the Temple: "My Father's house," Jesus says in 2:49. The house of God (1:32 and 35) is the house of the Father. The Son, like the Father, is "Lord." Therefore, this title was given to him in 1:43 and 2:11. Like him, he is Holy (1:35); he is glory. But the identification is affirmed by means of a distinction of persons, something which theology will take time to grasp. The Lord, revealed by the Bible, and this child, Jesus Christ, are mysteriously identified. Jesus comes into the Temple as glory (2:32). This apotheosis qualifies the Temple (deprived of the Ark of the Covenant) more than the child, who is qualified from the beginning by transcendent titles and properties (1:32-35, 43; 2:11).

The conjunction with the Temple thus manifests symbolically the identification of Christ with God (with the glory).

3. The conjunction of Christ with Jerusalem implies his identification with the people of whom he is the Messiah-Savior (2:11, 26) and the salvation (2:30). Luke signifies this arrival of Christ at Jerusalem as a purification (2:22) and a redemption (2:38), and alternately as the "consolation of Israel" (2:25). The conjunction with the people of Israel is realized in the person of a man and a woman, without official or hierarchical qualification. They are the type and the personification

of Israel. They represent more exactly the "small remnant," the people of the poor, represented also by Mary the Daughter of Zion. They wait for "the consolation of Israel" (2:25), in justice and piety (Simeon, 2:25), prayer and fasting (Anna, 2:37). Their conjunction is accomplished in the Spirit (2:26-28) and according to the prophetic charism (2:25 and 2:36). Simeon interprets the being and the future of the Messiah: his present glory and the passion. Anna spreads this Good News beyond the people of Israel. The prophecy of Simeon expresses the expansion of salvation, to all peoples. The Messiah will be a light for the nations.

The Human Axis and the Divine Axis

All these conjunctions are realized according to two axes:

1. A human axis: the human name of Jesus conferred in an atopic manner (before the ascent to Jerusalem), and the function of savior which it signifies. This salvation is brought first of all to Jerusalem and to Israel. Jerusalem is a symbol of Israel; Simeon and Anna the typical symbols and living representatives of all the people.

2. The divine axis is manifested by the titles, symbols, and convergent identifications which are encountered through the whole progression of Luke 1-2.

These two axes come together in the Temple and in Christ who visits it. This is the first symbolic stage of the identification which the abstract dogmatic approach will take centuries to express.[74]
These two axes progress in the narrative of the finding, the final sequence of Luke 1-2.

7. *The Finding in the Temple*

The second conjunction of the Messiah, Son of God (1:32 and 35; 2:49) with the Temple (designated here as the "house of the Father," as in Jn 2:16) marks a new stage, a transformation of the narrative, with the manifestation of hidden values. This concluding scene forms a transition to the Gospel which narrates Jesus' public life, and prefigures the final chapter of the entire Gospel (Lk 24).

It begins like the others with an elementary narrative program which opens out to unexpected conclusions, stimulating not only wonder (2:33), but also stupefaction (2:47-48) and incomprehension (2:50), which are only resolved in the long run.[75]

God in the Background, Jesus in the Position of the Principal Actant

There is now a significant actantial shift: in the narrative of the presentation (2:22-40), God was constantly named as the addresser:
—Lord (2:22-24, 39),
—Holy Spirit (2:25-27),
—God (*Theos*, 2:28, 38, 40),
—Master (*despota*, 2:29).

None of these words return in the final episode (2:41-51). God is not explicitly named except in the mysterious word of Jesus and with a new (relational) name, "Father" (2:49), introduced in reference to the ambiguous mention of the adoptive father (2:48). God emerges only from within, in the conscience of Christ, according to a mysterious identification which tears him from his human family (2:43-48). The discretion and restraint of the text is admirable and manifests the future of Christ in the veiled light of his humble childhood.

An explicit mention of God recurs in the final refrain (2:52) to remind us that he is the omnipresent addresser and guide of the events, above and within Christ, stimulating liberty, creativity, communication, orienting the topographical and other conjunctions and disjunctions. God appears explicitly only late in the last episode, because at the moment when the child Jesus acts and speaks as a master, the addresser is not so much God in heaven (God transcendent) as the child himself. The Son of God on earth assumes for the first time the function of subject-operator.

The Program of Custom (Lk 2:41-42)

The elementary narrative program which opens the sequence is not that of the Law which emphatically governed the preceding episode (2:22-24, 27-39). Here it is only the custom (*ethos*, 2:42) every year (*kat'etos*) to go to Jerusalem for the feast of Passover (2:41). They go up, not only in view of the altitude, but because it is the capital and unique place of worship, the Temple, where the conjunction of God with his people, signified since Luke 1:9-10, is realized.

This ascent is set for the celebration of the feast of Passover (2:41-43):

> Now his parents went to Jerusalem every year at the feast of the Passover.

The Search (Lk 2:43-45)

In the second verse, the principal subject changes. It is no longer the parents, but Jesus, the virtual (passive) subject, who becomes here an actant, who performs an act contrary to the custom followed by his parents. This verse, in which the "new" bursts forth, opens with an *egeneto* which brings out the surprising transformation of the narrative. However, this *egeneto* is integrated (like that of 2:2) to signify the coming of Jesus to the age of twelve years:

> And when he was twelve years old, they went up according to the custom; and when the feast was ended, as they were returning, the boy Jesus stayed behind in Jerusalem. His parents did not know it (2:42-43).

With the topographical shift of the parents, the new program implies a disjunction between them and Jesus:
—a physical disjunction; they leave, he remains;
—a disjunction in the order of knowledge: they did not know (*ouk egnōsan*). He did not forewarn them. They are in ignorance.

While the program of the parents was characterized by custom (2:42), Jesus' program develops according to another, a mysterious power, which the end of the narrative will only partially reveal.

The opposition of the two verbs "to return" and "to remain" outlines the situation. Jesus is designated neither as a *brephos* (2:12 and 16) nor as a *paidion* (the neuter noun indicating a little child or a young slave), but as a *pais*, a word which indicates a child or young man and designates also the servant of God (Israel in 1:54, David in 1:69, a parallel worth studying). Jesus is at the point of revealing himself as the son and servant of God *par excellence*, the title of the Messiah since Deutero-Isaiah (chapter 42ff.).

The insistent mention of the fulfillment which governed the preceding sequence returns here with a new verb (no longer *pimplē*-

mi, 2:21 and 22, nor *teleō*, 2:39, but *teleioō*, 2:43).[76] The completion of the ritual program of the parents leads here to the beginning of another program, that of Jesus poised toward the most distant future.

The following two verses manifest the search of the parents and the evolution of their ignorance:

> Supposing him to be in the caravan (*sunodia*) they went a day's journey, and they sought him among their kinsfolk and acquaintances (2:44).

They interpret the custom: the caravan was a large family where each could trust the solidarity of the group. He should have been there. But this interpretative knowledge is wrong. It is necessary to return:

> And when they did not find him, they returned to Jerusalem, seeking him (2:45).

The Finding (Lk 2:46-47)

The following verse begins, for the fourteenth and last time in Luke 1-2, with an *egeneto*, which always brings out a new stage, the finding of Jesus in the Temple.

> And it happened that after three days they found him in the temple, sitting among the teachers, listening to them and asking them questions; and all who heard him were amazed (*existanto*) at his understanding and his answers (2:46-47).

The narrative does not stop with the parents. The fact that they "find" Jesus is indicated by a word, without description of their joy or feelings, which Mary will express later, despite the long delay (2:48). "After three days" supposes a day of the journey, another for the return, and another for the fruitless search in Jerusalem.

Here again the narrative develops only on the level of knowledge. Jesus is among the *didascaloi* (teachers), he who will be the *didascalos par excellence*, according to a title which is frequently given him in the Gospel of Luke.[77]

He listens, he responds, and the listeners (Luke does not specify formally that they are *didascaloi*) are amazed at his "understanding" and his responses. His future qualification as *didascalos* is thus recognized, a glorifying test which prefigures the future.

His position as *didascalos* is discreetly accented by the choice of words:

—He sits: the word *kathezomenon* signifies the seated position, thus a stability. The word suggests that he was not standing (as represented by painters), cognizant of the fact that sitting was the proper position of official teachers, the *didaskaloi*.[78]

—The expression "among" (*en mesōi*) situates him in the center, in that position in which we will see him during his public life, surrounded by his disciples, on whom he casts a circular look, particularly when his family intervenes from outside.[79]

Luke, however, avoids the exaggerations of the Apocrypha. Jesus performs no miracle. Nor does he proclaim new revelations. He does not refute the teachers. He does not dispute. He is not even presented as a "one-way" teacher. On the contrary, he listens and questions. These words of verse 46 leave him in his role as a child. In such a picture, Luke expresses the astonishment of the listeners, characterized by the verb *existanto* (2:46-47). This word, from which we get the noun *ecstasy*, signifies "being outside of oneself." It is more than surprise, it is a stupefaction. Two words indicate the reason for this:

—His intelligence (*synesis*): the same root serves, by contrast, to describe the parents who "did not understand" (*ou synēkan* in 2:50). They had not reached the fullness of understanding and wisdom which the child Jesus already manifests.

—His responses (*apokrisesin*): with this last word of the verse, Jesus goes from the simple receptive attitude of the listener and questioner (suitable for his age as a child) to responses, where his teaching mission begins to appear, but still not exceeding the tone of modesty or probability.

These two verses, 2:46-47, serve to signify the qualifying and glorifying test of the child-Messiah as the future teacher (*didascalos*). He begins to function as a subject, as a hero, defined no longer by divine oracles, but by his actions, recognized for what he is by listeners.

The Dialogue and the Lack of Understanding (Lk 2:24-50)

The disjunction thus ends on the physical level. The parents have "found" Jesus, but they arrive from the outside, characterized by negative sentiment in a basically positive circle. They "see" (the first word of the following verse) without understanding. The disjunction thus continues on the level of knowledge:

> And when they saw him they were astonished; and his mother said to him, "Son, why have you treated us so? Behold, your father and I have been looking for you anxiously" (2:48).

The trial of the parents is indicated by two words which follow in the wake of the amazement of the listeners, but with a sorrowful note:
—*exeplagēsan*, they were astounded. This word emphasizes their surprise before the incomprehensible flight of Jesus.
—*odynōmenoi* signifies likewise a suffering, and even a torture. The word is used to indicate the torture of the rich man in the flames of hell (16:24-25), the suffering of Paul's disciples when he announces to them his death (Acts 20:38), and Paul's own deep suffering for the Jewish people (Rom 9:2).

The translation "anxiously" fits here because it describes an uncertain search. Anxiety is a form of fear without precise object, which impels the spirit to expect the worst. It is most descriptive of the fear of parents who are attached to their child. We have seen how the shadow of death hovers over this narrative.

This emotive vocabulary is used here to indicate the first realization of the sword (2:35) which will "pierce the life of Mary." Likewise, 1 Timothy 6:10 specifies the signification of the word *odynē* as a piercing, similar to Luke 2:35 and 48. We have seen how this detail appears in a coherent series of allusions to the future passion of Christ.

Mary's question is asked with authority. The word "child" (*teknon*, from *tiktō*, to give birth) which here replaces *pais* (2:43), indicates the dependent relationship of a child to the one who gave him birth. Mary, nevertheless, does not utter a formal reproach. She questions Jesus on the cause of his surprising conduct. She simply expresses the fact of this search and this sorrow.

Jesus replies to the question with a question: the surprise he counters with a surprise.

> And he said to them, "How is it that you sought me? Did you not know that I must be in my Father's house?" (2:49).

Jesus thus seems to justify the disjunction with his parents by the obligation to a definitive conjunction with the house of his heavenly Father, the Temple. If the rest of the narrative were lost, the reader could suppose only one thing: Jesus would remain in Jerusalem. By saying to his parents that he *had* to be there (2:49), he dismisses them. One would assume that they would return alone to Nazareth.

The Return and the Submission (Lk 2:51)

What follows, however, is the exact opposite:

> And he went down with them and came to Nazareth, and was obedient to them (2:51).

Descent[80] (*katebē*) and submission (*hypotassomenos*) are two parallel words. They create a striking contrast with what has just occurred. Jesus had remained in Jerusalem, he now descends to Nazareth. Not only does he join them, united in their descent (abasement), but he, who placed himself above them by leaving them in following the higher order of his heavenly Father, now submits to them. He shifts again to being subject to them. The isotopy (descent and submission) is striking and significant.

By this unexpected reversal, the disjunction realized and confirmed by Jesus is transformed into a conjunction. Jesus rejoins his parents after having left them. The disjunction, however, remains on the level of knowledge, on which level this whole scene developed:

> And they did not understand the saying which he spoke to them (2:50).

This negative statement is completed by the recurrence of the refrain concerning the meditation of Mary:

> And his mother kept all these things [words-events] in her heart (2:51).

This meditation implies a long-term growth in knowledge. According to the analysis of Serra, "all these things" (an expression which occurred already in 2:19), refers here to the whole of Luke 1-2.

The Growth of Jesus (Lk 2:52)[81]

The narrative ends with the refrain concerning growth, some of whose variations we have already studied. From the semiotic point of view, the most important variation is that Jesus is no longer designated as *paidion* (little child), nor even as a *pais* (child, servant, as in 2:48), but only by his name, Jesus, as the hero and subject of this last scene. His development "before God and men" (this final note is likewise new) prepares us to find him as an adult in 3:21. This last verse thus functions as a transition, a final reference to the addresser (God) and to the addressees, who have a constant and primary importance in the Gospel.

Conclusive Function

The first two visits of the child Jesus to the Temple of Jerusalem have a conclusive character. Both signify less the tranformation of *Jesus* than that of the *Temple*. From the beginning, Jesus is already fully defined in his being in a theophanic manner. When he leaves the Temple the element of value (the presence of God) is associated with him and moves with him. This is the meaning of the two returns to Nazareth, especially the second, where this value is hidden in humility, and brought out with insistence, in contrast with the preceding context.

The two visits to Jerusalem, however, have differentiated functions. The first was, as we saw, the fulfillment of the biblical prophecies of Daniel 9 and Malachi 3:1, "The Lord whom you seek will suddenly come to his temple," of the oracles of Luke 1:32-35, and of the Law (understood typologically) according to the newness of the Spirit (2:24-27).

The finding in the Temple is no doubt a second fulfillment of Malachi 3:1. The word "to search" recurs three times.

The episode of the finding is likewise programed by the prophecy of Simeon in 2:35. The piercing of Mary, indicated for a distant future, finds a first realization in this sorrowful loss of the child.

Finally, the function of this last episode is original (it was studied in the literary analysis).

Jesus manifests his consciousness of his divine filiation, declared in the message of the annunciation (1:32 and 35). This constitutes, in the infancy Gospel, a final theophany, for which Christ, having become subject, is himself the single and distinct actant. It involves the first words of Christ and his first self-confession on earth. It is no longer the angel nor the Spirit who pronounces the oracle, but Jesus himself.

The basic purpose of the episode lies especially in its openness to the future, not only in the final reference to his growth toward adulthood (2:52), but also in the announcement of the passion and the Resurrection. The infancy Gospel appears as a Gospel in miniature. It concludes on the themes which complete the entire Gospel. The first words of Jesus (2:49) unite with his last (23:46). It is this proleptic openness that is intended by the enigmatic word of 2:50, "They did not understand."

Formalization

The play of conjunctions and disjunctions is extremely rich and meaningful in the episode of the finding in the Temple. They can be schematized in the following way (→ signifying conjunction and ← signifying disjunction).

1. Jesus → parents (at the beginning, 2:42).
2. Jesus ← parents → heavenly Father (2:43 and 49).
3. Jesus → parents (but ← on the level of knowledge, 2:48 and 50).

The disjunction with the parents is correlative with the conjunction with the Father which motivates it.

This play of conjunctions and disjunctions takes place subtly on two levels: somatic (bodily) and cognitive, human and divine, which are woven together in the narrative.

Jesus appears first of all in physical and social conjunction with his parents for the ascent to Jerusalem, according to the program of custom.

He then poses a disjunction at once somatic and cognitive (2:43) with his parents, in order symbolically to place a conjunction with his Father in heaven, which he himself expresses at the end of the narrative (2:49).

The disjunction is temporary (three days) and extends on the cognitive level, since the amazed parents (2:48) did not understand what he said (2:50). Mary, however, is in search of a progressive solution by her meditation (2:51).

Jesus' act of independence is temporary, thus symbolic. His return, however, to conjunction with his parents (apparently contradicting his word in 2:49) does not change his conjunction as Son to his Father, which will be manifested throughout the Gospel. The Temple is only the symbol of this conjunction. The conjunction itself is ontological. It is linked to his person, to his body, whose topographical movements form the symbolism of the scene. It is affirmed from the beginning (1:32-35).

The suffering of the parents, from whom Jesus separates himself, prefigures that of his death. The ultimate meaning of this disjunction is the definitive conjunction with his Father, to which Jesus will in the end call his disciples. They also will be "continually in the temple" at the end of the Gospel (24:53) as in the Acts of the Apostles (thirteen times from Acts 2:46 to 5:4), until the moment when Stephen challenges this Temple "made with hands," as were idols (Acts 7:48), and the persecuted apostles are "dispersed." The Holy Spirit and the Lord, however, are with them to announce "the good news of the word" throughout the whole world.

The mainspring of the narrative of the finding (2:41-52) is the apparently subtle yet profound articulation between ordinary life (the observation of the Law and common custom) and the transcendent level on which the being of the Son of God is defined by an absolute reference to him whom Jesus calls "my Father" (2:49), and the mission which violently tears him away from his own for a return to the Father, to whom he calls his disciples. This tearing away caused by death, already signified at the presentation by the contradiction and the sword (2:34-35), finds its first realization and a new long-term significance at the moment of the finding. The poignant sorrow expressed by Mary (2:48) is the first blow of the sword and an announcement of the last blow, the *triduum mortis*, prefigured by the three days of the first paschal separation.

F. THE MODEL

The model underlying the narrative program is easy to synthesize according to the remarkable operational schema established by Greimas:

Addresser (A)	Object	Addressee (A2)
	↑	
Helpers	Subject	Opponents

The schema can be verified, although it is quite complex.

Subject

In each sequence, and sometimes in each scene within the sequences, the birth and the presentation, for example, we saw the subject change. We noted several times the disappearance of a subject who has been presented: Zechariah, who becomes mute, Joseph, who disappears, the parents, in 2:21-26. In 2:21-26 all the subjects disappear before the transcendent God, who is Principle and the ultimate reference of each scene, and who becomes "the subject of doing." We do not need to repeat the details of this analysis: Elizabeth disappears in favor of Zechariah in 1:8, then Zechariah in favor of Elizabeth in 1:24. . . until the last scene where Jesus becomes the subject.

Two important observations follow:

1. The identity of the successive subjects is finally referred to God, the exclusive subject of "doing," as we saw (1:25, 35, 37, 49, 51, 68, 72; see 1:20, 45, 65). The verb "to do" was attributed only to the parents regarding the accomplishment of the Law in 2:39. However, God does not eliminate human subjects. He does not overrule and circumvent them. They appear, rather, as living and free. They are referred to God, not as robots, but as servants who find their liberty in adoration and love (cf. 1:46-55, 68-79; 2:30-32). Thus we saw Mary and the shepherds depart "in haste" of their own initiative in harmonious adhesion to the project of God (1:39 and 2:16).

2. There is another permanent subject (1:2-56; 2:1-52), already programed, recognized, and qualified by important titles: Son of God, Christ, Lord. This subject, intermediary between God and human subjects, is the child Jesus. Already he is revealed as transcendent on the level of being. But he is still hidden in the womb of his mother, then in the manger, or curled up in the arms of Simeon. He is the subject of a state of being, not the subject of doing, we would say in

semiotics; he is passive, not active. He is, however, the virtual subject of the program of the whole Gospel, which early Christian preaching saw as beginning with the baptism by John, with the coming of the Spirit and the qualifying declaration of the addresser-Father, "This is my Son. . . ." These two traits are affirmed in 1:35 at the annunciation from the moment of the conception of Jesus. The Holy Spirit is upon him and he is already designated Son of God. Furthermore, he moves into the role of virtual subject (effective but not explicitly indicated as such) at the visitation, and that of active subject, independent of his parents and breaking with them, at the last scene of the infancy narrative, the finding in the Temple. This removal from hiddenness begins with projections towards the most distant future, which form a remarkable transition to the narrative of his public life (Luke 3).

In short, the particular subjects of each scene are referred to:
—the transcendent subject who is God the addresser;
—the principal virtual subject who is the Messiah.

In the measure in which this Messiah is the virtual subject, the particular subjects appear as his helpers.

Object

The principal virtual subject is Jesus-Savior. The corresponding object is salvation. There is a strong correlation between the name of Jesus, which signifies savior (the meaning deciphered in 2:11) and *salvation*, often mentioned with certain etymological allusions in the canticles (1:47, 69, 77; 2:30). Parallel (isotopic) expressions likewise appear: the consolation of Israel (2:25), the redemption of Jerusalem (2:38), even the purification of Jerusalem (2:22) which Luke relates to the addressed people by the plural pronoun, "their" purification.

It is important to note that God is not an object in Luke 1-2. He is more important than his gifts, which, however, establish a link, even union with him. Reciprocally the "people prepared" (1:17) are not an object for God, who establishes them in communion, in grace, and in sharing. The highest expression of this communion is 2:14, a cycle of praise rising toward God and of peace descending toward the people he loves.

What surfaces in Luke 1-2 is the identification of the savior and salvation. Jesus is designated as *sōtērion* in 2:30 and *sōtēria* in 1:69, 71, and 77. He is at once subject and object, as he is in the Eucharist, where he says, "This is my body" (the object identified with the subject). The convergent use of the two words, *savior* and *salvation*, the concrete and the abstract, testifies that salvation is the person of the savior with whom the people will identify as "a single body," as the apostle Paul will say; "a single vine," according to John 15.

Helpers-Opponents

It is not necessary to spend a great deal of time on a subject that would yield a very sparse harvest, that of helpers and opponents. Opponents are practically non-existent in Luke, who avoids conflicts. The program is not conflictual.[82] The helpers, likewise, find no important place except in reference to the virtual program where Jesus Christ is already the (hidden) subject of the Gospel. This confirms the recent analyses of Greimas, according to which helpers and opponents are not *actants*, but modalities of the subject.

Addresser

The major and final role is that of God the addresser. He holds a considerable place under the following names:
—God, twenty times,
—the Lord, twenty-six times,
—the Most High, three times,
—Savior, twice, identified with Christ,
—Mighty, 1:49,
—Master, 2:29,
—Father, 2:49,
—Holy Spirit, seven times.

No other character appears with such frequency. The most often named, Mary, appears only twelve times ("his mother," four more times). These statistics are significant.

God the addresser is always subject of a verb of doing, with one exception, as we saw. If, however, he appears here as the subject of "doing," he is a transcendent subject. He does not join but stirs up the action of human beings. The biblical practice of attributing to the first cause what comes from second causes does not deny the latter but signifies that all eventually comes from the Creator, in whom "we live and move and have our being," according to Acts 17:28.

The addresser, however, is not the subject who does everything. He inspires, directs, and stimulates the initiatives woven by human beings. He intervenes visibly only once in Luke 1-2 when his glory surrounds the shepherds. The glory here designates God himself, through a mediating formula. The angels (etymologically those sent by him) have the same mediating role. While speaking of God in somatic terms (his hand, his arm, his glance, the bowels of his mercy, as we saw), Luke accentuates his transcendence in continuity with the biblical tradition. In contrast to Caesar (Luke 1-2), God is not a manipulator. He influences by attraction and inspiration; in the form of the Holy Spirit, directing from within the freedom of human actions toward that communion which pleases God, where man finds his fulfillment and happiness. This conjunction with God, the gratuitous result of his plan of love, is celebrated spontaneously in the form of canticles (extremely important in the structure of Luke 1-2, as demonstrated by A. Gueuret).

Jesus, Savior and Salvation, Virtually Identified with the Addresser

It is also important to observe that several names of God are given to Christ. This transference, with which the revelation of the divinity of Jesus begins, is difficult to define, since it remains ambiguous. Thus, the name of Lord, applied to God twenty-four times, is applied to Christ twice (1:43 and 2:11). The representative significance of "Son of the Most High" (1:32) and "Son of God" (1:35) has also been discussed. The context of 1:35 clarifies the transcendent nature of Jesus which would in no way be evident if the text stopped with 1:32. But ambiguity is the very medium through which the divinity of Christ is gradually revealed throughout the NT. Here as elsewhere it is affirmed by the transference to Christ of texts and titles specifically related to God in the OT.

The title of Savior (2:11) is given to "Christ-Lord" in the strict and universal sense which the Bible reserves for God. Where at the beginning of the Magnificat Mary says "my spirit rejoices in God my savior" we might ask if it is not Jesus himself, God and Savior, to whom she is referring (see Hb 3:13, Vulgate). That Christ is abstractly and superlatively called "salvation" (*sōtērion* in 2:30 and *sōtēria* in 1:69, 71, 77 with an etymological allusion) also leads us to identify him with God himself.

In short, the semiotic analysis tends to confirm, in a structural way, his identification with God the addresser, an identification manifested also by the literary analysis of the application of theocentric texts and titles to Jesus in Luke 1-2.

Addressees

The position of addressee is also clearly supplied here: it is the people of God. The word "people" (*laos*) occurs eight times in Luke 1-2 (1:10, 17, 21, 68, 77; 2:10, 31, 32). From the beginning to the end the people do not cease to be present, in varying states of participation, which we have differentiated at each step.

They appear first as the liturgical assembly (in great number: *pan to plēthos*, 1:10, the same word used for the multitude of angels in 2:13). They pray in union with the priest. The joy announced by the angels is for them (1:14), since the converting precursor makes "ready for the Lord a people prepared" (1:17). They wait; they wonder and interpret correctly the priest's loss of speech: "He had seen a vision in the temple" (1:22).

They seem to disappear during the intimate scenes of the annunciation and the visitation. They are present, however, their presence and their history interwoven as addressees of the messianic salvation. They are designated as Israel, child of the God of mercy in the Magnificat (1:54).

They reappear at the birth and circumcision of John the Baptist, first in a small group, of neighbors and relatives (1:58), and then growing progressively with the repetition and amplification of the word "all," involving finally "all the hill country of Judea" (1:65).

They are absent during the intimate scene of the birth (2:6-7), but reappear with the shepherds, i.e., the poor, who are eminently symbolic of the people both according to the prophets and the Gospel. The canticle of the angels announces "peace among men with whom [God] is pleased" (2:14).

In the following development the people seem to disappear, but they are represented by Simeon and Anna, figures of the small remnant who wait for "the consolation of Israel" (2:25). The prophetess, Anna, announces to all the redemption of Israel.

It is important to note that the principal characters of Luke 1-2 are representative types of the people. This is true not only of Mary, shown as Daughter of Zion in reference to Zephaniah 3 and by the very structure of the Magnificat; it is true also of Zechariah and Elizabeth, then of Simeon and Anna, prototypes of the transition from the Law (1:5-8; 2:22-24) to the Spirit (1:41, 67; 2:25-27).

To this group can be added the representative figures of the "fathers" (1:55 and 72), of Moses (2:22), and especially of Abraham (1:55 and 73), who form a counterbalance to Mary at the end of the Magnificat, which she began in thanksgiving for the arrival of the long-awaited realization of the promises of God in herself, and ended with Abraham, who was the first to receive those promises (1:55).

In short, the model of Greimas is verified in an obvious and ample manner in Luke 1-2, but with instructive and surprising features. Christ fills all the important positions of the model in an unusual way, which I have never seen elsewhere. Not only is Jesus at once the subject and object (savior and salvation) but he is identified at once with God as addresser and with human beings as addressees:
—God with God (Lord, Holy, Great, son of God);
—a human with human beings (as baby, child, as a growing boy, as one of the poor).

In this new area of research, other surprises await us.

G. FUNDAMENTAL STRUCTURE AND SEMIOTIC SQUARE OF LUKE 1-2

Should we now attempt the final stage of semiotic analysis—the identification of the organic model of Luke 1-2, in the form of a "square"? This operation seeks to identify the true motives of the text, its coherence and unity, according to certain objective criteria.

The operation is limited: it is hypothetical, and it cannot claim to offer an adequate explanation. It is a fact that different scholars, studying the same text, often come up with different squares, depending on their perspective, presuppositions, methods, insights, and the

The Date of Christmas

The Year

At one time, the consensus about the date of the birth of Christ posited that it took place in 4 B.C., shortly before the death of Herod, which is situated before the Passover (Josephus, *Antiquities*, 17, 9, 3 no. 213 and *Jewish Wars*, 2, 1, 3, no. 1), thus probably in March or April, after thirty-seven years of a reign which began in 40 B.C., i.e., between the first and the fourteenth of Nisan of the year 4 B.C. This seemed to be confirmed by a lunar eclipse (*Antiquities* 17, 6, 4, no. 167) which is situated in the night of the twelfth or thirteenth of March (a conclusion clearly summarized in the last edition of E. Schürer (*The History of the Jewish People*, revised by G. Vermes, Edinburgh, T. Clark, 1973, I, pp. 326-328, and notes 165-166; J. Finegan, *Handbook of Biblical Chronology*, Princeton University, 1964, pp. 230-259, nos. 362-408; S. Dockx, *Chronologie néotestamentaire*, Gembloux, 1976, pp. 3-4).

But new hypotheses have been presented in the last few years which place the death of Herod in the year 1 B.C. (W. E. Filmer, "The Chronology of the Reign of Herod the Great," in *JTS* 7, 1966, pp. 283-298, refuted by T. D. Barnes, *ibid.*, 19, 1968, pp. 264-269). This hypothesis has been restated in a new analysis by E. E. Martin (*The Birth of Christ Recalculated*, Pasadena, 1969) and Ormond Edwards (*Chronologie des Lebens Jesu*, Stuttgart, Verckhaus, 1978, and "Herodian Chronology," in *Palestinian Exploration Quarterly* 114, 1982, pp. 29-42). The wavering of Flavius Josephus (*Wars* 1, no. 665 and *Antiquities* 17, no. 191, etc.) is understandable, as he was calculating according to two calendars, one civil and the other religious. Herodian coins argue in the direction of a later death. This would lead us to fix the birth of Christ either on January 4, 1 B.C., according to the data of Matthew, with the visit of the royal magi on January 6th, or on the 25th of December of the same year, according to Luke.

In his article Edwards states his surprise that this point of view of a vociferous minority has not overturned the traditional consensus. It seems to us premature to make a decision on this complex debate, which deals with multiple and overlapping textual, numismatic, and astronomical data.

The Month and the Season

The date of Christmas has been fixed in a variety of ways since the time of Clement of Alexandria (*Stromateis* 1, 21, second century), according to a pluralism of traditions, none of which has been historically compelling:

—The Eastern tradition places the feast of the birth of Jesus on January 6 (perhaps to replace a pagan feast previously held on this date in honor of the goddess Koré giving birth to Eon [Finegan, 255]).
—The Western tradition situates it on December 25 (probably to replace the pagan feast of the solstice, *sol invictus*, by a Christian feast of the Sun of Justice).

Both probably arise from an ancient Christian tradition holding that "Jesus was born in the winter" (S. Dockx, 1976, p. 4). The proofs drawn from the custom according to which shepherds spent the night in the fields from March to November have not been conclusive (R. E. Brown, 1977, 401-402).

The Hour

The hour of midnight was inspired by Wisdom 18:14-16:

> For while gentle silence enveloped all things, and the night in its swift course was now half gone, thy all-powerful Word leaped from heaven, from the royal throne, into the midst of the land that was doomed, a stern warrior carrying the sharp sword of thy authentic command, and stood and filled all things with death.

Both Luke and Matthew place the birth at night, by the star of the wise men (Mt 2:2) and especially by the revelation to the shepherds watching at night (Lk 2:8).

options which they choose. This has certainly happened in the study of the text of Luke 1-2 where three squares have been proposed.

1. Status Questionis

The Lyons group (CADIR)[83] have, for economic reasons, produced a very complex square without commentary. I shall not reproduce here the explanation which I have attempted in *Ephemerides Mariologicae* (1982, 59-62).

The fundamental level of this square is as follows:[84]

A. To be born of woman + man on the biological level (to be born in the world) (to be born for the mother)	B. To be born of the Word on the divine level (to be born to the Word) (to be born for God, for the Father)
B* Not to be born of the Word	A* Not to be born of woman + man

This square is centered on birth (both of John and of Jesus) and puts much weight on the opposition between biological birth (physically impossible in the case of Zechariah, and contrary to Mary's expressed wish not "to know man," 1:34) and the Word of God which begins the history of salvation with the births of the precursor and of Christ. The two births are valued as the fruit of the Word and not as ordinary biological processes. In this measure there comes to light a process of birth to God, to salvation.

We will not spend too much time with this square. It is quite complex, the result of a collective and rather hasty research. There may be material here for several squares. This analysis centers only on the notion of birth, which, in fact, covers only a relatively limited part of the text and its functioning. Furthermore, the axis of contradictories and even of correlatives is hardly verified in the development of the narrative. This limited focus manifests the contrasting tension between birth and word. It is strange to note, however, that this tension is made even more clear in the Johannine prologue, where Christ is called "the Word," and where birth is explicitly referred to "nor of the will of the flesh nor of the will of man, but of God" (Jn 1:13-14; see below, pp. 406-407).

All this invites us to look for a square which deals more completely with Luke 1-2, and corresponds more to the essential issues—salvation by communion and communication between God and humans—issues which the analysis of the model have manifested to us.

The Association of Roche-Colombe (Paris)[85]

M. Rosaz and E. Pousset also propose a limited square for the infancy narratives, one which centers on the last episode, the finding in the Temple.

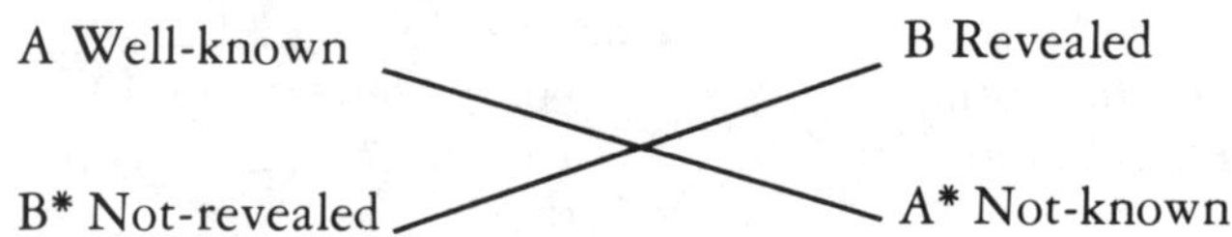

This perspective is limited to the dimension of "knowing" which, we have seen, is the dominant factor in the finding sequence. Jesus, known on a superficial level, reveals himself in depth by an act of independence which provokes astonishment, search, anxiety (2:48). The negative aspect (not-known) of the schema is verified in the incomprehension of the parents (2:50). This is, however, a limited view point.

Agnes Gueuret[86]

Agnes Gueuret constructs her square from the canticles wherein she discerns, in a penetrating way, the profound meaning of the text.

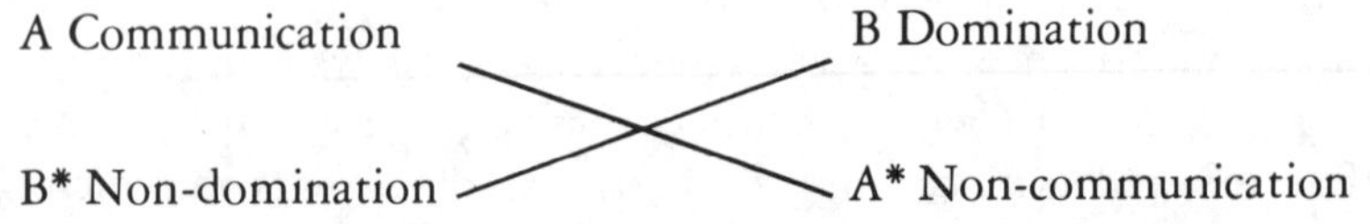

This square, established in a methodical and detailed manner ("*la composante sémantique*," pp. 189-303 of the typed thesis), manifests clearly a fundamental opposition around which the others are organized.

Gueuret identifies the model in the Magnificat, where Mary magnifies God who magnifies her, where the Most High regards the lowliness of his servant, where the Powerful One fills the weak and casts down the powerful from their thrones (1:51-53). The latter manifest domination which is defined by discrimination (between rich and poor, powerful and weak) and exclusivism (unilateral relation), while bilateral communication is defined by differentiation (the Most High and the servant who remains servant) and by reciprocity (the gift of God and praise).[87]

What is verified with the greatest amplitude is the pole of communication characteristic of Luke 1-2 (almost absent in Matthew 1-2).

The notion of domination has only a limited place here. In a strict sense it appears only in the passage cited from the Magnificat (1:51-53) and by way of mere allusion in the Benedictus (1:68-76), speaking of the relations of Israel to its enemies; and finally in Caesar Augustus' decree compelling Joseph to be enrolled (2:1-2). To this we could add the role of the Law, which the parents of John the Baptist (1:5-10) and the parents of Jesus obey in the last two scenes. In Luke 1-2, however, the Law does not appear so much as a form of domination. In the perspective of Psalm 118, the Wisdom books, and Luke 1-2, the Law is practiced in a spontaneous way, as an intimate contract, as it was lived by the Judeo-Christians, whose faith formed the source of this sequence.

The weak point of this square, otherwise enlightening and methodically well-established, is the fact that this concept of domination is relatively inadequate and occupies a small place in the essential development and progression of the text.

Should we add that the words "communication" and "domination" do not appear in the text of Luke? This is not an objection, for abstraction is legitimate in this matter. Nevertheless, it is desirable that a square assume objectively the terms of the author. According to this inductive option and in reference to the very thrust of the text, we propose a square whose terms belong to Luke himself.

2. *The First Proposition: Law and Grace*

The first square is based on the contrast between Law and grace, according to the following schema:

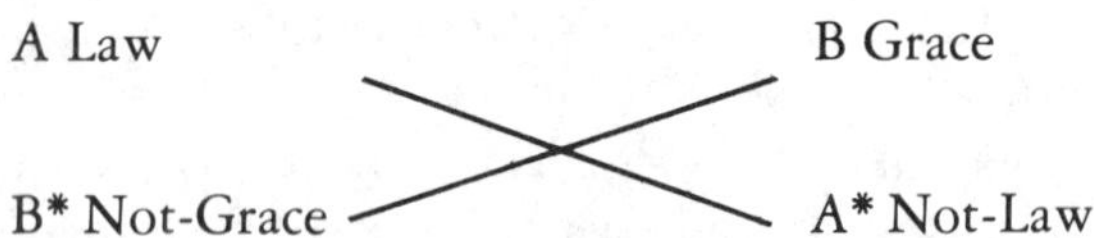

The frequency of the two words in Luke is relatively important: Law in 2:22, 23, 24, 27, 39; grace (*charis*) in 1:28 (*kecharitōmenē*) and 1:30, "You have found grace," which is the commentary on this name given from above.

The word "grace" forms a sort of inclusion in Luke 1-2, from the annunciation to Mary (the major sequence which introduces Christ) to the last verse indicating Jesus' growth in grace (2:52). (This inclusion is particularly important given that Mary appears "as a representative of her son," according to the semiotic analysis of Gueuret.)

Isotopies (Parallel Analogies)

The two words, Law and grace, are significant in Luke 1-2.[88]

A. There are several mentions of the Law:

—The ritual observances and the justice of Zechariah and Elizabeth at the beginning of the narrative (1:5-7).

—The allusion to the law of the *nazir* (ritual consecration to God, 1:15).

—The fulfillment of the liturgy (1:8-10;23).

—The two circumcisions (1:59 and 2:21).

—The fulfillment of the rites concerning Jesus as first-born where the Law is explicitly mentioned five times (2:22-27, 39).

—The customary observance of the paschal pilgrimage (2:41-42) according to Deuteronomy 16:16.

To these manifestations of the religious law we can add those concerning the secular law of the census imposed by Caesar Augustus (2:1-3).

B. Concerning grace, the principal connections are:

—The benevolent regard of God on Elizabeth (*epeiden*, 1:25) and on Mary (*epeblesen*, 1:48).

—His presence to those whom he loves: presence upon (1:35; 2:25, 40); presence among (1:35b, 38, 58, 66, 72; 2:25, 26); his enveloping presence which surrounds the shepherds (2:9).

—The act of going "before him," which characterized the precursor (1:15, 17, 19, 75, 76).
—*eleos*, the mercy or tenderness of God. The Hebrew word is more often translated by *charis* in the LXX and seems to be the substratum for *kecharitōmenē*.
—Salvation (*sōtēria*, 1:69, 71, 77 and *sōtērion*, 2:30) and Savior (*sōtēr*, 1:47; 2:11) which always appears in relationship with the name Jesus ("a Savior, who is Christ the Lord," 2:11), likewise connote gratuity.
—The consolation of Israel (2:25).
—Light (1:79; 2:32) and glory (enveloping and illuminating in 2:9; identified with Jesus in 2:32) are the radiating manifestation of God and of his grace communicated to humans.
—Grace (freely given from above) in response to which is thanksgiving, the praise of God (*aineo*, 2:13, 20), which abounds in the five canticles of Luke 1-2 (1:25, 46-55, 68-79; 2:14, 29-32; cf. 1:42-45; Elizabeth's thanksgiving, 1:58 and 64). The isotopy between the gift of grace and thanksgiving does not appear in the Greek of Luke 1-2; however, it is inherent in the reciprocity of the double movement, ascending and descending, which is a recurring motif in these two chapters. This parallel appears in the double meaning of the word "benediction," used in an ascending form to bless God (1:64 and 2:28; see 1:68) and in a descending form to bless human beings, who are thus filled with grace (1:42 and 2:34). The isotopy suggests the unity of the cycle according to a reciprocity between the actions of God and of human beings.
—The Holy Spirit, the spirit of Pentecost, the source of freedom, of charisms, of joy, who appears in a significant manner throughout Luke 1-2 (1:15, 35, 41, 67; 2:25, 26, 27) as a source of inspiration, revelation, prophecy (1:42, 67, 70, 76; 2:28 and 36), and prediction (1:48, 76; 2:29, 32, 34-35). In Acts 15:8 (see Lk 1:15, 28) the Spirit, in contrast to the Law (Acts 15:8 and 10), is identified with grace (15:11). The same connection appears in the narration of the annunciation (1:28 and 35). It is by the Holy Spirit (1:41 and 67) that Elizabeth and Zechariah pass from the Law to grace, and that the fulfillment of the Law (2:22-24) issues forth in grace (2:25-32). Luke speaks of the Holy Spirit according to the charismatic experience of Pentecost which he describes in Acts.

Law and grace have a structural position in each episode. Luke begins with an ordinary program, regulated by law, religious (1:5, 59-62; 2:21-22) or secular (2:1-2), and by custom. Grace, however, causes the eschatological newness to burst forth by a gratuitous act of the Lord. We have seen this movement in each of the sequences (or sub-sequences).

In line with the optimistic perspective of Luke, the positive poles, A (law) and B (grace) occur more frequently than the contrary negative poles, which are nevertheless represented.

The Negative Poles

B*: At the 'not-grace' pole we find:

—Zechariah's lack of faith. This man, although exemplary in his relation to the Law (1:5-6), did not know how to recognize the free nature of the gift and asked for a proof from God (1:18): lack of faith (1:20) in contrast to Mary (1:45).

—The proud, powerful, and rich, whose disgrace is outlined in the Magnificat (1:51-53).

—Those who live in the shadows, mentioned in the Benedictus, for whom Christ will be a light (1:79 and 2:32).

—The adversaries of Christ, who appear in the prophecy of Simeon (2:34-35).

A*: The 'not-law' pole applies to the pagans, alien to the Law (as to grace):

—The enemies of the pious people (1:71 and 74), occupiers or oppressors, characterized by hatred (1:71).

This 'not-law' pole, however, also applies, in a paradoxical sense, to those who are freed from the Law by grace: Mary, who intends not to know man (1:34) although legally married (1:27 and 2:5), and Jesus, who evades his parents because of the superior attraction of his Father in heaven (2:43-49). Here we have one of the most paradoxical and most significant dimensions of Luke 1-2.

The most important task in establishing a semiotic square is to grasp the scope of the narrative processes accounted for by the schema, according to the diverse axes: horizontal, diagonal, and vertical.

The most significant narrative processes are those which manifest the transcending of the Law (and customs) by the eschatological gift of grace. This going-beyond the Law asserts itself in a significant manner with the parents of John the Baptist, who, though qualified according to the Law (1:5-7), receive the new gift of God under the sign of punishment (Zechariah), of secrecy, and of shame (Elizabeth in 1:25), until the time of the twofold triumph of the Spirit. The same phenomenon is manifested in an entirely positive way in the case of John the Baptist, an intermediate figure of a prophet (1:67) connected with the Law by his asceticism (1:15; see 1:80) and with grace by his name (root: *ḥānan*) and by the Holy Spirit, who fills him from his mother's womb (1:15b). The word grace (1:28) inaugurates the essential message of the annunciation in order to introduce Christ (1:31-32) under the sign of perfect conjunction with God (1:28-30; celebrated by the visitation, 1:39-56). Mary prefigures Christ, who is characterized also by grace in 2:40 and 52.

In chapter 2, grace, or rather glory, makes use of the secular law of Caesar Augustus, which occasions the qualification of the Messiah in the city of Bethlehem. This grace appears suddenly in an exceptional burst of glory (2:9). It invests the poor shepherds who hasten to realize their conjunction with the Messiah-Lord and to spread this Good News and this praise (2:8-20).

At the presentation, the Law, which would seem to provide the program for the first coming of Jesus into the Temple, receives an unexpected typological-eschatological fulfillment, theophanic and complete (2:25-27). The Holy Spirit manifests Jesus internally to Simeon and Anna. Subjecting himself to the Law, Jesus brings to the subjects of the Law (typical representatives of the people's hope) the consolation and the fulfillment which they are waiting for (2:22).

At the finding in the Temple, the Holy Family, having made a pilgrimage in accordance with custom (2:41) and the Law (Dt 16:16), underwent a test of great moment, ending on a note which prefigures Jesus' return to the Father. The sword of sorrow, predicted for Mary by Simeon, was realized for the first time when Jesus disappeared during three days in that same Jerusalem to which, during a future Passover, he will return. But the infancy Gospel does not close on this Mount

Tabor. Jesus returns to the lowliness of Nazareth and to submission in order to grow in grace.

Let us verify more carefully the three axes of the square.

1. The horizontal axes of contraries:

AB: Are 'Law' and 'grace' really contraries? Yes, in the sense that they are opposed as exterior and interior norms, as rule and freedom, as framework and impetus (the haste of Mary at the visitation or of the shepherds at the birth of Jesus, the determination which moves Jesus to remain in Jerusalem [2:43], or Mary to refrain from knowing man, 1:34). But the dramatic opposition described by Paul (Rom 7:1-5) is here resolved in a joyous and serene transcending of the Law. This "moving beyond" is the motive of the progression of Luke 1-2.

A*B*: The lower horizontal, 'not-Law'/'not-grace', seems to be realized among the hateful enemies mentioned in the Benedictus (1:71) and with those characterized by "darkness and the shadow of death" (1:79). They are the antithesis of the people of God who are characterized by piety and justice. They seem to be defined by impiety and injustice, the contraries of grace and Law. But this double negative horizontal has very little importance in the program of transcending the Law, which is essentially non-conflictual.

2. The diagonal axes of contradictories appear in the same atmosphere of serenity:

BB*: 'Grace' and 'not-grace' manifest their conflict in diverse ways. We see the revolution of God (of grace) in favor of the poor, against those who triumph according to the law of the world by knowledge, possession, and power (1:51-53). We see Zechariah's resistance of grace and his punishment. We see the opposition between the eschatological light and those who live in "darkness and the shadow of death." The same contradiction appears in a more dramatic way in the prophecy of Simeon. Christ will be an occasion of falling (for those who do not accept grace), a sign of contradiction in Israel, revealing the hearts imprisoned in legalism (2:35).

AA*: 'Law' and 'not-Law' concern the opposition between the people of God and the pagans to whom the Messiah will bring light (1:79; 2:32a). This opposition will be overcome by grace.

3. The vertical axes of correlations:

AB*: The correlation between 'Law' and 'not-grace' concerns the case of Zechariah, who is just according to the Law, but, failing at first according to grace (and the Spirit), enters into grace by passing through the test of punishment.
BA*: The correlation 'grace' and 'not-Law' sheds light on the most unusual paradoxes of Luke 1-2, where the impetus of grace and the motions of the Spirit overturn norms and customs. Mary's resolution ("not to know man," 1:34) which is contrary to the marriage in which she is legally engaged, finds its fruitfulness according to a plan of grace (1:35).

Likewise, the name "John," prescribed for the precursor, contradicts the custom of giving a child the name of its father (1:59-61). The enrollment of Christ, according to the law of the emperor (2:1-2), programs the coming of a subversive king seen as "subversive," who, according to Luke (23:2-3, 37, 38), will one day be crucified under this very pretext. Unlike Matthew, however, Luke does not bring out in his infancy narrative this conflict between "the King of the Jews" and the earthly "King" (cf. Mt 2:1-2). The presentation of Jesus in the Temple alters the essential points of the fulfillment of the Law (the purification of the mother and the redemption of the child) in order to transfer them to the people according to grace. In the scene of the finding in the Temple, Jesus' impulse toward his Father prompts him to leave his parents and violates the rules of "custom" (2:42) and of the caravan (2:43).

All the theoretically possible narrative processes are thus illustrated in a significant way.

The relationship of Law to grace is subtly delineated in these narrative processes:

We have already asserted that John the Baptist belongs to the Law, through his parental lineage as well as by his abstinence. However, in the dynamic line of the precursor prophets (in whom the Spirit was already manifested), this child, filled with the Holy Spirit from his mother's womb, is clearly situated in the line of Pentecost and of grace. Luke 1-2 thus illustrates in a remarkable way the mediating position of the precursor between Law and grace.

Jesus is situated wholly on the side of grace and glory. Thus we might be surprised to see him subject to the Law in 2:22-25, 27, 39. In this respect 2:1-2 seems to illustrate the saying of Paul in Galatians 4:4, "Born of woman, born under the law." This respect for the Law (see Mt 5:17) brings about a transcending of the Law (cf. the incident of the finding in the Temple). We have put our finger on the subtle and positive relationship between the Law and grace, according to Luke. Jesus is subject to the Law and transcends it. He does not abolish it but fulfills it by up-dating and transferring its meaning.

Topographical Implications

This square takes into consideration the organic topography of Luke 1-2 and its narrative ranges:

—Nazareth is the place where the word "grace" (*charis*) is exclusively situated: three times in 1:30; 2:40 and 52; in addition, *kecharitōmenē* in 1:28.

—Jerusalem is the place where the "Law" is exclusively situated (2:22-24, 27, 39) along with the legal and cultural vocabulary (1:5-11, 23). Twice when the parents of Jesus had accomplished all that was prescribed by the Law, they left Jerusalem (2:39 and 43).[89] The Law is seen in relationship to Jerusalem; grace, in relation to Nazareth. This grouping of occurrences is organic.

—Bethlehem (2:4 and 15) is situated in the contradictory pole: in contradiction to customary usage, Luke uses the title "city of David" not for Jerusalem, where David placed the Ark, the sign of God's presence, and reigned as king and supreme pontiff (2 Sm 6:17 and 20), but for his humble place of origin.[90]

—"Darkness and the shadow of death" (1:79), the pagan places in which the light of the Messiah would shine (1:79 and 2:32), constitute the fourth pole, in contrast to Nazareth, the place where light arose.

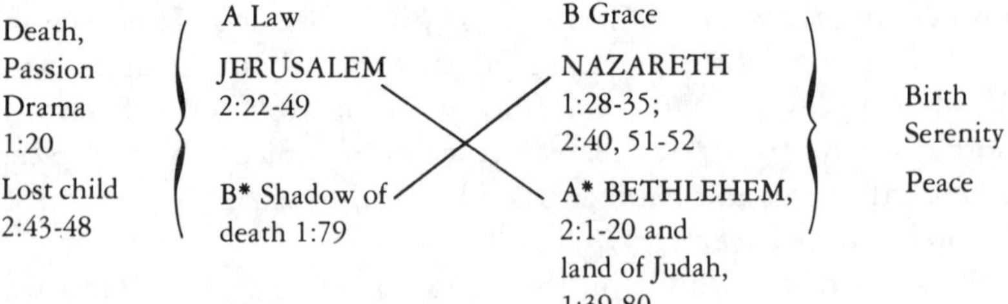

The opposition of the contraries AB (Jerusalem-Nazareth) is clear. In Jerusalem, the place of the Temple (2:27, 37-46) and of the Law (2:22, 23, 24), the fulfillment of grace comes from Nazareth where Jesus was conceived (1:31-38) according to grace (1:28 and 30). This arrival of the Lord, which involves a social revolution, the reversal of the high and the low according to the Magnificat (1:51-53), involves also a reversal of topographical hierarchies. The Law is fulfilled because it is transcended when Christ comes to fulfill the Law in the Temple. This sense of "moving beyond" is the root of all the transfers of meaning which we discussed earlier. No longer is it the mother who is purified, but Jerusalem itself. No longer is it the "first-born" (2:7 and 23) who is redeemed, but the people of God, because his coming is "the redemption of Jerusalem" (2:38). He who comes from below is the "glory of Israel," his people, and the "light for revelation to the Gentiles" (2:32). In the process, Bethlehem is promoted to being "city of David" when Jesus is born there (2:4 and 11), appropriating the title given to Jerusalem.

When Jesus returns to Jerusalem as an adolescent, coming up from Nazareth where he had returned, he breaks with the custom which called for his return with his parents. He remains in Jerusalem to demonstrate that his Father's house is his dwelling. He confers on the Temple the plenitude with which he had filled it at the moment of his presentation (2:22 and 32). However, this place is only a temporary symbol of a reality beyond Jerusalem, of what will later be called the "heavenly Jerusalem," and his lingering in the Temple, a temporary symbol of the return to the Father which Jesus alludes to (2:49) and which will be achieved by the *triduum* (2:46) of his death.

In the humility of this place of grace (Nazareth), the humble topography of the infancy ends, under the sign of grace (2:52).

The lower register of sub-contraries (B*, the shadow of death and A*, Bethlehem) is not made explicit. Luke merely sketches this relationship from the fact that the shepherds, submerged in the watchful night of the poor outside the city (2:8), are the first ones to be touched by the light (2:9). They announce this light for the admiration of all (2:18), and Luke presents them as the prototype of the pastors of the Church (*poimenes*, 2:8, 16, 18, 20; see Eph 4:11; and Jn 10:11, 14-16;

Heb 13:20; 1 Pt 2:25). This well-constructed vocabulary was correctly pointed out by A. Serra (1982, 220-221).

In the contradictory poles:

AA*: Jerusalem-Bethlehem. The rituals of the Law are explicitly situated only in Jerusalem. This is no doubt the reason why the topography of the circumcision, normally fulfilled in Bethlehem, is hidden from view, to the accompaniment of the fulfillment refrain which connects this verse and this rite to the Jerusalem sequence (2:21-22). We find here an explanation of an ambiguity which has thrown off many exegetes. Historical factors would urge one to situate 2:21 in the Bethlehem sequence. But the literary and semiotic reasons agree in linking this verse with the following, the Jerusalem sequence.

BB*: Nazareth-shadow of death. This insignificant and marginal village of Galilee is chosen by grace (1:26-30). It is possible that Galilee, on the frontier of Israel, was also for Luke a symbol of the Gentiles who would receive the light, as Matthew 4:15-16 states: "Galilee of the Gentiles—the people who sat in darkness have seen a great light."

The correlative poles are likewise significant:

AB*: Jerusalem-shadow of death. The relativity of Jerusalem, according to Luke, is registered here. The capital is flooded with a light which comes from elsewhere, from the Messiah conceived in Nazareth and born in Bethlehem. Jerusalem, placed under the Law, is enlightened by the Messiah (2:32), but Jesus does not remain there. He leaves Jerusalem and the Temple (2:39 and 51), having brought purification (2:22), consolation (2:25), and redemption (2:30). For this reason the ascent to Jerusalem is not the conclusion of Luke 1-2 which ends with the descent (the *kenosis*) of the son of God.

Also on this vertical axis, Jerusalem-shadow of death, is the passion of Christ, predicted by Simeon, typologically announced by the episode of the finding in the Temple. Jerusalem is the place of the contradiction and the sword (2:34-35), of the "three days" (2:46) of the death of Christ (2:34) for the salvation of the nations (1:78-79).

BA*: Nazareth-Bethlehem. These are two places of humility, in contrast to Jerusalem and to the shadow of death (where the glorious reign of Caesar Augustus is situated [2:1-2] as well as that of his henchman, Herod). It is here that "the day shall dawn upon us from on high" (1:78).

Modalization: Being-appearing

The classical square, 'being-appearing,' manifests an essential dimension of Luke 1-2, the progressive revelation of the being of Christ, from hiddenness to the manifestation of his public life (Luke 3).

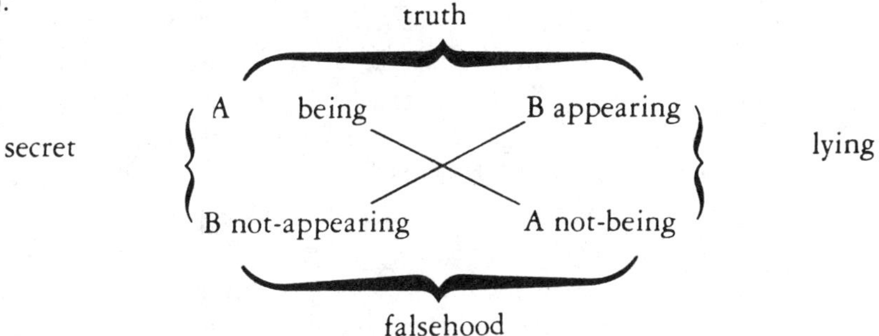

This square partially coincides with the preceding, Law-grace. The Law corresponds to appearing (the visible signs of the liturgy); grace (which characterizes Christ, 2:40, 52 and Mary 1:28, 30) to being. It will suffice here simply to sketch the essential lines of the narrative processes which illuminate the being of Christ. The manifestation of being under the appearing identifies with and is largely integrated into the manifestation of grace in the framework of the Law. There is some accord here with the square proposed by Gueuret, where communication is realized under domination. This square is thus a supermodalization (modal reinterpretation) of the preceding one, according to the square of truth (veridiction), that which articulates being and appearing.

In short, the revelation of the birth of the precursor, herald of the eschatological times (being), is given to Zechariah in the "appearing" of the legal liturgy, which is interrupted by this revelation (1:11, 20-22). The priest, speechless (1:20, 22), leaves the scene lessened in his "appearing" as priest. Mary receives, in an equally secret and intimate manner, the revelation of the Messiah, a transcendent being who has no "appearing." The realization of his conception is not even described, but rather known by its effects.

Such is the meaning of the visitation which manifests the radiance of Christ ("appearing") in the intimacy of the two women in whom the two infants remain hidden. Thus the narrative paradoxically seems to make them prevail ("appearing") over their children, who in the context of "being" are far more important.

The birth and circumcision of John the Baptist manifest the precursor, but in an enigmatic way. His "appearing" does not explain his "being."

The legal census which causes Jesus to be born in Bethlehem manifests his Davidic label (topographical identification with David). The triumphal "appearing" of the glory leads the shepherds to the humble "appearing" of the Messiah, a baby laid in a manger (2:16). The Messiah is recognized, but his being, already proclaimed (2:11), remains secret, hidden in humility.

At the presentation, where he comes under the externals of the Law (an "appearing" filled with hidden typological meaning, signified by the implicit references to Scripture), Simeon, inspired by the Spirit, reveals Jesus as "salvation" (2:30), "light and glory" (2:32), but also in the mystery of contradictions and of his future passion, which forms the counterpart to the humility of the infancy. He "appears" to be a son of Joseph (2:48), but he is the Son of God (1:32, 35).

In the last pericope (the finding), Jesus himself reveals his being, although discreetly. In the Temple, he manifests his understanding which provokes the admiration of his listeners (2:47). His "being" appears also when he reveals to his disturbed parents his consciousness of being Son of God, and typologically, his mysterious future return to the Father. He does this enigmatically. At first they "do not understand" the meaning of his answer (again the constant dimension of secrecy). He goes down again toward the submissive and hidden life of Nazareth. However, in contrast to John the Baptist (in the desert, 1:80), his growth appears not only before God but also before men (2:52). These are the last words of the infancy Gospel, before the revelation of his public life.

The positive processes, truth and secrecy, are made clear, but the ranges of lying and falseness do not really appear in Luke 1-2, which dwells on lights rather than shadows.

This square clarifies significant aspects of Luke 1-2. The first revelation of Christ is the eschatological fulfillment of the prophecies reworked in the text. But this revelation remains discreet. In contrast with John the Baptist, who is characterized especially by his function, Christ, who does not act, is characterized by his being (not yet manifested). This explains the paradoxical fact that the ontological titles of Christ are numerous in the infancy Gospel in contrast with the rest of the Gospel.

3. The Second Proposition: Glory-Humility

Theophany and Poverty?

Analysis of the text suggests to us another square, founded on opposition between two contrary poles: theophany-poverty.

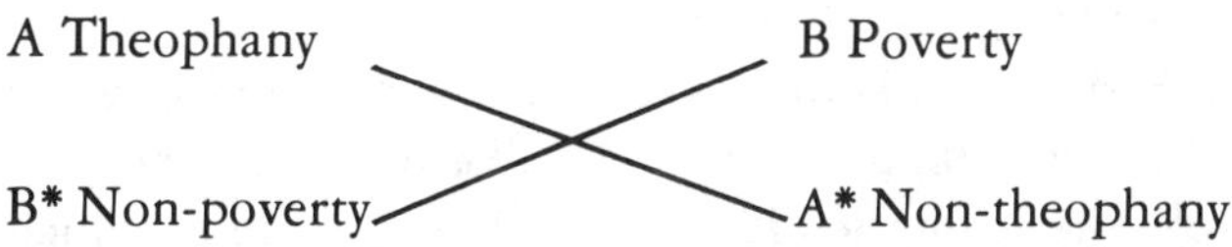

A. The theophanies (manifestations of God; cf. the verb *epiphainō* in 1:79) appear according to a meaningful gradation.

The manifestation of the angel Gabriel to Zechariah in the Temple (place of God) is only a prelude, an indirect theophany through the mediation of angels, which announces the precursor.

The series of theophanies actually begins with the annunciation to Mary. The Son of God is announced in the future tense under the figure of the shekinah. The resplendant theophany of Christmas begins with a direct manifestation of the glory of God which surrounds the shepherds (in order to invite them, however, to discover the child in his poverty). The theophany of the presentation, which has been studied in detail, is a major one. The paschal theophany where Jesus manifests himself (at the finding in the Temple) is realized in extreme poverty and is fulfilled in humility (2:51).

B: Poverty (*tapeinōsis*, explicit in 1:48 and 52) provides the framework of these theophanies, which causes a transformation of apocalyptic, in discretion and humility, as Legrand has correctly noted.

We see this poverty first of all in the lowly and marginal situation of Nazareth, the paradoxical place of the conception of the Messiah and of the humility of Mary, glorified in and because of her poverty (1:48), a prototype of what God the Savior will do in raising the poor (1:52).

We see it next in the poverty of the Holy Family at Christmas: displaced persons, without lodging, without a crib for the child, who is reduced to an animal habitat. (It is against this background that the manifestation of glory bursts forth.)

The presentation is a humble submission to a law of purification. For him who will be described as Holy (2:23), savior (2:30), light and glory (2:32), only the offering of the poor is made. The divine self-confession of Jesus in the Temple occurs in humble submission to a legal custom. After his sublime and yet trenchant self-declaration as Son of God (2:49), Jesus returns to the humility of Nazareth and to submission (2:51).

In short, the theophanies take place in the context of a poverty which is in no way abolished, but rather becomes the new sign of God. For Luke, glory is implied in poverty. This is a theme which has its roots in the infancy narrative, and is developed throughout as the paradox of the Gospel.

The two negative poles of the square can be identified in the following manner:

A*: In the non-theophanic poles we find kings of the earth in contrast with their pretentions to be divine (cf. Acts 12:21-22): Herod (1:5) and especially Caesar, who was called Augustus (= divine, 2:1-2).

B*: In the non-poverty poles we find the powerful and the rich (1:51-53).

This square offers interesting lines of development.

1. On the contrary axes:

On the upper level, AB, there takes place a reconciliation of these apparently opposite poles. God chooses poverty. Because of his condition as "poor," Jesus is subject to the census, and yet this servitude manifests him as the Messiah, son of David, in the city of the great king (2:1-7), where he will be enthroned from heaven (2:9-14).

On the lower level, B*A*, we see a similar coincidence between non-poverty and non-theophany with the kings and the powerful cast down from their thrones (1:52). It is not in them that the divine Glory manifests itself, for it belongs to the poor. In the same way, Zechariah, officiating in the glory of the Temple, is not glorified but punished (1:20-23).

2. The contradictories are enveloped in discretion, as always with Luke, who tends to smooth out the negative poles. However, at close examination, we find them on a deeper level.

On the axis non-theophany, opposed to theophany (A*A), the emperor unwittingly promotes the theophany of Christ in the humility of the manger. The same contrast appears between the submission of Jesus to the Law and the theophany which the coming of Christ the Lord brings to Jerusalem, to the Temple and to the people. Jesus himself is recognized as the source of the glory which he will radiate over the people (2:32).

The opposition between the poor and the non-poor (BB*) is striking in the Magnificat, where God reverses the hierarchies of this world. God manifests himself (theophany) by exalting the poor and bringing down the non-poor. This begins with Mary (1:28-55, especially verse 48) and extends in various ways to the shepherds, and to Simeon and Anna at the presentation.

3. According to the double vertical axis of correlations, the narrative processes are, at first sight, more subtle. This is due to the paradoxical coincidence of the contraries, theophany and poverty, which is the most profound revelation of Luke 1-2. These correlations become clear in the progression of time.

The correlation poverty/non-theophany (BA*) is the test of the poor, in conflict with their enemies (1:41-53, 71-74), the poor who are still waiting for the "consolation of Israel" (2:25), which is the coming of the Messiah. The poor seemed to be abandoned, crushed by the domination of the rich and powerful on their thrones (1:51-53). This is the tragic situation of the subjects of the Benedictus. Likewise, the shepherds watched in the night, without shelter in the fields (2:8), and Simeon waited at the threshold of his death (2:26) for a divine manifestation. This tension of hope and the "not yet" is correlative to the eschatological theophany that fulfills it.

The correlation theophany/non-poverty (AB*) shows the other pole of the history of salvation. This is no longer the long wait of the poor before the manifestation of God in a land occupied by a foreign power (2:1-2; see 1:5); it is transformed into eschatology. The glorifying theophany eliminates the suffering and oppressive aspects of poverty. The prophetic affirmation of the Magnificat looks with assurance at a future not yet realized as though it were already present. It anticipates the eschatology that is in the process of being fulfilled. That is also what is prefigured by the glory which envelops the shepherds (2:9). It is a pledge of salvation (2:11) and of peace which God brings to the people he loves (2:14). The eschatological perspective of light and glory, celebrated by Simeon, moves in the same direction.

But we must go further. Under this form the square is inadequate, from the point of view of a properly semiotic analysis. The principal defect is that it links the glorious pole, God, with his manifestation, which is revealed across the range of the square rather than in a single term.

Glory-Humility

The elimination of the manifestation, a result of the supermodalization 'being-appearing,' leads to the following square:

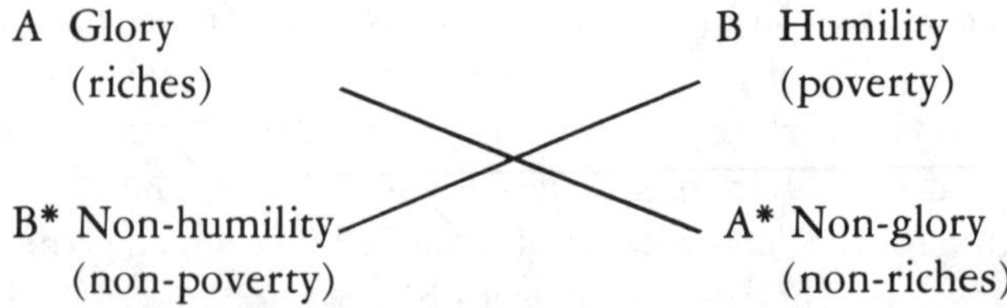

The word glory (*doxa*) occurs strategically in 2:9, 14 and 32 to manifest the glory of God. "Glory" is, as we know, one of the most expressive words used to designate God in the OT.

This square coincides in a certain way with the first, Law-grace, because law expresses submission, humility, the obedience of the child Jesus to his parents (2:51), while grace signifies the love and the gift of God, and the grace of God radiating in glory (2:9 and 32). The continuity between grace and glory is obvious in biblical theology as in classical theology.

At the same time we can pick up the modalization "being-appearing."[91] Glory (the manifestation of God) is on the side of appearing; poverty, on the side of being (although hidden, secret). Luke 1-2 describes the manifestation of the divine glory in human humility in such a way that the glory is tempered, without human display or triumph. In this sense, humility-glory extends further than Law-grace, which remains on the level of obligation and gift. This new square gives the key to an ontological level, not yet explicitly formulated in Luke 1-2, but which determines the significance and the connection of the acts and signs of the narrative. Let us see how the axes of the square are verified.

1. The axis of contraries:

AB: Glory (2:9, 32) and humility (1:48 and 52), riches and poverty (1:53), are evident contraries. The whole paradox of the square, however, is that this contradiction is made void in Christ: the glory of God manifests itself in human humility. Here we have a paradox which takes our logic by surprise and breaks open the ordinary modes of semiotics, because the Gospel expresses an unheard-of newness: a reconciliation of those things that seemed to be contraries. This, indeed, is the challenge of the Gospel.

The contrariety between wealth and poverty is indicated with a particular insistence in the Magnificat. The contrariety between non-glory and non-poverty (A*B*) implies the same paradox, that between the proud who are confounded (deprived of their false glory) and the poor who are filled, rescued from the negative element of their poverty. The revolution of the Magnificat correlatively makes void the privations of poverty and the false glory of the rich and proud. In this way, God is linked not to the rich, but to the poor of this world.

This proclaimed revolution, however, is the revolution of God. It is not yet manifest in the appearances of this world, where the kings (Herod in 1:5; Augustus in 2:1) have not yet come down from their thrones, where the Messiah does not yet have any glory or even a place on earth and is reduced to the condition of the poor (cf. the manger, 2:7; the offering of the poor, 2:24). This paradox is the heart of Christianity. God becomes poor in our humanity. Man is glorified by

God himself. A conjunction takes place between God and man's humility, between man and the glory of God. The Fathers of the Church called this "an admirable exchange," and the canticle of Christmas puts together "the glory of God" with "peace among men with whom he is pleased" (2:14). The "highest" (in heaven) is identified with the lowest on earth.

This paradoxical connection between glory and poverty, the very essence of the salvation brought by Christ, manifests itself at every stage, confounding the wisdom of this world and the perspicacity of the exegete.

2. The axis of contradictories:

AA*: Divine glory and non-glory manifest their maximum paradox at Christmas, where the radiating glory of God clothes the shepherds (2:9) but not the child in the manger. In the same way, Jesus' sojourn in the Temple, in the house of his Father, is not described either as a radiating theophany or as a sublime mystical experience, or as a triumph over the doctors, but as a humble dialogue between a child and his teachers and then with his mother, who chides him. (The Apocrypha reverse the paradox and show the child Jesus imbued with the totality of the human sciences and confounding the doctors by the glory of his omniscience.)

BB*: Poverty and non-poverty. This contradiction bursts forth between the rich and the poor, in the revolution of the Magnificat. The salvation in Jesus Christ will identify the poor with God and confound the rich of this world.

As to the correlatives:

AB*: Divine glory and human non-poverty. It is God who confounds the rich of this world, calling them, however, to share the condition of the poor and thereby the grace and glory of God.

BA*: Poverty and divine non-glory. We see this correlative in the Son of God who lives apparently without glory at Nazareth as in the manger of Christmas and in the modest mode of his manifestation in the Temple.

The radiance of the Messiah, who is light and glory (2:32; see 1:78) for his people and his Temple (and who glorifies them both), abolishes the oppositions and the violence to which the poor are subject

(1:51-53), but does it under the veil of the poverty with which the Son of God became identified. This is the point of Luke's entire Gospel, beginning with the first beatitude, "Blessed are you poor, for yours is the kingdom of God" (6:20; Mt 5:3).

Seen in this way, poverty is the fulfillment of the inner value of those without possessions, without power, without knowledge, according to the gift, the power, and the light of God.

The theophanic crescendo of Luke 1-2 moves from an angelic mediation in the glory of the Temple (1:11) to the major theophany of Christ himself, which begins at Nazareth in Galilee (fundamental theophany) and gradually to the manifestation in the Temple of Jerusalem. The one who is revealed is by no means distinct from mortals and the community of the poor (2:24), except by his assurance of being the son of the Father (2:49) and by the grace-filled aura of "wisdom" which begins to radiate from him (2:40 and 52) in the humility of Nazareth. The Messiah-Lord shares the condition of the people of the poor, the first addressees of salvation, since it is given to them and to those who resemble them (10:21-22).

These narrative processes are apparently subtle. They are easily perceived and lived by those who see in this infancy a prefigurement of the passion. Luke proposes this symbol in the three scenes of chapter 2: the birth scene (where the manger and the linens prefigure the tomb of 23:53 by the use of analogous vocabulary), the presentation (where Simeon, in 2:32, predicts the glory, and in 2:34-35, the contradictions, divisions, and the sword of sorrow), and the finding in the Temple (where the sorrow touches Mary—a sign which anticipates the "three days" of his death—while Jesus contemplates the absolute future of his passing to the glory of the Father, 2:49, before subjecting himself to obedience and to the descent to Nazareth 2:51).

CONCLUSION

From the Law to Grace by the Spirit

Semiotic Evaluation of Luke 1-2

Can we now summarize in simple terms our evaluation of this long semiotic study and of the squares which radically sought to explore it?

The ongoing movement of Luke 1-2 consists in surpassing or

transcending the ordinary and earthly program by a divine supernatural program. This occurs in each sequence. What is true of each sequence, furthermore, is true for the three major movements. This is the principal contribution which semiotics brings to our study of the dynamic of Luke 1-2.

The first sequence begins under the Law, with Zechariah, and is gradually moved by the Spirit towards the new form of God's presence, the *generation* of the Son of God (chapter 1).

The second sequence begins under the earthly law (of Rome) and yet ends in the radiance of God's proclamation to the shepherds of the divine paradox of glory in humility (2:1-20).

In the last sequence the Law is surpassed by being fulfilled. The child is brought into the Temple only to be seen as the Lord of the Temple; later on he is found in the Temple, where he declares God to be his Father. But this glory ends in humility. In the abasement of Nazareth he grows up. Upon him and in him resides the grace of God which the rest of the Gospel will seek to communicate (2:21-52).

Two modalities give this dynamic all its significance. First of all, the transcendent being of the Son of God is signified from the beginning of the narrative (1:32-35) and appears in progressive manifestations (annunciation, visitation, birth, theophany at the Temple). In the final scene he himself expresses his very being and his mission as Son of God. The movement proceeds from being to "appearing," which will have its full manifestation in the rest of the Gospel.

Secondly, these theophanies of the infancy (manifestations of God in Jesus Christ) occur without the trappings of human glory. They take place in the poverty with which the Son of God identifies himself. Thus, from the very beginning, the unfathomable newness of the Gospel revelation is affirmed.

Part II
Matthew 1-2

Christian memory has spontaneously synthesized Matthew and Luke in the popular tradition. Nativity scenes tend to include both shepherds and wise men. Matthew, however, does not mention the shepherds and the manger, nor does Luke mention the wise men and their gifts. We often overlook the degree to which Luke 1-2 and Matthew 1-2 differ. An exegesis of Matthew is necessary, therefore, before we look at the question of the historicity of the Gospel narratives concerning the infancy of Christ.

I
TEXTUAL CRITICISM[1]

Text-critically, the problem which has caused the most ink to flow is the variant which concerns the question of Mary's virginity (1:16). At the end of the genealogy, three readings are attested to, with varying degrees of importance:

1. Practically all the manuscripts, versions, and citations read: "Joseph, the husband of *Mary, of whom was born Jesus*, called the Christ."

2. However, a small group of manuscripts (Θ and the Ferrar group) give a quite different reading: "Joseph, *to whom* his betrothed, *the virgin Mary, generated* [or gave birth to] *Jesus* who is called Christ." This reading stresses that Jesus belonged to Joseph, in the sense specified by the following pericope of Matthew (1:18-25). According to the contemporary mentality, a woman gave birth "for her husband" (cf. Lk 1:13). This reading, therefore, specifies that Mary bore a child who belonged to the head of the family, as confirmed by God himself (1:20-21). This awkward reading, however, involves some incoherences, which the copyists avoided by a third reading.

3. "*Joseph*, to whom Mary the virgin was espoused, *generated Jesus* who is named the Christ" (the Sinaitic Syriac version).

Some have tried, in line with rationalist presuppositions, to capitalize on this last reading as a witness to the primitive text. This reading, "Joseph generated Jesus," relies on a historical likelihood, since the genealogy preserved in Nazareth or in the family of Jesus (a numerous clan, which supplied Jerusalem with its first two bishops), must have described him as son of Joseph, since his virginal birth was kept a secret between Joseph and Mary. It may have been circulated merely as a rumor; it was not recorded in the archives.

In answer it should be said that, apart from the fact that this reading is an evident corruption of the text (more precisely, a corruption of the second reading), it nevertheless avoids calling Joseph "the husband of

Mary." It refers to her merely as "espoused" (in the same paradoxical manner as Lk 2:7; see above, pp. 11-12), and it continues to call her "virgin."

The reading "Joseph generated Jesus" is obviously an attempt at homogeneity (which the rules of criticism urge us to set aside). After thirty-nine occurrences of the verb "generated," for each generation, the scribe could have been drawn into repeating it for the fortieth time.

We shall avoid, therefore, any attempt to trace the probable derivations of the awkward readings, since this has been very aptly done by Lagrange[2] and by R. E. Brown, who agree in concluding that the Sinaitic Syriac version understood Joseph's fatherhood of Jesus "not in a biological way that would contradict Matthew's emphasis in 1:18-25 but in terms of legal paternity" (1977, 64).

These two first-rate authors, so different in their approaches, hold to the first reading, which is attested to by nearly all of the manuscripts, and explain the other two as merely two stages of corruption.

II
LITERARY CRITICISM

A. COMPOSITION

The literary criticism of this text was expounded in its most penetrating form by A. Paul (1968). It divides the pericopes into two groups corresponding to the two chapters:

1. The genesis of Jesus in Matthew 1.
   a. The genealogy of Jesus (1:1-17).
   b. The means of this genesis (Joseph's first dream 1:18-25).
2. The manifestation of Jesus in Matthew 2.
   a. The visit of the wise men (the first episode involving Herod, 2:1-12).
   b. The flight into Egypt (Joseph's second dream, 2:13-15).
   c. The massacre of the infants (the second episode of Herod, 2:16-18).
   d. The return from Egypt to Nazareth (Joseph's third and fourth dreams, 2:19-23).

Matthew 1 appears as a diptych. Each of the two pericopes begin with the title, "The genesis of Jesus Christ" (1:18). The use of this word is striking, placed at the beginning of a genealogy. Thus the Vulgate translated it as "The book of the generation." Generation, however, would have been expressed by the word *gennēsis*. Yet it is clearly *genēsis* which Matthew repeats at the beginning of both pericopes:

> The book of the genesis of Jesus Christ (1:1).
> The genesis of Jesus Christ took place in this way (1:18).[1]

The use of this word signifies that the Gospel is a new beginning, a book of genesis, like the first book of the Bible known under this name, according to the LXX where the word *genesis* concludes the narration of creation:

> This is the book of the genesis of the heavens and the earth (Gn 2:4).
> This is the book of the genesis of Adam (Gn 5:1).

Jesus the Messiah realizes the new creation promised by the prophets for the eschatological times. God, the master of history, inaugurates the time of the savior and of salvation.

Matthew 2 is composed of shorter sequences alternating between Herod (2:1-12 and 16-18) and Joseph (2:13-15 and 19-23). (The narration suggests an analogy between Joseph, the adoptive father of Jesus, and Joseph the patriarch. Both are sons of Jacob [1:16], both have dreams, and both are exiled in Egypt by threats of death.[2]) These are analogous in style and structure. They would fit well if grouped together instead of in alternating segments. This could be an indication, if not of two sources, at least of two traditions centered respectively on the two characters.

The structure of Matthew is signaled by the repetition of key words from one episode to the other. Nearly always, the last word of each episode is repeated at the beginning of the following.

The first pericope begins with the words, "The book of the genesis of *Jesus Christ*." It ends with, "*Jesus*, who is called the *Christ*" (1:16). The word "Christ" recurs in verse 17 (recapitulating): "From the deportation of Babylon to the *Christ*, fourteen generations."

The second pericope (1:18-25) begins: "The genesis of *Jesus Christ* took place in this way." Matthew specifies there why the title *Christ* is given to Jesus. The section ends with these words, "He called his name *Jesus*."

The third pericope (2:1-12) begins with the same word, "Now when *Jesus* was born in Bethlehem of Judea." It ends thus, "They *departed* (*anechōrēsan*) to their own country."

The fourth pericope (2:13-15) begins with the same key word, "When they had *departed* (*anachōrēsantōn*)." It ends with, "He... remained there until the death of *Herod*."

The fifth pericope, the slaughter of the infants (2:16-18), begins with the words, "Then *Herod*, when he saw that he had been tricked. . . ." It ends with a biblical citation.

The sixth and last pericope (2:19-23) seems to be an exception to this verbal linkage. That could be one indication, among others, that the preceding pericope (the fifth), about the slaughter of the infants, was a later addition. The first words of the sixth and last pericope, "when *Herod* died...," pick up literally the last verse of the fourth pericope concerning the flight into Egypt.

B. THE FUNCTION OF BIBLICAL CITATIONS

Another significant element of the literary composition is the fact that each of the narrative accounts, leaving aside the genealogy for a moment, ends with an explicit biblical citation:

> All this took place to fulfill what the Lord had spoken by the prophet [Is 7:14]: "Behold, a virgin shall conceive" (1:23).
> For so it is written by the prophet (2:5, an abbreviated form; Mi 5:2, 3; completed by 2 Sm 5:13).
> This was to fulfill what the Lord had spoken by the prophet, "Out of Egypt have I called my son" (2:15; Hos 11:1).
> Then was fulfilled what was spoken by the prophet Jeremiah (2:17; cf. Jer 31:15).
> That what was spoken by the prophets might be fulfilled, "He shall be called a Nazarene" (2:23; Jgs. 13:5, perhaps combined with Is 4:3).

These formulas were studied by G. M. Soares Prabhu, (*The Formula Quotations in the Infancy Narrative of Matthew*).

The pericope of the wise men is only a partial exception to the rule because it implies a use of Isaiah 60:6 and Psalm 72:10-11, 15.

Isaiah 60:6	*Matthew 2:11*
All those from Sheba	They
shall come,	
They shall bring	offered him
gold and frankincense.	gold and frankincense
	and myrrh.

Psalm 72:10-15	
The kings of Tarshish...	They [the wise men]
bring gifts	offered gold, frankincense
kings will fall down	they fell down
before him	they worshiped him
may gold of Sheba	They offered him gold.
be given to him.	

The reworking of these texts in the very body of the narrative could have dissuaded Matthew from repeating them in the form of a citation at the end of the pericope. He reserves the explicit citation with the solemn expression "to fulfill" for the five biblical texts using the word *son* (C. Perrot, 1983).

C. LITERARY GENRE

The literary make-up of Matthew is less varied than that of Luke: a genealogy followed by a series of narratives, each of which ends with a biblical citation which clarifies the baffling event. For this reason, some have seen here an apologetic intent. But apologetics is not exactly the right word for this genre, for Matthew seems to be seeking justification of a contemplative rather than a demonstrative nature. In contrast to Luke, Matthew himself defines his own literary genre, "genesis" (1:1 and 18), an account of the origins of this new creation which is the birth of Christ. This is his trademark; it characterizes the first chapter. One might argue whether it extends to the second, but that is not important. The narratives of Moses' infancy from Jewish literature might have served as a model or influence for the second chapter, but only remotely, as one allusion among others which manifests Christ as recapitulating the history of salvation.[3]

Matthew 1-2 is, like Luke 1-2, an infancy narrative composed in the light of the Scriptures—and in Matthew (in contrast to Luke) this is done explicitly. In Matthew, as in Luke, however, the *midrash* is turned around: the Christ-event sheds light on the Scriptures. As with Luke, the titles of Messiah and Son of God (Mt 2:15) prevail over the actions, since the child remains passive and silent, even more radically in Matthew than in Luke. Matthew, to whom the glorifying fables of the Apocrypha remain totally foreign, merely indicates that this childhood, threatened by death, prefigures the passion. Like Luke (but from a different perspective), he elaborates his own literary genre in continuity with tradition, yet assimilating the baffling newness of Christ.

In short, the structure of Matthew 1-2 can be summarized as six sequences of different kinds:

1. The genealogical genesis of the Messiah: the human recapitulation of the history of salvation down to the "break" in 1:16 (1:1-17).

2. The genesis (= origin) of the *how* of the Messiah's birth: the divine dimension (the Holy Spirit, of whom the virgin is the sign) and the human dimension: adoption by Joseph (1:18-25).

3. Journey of the wise men to Jerusalem under the guidance of the star; intrusions into their program by the program of Herod; homage to the Messiah-King; return (2:1-12).

4. The flight of Joseph (led by a dream) into Egypt: exile of the Messiah (2:13-15).

5. Herod's program and the massacre in Bethlehem (2:16-18).

6. The death of Herod; dream; return from Egypt; another dream; exile in Nazareth (2:19-23).

These elements of literary analysis shed light on the order of the discourse, its form, and framework. They do not, however, lead us to the internal organization and functioning of the meaning, the specific domain of semiotic analysis. This will be the object of our second stage.

III
SEMIOTIC ANALYSIS

1. GRAMMAR

The future tense is used in Matthew to program the future, in biblical prophecies ("He shall be called a Nazarene," 1:23; 2:6 and 23) and in the commands given in dreams ("You shall call his name Jesus, for he will save his people from their sins," 1:21; and 2:13, where *mellei* signifies an imminent future event). It is God who leads history from the distant past by prophetic predictions, or through current experience, by the oracles of angels, which are also commands.

The verb *egeneto*, which emphatically introduced the events in Luke 1-2 (fourteen times), is absent in Matthew 1-2. In contrast with Luke 1-2, the subject of active verbs is not Mary, but Joseph; the wise men and King Herod, the adversary of Christ, are also subjects.

2. SPACE (topology)

Matthew's narrative begins without any mention of place. The only located event which appears in chapter 1 is of the Babylon captivity, and this appears three times (once in 1:11 and twice in 1:17). It provides the only background for the origin of Jesus: a dynastic failure. In contrast, chapter 2 begins with topology. The first verse situates the birth of Jesus in Bethlehem of Judea. The last verse, after the flight into Egypt (2:13-19), situates Jesus in Nazareth, which Matthew highlights with a confusing biblical citation, "He shall be called a Nazarene" (2:23).

The topography concerning Jesus (Bethlehem, Egypt, then Nazareth) runs counter to that of Herod, the murderous king who is enthroned in Jerusalem, and that of the wise men coming from the East.

The topology of Matthew 1-2 is marked by journeys:
—The wise men, coming from the East to Jerusalem (2:1) and return-

ing "by another way" (2:12). They provide a framework for the key incident: the visit to Bethlehem (1:9-12).
—Joseph (2:14-15): The flight into Egypt, which anticipates prophetically the return in 2:15: "Out of Egypt have I called my son," and 2:19-22. The return is in two stages.

3. DURATION

The first chapter has no chronology other than the succession of the generations. The dating of the ancestor-kings is to be supplemented by the Bible. The annunciation to Joseph, however, begins atemporally (1:18) in the shadow of the only event mentioned (1:17), the Babylonian captivity, where the points of reference for the royal chronology disappear. Chapter 2 takes its reckoning from another royal dynasty, "in the days of Herod the king" (2:1), then, after his death (2:15 and 19), from Archelaus his son, who succeeds him (2:22). Kings were the measure of time and history. Jesus, the "king of the Jews" (2:2), inaugurates a new time and a new history.

The time of the kings interacts with the "time the star appeared" (2:7 and 16). This time is referred to God, the master of time and of the prophets who announce the future at the end of each sequence.

4. SOCIOLOGY

The principal social reference point is the royalty which gives the genealogy its structure according to three series: non-kings, kings, non-kings leading finally to the Messiah. Matthew 2:1-2 specifies the opposition between "Herod the king" and "he who has been born king of the Jews."

The clash of king against king dominates the entire narrative program. Prestigious foreigners—wise men from the East—are received with honor by the king himself (2:1).

"The chief priests and scribes of the *people*" (2:4) are consulted by the king. The people appear here in the orbit of the priests and scribes; they are also mentioned independently of them in 1:21 and 2:6.

Modal Categories

5. HAVING appears not only in the rich gifts of the wise men, but also in

a genealogical meaning: Joseph does not wish to appropriate the posterity which comes from the Spirit and not from him (1:19), but he is invited by a heavenly mandate to "take" the child and his mother. The verb *paralambanō*, to take, recurs six times in Matthew (1:20, 24; 2:13, 14, 20, 21).

6. WILLING: that of the cunning and homicidal Herod is opposed to the transcendent will of God who guides the events from above by means of prophecy and of warning dreams.

The search of the wise men likewise indicates a "willing" to render homage to the King-Messiah (2:2).

Joseph wants (*eboulēthē*, 1:20) to repudiate Mary, but obeys the contrary will of God the addresser. Afterwards, only his concern about coming back to "the land of Israel" (2:21) witnesses to a personal deliberation. The divine mandate moves in the line of his hesitation and directs it into action (2:22-23).

7. OBLIGATION appears at the same time in Joseph, the just one, whose decisions are regulated by justice (1:19) or by the orders of God himself.

8. KNOWING, which acts as an organizing principle in Matthew 1-2, belongs to God, who leads the "genesis" to its completion (despite apparently chance events, like foreign or inexplicable women in the genealogy), i.e., exile and persecution of the Messiah. All this was predicted long ago in Scripture, the hidden significance of which is revealed by events. The oracles of God remedy the incidental deviations of events.

The "knowledge" of God thwarts King Herod in gathering information and keeps him from identifying the Messiah and locating him.

The star of the wise men also pertained to God, according to the ideas of that time. Legrand wonders if the star of Matthew was meant to signify, not just an astral event, but the manifestation of the very glory of God (as in Lk 2:8-9).[1]

The "knowing" which guides Joseph comes to him from God, who corrects his "just" decision to leave Mary. But since God's "knowing" differs from that of men, Joseph is reluctant to return to Judea according to the information which he has "heard" (2:22). This obliges God to give him a fourth dream, which takes account of his objection. God's "knowing" is royal and theocratic, but it comes to terms with earthly realities.

9. POWER: that of Herod appears formidable and totalitarian, skillful and manipulative, in all the meanings of that word. However, the power of God (exercised by means of dreams sent to men of good will) reduces Herod to helplessness, culminating in his death (which is referred to several times: 2:15, 19, 20, 22). God does not act directly on the events; he informs and guides them through men. God has need of human beings.

10. BEING: that of the Messiah, expressed first by his quality as son of David (1:1-17, 20; see 2:6), is signified by three types of titles which characterize, respectively, his humanity (a child, *paidion,* with the passive humility which this neuter word, often repeated in Matthew 2, suggests), his messianic attributes (1:23; 2:4, 6, 23), and finally, his transcendent attributes (God with us, 1:23; Son of God, 2:15). This gradation is significant.

The transformation and qualification of the other subjects arise clearly from the narrative, notably in the case of Joseph, who is chosen to assume the relationship of father. The wise men are chosen to manifest the universal royalty of the new "king of the Jews."

11. DOING and "causing to do" (or mandating) have as subjects the addressers, terrestrial and celestial:

—Herod, who uses priests, wise men, and soldiers in the arena of the powers of this world.

—God, all powerful, the inspirer of dreams, who directs the action, as foreseen by the prophecies which conclude each pericope. In contrast to Herod's action, which is exterior, deceiving (2:8), and violent (2:16-18), that of God is interior, informative, inspiring. It excludes the current sense of the word "manipulate," popularized by semiotics in similar cases.

SEMIOTIC DIVISION

The semiotic division of this text coincides with the division which we have already established by literary analysis. Semiotic analysis, however, brings out more clearly the unity of each of the two chapters and their progression.

The genealogy (1:1-17) and the story of the conception and birth of Christ are two expressions of one and the same central fact. Jesus is born of the human race; not of Joseph (who is accounted his father), but of God: of the Holy Spirit through the virgin Mary.

The topological features of the sequences must yield priority to the actantial changes. Indeed, the second sequence (Matthew 2) begins in Bethlehem and ends in Nazareth. Like the first sequence, it ends with a name being given to Jesus (1:25; 2:23).

In the interval between Bethlehem and Nazareth the apparently stereotypical biblical citations appear which conclude most of the sequences. There is no concluding citation in 2:12, at the end of the sequence concerning the wise men, who are caught between their search for the "king of the Jews" (2:2) and King Herod (2:3). The formula which introduces the final citation shows some variants. The final sequence (2:12-23) shows us the antiprogram of Herod and the double exile of the Messiah: first in the south, then in the north, far from the throne of David. The whole is punctuated by dreams in which God asserts himself as addresser.

Let us try to grasp the narrative program that is at work in these subtly articulated sequences and subsequences, whose symmetries are not mechanical but rather give expression to the unity of meaning.

NARRATIVE PROGRAM

We are now in a position to analyze, in bold outline, the program of Matthew 1-2. It is inaccurate to speak of a narrative program in connection with the first pericope, since the "genesis" of Jesus is expressed in the form not of a narrative but of a genealogy. Nonetheless, this firmly structured chain of generations implies a program. In concentrated fashion it recapitulates the history of the chosen people by means of a line of descent from Abraham to Christ. It brings to a head, in striking terms, a problem which was a source of perplexity until the evangelist found the solution to it, given in the second pericope (1:18-25). Let the reader be the judge.

The structural program of the first pericope is clearly set forth in the opening verse:

> The book of the genesis of Jesus Christ, the son of David, the son of Abraham.

FIRST PROBLEM: JESUS, SON OF DAVID?

What is stated here is, first of all, that Jesus is Christ (Matthew does not yet add the further determination, Son of God), then, that he is son of David, a title essential to the messianic hope.

This datum must have had its source within the Jewish culture, in which genealogies had an important place as a qualification of identity or functional legitimation for priests and so, all the more, for a King-Messiah. The point which serves to provide the focus of Matthew's genealogy is that Jesus is said to be the son of King David (1:6), the founder of the royal dynasty whose monarchs are recalled in 1:7-11. It was David to whom the promise of the Messiah was given (2 Sm 5-17; cf. Is 7:14; Mi 5:1). The awaited Messiah was to be "son of David," and it was by this popular title that he was acknowledged, invoked, and acclaimed by the crowds.

The first verse of Matthew (1:1) is an abridged genealogy which moves back from Christ to David and to Abraham, the father of the chosen people and the first link in the chain. The ascending path was developed in Luke 3:23-38. Matthew, however, uses it only in stating the program; he then follows the descending path from Abraham to Christ in three series of fourteen generations to which he calls explicit attention in (1:17).[2]

The abridged ascending genealogy in Matthew 1:1 is thus the statement of a narrative program, the details of which are filled in by the descending genealogy in 1:2-17. The first verse sums up the entire genealogy, starting with the person who is its end and essence, Jesus Christ, and then moving backward to reach the two most important links: Abraham, the starting point, and King David, the ancestor whose line leads to Jesus the Messiah.

Genealogy

The descending genealogy advances through three patterned series of equal length:

1. Fourteen *non-kings* from Abraham to David, the founder of the dynasty (1:2-5).

2. Fourteen *kings* from David to the Babylonian exile, which brought the dynasty to an end (1:6-11).

3. Fourteen *non-kings* from the Babylonian exile to Christ (1:12-16).

David is the pivot of the entire genealogy:

—He alone is given a title, king (1:6).

—His name occurs the most frequently: five times in the genealogy, whereas other names each occur twice, except for Abraham, who is mentioned three times (1:1, 2, and 17) and Joseph, who is mentioned only once, at the end which also serves as the point of a new beginning.

—The importance of David is also brought out by the organization of the genealogy into three series of fourteen links, since fourteen is the number represented by David (DWD) in Hebrew (where the letters of the alphabet provided the only way of signifying numbers): *Daleth* + *Waw* + *Daleth* = 4 + 6 + 4 = 14.[3]

But this program, so carefully organized in order to show that Jesus is son of David and therefore Messiah, ends in a break that requires an explanatory narrative (1:18-25).

The genealogy moved along from begetter to begotten in strict sequence, each begotten becoming the begetter of the next link in the chain. However, it begins with a begetter who is not begotten, Abraham, and ends with two "begottens" who do not beget: Joseph and Christ himself.[4]

Now, after thirty-nine stereotyped repetitions of the verb *begot*, at the point at which we would automatically expect "Joseph begot Jesus," the chain breaks. The name Joseph is not followed by "begot"; it is followed by ten extremely important Greek words that determine all that follows: *ton andra Marias, ex hēs egennēthē Iēsous ho legomenos Christos* ("The husband of Mary, of whom Jesus was born who is called Christ," 1:16). Let us reflect on them.

The fact that Christ, who closes the genealogy, is begotten and does not beget is not significant in itself. The reason might be simply that he was the last link in the chain, that he did not in fact beget anyone, or that there is no interest in his descendants. But the Gospel, written long after his earthly life had ended, is clearly intimating that he did not beget anyone.

The King-Messiah left this world without begetting anyone—this statement is highly significant. It means that this king without a kingdom, born when the dynasty had vanished, is a successor-king but not of a dynastic or political kind.

He has no son because he has broken with traditional ideas and shifted kingship to a new level. What he initiates, after the dynasty has expired, is a transcendent kingship that is not subject to change and "will have no end," as the prophecy of Nathan had already hinted (2 Sm 7:11, 16) and as Luke 1:33 makes emphatically clear. Matthew may not be as explicit but his thought moves in the same line: his first prophecy concerning Jesus speaks of him not as a Davidic king but as Emmanuel, God-with-us (1:23). His Gospel ends with an identical statement by Jesus to his disciples, "I am with you always, to the close of the age" (28:20). It is therefore natural for this King-Messiah not to be described as a begetter. He is not a link in a dynastic chain, but the new and divine fulfillment of the kingdom, as the rest of the Gospel manifests. He is with us forever, because he is "*I am.*" In varying degrees the evangelists were making the revelation of the divine name to Moses (*I am*) a reality in Christ (Ex 3:14; Mk 6:50; 14:62; Jn 6:35; 8:24, 58; 13:19).

The fact that Joseph, the last descendant of David, is not a begetter is more disconcerting. It would appear to break the messianic chain.

Are we to say that, unlike the preceding links in the chain, the Messiah is not begotten? Matthew asserts that Jesus was indeed begotten; he says so three times[5] (the verb *gennaō*, in the passive voice). But then, who begot him? Matthew 2:1 says nothing on the point, while 1:16 only says, "Joseph, the husband of Mary, of whom Jesus was born, who is called Christ." The passive form of the verb makes it unnecessary for him to specify the begetting subject. In any event, the begetter of this begotten is not Joseph, and this break in continuity causes the program to make a fresh start in 1:18-25.

Nor is Mary the begetter. She does not take Joseph's place in the role of father. She is not a begetter in his stead. Throughout Matthew 1-2 she is always passive, never active. She is not the subject of the verb beget which Matthew reserves for males.

Jesus is linked to Mary (his sole biological source) by the particle *ek* which describes the role of women (who are dependent on their husbands) throughout the genealogy:

> Judah the father of Perez and Zerah by (*ek*) Tamar (1:3).
> Salmon the father of Boaz by (*ek*) Rahab, and Boaz the father of Obed by (*ek*) Ruth (1:5).
> David was the father of Solomon by (*ek*) the wife of Uriah (1:6).

This series of four women paves the way for the fifth, Mary, to whom Jesus is linked by the same particle but, this time, without a father being named: "Mary from (*ek*) whom was begotten Jesus who is called Christ."

Can we say, then, that the begetter is the Holy Spirit, who is twice mentioned in the following pericope (1:18 and 20) as being the origin of the Messiah? He is not presented here as the begetter or father of Christ. Jesus is linked to him by the same particle *ek* that describes the connection of children with their mothers. The word spirit, which is feminine in Hebrew and neuter in Greek, excludes any notion of a theogamy. For Matthew, the Holy Spirit does not serve in any way as Father of Christ or "Spouse of Mary".[6] This poetic formula (which would be pardonable in mystic poetry) belies the nature of the two infancy Gospels, which are on guard against any form of theogamy.[7]

There is another confusion to be avoided: we must not translate "Jesus whom *they* call Christ" (as is too often done) but rather "Jesus *who* is called Christ" (1:16). In this verse in which Jesus is begotten and called, Matthew does not tell us either who begets or who calls. The passive form enables him to keep the subject of the active verb hidden. This subject is gradually revealed as being a transcendent one. According to the Gospel, this unusual begetting which has no biological agent refers by implication to God, the sole Father of Christ. The Father does not have to beget Christ anew but only to assume him (transcendentally) in his new human condition. It is this that seems to preclude any human begetter. The divine sonship is revealed at the beginning of the infancy Gospel (2:15, "Out of Egypt have I called my son"). John 1:13 speaks of Christ as "born of God" (see below, p. 406). Matthew confines himself to explaining that Christ has no father but God. Luke renders this view more explicit in his genealogy, if we are to understand him as saying that "Jesus . . . the son (as was supposed) of Joseph" is in reality the son "of God" (Lk 3:23-38). If Jesus is called Christ, as Matthew 1:16 tells us, then it is God, again, who does the calling. Where Paul says that he is called "an apostle," we really ought to translate the words with Osty's felicitous formula, "an apostle by calling," i.e., by the call of God (Rom 1:1).[8]

The genealogy ends (1:16) as it began (1:1), with the name of Jesus who is called Christ. But this title, whose full importance is highlighted by the device of inclusion, has been preceded by a break. The program of 1:1, which set out to establish the Davidic filiation, is broken off by the fact that Joseph does not beget. This break is the most significant and central element of the narrative.

How, then, is Jesus the son of David? This is the disconcerting problem which the second pericope develops. In order to show that this pericope has the same object and the same narrative program as the first, Matthew begins with the same formula as in 1:1:

> Now the birth [genesis] of Jesus Christ took place in this way (1:18).

Joseph's Program

Joseph's program is set out as a twofold problem: the fact of Joseph's Davidic heritage is linked with the situation which deprives him of any posterity. Mary is presented as the primary subject:

> When his mother Mary, being given in marriage to Joseph (*mnēsteutheisēs*), before they came together she was found having in her womb (*en gastri*) from (*ek*) the Holy Spirit (1:18) [I translate literally the veiled formulas of the Greek text.]

This verse states the problem set for Joseph: not the simple fact that Mary was pregnant, but the transcendent cause of this outstanding event, namely, the Holy Spirit.

The next verse describes as follows the reaction of the heir of David:

> Her husband Joseph, being a just man and unwilling to put her to

shame, resolved to send her away quietly (1:19).

This account by Matthew contains no hint of any suspicion on Joseph's part. His decision is explained by the fact that "he was a just man." If he had considered his wife to be guilty, justice would have demanded that he apply the Law to her; the Law, however, acknowledged no private proceedings but only an official writ of divorce (Dt 24:1).[9] What Joseph knew, according to Matthew 1:18, is that this child belonged to God alone. Justice required that he not seek to make his own either the holy offspring that was not his or this wife who belonged to God. He therefore withdrew quietly to avoid putting Mary in an awkward situation. He left the resolution to God, the author of the event. The account gives no further details, as they are of no importance for the meaning.

The Commission Given to Joseph

In response to Joseph's action the angel of the Lord appears to him in a dream. Any translation must respect the operative Greek particles (*gar. . . de*), the function of which A. Pelletier has carefully analyzed.[10]

> Joseph, son of David, do not be afraid to take Mary your wife into your home, for *although* that which is begotten in her comes from the Holy Spirit, it is you who will call the son she bears by the name of Jesus, for he will save his people from their sins (1:20-21).

At the very outset Joseph is described as son of David, a name essential to the narrative program. The Davidic program, which was broken by the genealogical gap in Matthew 1:16, is re-established by the commission given to Joseph: although Joseph is not the begetter (1:16) and although the begetting has a divine origin (from the Holy Spirit, 1:18 and 20), it is nonetheless he, Joseph, who will play the part of father. He will "take to himself" Mary his wife (Mt 1:20 and 24). He also takes the child as his adopted son (2:13, 14, 20, 21). He will act as father by bestowing the name on the child.

Matthew thus solves a problem which was unknown to the Jewish tradition (which did not look for a virginal conception). He finds justification for his solution in the prophecy of Isaiah 7:14:

> All this took place to fulfill what the Lord had spoken by the

The Motives of Joseph the Just Man

The situation seems to be defined by the law given in Deuteronomy 22:23-25: "If there is a betrothed virgin, and a man meets her in the city and lies with her, then you shall bring them both out to the gate of that city, and you shall stone them to death with stones, the young woman because she did not cry for help though she was in the city, and the man because he violated his neighbor's wife." But verse 25 excuses the young woman if the incident took place in the open country where she could not cry out nor call for help (2:25-27).

With this as background, three explanations have been given:

1. Joseph is called "just" because he obeys the Law (like Zechariah and Elizabeth in Lk 1:16). This view became prevalent under the influence of *The Protoevangelion of James* 14, 1, where Joseph says: "If I conceal her sin, I shall be found opposing the Law of the Lord. If I expose her to the children of Israel, I fear lest that which is in her may have sprung from the angels and I should be found delivering up innocent blood to the judgment of death" (Strycker, 126-129). The outcome is that Joseph solves the problem by privately dismissing Mary. This interpretation was dominant in exegesis from the time of Justin, Ambrose, Augustine, Chrysostom, onward. It developed in the direction of "Joseph's suspicion."

2. According to R. Pesch ("Ausführungsformel," in *Biblische Zeitschrift* 11 [1967] 91), and C. Spicq (*Revue Biblique* 71 [1964], 206-209), the "justice" of Joseph consists in his determination to be merciful and in his moderation, in accordance with Ps 112:4, which urges that kindness be joined to justice (cf. Ps. 37:21 and Wis 12:19; Philo). But if this were so, Joseph should be described as "clement" rather than "just"; it is also difficult, in this explanation, to understand why the angel should say, in trying to overcome Joseph's scruples, "Do not be afraid to take Mary your wife . . ." (1:20).

3. With Xavier Léon-Dufour and A. Pelletier (who add strictly grammatical arguments), we must conclude that Joseph is just because he refuses to take as his own an offspring that comes from God and does not belong to him. He acts justly out of respect for the plan of God, the secrecy of which he preserves. This solution seems to be required by Mt 1:18 which from the outset states clearly the terms of the problem Joseph faces: Mary is pregnant due to the transcendent, mysterious action of the Holy Spirit. This is the explanation given by Eusebius, Ephrem, and Theophylactus. Joseph acts out of fear of God, in order not to usurp a posterity that belongs to God alone and

not to take a wife whom God has drawn into his sacred orbit (in an utterly nonsexual way, as Matthew's redaction makes clear).

The logic of this convincing solution is buttressed by the fact that at this period a husband was forbidden to have sexual relations with a wife who had committed adultery. This same attitude applied to virgins consecrated to God, and to Mary in her virginal conception of Jesus.

R. Gundry (*Matthew*, pp. 21-22), refers to various rabbinical texts which show how complex the substratum is. In Jewish legislation a marriage agreement was much more than an engagement; it even considered the man a widower if the woman died. On the other hand, the interpreters of the law tended to eliminate stoning (Strack-Billerbeck, vol. 1, pp. 50-53) unless a culpable male could be identified. According to Gundry, Joseph feared "to do wrong by taking Mary to wife when she was pregnant by divine causation." Mt. 1:18 is not "a piece of advance information to the reader" but states the terms of the problem Joseph faced, the information on which his "justice" based its reasoning. Consequently, the formula by which the angel sets aside his scruples, "Do not be afraid. . ." (1:20; cf. vv. 16-21), speaks of Mary both as betrothed (1:18) and as wife (1:20-21). Joseph is called her husband in 1:16, two formulas (wife = woman with possessive adjective; husband) which are avoided by Lk 2:5 with its greater reserve.

> prophet: "Behold, a virgin shall conceive and bear a son, and his name shall be called Emmanuel," which means, God with us (1:22-23).

This prophecy had not hitherto been understood in this way. The Hebrew text speaks of a young girl, not necessarily a virgin, and it is she who will give the child its name. In translating "young girl" as virgin (*parthenos*) Matthew was perhaps following the LXX translation. In the LXX, on the other hand, it is King Ahaz who is asked to bestow the name: "You shall call him." Matthew however adopts a vague passive translation, "He will be called," and makes the prophecy relevant to the unexpected event of the virginal conception.

Verse 24 tells of Joseph's implementation of the divine command by which Jesus is qualified as Messiah, son of David:

> When Joseph woke from sleep, he did as the angel of the Lord commanded him; he took his wife, but knew her not until she had borne a son; and he called his name Jesus.

The word *egertheis* (from *egeirō*, "to awaken"), which is also used for the Resurrection (Mt 27:52, 63, 64), occurs four times, at the end of each of the dreams. The word emphasizes Joseph's active clarity of mind. He takes the wife whom he had been planning to divorce. This cohabitation of Joseph and Mary is important since it gives the Messiah not only a name but a normal home and family.

But Matthew adds, Joseph "knew her not until she had borne a son." The word "until" contains no implication as to what happened after that point. In semitic usage "until" designates the *duration* and *limits of* the writer's or speaker's *interest*. Thus when 2 Samuel 6:23 says that Michal had no child "until the day of her death," it is likewise clear that she did not have any later on.[11]

The important thing from the standpoint of the narrative program is the conclusion of the pericope: Joseph bestows the name "Jesus" (1:25). This is the qualifying test that entitles Joseph to exercise a protective authority throughout chapter 2.

The aim of the entire narrative program is thus to show how Jesus is a son of David even though Joseph did not beget him. In so doing, a difficulty is overcome that was of no small moment to the people of that time: the use of the messianic title "son of David" is justified.

Formalization

If we want to formalize all this in semiotic terms, we may say: the Messiah (the virtual subject) must be conjoined to King David (1:1 and 6) through "Joseph son of David" (1:16 and 20). The genealogical disjunction (Joseph does not beget Jesus) is bridged by God the addresser who bestows an adoptive fatherhood on Joseph.[12] This paradoxical disjunction is the obverse of a transcendent conjunction of the Messiah with God, a conjunction that will shortly be specified as divine sonship (2:15). The pericope before us says only that the origin of Jesus is from God alone: from the Holy Spirit (1:18, 20). The messianic kingship (brought into existence under the sign of dynastic collapse and captivity, 1:17) is thus shifted onto a transcendent plane.

Joseph, joined to Mary by the bonds of marriage, decides on dismissal (disjunction) because the child belongs to God and not to him. At the command of God himself, Joseph maintains the conjunction of marriage, but without "knowing" his wife: the conjunction will be conjugal but not sexual (1:24). He thus gives the Messiah a legitimate family and a place in the dynastic line that has been established by God himself.[13]

A SECOND PROBLEM: NAZARETH

Chapter 2 takes up and resolves a second problem: Matthew faced the difficult task of reconciling the idea of Jesus as the Messiah with his origins in the proverbially despised Nazareth of Galilee (cf. Jn 1:46 and 7:41, 52). The disrespect lasted beyond Jesus' lifetime: Paul's adversaries scornfully described him as a leader of "the sect of the Nazarenes."[14]

Matthew solves this difficulty in the same way as he did the first: he states at the outset the quality which the rest of the chapter will seem to negate. The words of the first chapter began, "The genesis of Jesus Christ, the son of David." Now the first verse of chapter 2 proclaims, "Jesus having been begotten (*gennēthentos*) in Bethlehem of Judah."

Contrary to what was seemingly a well-known fact (2:23; 21:11; 26:71; 27:55; cf. 3:13; 4:13), Jesus was a native not of Nazareth in

Galilee but of Bethlehem in Judah, the birthplace of David himself (2:1). This confirms the Davidic connection upon which doubt was cast by the virginal conception (topographic conjunction with King David).

Unlike Luke, Matthew says not a word of the Holy Family's previous history in Nazareth.

How then did the impression arise that Jesus was a native of Nazareth? How did it happen that he first came before the public in that "Galilee of the Gentiles" which was so unsuitable for a Messiah (4:15)? The narrative provides a twofold explanation, one historical, the other prophetic (2:13-23).

First, the narrative elaborates the recognition of the Messiah. In Matthew it is the wise men who provide this: foreigners act as a universalist counterpart to the Hebrew shepherds of Luke 2. Persecution (which foreshadows the passion) then explains the humiliating exile of the Messiah-King to a village.

The Program of the Wise Men (Mt 2:1-2)

At the level of the basic narrative (which, as we shall see, is integrated into a more comprehensive program), the program of the wise men is presented first. These men play the role of a collective subject that seeks the "king of the Jews." They describe him in this manner in accordance with the star which they have seen. With their knowledge of astrology they have been able to decipher its meaning.

> Now when Jesus was born in Bethlehem of Judea in the days of Herod the king, behold, wise men from the East came to Jerusalem, saying, "Where is he who has been born king of the Jews? For we have seen his star in the East, and have come to worship him (*proskunēsai*, 2:1-2).

The striking thing about this opening is the repetition of the word king applied both to Herod and to the child. The latter is still unknown to the wise men. They therefore describe him by his functional title. This establishes a polemical program: the conflict between the political monarch set over the Jewish people and the new Jewish king who has just been born.

Herod's Program (Mt 2:3-18)

It will come as no surprise, then, that King Herod should be disturbed by the undisclosed birth of a rival:

> When Herod the king heard this, he was troubled, and all Jerusalem with him (2:3).

What seems odd is that Herod's negative disturbance is shared by the whole of Jerusalem: the entire city is conjoined with him (by means of the conjunctive preposition "with"). This fact fits well within the perspective of Matthew, for whom "Jerusalem kills the prophets" (23:37; cf. Lk 13:34).[15] Unlike Luke, Matthew does not record any of the appearances of the child Jesus in the city in which he was put to death. The capital city is thus seen from the beginning in a negative light. Matthew presents the infancy in the perspective of all that is to follow, including the passion.

Herod, the primary opponent, develops an antiprogram (which runs counter to the programs of the wise men and of God himself): to get rid of the king of the Jews (2:2), his rival. He mobilizes the religious authorities (2:4-6).

> And assembling all the chief priests and scribes of the people, he inquired of them where the Christ was to be born (2:4).

As possessors of biblical knowledge (at the moment when the astrological knowledge of the wise men seemed deficient), they answer by citing Micah 5:2:

> In Bethlehem of Judea; for so it is written by the prophet: "And you, O Bethlehem, in the land of Judah, are by no means least among the rulers of Judah; for from you shall come a ruler who will govern my people Israel" (2:5, 6).

This citation from the Bible, quoted by the priests, forms the oracular conclusion of the pericope.

In the next sequence[16] Herod pursues his antiprogram by drawing upon the astrological knowledge of the wise men. He calls them together secretly (*lathra*, 2:7). This malevolent secretiveness of Herod is contrasted with the compassionate secrecy of Joseph the just man

(1:19). Herod makes careful inquiries (*ēkribōsen*) regarding "the time when the star appeared" (2:7); this chronological guide programs his murderous activity later on (2:16). He "sends" them (manipulation) to the place identified by the learning of the priests and urges them to make careful inquiries as a service to him:

> Go and search diligently (*akribōs*) for the child, and when you have found him [we are still involved in the quest theme] bring me word, that I too may come and worship him (2:8).

Herod makes hypocritical use of the wise men's own expression, claiming that he too would adore the Messiah.[17] He adds a pretended fervor to his power of setting events in motion. The story has not yet brought to light his murderous plans. His hypocrisy is exposed after the event.

The wise men, who had been started on their journey by an astral sign which, according to the cultural code of the time, came from God, continue their journey at the suggestion of Herod: they are now caught up in his antiprogram. But the information he has given them proves unnecessary because the divine star once again guides their steps. This means a return into the orbit of God and a first disjunction from Herod:

> When they had heard the king they went their way; and lo, the star which they had seen in the East went before them, till it came to rest over the place where the child was (2:9).

In its short path the star no longer moves in normal fashion from east to west (2:2) but moves paradoxically from north to south (2:9), thus emphasizing its specific function as a sign from God. The narrative had not previously said anything about the star disappearing. We learn of this after an odd delay (2:9). After the arrival of the wise men in Bethlehem the narrative tells us that the star reappeared as soon as they had set out:

> When they saw the star, they rejoiced exceedingly with great joy (2:10).

We learn of their frustration only through their joy at rediscovering the guiding star. The synchronization of their conjunction with the Messiah and their conjunction with the star tends to identify Messiah and star, in keeping with the prophecy of Balaam (Nm 24:17; cf. Rv 22:16) which seems to lie behind the passage.[18]

Having reached the goal, they carry out the program stated in 2:2:

> And going into the house they saw the child with Mary his mother, and they fell down [*pesontes*, aorist participle of *piptō*] and worshiped him (2:11).

Mary, who plays such an unobtrusive role, reappears here as a sign of the child-king who has just been born. Joseph does not appear in connection with the birth.

The adoration of the wise men is continued in their offering:

> Then, opening their treasures, they offered him gifts, gold and frankincense and myrrh (2:11).

In identifying the king by the heavenly sign and paying him homage, they have fulfilled their program. The antiprogram in which Herod had involved them should have led them to return to Jerusalem in response to Herod's request so that they might supply him with information. The story has not yet told us of his plans, which are still hidden in the "secretiveness" mentioned in Matthew 2:7. But God, the addresser of the messianic program, guides the wise men by the same means with which he guided Joseph.[19]

> And being warned in a dream not to return to Herod, they departed to their own country by another way (2:12).

The divine information completes their disjunction from Herod. After their fervent conjunction with the royal child, they disappear into the exclusive orbit of God (disjunction from Herod and disjunction from Jerusalem).

The Flight to Nazareth

The next pericope (2:13-15) brings us back to Joseph, whose name appears here for the first time in chapter 2. He is again given warning in a dream. The message from the Lord-addresser orders him to flee to

Egypt "for Herod is about to search for the child, to destroy him" (2:13). We learn only now, through a revelation, of Herod's plan. Thus the opposition between the fervent quest of the wise men and the malevolent quest of Herod is finally made clear.

The exile is connected with the Exodus, through reference to Hosea 11:1:

> And he rose and took the child and his mother by night, and departed to Egypt, and remained there until the death of Herod. This was to fulfill what the Lord had spoken by the prophet, "Out of Egypt have I called my son" (2:14, 15).

The prophecy states at one and the same time the test, the termination, and the deeper meaning of the qualification of Christ as Son of God. This title, which had not previously appeared explicitly, becomes a central feature in the public life of Christ (3:17; 4:3, 6; 8:29). The Messiah has already been described as God-with-us (1:23) and as having no other father than God (1:16, 18-20). The prophecy of Hosea formally states his connection with God in a title that describes him and will cause his execution (22:45; 26:64).

The Massacre of the Innocents (Mt 2:16-18)

The fourth pericope (2:16-18) returns to Herod, and in so doing disturbs the natural connection there would otherwise have been between the third pericope and the fifth and final pericope:

> Then Herod, when he saw that he had been tricked by the wise men, was in a furious rage, and he sent and killed all the male children in Bethlehem and in all that region who were two years old or under, according to the time which he had ascertained from the wise men (2:16).

Herod, the addresser of the antiprogram, has been discomfited. This expert in diplomacy and police work has been "tricked" by the wise men. He realizes this and is enraged by it. But he does not realize that it has been accomplished under the influence of God, the addresser of the infallibly victorious messianic program. He begins again his own program: the death of the rival king. He leaves nothing to chance. He does his killing not only in Bethlehem but "in all that region," and he extends the killing to all the children up to the age of two years "according to the time of the star," which he had *carefully* learned from the wise men (2:16 repeats the words used in 2:7, *chronos* and *ēkribōsen*).

Herod seems to set the time-frame so as to allow a good margin of security. His knowledge and his craftiness are never lacking. Nonetheless he is once again confounded by God. A dream causes the departure of Jesus. The Messiah does not die, it is Herod who dies (2:15, 19, 20, 22; note the emphasis on this point). Jesus is being saved for a different death.

The concluding prophecy, from Jeremiah 31:15, underscores the disphoric meaning of this cruel and scandalous event; not the happy rescue of the Messiah, but the grief for these dead children:

> Then was fulfilled what was spoken by the prophet Jeremiah: "A voice was heard in Ramah, wailing and loud lamentation, Rachel weeping for her children; she refused to be consoled, because they were no more" (2:17, 18).[20]

Herod's antiprogram is a failure. It brings about the exile of the Messiah who is removed from the place which qualified him. Luke explained this (humiliating) descent to Nazareth as a voluntary act of humility on Jesus' part. Matthew explains the descent as a way of parrying Herod's murderous plans. The infant Messiah escapes death only through flight and obscurity.

The Return

> But when Herod died, behold, an angel of the Lord appeared in a dream to Joseph in Egypt, saying, "Rise, take the child and his mother, and go to the land of Israel, for those who sought the child's life are dead" (cf. Ex 4:19). And he rose and took the child and his mother, and went to the land of Israel. But when he heard that Archelaus reigned over Judea in place of his father Herod, he was afraid to go there, and being warned in a dream he withdrew to the district of Galilee (2:19-22).

The new program which begins here—the return of Jesus to Israel—comes from God. It is carried out in two stages, by two

He Shall be Called a Nazarene (Mt 2:23)

"He went to live in a town called Nazareth, in order to fulfill what had been said by the prophets: 'He shall be called a Nazarene.' "

This verse has been an exegetical bugbear. C. C. Torrey, in *Documents* (1941, p. 53), called it an "insurmountable problem."

Nazōraios evidently refers to the fact that Jesus was known as a resident of Nazareth, a fact which won him the seemingly current appellation "Jesus the Nazarene" (*Nazōraios*: Mt 26:71; Lk 18:37; Jn 18:5, 7; 19:19; Acts 2:22; 3:6; 4:10; 6:14; etc.). The form *Nazōraios*, "Nazarene," occurs twice as frequently as *Nazarēnos*, "of or from Nazareth," which is found in Mark and in Luke 4:34 and 24:19.

Is this a biblical reference? The problem is to identify the alleged prophetic statement. Exegetes have come up with four possible explanations:

1. That Matthew did not intend to cite any particular text; the quoted words are a creation of his own (A. Paul, 1968, p. 168). The reference would not be to a text, but rather to the fact that Jesus was a Nazarene.

This hypothesis is open to two objections:

—The use of the future tense: "He shall be called. . ."

—The expression *to rhēthen* ("what had been said"), which Matthew always uses (thirteen times) in connection with a citation.

2. That Matthew was citing from memory and instinctive knowledge a text which he did not identify for himself. But this is not his customary way of acting and is not appropriate at this juncture, which is a kind of climax.

3. That we are dealing here with a lost canonical text. This is a rather desperate attempt at a solution.

4. That it is a free citation of one text or several combined texts.

What text did Matthew mean to cite?

I shall not delay over a few short-lived attempts:

—*Nōṣēr*, "watcher," according to Jer 31:6. (E. Zolli, *ZNW* 49 [1968], 135).

—*Nāṣûr*, "secret, hidden, obscure, marginal," according to Is 11:1. (W. Caspari, *ZNW* 21 [1922], 122-127).

Two solutions still have their supporters:

—*Nēṣer*, "branch" (of David), according to Is 11:1. This solution may have been influenced by Moulton's concordance (which gives this reference for Mt 2:23). It had already been the view of Maldonatus. Schanz, Weiss, Holtzmann, Schmid, and R. Gundry likewise offer this solution. Lagrange regarded it as simply "a rather whimsical play on words" (*Matthieu*, 1927, p. 39).

—*Nāzir*, "consecrated," the reference being to Jgs 13:5: "The boy [Samson] will be *nāzir* from his mother's womb, and it is he who will begin to *save* Israel. . . ."

Thus Loisy (*Synoptiques*, vol. 1, p. 376). McNeil, Schaeder, Schweitzer, Sanders, (*JBL*, 84 [1965], pp. 169-172), S. Lyonnet (*Bib* 25 [1944], pp. 196-206). It was also the solution adopted by St. Jerome after mature reflection. To the detailed arguments of G. M. Soares Prabhu (1976, pp. 205-207, 215-216), who adopts this solution, may now be added this one of C. Perrot (in an unpublished article): The five explicit and solemn citations in Mt 1-2 refer to texts which all contain the word *son*. Matthew is thus using a collection of texts which have this key word as their focal point. This fact argues that he is here referring to Jgs 13:5: "Behold, you will conceive and bear a son. . . . The boy will be *nāzir*." The fact that Matthew attributes the citation to the "prophets" is not an objection, because the scrolls of Joshua, Judges, Samuel, and Kings (which followed upon the Pentateuch) were called the earlier prophets, a designation which explains the expression "the law and the prophets."

Matthew is thus taking the name Nazarene which had been given to Jesus because of his town, and giving it meaning and relevance in function of the holiness signified by the word *nāzir* in Jgs 13:5.

This procedure may seem strained. But *nāzir* is quite simply equivalent to "consecrated" or "holy" in Jgs 13:5. Thus the Greek *Codex Vaticanus* translated the word *nāzir* by *hagion* in 13:7 and 16:17 (but not in 13:5 where it retains the Hebrew as *nazir*, while *Codex Alexandrinus* interprets *its* version, *naziraios*, by *hēgiasmenos*, "sanctified"). This shows how easy it was to pass from the ritual term *nāzir* to "holy," which expresses the meaning and profound intention of that term. In 13:5, then, the word *nāzir* is explained by the verb *sanctified*: "He will be *nāzir*, i.e., sanctified (*hēgiasmenos*) for God.

This identification of Matthew's citation seems to be called for not only by the analogy between the announcement to Joseph and the announcement to the parents of Samson, but also by the attraction exerted by the title given to Jesus in the Gospel: "You are the Holy One of God" (Mk 1:24; Lk 4:34; Jn 6:69).

It implies a further point of contact between Matthew 1-2 and Luke 1-2, since Luke gives such surprising emphasis to the expression *hagion klēthēsetai* (he shall be called holy), making it signify, typologically, the transcendent holiness of Christ the Lord. The intention is the same in Mt 2:23 with regard to Christ as God-with-us.

Confirmation: This (objectively valid) connection between nazirate and holiness has been interpreted by reductionist criticism as implying a leveling-down; this is in keeping with the tendency of such criticism to explain the higher by the lower and to reduce anything new to factors present in the environment. Sahlin and others suppose that a procedure exactly the opposite of that in Matthew was followed in Luke 1 and that the clear and solemn formula in Lk 1:35, "He will be called holy," would have been in Hebrew Proto-Luke: "He will be called *nāzir*" (Sahlin, 1945, 132-136). The firm, clear context in Luke forbids such a reduction. It is John the Baptist who is promised to the nazirate in Lk 1:15, whereas Jesus is characterized by a divine holiness which the shekinah makes manifest. Matthew alone gives meaning and relevance to the text in Jgs 13:5 (Samson *nāzir* and holy).

Confirmation that Jgs 13:5 is indeed the passage being referred to in Mt 2:23 is to be seen in the detail that the consecrated child (Samson) "will begin to save Israel." Salvation, of which Samson was a "beginning" and a first prefiguration, is completed in Jesus, whose very name means savior, as Matthew had detailed in 1:21.

N.B.: It may be that in 2:23 Matthew is combining Jgs 13:5 with Is 4:3, which reads: "Then the remnant of Zion . . . will be called *holy*." This might be suggested by the fact that Matthew refers chiefly to Isaiah: almost half of the citations in his Gospel are from this prophet.

By means of this second reference Matthew would be applying to Christ what is said of the captive people, just as he does in 2:15 when he cites Hosea 11:1. The odd thing is that Is 4:2-3 combines the ideas holy (*gādôsh*; cf. *nāzir*) and branch (*ṣemaḥ*, cf. *nēṣer*): "On that day the branch of Yahweh will become ornament and glory . . . the remnant left in Zion, surviving in Jerusalem, will be called holy. . . ."

Although this joint allusion to Is 4:2-3 is difficult to prove, Matthew may have used it in order to reinforce what he wants to say: that Jesus, Emmanuel and Son of God, was predestined to be holy (a remarkable convergence with Lk 1:35 and 2:23), but also to be the messianic branch promised to the root of Jesse.

Matthew gives relevance and thus transfigures the obscure title *Nazarene* by making it mean both *nāzir* and holy. He does it at an appropriate place, at the end of his infancy account. It was similarly centrally placed in Lk 1:35.

The lowly (Nazarene) origins of Christ take on, for the evangelists, a meaning analogous to that of his passion. Matthew chooses this trait as the curtain-fall of his infancy gospel. It is pregnant with meaning.

Here as elsewhere we get a glimpse of the paths traveled by the Christian consciousness in its first efforts to express the divinity of Christ.

commands from God that are given to Joseph in two dreams.

The first bids him to return "to the land of Israel" (with no further specification of place) because the child will now be safe (2:20). The murderer is dead (2:19 and 20), and his cleverness has been confounded (2:16). This twofold contrast is part of the meaning of the story. The third dream is characterized by a refrain: Joseph arises and takes the child and his mother. This new action highlights the mission of fatherhood which he received as heir to David (1:20-21).

A fourth and final dream removes Joseph's perplexity by separating the Messiah from his royal and Davidic home, Judea, and exiling him to the north:

> And being warned in a dream he withdrew to the district of Galilee. And he went and dwelt in a city called Nazareth, that what was spoken by the prophets might be fulfilled, "He shall be called a Nazarene" (2:22, 23).

The fact that the Messiah has come forth from this despised place is thus explained in three ways:

—It is the result of death threats which prefigure the passion.

—It is at the bidding of God.

—Finally, it fulfills a prophecy which likewise comes from God as addresser.

The conclusion of chapter 2 closely resembles the conclusion of chapter 1. Both involve the naming of Christ: "And he called his name Jesus" (1:25); "He shall be called a Nazarene" (2:23). The words and modalities are different, but the parallel is beyond doubt. The importance given to the *name* (the word "name" occurs three times and the verb "called" six times in Matthew 1-2), and the very meaning of the name as explained at the end, link these chapters with Luke 1:35 and 2:23: "He shall be called holy." We have our finger here on a procedure that is an essential motive of the two infancy Gospels: the explanation of the names which describe, express, and manifest the very being of the Messiah-Savior.

Formalization

Let us sum up in semiotic terms the program of this second chapter.

The narrative establishes, first of all, the conjunction of Jesus with Bethlehem, the native city of King David.

The wise men, whose quest takes them to the royal city of Jerusalem, carry out their program (enunciated in 2:2, accomplished in 2:11): conjunction with the Messiah.

The quest of the wise men sets in motion the murderous program of Herod. He too "seeks" Jesus (cf. 2:13 and 20), not, however, in order to adore him but in order to kill him. As king of Jerusalem (2:3-9) he plays the leading role. He is addresser of the program which mobilizes the priests, the wise men, and then the soldiers (2:4, 5, 8, 16).

Herod's program as addresser (which is effectively countered by the program of God, the true addresser) necessitates a disjunction of the Messiah from his Davidic place: first, an exile to the south, in Egypt, a foreign land; then a semi-exile, away from Judea, the homeland of David (2:22), but in the peripheral province of Galilee.

But this marginal conjunction has been programed by God himself. He sent the dreams which rescued the Messiah from the murderous enmity of Herod's men; he causes the typological fulfillment of an ancient prophecy (Jgs 13:5, perhaps combined with Is 4:3): "He shall be called Nazir," that is, holy. The entry into Galilee prefigures the exclusively Galilean appearances of the risen Jesus: Matthew 28 closes his Gospel where he began it in 2:23.

From a semiotic viewpoint then, the infancy Gospel of Matthew takes the form of two series of stories which are meant to explain and defend the two problematical aspects of the infancy and childhood of Christ:

1. The virginal conception, which seemed to remove him from the Davidic descent foretold by the prophets (Matthew 1).

2. The lowly childhood spent in an environment that seemed wholly wrong for the Messiah: Nazareth in Galilee (Matthew 2).

The answer given to each difficulty follows a divine logic: each fulfills the prophecies and the commands of God. Each reveals the true being of Christ-Messiah as God-with-us (1:23) and Son of God (2:15)—truly such, though hidden. Each contains prefigurations of the future: the manifestations of the paradoxical Messiah in Galilee and the passion in the royal city of Jerusalem.

THE MODEL

Through narrative analysis we have identified two levels in the story, the earthly, anecdotal events and the plan of God that guides these events: a mysterious program that explains the seeming anomalies attached to the infancy of Christ.

These two clearly articulated levels must be kept in mind as we inquire how Matthew 1-2 matches Greimas' model of actants: subject-object, addresser-addressee, and helpers-opponents.

Subject

At the anecdotal level, we find a number of subjects appearing in succession.

In the genealogy (which is not a narrative) there is David, founder of the royal dynasty and addressee of the messianic prophecy (2 Sm 7:14) fulfilled in Christ his heir. Since the genealogy is interrupted, there is apparent disjunction: Jesus seems no longer to be son of David (object of this subject).

In Matthew 1:18-25, therefore, Joseph, "son of David" (1:16 and 20), comes into the foreground and is commissioned to connect the Messiah with David by adopting him. Joseph is doubly qualified for this mission, by reason of his own justice (1:19) and by divine mandate (1:20). In the first chapter Joseph is portrayed as a passive heir of David. In the second, David's name does not occur; he is only alluded to implicitly in the topographical mention of Bethlehem, his birthplace (2:1 and 6). As subject, Joseph assumes responsibility for a project of dismissal (1:19-20) and then for the program of which God is the addresser. Mary does not take the position of subject. She appears only as a maternal sign in 2:11, during the adoration of the wise men.

The wise men appear as subjects of their own program in the first two pericopes of chapter 2. Herod too appears as the subject of his own program.

Joseph moves into the foreground again as delegated agent of God (2:13), being assigned an active but stereotyped role: he "takes" the Messiah and his mother. He saves the Savior from death, although this important role is not explicitly presented as a glorifying test. His role remains a modest and unobtrusive one.

Above and beyond these particular subjects the true subject of the Gospel is Jesus, already hidden yet defined as hero by the titles which bring out the meaning of each scene:
—Christ-Messiah (1:16, 17, 18; 2:4),
—Savior (1:21, the very meaning of the name Jesus),
—Emmanuel (God-with-us, 1:23),
—King of the Jews (2:2, in accordance with the astral learning of the wise men, in opposition to King Herod, 2:1),
—Ruler and Shepherd (2:6, citing Mi 5:1, which is made more explicit by 2 Sm 5:2, "From you shall come a ruler who will be shepherd of my people Israel"),
—Son of God (2:15 by reference to Hos 11:1),
—Nazarene, understood in the sense of holy one (separated, consecrated, 2:23).

Through the use of these titles, Jesus receives the homage due to a king (2:2, 8, 11). Does Matthew intend to say that this homage is due to him from the very kings of the earth? Tradition has represented the wise men as kings. The story itself suggests this without stating it explicitly.[21] Herod himself acknowledges his duty of adoring the child (2:8). Jesus is presented as royal and divine from the outset.

As in Luke, there is a striking contrast between the transcendent titles bestowed on the hero, Jesus Christ, and his modest manifestation. He appears first in the form of an object (the reference to him in 1:18 and 20 uses not a masculine noun but a neuter phrase). Did the Holy Spirit remove him from the Davidic line in order to locate him in a sacral realm apart from the world? No. The child is linked with the genealogy by means of the mission given to "Joseph, son of David" (1:20). The very paradox of the Incarnation emerges here. Will the child be triumphantly qualified as king by the adoration of the wise men (2:1 and 11)? Or will he instead be killed by Herod (2:13-17)? At this stage, neither of these things occurs, but he is threatened, hidden, and exiled until the time for his manifestation as an adult (Matthew 3). Beyond the narrative programs operating on the surface, Jesus is the virtual subject of the Gospel. From this point of view the other actants appear as helpers or opponents. They gravitate around him.

There is thus a kind of tension between the transcendent titles of the Messiah and another series of traits which conceal him: the powerlessness of his infancy, his exile, and the Nazarene-Galilean problem. This is the paradox which Matthew 1-2 accepts and resolves.

Object

What is the object? At a superficial level it is doubtless Jesus who is the object of the infancy narrative. Joseph (and through him David) is given Jesus as his child, his possession which he "takes." The wise men find (2:11) him at the end of a lengthy search (2:2, 3,9-12). But at a deeper level the object is the welfare of the "people" whose shepherd the Messiah is to be (2:6). More particularly, the object is salvation. Salvation is the virtual object to the extent that the Messiah is the virtual subject. We already sense that salvation is identified with the person of the Savior.

Addresser

Who is the addresser? In Matthew 1-2 there are two addressers at two levels, and their narrative programs are opposed and in conflict.

Herod seeks to kill the Messiah. But his consummate craftiness is confounded. (This last word expresses the sense of incongruity evoked in the NT by the name Herod and the individuals who bore it; cf. the realistic end of the narrative of the other Herod in Acts 12:22-23.) He assumes the role as addresser and, on the level of appearances, is successful in this role. He exercises it with various modalities: with secretiveness and cleverness (2:8), with anger and violence (2:16).

The only genuine addresser is God, with his infallible omniscience. Herod's great power, so craftily exercised, is thwarted by nocturnal communications from God and confounded by failure (2:16-17) and death (2:15, 19-20, 22). God's role is so important that he appears as the principal subject of what is done, the one who transcendentally effects the conception of Emmanuel by the power of the Holy Spirit, and the program which protects the child.

But unlike Herod, who acts by manipulating human beings, God acts through interior, mysterious mediations.

—*The angel of the Lord* (1:20, 24; 2:13 and 19). But the Lord of the angel is more important than the angel of the Lord, who is sometimes little more than a literary device used out of respect for God's transcendence.

—*Dreams*, described (1:20; 2:13, 19) or implicit (where the formula is simply "having been warned in a dream": the wise men in 2:12, Joseph in 2:22) are also a mediation that safeguards transcendence.

—The explicit *prophecies* which conclude each scene show that the divine program and knowledge are anterior to the events (1:23; 2:6, 15, 18, 23).

—To these must be added two implicit and typological prophecies: the star, which seems to bring up-to-date the messianic prophecy of Balaam; and the gifts of the wise men, which are those of the kings of Tarshish according to Psalm 72:10-15.

In these ways the addresser guides events despite vicissitudes and contradictions.

Addressee

Who is the addressee? Here again, we may make an identification at several levels.

At the first level it is Jesus. He is a fatherless child who must be connected with David in order that he may be rightly designated; he is a child hunted and threatened with death, who must be rescued. He is addressee of the immediate protective activities which God assigns to Joseph. But at a deeper level the addressee is the people whose savior (1:21), king (2:2), ruler and shepherd (2:6) the Messiah is meant to be.

The people are mentioned explicitly in 1:21, where the etymology of the name Jesus is explained by the angel, "For he will save the people from their sins" (an essential text); and in 2:6, "He will govern my people Israel" (citation of Mi 5:2, which is made relevant by conjunction with 2 Sm 5:2).

But this addressee is hidden by the fact that the narrative in Matthew (2:3) joins "all Jerusalem" (the people of the capital) to Herod, the addresser of the anti-program. The word people appears a second time in the negative orbit of a hostile Jerusalem ("the scribes of the people," 2:4).

This hiddenness is carried so far that the concrete addressees in Matthew 1-2 do not belong to the people of Israel (unlike those in

Luke 1:2); these addressees are the wise men from the East. These foreigners are the only ones to symbolize the addressee-types on the larger scale. While Jerusalem, with Herod, is "disturbed," the foreigners worship the Messiah.

The gifts offered by the wise men present a glorifying test of the child. At the hour of the Messiah's birth these foreigners symbolize the Gentile peoples. It is they who take possession of the promise. This universalist opening is reinforced by the implicit reference to prophecies (Is 49:23; cf. 60:6; Ps 72:10-15, and Mt 2:11).

The fact that the Gentile nations are addressees of salvation is not made clear until the end of the Gospel. During his public life Jesus says that he has been sent only "to the lost sheep of the house of Israel" (a text peculiar to Matthew, in 15:24; cf. 10:6). It is only at the very end of the Gospel (28:19-20) that salvation is extended to "all nations." By prophetic anticipation the episode of the wise men suggests universalism. Here again we find the prefigurative character of the infancy narratives. The pagan peoples, represented by the wise men (as Joseph represents the Israelite people) are still only virtual addressees, to the same extent that the Messiah is a virtual subject.

Helpers-Opponents

In an examination of the essential components of the narrative, the role of the helpers and opponents is secondary. Since I have explored this role in detail in *Mélanges Cazelles*, I shall only summarize the two levels on which the helpers and opponents are situated, and add a few further considerations.

The persons of Joseph, Mary, and the wise men appear as helpers in relation to the Messiah, the hidden virtual subject (God remaining principal subject of the action from above).

The opponents are those whom, in varying degrees, Herod uses to serve his program: his soldiers and, in a sense, also the "priests and scribes of the people" who make their appearance in his orbit, and the wise men over whom he gains ascendency until God frees them from his influence (2:12).

Places also function as helpers and opponents. On the earthly level there are:

—Bethlehem on the side of the helpers (2:1, 5, 6, 8, but with the tragic reversal in verse 16).
—Babylon on the side of the opponents (1:11, 12, 17—twice).
—Egypt, mentioned four times (2:13, 14, 15, 19), which might be regarded as an opponent since it effects a disjunction of the Messiah from his proper place, but in this text plays the helping role of refuge and sign of sonship by reference to Hos 11:1, cited in Mt 2:15.
—Nazareth in Galilee (2:22-23) with characteristics similar to those of Egypt, even playing a positive helping role in 2:23 as a place which qualifies the Messiah in accordance with the prophecy cited there.

On the heavenly plane there are only helpers:
—The star of the wise men (2:2, 7, 9, 10) seems to verify the prophecy of Balaam.
—The five dreams (place of the angels): the dream of the wise men and the four dreams of Joseph make known the commands of the Lord.
—The biblical prophecies which are the expression of the plans of God are also helpers since they direct events from afar.
—The Holy Spirit, author of the virginal conception, would seem to be located initially in the category of opponent since he interrupts the Davidic line and brings about the decision of "Joseph the just" to divorce his wife (1:19). But the dream given to Joseph and the prophecy in Isaiah 7:14 show that the obstacle created by the Spirit fulfills a prophetic oracle (1:22) in order that the Messiah may come not as an ordinary human descendant and by human generation, but from on high as "God-with-us." It is from God alone whose son he is (2:15; 3:17) that the Messiah derives his origin and his royal anointing as Messiah. The Holy Spirit, through whom his anointing as Messiah occurs, is the hypostasis of God the addresser.

Semiotics thus sheds light on the exegesis of Matthew 1-2 and on the coherence-through-contrasts of these two chapters. It brings out not only the progression of the narrative but also the underlying structure in which the narrative is inscribed. We have gone beyond the elementary models to be found in fairy-tales. The narrative refers to God (addresser) who programs salvation (object) through the Messiah (subject) for the people of Israel and the pagans (with the wise men as the first addressees). The model identified in Matthew 1-2

(God as addresser, the people as addressees, salvation as the object) comes from biblical revelation, but there is a new factor: Christ is inscribed in it as the basic subject who proceeds from God himself and is identified with God (1:23 and 2:15). It is to him that all the superficial subjects are related.

Conclusion

Summing up the results in abstract terms that are closer to life and faith, I would say the following. Semiotics helps us to grasp the problems and solutions of Matthew. Disturbed—as others were—by the virginal conception (which certain Jewish circles stigmatized as adulterous) and by the idea of the Messiah's coming from Nazareth, he does not hide this double paradox and does not invent a *theologoumenon* to disguise it. Instead he incorporates these facts. They had confounded the wisdom of the wise and dismayed those who awaited the Messiah, since people hoped for a Messiah who in the time of Roman occupation would gloriously restore the political kingship of David. Meditating on it in the light of faith, Matthew came to understand the meaning of the obscure infancy of this hunted Messiah: his kingship is transcendent but powerless, and not political. Matthew integrates this new and original understanding of the Messiah into the traditional structure derived from the OT, which thus takes on a new dimension. The Messiah, the Son of God, inaugurates the eschatological age unobtrusively and humbly.

Here (as in Luke) Christ, the virtual subject, takes over all the key positions in Greimas' model: he is *subject* and *object*, being *savior* and *salvation*, and he is identified with the *addresser* and the *addressees*, being *God* with God and *man* with humans.

What part does the information available to Matthew play in this narrative? I shall discuss this question in the chapter on historicity. At the level of semiotic analysis (which ignores the question of historicity) let us note only the coherence and concentration of meaning: Matthew makes us read the infancy of Jesus from the standpoint of God and in the light of revelation. It is a marvelous icon and a source of icons, and has inspired the liturgy and its feasts down to the present day.

SEMIOTIC SQUARE

The structure of Matthew 1-2 is perhaps clearer and more one-dimensional than that of Luke 1-2. The square takes shape in relation to two poles which are always linked: generation and kingship.

Generation

The verb *beget* occurs forty-three times, thirty-nine times in the third person singular of the aorist active. As we have seen, the names of the ancestors of Jesus are linked, with each begotten becoming the begetter of the next link in the chain. But after the thirty-ninth occurrence the chain breaks: Joseph does not beget Jesus.

The verb *beget* continues nonetheless to be the key-word. It occurs four more times (1:18, 20; 2:1, 4), but in the passive voice: Jesus is begotten. The use of the passive makes it possible to hide the active subject of the verb. The actant in this begetting remains shrouded in mystery, because (as we have seen) the begetting takes place in a quite different and transcendent way. The actant is an *addresser* who does not act after the manner of ordinary subjects and actants (or, to put it in theological terms, he is the first cause and utterly different from second causes).

The verb *beget* does not appear after 2:4, but the idea of generation or begetting is nonetheless implied in the relation of sonship (referring to Jesus, 1:20, 21, 23, 25; 2:15) and of fatherhood (referring to Herod, 2:22). Finally, death, which is inherent in a succession of generations, occurs four times, in connection with Herod (2:15, 19, 20, 22); the mentions of his death are closely connected with his plans to destroy the King-Messiah.

The two opposing genealogies, that of the Messiah (1:1-16) and that of Herod (2:22) are both dynastic and connected with the correlative idea of kingship.

Kingship

The word king (five times: 1:16; 2:1, 2, 3, 9) and the verb reign (2:22) do not occur as often as the verb *beget*.

The word *messiah*, however, is an exact synonym. In Hebrew (*meshiah*) and in Greek (*christos*) it signifies the king by means of the anointing that establishes him as a king: he is the Anointed One.

Jesus acquires the status of Messiah in an unexpected way, because he is not anointed king with oil, as Saul and David were. His anointing seems to be indicated in the originating action of the Holy Spirit (1:18 and 20). The isotopy, Spirit = Anointing, which is explicit in Luke, seems to be really implied in Matthew.[22]

The title Messiah therefore signifies king and, at a time when kings claimed divine status (including Caesar when he displayed the title Augustus), it also had a divine significance. The word Messiah appears:

—First in the form of an inclusion, at the beginning of the genealogy ("The genesis of Jesus Christ," 1:1), and then at each of the final two verses of the genealogy (1:16 and 17).

—It opens the second sequence ("The genesis of Jesus Christ," 1:18). This sequence ends with the citation of the messianic prophecy addressed to King Ahaz, and with the transcendent title bestowed on the King-Messiah when he is mysteriously described as "God-with-us" (1:23). The sememe of kingship plays a determining role. It underlies the entire narrative with its significant contrasts (see above, pp. 262-263). He is king, then, less because he is son of David, since he is connected with David only by adoption and topographic coincidence, than by divine investiture (anointing by the Holy Spirit) as Son of God.

The next sequence (Matthew 2) opens with an opposition between "King Herod" (2:1) and "the king of the Jews who has just been begotten" (2:2). The Messiah is presented as a hidden rival of Herod, and this determines Herod's program of chapter 2. The title king occurs twice to describe Herod, who defends his kingship (2:3 and 9). The threat represented by Herod is continued by his son Archelaus who "reigned in place of his father Herod" (2:22). It should be noted, however, that Herod ceases to be described as king once his evil intentions are made known in the course of the narrative. From the moment when Herod has identified Jesus, the word Messiah (Christ) also disappears as a designation for this hidden, hunted and exiled infant. Herod is not mentioned again except in reference to his death, nor the "messiah" except in reference to his exile and as a Nazarene in the sense of *nazir*, holy.

I have used the abstract words *generation* and *kingship* for these two sememes, though Matthew tends to use concrete terms: the verbs *beget* and *reign*, and the nouns *king* and *messiah*. Why this shift? The verb *beget* is used actively in the genealogy, and then passively in a significant shift that refers it to God who becomes the mysterious "father." The abstract noun "generation" provides a suitable means of covering the two voices (active and passive) of the verb beget. In fact, Matthew himself uses it four times (1:17). Furthermore, these reigns which end either in death or captivity (1:11, 12, 17) and which in Matthew 2 are the reigns of those opposed to the Messiah, are of such contrasting diversity that only an abstract noun can adequately replace all of them.

The ideas of kingship and generation are implied each in the other, since it is always a question of a dynastic kingship, whether in regard to the Messiah or in regard to Herod. These ideas are as it were the warp and woof of Matthew 1-2. As the narrative advances, kingship is embodied in ways marked by disconcerting contrasts: the foundation of the dynasty in the person of David (1:6), its downfall through captivity (1:11), and its re-establishment in Jesus, which is not a restoration, but a paradoxical new beginning that does not involve genealogical continuity and is not political. A different pagan dynasty hunts for him and compels him to flee when he has just been born; it "reigns in his place" (cf. 2:22). His royal anointing is transcendent but hidden; it is the work of the Spirit (2:16 and 18), and as such has a spiritual character.

The concept of kingship-generation is a philosophical and theological as well as a dramatic touchstone. It brings out the extraordinary newness of this Messiah who comes in a wholly unexpected manner. How could this marginal, obscure, hunted Jesus be the King-Messiah? Matthew shows that his messiahship is proved first by the transcendent action of the Holy Spirit. He describes his origin and divine kingship by pointing to the Davidic location of his birth, Bethlehem, and by adducing three kinds of oracles: the sign of the star, which was apprehended by the astrological learning of the wise men; the prophecies, which were understood by the priests (2:5-6) or identified by the evangelist (2:15, 18, 23); and the direct providential action of God which takes oracular form in the dreams of Joseph and the wise men (1:20; 2:12, 13, 19, 22).

Matthew answers the question of Christ's origin by saying that the Messiah is from God, who is the sole source of his generation and his kingship (1:16, 18, 20). The rest of the Gospel reveals the transcendent sense in which he is God-with-us (1:23; 28:20), namely as Son of God. His divine sonship is signified by means of the prophetic realization in Matthew 2:15, before it is proclaimed from on high in 3:17 at his baptism (then in 4:3, 6 and throughout the Gospel). In this way a transfer was made from human and political kingship to divine kingship and, at the same time, from human generation to divine sonship.

All this leads us to suggest the following square:

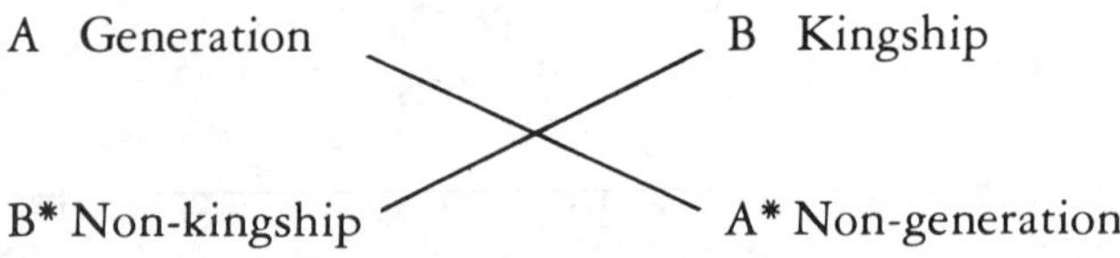

The positive terms (generation and kingship) have already been justified. We must now define the negative terms on the lower level.

Non-kings make up the first and the third series of fourteen generations: before David (1:1-5) and after the Babylonian captivity (1:12-16). (I have also pointed out that after being repeatedly described as a king in 2:1, 3 and 9, Herod loses this title after 2:9, from the moment when his evilness is brought to light. Then he is very emphatically described in reference to his death.) The Messiah himself is inscribed in the genealogical series of non-kings, kings who are fallen and without political power. The dialectic of non-kingship is subtle but far-reaching.

The *non-generation* pole is represented symmetrically at the beginning and end of the genealogy which moves from the non-begotten begetter, Abraham (1:2), to two non-begetting begottens: Joseph and Jesus, as shown in our earlier analysis. This inclusion is significant.

To this negative pole may be linked the slain children of Bethlehem (2:16-18); they represent Christ inasmuch as they are non-begetting begottens, but also by their violent deaths, which prefigure the passion of Christ.

The four terms of the square are thus solidly based. The chief apparent difficulty of this hypothesis is that generation and kingship do not seem to be contraries, in the sense required for a square.

On examination, this contrariety actually proves to be the key to the meaning of the whole: it permeates human kingships, woven as these are of deaths and changes by which the messianic kingship is not affected.

Generations, after all, are inherently ephemeral, subject to the cyclical repetition of life and death. Thus each begotten king becomes a begetter and at his death disappears to make way for the new begotten. Kingship is perpetuated only through an alternation of generations and death. In order to protect his own kingship Herod slaughters the children.

But while men die the kingship continues on ("The king is dead, long live the king!" as the common saying has it). It is the function of a dynasty to ensure this permanence.

The kings of that past age used to try to avert this catastrophic change by claiming divine status. This was the case with the Roman emperor. It was also true, Luke tells us, of Herod Agrippa. The people went along with his illusory claims and acclaimed him:

> On an appointed day Herod put on his royal robes, took his seat upon the throne, and made an oration to them. And the people shouted, "The voice of a god, and not of man!" Immediately an angel of the Lord smote him, because he did not give God the glory; and he was eaten by worms and died (Acts 12:21-23).

Luke ironically points out here the illusion represented by this claim to deathless divinity that is given the lie by death (in contrast to Christ who lives and reigns eternally). Generation and dynastic eternity are thus contrasted as succession and permanence, mortality and immortality, humanity and divinity.

The analysis thus bids us replace generation-kingship, the terms which emerge from the text itself, with more abstract terms that can give a better account of its logical structure in the light of semiotics.

renewal
through generation

dynastic permanence

non-dynastic
non-permanence

non-renewal
through generation

The essential point being conveyed is that Christ overcomes this contrariety between dynastic permanence and renewal through birth. Jesus does not beget a son to succeed him, because his dynasty is achieved in a different way, in his eschatological existence as Son of God.

The Messiah thus transcends the dynastic model in two ways:

1. In political terms: The downfall of the Davidic kings as a result of the Babylonian exile means that Jesus, as a member of the dynasty, is powerless in contrast to Herod who threatens him with his might. In this respect, Jesus is not the restorer of the Davidic reign; he is the last of the non-kings, born under the sign of non-power and of the Babylonian captivity (1:11, 12, 17): he is caught up in this political collapse. His kingship will be a source of mockery for his enemies (27:29 and 42), as are also his titles of "Savior" and "Son of God" (27:42-43). In the helplessness of an ignominious death, as in his infancy, it is another kingship that asserts itself: a kingship which comes into this world but is not of this world (cf. Jn 18:36). The kingdom is the central object of Matthew's preaching, but it is the kingdom of God that is proclaimed to the poor. This is what is beginning to emerge in Matthew 1-2.

2. There is a two-stage break in the chain of generations. Joseph does not beget; Jesus' generation is due solely to God, and is not a part of any dynasty. Jesus is the definitive, eschatological fulfillment of the generations of the dynasty. He gathers up everything in his own person, as "Savior" of all (1:21) rather than as father of a ruling dynasty. The Davidic dynasty changes its character as it reaches its

fulfillment. The anointing of the Holy Spirit is upon the Messiah from the very beginning (1:18 and 20). This anointing is renewed or, more accurately, is manifested at his baptism, when the Holy Spirit comes upon him and when the heavenly Father proclaims him as his son (3:16). He will effect salvation, not through a succession of temporary mortal heirs but by bringing definitive salvation to all human beings (1:21), who are identified with him as son of God, a theme which Paul (with symbols of the body and the building) and John (the vine) develop. Cyclical perpetuity, in which death is temporarily conquered by the coming of a new generation, is replaced by eternal life. Human origins are replaced by a divine origin.

The infancy Gospels do not make all this explicit, but this is nonetheless the intuition that controls their symbolic structure. The expression of it is there in germ—a term we must take here with all the dynamic power it implies. It remains under the surface because Jesus is as yet only a virtual subject. The pattern of transformations is as follows. Being king from the very beginning (by anointing of the Holy Spirit, 1:18 and 20), Jesus is acknowledged at his birth by the wise men (who call him "the king of the Jews," 2:2) and, in some sense, by King Herod himself (2:8). But despite his apparent power and craftiness Herod is in fact only a puppet and doomed to failure and death (2:15, 19-22). Beyond the outward semblances of power stands Jesus, the true king, born of God. The virginal generation is the sign of his transcendence over the kings of earth. It prepares the way for the revelation of his being as Son of God.

This definitive break in the ongoing succession of generations also takes us out of the cycle of death which controlled David and his heirs as it did Herod and his descendants (2:19-22). Jesus will manifest even in his death and Resurrection the kingship of salvation that is signified by his name (1:21; cf. 14:36; 16:25; 19:25-26; 27:18-20, 29, 37, 40, 42, 49).

In the background of this model we glimpse the impetus that led to the sacralization of dynasties and to the divinization of kings. For Jesus, however, the sacralization and divinization are of a different order, one which as Son of God he derives from the source of all divinization and which he shares with all human beings, whom he makes sons of God in his "kingdom." These are not projections made onto the text, but the result of an internal evaluation of the lines of force that lie behind Matthew 1-2 and will be developed throughout his Gospel.

It is the mystery of God made man that is at work here and seeks expression in the basic but prestigious categories of generation and kingship. The square we have just seen explains the astonishingly varied and contrasting narrative ranges which we find on the horizontal, diagonal and vertical axes.

Horizontal Axes of the Contraries

On the upper horizontal AB, generation-kingship, the contrariety is between the chain of successions, each doomed to death, and the permanence promised to David, that is, the messianic kingship which becomes real in a transcendent manner in Jesus Christ.

On the lower horizontal B*A*, non-kingship/non-generation, the contrariety is between non-kingship from Abraham to Jesse, the father of David, and especially from the Babylonian captivity to Jesus, a non-kingship implied in the fall of the dynasty; and non-generation, due to which the dynasty becomes biologically extinct, only to become real in a transcendent manner through the virginal conception of the Messiah, the God-with-us.

On the Diagonal Axes (Positions of the Contradictories)

The contradiction between kingship and non-kingship (BB*) becomes clearly visible in the relationship between the three groups of ancestral kings and non-kings (1:1, 12, 17); Jesus is part of the latter group, since he is a non-king according to power and appearance.

The contradiction between generation and non-generation (AA*) which is suggested at the very beginning of the genealogy by the abrupt introduction of Abraham (begetting but seemingly not begotten), is brought into the open at the other end of the chain in the two begottens who do not beget: Joseph and Jesus, with Joseph prefiguring Jesus insofar as he is placed beyond the condition of begetter.

Vertical Correlations

Do the vertical correlations make an appearance within the narrative? Generation without kingship (AB*) describes the condition of Jechoniah and his brothers, at the collapse of the dynasty at the time of the deportation (1:11). They were followed by the successive generations of a non-reigning royal line, up to and including Jesus.

Kingship without generation (BA*) belongs to the Messiah, who is not begotten and who does not beget. His mission is to save and to gather up human beings in his role as ruler and shepherd. He gathers them by a new process which is neither dynastic nor domineering. In short, the termination of the generations in 1:16 simply puts a biological end to a kingship that had already fallen politically. It is within this fallen state that the kingdom preached by Christ takes on a new and divine meaning, as Jesus reveals himself to be Son of God and Savior. This is the meaning of his kingship in the kingdom which plays such an essential role in the Gospel of Matthew (3:2).[23]

Topographical Aspect

The square I have been analyzing[24] accounts for the topography of Matthew 1-2. The towns and countries which he mentions find their place according to the four poles of the square:

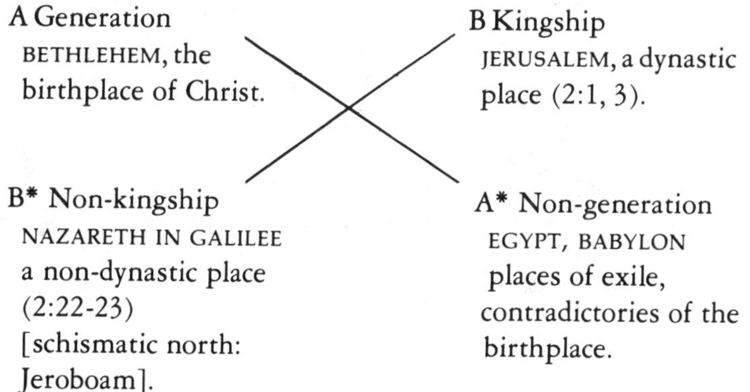

A. Generation: Bethlehem is formally given as the place where Jesus was begotten (*gennēthentos*, 2:1). As the birthplace of King David, it qualifies the Messiah. Luke 2:1-5 asserts this more explicitly than does Matthew, who expressly fastens this qualification only on to the divine oracle: "But you, O Bethlehem. . . from you shall come a ruler who will govern my people Israel" (Mi 5:1 quoted in Mt 2:6). At the topographical level, therefore, Matthew shows a reserve with regard to the Davidic definition, which he saw as essentially transcended rather than merely fulfilled.

B. Kingship: Jerusalem is the dynastic place, the "city of David" in which the first anointed one (the Messiah) established his dynasty. It is there that the wise men look for "the king of the Jews who was just born" (2:2). But they find only King Herod (2:1) who plots the death of the Messiah-King (2:16-19) and is succeeded by an equally evil progeny (2:22).

A* Non-generation: Egypt (four times in 2:13-15 and 19) comes into the picture as the Messiah's place of exile, a foreign land, in contrast (contradictory) to the royal birthplace. We shall see that this foreign place (the place of exile of the chosen people according to 2:15) is the counterpart of Babylon (likewise mentioned four times, in 1:11-12 and 17) as the place of exile for the people and their fallen kings.

B* Non-kingship: Nazareth in Galilee is a true contrary. It is another place of exile, not in a foreign country but in the marginal, paganized outskirts (Galilee of the Gentiles, 4:15). This northern province is seen as an anti-dynastic place (2:22-23): it was the schismatic place where Jeroboam established an alternate kingdom.

The topographical range in Matthew 1-2 is thus clear.

The only place mentioned in the genealogy is the Babylon of the captivity, where the kingship (the dynasty) came to an end.

The second sequence, the origin of Jesus, who is born of the Spirit, is strictly atopical. Matthew says nothing about the localization of this origin at Nazareth, a localization which was clear in Luke (1:26-27). From the semiotic viewpoint, this silence shows that Matthew had moved beyond the cultural ideas of the age: the kingship of the Messiah is not seen as topographical or political. Its location is unimportant. This atopy helps to underscore the basic assertion that the kingship of Christ does not depend on generation from David through Joseph but on God alone: on the anointing of the Spirit who alone qualifies Jesus as the Messiah, the Son of God (1:18 and 20; cf. 2:15).

The third sequence, which begins with a topographical connection with Bethlehem, therefore, has only the value of a superficial sign as far as Matthew is concerned. This is why he does not call attention in any way to the fact that Bethlehem is a Davidic place (unlike Lk 2:1-4). The conjunction Jesus-Messiah → Bethlehem does interest Matthew as being the fulfillment of a messianic prophecy (Mi 5:2, cited in 2:6).

The point which is given primary emphasis, however, is the disjunction Christ ← Jerusalem. Not only is the dynastic city on the whole opposed to him (2:3), it even threatens him. Through its anti-king it would kill him were it not for God's protection. When it becomes possible for Jesus to return to Israel after the death of Herod, the threat represented by Archelaus, the dynastic successor of Herod, keeps him out of Judea (the king's province).

The topographical range of the infancy Gospel, which begins with a significant atopy, ends then with two places of exile. Egypt is the counterpart of Babylon, the place of the dynastic downfall, while Bethlehem is transformed into a place of carnage and desolation (2:16-18).

This topography is in accord with the topography of the rest of Matthew's Gospel, in which Jerusalem, which is viewed as the city of death, the city that kills the prophets and the Messiah, is neither the place of preaching nor the place where the risen Christ manifests himself. The classic topographical values are both revolutionized (an inversion of values between Jerusalem and Nazareth) and transcended. Galilee of the Gentiles becomes the place of the Messiah's manifestation (4:15), of his post-resurrection appearances (28:10 and 16), and of the missionary sending of the apostles (28:16-20). This is what is new about Matthew 1-2. The Messiah transcends the accepted genealogy and topography. The Gospel overturns the established values of the culture.

Being-Appearing

The square which we have proposed can, like the one in Luke 1-2, be modalized by the square of veridiction:

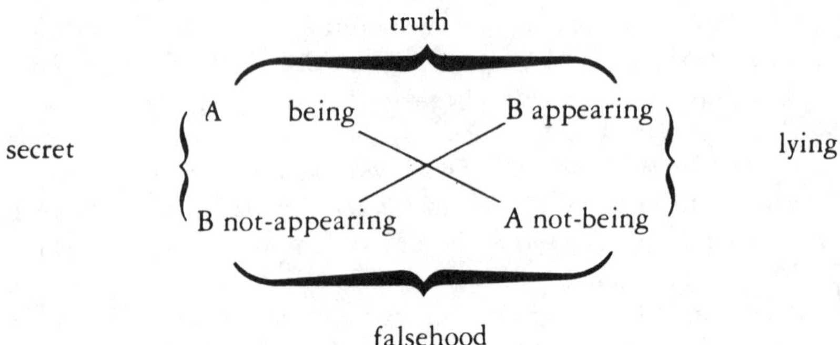

The operation is a simple one, since there are isotopic parallels between being and generation and between appearing and kingship.

The being of the kings of earth is destined to turn into the non-being of death, as transpires with Herod.

The appearing of their kingship dies out and disappears for them, passed on with difficulty through the dynastic institution and destroyed by the ceaseless erosion of time.

The Messiah is the fulfilled being who does not pass away and who renders ineffectual the appearing of human kingship, at the time when the dynasty of David lies in the shadows and when the awesome appearance of the tyrant is enthroned in Jeusalem. Christ is the Son of God and God-with-us, but his being is hidden and threatened by the apparently powerful kingship of Herod.

This kingship (appearing without being) ends for Herod in death, which brings to light the provisional, misleading, condemned character of his being. His kingship is a lie.

The kingship of the Messiah, on the contrary, exists but does not appear. It is secret. The function of the narrative is to manifest this hidden kingship: to declare the titles which reveal his being (Son of God, and so on), his signs, his victory over threats of death, a victory infallibly guaranteed by God. There is a gradual elucidation of the symbol of new creation signified by the word *genesis* (1:1 and 16), and of the role of the Spirit, who is connected with the origin of creation.

All this illustrates how Matthew decodes the prophetic program hidden in insignificant or disturbing incidents. The transcendence of the Messiah is hidden in the disconcerting virginal conception. But the begotten one is the Savior, God-with-us (1:22-23); the promised kingship has come via this obscure birth, the birth of the Son of God, this hunted exile (2:15)—the holy one, this obscure Nazarene (2:23) whose name, lacking in glory, reveals his holiness.

The modalization of the generation-kingship square by the square of veridiction is extremely revealing, because it is indeed a revelation that is set forth in Matthew 1-2: the truth of God, communicated in the vicissitudes of this world is the basis of an utterly different, non-political, non-dynastic kingship. Thus the contrariety between generation and kingship (vicissitudes and permanence) is overcome, not at the level of appearing but at the level of the revealed being who transcends appearing and brings about a new reconciliation of being and appearing. The key to all this is this wholly different king, who is unknown to the powers of this world and whom the Scripture defines as "God-with-us," the image which begins and closes Matthew's Gospel.

IV
MATTHEW AND LUKE

Concordantia Discordantium

Before turning to a final problem, the problem of historicity, I must compare the two infancy Gospels.[1] Some exegetes have emphasized the similarities between them; Resch has done so to the point of making them two fragments of a single original text. Others have emphasized the differences to the point of making them seem wholly contradictory. To what extent is there disagreement? To what extent agreement? And how do the two fit together? These are the questions to be answered here.

A. DIFFERENCES

The first point to be made is that the events narrated differ through almost 99% of the text. In the 132 verses of Luke 1-2 and the 47 of Matthew 1-2 the (scattered) details they have in common occupy the space of about a single verse.

The episodes are entirely different. In Matthew we find a genealogy, the announcement to Joseph, the visit of the wise men, the persecution by Herod, the slaughter of the Innocents, and the flight into Egypt. In Luke we find the two announcements to Zechariah and Mary, the visitation, the birth of John the Baptist, the census which brings the Holy Family to Jerusalem from Nazareth, the visit of the shepherds, the two presentations in the Temple.

The point of view, the atmosphere, and the organization are likewise different in the two narratives. According to Matthew the birth is announced to Joseph alone; according to Luke, to Mary alone. (Joseph is as much in the background in Luke 1-2 as Mary is in Matthew 1-2.)

The typology and chronology are organized differently in each of the two Gospels. Luke locates the conception at Nazareth. Matthew says nothing about the place of the conception (an atopic sequence) and presents everything as beginning with the birth at Bethlehem;

according to Matthew, the birth takes place in a house (*oikia*, 2:11), whereas Luke emphasizes the uncertainty with regard to lodging ("no room for them," 2:7; the birth in a manger, 2:7, 11,16). Luke assesses the chronological magnitudes: the seventy weeks (in detail), then the twelve years of Jesus' boyhood. Matthew gives no such temporal indication, except for the synchrony with the age of Herod (common to Mt 2:1 and Lk 1:5).

In Matthew, the Messiah is made known to wealthy foreigners who bring gold; in Luke, he is made known to poor Jewish shepherds. In Matthew, the story is told from the outside and schematically; in Luke, from within. In Matthew, the characters are guided by orders from heaven; in Luke, the dynamism of the Spirit—initiative, freedom—directs their participation in the events; there are few orders issued. The charisms, in their incipient stage, are what bring events to pass, rather than guidance from heaven.

Matthew disparages Jerusalem, a threatening city which the coming of the King-Messiah seems to disturb as much as it disturbs Herod himself. For Luke Jerusalem is the place of "value" where Jesus is acknowledged (Lk 2:22-49): he goes up to it twice, whereas Matthew says nothing of these visits and may even give the impression of excluding them.

In Matthew 2 the program is conflictual: King Herod against the King-Messiah (2:1-2). In Luke, there is harmonious agreement. There is violence and the wailing of children in Matthew 2:13-18; in Luke a serenity in which the shadow of Christ's death is only dimly seen far in the future (Lk 2:35 and 48).

In short, these two narratives seem alien to each other.

B. AGREEMENTS

These differences, however, are rooted in surprising and basic agreements which have been insufficiently appreciated.

The Same Essential Data

To begin with, the factual data are the same in both accounts:

—The principal characters are the same: Jesus, Mary, Joseph, along with Herod, who serves as a chronological guide (Mt 2:1-22; Lk 1:5).

—The birth of Jesus was announced by a divine message which both evangelists assign to "the angel of the Lord"[2] (Mt 1:20-23; Lk 1:26-38). The name Jesus was meaningfully prescribed (Mt 1:21; Lk 1:31), for he is salvation for the people of Israel (Mt 1:21; Lk 2:11, 30, 32a; cf. Lk 1:47, 68-69); a light for the nations (Mt 2:1-12; Lk 1:78-79; 2:32); and he brings forgiveness of sins (Mt 1:21; Lk 1:77).

—By genealogy Jesus is a son of David (Mt 1:1; Lk 1:32; 2:4-5; 3:32) but he is not born from Joseph (Mt 1:18-23; Lk 1:34-35; 3:32). His origin is entirely from the Holy Spirit (Mt 1:18-20; Lk 1:35) and a virgin (Mt 1:23; Lk 1:27).

—Having been conceived before the stage of cohabitation which sealed a Jewish marriage (Lk 1:27; 2:5; Mt 1:18-25), he was born after Joseph "took Mary into his home."

—He was born in Bethlehem (Mt 2:1; Lk 2:1-4, 11, 15—a very Lucan trilogy) and variously associated with Jerusalem.[3]

—The unusual birth of Jesus is explained by a transcendent (and not theogamic) intervention of God. It is an eschatological intervention which renews creation and the course of history.

—This birth is a light in the dark (Mt 2:9-10; Lk 2:7-14) and a source of joy (Mt 2:10; Lk 2:10; cf. 2:44, 47).

The Same Questions, The Same Answers

The two Gospels were clearly answering the same question: Who was Jesus at the beginning of his life, before his manifestation at his baptism? Both confront two major difficulties: How is it that the Messiah was not born from Joseph, son of David? How is it that he came from Nazareth in Galilee, a place traditionally held in contempt? Both accept this twofold paradox and incorporate it into their narratives. Both attribute the virginal conception to the Holy Spirit and assign Joseph the same role as adoptive father, though only Matthew formally explains it. They are in agreement that the birth took place at Bethlehem, and both give a positive evaluation of Nazareth, although from different arguments. According to Matthew, residence there is the result of mortal danger and fulfills a prophecy which cannot be identified. According to Luke, the family was already resident there (1:26-27), a fact which points to the humble station that is essential to the Messiah; this is a much more profound approach. For both evangelists Jesus is seen as a son of David; this explains the emphasis they place on Bethlehem, the "city of David" according to Luke 2:4 and 11.

In both infancy Gospels Jesus is portrayed as the Son of God from the outset. According to Luke, this title formed part of the announcement of the angel and defined Christ from his very conception (1:32, 35; 2:49); Matthew avoids using the title in connection with the origin of the Messiah (although he assigns him an analogous title, Emmanuel, God-with-us). It would seem that he avoids the term Son of God in this context in order to remove any suggestion of a theogamy. Only later on and in a different context does he introduce this fundamental title (2:15).

The two evangelists accept the hidden life of Jesus. They do not indulge in the miracle-ridden mythology of the Apocrypha. They see in the origin of Christ a new act of creation, that eschatological condition announced by the prophets. According to both evangelists, the Spirit hovers over this new creation in Jesus Christ as he did over the first creation in Genesis 1:2. Matthew alone makes this explicit reference to the "genesis" (1:1 and 18). The Spirit confers—this is certainly the case in Luke—that anointing of the Messiah which early catechesis located at the baptism of Christ (Acts 10:38, which implicitly cites Is 61:1, "The Spirit of the Lord is upon me, because the Lord has anointed me," which is cited in Lk 4:1). According to Luke 1:35 and Matthew 1:18, 20, this anointing is bestowed on Christ at the very beginning of his human existence.

In both evangelists this eschatology is unpretentious and unobtrusive. The shadow of the passion hovers over the infancy of Jesus: persecution and slaughter by Herod in Matthew 2; in Luke the prophecy of Simeon (2:35) and, later on, the prefiguration of death which can be seen in the disappearance of the child Jesus at Passover (2:49).

Symbolic Convergences

At the symbolic level the two evangelists agree in situating the origin of Christ against a backdrop of darkness: in Matthew, the star of the wise men (2:2, 9-10) and the flight of Joseph at night (2:14); in Luke, the night which surrounded the shepherds at Christmas (2:8).

This night or darkness underscores the light: the glory of God himself in Luke 2:9; the star of the wise men in Matthew 2:10. Both writers seem to identify Jesus with the star coming from the East (Mt 2:2; Lk 1:78) and with the messianic star of Balaam's prophecy in Numbers 24:17.[4]

The Same Midrashic Use of Scripture

Matthew and Luke both adopt the same literary technique, the up-dating of Scripture in the midrashic tradition. Both renew this tradition by focusing Christ as the one who gives ultimate meaning and relevance to the Scriptures, the *pesher* of all fulfillment.[5] But this was not achieved without some tension. It gave rise to the exercise of creative originality on the part of both authors.

While biblical references are for the most part explicit in Matthew 1-2 and implicit in Luke 1-2, the latter does explicitly cite two texts of Scripture in 2:23-24 (Lv 12:1-8 and Ex 13:1-2). Matthew, on the other hand, has an implicit citation of Psalm 72:10-15 (and Isaiah 60:6) in 2:11.

The references are explanatory and apologetic in Matthew, allusive and meditative in Luke, but both manifest the same concern to shed a retrospective light on the Scriptures through the person of Christ, rather than on Christ through the Scriptures.

The scriptural references made by the two evangelists are for the most part different. Both, however, do refer to Micah 5:1-5 and Isaiah 7:14 (explicitly in Mt 1:23, by way of allusion in Lk 1:30-33). Brown thinks that there is a reference in both to Balaam's prophecy (Nm 24:17) regarding the Messiah as the "star of Jacob," a prophecy which received important attention in the Qumran texts.

Unexpected Agreements

A careful study of the two infancy Gospels shows a number of theological points of convergence:

—At first sight, Luke alone offers an ascending genealogy, while Matthew has a descending chain of generations. But Matthew in fact begins with a short ascending genealogy in 1:1.

—Luke alone goes back to Adam, while Matthew begins with Abraham. But J. Chopineau points out that the initials of the three persons mentioned in this abridged genealogy (1:1) form the name Adam (in the Hebrew substratum which, as far as this genealogy is concerned, certainly existed).[6]

Abraham = *Aleph*
David = *Daleth* ADAM
Meshiah = *Mem*

These three key names, which sum up the genealogy and give shape to the descending series, are in proper order. Can this be pure chance? Did not Hebrew culture cultivate "accidental" phenomena of this kind?

Matthew's final reference, "He shall be called a Nazarene" (from Jgs 13:5 and Is 4:3) stresses the holiness implicit in this title. This accords well with Luke's oracle at the annunciation, "He shall be called *holy*" (Lk 1:35).

The similarity is so well established that a number of experts on the subject of biblical substrata tend to reduce the texts to one another, and this in either direction, that is, by seeing in the second the fuller meaning (*sensus plenior*) of the first, or by reducing the meaning of the second to that of the first.[7]

Same Semiotic and Theological "Model"

Semiotics has brought to light a more surprising and more fundamental agreement that involves a deep thought-structure.

While the "squares" show very different motifs, generation and kingship in Matthew, Law and grace in Luke, we have seen to our surprise that they operate nonetheless within the same model. In Luke as in Matthew, God is the addresser; the Israelite people and the Gentiles are the addressees. Christ is the (hidden) virtual hero standing behind the other subjects; he is defined in ontological fashion as savior (Mt 1:21), the same identification being made between savior and salvation.

In both evangelists Jesus is given important titles which are to some extent common to both Gospels: Christ, Son of God, Savior.

The other titles differ in the two Gospels but are nonetheless convergent: Emmanuel, King, Ruler, and Shepherd in Matthew; Lord, Light, and Glory in Luke.

From all this it can be seen that the *concordantia discordantium* extends to all areas:

—From the structural perspective, the elements which the two narratives have in common are basic ones: date, topographical framework, characters, and an unusual birth, an account of which has been transmitted according to different traditions and in different forms and recounted through different narratives.

—From the point of view of meaning, the symbols and theology of the two infancy Gospels are rooted in the same Scriptures, the same tradition and the same frameworks, that is, not only the same culture and references to the OT, but the same major axis of a revelation which enters a new stage in the same way, namely, through the coming on the scene of a humble Messiah who is transcendent but at the same time strangely obscure.

Making use of strong biblical expressions, the two very different evangelists begin to bring out the deeper reality of this Messiah and his identification with God as God's Son (Lk 1:32, 35; 2:49; Mt 2:15). The remainder of the Gospel will make clear the meaning of this title. Divine sonship is the indispensable means of safeguarding the transcendent unity of God within the distinction of persons. Matthew and Luke had not yet arrived at this explanation, but even in the infancy Gospels they present it in existential terms.

In short, the two Gospels are different, but they are neither incompatible nor contradictory. They converge and are coherent. The *concordia* between them exists in matters that are truly important: essential historical guide-marks; reference to God, to human beings, to the salvation that has made its appearance as free gift in Jesus Christ; convergent interpretations of events within the framework of biblical revelation and tradition that are structured in parallel ways.

We must now examine more closely the consequences of this pluralism for a historical, symbolical, and theological evaluation of the two infancy Gospels.

Part III
What Kind of Historicity?

The Gospels are not divergent
in their substance,
even though one mentions
what the other passes over in silence
or reports it differently.

(St. Augustine, *Letter* 199,
To Hesychius, no. 25 PL 33)

When truth is lacking
edification achieves nothing....
Let the meaning
not diverge
from historical truth.

(St. Gregory the Great, *Moralia*
XXXV, 20, 48 PL 76:779d)

Having subjected the texts to a critical examination in the light of exegetical norms, we must now subject them to a critical examination according to the norms of history.

Exegesis analyzes texts. History inquires into the reality of what the texts relate. This second task is not marked by the same translucent homogeneity, and it proves challenging on two counts.

First of all, we do not reach the event except through the text, where it has undergone a twofold transposition due to the intentionality characteristic of knowledge and to the expression which builds a text. We have at our disposal only the end result. We can establish contact with the event only through a subtle relationship.

Furthermore, when we deal with history, the event has ceased to exist. It is an illusion to think of the past as a kind of spatial domain that is located behind us. We know the past only in a new present and through the lasting traces it has left. But then, what kind of operation can it be that refers back to this "thing which is not" in order to perpetuate the memory of it? Is not the attempt a presumptuous one?

Nonetheless the human person, caught up in the movement of time, constantly stakes a great deal on memory, and does so with a legitimate assurance. All human undertakings are based on memory, one of the major concerns being not to fall into some form of illusion. In fact, the control of witnesses is carried on in a fairly satisfactory way. This is the ongoing work and justification of knowledge, which is defined by intentionality or the ability to contact the other as other, whether in the past or in the present. This twofold reference is essential, and it proves important when dealing with the Gospel.

Fiction or fact? The Bible does not shrink from using fiction (as the books of Judith and Esther, as well as the parables, make it clear), but it is, above all, the history of salvation. This is especially true of Matthew

1-2 and Luke 1-2. Is this history, then, truly historical, that is, in conformity with the events themselves?

Three questions may be asked:

1. Is the narrative an imaginative invention of the author?

2. Is it a copy or adaptation of an earlier narrative? If so, what is the value of that earlier narrative?

3. Is it a more or less direct expression of the event, based on the testimony of eyewitnesses? To what extent do the narratives in Matthew 1-2 and Luke 1-2 reflect what the infant Christ and his fellow actors experienced and did? This question is asked without any intention of challenging the importance of studying the expression itself, in its genesis and structure.

Exegetes are reluctant to raise these questions because the object of their study is the text. It is difficult for them to lay hold of what lies beyond the text, and they tend to avoid any attempt to do so. The ideal situation for them is when a text can be explained by another text which is the source of the first and makes a homogeneous comparison possible. When another such text is lacking, they may suppose that the text before them represents an ideological or mythological creation in which the author expresses a doctrine in narrative form. It is "more fruitful" to regard Mary as a symbolic than as a historical figure, says R. E. Brown, one of the leading protagonists of this method.[1] One must not be surprised that semiotics, which has a different orientation, nevertheless inclines to the same type of thinking and produced the adage, "It is not the author who creates language, it is language which creates both the author and the event." The convergence of two widely differing disciplines (the one which reduces itself to history, and the other which is "allergic" to history) stems from the methodological demand common to both: in the study of texts—from the literary or the semiotic point of view—language is everything. The rest is unknowable; to linger over it is to abandon objectivity. The idealist philosophy of Kant and Hegel, which has dominated modern thinking and the birth of scientific exegesis, has brought out this tendency even more radically.

The exegetes who proceed down this slippery slope and interpret the Gospel narratives as fictions or personal or communal creations (those of the so-called "creative community") put themselves at odds with their faith in saying that while symbolism is not history, it has its own value. Whether the narrative is historical or not, according to this logic, the symbolism is the same, the meaning is identical. But this conviction, cultivated with such aplomb, is hardly satisfying. People who take something seriously, be it love or money, must avoid confusing fiction and reality. On this point, exegetes have often been heavily influenced by the "teachers of suspicion," promoting a disintegration of history which inevitably leads to a disintegration of faith, since Christianity is a historical religion, based on the entry of God into history. A further consequence is the assumption that religion is unrealistic and built upon fiction in the form of fables and myths. There is a kind of catechesis, for example, which has gone so far as to present the miracles of Christ as "parables." What we must hold on to (we are told) is the meaning, not the reality. But is this not to grasp at shadows, and let the real prize slip by? And if this is all there were to Christianity, would it not indeed be an "opiate of the people"? Those who get themselves bogged down in philosophical positions so alien to Christian revelation are little inclined to preach it, or else preach it in a way that is deceptively unrealistic and literary.

In this climate of opinion (which, happily, is changing), an objective inquiry into historicity means swimming against the current. The operation is a difficult one: the purpose is to evaluate the relation between the text and the event. However, only the text is available to us. History, therefore, operates in an atmosphere of pervading relativity. But this relativity must not degenerate into an unhealthy and disintegrative relativism. The relativity in question is a relatedness to the reality of the event.

In this third section, our task is to assess this relatedness or reference while avoiding factitious presuppositions that would distort it, and to strive to evaluate the facts thoroughly and impartially.

Such an effort requires strict attention to the text, its literary genre and its cultural milieu, because every age (including our own) has its own way of writing history. The question, then, is this: What conception of historicity guided the writing of the infancy narratives, if indeed they are dealing with history?[2]

On the one hand, we must reject the presupposition that the infancy Gospels are different in character from the rest of the Gospels, a kind of legendary preamble created from whole cloth after the event. Objectivity compels us, moreover, to recognize (as indeed we have already) that Matthew and Luke are truly the authors of Matthew 1-2 and Luke 1-2 and that they wrote these sections with the same concern for truth which they show elsewhere. On the other hand, we must keep in mind the special handicap under which we labor in dealing with the infancy Gospels. The events date from a time thirty years before the rest of the Gospel. The facts narrated are those of private life. At the time of writing there was in the Christian community a scarcity of eyewitnesses of those early years; therefore access to the testimonies is often more indirect. While these testimonies are part of the storehouse of memories of particular Christian communities (those in which the brothers of Jesus and Mary his mother lived, Acts 1:14), they are not part of the basic common memory which from the outset gave structure to the kerygma and catechesis of the Church.

In order to carry out this necessarily difficult verification, we must, on the basis of identifiable signs, examine successively:

1. The historicity of Luke 1-2,
2. The historicity of Matthew 1-2,
3. The convergences (or divergences) of the two infancy Gospels among themselves, with the remainder of the NT, and with extra-biblical data, since the criterion of historical truth is not mathematical but is a matter of convergence.

We shall then be in a position to evaluate the historicity of the various elements that constitute the infancy Gospels: genealogy, narratives, dialogues, canticles. Because of the intrusions which have distorted the study of the miraculous, we must treat this aspect separately: the appearance of stars and angels, supernatural revelation, and the virginal conception.

This evaluation of the text's reference to events calls for a corresponding examination of the meaning and symbolism inherent in this reference to the historical reality of the infancy of Christ.

I
LUKE 1-2

Declaration of Intent (Luke 1:1-4)

From a historical perspective, the major datum in Luke lies in his prologue, in which he clearly states that he wishes to recount with accuracy (*akribōs*) the real and recent events as reported by eyewitnesses:

> Inasmuch as many have undertaken to compile a narrative of the things (*pragmatōn*) which have been accomplished among us, just as they were delivered (*paredosan*) to us by those who from the beginning (*oi ap' archēs*) were eyewitnesses (*autoptai*) and ministers of the word, it seemed good to me also, having followed (*parēkolouthēkoti*) all things closely (*akribōs*) for some time past (*anōthen*), to write an orderly account (*kathexēs*) for you, most excellent Theophilus, that you may know the truth (*asphaleian*) concerning the things of which you have been informed (*katēchēthēs*).

This prologue expresses both a concern for and an assurance of (*parrhēsia*) the truth. The commentaries unilaterally and systematically emphasize that what is meant here is religious truth. Luke speaks of a "tradition" (cf. *paredosan*), drawn from the ministers of the Word, a Word set down (1:1) in an ordered fashion (1:3), which has the apologetic concern of confirming the certitude of a catechesis (cf. *katēchēthsēs*, verse 4; the term "ministers of the Word" appears twice, verses 2 and 4). These terms and this apologetic dimension must be taken into consideration. Luke was writing in and for a community of faith, with concern for the meaning which vivified the community. The "account" which he proposes (verse 1) is not purely factual or anecdotal. It is a holy history, and would have been perceived as such.

However, this does not exclude Luke's fundamental concern to conform to the actual events.[1] Actually, he intended to present "things which have been accomplished among us" (*tōn peplērophorēmenōn en hēmin pragmatōn*).[2] He began there and referred himself to those contemporaries who were still able to verify or contest the materials. He remained the historian of a living reality and not of a dead past.

He was anxious to base his work on "eyewitnesses" (verse 2); those who were such "from the beginning." Many exegetes have been bent on restricting this word "beginning" to the baptism of Jesus. Is it not there, in fact, that the primitive kerygma began, according to both Acts 1:22 and 10:36-40, and as Mark's Gospel attests? Certainly. But Luke wanted to make the starting point of the kerygma clear. So he stressed the true point of departure of the Gospel—not the public baptism of Jesus, but his very origins, his conception and birth. Luke took this innovation to heart. This clearly explains his pleonastic insistence, "from the beginning" (verse 2), starting at the beginning (verse 3: isotopy). Usually these expressions refer to the very opening of a narrative, and indeed that is the case here: the beginning, as Luke expresses it, is the infancy Gospel which this prologue introduces.

Numerous attempts have been made to account for these first two chapters as an interpolation or insertion. Luke 1:1-4 would then be affixed to the opening of chapter 3, and would only refer to the Gospel of the public life. These unfounded hypotheses are generally discounted and abandoned today.[3] Indeed, the infancy Gospel is an organic part of Luke's Gospel. It bears the mark of his style, his vocabulary, and his theology. It links perfectly with the rest.

The concern Luke showed to refer to the eyewitnesses is affirmed explicitly in the infancy Gospel, where Luke refers on three occasions to the witnesses who "keep these words/events" in their hearts[4]—namely, the witnesses of the infancy of John the Baptist (1:66), and especially Mary, the mother of Jesus.

More so than the other evangelists, Luke refers to women, for they are attentive to the first origins of life (cf. Lk 8:1-3; Acts 1:14). He gives a place of honor to the "brothers of Jesus" (scorned in Mk 3:31 and Jn 7:5) who were the eyewitnesses of his life in Nazareth.[5] He has not limited his sources to the official testimony of the Twelve. He says that these witnesses—the apostles during Jesus' public life, Mary in his infancy—"did not understand" certain acts or words of Jesus. This apparent misunderstanding serves to stress the ongoing effort that is necessary to achieve understanding—a difficulty which the first "eyewitnesses" themselves had to overcome.

Mary's meditation is characterized by a thorough acquaintance with the events (as is apparent in the repetition of *panta* in 2:19 and 51) as well as by an active reflection (*symballousa*, 2:19) in which the events are confronted with the Scriptures and thus yield their true meaning. In this context, inquiry and research into the meaning, truth, and symbolism are presented as strictly correlative.

The word *asphaleia* (Lk 1:4) which has at times been rendered as "religious certitude," also has a twofold significance. This word indicates an assurance or steadfastness which can be relied on, whether it is a question of the bolts on a prison door (Acts 5:23), a prisoner's shackles (*asphalizō*, Acts 16:24), the seals of a tomb (Mt 27:64-66), or, on the other hand, of an accurate deposition in an inquest (Acts 21:34; 22:30; 25:26—*asphales*). Luke intends to give an assurance of faith. But his Gospel does not do this by yielding abstract dogmas, rather, it sets out the very history of Jesus. It is of the utmost importance that this history be true; otherwise, it would have no meaning. The assurance with which certain exegetes disassociate the symbolic from the historical stems from a culture and a philosophy altogether different from that of our evangelist. He intends to pass on a truth that is understood, meditated upon, competently interpreted, solidly grounded in fact as well as in meaning. This is what Luke means by the art of composition which he mentions (1:1-4) and which he practices with such dedication and talent.

Luke insists on the *akribeia* with which he has done his research. The adverb *akribōs* is peculiar (within the Gospels) to the infancy narratives. It is found in Matthew (2:8; cf. 2:16), where it characterizes the meticulous exactitude with which Herod inquires about the infant Messiah.[6]

Luke conformed to the cultural standards of historians of the period, not only Polybius, but also Lucian the sceptic who said that history ought to be written with candor and truthfulness (*parrhēsia kai alētheia*).[7]

He took his inspiration from these pioneers of recorded history, even to writing his prologue according to the most classical model. He brings out other (i.e., religious) dimensions, but this is entirely in keeping with his concern to be in conformity with the events. His prologue expresses his thorough concern for historical authenticity. It is the most explicit declaration of historicity we have in the Scriptures.

This evident concern for historicity can only be contested by projecting upon Luke and his era the philosophical presuppositions of the nineteenth century which treated religious discourse as fiction. To the extent that this hypothesis has gained credence, it falsifies the interpretation of the infancy Gospels and undermines their value, even their religious value.

Once again, we are not contesting the religious intent of Luke, but this intent cannot be dissociated from a concern to express the truth about events relating to the real person of Christ.

For the evangelists, truth and meaning do not oppose each other. They are correlative. It is a question of discovering the meaning in factual truth. This does not lead to a preoccupation with handing on a detailed chronicle, despite the word *panta* (1:3; cf. 2:19, 51) which Luke uses frequently, (twenty-five times in Luke 1-2 alone); rather it leads to a process of selection, whose guiding principles we will see later.

Luke adhered to the significant elements, reduced to their essentials. He allowed himself the right to present, not to deform or betray. He wanted his history to be truthful, solid, and rigorous (1:1, 3).

Marks of Historicity

The indications that his Gospel adheres to this purpose are both numerous and convergent. He faithfully recorded the unexpected modesty, poverty, and humility of the birth of Christ; it was among the poor and not in lofty circles that faith and its charisms first blossomed.

The detail of his narratives shows his scrupulous concern for exactitude and accuracy:

In the account of the visitation, which he wrote in the mode of the Ark narrative of 2 Samuel 6, he speaks of the three months that Mary spent in the house of Zechariah, paralleling the three months that the Ark spent in the house of Obededom (2 Sm 6:11). But he does not force the comparison, adding the nuance "approximately."[8]

James, "The Brother of the Lord" Source of Luke 1-2?

Some have considered James, the "brother of the Lord," the first bishop of Jerusalem, to be the source of the infancy gospel.

According to Acts 21:18, Luke met him: "The next day, Paul went with us to James" (cf. 21:12-17; 15:14). James was not martyred until the year 62, according to Hegesippus (cited by Eusebius, *Church History* 2.23). Thus he must not be confused with James the Greater, "the brother of John," one of the two "sons of thunder" (Mk 3:17), a hot-tempered personality whom Herod Agrippa I had killed in A.D. 42 (Acts 12:2).

However, if Luke did know James and spoke to him about his memories, he never refers to them; he refers only to those from Mary (Lk 2:19 and 51), the best "eyewitness" concerning the origins of Christ (see below, pp. 461-463).

James the Less is called "the brother of the Lord" in the broad sense of the word, abundantly attested to in the Bible (Gn 13:8; 14:14 and 16; 29:12 and 15; other references in R. Laurentin, 1967, p. 176).

The "brothers of Jesus" constituted a group of some importance: the family clan of Nazareth stands out notably in Acts 1:14 and Mt 13:55-56, where "all his sisters" are mentioned. "*All* is not said, except of a crowd," wrote Jerome (*Adversus Helvidium*, PL 23, 200). Several of these were known to believe in Christ, but the majority "did not believe in him," according to Jn 7:5 (cf. Mk 3:21).

Mt 13:55 mentions four "brothers of the Lord" by name. But his list is not exhaustive since, from other sources, we know of Simeon, the second bishop of Jerusalem, another "brother of the Lord" (Hegesippus, cited by Eusebius, *Church History*, 4, 22, 4. J. Blinzler, *I Fratellia*, Brescia, 1974, pp. 116 and 125-128).

The first of the four "brothers" whom Mt 13:55 cites is James the Less, the subject of the present note. He is the son of Mary who cannot be identified with the Virgin. While the latter is generally called "the Mother of Jesus" (Jn 2:1, 3; 19:25; Acts 1:14), "the other Mary" is always designated as "the Mother of James and Joses" (Mk 15:40 and Mt 27:56), or "the mother of Joses" (Mk 15:47), or "the mother of James" (Mk 16:1), precisely to avoid confusion. Furthermore, this woman is always named *after* Mary Magdalen. Other indications that strengthen this evidence can be found in R. Laurentin (1967, pp. 176-177), and in the monograph by J. Blinzler already cited, J. McHugh, (1977, pp. 244-298), and H. Cazelles (in *Catholicisme* 4, 1630-1633).

He did not define Mary as a daughter of David, which would have helped to justify Jesus' Davidic lineage.[9] Church tradition did not adopt a similar scrupulosity. From the second century onward, it attempted to deduce or invent what Matthew and Luke were not able to say. The imperative which manifested itself less than a century later existed already at the time of our evangelists (see below, pp. 342-345).

Moreover, Luke did not suggest that Mary was a descendant of the priestly tribe, although the tradition of the priestly Messiah stemming from Aaron, attested to by Qumran (and the very same text, Mal 3, on which it depends), might have led him toward this view. He restricted himself to saying that Mary was related to (*suggenis*) Elizabeth (1:36), "a descendant of Aaron" (1:5).[10]

He did not project the glory of God over the manger in Bethlehem, but only over the shepherds, leaving the infant Jesus in the starkest privation.

Simeon's prophecy, which is today still something of an embarrassment to exegetes, is allowed to stand in all its confusing obscurity, while the passion and Resurrection of Christ, the object of chapters 23-24, might have facilitated its clarification.

We find the same moderation in the story of the finding in the Temple: the apocryphal Gospels show the doctors confounded by the exhaustive knowledge of Jesus; Luke keeps to the humble questions and replies of the child, only hinting at his future role as a teacher (2:45-47).

Luke did not write history like a modern historian. He collated narratives of a simple, direct, colloquial character which had already been elucidated, interpreted, meditated upon. In keeping with his policy, he respected their meaning and scope. He restricted himself to perfecting them, making them explicit, or sifting them within the limits which his use of Mark[11] or other texts allowed him; and we see that he did it to his credit.

Luke was not an ideologue. His theology is not a *theologoumenon*.[12] It is a contemplative meditation which adheres to the events and, by the light of faith, discerns in them a living light.

This is the finding of our analysis concerning the historicity of Luke, as it is attested to by his declaration of intent, and confirmed by various converging indications.

II
MATTHEW 1-2

Matthew 1-2 yields the historian fewer guarantees and indications than Luke 1-2. We find in the text no declaration of historical intent (Luke's is a rarity, a *hapax* in the NT).

Character of the Narrative

Matthew's narrative is more schematic, structured, stylized; this could put us on our guard, although the miraculous element is very discreetly included. God's intervention by means of dreams places the supernatural at the lowest possible level: a dream is not a miracle. He does not portray the wise men as kings, although the logic of the narrative and some biblical allusions lead in the direction of such an interpretation. Matthew shuns the spectacular. The nativity unfolds without miracles, without human triumphs. His genealogy manifests a conscientious documentary concern (which we will examine later). It is clear that he was concerned with writing for his contemporaries (among whom adversaries were not lacking), not a legend or novel, but a stylized account of real, credible events.

Several details cut across the historical data: there were in fact traveling astrologers in the East. Qumran has preserved a horoscope of the Messiah. It is generally known that Herod was a cunning and cruel king. We will return to this historical background.

Manner of Using Scripture

Perhaps the best sign of Matthew's historical rigor is his reluctance to make the events conform to the corroborating prophecies which he cites. If these narratives had been fiction, he would have made them fit the very letter of Scripture. He would also have used prophecies that were current and would have illustrated them with the great care of a novelist. However, he cites obscure, less significant, even at times unidentifiable prophecies. He laboriously adapts their vocabulary in order to make them fit the disconcerting events of the infancy, which could not have been foreseen in the Bible.

The notion that Jesus was not begotten of Joseph, and therefore of the Davidic line, might have jeopardized his qualification as Messiah. Matthew demonstrates historical exactitude by assuming this paradoxical datum and by justifying it by painstaking expedients. He turns to the prophecy of Isaiah 7:14, and in so doing, gives it a new and unexpected meaning.

Matthew achieves his goal only with difficulty, for the prediction does not fit the event on all points: the name Emmanuel, given to the Messiah according to Isaiah 7:14, does not coincide with the name Jesus. The Hebrew *'almāh* (or *parthenos* in the LXX) is reinterpreted. The impersonal reference to those who named the child differs from both the Greek and the Hebrew texts (the latter attributing it to the mother, the former to King Ahaz). If Matthew took the trouble to reinterpret and modify the text, this was because he did not have the right to modify the event.

Similarly, he rearranges the prophecy of Micah 5:1-3, integrating it with 2 Samuel 5:2, in order to explain the function of shepherd and the reference to David.[1]

He could have tried to model Jesus after Moses; certain allusions show that he considered doing so. Had he wanted to construct a *theologoumenon* on this basis, he would have had to recount a tale of Jesus saved from the water (Ex 1:22 and 2:1-6). Must we see a reworking of Exodus 2:15 in Matthew 2:13?

Exodus 2:15	*Matthew 2:13-14*
Pharaoh. . . sought to kill Moses.	Herod is about to search for the child, to destroy him
But Moses fled from Pharaoh,	(Joseph). . . took the child. . .
and stayed in the land of Midian.	and departed to Egypt.

The analogy is slight: Moses himself flees as an adult because he knows that Pharoah is going to kill him. Jesus is taken into Egypt by

Joseph to whom an angel has appeared in a dream. Moses flees from Egypt and Joseph takes refuge there. The Exodus narrative does not determine Matthew's model in any way.

The literal analogy is more striking between Exodus 4:19 and Matthew 2:20.

Exodus 4:19-20	*Matthew 2:19-21*
The Lord said to Moses	An angel of the Lord appeared in a dream to Joseph, saying
"Go back to Egypt	"Rise. . . go to the land of Israel,
for all the men who were seeking your life	for those who sought the child's life
are dead."	are dead."
So Moses took his wife and his sons and	And he rose and took the child and his mother, and
went back to the land of Egypt.	went to the land of Israel.

But here again the two journeys proceed in opposite directions: Moses returns to Egypt and Jesus leaves it. Moses takes his wife and his child. But Jesus is the child in Matthew's narrative. Joseph would seem to be the counterpart to Moses, a comparison which has little significance.

For the return journey to Israel, Matthew does not compare Christ with Moses, but with the people adopted by God, by citing Hosea 11:1: "Out of Egypt I called my son" (cf. Ex 4:22). Jesus is likened to Israel, not to Moses. Even if one were to collate the lesser details from the abundant Jewish tradition concerning the childhood of Moses, nothing would be found there that could have served as a model for Matthew's narrative. The minor and limited comparisons have value only as allusions, and we have pointed out the more striking ones with the patriarch Joseph, the man of dreams (Gn 37-41), a homonym of Jesus' adoptive father. The very fact that these analogies are scattered takes away any value they might have for explaining the text.

The prophecy of Jeremiah 31:15, used to illustrate the slaughter of the Innocents, does not bear the slightest characteristic which could have determined or even inspired the narrative (as R. T. France, 1979, 98-120, has meticulously demonstrated).

The final case is the citation which closes the infancy Gospel: "He shall be called a Nazarene" (2:23). Matthew searched out this word "Nazarene," and it was only by way of midrashic updating that he was able to justify the highly paradoxical event of a Messiah who appeared in Nazareth in Galilee, against every expectation and prediction, in such a way that this name, Nazarene, was attached to his person much like a nickname.[2]

In short, Matthew has maintained the jarring details which caused difficulty and even scandal for the contemporary mentality, the virginal conception and Nazarean origin of Jesus. He did not believe he had the right to eliminate them in order to satisfy the cultural and religious expectations of the people of his time. On the contrary, he assumed the right to modify the scriptural texts in order to furnish a biblical proof of the events. He felt therefore more bound by the event than by the letter of the Scriptures. These indications give Matthew's narrative serious credibility.

III
CONVERGENCES

A. LUKE 1-2 AND MATTHEW 1-2

Certain critics have attempted to find insurmountable contradictions between Matthew 1-2 and Luke 1-2. They have only succeeded by twisting the meaning of the texts.

It is true that the two infancy Gospels are very different and that we are frequently at a loss as to how to put them together. How, for example, do we reconcile the crib and the "homeless" nativity of Luke (2:7) with the "house" which we find in Matthew (2:11)?[1] How does one reconcile Jesus' Nazarene ties with the incidental character of his setting in Galilee, as Matthew reports it? Where, in Luke's infancy schema, do we place the astrologers' visit and the flight into Egypt? The texts give no answer to these questions, but neither do they present contradictions.

By the second century the *Diatessaron* had harmonized them without difficulty and in a plausible fashion, by placing the story of the wise men after the presentation in the Temple, a judicious solution adopted down to the present day by exegetes concerned with concordism.[2] After the birth in the manger, the Holy Family was able to find a house. The wise men could only have come after the shepherds. One can also find reasons explaining why the Holy Family would have stayed in Bethlehem for a period of time (Matthew would give us a margin of about two years, 2:16). But these are only hypotheses. Critical rigor bids us not to treat the episodes in Matthew and Luke like pieces of a puzzle which have to be fitted together, since the fitting of the pieces together is not a "given." Rather, we are dealing with recollections which have been written down, preserved, interpreted, and organized from greatly differing perspectives. They are like photographs taken at different angles around a building. The whole effect would be distorted if they were combined into a single picture. What results from analysis is that Matthew 1-2 and Luke 1-2 embody one of the best indicators of historical truth: the agreement of independent and divergent witnesses, *concordantia discordantium*.[3]

B. AGREEMENT WITH THE REST OF THE NEW TESTAMENT

The Gospels

Luke 1-2 and Matthew 1-2 converge along many lines with the rest of the NT.

In both infancy Gospels as well as in the rest of the NT, Jesus is presented as a Nazarene (see above, pp. 277-279) and as son of David, a title which recurs twelve times in the NT, not including numerous references to Davidic lineage. The evangelists avoid calling him "son of Joseph," except when this expression is used by his adversaries (Mt 13:55; Jn 1:45; 6:42) or in certain contexts in which this everyday manner of speech offers its own correctives (Lk 2:33, 48-49). We will see that they consistently avoid referring Jesus to a father other than God.

Likewise, the objections of those who charge Jesus with not being born in Bethlehem (the traditional birthplace of the Messiah) are cited ironically as objections from obtuse adversaries (Jn 7:42).

The body of the four Gospels confirms the obscurity of Jesus' first years. He was unknown at the beginning of his ministry. He was a common layman (not a priest). Luke's insinuation that he may have been related to the priestly families (1:5 and 36) does not contradict this datum but respects it. Jesus did not receive the education of a scribe. However, he speaks "with an authority" which asserts itself.[4] The mentality of that time would have preferred that the Messiah have impeccable credentials or a miraculous origin. A *theologoumenon* satisfying the aspirations of the people of that time would have had him come down from heaven. Such a tendency clearly appears in John 3:13; 6:33.[5] The evangelist attempts to apply this dazzling expression to Jesus in a spiritual sense, not as the full grown man of Daniel 7 who comes down from heaven with a heavenly body, but as the "Word made flesh," born of a woman (Jn 1:14).

Luke 1-2 and John 1

The points of contact between the infancy Gospel of Luke 1-2 and John's prologue (1:1-18) are particularly numerous and significant; the prologue seems to refer to Luke at each step.

Like Luke 1-2, the prologue is structured around the contrasts between John the precursor and Jesus, the Son of God (Jn 1:6-8). Jesus is the light (Lk 1:79 and 2:32; Jn 1:7-9), John is only a witness to the light (Lk 1:76-78; Jn 1:7).[6] Jesus comes "to his own" and "his own received him not" (Lk 2:7 and Jn 1:11), a cross-reference which concerns historicity.

Above all, John 1 takes up the theology of Luke: Jesus is presented as the Son of God (Lk 1:32 and 35; 2:49; Jn 1:14 and 18). The virginal conception is a sign of his divinity (Jn 1:13 and Lk 1:35): I do not know man, Mary says in Luke 1:34; Jesus is "not begotten by man's desire" in John 1:13. (We will explore this reading of the verse in the singular, below pp. 406-407.)

The divinity of Christ is further revealed through the image of the shekinah, the presence of God in the Ark of the Covenant, echoed in John 1:14, the image of the Word which "dwelt amongst us."

In Luke 1 as in John 1, the theology of Christ is developed on the basis of grace (Lk 1:28, 30; 2:40 and 52; Jn 1:14, 16, and 17) and glory (Lk 2:9 and 32; cf. 1:35; Jn 1:14).

In John 1:1-2, as in Luke 1:32a, affirmation of divine origin precedes that of human origin. Jesus is called "Son of God" in Luke 1:32a before he is called "son of David" in 1:32b, a sequence which announces the Johannine notion of pre-existence. We will not go into more detail concerning the analogies of terms, of themes, and of theology, which have been so meticulously catalogued by Resch.[7] As has been observed, the parallels have at least as much to do with the theological manner of understanding the data as they do with the actual data, such as references of Jesus to his precursor, the virginal conception, the poor welcome accorded to Christ. At each step along the way we are made vividly aware of the impossibility of separating the verification of the facts from the interpretation which gives them their meaning.[8]

Paul

Paul took no interest in the infancy of Jesus. From his very first experience of Christ, on the road to Damascus, it was the resurrected Christ, as related to his passion and death, that Paul encountered. It is only rarely and not without some embarrassment that he refers to the human origin which John calls the Incarnation. But Paul, like Matthew and Luke, presented Jesus as "coming from the line of David" (Rom 1:2; 2 Tm 2:8) and reference is never made to his having a human father. Paul says only "born of woman" (Gal 4:4). Later, we will evaluate these remarkable, albeit implicit, references to the virginal conception (pp. 408-409).

C. AGREEMENT WITH THE EXTRA-BIBLICAL DATA

Secular History

Verifications of the infancy Gospels from secular history are (as for any childhood history) scant. References to the reign of Herod by both evangelists (Mt 2:1 and Lk 1:5), and to the reigns of Archelaus (Mt 2:22), of Augustus and of Quirinius (Lk 2:1-2), offer concurring chronological guideposts. The difficulties which have been raised regarding the census of Quirinius show how fragmentary is our historical information concerning the administrative backgound of the period. They are by no means insurmountable, as Benoit has demonstrated.[9]

Quirinius became governor of Syria in 6 A.D. and presided over the property census which took place when Judea was reduced to the status of a Roman province. (Several historians think that Quirinius could have been given charge of Roman affairs in the Near East some ten years before being named governor of Syria.) The two evangelists locate the birth of Christ at the time of Herod the Great, who died in 4 B.C. (1 B.C. according to another hypothesis). According to this theory, the birth must have taken place earlier.

But a census of persons could have been made as early as the period of Herod the Great, in the wake of his oath of allegiance to the Emperor, according to custom (Josephus, *Jewish Antiquities* 18 and 124). Furthermore, the process of taking the census seems to have been gradual. It was taken every twelve years in Syria, which provides another cross-reference. In describing the census which we are concerned with as the "first" (*prōtē*), Luke might have meant to indicate that it preceded the one which Quirinius had taken as governor of

Syria. Lagrange found a basis for this meaning of the word in Sophocles (*Antigone* 637-638; RB, 1911, 83). This solution, recognized by several grammarians, but rarely followed by exegetes, is nonetheless quite probable.

The census could have taken place in the city of origin. This does not pose any difficulty. It was the rule for censuses in Egypt concerned with regulating family property taxes.

The texts are too fragmentary to allow a reconstruction of the event or to shed light on it. To what extent has Luke, who seems to have known of only one census (Acts 5:37), combined two different censuses, or even put together a whole series of population studies made between the years 6 B.C. and 6 A.D.? To what degree does he reflect little-known aspects of the long and complex process of Roman integration?

The discussion remains open. The mention of the "first census" of Quirinius, inserted as an additional but unnecessary clarification, attests to Luke's concern for exactness. He made inquiries according to the methods of his time. Documents had less importance then than they do today, memory and the spoken word had more. He is not any less reliable for that. It was not through imagination, but by relying upon complex data (not yet mastered in our own day) that he based his account of Christ's birth. His information is justified at least in substance. He rightly discerns in it the plan of God, who established the association of Christ with the "city of David" and was preparing, in a unified world that had become an *oikoumenē*, the spreading of the Gospel. His historical theology is excellently founded. Bossuet did not do better, and we have not sufficient material to know to what extent Luke is accurate.

The critical analysis of the episodes will show us how the portrait of Herod as a cruel, unscrupulous, and clever murderer squares with the historical data.

The Apocryphal Gospels

In their sobriety, the infancy Gospels of Matthew and Luke sharply contrast with the Apocrypha, which multiply the miracles of the infant Jesus.

Even the most noteworthy of them, the *Protoevangelion of James* (mid-second century), which inspired several liturgical feasts, like Mary's nativity and presentation, as well as much Christian iconography, strongly contrasts with the canonical Gospels in its ignorance of the Palestinian milieu and culture and by its gratuitous inventions that are contrary to the customs of that time. It has miracles abounding at the birth of Mary. Her mother does not nurse her at all until she has been purified on the fortieth day. The child's feet are kept from touching the ground until she is brought to the Temple, where she climbs the steps and heads straight for the Holy of Holies, into which the priests bring her. Then there is the marvelous account of the marriage with Joseph, arranged by the priests. Joseph's staff blossoms forth, while those of the other suitors do not. Thus is he chosen as Mary's spouse. At the birth of Jesus, a midwife is present to confirm Mary's virginity after delivery; the birth in turn is the occasion of further miracles. Luke proves himself infinitely more prudent and more sober when he presents Mary in perfect self-control, clothing the child herself before placing him in the manger.

When the *Infancy Gospel of Thomas* takes up the story of the finding in the Temple (2:41-52), it does not maintain Luke's sobriety. The doctors are aghast with wonder at the knowledge of the child:

> And all paid attention to him and marvelled how he, a child, put to silence the elders and teachers of the people, expounding the sections of the law and the parables of the prophets. . . .
>
> But the scribes and Pharisees said [to Mary]: "Are you the mother of this child?" And she said: "I am." And they said to her: "Blessed are you among women, because the Lord has blessed the fruit of your womb [cf. Lk 1:42]; for such glory and such excellence and wisdom we have never seen nor heard" (*New Testament Apocrypha*, E.Hennecke, ed. by W. Schneemelcher, tr. by R. Mc L.Wilson, Philadelphia, 1963, 398-399).

Luke never indulges in such triumphalism, which even Flavius Josephus used, recounting his own adolescence:

> While still a mere boy, about fourteen years old [51-52 A.D.], I won universal applause for my love of letters; insomuch that the chief priests and the leading men of the city used to come to me for

precise information on some particular in our ordinances (*The Life*, 2 no. 9, tr. by H. St. J. Thackeray, Loeb Classical Library, Cambridge, 1956, I, 5).

Luke does not even accord Jesus an intellect exceeding that of childhood, as Flavius Josephus records for Moses: His growth in understanding was not in line with his growth in stature (*hēlikia*), but far outran the measure of his years (*Jewish Antiquities*, II, 9, 6 Loeb Classical Library IV, 265).

The Arabic infancy Gospel pushes the triumphalist extrapolations even further. To a scribe's question, "Hast thou read the books?" Jesus answers that he knows everything:

> Both the books and the things contained in the books. And he explained the books, and the law, and the precepts, and the statutes, and the mysteries, which are contained in the books of the prophets—things which the understanding of no creature attains to ("Arabic Infancy Gospel," *The Ante-Nicene Fathers,* tr. by A. Walker, Grand Rapids, 1951, vol. VIII, 415).

To a master astronomer, he responds with the same assurance, telling him:

> The number of the spheres, and of the heavenly bodies, their natures and operations; their opposition; their aspect, triangular, square, and sextile; their course, direct and retrograde; the twenty-fourths, and sixtieths of twenty-fourths; and other things beyond the reach of reason (*ibid*, chap. 51).

To a philosopher "versed in medicine," he responds in similar fashion:

> [He] explained to him physics and metaphysics, hyperphysics and hypophysics, the powers likewise and humors of the body, and the effects of the same; also the number of members and bones, of veins, arteries, and nerves; also the effect of heat and dryness, of cold and moisture, and what these give rise to; what was the operation of the soul upon the body, and its perceptions and powers; what was the operation of speech, of anger, of desire; lastly, their conjunction and disjunction and other things beyond the reach of any created intellect. Then that philosopher rose up, and adored

> the Lord Jesus, and said: "O Lord, from this time I will be thy disciple and slave" (*ibid.*, chap. 52, 63).

The contrast between this amazing prodigy and the humble child of Luke 2, shows more clearly than any commentary the difference between fiction and historical realism.

The *Infancy Gospel of Thomas* attributes to Jesus in his childhood a number of childish and magical miracles. These are enlarged upon in the Syriac, Arabic, and Armenian versions.[10] Jesus makes clay birds to amuse himself, then makes them fly away. He alters some furniture which Joseph makes for Herod's palace which is found to be too short. He heals many sick, raises the dead, and so on.

Had Luke been an inventor of fiction (*theologoumena*), the tendency of infancy narratives to make some intimations or prefigurations of adulthood would have led him to recount at least one cure or miracle. He did nothing of the sort. This indicates the degree of his seriousness and of his concern for historicity. It is this honesty which led him to portray the poverty of the infant Son of God, an unexpected, undreamed of marvel, revelatory of the Gospel itself. (It is this that was unfathomable, and not the knowledge or the marvels which the Apocrypha multiplied.)

We are now in a position to evaluate the data contained in the infancy Gospels: first of all, the genealogy, which allows us to lay direct hold on the historical painstaking labor of the evangelists; then, the various episodes.

IV
THE GENEALOGIES

The genealogies of Matthew 1:1-16 and Luke 3:23-38 have sometimes been considered fictitious, given their symbolic schematization and their considerable differences. We will evaluate these two traits. They will lead us to examine the sources, the documentary support and the historicity of both genealogies. Since their historicity is inseparable from their meaning, we will conclude by attemping to evaluate the meaning of the genealogies.

A. TWO TREATMENTS

The synoptic table of the two genealogies provided here will help to clarify the points made in this chapter.

The two genealogies are placed differently: Matthew situates his at the very beginning of the infancy Gospel (1:1-16); Luke's comes after and outside the infancy narrative (3:23-38). Matthew's genealogy descends from Abraham to Joseph; Luke's ascends, from Joseph to Adam and to God. But this difference is relative, since Matthew begins with an ascending resume of three fundamental links ("The genealogy of Jesus Christ, the son of David, the son of Abraham," 1:1), before descending again from Abraham to Jesus.

The linking of the generations is expressed differently: Matthew constructs as many sentences as there are generations, with a rhythmic repetition of the verb "begot."[1] Luke avoids all sentences and verbs. The name of each ancestor is connected to the preceding one merely by the article in the genitive. This was one advantage of the ascending route. Thus his genealogy is nearly half the length of Matthew's, although it contains nearly twice the names (seventy-eight instead of forty-two). It also dispenses with any explanatory clauses. This uninterrupted chain unfolds between two affirmations of divine sonship which introduce and close the genealogy:

The Two Genealogies of the Gospel: Mt and Lk Synopsis

This synopsis of the genealogies of Mt and Lk shows:
1) The names of ancestors: 17 are common to both.
2) The main *Biblical references* concerning the ancestral figures. Others are drawn from non-biblical sources or archives.
3) The *differences* and *missing linkages*.
4) The *septenary rhythm*:
— Matthew: 3 series of 7 x 2 or 14 x 3 = 42
— Luke: 1 series of 7 x 2 plus 3 of 7 x 3 = 21
Total: 77

Matthew's *Enumeration* is descending (left-hand column), while Luke's is ascending (right-hand column).
To facilitate comparison with Mt., we have put a descending enumeration to the left of Luke's column.

[Spellings of proper names have been conformed to the English version of the Jerusalem Bible — tr.]

Matthew 1:1-16

1	Abraham: Gn 11:26; 25:11
2	Isaac: 1 Ch 1:34
3	Jacob: 1 Ch 1:34
4	Judah, by Tamar: 1 Ch 2:1-8

Luke 3:23-38

	0	GOD	77	11 x 7
	1	Adam: Gn 2-3	76	
	2	Seth: Gn 4:25	75	
	3	Enos: Gn 4:26	74	
	4	Cainan = Kenan: Gn 5:9-14; 1 Ch 1:2	73	
	5	Maleleel = Mahalalel: Gn 5:12-17; 1 Ch 1:1	72	
	6	Iaret = Jared: Gn 5:15-19; 1 Ch 1:2	71	
1 x 7	7	Enoch: Gn 5:21-24	70	10 x 7
	8	Methuselah: Gn 5:25-27	69	
	9	Lamech: Gn 5:28-31	68	
	10	Noah: Gn 5:32	67	
	11	Shem: Gn 5:32; 11:10	66	
	12	Arphaxad: Gn 10:22-24; 11:10-13; 1 Ch 1:17	65	
	13	Cainan II: Gn 11:12; 1 Ch 1:8, 24 LXX	64	
2 x 7	14	Sala = Shelah: Gn 11:12-15	63	9 x 7
	15	Eber: Gn 10:24; 11:14; 1 Ch 1:18, 25	62	
	16	Phalec = Peleg: Gn 10:25; 1 Ch 1:19	61	
	17	Ragau = Reu: Gn 11:18-21; 1 Ch 1:25	60	
	18	Serouch = Serug: Gn 11:20-23; 1 Ch 1:26	59	
	19	Nachor = Nahor: Gn 11:22-25; 1 Ch 1:26	58	
	20	Thara = Terah: Gn 11:24-26; 1 Ch 1:26	57	
3 x 7	21	Abraham: see opposite = Mt 1:1	56	8 x 7
	22	Isaac	55	
	23	Jacob	54	
	24	Judah	53	

	5	Perez: Gn 38:27-30
	6	Hezron: 1 Ch 2:9
	7	Ram: 1 Ch 2:9
	8	Amminadab: 1 Ch 2:10
	9	Nahshon: 1 Ch 2:10
	10	Salmon, by Rahab: Jos 2
	11	Boaz, by Ruth: Rt 1-4 and *ibid.*
	12	Obed: 1 Ch 2:12
	13	Jesse: 1 Ch 2:12
2 x 7	14	DAVID, by Bathsheba: 2 S 11-12, *ibid.*
	15	Solomon: 1 Ch 3:5
	16	Rehoboam: 1 Ch 3:10
	17	Abijah: 1 Ch 3:10
	18	Asa: 1 Ch 3:10
	19	Jahoshaphat: 1 Ch 3:10
	20	Joram: 1 Ch 3:11
	Omissions	1 Ch 3:11-12 Ahaziah 842 Joash 2 Ch 22:11 Amasias 800-783
	21	Azariah: 1 Ch 3:12; 2 K 15:1
	22	Jothan: 1 Ch 3:12
	23	Ahaz: 1 Ch 3:13
	24	Hezekiah: 1 Ch 3:13
	25	Manasseh: 1 Ch 3:13
	26	Amon
	27	Josiah [*Omission of Jehoiakim*: 2 K 23:34]

	25	Perez	52	
	26	Hezron	51	
	27	Arni	50	
4 x 7	28	Admin	49	7 x 7
	29	Amminadab	48	
	30	Nahshon	47	
	31	Sala	46	
	32	Boaz	45	
	33	Obed	44	
	34	Jesse	43	
5 x 7	35	DAVID	42	6 x 7
	36	Nathan: 2 K 5:14; 1 Ch 3:5; 14:4	41	
	37	Mattatha [19 *linkages of obscure descent, unknown to the Bible*]	40	
	38	Menna	39	
	39	Melea	38	
	40	Eliakim	37	
	41	Jonam	36	
6 x 7	42	Joseph I	35	5 x 7
	43	Judah	34	
	44	Symeon	33	
	45	Levi	32	
	46	Matthat I	31	
	47	Jorim	30	
	48	Eliezer	29	
7 x 7	49	Joshua	28	4 x 7
	50	Er	27	
	51	Elmadam	26	

4 x 7	28	"Jechoniah and his brothers": 1 Ch 3:16-17 in whom Solomon's line becomes extinct (according to Masson)
	29	Salathiel: 1 Ch 3:17
	30	Zerubbabel: 1 Ch 3:19
		Omissions: 9 *linkages of obscure descent follow*:
	31	Abiud
	32	Eliakim
	33	Azor
	34	Zadok
	35	Achim
	36	Eliud
	37	Eleazar
		Linkages omitted according to J. Masson
	38	Matthan
	39	Jacob
	40	Joseph, husband of
	41	Mary of whom was born
6 x 7	42	JESUS who is called CHRIST

	52	Cosam	25	
	53	Addi	24	
	54	Melchi I	23	
	55	Neri	22	
8 x 7	56	Salathiel = Shealtiel: 1 Ch 3:17, etc.	21	3 x 7
	57	Zerubbabel: 1 Ch 3:17-19 + Ezr/Neh/Hg 1:2	20	
	58	Rhesa [16 *links of obscure descent*]	19	
	59	Joanan	18	
	60	Joda	17	
	61	Joseph II	16	
	62	Semein	15	
9 x 7	63	Mattathias I	14	2 x 7
	64	Maath	13	
	65	Naggai	12	
	66	Esli	11	
	67	Nahum	10	
	68	Amos	9	
	69	Mattathias II	8	
10 x 7	70	Joseph III	7	1 x 7
	71	Jannai	6	
	72	Melchi II	5	
	73	Levi	4	
	74	Matthat	3	
	75	Heli	2	
	76	Joseph ("as was supposed": 3:24)	1	
11 x 7	77	JESUS	Outside the count: 0	

> Jesus had been baptized and was praying. . . A voice came from heaven, "You are my Son, today I have begotten you" (citation of Ps 2:7; Lk 3:22).
> Jesus, beginning [his work, *archomenos*] at about thirty years of age, was the son, it was thought, of Joseph, of Heli [i.e., in reality], of God (Lk 3:23).

This inclusion between God's word, "You are my son," and the conclusion, "son of God," invites an understanding of these intermediary links (Lk 3:23b-38a) as an extended parenthesis referring to the designation: Son of God.

This is a suggestion and not a thesis. The suggestion prompted by the inclusion is reinforced on two accounts. The genealogical principle, "the sons of the sons are considered sons," (see below, Part III, ch. 4, n. 18) takes on a striking application if one compares the two ends of this long continuous chain. On the other hand, it is clear that Adam is only figuratively presented as "son of God" (the last word of the genealogy, 3:38) and that these words are literally true of Christ, the first link of this long ascending lineage.

One could debate the modalities of this meaning, but before the mention of the putative descent from Joseph, Luke strongly affirms three times (1:32, 35, 43) that Jesus is the Son of God, by a claim far superior to Adam's, one that is different, exclusive, a title which the heavenly Father declares at the very threshold of the genealogy.

The number of links differ: forty-two from Abraham to Jesus, according to Matthew; seventy-seven from Joseph to God, according to Luke. Their calculations do not lend themselves to a clear comparison because of dissymmetry: Matthew mentions (and counts) Mary and Jesus in his reckoning. Luke does not mention Mary in his genealogy, and does not count Jesus as the first link: he places him outside the series, which is quite in agreement with the hypothesis of the "parenthesis."

Luke extends the genealogy back to the origin of humanity,[2] which gives us an additional twenty links. The remaining fifteen are added by him within the period common to both genealogies, producing a greater number of generations. From Abraham to Joseph, there are forty, according to Matthew, and fifty-six according to Luke, only seventeen of whom are identical. From Abraham to David fourteen are the same, except for a fifteenth, Admin, whom Luke adds right in the middle. With Zerubbabel and Shealtiel (2) and Joseph (1), the total is seventeen. If Jesus is included in this calculation (Matthew includes him; Luke does not), the total would be eighteen.[3]

B. FASCINATING SEPTENARY RHYTHM

The detailed breakdown of the links is not without some problems, not because of the insignificant variants of some manuscripts,[4] but for reasons of interpretation. Analysis of the septenary rhythm which characterizes both genealogies allows us to clear up these difficulties. The two genealogies are given their structure by the number 7 which reappears in different series in its multiples (7 x 2 or 7 x 3):

Matthew:	3 x (7 x 2)		42
Luke:	1 x (2 x 7)	14	
	3 x (3 x 7)	63	
		Total in Luke:	77

Matthew: 3 x 14 = 42

Matthew openly states the number of names in his genealogy, and he does it with some emphasis in verse 17; 3 x 14:

> 14 from Abraham to David,
> 14 from David to the deportation to Babylon,
> 14 from the deportation to Babylon to Christ.

This makes a total of forty-two. But let us verify this. The count is accurate for the first two series; both David and Jechoniah are in fact the fourteenth of their respective series. David symbolizes the foundation of the royal line, and Jechoniah, its downfall. In the third series, however, from Shealtiel to Joseph, there are only twelve links. The fourteenth is easy to identify: it is Christ himself. He has, according to 1:17, David's number, fourteen, a set figure—"fourteen from the Babylonian exile to Christ."

Where is the thirteenth? It is so hopelessly missing that certain exegetes have accused Matthew of an error in calculation. But he could not be mistaken about a figure which plays such an essential part in his genealogy. It would have been easy for him to have added names to this series, for which Luke has twenty (six more covering the same duration).

Others have tried to come up with the missing link in the second set, before the Babylonian captivity, where Matthew has omitted Jehoiakim. This king, who persecuted Jeremiah, was the father of Jechoniah (Jer 24:1; 27:20; 28:4; 29:2; Est 2:6; 1 Chr 3:16-24, also called Coniah: Jer 22:24-29; 37:1 and Jehoiachin: 2 Kgs 24:6-15; 2 Chr 36:8ff and 2 Kgs 25:27-30; Jer 52:31-32). His name, Jehoiakim (Greek, Ioakim: 1 Chr 3:15; 2 Kgs 23:36 and 24:6; 2 Chr 36:5), looks a great deal like his son's, and it has been said that this could account for its omission. But this ingenious solution changes the structure of the received text, articulated in Matthew 1:17. It necessitates counting Jechoniah twice (which Matthew does not do with any name, even David) and placing him in another series, thereby destroying the symmetry that contrasts him to David. Those who attempted to re-establish this link have realized that they were falling under the accusation of "violating all the rules of criticism" (Masson, 50), for there is a great risk involved in rewriting a text with no textual support.[5]

The solution, then, should be sought in the text itself. It is necessary simply to count all the proper names mentioned by Matthew. After Joseph, the twelfth, and before Jesus, the fourteenth, Mary is the thirteenth, as A. Paul has noticed (1968, 26-28).

One hesitates to draw this conclusion, as women had no place at all in the genealogies of that time. They were not considered as "begetting," nor did they count as a "generation." It was reported merely that they conceived and gave birth; at most, that they begot for the husband, and by way of reference to him (cf. Lk 1:13, as we explored above).

In this instance, Matthew is unusual and differs from Luke. Though the latter has brought the women of the Gospel into broad daylight, he does not, strangely enough, breathe a word about Mary in his genealogy (3:23-38): it is a genealogy without a mother. He who has spoken better of Mary than anyone else (Lk 1:26-56; 2:5-7) does not name her at all in this context, and omits any reference to her lineage, in contrast with Elizabeth, whose priestly purity he mentions in 1:5, and with Anna, whose ancestry he gives in 2:36.

Why then does Matthew, who seems more inclined to masculine prejudices, give Mary a key position? And why does he include four other women, Tamar, Rahab, Ruth and "the wife of Uriah," Bathsheba, who became the wife of David? (The questions are related.) Why has he chosen these women and not Sarah, nor Rebecca, nor Leah, nor others who figure more prominently in the history of the origins of the chosen people, in accordance with Jewish tradition?

It has been said, following St. Jerome (*In Mt*, 9 PL 26, 22), that Matthew chooses sinful women. However, this is not the case with Ruth, nor does Jewish tradition recognize Tamar as such. She disguised herself as a prostitute so as to take up with Judah, her father-in-law (Gn 38:15-30). She did this in order to raise up posterity to him, to ensure the continuation of the dynastic line. Judah acknowledged this, saying, "She is more righteous than I" (Gn 38:26). Jewish tradition glorifies her holiness with amazing excess and insistence:

> Holy Tamar sanctified the divine name; she who desired a holy offspring deceived but did a holy work.[6]

Rahab the prostitute is hailed as a heroine (Jos 2:1-21; 6:17, 22-25): she is incorporated into the people of the promise because of the immense service that she rendered to Israel. As for Bathsheba, since she was only a woman, she was helpless when the king sent the masters of his harem to fetch her (2 Sm 11:3). The sin was unilaterally masculine. This misogynous slogan "sinful women" turns out to be misleading.

Should we conclude that Matthew has retained the foreigners? This is the case with Tamar, Rahab, and Ruth. The first two were Canaanites and the third a Moabitess. Bathsheba, whose own origin is not at all clear, was the wife of Uriah, the Hittite. We have here a common trait which fits well with the universalist approach of Matthew 1-2.

A. Paul sees irregularity as the common point. This he justifies in the case of Ruth, from Jewish traditions.[7] In this perspective, these women prepared the ground for an understanding of the apparently irregular position of Mary, the virgin mother (Mt 1:16-17).

A fourth motif, however, (which does not exclude the preceding one) seems to be no less important. Each of the four women cited played an extraordinary, personal role in the history of Israel and, more specifically, in the history of the dynasty.[8]

Tamar prevented the tribe of Judah from becoming extinct. It was announced that the Messiah would descend from it, according to Genesis 49:10. She had married Judah's oldest son, who died without an heir. The Law was that his brother should marry the widow in order to secure a posterity (Dt 25:5-10; Mt 22:24). This the second son did. However, he displeased God and died. Judah, now the father of two dead men, did not wish to give his third son to Tamar, fearing superstitiously that he too would die. In this he was disobeying the Law. Deprived of her statutory right, Tamar resorted to a strategy: she disguised herself as a prostitute and seduced Judah himself, who was still without descendants, so as to raise up posterity to him as required by the Law of God, the messianic posterity already promised to his line (Gn 49:10). She was performing her duty; whence the unreserved praise which Jewish tradition accords her.

Rahab, who declared her faith in Yahweh (Jos 2:9-10) and received the spies from Israel, thus secured the entry of the people into the Promised Land, which had been hitherto blocked by the fortress of Jericho. She was incorporated into the people of God for having opened the gates of the kingdom.[9]

Ruth, the Moabitess, followed her mother-in-law to Israel, and married the one ordained for her by the Law in order to raise up children to her dead husband by marrying a near relative, Boaz (Ru 3:2). Thus Obed, the grandfather of David, was born.[10]

As for Bathsheba, the importance of her dynastic role is not in reference to the birth of Solomon, but to her intercession with David that he become (in the place of Adoniah, the older son) the heir promised by God, according to the prophecy of Nathan (2 Sm 7:8-16).

Matthew, who usually gives women such a marginal role, mentions these four at the beginning of his Gospel that they might prefigure the unexpected and different role of Mary: she conceives, and it is a peculiar conception, but it ensures the dynastic fulfillment. God alone is the principle of this human peculiarity, by which God puts all things back into order: this genealogy, filled with sinners (male and female, above all, kings), directs history toward the salvation of mankind.

Was Mary a Descendant of David?

Mary's Davidic ancestry has been eruditely defended by Denise Judant, *Maria, figlia di Levi o figlia de Davide*, in *Renovatio* 2 (1975) pp. 302-329, 451-471; *Marie descendait-elle de David?* in *La Pensée Catholique,* no. 175, pp. 15-34 and no. 176, pp. 39-60; J. Masson, *Jésus*, (1982), pp. 484-498. Cf. J. deAldama, *Maria en la patristica*, Madrid, *BAC* (1970), pp. 78-80.

Arguments "Pro"

According to the biblical texts, Jesus is descended from David, without being the son of Joseph (Heb 7:14; Rev 5:5 and 22:16; Jesus is from the family of David. He is even *ek spermatos* as Rom 1:5, 2 Tim 2:8, and Jn 7:42 put it).

However, *sperma* does not have the biological sense of its English equivalent. It means "posterity," "lineage," "descent" in a very broad sense: according to Levirate law, a brother would marry the widow of his brother in order to raise up a posterity to him (*sperma*, as per Mt 22:24-25; Mk 12:19-22; Lk 20:28). The sense is juridical, not biological. Thirty-six uses of the word in the Bible demonstrate the broadness of the meaning; Rom 9:7-8 seems at first to accentuate the biological sense, but the juridical sense is immediately reestablished.

St. Augustine's argument was a biblical one (*Contra Faustum* 9, 10, PL 42, 171-172: "Christ was of the seed of David according to the flesh. Now he was born of the Virgin Mary without the assistance of a man, thus... Mary belonged to the family of David"). The syllogism was foreign to the Apostle Paul; he confined himself to citing an (established) ancient profession of faith, coming from Judeo-Christian milieux (note from TOB on 2 Tim 2:8, p. 648; cf. Acts 2:20 citing Ps 132:11). These texts only reformulate the messianic title "Son of David," which the crowds recognized as pertaining to Jesus. They concern the official, legal descent owing to adoption by Joseph (Mt 1:18, 25), but in no way focus on the biological connections, nor on the virginal modality.

In the patristic literature, since the second century, Mary has been presented as the daughter of David: the *Protoevangelion of James* and other apocryphals, Ignatius of Antioch (Ep 18, 2; ed. Sources Chrétiennes, p. 119, Trall. 9, 1 and above all, Smyrn. 1, 1), Justin, Irenaeus, Origen, Tertullian, Eusebius (who refer to the previous traditions), Augustine, and so on. But this ancient affirmation merely confirms the use of the title "Son of David." Origen, Aphraates, and Ephrem justify it by referring to Mary the clause that

Lk 1:27 uses in reference to Joseph, "from David's lineage" an exegetically worthless transposition.

There is an argument based on "appropriateness": Num 36:6-9 prescribed that young women marry within the tribe of their father. Nevertheless, as D. Judant recongizes (p. 24), the NT (Lk 1:5 and 36) implies that there might have been (within Mary's family) "a marriage between members of different tribes," either because Mary "may have been from the tribe of Levi, or, being from the tribe of Judah, she may have had a male or female ancestor who had married a member of the family of Levi (. . .). In any case, the old law forbidding marriage between different tribes (. . .) allowed some exceptions at the very least."

Another patristic tradition, influenced perhaps by the *Testament of the Twelve Patriarchs* (ed. Charles, p. 294), and the Qumran texts (*Rules of the Community* 9, 10, 11; *Damascus Document* 7, 18, 21, etc.) posits that Mary descended from both the tribe of Judah and the tribe of Levi (Hippolytus, Epiphanius, Ambrose, etc.).

Reconstructions

Some attempts have been made to reconstruct the genealogy of Joseph and Mary. We will not discuss the hypothesis of Annus of Viterbo (c. 1490) who made the Lucan genealogy apply to Mary. It is not maintained by anyone today. Neither will we take in H. A. Blair's theory (in *Stud evangel*, 2 *TUU* 87, 1954, 149-154) in which the Joseph of Mt 1:16 would seem to be the father of Mary; it is a desperate attempt to establish Davidic descent by a biological route. The attempts by Julius Africanus (3rd century), recounted by Eusebius (*Church History* 1 7) and of John Damascene (*De fide orthodoxa*, book 4, p. 14, PG 1156-1157) do not agree with each other; J. Masson makes use of them only by first rectifying them. He takes up the proposition of John Damascene according to which Joachim, the father of Mary, according to the *Protoevangelion*, descended from Levi (Joseph's third ancestor in Luke's ascending genealogy) in the following five generations:
1. Heli (Lk 3:25), 2. Panther, 3. Barpanther, 4. Joachim, 5. Mary.

Objections

First, this "information" is rather late (8th century) and is of uncertain origin. Second, the name *Panther* could well have come down from the legend of the Roman Legionnaire whom Celsus calumniously claimed to have been the father of Jesus (see below, p. 406). Third, the objections to Mary's Davidic descent stem from the infancy gospels themselves: Mt 1 and Lk 1 are silent regarding Mary's lineage, and this seems to be because they were not able to call her a descendant of David. Had this been possible, it would have solved their difficult redaction problem, and they would have referred to it, as they were always seeking qualification.

This is particularly clear in Luke: his genealogy is completely silent about Mary, despite the importance he accords her in chapter 1:26-56; cf. 2:5-7, 19, 34-35, 48, 71). At the threshold of the two parallel introductions, where he presents the parents of John and Jesus (Lk 1:5-6 and 1:26-27, respectively), Luke is precise about the priestly lineage not only of Zechariah, but also of Elizabeth, "of the daughters of Aaron." By striking contrast, the parallel presentation of Joseph and Mary (1:26-27) is specific only about Joseph's Davidic ancestry (although he is merely a secondary character in this pericope), and is silent concerning Mary's ancestry. This is so astonishing that grammatically unacceptable solutions have proliferated since the time of Origen in attempts to attribute the expression "from the line of David" to the mother of Jesus. The silence of Luke 1:26-27 creates a dissymmetry that is all the more remarkable since Luke later mentions Mary's blood tie to the priestly line of Elizabeth (1:36). By mentioning this blood relationship, he seems to wish to respond to the contemporary expectation of a messiah rising up from both the line of David and of Aaron. Luke tries to satisfy this double requirement by mentioning a priestly affinity without being precise about it. But above all, he rejects the interpretation by which John (who is from the pure priestly family) could be seen as the Aaronic messiah, stressing the fact that he was only a precursor (1:17 and 76), and not the messiah that the Johannites (encountered in Acts 18:25 and 19:3-4) proclaimed him to be.

The two evangelists justify Jesus' descent, without any recourse to Mary, by invoking only the adoptive paternity of Joseph (very explicit in Matthew, implicit but clear in Luke 1:26; 2:4-5, 27, 33, 41, 48-49) and the birth of Jesus in David's city of origin (Bethlehem, Mt 2:1 and Lk 2:4-5, 11). Seeing that they sought to multiply Jesus' ties to David, including this minor topographical connection, they would have been happy to produce a maternal bond if there had been one.

Conclusion

The hypothesis of a Davidic filiation with regard to Mary is foreign to the two evangelists; indeed, it is to a certain extent ruled out by Luke.

The two evangelists have gone beyond the Davidic label which was so important for their contemporaries. What is essential to them is that Jesus, the Son of God, is messiah by a divine and transcendent title (Lk 1:32, 35; Mt 1:23), anointed by the Holy Spirit himself (Mt 1:16 and 18; cf. Lk 1:35).

Moreover, Matthew seems to have thought that the sin deeply engraved in the lineage (most importantly in the royal line of David and his descendants, from which he has eliminated the three links springing from Athalia), demanded a genealogical distancing from the messiah; his ancestry is not at all biological, but legal: the legal paternity is juridically prevalent, acccording to the received values of the time.

Nothing is truly lost in Mary's not being biologically the daughter of David. The rigor with which the evangelists have avoided this easy solution gives a new indication of their exactitude. They do not invent in order to appease current expectations, as those who came after them did. On the contrary, they accepted the paradoxes which caused the difficulty. This honesty led them to a great theological profundity.

This explanation may seem quite satisfactory, but Matthew does not in fact count the four women of the genealogy, not only because of the genealogical norms of the period, but because they are counted as one with their spouses who beget: each couple forms one link, one generation.

How is it that Mary is counted? The case of Mary is different and Matthew perceived it as such. He had to name Joseph, according to the tables of the official genealogies which he had gathered, for the sake of form and credibility, since Joseph was a biological heir of the dynasty, and it was by this title that the crowds had greeted Jesus as son of David. Joseph assumed this role under the rubric of adoptive paternity which had been entrusted to him from on high, as Matthew reveals in the second pericope (1:18-25). In the genealogy, legal paternity (by adoption or levirate) prevailed over biological paternity. But Joseph is not described as a begetter. At this point, Matthew breaks the genealogical stereotype and only speaks of the generation in the passive with the meaning we have seen: "Joseph, the husband of Mary, from whom was begotten Jesus, who is called Christ" (1:16).

Matthew does not present Mary as a begetter or a dynast—in his cultural milieu these roles were strictly a male prerogative. Neither does he present her as a member of the Davidic line: this would have been foreign both to his information and his perspective. Luke dismisses this solution even more specifically. Literal-minded piety very quickly improvised on this theme, abandoning the historical and theological exactitude of the two evangelists (see the special note on pp. 342-345).

Matthew mentions Mary in a singular role which characterizes the singularity of the "generation"—a role of central importance at the center of salvation history. He includes her in his calculation in order to affirm the bewildering fact (which was scarcely credible to his contemporaries) that Mary was the sole human origin of Christ—his sole biological origin, as we would say today. But he mentions her with every respect for the established norms, which Christ came not to abolish but to fulfill (5:17). The norms do not need to be reexamined in the light of this exceptional case. Matthew's formulation is truly remarkable.

Matthew does not say that Mary begot Christ; when he mentions her, it is less as the biological origin of Christ than as a sign and witness of God's transcendent action (1:18 and 20). In this capacity he clarifies her role, without telling us anything of her person, her grace, her feelings, or her merits, in contrast to Luke 1. He presents her as a sign of God and sole human origin of Christ, not by stating this explicitly, but by bringing it out in a significant manner.

According to Matthew, Jesus was begotten by God. He could not have another father. God alone is the principle of his very singular human origin.

Matthew takes care not to make of God a human begetter, although he says that Jesus is "begotten" (in the passive, on three occasions: 1:16, 20; 2:1, always with the verb *gennaō*). He attributes the principle of this generation to the Spirit. But Matthew avoids all causal terminology. He only formulates a relation of origin by the particle *ek* ("sprung from"). For him, Mary is not the spouse of God, nor of the Holy Spirit.

Matthew leaves the place of the begetter blank, so as to refer Christ only to his Father, God. This is done, not while speaking of his miraculous human origin, but in an entirely different context, on the occasion of the flight into Egypt (2:15 in reference to Hos 11:1), then at the baptism by John (3:17; cf. 4:3, 6 and above all 14:33; 17:5).

It is more as a human sign of this exclusive divine paternity than as the human and biological origin of Christ that Mary is mentioned and counted in Matthew's genealogy in a singular way and for profoundly theological reasons. She is counted as the second last of the fourteen links between the two begotten non-begetters; Joseph, the legal father, and Christ, the last link. She is another unusual link (disconnected from Joseph, referred to God alone, 1:18-20), indispensable to the manifestation of a mystery that bewilders the wisdom of the sages and the order of this world.

Luke: 7 x 11 = 77 + 1

Luke does not make an explicit calculation, but he has given 77 links, and his genealogy is obviously divided into groups of 7: names of special value or significance are situated at multiples of 7; first of all, those which Matthew highlighted by placing them as 1st and 14th:

—David (Lk 3:31)	no. 42 (6 x 7)
—Abraham (Lk 3:34)	no. 56 (8 x 7)

But also:

—Joseph II	no. 7 (1 x 7)
—Shealtiel, at the time of the Babylonian captivity	no. 21 (3 x 7)
—Jesus, the ancestor of Jesus	no. 28 (4 x 7)
—Joseph III	no. 35 (5 x 7)
—Admin (which Luke adds)	no. 49 (7 x 7)
—Enoch	no. 70 (10 x 7)
—God	no. 77 (11 x 7)[11]

Among the 10 names situated at the multiples of 7, only two do not offer remarkable peculiarities: Shela in 9 x 7 and Mattathiah in 2 x 7. Yet it is clear that Luke draws attention to this last name, which abounds in his genealogy whether it be under this form, Mattathiah, in the 8th and 14th positions (in ascending order), or under derivative forms: Matthat (in the 3rd and 31st positions), Mattatha (in the 40th position), or Maath (in the 13th position), just before Mattathiah. This proliferation is not artificial. It seems to be due to the fact that certain names reappear in certain families by tradition. Masson noted the presence of "Davidic" names between Nathan and Neri in the Lucan genealogy.

This septenary ordering is obvious because of the names which it highlights. It is coherent and conforms to the gematric rhythms of that period. It confirms that the first link, Jesus, must not be counted. The genealogy clearly sets him apart. At the same time, it distances him from Joseph, by the sentence concerning his beginnings and his being thirty years old (Lk 3:23), while the other links of the genealogy are mentioned only by their name; and by the insertion of "it was thought," which relativizes his bond with Joseph.

Thus it is Joseph that is the key link in Luke's chain. Jesus is positioned outside the series, at the starting point, undoubtedly to manifest his transcendence and his identity with his source and at the end (3:38) of this genealogy, which acts as a chain connecting these two mentions of the divine sonship. It seems significant that the last septenary step before God, Enoch, is the one whom God took at the end of his days (Gn 5:24). Whatever the case may be with these last two observations, Luke has certainly reckoned in the manner we described.

This is easily verified: if one tries to count differently, placing Jesus in the first position, the well-cadenced construction breaks down. Abraham, David, and the others lose their septenary place. It is strange how good exegetes, beginning with F. Prat, have fallen into this trap. But as he indeed saw the necessity of placing Abraham, Enoch, and God in a position that would be a multiple of seven, Prat eliminated Admin so as to regain a link. Fitzmyer takes the same point of departure more coherently, but breaks the genealogical rhythm in such a way that David (#43), Abraham (#57), and Enoch (#71) lose their rhythmical position and are assigned numbers that are insignificant for the accepted norms of gematry: none of the three numbers is used in the Bible. Instead, their real position in Luke corresponds to numbers which frequently hold some significance: 42, 56, and, above all, 70.

Confirmation

If one wishes to read this genealogy of Luke in descending order, a surprising problem surfaces: in order that the important figures (Enoch, Abraham, and David) find their septenary place, it is necessary, that the first (and transcendent) link, namely God, *not* be counted.[12] If God is given the first position, we fall back again into numerical and gematrial chaos. Was this inverted descending order calculated, intended, perceived by the author of the genealogy (Luke or his source)? Not necessarily. He chose the ascending order. It is not evident that he also thought about a descending order which is simply symmetrical. If the septenary rhythms reappear here, according to the same rule, it could simply be that holding to the laws of numerical ordering necessitates what we would call today a "zero link" being placed at the beginning of a cadenced series (in both the ascending and descending direction) so that the concluding element of each series finds its proper place (in this instance a multiple of seven).[13] Furthermore, those skilled in gematry, which was in widespread use in that period, would have been familiar with the rhythmical and other, more subtle properties of figures. This double effect, then, is not purely accidental. It could be the secondary consequence of a well-conceived ordering whose symmetry allows for all kinds of coherent and ordered schematizations.

The author of the genealogy did not consider the "calculations" as starting from the number zero, which did not exist in the numerical system of that time. But he considered Jesus, the first in the ascending order, as a link outside the series, as forming by himself a transcendent level. Thus the eleven series of seven are completed by a twelfth element of fundamental importance at the starting point: Jesus Christ, the Son of God. This starting point of the ascending genealogy is the eschatological destination, the last link. This twelfth element was important in the culture of that time: eleven, in effect, was not a significant number.

2 Baruch 53-74 divided world history into eleven periods: the twelfth was the messianic time. As the non-chronological terminus, Jesus occupies precisely this position in the genealogy. He is outside the series as the inaugurator of an absolutely new era, a new genesis, according to the symbolism of Matthew 1:1 and 18.

This ordering agrees well with Luke's predilection (especially in Luke 1-2) for the numbers seven and twelve.[14]

In spite of accidents in the manuscript tradition and various exegetical hazards, a numerical principle of organization in Luke's genealogy was recognized very early, notably by St. Augustine and the Cappadocians.[15]

It is clear that the genealogies of Matthew and Luke are both based on the number 7, organized in binary and ternary series—an explicit reckoning in Matthew and an implicit one in Luke which highlights the key characters.[16]

This schematization seems to form an objection to historicity: it might be said that the genealogies are artificial rather than historical. Have not the numbers determined a priori the construction of the two genealogies? Are they not a fictitious display of this symbolism?

We would contest this on two counts. First, the number 14, whose fundamental character we will examine, was not at all taken into consideration by the gematry of the period, as Brown observes (1977,

80-81). Second, this number 14 is a datum which both evangelists have drawn from the same source: the Bible.

If we count the generations mentioned by the Bible between Abraham and David (the fundamental series where we find the father of the Chosen People and King David, whose descendant is the Messiah) it contains exactly fourteen links.[17]

In making this calculation, Matthew recognized a posteriori the number for David and on this basis organized the remainder of his genealogy. It is a historical basis in the sense that it is documented and that Matthew has strictly respected the traditional documentation. This does not indicate a precise and exhaustive historicity according to our modern rules, but a serious reference to the documents best attested to by the tradition.

The fourteen links that the Bible mentions between Abraham and David are not a complete listing: there are necessarily more than two generations between Salmon (Sala, according to Lk 3:32: cf. 1 Chr 2:11; Ru 4:20), at the time of Joshua, and Jesse, the father of David, about two centuries later (i.e., from 1200 to the beginning of the year 1000).

Matthew was fully aware of this, but he made no attempt to compensate for these omissions which he found in a selective tradition. Luke, who was more sensitive to the chronological lack of balance, had no scruples about finding an additional name, for reasons of gematric ordering.

In order to maintain the number 14, Matthew has made some selections, in keeping with the same mindset. He has deliberately eliminated some generations.

For the kings, the OT records eighteen generations, from Solomon to Jechoniah. He retained fourteen of them (Mt 1:7-10). To do this, he eliminated the three generations springing from Athaliah (and Jehoram): Ahaziah (died 841), Joash (died 796) and Amaziah (died 781) (2 Kgs 11-14). He did this in accordance with accepted rules: Jewish tradition authorized the *erasio nominis* (erasure of the name) for idolaters. Their elimination was held to be harmless, according to the accepted adage: "The sons of sons are to be considered as sons."[18]

The suppression of Jehoiakim (1 Chr 3:15; 2 Kgs 23:34-36 cf. 2 Chr

36:4-5), the father of Jehoiachin-Jechoniah, could have been suggested by the oracle of Jeremiah 22:30 and 36:30-31, foretelling the extinction of Jechoniah's line: "He shall have none to sit upon the throne of David." Matthew might have been inclined to omit him as he did the three impious kings, for having burned the scrolls of the first edition of the oracles of Jeremiah 36:9, 16-32, as they were being read. He murdered prophets (Jer 26:21-23) and Jeremiah had the most severe words for this king (Jer 22:13-19; cf. 2 Kgs 23:37; 24:19; 2 Chr 36:8).

It seems that Matthew also eliminated names from the last (post-exilic) series. This conclusion is based on the duration of the exile and a comparison with Luke, who has five more generations for the same period.[19]

It seems clear that Matthew adhered to the biblical lists for the most part, except for some sufficiently motivated eliminations. In this he was following the example of the Bible, since the first series of fourteen (Abraham-David) which he found there is abridged in the source itself.[20]

These omissions explain why his three series of generations correspond to periods of very unequal duration:

—750 years from Abraham to David: In the 200 years between Solomon and David, there must have been more than 4 generations.

—400 years from David to the exile (in which Matthew deliberately omits 4 links).

—592 years (according to Masson), 575 (according to Brown) from the exile to Jesus, in which Matthew has 6 links fewer than Luke, whose number is better proportioned to the real number of generations: 21 for this last period, compared to Matthew's 14. Luke's number is consistent with the formula that a generation in that time was about 30 years.

Matthew invented nothing for any verifiable section of his genealogy, and there is every reason to believe that he did the same for the final links, of which only 5 are otherwise known to us: Shealtiel and Zerubbabel, through the Bible; Joseph, Mary and Jesus, through the other evangelists. Matthew clearly had additional documentation from other sources, however these are lost today.

In a different way, Luke used a pattern based on seven, a number which had considerable significance in a culture so taken up with gematry. When he composed his genealogy of three series of 7 for the opening and the end, he was being consistent with the 2 x 7 series that runs from Abraham to David. Luke, too, places these two names at key-places, 42 and 56—which are multiples of 7.

But why has Luke added the name Admin, which occupies the septenary place 7 x 7 = 49, right in the middle of this series of 14 which he has otherwise echoed faithfully, as has Matthew? This is in keeping with the mathematical laws of series-organization (see n. 14 above), i.e., with the very properties of numbers. For Matthew, who began his genealogy with Abraham, the father of believers would occupy the first position among the Chosen People. The first place gives him an honorable position, but this is not a multiple of 7. For Luke, who traces the genealogy right back to God, Abraham would not hold the first place. Had Luke not added a link, Abraham would have occupied an insignificant position, #55,[21] which is not a multiple of 7. Luke had to push him up a notch so that he would be in the 56th (8 x 7) position. Evidently, this rhythmic necessity motivated the addition of Admin. This is probably a distorted equivalent of the name Aminadab (the preceding link, 48). Did he go so far as to invent it? The care with which this genealogy has been written leads us to believe that in this difficulty, he sought the "missing link," as all genealogists do, and found it, thanks to one of the accidental variants that only too often abound in the material.

What Luke's genealogy demonstrates regarding his procedures makes it most probable that the author (Luke or his source) did not invent this name so as to re-establish the rhythm. He seems to have profited from some accident of genealogical recollections (deformation of names, dittography). This arrangement would be then a simple interpretation.

From the point of view of historicity, the object of our study, the major conclusion consists in this: these genealogies are not the product of ideologies or gematry, which would have created names. Twenty-eight names are drawn from the Bible in Matthew, and 37 in Luke, of which 34 are the most distant ancestors: from Adam to Nathan, the son of David. Only one ancestor from this series is unknown in the Hebrew Bible: Cainan II (#64). Might this be an invention or an accidental equivalent of Cainan I (#73)? No, Luke found it in the LXX which was the source of his genealogy, for both the names and their spelling.[22]

To these names from antiquity are added Shealtiel and Zerubbabel, who come from the time of the deportation and return. This last coincidence between Matthew and Luke, founded on the same biblical source, attests to the same documentary concern.

Convergences and Divergences

Are the two genealogies consistent with each other? Here is where the major objection to the historicity of the two genealogies surfaces; except for the last-mentioned two names, they are in disagreement about all the names between David and Joseph. It is frequently said that they are "irreconcilable," that attempts to harmonize them are vain and stem from "concordism."

J. Masson has taken on this challenge.[23] During his thirty years of fascination with genealogies, he has meticulously collated hypothetical reconciliations from Julius Africanus (second century) to Didon (1891), Fouard (1904), Prat (1903 and 1933), Holzmeister (1943) and so on, and has gone beyond them. His thesis, defended at the *Angelicum*, demonstrates quite well the errors of previous reconciliations. His own reconciliation substantiates its coherence by reliance on a precise knowledge of usages and a meticulous collection of the slightest evidences. Short of proofs in the strict sense, he brings out new convergences, which throws the burden of proof upon those who suspect errors in the two evangelists.

In a seriously documented approach, the two genealogies refer to the same event according to different sources and perspectives. It is thus necessary to describe their characteristics from the outset.

Matthew, whose universalist preoccupation is more restricted than Luke's, begins with Abraham, the father of the Chosen People. Luke traces the genealogy back to Adam, and even to God—which expands the perspective into the transcendent.[24]

For the pre-exilic descendants of David, Matthew chooses the royal line: from Solomon to Jechoniah, with the four omissions already mentioned.[25] Luke adopts another line, that of Nathan (3:31), the third son of David, born to Bathsheba at Jerusalem (2 Sm 5:14; 1 Chr 14:3-4; cf. 1 Kgs 4:5-6 and Zec 12:12, which puts "the family of the house of Nathan" in good standing).

Why did Luke make this choice? Did he perhaps identify Nathan with the prophet of the messianic oracle (2 Sm 7:15-17)?[26] He could have, since rabbinic tradition confuses these two characters. Did he see there a priestly line in accordance with the Greek manuscripts which record this Nathan as being a "priest"?[27] Did he wish to fill out Mary's affinity with the line of Aaron through her cousin Elizabeth (1:5 and 36)?

In any case, Luke seems to have carefully avoided the line of the kings, who in the Bible are so often portrayed as impious, to the point where Jeremiah finally predicted the extinction of Jechoniah's line (Jer 22:28-30; 36:30-31). In this perspective, Luke adopts a secondary line of Davidic descent.

This younger line of authentic Davidic extraction becomes dynastic precisely at the extinction of the line of Jechoniah, who dies "without a son."[28] The two Davidic lines springing respectively from Solomon and Nathan (two authentic sons) are rejoined in Shealtiel, the son of Neri, because, according to this hypothesis, Jechoniah, not having an heir, adopted Neri, his son-in-law (husband of his daughter), and thus made Neri's posterity his own.

Matthew thus assumes the juridical line through Jechoniah, the adoptive father; Luke assumes the natural and biological descent through Neri (J. Masson, 1982, 239-354).

The rest (from Zerubbabel to Joseph) once again differ, so that Joseph is assigned two fathers: Jacob (#39 in Matthew) and Heli (#2 in Luke). Masson finds a solution to this: Jacob is the legal father of Joseph, and Heli, his biological father (*ibid.*, 417-511). But here, double paternity would be in keeping with the Levirate law.[29] Julius the African, who refers to the testimony of the *Desposynoi* (Jesus' close relatives), made a mistake in calling Jacob the brother of Heli, but the law of the Levirate would indeed apply, because Eliud (#36 in Matthew) would seem to be the same person as Esli (#11 in Luke). This hypothesis is perfectly coherent, unlike those that have been proposed up to the present day. It relies, however, upon indications of lesser weight than does the preceding one, relative to Shealtiel.

The major point is established: no one can declare that the genealogies are fantasies, fictions, or even erroneous. Their divergences can be perfectly well explained by their different interpretations, which start from one and the same reality, and vary depending on differing choices regarding documentation. These can be partially explained by the fact that Matthew, under Jewish influence, chooses legal paternity, whereas Luke, under Greek influence, prefers natural paternity, which we would call real or biological paternity.

Such divergences should not be surprising; given the customs and materials of the first century (births recorded without birth certificates, often transmitted by oral tradition), Matthew and Luke could not have worked like the specialists of today. Their genealogies are in conformity with the cultural requirements and possibilities of their time.

They sought their information wherever it could be found. It is evident that sources were not completely lacking, in view of the care with which genealogies were preserved. These were collated by their authors with a concern for exactness and for a rhythmical and numerical order, which is not mathematical but gematric, i.e., symbolic. Their genealogies have a poetic dimension. Matthew's is apparently more so; Luke's, which is starker and closer to the biological realities, also betrays this artistic preoccupation, on the basis of a model furnished by the biblical sources themselves.[30]

In short, the two genealogies, developed in a milieu which cultivated this art with precision, have been documented and composed in a painstaking fashion as regards the sources and proper ordering. To question their accuracy in the more recent portion would be absurd on two counts: we have no external information with which to verify their statements, and it was precisely that portion for which the surrounding milieu would provide a superabundance of material. It is from this abundance that the evangelists have drawn their respective and coherent choices, each according to his culture. It is according to those norms, and not to those of our computerized civilization, that the genealogies must be judged.

There is no serious reason to fault the evangelists, belittle their work, or view it condescendingly, as though our limited resources could ever give us knowledge superior to theirs. They knew more than we do about their times, their customs, and the near-contemporaries about whom they wrote. The interpreters who look down on them will pass. But the witness of the evangelists will still be around in the third millennium. The difficulties of historical research ought to inspire modesty among those who practice the science.

Function and Meaning

The genealogical labor of the evangelists evokes, above all, admiration for their historical, literary and doctrinal achievement. These genealogies had the function of attracting not simply curiosity, but faith. Faced with the idealism of the Docetists and Gnostics, they offer a guarantee: the human reality of Christ—that which later came to be called the Incarnation of the Son of God.

In accordance with the culture and documentary resources of their time, Luke and Matthew established that Jesus, the Son of God, was indeed a man of human stock. This was difficult to express, since his origin was singularly marked by God through the virginal conception, attested to by the Judeo-Christian familial data. We must say "data" since so many ideologies of that period (gnosticism and its derivatives) would tend to lead in other directions.

Both evangelists have assumed this disconcerting fact, but in different perspectives: Matthew 1, in the context of ancestral origin and Luke 3, in the context of Jesus' baptism; Matthew, by reference to a "genesis" (1:1 and 18) and Luke, at the threshold of his baptismal manifestation, by reference to the beginning (3:23) of the history of salvation in Jesus Christ. Both, however, are concerned not with political criteria, but with sonship and the divine designation of Jesus. On the historical level, and even more on the doctrinal level, their independent genealogies realize a remarkable *concordantia discordantium.*

CONCLUSION

How Matthew and Luke Take Up and Go Beyond the Literary Form of Genealogy

We need not wait for the chapter dealing with symbolism and theological impact to indicate the meaning which Matthew and Luke have given this genealogy, nor how this meaning goes beyond the genealogy itself.

Matthew

Matthew gives us the most explicit key to this matter. He takes as his point of departure the problematical title attributed to Jesus, "son of David" (attested to as a historical datum in the three synoptic Gospels, where the crowds give this title to Jesus), and the genealogical rupture leads him to understand the messiahship of Christ in another, a transcendent manner, without having to adhere to dynastic lineage but within the humanity assumed by God.

It is clear that Matthew took his careful genealogical survey so as to verify and prove that Jesus was the son of David. It was a disturbing surprise for him to discover the final rupture of this genealogy. This search for the truth proved fruitful. Matthew did not go beyond his data iconoclastically. He did not proclaim: Jesus is not a true royal descendant, he is not king, he is not the son of David. Rather, he perceived a reality different from his initial purpose, a reality more humble, yet transcendent.

The Davidic line to which the genealogy links Jesus had, by Jesus' time, lost all political power and lapsed into obscurity. Not only did Jesus never reign, he was crushed, put to death by the kings of this world. He did not want to be king, even when the dynastic and political ambition of the people pushed him in that direction (Jn 6:15). He was not even the biological son of Joseph, the son of David. Matthew understood this gap perfectly, this shipwreck of political hopes, and integrated it into a profound new vision.

But he did not for all that eliminate the popular and traditional idea with which he had started nor the promise of God to David (2 Sm 7:14; Is 7:14). He justified it by a culturally solid expedient, since adoption (as well as Levirate fatherhood) was the basis for an authentic paternity.

According to Matthew, the adoption of Jesus by Joseph fulfills the promise made to David. The biological breach serves to manifest another facet of the salvation history which is essential to Matthew's perspective. The sinful ancestors and impious kings, alluded to in Jeremiah's prophecies of chastisement seem to account for the dynastic failure at the captivity (1:11) and for the final breach of the genealogy (1:16), at the point where the captivity eliminates Solomon's descendants along with the political reign of his dynasty.

This other facet has a profound bearing upon the relation between the infallibility of God's design and the crooked lines in which human frailty writes it, as well as upon the relation between these failures and the mercy of God which restores things in a new way. Matthew's genealogy illustrates this saying of Christ, found later in this Gospel: "I have not come to abolish, but to fulfill" (5:17).

The messiahship of Jesus is justified juridically (on grounds that would have been by no means insignificant in Israel). Jesus is indeed designated as the son of David, but according to a broken genealogy, a filiation by default. We will note that Joseph, the restorer, is recorded, not like the sinners, who perpetuated the race while vitiating God's plan, but as a "just man" (1:19). He pays the debt of a guilt-laden heredity: he is not the generator (the "begetter") of the Messiah. In this way, he prefigures his son, the Christ-Messiah, who does not beget either. The dynasty is closed; its political future is finished. Something else begins: a new kingship, in the new creation where one must be born of God, where celibacy for the sake of the kingdom and eschatology take priority over the basic human enterprise of self-continuation through generation. This was a profound new aspect of faith which demanded a radical cultural breakthrough.

This breakthrough is of utmost significance. It consists in this: it is a fact that Jesus was not a genealogical or political king. He is king, not on human grounds, but on divine ones, as Son of God.

His royal anointing as Messiah is not a ritual anointing; it is the anointing of the Holy Spirit. This anointing, connected to the virginal conception, attests that Jesus is the Son of God. For Matthew, it is not this anointing, not this action of the Spirit, which makes Jesus the Son of God. He is this absolutely, and always. His human generation merely manifests this to humans; it does not make him the Son of God ontologically. He already was the Son of God in a mysterious way, but Matthew had no adequate conceptual instrument to account for this mysterious sonship or even to express it (whence the difficulty in evaluating and formulating his position). Though Jesus was the adopted son of Joseph, he was not the adopted Son of God. His human generation is not described as a mythological process in which God played the role of a human father by substitution. Matthew refrains from attributing the human origin of Jesus to the Father. Jesus' spiritual generation is presented as a sign that brings the Son of God to the human race. The apostle Paul said this even before Matthew wrote his Gospel (Rom 1:3). Matthew says rather that it is a sign which brings "God with us" (1:23). This sign both manifests and gives to men the Son of God as a savior, re-emphasized through the name "Jesus" (1:21), the human and messianic name of the Son of God becoming man. But this name has a transcendent value, since "savior" is ordinarily in the Bible a name proper to God.[31]

On a level that is less conceptual than symbolic, Matthew brings out this intuition of faith, implicitly but resolutely attested to throughout the NT: that Jesus has no other father than God. Matthew transfers him from the dynastic genealogy to the transcendent order.

Mary, the mother of Jesus, does not belong to the transcendent order. Matthew perceives her as a sign of the gift of the Spirit (since the virginal conception is indicative of the new creation, of eschatology, which renews all things), and as the sole human origin of Jesus.

Thus, when Matthew includes Mary in the fourteen names of the last series, in a mediating position between Joseph and Jesus, the two begotten non-begetters, she is not a "begetter" (as our analysis demonstrated) and she is not a transmitter of royal claims. Rather, she is presented as a sign of the gift of God. In daring to name Mary in the same genealogy, Matthew makes vivid use of this paradox. The genealogy of the Messiah is not like any other. His kingship is not like any other, it is transcendent and divine. It is remarkable that Matthew, the least feminist of the evangelists, was thus led to mention women in his genealogy, altogether outside the established custom. He mentions them as a sign of God, in order to prepare for the different, exceptional case of Mary, at the beginning of Christ's human generation by God alone. Through these paradoxical breaches of human expectations, God's transcendent gift expresses the newness of Christ right from his origin. Matthew is not the only one to have perceived it.

Luke

Luke achieved the same breakthrough. It is even more remarkable that he does it differently, in a manner that is more radical and, at the same time, more explicit. It is apparent in his Gospel that Joseph is seen as Jesus' adoptive father, since he is not the biological father (1:34), and that Mary remains his betrothed (2:5), but that he is nonetheless one of the two "parents" of Jesus (2:27, 41), his human "father" (2:33), as Mary herself declares (2:48). But Luke does not highlight the relation of Jesus to Joseph, as Matthew does (Mt 1:18, 25). He does not make the adoption explicit. He says nothing to justify Jesus' Davidic ancestry according to adoptive paternity.

Why? Because he proceeds still futher. He has severed the genealogical chain to an even greater extent. Through topography he justifies the Davidic designation of Christ (2:1-5); his narrative, like his generation, is referred totally to God. At the very outset (1:32a), he posits divine sonship, before the Davidic lineage is established (1:32b). In his ascending genealogy, the human side is relativized from the very start, with the very deliberate "as was supposed" (3:23). This genealogy begins with a statement of Jesus' designation by the voice from heaven, at his baptism: "You are my Son; this day I have begotten you" (3:22). He continually traces Jesus' origins back to the source, without a clause or commentary, verb or sentence; he establishes a continued chain of ancestors (connected by the article in the genitive), culminating in God as the origin of Adam, in a sort of leap that depicts God less as the creator of Adam than as the father of him whom he has "begotten."

Mark

The leap is even more radically conveyed in Mark's Gospel, which was quite familiar with the title, "Son of David," given by the crowds (10:47-48; 11:10), but which opens concisely in this manner:

> The beginning of the gospel of Jesus Christ, the Son of God (Mk 1:1).

Mark presents Christ as Son of God without reference to any Davidic, or even human origin. Joseph is not named in Mark's Gospel.

John

The same breakthrough is found in John, who is dependent on Luke. Davidic descent has no place in his Gospel. It is invoked by Jesus' adversaries as an unfulfilled requirement, so that Jesus is disqualified in their eyes (7:43). Without excluding the human dimension, to which Matthew addressed himself, John makes the theology of this qualification explicit on another plane, beginning in his prologue. One would betray his perspective if one were to see in it "three generations" of the Word: an eternal, a temporal, and a baptismal generation. No such calculation exists for John. There is a single, eternal generation which progresses and manifests itself in time through the Incarnation and baptismal faith (1:14, cf. below, p. 407). This generation is entirely virginal at every step along the way, although in a very different sense from the concept of virginity in the synoptics, and this trait is portrayed with reference to the visible, human filiation of Christ wherein the Gospel perceives the glory of God (1:14 and 17).

This virginal nature is expressed in terms that are suitable, in a most obvious manner, to the human conception of the Son of God and would not make much sense outside of that context:

> Begotten [the same word as in Mt, and, likewise, in the passive, concealing the transcendent subject] not of blood, nor of the will of the flesh, nor of the will of man, *but of God* (Jn 1:13).

It is from this sign (which is at the high-point of his prologue), and also from the experience of the "children of God" (1:12, an equally central verse), that John makes explicit his theology of the pre-existence of the Son of God (present in all of the NT, although implicitly; see below, Part III, chapter 8, footnote 9).

Like Mark 1:1, John 1:1 opens with the word *archē* (the beginning is analogous to *genesis* in Mt 1:1). However, his affirmation of the divine origin does not omit reference to the human origin of the "Word made flesh":

> And the Word became flesh and dwelt among us, full of grace and truth; we have beheld his glory [manifested in his humanity], glory as of the only Son from the Father. . . . And from his fullness we have all received, grace upon grace. For the law was given through Moses; grace and truth came through Jesus Christ. No one has ever seen God; the only Son, who is in the bosom of the Father, he has made him known (Jn 1:14, 16-18).

The fact that John does not provide a genealogy, and brings up the human origin of Christ only through the objections of adversaries (1:46; 6:42; 7:42-52), manifests a breakthrough more radical than Matthew's. His eagle-eye perspective rises to the eternal pre-existence of the Son of God made man. Pre-existence is not his fabrication; it is the fruit of his contemplation, a gift of grace and truth. If indeed he needs to construct language to express it, it is the expression of a new perception, not of a fictitious idea. This divine filiation does not destroy the humanity of Jesus. Rather, in his humanity the evangelist has concretely perceived the glory of God:

> That which was from the beginning, which we have heard, which we have seen with our eyes, which we have looked upon and touched with our hands, concerning the Word of Life (1 Jn 1:1).

The pre-existence and the eternal filiation of Jesus do not destroy, but rather lay the foundation for his paradoxical coming into the human race. This is why the genealogies of Matthew and Luke maintain their importance.

The two evangelists display historical intentions as well as honest and conscientious methods, always with their own cultural coloring and different mentalities, but with serious reference to the same historical reality. All of these points demonstrate a remarkable convergence both as to fact and interpretation.

They assumed the genealogical norms of that time, only to surpass them; for the exceptional filiation of Christ profoundly relativizes Davidic filiation and the genealogical chains. The novel way in which he is born indicates that he is "God with us" (Mt 1:23) and Son of God (Mt 2:15 and Lk 1:32, 35; 2:49). This radical newness changes the very nature of kingship, history and salvation.

V
EVALUATION OF THE SEQUENCES

A. THE NARRATIVES

The infancy Gospels are based on narratives which constitute (as an extension to the history of the Chosen People) a sacred history, a history of the Messiah's childhood. The question before us is: Are these fictitious stories or true history?

As Luke 1-2 and Matthew 1-2 are accounts concerning a child who made no pronouncements and performed no miracles, one would be tempted to say that they do not on the whole pose a historical problem, except for some elements which we will treat later.

However, suspicion has been cast upon the infancy more systematically and radically than upon the accounts of Jesus' public life. Strauss classified these narratives and Bultmann defined them (rather summarily) as myths or legends. Some have wished to see them as simple projections, apologetical, biblical, or theological, in the form of *theologoumena*. Doubt has been cast on everything except the names of three principal characters: Jesus, Joseph, and Herod (who serves as a chronological reference-point).

None of the places has escaped suspicion. The very existence of Nazareth has long been contested. According to F. Burkitt (*The Syriac Form of New Testament Proper Names*, 17), this name, unknown in the Bible and in the Talmud, could have been created from the surname Nazarene (Mt 2:23), which was given to Jesus. Burkitt thinks that Jesus may have come from Chorozain. This "childish" thesis, as Lagrange called it (1927, 38) has been rendered obsolete today by archeological research. It has resurfaced, however, under a new form. J. S. Kennard (1946) and, later, H. Stegeman (1969) situated Jesus' origin in Capernaum, where he began his ministry. According to this theory, Nazareth was substituted for Capernaum from the pseudo-biblical text cited by Matthew 2:23 (Blinzler did not have difficulty in refuting these hypotheses, which raised quite a din in the German newspapers).[1]

Bethlehem has been the target of more subtle objections. Did not the two evangelists situate the birth of Christ in this city purposely, in order to provide him at all costs with a Davidic foundation? Have they not invented this label on the basis of Micah 5 and Jewish tradition?

Here again, the critics give in to extrapolation on the methodological principle which says that it is better to explain one text by another text (in this case, to explain a prophecy) than by an event. They add that the testimonies for the birth at Bethlehem remain isolated: only Matthew and Luke have them. Even they differ in their way of explaining Jesus' presence at Nazareth: in Luke 1, Jesus is there from the beginning; in Matthew 2:13-23, he only arrives later and under special circumstances. But the differences of interpretation only serve to uphold the independence of the witnesses. Such divergences are considered as signs of authenticity when it comes to examining testimonies.

The infancy Gospels are not alone in speaking of Bethlehem. John refers to it by citing this criticism on the part of Christ's adversaries:

> Has not the scripture said that the Christ is descended from David, and comes from Bethlehem, the village where David was (Jn 7:42)?

John cites these objections in an ironic fashion so as to transcend them.[2] The adversaries are wrong in taking materially what should be understood spiritually. The comparison is even more significant in the three cases where objections deal with the origins of Christ:

—"Can anything good come out of Nazareth?" says Nathaniel (1:46).

—"Is not this Jesus, the son of Joseph, whose father and mother we know? How does he now say, 'I have come down from heaven' ?" ask the Jews in the "bread of Life" discourse (6:42).

—"We were not born of fornication," the scribes reply to him, having been accused of not being "Abraham's children" (8:41, a text which we will take up later).

According to the structural study of these passages (de la Potterie, 1978, 53-55), John knew that Jesus was the son of Mary (whom he openly called his mother: Jn 2:1-12, 19, 25, 27), that he was not

Joseph's son, and that he was born in Bethlehem (see below, pp. 406ff.). He supposed that these facts were known to his listeners, and invited them to go beyond the level of appearances to the divine filiation of Christ (Jn 5:18). This process accounts for the anomalies. Writing after Luke, whose writing depended on the same tradition, he could not ignore the fact that Jesus was born in Bethlehem, "where David was" (Jn 7:42), as the majority of the manuscripts add, although he manifested himself at the place of his childhood in Galilee (cf. Jn 1:43 and 46).

For the fourth evangelist, the meaning does not lie in the realistic details that are evoked, but in the fact that they are transcended, in the awareness that Jesus is "something other": namely, the Son of God. This transcending of genealogy and topography, which we analyzed in Luke 1-2, was extended even further by John in his new perspective: he made explicit the notion of pre-existence of the Word, which was already implied, it seems to us, by the perspective of the two infancy Gospels.[3]

The silence of Mark (the only evangelist who does not speak of Bethlehem) is explained by the limits of his perspective, since he begins his account of Jesus' life, not at his birth, but at the baptism of John. He makes reference to the Nazarene origins of Jesus as to a known fact (1:9 and 24; cf. 6:1-3), with a curious ellipsis on the name Nazareth in these last two texts; he uses the name again in 10:47 and 14:67.

The historical question of Jesus' Davidic sonship, which has been widely debated,[4] poses no problem if we accept the way in which the two evangelists justify it, according to the genealogy passed on through Joseph, the adoptive father.

They did not even have recourse to the easy solution of justifying natural filiation, namely, making Mary a "daughter of David," a solution used as early as the first half of the second century. We have seen how Matthew and Luke take on the dynastic inheritance by way of a renewal in which biological descent and the figure of the "son of David" as a political-nationalistic figure are radically transcended.

The Lucan Narratives

Luke's narratives are composed within a format in which signs from

God emerge against a very ordinary background. The characteristics of "God's signs" will be examined in a later chapter. The basic background of the narratives harmonizes with the setting and customs of the period (in contrast to the Apocrypha), and does not give rise to any historical objections.

Zechariah may have gone up to the Temple to participate in the sacrificial worship of the Temple; this was decided by lot, and if Zechariah was a member of the line of Abijah, his turn would occur from time to time: these are unimpeachable facts. He may have been childless until his old age: this is a fact that Luke has evidently received and not invented. The varied administrative enterprises for the integration of the empire could have resulted in a journey by Joseph and Mary at the birth of Christ; this birth might have thus entailed precarious conditions, contrary to any expectations; the Messiah may have been badly received in his home town (a coincidence brought out by the convergence of Lk 1:7 and Jn 1:11); Jesus and John the Baptist would, as children born under the Law, have been submitted to the rite of circumcision on the eighth day (Lk 1:59; 2:21) and Jesus' mother to the customary rite of purification on the fortieth (2:22); the family could have made the paschal pilgrimage to Jerusalem "according to custom" (2:41-52)[5]: all this does not pose any problems, except for the census, which we discussed earlier (p. 328).

I. H. Marshall (1978, 125-126) makes the same diagnosis concerning the finding in the Temple:

> A story which tells of the unusual ability of a boy destined for a great future, or of the early insight of a future religious teacher, inevitably finds parallels in various cultures, even down to the detail of the boy being twelve years old. Bultmann (327f.) lists: Moses (*Antiquities* 2.230; Philo, 1.21); Josephus (*Jos. Vita* 2); Cyrus (Herodatus 1.113f.); Alexander (Plutarch, *Alex.* 5); Apollonius (Philostratus, *Vita Apoll.* 1.7); Si Osiris; and Buddha. There is nothing surprising about such parallels. . . . Hence these parallels cannot be used to show that the story in Lk. is legendary, but only that the motif is a common one. Dibelius (103-106), who is particularly insistent on the 'legendary' form of the narrative, emphasizes that the form does not necessarily determine the historicity of the story. . . van

Iersel rightly sees that the story is not basically about a precocious Jesus.

The Matthean Narratives

Matthew's narratives lend themselves to a greater number of objections. The very distinctiveness of the events (e.g., a startling visit by foreigners, the persecution by King Herod) raises questions. Here again, however, the background of the narrative does not preclude these events.

Joseph's deliberation of separation from his pregnant betrothed (1:19-20) is in the order both of normal reactions and of Jewish legislation. Later, we will examine the unusual event which provoked this momentous decision.

The episode of the wise men has been considered legendary. Some have wanted to see in it the reworking of biblical texts, implicitly referred to in the course of the narrative (Psalm 72, for example, in Matthew 2:11). But Matthew clearly does not present the wise men as kings, in the style of such biblical models; and these texts say nothing at all about myrrh. Thus they do not "create" the narrative. It is the event which suggests the biblical allusion, without extrapolation or exaggeration. Soares Prabhu, a renowned expert in the historical-critical method, considers that this narrative cannot be explained in this manner. A factual tradition seems the most probable source to him: a narrative usually stems from an event, from a fact, and not from a fictitious projection.[6]

Wise men may have come in search of a king, relying on the stars, says Xavier Léon-Dufour (who, in this instance, criticizes a certain radical approach by Brown). This is not absolutely impossible since, about the year 70, a magus came to adore Nero. Why not say, if all negative proof is lacking, that there still remains a factor of non-impossibility (cf. the recension of Brown, 1978, 131).

The Massacre of the Innocents

Of all the episodes in the infancy Gospel, the massacre of the Innocents is the one which meets with the most objections.

From its literary style, we have seen that it appears to be a later addition (p. 252). But this detrimental factor does not rule out the possibility of its having been taken from a genuine source.

It is surprising that Herod, a cunning and watchful king, did not have the wise men followed into Bethlehem, which was so near by, and that he did not know how to find the "house" visited by the wise men who, after all, must have been conspicuous, as they were foreigners laden down with treasure chests (2:11), luggage, and pack animals.

In this, the most suspect point of all, Soares Prabhu's rigorous historical-critical study has detected the possibilities of a historical kernel, the narrative being due neither to the style proper to Matthew, nor to the reworking of sources, biblical or otherwise.[7] R. T. France has devoted an excellent monograph to the historicity of this episode, the essence of which is as follows.[8]

On the plane of literary analysis, could the narrative of Matthew 2 be explained as a staging, an "enactment" of the biblical texts linked to each sequence? The citation of Jeremiah 31:15 does not have any explanatory value: Ramah is not Bethlehem; the tomb of Rachel in this city constitutes a tenuous connection between them indeed. The lost children she mourns are the exiles, according to Jeremiah 31:15, and do not at all incline one to think of the massacre by Herod. The citation has ostensibly only been given to shed light upon a pre-existing narrative which stems, like the others, from a popular source that belongs to the history of Jesus.

The attempts to explain the narrative as a patchwork of pagan legends or of Jewish traditions concerning Moses, Abraham, Jacob provide no clarification of the text (France, 105-108).

The congruence which might have arisen between the infant Moses under threat of death from Pharaoh and the children slaughtered in Bethlehem is not achieved by the narrative of 2:16-18. The single literary contact with the biblical story of Moses (Ex 4:19 and Mt 2:19) has no interpretive value (see above, p. 322).

France, who stresses the express influences of Jewish traditions concerning this point, concludes:

> But to establish that the story of Moses has served as a model for the wording of the narrative is not *per se* to explain the *origin* of the tradition. The question arises again: Which came first? Did the

> tradition derive simply from a Christian desire to clothe Jesus in the garments of Moses, or did an already existing narrative tradition suggest the parallel with the Exodus story, so that the later story was related in the light of the earlier? (108)
>
> If there was not existing tradition of Herod's killing of children, why was Pharaoh's massacre ever thought of in connection with Jesus? . . . The idea of Jesus as the new Moses is not prominent in Christian tradition as this explanation presupposes. While it is clearly presupposed in chapter ii, it is only a minor element elsewhere in Matthew [contrary to the views of W. D. Davies, *The Setting*, 1963, 25]. In the first two chapters of Matthew, moreover, the new Moses theme is in fact only one element in a mosaic of motifs . . . which . . . emphasized the Christ as a new creation, the Messianic King, who represents Israel and is Emmanuel (109-110).

Thus the explicit citation of Hosea 11:1 in Matthew 2:15 refers to Israel and not to Moses. This corresponds with the "fundamental typology of the chapter." It is not the texture of the narrative, but "the redaction and external expression" that is inspired by the narratives relative to Moses. These traditions are not the underlying principle of the narrative, but represent an element of interpretation.

> W. L. Knox judges correctly that "the fact that the typological correspondence is not more complete suggests that it has been superimposed upon the infancy narrative at a stage in its growth which is not primary." Chapter ii is not structured as a midrash on the Exodus stories but, as Stendahl has shown, as an apologia for the unexpected geographical origins of the Messiah (*The Sources*, Cambridge, 1957, 123 and R. T. France, *op. cit.*, 111).

In short, Matthew 1-2 has made use of midrash, in the broad sense where this word means an updated exegetical application: drawing the events of Scripture together, but not in the strict sense that Scripture is the source of legendary constructions (*theologoumena*).

To explain the massacre of the Innocents as an apologetic construction (as does J. D. Kingsbury, 1975, 89-92) is even less convincing. To say that the episode was created as a sign of judgment against Israel for having rejected the Messiah seems quite artificial, and it is not clear how a Christian apologetic would have fabricated a narrative that made Jesus responsible (albeit indirectly) for the unjust suffering of Jewish infants in Bethlehem (*ibid.*, p. 113).

The narrative does not present the characteristics of Matthew's own style, and makes use of a number of words that are only found there.[9]

Finally, the precise detail relative to the children's age, "two years old and under," is "neither essential to the narrative nor suggested by any . . . literary models," which "does indeed suggest that what is presented is a reminiscence of some actual event," concludes Soares Prabhu.[10]

Historical criticism exhibits evidences in the same direction. The background of the presentation conforms perfectly to known historical facts. Herod was an atrocious murderer. The most noted of his killings are dated during Herod's final years, precisely those around the time of Jesus' birth, in frantic reaction to a prediction that his dynasty would lose the throne.[11] His policing skills, his murderous plot, his violent reaction when his plan failed—all these, as reported by Matthew, do in fact correspond to his character. The obsession with threats to his throne which characterized the end of his reign, lends credibility to Matthew's account, as does Flavius Josephus' account of the reign of Archelaus. In view of the sinister character of this reign and this period, Joseph, the adoptive father, just returned from Egypt, had good cause for concern (see *Antiquities*, 17, 13, 339-355; *Jewish Wars*, 2, [c. 6], 111).

The Bethlehem massacre was overlooked by Josephus. This omission does not constitute an objection.[12] His chronicle is filled with the massacres committed by Herod, in his own family, among his officers, and among the Jews on a greater scale. In comparison to these major acts of violence, the Bethlehem massacre could have been passed over unnoticed. The village and its environs numbered about 1,000 persons, which would include at most about 20 boys under 2 years of age, an insignificant figure within Herod's full tally of massacres. It is hardly surprising, then, that Josephus, whose account is overloaded with such episodes, should make no mention of this. His silence is in no way significant.

Do we have any way of cross-checking this slaughter of the Innocents? E. Stauffer (1960, 38ff.) cites in this connection *The Assump-*

tion of Moses (6, 4 and 6), written shortly after the death of Herod (between the years 4 and 30). We find here a prediction (after the event): an impudent and wicked king "shall slay the old and the young. . . he shall execute judgements on them as the Egyptians executed upon them, during thirty and four years he will execute judgements on them as the Egyptians did on their fathers" [the length of Herod's reign]. This massacre "of the young" could be an allusion to the slaughter at Bethlehem. If this is a convergent witness, it is one which is independent of the Christian tradition.

Likewise Macrobius (cited above) supplies this context to Augustus' remark that "Herod's pigs" were more fortunate than "his sons," "when he [Augustus] learned that among the children under two years of age, killed in Syria by order of Herod, king of the Jews, Herod's own son had been killed" (Saturnalia 2, 4, 11). We have here a strange mixture of traditions relative to two massacres by Herod: that of his own children who were killed as adults, and that of children "under two years of age," which corresponds to an apparently factual description of Matthew 2:5. Since Macrobius was a pagan who otherwise "gives no indication of Christian influence" (France, 118, n. 87) the hypothesis that he is echoing Matthew seems hardly probable, particularly since he situates the massacre in Syria.

These texts may amount to historical confirmation, but this is not proven. They provide neither direct evidence, nor certain convergent testimony—only probability. France is right then in concluding with reserve:

> Our conclusion from a literary point of view was that it was easier to explain the origin of the tradition of Herod and the children of Bethlehem on the assumption that it recorded an actual event, and our study of the historical question has shown that it is not improbable that such an event could have occurred in the last years of Herod's reign. . . . This incident should not be cited without more ado as evidence that the nativity stories were simply "made up" in the interests of Christian hagiography or apologetics, or evolved without an historical basis from reflection on scripture and Jewish tradition.

Objective analysis, therefore, invites us to consider Matthew's account not as an imaginative creation but as a datum of history—which led Matthew to think of a number of biblical analogies. If this were not the case, his procedure here would make no sense, given his perspective and overall purpose.

> Matthew is not simply meditating on OT texts, but claiming that in what has happened they find a fulfillment. If the events are legendary, the argument is futile. Of course, Matthew could be mistaken, and could have accepted as fact what was in reality pious legend. But we have seen reason to doubt whether this was the case (p. 120).

The Flight into Egypt

According to Bonnard in his *Commentary on Matthew* (1970, 28), the flight into Egypt is also not historically "unlikely":

> The flight of suspect Jewish families into Egypt, Herod's acts of violence, and above all the settling in Galilee in order to escape the terror which characterizes the nine years of the ethnarchate of Archelaus, son of Herod and Malthake—all this corresponds to what we know of this sad period (cf. Flavius Josephus, *Antiquities* 17, 9-13 #206-355).

J. Klausner (1933, 216) describes the situation:

> Herod had scarcely closed his eyes when trouble and confusion broke out such as had never before been seen in Judea. . . . Archelaus who had not dared to punish Herod's counsellors before his authority had been confirmed by Rome, did not hesitate to send his entire army against the people gathered together in the Temple and to have 3,000 persons massacred like sheep in a single day, side by side with the victims destined for sacrifice; the Temple was filled with corpses (1933, 222).

Egypt was a journey of some five or six days away, and was traditionally a land of refuge, even in the time of the kings (1 Kgs 11:4) and particularly during the Maccabean period. Its conquest by Octavius, the future Augustus, in 30 B.C., had annexed it to the Roman Empire as an imperial province in the time of Christ.

On this point, France examined two Jewish traditions of the first century which may provide independent testimony. One connects the childhood of Jesus with Egypt, where he was said to have learned magic,[13] the other[14] explains the journey to Egypt as a flight that took place "when King Jannai slew our rabbis."[15] But one might ask whether we are dealing with an independent tradition or with direct influence of the Gospel itself.

If, then, we do not have arguments that weaken the accounts of Matthew, neither do we have decisive proofs that confirm them—only clues. This is not surprising for the obscure history of a child who passed unnoticed. The least we can do is to establish a conformity, not marred by anachronism or distortion, with known history and a number of possible or probably independent witnesses from literary sources which everyone will have to evaluate for himself or herself. This does not allow us to determine with precision what belongs to historical reality and what to the creative contribution of the redactor. However, the mass of convergent indications imposes the hypothesis of substantial historicity. Where such a hypothesis is lacking, experience proves that objections abound.

As to the attempts to explain these accounts as fiction, they are divergent and contradictory because they proceed from a priori assumptions. Historians (however exacting they may be) never cultivate doubt to this extent when they are not dealing with the Gospel. After a stage of absolute doubt, which has been very helpful in that all possible false trails have been investigated, it is healthy for exegesis to return to a serious evaluation and to grant a favorable presumption to the qualified witness (in this instance, Matthew) as long as there is no substantive argument to the contrary.

This does not guarantee all the details of the account. Must we then reinterpret it by eliminating what makes it characteristic, in order to render it "more plausible"? In one sense this would be legitimate, since every narrative tends to heighten the significance of a particlar event. This is one of the laws of communication. The background would justify caution in magnifying the episode. In any case, the flight into Egypt was of short duration, since Jesus was born shortly before the death of Herod, and he returned at the beginning of Archelaus' reign. Therefore the exile would have lasted, at the most, one or two years; at the least, a few days. (Is it necessary to assume, as is sometimes said, that the Holy Family withdrew only as far as the borders of Egypt?) The speculations aimed at "reworking the narrative" into a minimal form on the basis of mere likelihood, without new documentary support, are unfortunately artificial. We are less likely to stray from the truth if we simply stick to the data of Matthew, in the sobriety they already possess. Anything else too often amounts to empty speculation.[16]

Conclusion

In conclusion, the events reported by the narratives of Matthew 1-2 and Luke 1-2 are modest and not spectacular. For Luke, the great symbol of Christmas is the crib. Is it so very unlikely that people on the move and without lodging should put a baby to bed in a place like this? The prominence that Matthew 2 gives to the visit of the wise men in no way contradicts this modest setting; he has not overdrawn this private visit in the colors of a triumphal public pageant.

It is clear that Matthew and Luke ran up against the difficulty that historians often encounter when they seek to reconstruct the infancy of a personage who has become famous. Information is remote, spotty, transfigured with hindsight, but they intended it to be authentic as well as significant, so as to form a worthy complement to the first type of Gospel (Mark) where "Jesus Christ, the Son of God" (1:1) appears as an adult at the time of his baptism by John, without our knowing anything of his origins.

Luke's stylized portrait appears to adhere more closely to the events than Matthew, whose presentation is clearly schematic. The obscurities in his account testify to respect for historical data. The prophecy of Simeon remains enigmatic even after the event. The finding scene requires of the reader even today not so much intellectual perception as internal comprehension, one acquired through meditation and deep familiarity with the text.

Finally, the work of interpretation, not excessively hyperbolic, is a work of penetration rather than of extrapolation, a work of analogy and comparison rather than of metamorphosis, even if it necessarily gives prominence to what it chooses to express. The transfiguration of recollections is the law of all memory and all history. It is not necessarily betrayal. It is interior illumination of an event, and thus implies a degree of stylization. The positivist concern at the turn of this century and the return of the new historical technique toward everyday human realities have not abolished this profound law, which is of particular importance in the case of religious history.

B. THE DIALOGUES[17]

The function of dialogues, which appear along the course of a narrative, is to pass on the communication that occurs between persons. Here, as elsewhere, there is a striking contrast between the two infancy Gospels.

In Matthew, there is hardly anything but monologues. Biblical dreams generally have this character. The nocturnal messages of the angel to Joseph (1:20-21; 2:13, 19-20, 22) and to the wise men (2:12) are not exceptions. (We should also include here the order issued by Herod who "sent and killed all the male children in Bethlehem," 2:16.) Only two dialogues, those of Herod with the wise men (2:2-3, 7-8) and with the priests (2:3-4) are outlined in this sequence (which, unlike the others, does not conclude with a biblical citation).

In Luke, monologues are the exception; the annunciation to the shepherds is the only one (2:10-14). It too has the unilateral character of nocturnal communications. But dialogues predominate, either in an indirect style of presentation (1:66; 2:18; 2:38, 46, 47), or in a direct fashion—in the case of the first two annunciations (1:13-38), the exchange between Elizabeth and Mary (1:42-55), between Elizabeth and her neighbors (1:58-61), then between the latter and Zechariah (1:62-63), and between Jesus and his parents (2:48-49).

It is important to place these dialogues according to their function. Every day we hear and recount, or we hear reports of dialogues. This material belongs to the fabric of life. It has neither the character of shorthand nor of fiction. As a rule it summarizes, reconstructs, and interprets only the essential. We presume the reliability of such reports without stopping to determine, beyond reasonable limits, their substantial fidelity and their relativity. Matthew 1-2 and Luke 1-2 should have been accepted in the same way without confusing critical sense with systematic doubt. The presupposition that dialogues of this kind are a creative expression of the "author's ideas,"[18] and not a presentation of events, has become deeply rooted.

The annunciation (which, as revelation, presents special problems to which we shall return later on) has particularly been the object of such reductive treatment. We need not inquire here into "the psychology of Mary"; this has been done to excess. These narratives do not have an anecdotal character. They communicate the essential with the perspective which is the fruit of lengthy meditation, and are presented schematically. But to completely fail to see in them the expression of a real vocation which called forth Mary's response, is another matter altogether (as we shall see in the chapter where we examine the credibility that can be accorded visions and revelations).

As to the rest, the sober dialogues of the two infancy Gospels pose no special problems. The dialogues are to be seen within the context of sacred history, in accordance with the biblical model. The implicit or explicit use of biblical texts, which characterizes the Gospels, does not necessarily indicate the presence of fiction. These texts can act as catalysts for the Gospels. In every milieu where texts are highly regarded, citations become common currency. The meaning of the biblical passages used is determined by a religious reflection that seeks to capture the impact of God in history and in life. This was the technique that the "poor of Yahweh" spontaneously cultivated "in expectation of the consolation of Israel" (Lk 2:25). Luke echoes their searching (1:66), the spreading of the Good News (2:18 and 38)—things that always flourish where the faithful share the same quest for God. Exegesis without this essential element is a fruitless exercise.

These dialogues are evidently not shorthand reports. They summarize the essential. Their material reconstruction is not given to us because it is of little importance. What exactly was the conversation of Mary with Jesus when she found him in the Temple (Lk 2:48-49)? Might not someone who had witnessed the occurrence by chance have perceived it as the reproach of a distraught mother and the reply of an insubordinate child, or a child employing diversionary tactics? Could one have guessed more? In any case, anyone at all would doubtless have understood less than Mary, for whom the essential gradually became clear, and who was able to evaluate this enigmatic response by seeing the connection of this first heartrending experience to the prediction of the sword and, later, to the passion.

A stranger to poetry and to the experience of faith cannot but spurn or dismiss as artificial the concise and schematic expression of such dialogues, whose literal sequence is quite beyond the possibility of precise reconstruction (though they in no way invite suspicion). Their simplicity, their very ambiguity at the threshold of a future not yet disclosed are good signs of substantial authenticity.

C. THE CANTICLES

The canticles present an analogous problem of oral transmission, though in this case we are dealing with literary forms created for the purpose of ritual repetition according to a fixed format. Though none are found in Matthew, there are several in Luke's infancy Gospel: Elizabeth's miniature canticle (1:25), the Magnificat (1:46-55), the Benedictus (1:67-79), the Gloria (2:14), and the Nunc Dimittis (2:29-32).[19]

Contradictory Hypotheses

The Magnificat and the Benedictus have the form and structure of classical psalms or canticles. There has been a unilateral cultivation of the arguments that would deprive Mary and Zechariah of the authorship which Luke ascribes to them. The Magnificat has been transferred to Elizabeth (see above pp. 3-11) or even to Zechariah, against all exegetical probability, and the Benedictus to the prophetess Anna (Sahlin, 1945, 44).

These theories only reveal the inordinate passion of some exegetes for invention and novelty. More radical views have it that these are Maccabean psalms (Winter) or, on the contrary, that they are late, post-resurrection hymns (Brown and others).[20] Both theories are historically untenable. Both fall outside the period in question, the first being prior, and the second posterior to the event. These diagnostic assertions can both be ruled out as unsatisfactory. But we may retain one important element of Winter's theory: the archaic character of these psalms. They are completely within an OT ambiance and are in no way anachronistic to the time in which Luke situates them. As to the second assertion, our reaction can only be one of surprise, since one looks in vain in these canticles for any allusion to the Resurrection.

To declare that the Magnificat is "too developed" for Mary, and to attribute it to Christians suffering from poverty and hunger in the first generation of Christianity (Brown, 1977, 363-364), represents no progress in literary criticism. Rather, it seems to be a step backward, since this theory departs from the precise data of the text (Lk 1:28-46), in the interest of a contrived and groundless hypothesis. Hunger was a chronic social condition in that milieu, and, in itself, offers no indication for dating the background of the canticle. "The hungry" of the first Christian generation (who are completely unknown to us) have not left us any hymn which we could compare to the Magnificat. Moreover, Mary (to whom Luke attributes the canticle) was a real person; and the Magnificat is eminently appropriate to her personality and her circumstances as we perceive them through the Gospels. The few verbal similarities that have been noted between the Acts of the Apostles and the canticles have no bearing on the question of their authorship.[21]

It is pure projection to attribute to the canticle of Mary a "universalist" character. The Magnificat refers only to Israel. It is only at the end of the Benedictus (1:79) that a universalist perspective begins to emerge. It does not become explicit until the Nunc Dimittis of Simeon and, when it does, it shows nothing of a post-resurrection nature. Such universalism is expressed with reference to Isaiah (as we have seen, and as Brown himself has perceived). Why not then evaluate these texts according to their content rather than according to fragile presuppositions which seek to attribute the canticles to the "creative Christian community" (itself a lovely myth, generously exploited by the *Formgeschichte* school)?

We say this without wishing to fall back into another simplistic outlook which would maintain that this canticle must have been taken down by a secretary, or that Mary (who was probably illiterate as were virtually all women of her era) must have sat down at her desk to write. I don't know that such a position has ever really been held. This type of thing is usually no more than a contrived caricature whose purpose is to discredit what is really a very different, and highly probable, explanation.

In the oral transmission of the prayer, ecclesial and communitary mediation has, without doubt, played an essential role in the way this text has been handed down. But to transmit is not to create. Only systematic presuppositions would justify moving from the first hypothesis to the second.

What "critical" analyses often lose sight of is the fact that the prayer of those times lies within the framework of a living tradition. Its roots lay in past models that lent themselves to successive layers of updating which almost went unnoticed. The important thing, then, is to situate these canticles within their tradition, a tradition which was characterized by a faithful and retentive memory—a phenomenon totally unknown to us.

This memory was spontaneous, interior, open to creativity. It did not follow the pattern of rote-learning under the supervision of a master, which would guarantee material conformity of formulas and rubrics. The people had neither missal nor psalter, but they had memories that were alive. It was within this living environment that Luke recorded the canticles.

There are no canticles anywhere else in his entire work (Luke and Acts). This is not then merely a characteristic of his style as an author. There is no doubt that what we have here is quite simply a new indication of his fidelity in following his sources in accordance with their distinctive character.

The Tradition of the Magnificat

The tradition of the Magnificat is in no way contrived. Its existence may be readily accounted for. Continuity is discernible. The first link, the prototype, is the canticle of Hannah, mother of Samuel, from a thousand years earlier (1 Sm 2:1-10). It too was a prayer of thanksgiving for a birth recognized as a gift of God, and this act of thanksgiving already extends to include the poor whom God lifts up, even as he puts down the rich and the powerful.

1 Samuel 2:1-10 *Canticle of Hannah*	*Luke 1:46-55* *Magnificat*
My heart exults in the Lord;. . . because I rejoice in thy salvation. The bows of the mighty are broken, but the feeble gird on strength. Those who were full have hired themselves out for bread, but those who were hungry have ceased to hunger.	My soul magnifies the Lord; and my spirit rejoices in God my Savior. He has put down the mighty from their thrones and exalted those of low degree; He has filled the hungry with good things and the rich he has sent away empty. [= 1:52, he raised the lowly].
The Lord kills and brings to life;	He has shown strength with his arm,
The Lord. . . will give strength to his king.	He has helped his servant Israel, in remembrance of his mercy.[22]

Given the climate of oral tradition, is it impossible to imagine Mary adapting the biblical canticle of Hannah to her own experiences, which she lived in the depth of her being, both in accordance with God and, by Luke's own testimony, in vital reference to Scripture?[23]

There is no way for us to reconstruct the stages between the visitation event in which Luke situates this canticle and the form he has given it in his Gospel. Its transmission, which must have entailed adaptations to living circumstances, in line with the practice of the time, must have involved Mary herself, as she lived and worshiped in the primitive community of Jerusalem where Luke himself places her (Acts 1:14). Between the prayer of this Judeo-Christian community and Luke, a translation necessarily intervened, hence its adaptation in Greek. It should cause no surprise that the final written form should bear the mark of Luke. The final redaction of the Magnificat by Luke may have benefited from the light of the Resurrection, but it has done so without anachronism or evident transformation, and undoubtedly in literal contact with the transmitted canticle.

When all is said and done, this thanksgiving prayer is its own best authenticating evidence. Here again the reasonable solution is to accept the datum as it presents itself, since we lack the means of reconstructing the stages of the community tradition which probably intervened between Mary and Luke (direct contact between these two being improbable though not impossible).

The affinities of this canticle with the annunciation scene that so many ignore have been brought out above. Mary reiterates here that she is a servant. This is the term by which she defines herself in 1:48 as well as in 1:38.

The Other Canticles

The principles of oral tradition must be kept in mind regarding the prehistory of the other canticles reported by Luke. But these last do not benefit from as many distinct echoes and allusions to the surrounding narrative as does the Magnificat.

The Benedictus and the Nunc Dimittis[24] are ascribed to old men, long since dead by the time of the writing of the Gospels—in contrast to Mary, who was able to perpetuate the memory of her hymn beyond Pentecost within the first Christian community, which evidently formed the immediate source of Luke 1-2 and Acts 1-2. The reference of Luke to the recollections which the witnesses of the infancy of John the Baptist preserved in their hearts is more vague. The mediating role of the community here appears to be a more important factor.

The Benedictus: Likelihood of its Historicity

The Benedictus (Greek *eulogētos*, 1:69) occurs as a revival of the *eulogōn* of 1:64, in which Zechariah blessed God. However, no argument can be deduced from this similarity regarding the origin and genesis of this canticle.

The first part of the Benedictus takes up the theme and the terms of the Magnificat, as we have seen. This is an indication of derivativeness. But no deduction is possible from this indication. It may be held that Zechariah echoes Mary's thanksgiving in his explicit praise of the Savior-Messiah (1:69-75), to which he adds an original prophecy regarding the newborn John the Baptist (1:76-79). Oral tradition, so much alive in that epoch, furnishes serious support for this hypothesis.

The attribution of the Benedictus to Zechariah nevertheless presents less of a probability than the attribution of the Magnificat to Mary: Zechariah disappeared from the scene several decades before she did, and Luke does not refer to him as an exemplary witness, as he does with Mary.

Does the fact that the first part of the Benedictus follows the schema of the Magnificat oblige one to conclude that Luke has refashioned the Magnificat in order to put it on Zechariah's lips (as a widely held opinion has it)? There are a good many arguments against such a theory. Luke was not a writer of canticles: they do not appear anywhere else in his writing. He reported such material as he gathered it, merely putting his mark upon the translation, or the rewriting of a translation, and on the final form.

Like the Magnificat, this canticle gives indications of having behind it a Hebrew original (into which it is easily re-translated). Among the most striking indications of this original are the traces of etymological allusions, which abound in all translations back into Hebrew.

Here is a remarkable fact: The Greek text of the Magnificat has clearly retained the obvious words corresponding to the Hebrew names of the first three characters mentioned: Jesus, John, Zechariah. But it softens the word "swear" (called for by the context and corresponding to the root of the name Elizabeth) into "speak." On the other hand, the Benedictus, in which *horkon hon ōmosen*, "the oath he swore" appears (well rendered by the Latin *jusjurandum quod juravit*), contains a word that usually corresponds to the root of the name Elizabeth: *sb'* (twice).

A double conclusion imposes itself: The deletion of the allusive word in the Magnificat (without loss of meaning, as the promise in 1:55 clearly shows) is attributable to Luke, a Greek writer who would not have been very sensitive to etymological allusions. But if, after all, he had created the Benedictus in Greek, as some say, how could he have reinforced (indeed, doubled) the words which create etymological allusions in the Hebrew re-translation? That would be very difficult to explain.

If, then, the Benedictus is based on the Magnificat, it is not the work of a hellenic writer and must be placed at the older level of a Semitic tradition, probably oral. From this perspective, the Benedictus has simply taken up the same theme as the Magnificat, adding to it the prophetic thanksgiving for the birth of John the Baptist (1:76-79).

On this hypothesis, it is obviously not the memory of Zechariah, an old man soon to die, which preserves the Benedictus, but the memory of Mary. In effect, according to the interpretation to which Luke 1:56 lends itself (see above pp. 157-158), she stayed in the house of Zechariah until the birth and circumcision of John. Zechariah, mute witness to the Magnificat, could have adopted that same thanksgiving (1:68-75), adding his own development on the subject of John the Baptist (1:76-79). In this case, the prayer of the priest could easily have been preserved by Mary, who recognized her own theme in this reiteration.

We do not pretend to furnish proof of this hypothesis, but it is one which concurs with the admitted facts and the multiple indications which oppose bookish hypotheses. On that basis, it merits retention. It is the only hypothesis which accounts for the texts and facts, and which takes into consideration the massive fact of oral tradition.

VI
THE WONDERS

The ancients were given to projecting wonders onto the sacred.[1] Historical criticism has been right in trying to purify the legends of the saints and the stories of sanctuary origins. The Gospels cannot, on principle, be shielded from the exigency of truth. They are in no privileged position in this regard. But this critical exigency should not be confused with systematic distrust. Properly conducted critical work does not always destroy everything.[2]

A. MIRACLE, CHALLENGE OR PROVEN FACT?

We treat the miraculous aspect of the infancy Gospels separately, with some regret, for these aspects are not disconnected from the rest. They are an integral part of a global experience and communication. Separate treatment is necessary because this aspect of the Gospels is not often examined according to the ordinary rules. Criticism most often alters the criteria at this point. It disregards the criteria customarily applied to factual reports and resorts to a priori presuppositions.

Often it does this without warning. We may be grateful to reductionist exegetes who have frankly described their principles. This is the case with Hugo Gressmann:

> When angels descend from heaven and appear to men, we no longer have an historical account, but a legend...depicted in the colors of creative imagination.[3]

Christian Hartlich is clearer still (*Concilium*, 58, 1980, 11-18). Every miracle, he declares *ex professo*, is without historical value:

> A man walking on water (Mt 14:25-33) contradicts every known law of experience.... Objective reality of events is not demonstrable except to the degree that they harmonize with the general conditions of authentic...knowledge, unlike reality that is simply presumed....

This a priori exclusion governs the following hermeneutic:

> Starting from, and relying on, the notion that miraculous events did not really happen, the critical historian poses the following question: what conditions must have been present *subjectively* in the minds of the narrators of the sacred history for them to be able to recount miraculous "events" as though they had really happened?
>
> One responds to this question by showing that the phenomenon of sacred history only appears in such eras and such societies where no incisive critical reflection has yet been arrived at concerning the conditions which underlie assertions bearing on these allegedly true events. [. . . When this does arise, one] gets to the root of the traditional understanding of Christianity. . . these assertions are doubtless cast in the forms of history, but they do not reconstruct any verifiable, real history. . . .
>
> The evangelists make use of the form: history. . . in order to stimulate faith. . . . To this end they employ stories that have been transmitted and that constitute a plastic material capable of being molded. . ., in accordance with the specific literary purpose of each—a purpose in any case not directed toward the idea of establishing facts. In other words, their objectifying assertions function in varying ways, subject to their basic underlying intentions, which are not addressed to the hearer's cognitive faculty, but which rather summon him to acknowledge the possibility of new life. Thus, anyone who would transform the apparently historical assertions contained in the Gospel miracle-accounts into affirmations of facts commits a fatal theological error: he is transforming sacred history . . . into a primary object of faith. In an era which no longer employs myths, a Church or a theology which would require that mythical assertions be held as true. . . would pervert Christianity into a mythodoxy.

These are not "arbitrary presuppositions," the author concludes: "the historical-critical method is based upon the cognitive make-up of man." It supports a radical understanding of Christianity.

According to this system, every miracle is eliminated a priori and scientific exegesis is authorized to explain them as the expression of an idea, whose origin one may conjecture *per fas et nefas* (by fair means or foul).

These explanations are purportedly based on the difference between the mythological mentality of the past and the critical mind of today. To be sure, cultural changes have been considerable and ought to be taken objectively into account. But this school's presuppositions falsify this objectivity into a system, and perpetuate the law of the three stages of which Auguste Comte was so fond—the mythological, the metaphysical, and the positivistic. The first two have supposedly been abolished, and only the third survives. But evolution is not so simple. The new strata of intelligence do not abolish the primitive strata: "The paleocephalic subsists beneath the neocephalic" (the old brain beneath the new brain), as J. Fourastié says.[4] It remains essential for our humanity, for love, for the perception of meaning, and of destiny. All human thought begins and is thoroughly steeped in a basic symbolism which we experience every night, in every dream. Even though this thought acquires refinement and development thanks to critical reason and the positivist spirit which bases truth on experience, nevertheless we still preserve our roots, for without them everything else would die.

Contrary to the radical evolutionary theory, poetry remains irrepressible, as does love, human or divine. The symbolic stratum is primary in human awareness. It precedes reflection and language. It never really disappears; instead it haunts our dreams. It remains the antenna through which we apprehend our ties with the world and with what is beyond this world. It is at this level that the Gospel expresses itself, in the language of the poor. This level endures, with its antennae only dimly identified. Those who have apparitions experience them as real events, not as imaginary or literary creations. If it should happen by the year 3000 that all the Lourdes documents had been destroyed, it would be easy to explain the account of the apparitions as a literary construction, the translation of an idea into the form of a *theologoumenon.* Such a reconstruction would be in contradiction to the numerous oral cross-examinations involving Bernadette, the substantial content of which she never changed, rarely even resorting to synonyms. After this, one may still ask about the nature of her experience. But, it is impossible to evade this primary evidence which is well documented—this in contrast to the case of the Gospel, where the field remains open to the inventions of criticism.

It is difficult to reach agreement here, because socio-cultural presuppositions have changed rapidly on the matter, so that few people really know where they stand. For the dogma which affirms the reality of miracles there has been substituted the dogma which excludes them. The First Vatican Council (1869-1870) defended miracles as the basis of faith, against the denials of rationalism. Today, rationalist presuppositions have won over a good part of the ecclesiastical intelligentsia. Vatican I held that it was necessary to believe *because* of miracles. The enlightened Christian today says that he believes in spite of miracles.[5]

It is ironic that this opposition to miracles has gained ground within the Church at the very time when the scientific world has outgrown the naive views of scientism that ruled out miracles on principle. For twentieth-century science has made progress in its acceptance of baffling facts that have demanded more complex explanations: relativity, the principle of uncertainty, statistical evaluation of certain facts, and so on. Science today is willing to look into phenomena that are difficult to explain, which were formerly either ignored or denied a priori. The science of the age of enlightenment won its freedom through its struggle against theological obscurantism in the name of pure reason. The clergy, who are often behind in the matter of revolution, have become "open" to scientific rationalism at the very time when science has gone beyond it.

Systematic skepticism has replaced credulity in the area of religious history. It is necessary to go beyond simplistic positions. In this regard, one may distinguish three levels on which confusion may muddle the debate:

1. The assessment of literary influences: sources are an element of explanation of texts.

2. The reference to facts, which are also an explanatory factor. They must be weighed according to the normal rules of historical criticism: sincerity of the witness, coherence of testimony, cross-checkings for convergences, and so on.

3. Finally, the presuppositions that function at two levels: those that prevail in the culture of the evangelists; and those indigenous to our culture today, as we evaluate the Gospels. This is a complex domain.

Methodological presuppositions tend to reduce reality to the assimilative capacity of the method employed, or at least to grant privileged status to the object that comes within their scope. Every human being has a tendency to consider things only according to the particular light at his or her disposal.

To this must be added the philosophical presuppositions, predominantly idealistic and rationalistic, derived from Kant and Hegel, to which Strauss gave form in the middle of the nineteenth century, at the time when the historical-critical method was being developed.[6] According to these presuppositions, it was tacitly admitted that every miracle or every communication with God is illusory and should be explained as a creative invention of the author: mythology or *theologoumenon*. This principle prevails, even today, in a notable segment of Catholic exegesis. We have just noted how one of the theoreticians of the historical-critical method assures us that such facts were admitted only in a precritical stage of culture. To be sure, it is necessary to be attentive to the differences between the original milieu of the Gospels and our own: each has its own linguistic and cultural baggage, its own memory, its guideposts and standards. What is regrettable in reductionistic exegesis is not critical exigency, but precisely the reduction of the *objective* data.

When a scienctific method addresses the problem of evaluating cultural confrontations, impacts, and evolutions, it is performing an objective and necessary task which is one stage in the work of every exegete. But to eliminate every supernatural fact, miracle, or revelation, and to explain it as a *theologoumenon*, is to substitute an ideological system for objective study. These spiritual phenomena have existed from OT times down to our own day, despite cultural changes which have the effect of a kind of refraction that produces superficial but not substantial differences. They exist in a *chiaroscuro*, which is as foreign to magic as it is to the closed world of the laboratory or to the creations of novelists. To reduce this body of original phenomena to a series of literary creations is to ignore the fact that these Christian experiences continue according to the same laws and the same element of unpredictability, even if today they are discredited and often repressed. Objectivity demands that we evaluate them for what they

are. This ought to be done with critical judgment on two accounts:
—The authenticity of these exceptional facts calls for painstaking discernment or evaluation.
—We must take into account the illusions or extrapolations which are frequent in these matters.

The living seers with whom I am acquainted, and who lead a completely normal life—not only priests or religious but fathers or mothers of families, practicing their professions like anyone else—speak of their experience with great concern for objectivity, one might even say for precision. They refuse to allow what they have seen or heard to be doctored up, however slightly, even for the sake of edification. If one explains to them how reductionist methods work in these matters, they really light up, for they then understand why, in the event of an interrogation, they are subjected to so many questions, objections and suspicions which seem strange to them.

B. REVELATIONS AND COMMUNICATIONS

What we have said above dispenses us from spending too much time on the mystical communications reported in the infancy Gospels. They are of two kinds: messages attributed to angels and inspirations of the Holy Spirit.

Audial or visual communications received from God are hardly frequent, but they have never ceased, throughout the centuries, from the time of the prophets up to our own day. They remain very much alive, but today they are becoming more discreet than ever before, in view of the poor reception accorded to them. So they may appear more exceptional than they are in fact.[7]

If Francis of Assisi, Teresa of Avila and so many others, right up to the time of St. Catherine Labouré, St. Bernadette and the children of Fatima, Beauraing and Banneaux (who are still alive), have had visions, or heavenly communications, why exclude these phenomena from the founding experience of Christianity? Why couldn't the mother of Christ have received from God the call so necessary to her mission?

The revelation she received at that time, according to Luke's Gospel, is in keeping, without anachronism, with the language of the OT. In retrospect, we realize that this was the only possible line of approach for such a novel announcement—to a woman, possibly illiterate, who knew only Scripture. The inner quality of this revelation is the best proof of its authenticity. God would hardly have acted in accord with his own self-revelation and the relationship he sustains with human beings, even today, had he used this woman as an object, an instrument, totally unaware of his plan to integrate his Son into the human race.

The stylization of this account is significant. It diverges from the model of birth narratives which characterize the annunciation to Zechariah, fitting instead the vocation narrative model—this in spite of the concern for parallelism that governs the composition of the two annunciations.

Here again, there is doubtless no way we could reconstruct in its exact content an experience that was surely ineffable. The Gospel refrains from telling us that Mary was favored with a visual apparition, presenting her experience as something heard. Was it sensible or purely intellectual? We have no way of judging. How did this intimate experience take shape? How was it transmitted? We do not know this either. But here again Luke's explicit reference to the memories which Mary pondered in her heart should caution us against viewing the account in Luke 1-2 as literary invention. How could this historian, whose faithfulness to sources was greater than his originality, have created a text of such depth, such extraordinary coherence? More than anyone else, he is in himself the best proof of his own authenticity.

The same basic principles govern the interpretation of other revelations of Luke 1-2, those to Zechariah (Lk 1:11-20) and to the shepherds in the account of the birth (Lk 2:9-17). In these cases, we no longer have the benefit of the same cross-references. Neither does the Gospel furnish us with information about the mode of transmission. The more anecdotal form inclines one to allow more scope for literary elaboration here. However, we still cannot get away from the basic question: If Matthew and Luke were looking for what might have been God's revelation at the beginning of Christ's life, how could they possibly have found nothing? And if, in fact, they had found nothing, why would they have had recourse to fiction? Such a revelation would not have been necessary in itself to establish faith which is founded on the Resurrection. What they inherited regarding the *kenosis* of Christ, they received in great freedom of spirit.

To be sure, questions may be asked. Serra, who methodically analyzed the correspondences between the vocabulary of Luke 1-2 and that of the Passion-Resurrection narrative in Luke 23-24 according to accepted modern methods, tries to distinguish, on the basis of this comparison, the historical content of the infancy narrative according to Luke (its factual nucleus) and the interpretation or retrospective extrapolation. The titles of Savior, Christ, Lord (Lk 2:11) would, according to this analysis, seem to be a post-paschal projection, as would the angelic manifestations. The factual nucleus would have been a visit of shepherds (who were numerous in this country) to the Holy Family. The rest would seem to derive from retrospective modeling. From this analysis, we would assume that Luke 2 testifies to the light of Easter in which meditation of the infancy took place (2:19 and 51). But none of the words Luke employs are alien to the OT, none defy probability or modesty. If revelation and communication with God are an enduring fact of Christian experience, need one hasten to conform with the presuppositions of a critical methodology according to which creative imagination must be accorded maximum probability since religion is a matter of subjectivity?[8] Certainly the factors of transmission, style of expression, selection, transposition, and elaboration do stand between the event and Luke's narrative. But do we necessarily arrive at greater truth when, in striving to reconstruct this unverifiable genesis, we systematically favor the authors' creativity over objective reference to events? Is not the credibility one is intent on gaining relative to modern prejudices more than to objective truth?

What must be emphasized is the fundamental sobriety of the revelations reported by Luke, whatever conventional imagery these may display, especially in the annunciation to Zechariah and to the shepherds. On these two points it is difficult to distinguish between the reported experience and its mode of expression, the criterion for which we shall see later (p. 432-448). As for the communications of the Holy Spirit reported throughout Luke 1-2 (to Mary, 1:35; John the

Baptist and Elizabeth, 1:15 and 41; to Zechariah, 1:67, to Simeon, 2:25-27 and to the prophetess Anna, 2:36), one is dealing with a divested form of the supernatural which does not involve the miraculous or improbable. For, according to Christian experience and theology, it is characteristic of the Holy Spirit not to appear objectively but to awaken each individual to the challenge of his or her freedom, from within. It is worth noting that Luke 1-2 locates divine communication chiefly at this profound level of the Spirit's influence, in line with the prophets and prefiguring the Pentecost event.

C. THE STAR, ANGELS AND DREAMS

What are we to make today of the stars, angels, and dreams that pervade the infancy Gospels? With these we move from the realm of existential communications between human beings and God to that of miraculous or providential signs. Media such as these run directly up against the objections prevalent today. Above all it is important to consider them in terms of their essential meaning: the relation with God which they manifest.

The sign set forth is a means. As such it is relative. It is often formulated in function of a particular culture. Thus, refinement in the manner of referring to God led the authors of the biblical tradition to attribute to the angel of the Lord what they had originally attributed to God himself (see below, p. 439). Signs, which, in their great variety, are the fabric of human communication with God, receive particular determination through the culture of the recipient, whether this be viewed as God's adapting *ad modum recipientis* (to the capacity of the recipient) or as the subject's refracting or interpreting, in his or her own way, an ineffable divine communication. Moreover, the border line between these two factors is most difficult to discern.[9]

To speak of signs, then, is to affirm that a human experience comes within the scope of scientific study, without excluding the possibility that signs are a way of entering into vital relationship with God, without reducing them to our standards of measurement.

The Star[10]

Divergent as their narratives are, both Matthew and Luke speak of stars. But they do so in totally different contexts.

For Matthew it is the star of the wise men who come from the East (*apo anatolōn*) saying, "We have seen his star in the East" (*en tē anatolē*), the star of the Messiah, king of the Jews (2:1-12).

For Luke it is the star of the canticle of Zechariah in which the Messiah is represented as the one "who has visited us," (a star) rising (*anatolē*) from on high (1:78).

Some have sought to explain this as a *theologoumenon* based on the prophecy of Balaam:

> A star shall come forth (*anatelei*) out of Jacob, and a sceptre shall rise out of Israel (Nm 24:17).

It is possible that the two evangelists are drawing on this prophecy, which was frequently cited at Qumran.[11]

However, the contacts (terms and themes) could hardly be more tenuous—specifically, the single root *anatellō*, meaning the Orient, the East, or the rising of a star. This root is employed in its verbal form in Balaam's prophecy, according to the Septuagint, and as a substantive signifying, in an ambiguous way, the East, in Matthew 2:1. The wise men came from the East (*apo anatolōn*); this same word serves to designate the star in its rising on the horizon in Luke 1:78. Luke does not use the word "star," and Matthew uses it in the form *astēr* (2:7, 9, 10) whereas the LXX uses *astron* for the prophecy of Balaam. Matthew was describing the journeying quest of the astrologers and Luke was suggesting the imminent manifestation of the Messiah in lyrical terms, none of which coincide with those of Numbers 24:17.

If, then, it is possible that both evangelists had the image in mind, still, this prophecy cannot be the explanation for their widely different texts. It is not necessary that the mention of "star" had any connection to Balaam. This was a classical and polyvalent symbol for evoking, among other things, a god or a divinized king, or the Messiah. We shall return to this point in the chapter on symbolism.

If the lyrical prediction of Luke 1:78 poses no problems of historicity, Matthew leaves himself open to criticism, because his account seems at first to suggest an astronomical datum; this star appears in the East (*en tē anatolē*) and draws the wise men toward Jerusalem, in accordance with the apparent direction the rotation of the earth gives to the stars (2:1-2). But after this the star follows a north-south route and "stops over the precise spot where the infant was." Do we have here a miracle of the first order? John Chrysostom did not think so at all. He wrote:

> We learn from scripture that this star is by no means just one of the stars. It wasn't even a star, it seems to me, but some invisible *dynamis* (a sign of God) which took on the appearance of a star. And one can prove this by the route it took, for we see the sun, the moon and the other stars travel toward the west but this one went north to south. It did not appear at night but in the full light of the sun. . . . It did not have a course of its own but went and stopped where it had to stop, according as the occasion demanded, much like the pillar of the cloud which appeared to the Jews when they had to move on or set up camp.[12]

As regards Matthew 2, we do not have the means of cross-checking and so evaluating to what extent an ordinary or extraordinary astral phenomenon—or something altogether different, as St. John Chrysostom thought—is involved. Nor do we know what might have been the interpretive criteria for the wise men, nor what is to be attributed to the freedom proper to this literary genre or to the symbolization that intervenes in every narrative.

The symbolic factor is more visible in Matthew than in Luke. We shall see later how this influenced the evangelists in their use of, and in the peculiar value they attached to, stars and angels. These two symbolic forms, in the cultural code of that period, functioned somewhat analogously as signs of the transcendent action of God. The efficacy of astral signs as catalysts of man's reflection upon his destiny, in both his cosmic and his divine relationships, requires us to exercise caution in trying to unravel the element of cosmic phenomena from that of projections or interpretations.[13]

Angels

Must the angels of Matthew 1-2 and Luke 1-2 be accounted for in terms of this cultural code? We will have to elucidate this aspect of the narrative in our chapter on symbolism. The Gospel itself makes us aware to what degree the term *angel* functioned as a key word for describing an extraordinary phenomenon. "A voice came from heaven," interpreted by the evangelist as the voice of the Father (Jn 12:28), is interpreted differently by the crowds, "An angel has spoken to him" (12:29). Likewise in Acts 23:9 when Paul is speaking to the Sanhedrin, the Pharisees, fascinated with his discourse, offer their interpretation, "Perhaps an *angel* or a *spirit* has spoken to him" (Acts 23:9).

It was considered very disrespectful to identify the transcendent God with a minor phenomenon. The terminology is fluid here and it is difficult at times to discern its real significance. But a relativizing interpretation should not lose sight of an imposing fact that argues the opposite meaning: the fact that many individuals throughout history, even some contemporaries whose credibility and psychological balance cannot be impunged, have testified to what they described as an encounter with an angel. We have already seen how, in the cultural expression of the evangelists, angels, like stars, were a means of expressing a relationship with God without compromising his transcendence. In this perspective, stars and angels have the same function in apocalyptic literature (see especially Job 38:7 and Baruch 3:34, cited below, p. 439).

Dreams

To admit the existence of angels is a veritable challenge in our contemporary socio-cultural system. The "man or woman of our times" can be grateful then to Matthew for situating the communications of angels exclusively in dreams.[14] Dreams situate divine revelation in the ebb and flow of impulses that traverse our most unreflective activity which, after all, occupies a third of our lives. Our dreams haunt us, although we often take no note of them. They help us to escape the restraints and limits of ordinary life. At times we are tempted to concede to them a mysterious, subtle significance, requiring interpretation. These intercultural phenomena testify to the fact that knowledge goes beyond the limits of our "codes" and our cultures. This resource remains a source. Communication through dreams has structural modalities that are proper to the Bible; a nightly vision does not entail dialogue. Only the celestial messenger speaks, and he commands with authority (see, for example, Acts 5:19; 12:7-8).

By reducing divine communication to dreams, Matthew presents the supernatural dimension of the infancy of Christ in the most modest way possible, not resorting to the miraculous, remaining on the common ground of dreams, as opposed to anything spectacular that might shock reason.

Conclusion

To sum up: In the cultural milieu of this time, in a religious environment where charisms flourished, it is altogether natural that the fabric of events should include three points of reference that played a role in the daily life of the people of that era: the watching of the *stars* which were believed to be closely bound up with the life of this world; *private messages* from God, which were not attributed directly to God, but to his angelic envoys, out of respect for his transcendence; and *premonitory dreams*. It really would be surprising if we were to discover no such elements in the religious experience of those times or that such phenomena were not viewed as important by the redactors of the Gospels.

VII
THE VIRGINAL CONCEPTION

The most difficult problem posed by the infancy Gospels is that of the virginal conception.[1] What is at issue in the case of angels, the star, and dreams is merely the mode of communication (necessarily symbolic) between God and men. This is an area where the subtle dialectic of the relationships between the sign and the reality (mode and term of knowledge) leaves room for a large range of hypotheses. Different outlooks can meet here and still keep the basic historical value of Luke 1-2 and Matthew 1-2 intact.

A. THE PROBLEM

In the case of the virginal conception, the evangelists are asserting a biological fact and there is no escaping the alternatives: fiction or reality.

The response is not a matter of indifference. It concerns the very manner of the arrival of the one who is God among humans: his origin, his initial relationship to humanity and, concretely, to his mother and his father (adoptive father according to Matthew). The problem is in some ways analogous to the problem of the Resurrection. In both instances, the Gospel declares a fact that is both historical and corporeal: historical, because it is an event; corporeal, because it concerns the body of Christ. In both cases, the evangelists do not describe the phenomenon itself. Much less do they provide scientific documentation commensurate with such an extraordinary happening. The events are accepted on faith at a deeper level, as they represent what might be viewed as limit-testimonies of God occurring at two key moments of salvation, at its beginning and its end.

The difficulties which the Resurrection presents to scientific determinism can be tempered, even eliminated. Some theologians believe they have done this successfully. They situate the Resurrection outside the laws of our cosmos. It is not a reanimation, they insist, and the Resurrection does not require that the elements of the body be taken up again by the resurrected subject. The resurrected body no longer belongs to our space-time structure. It is a "spiritual body," according to the apostle Paul (1 Cor 15:44), the object of a truly transcendent experience. Those who have carried this explanation to its extremes sometimes say, "The difficulty is the empty tomb," because this datum of the Gospel claims that Christ took up again his own body (scourged, crucified, pierced). They eliminate the empty tomb and interpret it (not without doing some violence to the texts) as a literary fiction. They think that they are thus providing a surer affirmation of true resurrection, since it is the soul, and not the physical particles, which constitutes the identity of the body.

Another hypothesis is that this Resurrection is similar to the resurrection of all the elect, because everyone experiences resurrection at the moment of death by passing from our space and time into the eternity of God, where the material constituent of the body is of little significance. The Judgment is merely the final recapitulation of these instantaneous passages into God's eternity (Rahner's thesis, refuted by Schillebeeckx). It is thus thought possible to bypass the cosmic dimension of the Resurrection without denying its essential meaning.

The virginal conception does not offer an analogous escape-route. If one does not acknowledge that Jesus was conceived without a father, miraculously, if one reintroduces the role of a human father, then Mary can no longer be presented as a virgin, and it is then necessary to enter upon a round of hypotheses which alter the human conditions of the Incarnation.

Ought we then to think that there may have been pre-marital relations between Mary and Joseph? Or extra-marital, therefore adulterous relations? These questions have been asked by the Spanish Catholic theologian X. Pikaza.[2] He goes to great lengths to show that all these hypotheses would have an equal symbolic value; for example, a Magdalen-like mother of God would more effectively demonstrate mercy.

This would mean, however, that the evangelists have lied; even if in good faith, they would have lied, and Christian tradition has been consequently deceived. Only through an illusion could Mary have been held to be a model and inspiration of virgins. The rejection of this model, considered dangerous (even morbid and repressive), is in fact one added reason for criticising the virginal conception. Denise Boucher, author of a feminist play which caused quite a stir in Quebec (*Les fées ont soif*), gives a radical and truculent expression to this denunciation:

> Why did the Middle Ages make a virgin out of the mother of a revolutionary who bore a message of love and liberty? Why was it necessary right up to our own times to destroy the real womb of this woman? Why was it necessary to propel her into the virgin category? It is an insult to all women, hurled by the Fathers of the Church, who were bachelors obsessed by celibacy. . . . They were celibates; therefore they needed virgins.[3]

On several scores the virginal conception has been a favorite target of criticism for more than a century and a half. But our aim is not to caricature the quite understandable prejudices which are opposed to the virginal conception.[4] Even if it is necessary to challenge rationalism as a system which would prevent God from working a miracle in this area, the legitimate demands of reason ought to be taken into consideration, because faith is neither unreasonable nor absurd. The degree of improbability of such a fact ought to be evaluated.

On the scientific plane, parthenogenesis is not a miracle against nature. Long ago, Origen (*Contra Celsum*, 1.37) defended its probability, pointing to the natural phenomena of animal parthenogenesis. Today, parthenogenesis is the object of experimentation, and there has been some success with it in certain mammals. But the scientific advances which make such a phenomenon more probable cause a new difficulty: due to a lack of chromosome Y, the product of parthenogenesis would be of the female sex. It is not to be ruled out that scientific experimentation may find a way of compensating for this absence of chromosome Y. But the solution of our problem does not lie in reducing the virginal conception to a natural phenomenon.

The efforts of exegesis to measure each of Christ's miracles by this yardstick are often forced: for example, when the multiplication of loaves is turned into "a mere miracle of sharing" by multiplying the little boy who had five loaves in order to avoid the multiplication of loaves. Here Brown quite rightly remarks:

> These attempts, though often well-intentioned, represent a misunderstanding of what Christian tradition intended by the virginal conception. It was an extraordinary action of God's creative power, as unique as the initial creation itself (and that is why all natural science objections to it are irrelevant, e.g., that not having a human father, Jesus' genetic structure would be abnormal). It was not a phenomenon of nature; and to reduce it to one, however unusual, would be as serious a challenge as to deny it altogether.[5]

Confrontation with science only serves to show that a miracle is in continuity with the natural order, not in contradiction to it. This is in line with the thinking of St. Thomas Aquinas, who stated that the wisdom of God would limit itself to miracles *praeter naturam* (and not *contra naturam*). To evaluate this difficult question, it is important therefore to clearly distinguish two programs that are often confused: the exegetical determinations arrived at according to the rules of historical criticism, and the establishing of presuppositions[6] which guide, determine, and govern interpretation.

Let us examine these two factors successively, as their interference triggers so much confusion and illusory consensus.

B. THE EXEGETICAL ARGUMENTS— AN IRREDUCIBLE GIVEN

If one keeps to the usual and objective rules for evaluating any given testimony (keeping aside any a priori prejudice concerning the possibility of a given occurrence), the virgin birth stands as a serious and solid datum. It is affirmed in an independent way, as we have seen, by the two infancy Gospels. Their divergencies at other points corroborate this remarkable agreement.

This datum occupies, in very different ways, a central place in the two Gospels which the semiotic study has confirmed: this piece of information shattered the Davidic genealogy, which was so important to the messianic ideal at that time, and so essential to their primary project. It forced them to reconsider everything anew.

The two evangelists managed to do this against the mainstream of their respective cultures. They accept this datum in spite of the absence of biblical antecedents. The only possible biblical link was the prophecy of Isaiah 7:14. But they had to interpret this prophecy in a sense that was totally different from that of the Jewish tradition, which saw in the text no trace whatever of a virginal conception.

This miraculous factor, embarrassing just from the cultural point of view, was as difficult to believe in the past as it is today. A virgin birth was just as much a target for skepticism and sarcasm then as it is now. Jewish literature testifies to this, as we shall soon see. If then the evangelists accepted this paradoxical datum, it is because it imposed itself as a fact. Some have sought in vain to find in some a priori assumption a compelling reason for the evangelists' retaining this fact. They have failed to do so, except by radically disfiguring the text and often their presumed sources as well. The radical distance the evangelists take with respect to the ideas of their times (the theogamies as well as the idealizations or obscure allegories so dear to the gnostics) is quite significant.

We shall not develop these observations, as they are already well established. It will be sufficient to examine the current watch-words which have assumed the appearance of a "scientific consensus" fatal to the Gospel realism regarding the virginal conception.

Authenticity of the Text

Radical criticism from Hillmann (1891) and Harnack (1901) to Grundmann (1961) has maintained that Luke 1:34 and Matthew 1:18-20 are merely cases of "interpolation." But the text has resisted such elimination, which stems from presuppositions foreign to its own outlook. Textual criticism does not supply any variant that would support such an elimination. The text is taken as it stands by all the critical editions.[7] The internal coherence of the text likewise forbids the elimination. Today the objection has become obsolete.

Multiple Convergences

The virginal conception, it has been said, is marginal, unique in the

NT. This conjecture, which has been repeated insistently since the end of the last century, does not square any better with the facts.

First of all, Matthew and Luke, as different in their information as in their theologies, witness to the virginal conception in a distinct and independent manner. On this point, their contexts differ considerably: for Matthew, Joseph was the "husband of Mary" (1:16) and Mary was "his wife" (1:20, 24); for Luke she was only his "betrothed," even at the time of the birth (1:27; 2:5). Matthew depicts the origin of the Son of God as a new creation, while Luke presents it as a new form of the eschatological presence of Yahweh to his people. However, the two Gospels converge in affirmations which are astonishingly new and unprecedented.

Jesus was really "begotten."[8] Both evangelists use the same verb *gennaō* which expresses the reality of this human generation. They use it in the passive, masking the subject so as to manifest the transcendent character of the paternal origin of Christ. Jesus was indeed begotten but one cannot say that God begot him the way a man would beget. He makes him to be born into the human race in an ineffable manner.

It was not Joseph who begot him (Mt 1:16, 18-25; Lk 1:31, 34-35; 3:24). Mary is the only human origin of Jesus, for Matthew (1:16, 18, 20-23) and for Luke (1:27, 35); both use the word *parthenos* in reference to Isaiah 7:14 (Mt 1:23 and Lk 1:27). The divine origin is not referred to the Father, but to the Holy Spirit (Mt 1:18 and 20; Lk 1:35). This significant datum, which radically excludes every theogamic model, has often escaped notice.[9]

The convergences, both historical and theological, of Matthew and Luke[10] in their totally different perspectives are the more striking since they cannot be attributed to a common source. This has been well demonstrated in different and converging ways by Xavier Léon-Dufour and L. Legrand. Luke and Matthew received the virginal conception, not in the form of a narrative (which would support the *theologoumenon* thesis) but as a "statement," according to the perceptive analysis of Legrand.[11] We would put it still more precisely: It is the statement of a fact which compels recognition even though it goes against the grain, since it involves a birth under strange circumstances which would seem to discredit the origin of Christ. Objectivity invites us to carefully evaluate this convergence, as coherent as it is striking, of two independent witnesses.[12]

Another poorly grounded statement that is often made is that the two infancy Gospels stand in complete isolation in the NT. The implicit cross-references to the rest of the NT are tenuous, it is true, but they are numerous and convergent.

The two other Gospels refer to this unusual birth, both within the context of presumed adultery. In Mark 6:3 the ironic and scornful question of the inhabitants of Nazareth, "Is not this the son of Mary?" seems to imply, "This carpenter, whose father we do not even know."

In John 8:41, the Pharisees, accused by Jesus of not being true sons of Abraham, make the following cutting remark, "We were not born of fornication (*ek porneias*)! We have one father, even God." This perspective seems to witness to the suspicion created by this unusual birth. The ironic tenor of the dialogue continues as Christ says of his adversaries, "You are of your father the devil" (8:44) and not "sons of God" (8:42). They go on to accuse him of being himself a son of the devil (i.e., possessed, 8:48, 52).

The underlying conviction of the evangelist is that they are wrong on all counts: Jesus alone is Son of God (cf. Jn 1:13). They are sons neither of God nor of Abraham. Their infidelity makes them sons of the devil, father of lies and of prostitution, which, in biblical terminology, is the name for infidelity itself.

These Gospel texts coincide with the ancient Jewish tradition according to which Jesus was born of adultery. Thus they tend to confirm the antiquity of this tradition. Celsus (ca. 177-180) explicitly accuses Jesus of having himself invented the story of his birth from a "virgin." Celsus is quoted as saying:

> [Jesus] came from a Jewish village and from a poor country woman who earned her living by spinning. . . . She was driven out by her husband, who was a carpenter by trade, as she was convicted of adultery. After she had been driven out by her husband and while she was wandering about in a disgraceful way she secretly gave birth to Jesus (*Origen: Contra Celsum*, tr. by Henry Chadwick, Cambridge, The University Press, 1953, 1:28, 28).

And again:

> The mother of Jesus is described as having been turned out by the carpenter who was betrothed to her, as she had been convicted of adultery and had a child by a certain soldier named *Panthera* (1:32, 31).

This name of *Panthera* is an anagram of *parthenos*, a virgin.[13] The one whom the Christians called "born of a virgin" (*ek parthenou*) Celsus calls "born of *Panthēr*." This tale may have originated in rumors circulating in Nazareth regarding the unseemly pregnancy of Mary of which we have just heard peculiar echoes.

The Gospel of John has been cited as proof against the virginal conception because he reports, in 6:42, the objection of the unbelieving audience, "Is this not Jesus, the son of Joseph?" and does not refute them. However, in accordance with the very structure of the polemic dialogues in John,[14] the objection of the unbeliever is not overcome by refutation, but by transcending it and by emphasizing ever more profoundly the essential message that Jesus is the son of the Father, "his own Father" (Jn 5:18). We analyzed other examples of this "ironic" dialogue of structure above.

Several objections specifically concern the origin of Christ: the adversaries reproach him with the fact that he was not born in Bethlehem (Jn 7:42). The readers of John (at the end of the first century) would have known that this reproach was groundless. In 6:42, the unbelievers deny the affirmation repeated by Jesus, "I have come down from heaven" (6:33, 38, 41, 50, 51, 58). No, they retort, he is the son of Joseph: "Is not he the son of Joseph, whose father and mother we know? How can he now say, 'I have come down from heaven' ?" (6:42). Jesus reproaches them for this idle murmuring: he has not fallen out of the sky like a meteorite; rather he has come from God as the pre-existing Word. He became flesh (1:14) without the "will of the flesh" (Jn 1:13).[15] The virginal conception is explicitly referred to in this verse (if this reading is accepted):

> He who is born, not of blood, nor of the will of flesh, nor of the will of man, but of God (1:13).

This reading in the singular, attested by the most ancient patristic citations, has been retained in the latest monographs on this verse: Galot,[16] Hofrichter,[17] and de la Potterie,[18] (who carries their thinking even further).

This interpretation is confirmed by the dependence of the Johannine prologue on Luke 1-2. The contacts of thought and of terminology are numerous, as Resch showed at the beginning of this century. The two prologues (Luke and John) are built on the same contrast between John and Jesus, who is called light and glory (Lk 2:32; Jn 1:9, 14) within the framework of a law-grace opposition (Lk 1:15-30; 2:40, 52; Jn 1:16-17), Jesus being given a bad reception (Lk 2:7 and Jn 1:ll).

They share the same reference to the mystery of the virgin birth:

Luke 1:34-35	*John 1:13-14*
I do not know man. How can this be, since I have no husband? And the angel said to her, "The Holy Spirit will come upon you, and	Born, not of the will of man,
the power of the Most High will overshadow you;	but of God. He has pitched his tent among us.
therefore the child to be born will be called	. . . the only Son of God;
holy, the Son of God."	full of grace and truth.

The substantive agreements go beyond those of terminology: Jesus comes from God alone and, in both texts, his bodily presence is signified by the expressions usually used to designate the presence of God in the Ark of the Covenant, the shekinah imagery.

The textual tradition has hesitated between singular and plural, he who is born, Christ, or those who are born, the believers. John does not make that distinction, but rather symbolically identifies the eternal birth of Christ, his birth in history, and his baptismal birth. He does not see these as separate births, but as the eternal birth of the Son of God unfolding in time, through the Incarnation (Jn 1:14) and among

Christians by faith and baptism (Jn 1:12). It is through the "power" given to Christians to "become children of God," by faith in him who was born of the will of God, that the eternal birth is known. The expressions of John 1:13 (exclusion of blood, of the flesh, of man), in their more obvious sense, imply the virgin birth, in reference only to the eternal birth and to the birth of the "children of God" (1:12) which is the Christian experience. The wavering of the textual tradition probably results from the way in which each of these births implies the others. It does not have great significance for the meaning of the text.

John 1:13 reinterprets the virgin birth affirmed in Luke 1:34-35 in terms of pre-existence and of the birth experienced by the Christian community.

In short, three Gospels out of four actually speak of the virginal conception, and even Mark, the only one who is not explicit about the virginal conception, seems to echo the tradition in 6:3. Moreover, his is the only one of the four Gospels which does not name Joseph.

More generally, in the whole of the NT, Jesus is never formally referred to Joseph by way of descent, although he is often called "Son of David" and Joseph is the guarantor of this descent. The rare exceptions are only apparent. In Luke's infancy Gospel, the twofold mention of Joseph as father (2:33, 48) is formally corrected by Jesus himself (2:49). Elsewhere, this expression is used by adversaries or objecting unbelievers who have not understood Jesus' origin. These mentions of Joseph as "father" are found only in the Gospels which explicitly speak of the virginal conception (2:48; cf. 1:34; 3:23, corrected by the phrase "as people thought": 4:22; Mt 13:55; Jn 1:45; 6:42). The other books of the NT make absolutely no mention of this human father.

The apostle Paul, who presented Jesus as being descended from the race of David (Rom 1:2; cf. 2 Tm 2:8) evoked the Incarnation in terms which do not conflict with the virginal conception but on the contrary suggest its exclusively feminine modality. As Vicent Cernuda has shown, Paul experienced difficulty in trying to express this mystery. He does not say that Jesus is "begotten" of the race of David, but that he has "come," "happened" (*ginomai*, not *gennaō*: Rom 1:3; Gal 4:4).[19] He says "come from" a woman, a quite striking expression, which refers him to a mother and not to a human father (Gal 4:4). It would have been more natural and more obvious to say "begotten of a man." Similarly in Romans 8:3 and Philippians 2:7, Paul speaks only of a human likeness or form, as if he is not quite willing to say that Jesus (who has thus "come" to human existence) was born a man.

In short, Paul's theology of Christ's origin contains nothing that conflicts with the idea of virginal conception, but in fact, contains some surprising traits which harmonize with it.[20] Cernuda attempts to demonstrate that they imply it. He concludes:

> St. Paul knew [about] the virginal conception and transmitted it. . . as an integral aspect of the Incarnation. If it is true that this mystery does not constitute by itself a characteristic moment of Pauline theology, it is nonetheless true that the stylized allusions (*analyzed above*) reveal the depth with which the apostle has meditated on this theme, according to its two aspects: the assumption of concrete humanity (by Christ), and the virginal mode of its fulfillment.
>
> He offers us. . . this Christology with remarkable delicacy. . . , as though in code. His archaic formulas confirm that (the virginal conception), often considered illusory in these times, did belong to the most ancient Christian tradition (1978, 289).

This reference to the virginal conception by way of omission is structurally verified throughout the NT. Except in the places where the evangelists have explicitly removed the ambiguity, Jesus is never referred to any father but God.

The virginal conception is indeed a fundamental datum underlying the NT. It surfaces in a sporadic and difficult manner because of its marginal position, in the quiet, unobtrusive infancy of Christ, where for a long time it was no more than a family secret, of less pressing concern than the Resurrection. There was also the difficulty of how to express this novelty regarding the origin of the Son of God. To eliminate these painstaking and difficult convergent witnesses would reveal an abysmal lack of understanding regarding one of the most profound insights that arose in the first generation of Christianity.

An Archaic Datum

This analysis dispenses us from delaying over another objection which has also taken on the appearance of consensus, namely, that explicit assertions of the virginal conception are a late development in the NT. This notion is a vestige of the dated theory that the infancy Gospels themselves are a late addition to Matthew and Luke.[21] The hypothesis has been discredited, but the slogan remains. Scholars still say that the virginal conception does not appear except "in two Gospels of the last third of the first century."[22] The word "late" is without significance in this perspective, since the books of the NT were all written during the second half of the first century. The difference of one or two decades is without any significance here. But is it even certain that the Gospels were written after the Pauline epistles and the year 70? Robinson has demonstrated the weakness of the previously-held consensus on this question, and no one has refuted his thesis, which places their composition between 50 and 60.

A closer investigation into the prehistory of the oral traditions or written sources of the Gospels reveals that there is no reason for considering the infancy Gospels as late. On the contrary, Matthew 1-2 and, above all, Luke 1-2 present an archaic, Judaic, old testamental character which has impressed all exegetes. They bear witness to ancient traditions, preserved in the first Judeo-Christian communities.

A Novelty

The coherent authenticity of the texts on the virginal conception having withstood the properly biblical objections, it became necessary to fall back on another hypothesis, derived from the same presuppositions; this new hypothesis addressed, not now the disintegration of the text of Luke as before, but a theory concerning the influences which would have determined such a construction, proposing that the virginal conception was a model so common at the time that the evangelists were constrained to adopt it. But the verification of this hypothesis was misleading. Scholars searched for determinant models in the pagan religions, not only in the Greco-Roman (Perseus-Romulus) and Egyptian (Horus and the Pharaohs) religions and among the philosophers (Plato, Apollonius of Tyana) but in the oriental religions as well (Buddha, Krishna, the son of Zoroaster). They even sometimes include Mexico in the discussion.[23]

The only example of an impressive terminological contact is a text of Plutarch:

> While a woman can be approached by a divine spirit [*ouk adunaton. . . pneuma theou*, as in Lk 1:35, 37] and made pregnant [*archas geneseōs*, cf. the *gennōmenon* of Lk 1:35].[24]

The conception of the hero is here attributed to the divine spirit and to the *dynamis* (the same term as in Lk 1:35 and 1:17). Plutarch specifies in his *Table Talk* (1969, 117) that God "does not beget by seed" (*dia spermatos*), but by another power (*dynamis*).

There is then an analogy here: for Plutarch spiritualizes the event and adjusts the theogamic model in the direction of transcendence; but this author, who was born in 48-49 and died c. 125, post-dates the Gospels. If any literary influence is at work, it is not that of Plutarch on Luke or Matthew, but rather the reverse.

The future Cardinal Ratzinger was merely expressing an already widely established concensus when he wrote two decades ago:

> Extra-biblical stories of this kind [concerning women who conceive by the action of a god] differ profoundly in vocabulary and imagery from the story of the birth of Jesus. The main contrast consists in the fact that in pagan texts the godhead almost always appears as a fertilizing, procreative power, thus under a more or less sexual aspect and hence in a physical sense as the "father" of the savior-child. As we have seen, nothing of this sort appears in the New Testament: the conception of Jesus is a new creation, not begetting by God. God does not become the biological father of Jesus (1979, 207-208).

The research pursued on the side of Jewish traditions was even more misleading. Isaiah 7:14 was cited. But Jewish tradition never interpreted this as a virginal conception. Isaiah 7:14 does not use the word "virgin," but "young girl." The LXX (two centuries before Christ) had, in the meantime, translated it by *parthenos*; this does not imply a development in the direction of the virginal conception. If this were the case, the Greek text would have retained the most significant factor of the Hebrew text, where it is the young girl who receives the mission of giving the name to the child. In the LXX this mission is given to Ahaz. This version then does not explain, but rather eliminates the more promising suggestion of virginal conception. The version of the LXX represents a regression with respect to the Hebrew text, and it is followed therein by Matthew, for whom it is Joseph who gives the name, and not the mother, as in the original text of Isaiah 7:14 and in Luke 1:31. Furthermore, the Greek word *parthenos* (virgin) is not all that significant: Dinah, the daughter of Jacob, was called "virgin" even after having been violated. The narrator remarks regarding Shechem, "His soul was drawn to Dinah the daughter of Jacob. He loved the maiden (*parthenos*) and spoke tenderly to her" (Gn 34:3). At the level of Jewish tradition, the mention of a virgin (in Is 7:14 and elsewhere) pointed less to the virginity of the mother than to the birth of the first-born son, who "opened the womb."[25]

In the Jewish tradition, the text which has appeared closest and most suited to elucidate the infancy Gospels is *De cherubim*, where Philo explains how the patriarchs, joined to Wisdom, conceive through it:

> The persons to whose virtue the lawgiver has testified, such as Abraham, Isaac, Jacob and Moses, and others of the same spirit, are not represented by him as knowing women. For since we hold that woman signifies in a figure (*tropikōs*) sense-perception, and that knowledge comes into being through estrangement from sense and body, it will follow that the lovers of wisdom reject rather than choose sense. And surely this is natural. For the helpmate of these men are called women, but are in reality virtues. Sarah, "sovereign and leader," Rebecca, "steadfastness in excellence," Leah, "rejected and faint" through the unbroken discipline, which every fool rejects and turns from with words of denial, Zipporah, the mate of Moses, whose name is "bird," speeding upwards from earth to heaven and contemplating there the nature of things divine and blessed.
>
> The virtues have their conception and their birth-pangs, but when I propose to speak of them let them who corrupt religion into superstition close their ears or depart. For this is a divine mystery . . . !
>
> Thus must the sacred instruction begin. Man and Woman, male and female of the human race, in the course of nature come together to hold intercourse for the procreation of children. But virtues whose offspring are so many and so perfect may not have to do with

> mortal man, yet if they receive not seed of generation from another they will never of themselves conceive. Who then is he that sows in them the good seed save the Father of all, that is God unbegotten and begetter of all things? He then sows, but the fruit of His sowing, the fruit which is His own, He bestows as a gift. For God begets nothing for Himself, for He is in want of nothing, but all for him who needs to receive (Philo, *On the Cherubim* 12-13, tr. by F. H. Colson and G. H. Whitaker, The Loeb Classical Library, 1950, 33-35).[26]

This brief extract suffices to show how far we are from the infancy Gospels. First of all, we find ourselves wholly in the realm of allegory. It is the virtues of the patriarchs, and not their genealogy, which is in question. There is no mention of the Holy Spirit, but rather of God who appears as the one who begets—this in stark contrast to Matthew—with the insistence of the text on the sowing of seed (spiritual, no doubt, but an element that Matthew and Luke carefully avoid). Philo concludes:

> I will give as a warrant for my words one that none can dispute, Moses the holiest of men. For he shows us Sarah conceiving at the time when God visited her in her solitude (Gn 21:1), but when she brings forth it is not to the Author of her visitation, but to him who seeks to win wisdom, whose name is Abraham.
>
> And even clearer is Moses' teaching of Leah, that God opened her womb (Gn 29:31). Now to open the womb belongs to the husband. Yet when she conceived she brought forth not to God (for He is in Himself all-sufficing for Himself), but to him who endures toil to gain the good, even Jacob. Thus virtue receives the divine seed from the Creator, but brings forth to one of her own lovers, who is preferred above all others who seek her favour. Again Isaac the all-wise besought God, and through the power of Him who was thus besought Steadfastness or Rebecca became pregnant (Gn 25:21). And without supplication or entreaty did Moses, when he took Zipporah the winged and soaring virtue, find her pregnant through no mortal agency (Ex 2:22) [13, 36-37]).[27]

The immense inquiry undertaken over a century ago to justify, *per fas et nefas*, the hypothesis according to which Matthew and Luke would seem to have been speaking about the virginal conception under the irresistible pressure of a cultural current, has thus far been fruitless. It has encountered a threefold difficulty which Brown has recognized.

First, there is no proof that first-century Christians were familiar with these traditions. Second, to the extent to which they might have been known, they exercised no real attraction. An aversion for pagan mythologies, attested to in Wisdom 14:24-27 (cf. Rom 1:24) is evident throughout the NT. It is clear that this governed the difficult formulation of Matthew 1-2 and of Luke 1-2, and prompted their radical distancing from any form of theogamy.

Further, the alleged models have no parallel in Matthew 1-2 and Luke 1-2:

> In short, there is no clear example of *virginal* conception in world or pagan religions that plausibly could have given first-century Jewish Christians the idea of the virginal conception of Jesus.[28]

Attempts have been made to find another Jewish model in the birth of Melchizedek according to the Slavonic *Enoch*. But this is a late text, very much later than our Gospels. The Jewish tradition which it echoes is the same one that inspired the Epistle to the Hebrews, where it says, more radically, that Melchizedek was "without father or mother or genealogy" (Heb 7:3), in order to make of him a "type" of Jesus Christ, "son of God, eternal priest." This text enables us to see clearly the kind of statement which the culture of the period might have produced, one in which Jesus would seem to have had neither father nor *mother*, but simply to be descended from heaven. This is the *theologoumenon* that was currently in use, had the evangelists been tempted by fiction.[29]

Once having accepted the fact of a mother and of a pregnancy, it would have been only fitting to shorten it to seven months as did certain Jewish traditions[30] or, better still, to lengthen it to "ten months" or more, as Virgil did for his messiah in the fourth *Eclogue*.[31]

In short, Jewish tradition was unaware of any virginal conception model (except Philo, in allegorical style).[32] What the Jewish or pagan traditions offer are not models that might have influenced the extraordinarily new texts of Matthew 1 and Luke 1, but rather antecedents, stepping-stones that offered a sort of archetypal substratum for these Christian novelties. These texts may have helped in perceiving the influence of God in an act of human generation.

A prime model is attested to in a text of Ras Shamra, six centuries earlier than Isaiah 7:14: "Behold! a maiden shall bear to a son" (poem of Nikkal, line 7, G. R. Driver, *Canaanite Myths*, Edinburgh, 1977, 128). The young girl seems to be a mother-goddess, called a virgin.

The Pharaohs were thought to be born from the union of their mother with a god (such texts are studied by H. Cazelles, "La mère du roi-Messie dans l'Ancien Testament," in *Maria Ecclesia* 5, 1959, pp. 39-56 with bibliography p. 140).

One finds an analogous theme in Genesis, where Eve attributes to God the births of Cain and Seth:

> I have gotten a man with the help of the Lord (Gn 4:1).
> God has appointed for me another child (Gn 4:25).

These antecedents offer more differences from than analogies to the virginal conception. Among the Egyptians, the action of the god did not exclude the possibility that Pharaoh "knew" his wife. The same is true in the Bible, where Adam "knew" Eve in the sexual sense (Gn 4:1 and 25). In brief, here as elsewhere, if the biblical authors were able to profit from prevalent themes, it is only at the price of radical corrections and reinterpretations. This process was employed from ancient times. It accounts for the difference between the Babylonian flood, which stemmed from a sordid quarrel among the gods, and the biblical deluge, where God, Creator and ultimate norm of ethical behavior, is in full control of the calamity, and uses it to chastise sin and re-launch humanity from uncontaminated stock. No less profound is the difference between the Egyptian hymn to the sun god and Psalm 104, which paraphrases it, reducing the sun to the level of a star created by God like the other stars (Ps 104, in reference to Gn 1:16).

Likewise, Matthew and Luke radically exclude any involvement with the flesh in the virginal conception, i.e., the Holy Spirit does not generate. They are fully convinced of the transcendence of God. The anterior texts that might have prepared the ground for the virginal conception are only stepping-stones to the completely new expression found in our two Gospels.

An Embarrassing Tradition

The avenue of literary influences having been blocked, the only way to eliminate the virginal conception was to see it as a *theologoumenon*, the imaginative expression of a theological idea. The reason given for this is that the divinity of Christ could not have been expressed at that time without recourse to this myth. For want of a pre-existing model, the mythological genesis of the idea would have had to be located in the brain of the evangelist. Contrived comparisons have attempted to demonstrate this.

J. de Freitas Ferreira has shown quite clearly that resort to this theory is not an exegetical but rather a philosophical exigency. It was in line with the presuppositions of Kantian idealism (applied to history by Hegel) that Strauss devised the model of the *theologoumenon* which has dominated exegesis ever since.

But far from being an exigency rooted in the environment, the virginal conception was, for Luke and above all for Matthew, a crucial difficulty, indeed a scandal. It ran counter to their apologetic concern, to establish that Jesus was the son of David, which was the very reason that had inspired Matthew to begin his Gospel with a genealogy. It was a tradition that came to them from reliable Jewish Christian circles, and nothing prepared our evangelists to resolve it. They managed to do so, however, in a more convincing way than Paul himself (Gal 4:4), not by choosing an easy route, but by accepting the very originality of this significant novelty.

Conclusion

After so many hypotheses, which have on examination turned out to be as many impasses, the obvious critical solution is to recognize that the virginal conception is a datum of tradition, handed down in Judeo-Christian circles. The two evangelists received it by different routes as a statement of fact. Mary appears to be its obvious source (Luke makes reference to her prayerful recollection). This is the conclusion to which an objective study of the text leads.

The tradition was indeed a scandal to the Jews, and folly for the pagans. On both sides, it triggered remarks of skepticism or irony, even as it does today. If Matthew and Luke had intended to construct a

The Intent of Virginity: Luke 1:34

"How will this happen since I do not know man?" (Lk 1:34). This saying has long been eliminated as an interpolation by rationalist criticism. Such a solution is untenable from the point of view of textual criticism (see above pp. 11-12), but at least it has the merit of recognizing the implication of the words: Mary's resolution to remain a virgin. This intention appeared to be unacceptable and invited the elimination of the text.

Today people seek to escape the obvious meaning in a number of ways: According to some scholars, Mary may have understood that she was already pregnant, although she had not yet lived with Joseph. But it is in the future tense that the angel announces, "Behold, you will conceive," and that Mary responds, "How will this happen?" Carmignac has clearly demonstrated that a substratum in the present tense is excluded (in his response to Dodd, in *Bible Translator* 28, 1977, pp. 327-330).

According to others, Mary meant, "Being no more than betrothed, I am not in a condition to be a mother." But why should an engaged woman, on the eve of her marriage, be astonished at the prediction of a child being born to her in the near future? Audet has attempted to invert the obvious sense of the text by translating it, "How can this happen, since now I must not know man (meaning, "I must remain a virgin," according to the prophecy of Isaiah 7:14), while I am already engaged?" This grammatically fanciful theory ignores the fact that Isaiah 7:14 had never been interpeted by Jewish tradition to indicate a virginal conception.

We can only fall back on the obvious meaning: Mary expressed the plan or the intention, the will or the resolution—qualify it as we may—to remain a virgin (*Structure*, 1956, p. 178). Under what conditions had she formed this plan? How did she intend to reconcile it with marriage, within the sociological norms of the time? The text doesn't tell us, and we will not indulge in unverifiable hypotheses here.

It has long been objected that an intended virginity would be anachronistic. But there was a precedent for this among the Essenes, women included, according to Philo, who speaks of a community of "aged virgins" (R. Laurentin, 1956, pp. 183-188). It is true that Mary renews the direction of such a manner of life. With her it is not a question of ritual abstention (such as the priests of Israel were bound to observe before performing the temple rites, an abstention which the Qumran community extended to the priest's entire life). It is, rather, an exclusive gift to God alone.

Some other precedents are pointed out by Sister Jeanne d'Arc in the collective volume *La chasteté* (Cerf, 1951, pp. 11-36). In the Bible, she calls attention to Tobias' three days of continence at the start of his marriage, according to certain versions of Tobias 6:16-22 (Vulgate: cf. 8:4, critical apparatus). More obvious are Jer 16:1, in which God says to the prophet, "Do not take a wife," and the Haggada, which attributes a perfect continence to Elijah and Elishah after their vocation. Rabbi ben Azzai, in the first century of our era, remained celibate without Christian influence. He nevertheless taught, in conformity with Jewish tradition, that the one who does not procreate diminishes in himself the image of God. To the objection, "You do not practice as you preach!" he would respond, "My soul is in love with the Torah, and so absorbed, that no time is left to me for the things of marriage. The world will continue through persons other than me" (Strack and Billerbeck, *Kommentar*, 1922, I, p. 807).

The anachronism some insist upon is surely relative, since a half-century later virginity flourished as a rule more than as an exception, following the counsels of Paul in 1 Cor 7:37. That text is susceptible to two interpretations: one, that the apostle was addressing himself to fathers worried about marrying off their daughters, and the other, that he was addressing Christians of marriageable age. In either case, Paul's response is the same: Marriage is a good, but "he who does not marry does better."

If someone was bound to make this discovery, or rather, take this step, who would be better suited for it than the woman destined to become the mother of the Savior? To avoid excessive length, we will not return to this subject of Mary's resolve of virginity (to which we devoted a chapter in *Structure*, 1956, pp. 178ff., a chapter found only in the French edition).

theologoumenon in line with the thought patterns of their time, they would have said that Christ had come down from heaven, or else that he was the son of David through Joseph. What they felt obliged to adopt instead ran counter to all prevailing notions.

The ancient opposition to the virginal conception was never motivated by a concern to restore a concept of ordinary birth and of descent from Joseph. It denied the humanity of Jesus the Lord. For the Gnostics (Cerdon, Cerinthus, Saturninus, the Carpocratians, Marcion) and the Manicheans,[33] the difficulty was not the virginal character of the conception, but the very fact that the Word should be made flesh. Hence the evasions: Docetism or a theory of pre-existence without earthly contamination. The virginal conception was, at the beginning of Christianity, the test against all who were inclined to deny the humanity of Jesus.[34]

The Virgin Mary as the human origin of Christ is the specific sign of the Incarnation. This sign has proved to be a stumbling block for all heresies which were devised to refashion Christ according to the tastes of the day, by denying either his humanity or his divinity. Should not these ancient lessons forewarn us against further repetitions of these errors?

W. Pannenberg (1968, 143) was convinced that an opposition could be seen between virginal conception (which he presents in somewhat caricatured form) and the pre-existence of Christ:

> In its content, the legend of Jesus' virgin birth stands in an irreconcilable contradiction to the Christology of the incarnation of the pre-existent Son of God found in Paul and John.

According to Matthew and Luke (and according to the whole patristic tradition, which captured its meaning), the virginal conception is the specific sign at once of Christ's transcendence *and* of the reality of the Incarnation. It signifies both his divine origin and the humble human reality of his conception, his life in the womb and his birth. The pre-existence of the Son of God is an idea already in the back of Luke's mind. It surfaces in the fact that he calls Christ "Son of the Most High" before he refers to him as son of David, and above all in his identification of Jesus with God,[35] whose theocratic coming was heralded by the prophets. Presented in the Judeo-Christian milieu, this theological clarification, which seems to have a Johannine thrust, goes farther than appears at first sight.

C. PRESUPPOSITIONS FOR REJECTION

According to the preceding analysis, the elimination of the virginal conception through the use of many successive and conflicting arguments, is not due to exegetical considerations, but rather to a presupposition which has tirelessly attempted to vindicate itself by heterogeneous and not entirely compatible means. Our analysis confirms the conclusion reached by Freitas Ferreira, in his painstaking analysis of liberal exegesis since the end of the nineteenth century.

The dominant presupposition which led to the elimination of the virginal conception and that of other miracles is determined by a rationalism that gives to reason the right to reduce and reinterpret whatever does not seem to fit with its principles. It was in compliance with this system that Strauss developed the procedures of demythologization through the use of *theologoumena*. The exegetes of this school assumed the right to eliminate a priori, and without further examination, whatever appeared to go beyond pure reason, and to reinterpret it, having reduced it "to its essential idea" according to the perspective of Hegel.

Here surfaces a second aspect of the presupposition, namely that of idealism, a philosophy poorly equipped to accept the mystery of the Incarnation, which does full justice to the body and to all sensible reality. This is not the place to take up the origins and mechanism of these presuppositions, which run counter to the virginal conception. It is a mystery that not only shocks rationalism but also offers considerable difficulties to reason.

In a sense, the believer finds himself in an awkward position because the virginal conception (like the Resurrection and miracles in general) has not been transmitted according to the procedures required by science. In such cases, particularly stringent procedures would be called for in view of the extraordinary character of the facts alleged. But here we are touching on the very nature of God's gift, which is offered to us neither according to the demonstrations of geometry nor by any method of strict experimental proof. God's revelation, which is love-language as much as it is truth, offers itself along lines analogous to those of human love, which does not address itself to pure reason, and indeed employs other avenues in its endeavors. The choice and the dynamic growth of a durable human love are not achieved by logical proofs. This is not without analogy to the love of God.

The truth of revelation, like the authenticity of human love, must be reasonable, but in accordance with reasons unknown to the logic of geometry—reasons which, for faith, pertain to the transcendence and the wisdom of God. Reason, which keeps its place, deals with signs within the light that God himself grants so as to make it clear to the believer that it is right for him to believe. It is in this sense that a believer cannot prove his faith to an unbeliever even if he is able to show that his faith is reasonable. This poses the basic (and neglected) question of meaning.

Revolution of Presuppositions

This question is unavoidable because the present crisis is, in large measure, connected with radical changes in presuppositions which have removed the structural support from under the Christian faith. In the cultural upheaval of the last few years, we have witnessed a massive alteration in the presuppositions relative to the virginal conception. They have quite literally been turned upside down at three points.

First of all, whereas Catholics used to believe "because of miracles," today they believe "in spite of miracles."

Secondly, it is no longer thought seemly to accord special privileges to Christ and to Mary. Formerly, theological Mariology and popular preaching alike never tired of adding to those privileges and of petitioning the Pope to promote them. Today, the tendency is to rule them out, for Christ as also for Mary—reserve in this area being regarded as a sign of authenticity. Christ appears more authentic if he is deemed to have only human knowledge. Even the best theologians, like Hans Urs von Balthasar, begin to challenge the theory of infused knowledges in Christ (which had been ever more generously conferred on him), as well as his possession of the beatific vision, which had been acknowledged unanimously throughout the centuries. Still more radically (and against the common faith), other theologians say, "If Jesus has a human father, he is more authentically man." How far can one go? To establish the human authenticity of Jesus it was indeed useful that he have an adoptive father. The process of human, psychological awakening calls for this relationship, which is not lacking in the Gospel. But is biological paternity necessary? A negative answer can be given, even if we are only considering Jesus' humanity. If we would consider his divinity, reasons of a transcendent order must also be applied.

Thirdly, there is another radical reversal: throughout the centuries, the unconditional exaltation of virginity left sexuality as such with an aura of shame. Today, sexuality has been erected into a fundamental value, as the principle and source of all other values; and virginity is viewed negatively as lack of fulfillment or as neurotic self-punishment.[36] The prototype of the celibate for the sake of the Kingdom, which the first Christians from the beginning recognized in Christ, and soon after in the Virgin Mary as well, has become widely contested or quietly eliminated. In the late 1960s there was a proliferation of books like W. E. Phipps, *Was Jesus Married?*, and of romanticized lives of Jesus, wherein his "marriage," a notion altogether foreign to the Gospels, stands in a place of honor.[37]

Likewise, she who was always called "the Virgin" is no longer being viewed as such except hypothetically. Differences between creeds are thus being leveled out, as we see Protestants reflecting seriously on certain basic doctrines, while Catholics are withdrawing their commitment to them.[38] We have often been told (since the mid- 1960s), that nothing would be altered in the Incarnation or in its significance if Jesus were born of Joseph and Mary. ("Not even if he were born of adultery," goes the less frequent comment of theologians like Pikaza.[39]) This disintegration of a tradition, unbroken since its origin, is partially explainable by a regrettable historical antecedent: Mariology celebrated Mary's virginity as a privilege and as a prodigy, without evaluating its significance. A growing lack of sensitivity to this issue which has been growing since the fifth century, has allowed this radical change of presuppositions, a change which has gone a long way toward eliminating the tradition of the Virgin birth.

A Respectful Disintegration

This quiet revolution has been accomplished tactfully and without provocation. The new hypotheses preserve the traditional language: Mary is a virgin, though not biologically, only spiritually. Progress has been made, it is said, when we pass from mythology to the order of faith and of ethics. The problem with this reinterpretation is that it divests language of meaning. If Mary is not a virgin biologically, but only spiritually, then the term virgin should also be applied to the holy mothers of families, who are legion. Where theology falsifies language, it alters the transmission of the faith and convinces no one. In spite of laudable efforts to harmonize the new with the old, Christian revelation thus loses something of its coherence and its integrity. The key problem is still that of meaning.

D. THE MEANING

An exegetical book is not the place to take a long and deep look at questions of meaning.[40] However, given the nature of the debate, the question cannot be properly clarified without recalling a number of relevant facts which have all too often been forgotten. The meaning of the virginal conception has been explicitly dealt with at three moments in the history of Christianity. The first treatment of this problem occurs in the Gospels. Luke and Matthew, as we have seen, provided a new formulation for this baffling notion. They saw in it a sign of the human reality of the Son of God, of his transcendence, and of the new creation promised by the prophets. This meaning was further defined in the fourth and fifth centuries, at a time when the rise of asceticism—the eremetical and monastic life—and the rise of associations of virgins, was nurturing an attitude favorable to the understanding of this fine point of the Gospels. The ascetical life of the Church at this time discovered Mary as a model.[41] Later ages lost sight of this understanding, confining themselves to a kind of mechanical wonderment at this prodigy and sometimes finding in it a rejection of sexuality, which attitude is actually antithetical to its true meaning.

Our age presents a twofold contribution. On the one hand, Barth and other theologians of liberal Protestant origin have reacted against this disintegration of faith and are rediscovering in Scripture a sense of the transcendence of God and the real meaning of the Incarnation, and, by this route, the challenge of the virginal origin of Christ. On the other hand, Catholic theologians who have attempted to play down the biological aspect of the virginal conception have tried to compensate for this by attaching some analogical meaning to the traditional affirmation. The concern and the arguments developed in this effort have not been entirely without value. Christ, they say, is a gratuitous gift of God, a gift that transcends the biological order. This is quite true, but not fully so unless the affirmation of the Gospels is not merely myth but reality.

Where these rays of light converge, the virginal conception becomes fully significant in three respects: above all, for the Incarnation itself (as the Gospel and the Fathers clearly perceived); then, for the special meaning of salvation in Jesus Christ; finally, for our perspective on Mary.

Significance for the Incarnation

In a very schematic way, the Fathers saw in the virginal conception a specific *sign* of the Incarnation:
—a sign of divine sonship and of its uniqueness.[42]
—a sign of the Creator at the starting point of the new creation.
—a sign of the pre-existence and transcendence of Christ.[43]

This is the essential point at issue here. It is not a question of "Marian dogma," but of a revelation of Christ himself.

Significance for Salvation in Jesus Christ

The virginal conception is an indispensable sign of salvation in Jesus Christ, a sign of its nature as free gift, which Barth has described with characteristic vigor:

> The man Jesus has no father. His conception does not come under the common law. His existence begins with the free decision of God himself. It proceeds from the freedom which characterizes the unity of the Father and the Son, bound by love, that is to say, by the Holy Spirit. This is the domain of the freedom of God, and it is from this freedom of God that the existence of the man Jesus Christ proceeds.[44]

This theologian, who had difficulty in coming to terms with the flesh, finds in this the triumph of *agape* over *eros*. He testifies to this in a striking way:

> In every natural generation, it is man, conscious of his power, strong in will, proud in his creative power, autonomous and sovereign man who is in the foreground. The natural generative process would not then be a sign adequate to the mystery that is here to be disclosed. . . . Sexual union. . .could never be considered a sign of the divine *agape*, which is completely disinterested love. The will to power and domination that is present in man and finds expression particularly in the sexual act, suggests something radically different from the majesty of the divine mercy. This is why it is Mary's virginity, and not the union of Joseph and Mary, that is the sign of revelation and knowledge of the mystery of Christmas.[45]
>
> The history of humanity. . . is in fact a history of males, a history of masculine exploits and undertakings. . . . In this perspective, one may better grasp the sign of the mystery of Christmas in all its significance. The fact that Jesus has no human father deserves attention. Man, conscious of his capacity to will, of his power—man, creator and master—would be incapable of participating in the work of God. . . . Consequently, the male must be excluded when a sign becomes necessary to reveal the inner dynamic of the Incarnation.[46]

Barth's incisive testimony should be put in its proper context. It highlights one aspect of the challenge of the Gospel message. Christ came to announce the Good News to the poor, and he used means that were appropriate to such an end. He deliberately renounced the means of this world with a radicality that the Church has found difficult to understand or to adopt throughout the ages. On the political level, he desired neither royalty (despite popular pressure), nor any power of this world (Jn 6:15; 19:11). He excluded money from the evangelical mission: "No money in your belts" (Mk 6:8-9; Lk 9:3; 10, 4). He renounced the learning of the scribes or of the Pharisees. He had not attended their schools and he spoke in a style that differed from theirs—one that enjoyed an extraordinary popular appeal (and which accounts for the enduring success of the Gospel). He practiced fasting at the very beginning of his ministry, and Christians were called to imitate him, when "the bridegroom is taken away from them" (Mt 9:15; cf. Acts 13:2-3). All of this is folly if viewed according to the wisdom of the world.

The virginal conception, the starting point of his existence, represents the most paradoxical element in evangelical poverty: celibacy for the sake of the Kingdom with all its eschatological significance. Jesus was perfectly aware that it would be difficult to make sense of this. To the questions of his astounded disciples, his final response was, "He who is able to receive this, let him receive it" (Mt 19:12).

Significance for our Perception of Mary, Mother of the Lord

Virginity also has a great significance for our view of Mary, whom tradition calls simply "the Virgin." For the Church and for Christians, she is the prototype of this choice, of this challenge (linked with vocation), which she expresses at the annunciation (Lk 1:34). Believers are very often referred to the example of Mary who "*conceived in her mind*" (adherence to Christ in faith) *before conceiving in her body*.[47] Mary commits herself to this charism at the very starting point of salvation. Her virginity is the sign of her faith. In her it is a twofold expression of the gift of God. Her absolute covenant with God according to grace (Lk 1:28-30) implies, in the very structure of the annunciation, an exclusive gift of self to God, a practice which spread very rapidly in Christian tradition.

She is also the sign of a new fruitfulness. The evangelical "hundredfold" found in her its fullest realization. This virgin enjoyed the fullest conceivable maternity: mother of the Son of God made man and mother of those who have become his brethren, according to the word of Christ on Calvary.[48]

In its inner meaning, thus defined, the virginal conception finds its structural support. It is not based on scientific findings or scientific methods. God never lent himself to such an approach when he freely bestowed the foundational miracles of the Gospel.

CONCLUSION

Reference to Events

The infancy Gospels' reference to real events is clearly established by analyses concerning historicity. Thus, Luke formally declares his *intention* to recount true events, compiled from eyewitness accounts. This declaration does not exclude, but rather includes, first of all, the infancy narrative which immediately follows this declaration of historicity. This is confirmed by the reference of Luke 1-2 to the eyewitnesses of the infancy events (e.g., 1:66), especially to the one best informed, Mary, to whose recollections he refers in 2:19 and 2:51.[49]

The agreement of Matthew and Luke, despite differences, confirms the major test for the critical examination of witnesses. In spite of a total divergence regarding episodes selected and perspectives adopted, they are in agreement on the basic factual data: on dating (at the time of Herod, Lk 1:5 and Mt 2:1), on places (Bethlehem, Nazareth, etc.), on principal figures, and on the extraordinary conception of Mary from which Joseph is excluded.

The evangelists were not interested in writing fiction. They took the birth and infancy of Christ seriously. Both infancy Gospels attest to a concern for serious investigation, which the genealogy has confirmed in the most thorough manner. Moreover, it was their concern to circulate a text that would not leave itself open to the criticism of eyewitnesses who were still alive—especially given the importance of the subject matter. They wrote not in the style of a chronicle or of a demonstration, but rather of a presentation of facts relating to the faith they lived in the Savior, Jesus Christ. It was the most illuminating facts, those most significant for faith, that they retained.

With this end in view, they collected a great diversity of materials, particularly varied with Luke; accounts of birth, journeys and encounters, genealogies and canticles, revelations and experiences of the first witnesses of Christ's infancy. This diversity reflects at once both the risks and the relative freedom of inquiry the evangelists enjoyed.

Some of the data, notably the obscurity of Christ's infancy, his Nazarene origin, and the extraordinary character of his birth, which distanced him from the biological lineage of David, presented real difficulties for the evangelists and for their readers. The fact that they included these data without evasion is a guarantee of their honesty. An examination of the episodes reveals their agreement with archeological and cultural data, a test which proves fatal with the Apocrypha. The selection of canonical writings was done with a genuine concern for historical veracity, not merely for edification.

The sobriety and true-to-life character of the episodes is remarkable. The only difficulty lies in the miraculous elements. However, these play a minimal role, much less than in the rest of the Gospels. In the entire account of the infancy of Christ, there is only one miracle: his coming to be without a human father. The other wonderful events of the infancy Gospel are not strictly miraculous in character. They belong rather to the categories of providential signs and of existential communion with God, such as have occurred from the time of the prophets to our own day. An understanding of the visionaries of the Middle Ages or of our own time can greatly clarify the matter.

The credibility of the one marvelous fact in the infancy Gospels depends on the presuppositions of the individual reader, of his or her philosophy and his or her particular lights of faith. We reach a point here where presentation in the form of factual statement becomes difficult. But the story of Jesus' human origin, like that of his Resurrection, has the frank appearance of historicity, together with a number of impressive convergences and cross-references which one cannot evade. They are based upon a number of coherent testimonies which imposed themselves on the evangelists. The multiplicity and incompatibility of the hypotheses resorted to for purposes of evasion, coupled with their innate fragility, have blocked the verification of any one theory, and their mutual inconsistencies (masterfully exposed by the work of Freitas Ferreira) are eloquent. In short, one would have to grossly misunderstand or caricature these remarkably coherent texts in order to escape the quality of their testimony. This is why scholarship has been able to disembarrass itself only at the price of contrivance.

The Infancy Gospels and Oral History

Research on the infancy Gospels is not unrelated to the preoccupations of "oral history," which today is coming back into vogue within the framework of the a new historical approach concerned with discovering the human and social realities behind the events. (The term "oral history" has won the day over the more modest "oral archives.")

The Gospel history began as oral history in the preaching that preceded Scripture. It began with an orientation set by faith, within a community experience and a profoundly Christian life style. It is the merit of the *Formgeschichte* school that it recognized this, but unfortunately it did so only to posit the creative community as a universal explanatory source—for miracles, even for the divinity of Christ. But this is not how lived faith functions. Faith in Christ is realistic because it is faith in God-made-man, in the realities of human history, the history of the poor. The contribution made by the community is not appropriately called invention, fiction, or legend (except for some quite marginal and particular elements), but rather discernment. Faith operates in this process as interpretative, not as inventive.

In the makeup of the infancy narratives, as in the rest of the Gospel, the oral element played an important role of expression and transmission, notably in the case of the four wonderful thanksgiving canticles of Luke 1-2. These were committed to memory, and the community loved to repeat them (as it does even today, for these hymns, along with Phil 2:6-15, are the most beautiful and the most popular of the Christian liturgy). It is not possible to ascertain the precise stages of this process. They have left traces, seams, but nothing that could really make a reconstruction possible. Those who have attempted this have achieved only an imaginative and rather futile work. How were the traditions brought together to compose Matthew 1-2 on the one hand, Luke 1-2 on the other hand? Did Luke discover an already written historical source, or only an oral tradition? We cannot say. Between the existence of a semitic and more probably a Hebrew substratum (to which the latest works on the subject lend new support) and the certainly Lucan Greek text, the intermediary links are not really accessible.

The contribution of "oral history" is that it lays hold of the real-life experience. The oral tradition behind the Gospels was not recorded on tape, in the manner of today's oral historians. Nevertheless, these Gospels preserve traces of a lived experience and of profound changes in style of expression taking place within the Judeo-Christian communities where the Gospels originated.

What is involved here is a hellenization of language. More profoundly, it is the experience of openness to grace and to new outpourings of the Spirit, and therefore to new community relationships whose vivid reality Luke attempts to capture (see further below, pp. 456-458). The change derives from a new historical fact—the coming of the Messiah, which changes all the axes of salvation history. It calls for the creation of new bonds—between the individual and God (cf. Lk 1:28-38) and within the community as a whole (Lk 1:40-79; 2:9-20, 25-39). It calls for a new reading of the Bible and of past events in the light of a new experience of the Holy Spirit—an experience that has not been without antecedents from the time of the prophets. Luke's experience of the Spirit (cf. Acts 2-4) expresses a new stage of faith calling for a new reading of the Scriptures of which Christ becomes the measure; hence this dynamic movement and the profound renewal of the OT literary genres which we analyzed above.

In this way, the study of the infancy Gospels coincides with the concerns of the new oral history method. For events so remote, these methods may be applied only indirectly. But this oral dimension is of fundamental importance and we shall endeavor to explore it further in the conclusion to our study.

Limitations of These Conclusions

Does methodical verification, conducted according to the objective historical criteria, allow us to isolate the source material of this history? Is it possible to extract it from its literary setting, as one might extract pure gold from the ore that contains it? This is not possible. The very nature of history makes it impossible; it is as fanciful to wish to capture an event without its account as to seek for thought without its language or for knowledge without symbols.

This impossibility is linked to the conditional nature of all knowledge and of all human expression. On the one hand, the event which takes place in the materiality of the world can only be reached by the awareness of a subject, at the level of intentionality which, though not factual, yet is related to the real. On the other hand, the event can only be transmitted by means of the expression that communicates it. The reference of the expression to the alleged event, its conformity with this event, as it is known from other sources, can be verified. But this event cannot be reached apart from the expression that refers to it. The expression is more than an inevitable means of access; it is the necessary medium of all historical knowledge. All criticism, therefore, remains inextricably involved in the indissoluble correlation between the *event* to which an account refers and the *account* which refers us to the event. This reference includes the community in which and for which the author writes, which provides a vast field for historical-critical investigation.

The fundamental question is: How does a narrative come into existence? How does history appear? It comes about where the dynamism of a questioning process lays hold of an event, by whatever available means, and gives it expression because it discovers therein a meaning. If meaning were lacking, there would be no history. Historical criticism would be unbalanced and ridiculous if it were to stick to material verification and forget this basic fact (this was the defect prevalent in apologetics at the beginning of this century). History attains its goal only if it takes into account the creative aspect of the narrative for which meaning serves as a catalyst.

The very word *meaning* already implies the use of symbolism. The symbolic is not something added on to the account, an extrinsic ornament, a superstructure. It is the very fabric of all knowledge.[50] It remains for us to identify the questions which gave rise to the infancy Gospels, the meaning the evangelists have explored therein, and the symbolic form in which they expressed themselves. This is the meaning behind the heading of this final section; we are not inquiring into the historicity of the infancy Gospels to discover whether they are historical or non-historical. Rather, the question is: As regards the infancy Gospels, what kind of historicity are we talking about?

VIII
SYMBOLISM AND HISTORICITY: A CORRELATION

Historical realities possess a profound sense and are to be understood in a spiritual manner: *historica pneumatikōs*; conversely, spiritual realities. . . are to be understood historically: *pneumatika historikōs*.

(Henri de Lubac, *Catholicism*, 1938, p. 108).

Mystery is what opens up temporality and gives it depth: that which endows it with a vertical dimension. It makes of it the time of revelation and of disclosure.

(J. La Croix, *Histoire et Mystère*, Tournai, 1962, p. 7).

What is it that guided the evangelists in their inquiry, their selection, their redaction of the infancy narratives? Fundamentally, it was their relationship to the obscure event of the infancy of Christ. They approached this event not with a spirit of scientific accuracy, but in order to understand the identity of Christ in this obscure portion of his life.

Who was this Jesus whose words, public life, death and Resurrection commanded such attention? Who was he, at the time when popular opinion had no interest in him?

A. THE QUESTION

Christ Before the Baptism

The questions that gave rise to the infancy Gospels are not those which arose in the first hour, those to which Peter had begun to respond on Pentecost day, according to Acts 2:14-36: Why is Jesus alive, risen, Savior, and Lord? Why did he have to go through his passion and death? It was, in fact, a prior question: How did this Savior, a gift from above, begin his existence in this world? Why did he remain unknown for such a long time? Why did he not simply descend from heaven or appear in the dazzling fashion that people were expecting, rather than in the humility of pregnancy and infancy? In what way did the first moments of his human existence show that he was already the Christ? How does his birth concern the new covenant between God and humanity, the eschatological era that begins with him? By daring to face this second difficulty, by refusing to say, in line with the pious hopes prevalent at the time, that Jesus had descended from heaven, Matthew and Luke are breaking new ground compared with Mark's Gospel and with the kerygmatic and catechetical tradition attested to in the Acts of the Apostles (1:21-22; 2:22-33).

Their inquiry and their compositional project are obviously aimed at confronting two disturbing factual reports concerning Christ's geographical and biological origins: he was known to be a Galilean; he was rumored not to be Joseph's real son. Both evangelists dared to take up this double challenge of the infancy, not unlike the challenge of the passion at the end of the Gospel. Their integrity was the same in the face of the initial scandal as it was with the final scandal. They themselves perceived this analogy, and they tried to discover in the infancy signs which prefigured the passion.

In this perspective, what they drew up was not a detailed chronicle. They made no effort to establish the particulars, the ins and outs of the matter such as scientific history would require (e.g., a medical report, for the virginal conception, as for the death and the Resurrection). They selected the events in accordance with the significance they discovered in them and only those which they deemed important. They were far from conceiving any disjunction between meaning and evidence, symbol and reality.

Was Christ Already the Son of God?

The primary question that directed their research and their compositional activity was the question of Christ's nature before his manifestation. Was he already the Son of God? By what title and in what way? Or did he perhaps attain this status at his baptism? They knew what the answer was, but they honestly sought for the evidence. They boldly accepted the fact of his lowly beginnings, and they subjected this to humble scrutiny in order to discover therein, with humble objectivity, the thread of God's action, the first revelatory signs, whose discreet character they did not violate.

B. THE SIGNS

EARTHLY SIGNS

The word "sign" (*semeion*) appears only in Luke, just twice, but in significant contexts—the sign of the manger given to the shepherds (2:12) and the sign of contradiction in the prediction by Simeon (2:34).

These are not heavenly but rather earthly signs, one referring to the lowliness of the infancy, the other announcing the paradox of the passion.

Topographical Signs[1]

Signs are deployed clearly on the topographical level. The evangelists refer to the same places: Nazareth, Bethlehem, Jerusalem; and in the same organic and coherent fashion which is reflected in their respective semiotic frameworks. For Luke, Nazareth is the place of grace and Jerusalem the site of the (superseded) Law; for Matthew, Nazareth is the symbolic place of hidden holiness and Jerusalem is the hostile place which threatens Christ's existence.

The approach of the two evangelists is different. Matthew begins with no local specification, and Nazareth appears only as the point of arrival (2:23). For Luke, Nazareth is the point of departure, Christ's very place of origin. But they agree in meaning on the essential point. Both aver that Jesus was born in Bethlehem, upholding the Davidic trademark of the Messiah, as sealed by the prophecy of Micah 5. Both situate Jesus' youth (up to the age of about thirty years, according to Lk 3:23) at Nazareth, the humble place from which he emerges to reveal himself as the Light. Matthew states this with singular emphasis in 4:15-16, by way of a reference to the prophecy of Isaiah 9:2: "Galilee of the Gentiles—the people who sat in darkness have seen a great light."

This paradoxical but organic topography has a clear meaning for them: the coming of the Messiah overturns, relativizes, and transcends the accepted symbolism of sacred places. For Matthew and

Luke, Jerusalem becomes "the city that kills the prophets" (Mt 23:37; Lk 13:34) because it was there that Christ was put to death. Luke continues to hold this holy city in honor, but not without making appropriate distinctions. Thus he calls Jerusalem at times by its glorious and sacred name *Hierousalem* and at other times by its profane and inglorious name *Hierosolyma.*

He does not conclude the infancy Gospel in the glory of the Temple (2:49, in contrast to the end of his Gospel, 24:53) but rather at Nazareth, in the self-emptying *kenosis* illumined by grace (2:21-52). He transfers to Bethlehem the revered title "City of David" (2:4 and 11). Nazareth also becomes the city of the Messiah ("their city," he says of the Holy Family in 2:39): it is the place where the Son of God grows to adulthood (2:40 and 52). He still holds the Temple in great esteem (2:49), nevertheless, but concludes with a hint that it has been transcended, which appears in the context of his Gospel as a kind of contradiction: the submissive return of Christ to Nazareth (2:51) contradicts the first saying of Jesus in 2:49, that he must be "in his Father's house" and not elsewhere. Luke goes as far as to record the iconoclastic formula of Stephen, who likens the Temple to idols "made with human hands" (Acts 7:48).

It is the Messiah who is of primary importance. Places, such as Jerusalem, or even the Temple, no longer have the same symbolic value. Their importance is relativized by Christ, Son of God. He is the principle of a new localization of the sacred; the new definition of salvation is to be found in Jesus and realized through his passion, the shadow of which already emerges in Matthew 2 and in Luke 2. Jerusalem is called to destruction (Lk 23:28; cf. 21:5-24), but a destruction that opens on to something else: Christ himself, the new place of the presence of God (according to Lk 1:35). The convergence of both infancy narratives on the passion is particularly pregnant with meaning. Both terminate in Galilee, which, according to Matthew, is the exclusive site of the risen Christ's appearance to his disciples.

The fact that Jerusalem has been transcended serves to enlarge the framework beyond the borders of Israel. But the universalism found in both these Gospels is expressed in differing signs. In Matthew we find the wise men from the East (in harmony with the foreign women of the genealogy, the reference to the Babylonian captivity, and Jesus' own exile in Egypt). In Luke, the ordered census is a census of the whole world (*oikoumenē*, 2:1). A more expressive word than this could not be found to denote the worldwide significance of the messianic event. Simeon's prophecy declares the Messiah as the "light of the nations" (2:32, referring to Is 42:6 and 49:6).

By way of converging symbols in an identical topography, both evangelists grasp and help others to grasp the striking newness of Christ, the incalculable and revolutionary novelty that he introduces.

Signs of the Times

This novelty also finds expression in time.[2] In his introductory genealogy, Matthew recapitulates the entire history of salvation from Abraham to Christ. Luke's recapitulation is still more radical, going back to Adam. We have seen that this radical focus on Adam and God is common to them both under different forms.

Both accounts are woven throughout with allusions to the principal characters and to the great moments of the OT. Matthew alludes to Moses and to the Exodus (2:20; Ex 4:19), but above all to David (1:1, 6, 17, 20), with an emphasis that recedes only in deference to Christ. Luke's narrative is a fabric of more numerous references, recalling Abraham (1:55, 73) and Sarah (cf. the use of Gn 18:14 in 1:37), Moses (2:22), Elijah (1:17), David (2:4 and 11), and, by allusion, Judith (Jgs 13:8 and Lk 1:42), Leah (1:48, alluding to Gn 30:13), but above all, the Daughter of Zion (1:28, 32 and Zep 3:14, 17) and the Ark of the Covenant (Lk 1:35 alluding to Ex 40:35; Lk 1:39-56 alluding to 2 Sm 6:1-11).[3]

In the infancy of Christ the evangelists perceived a typological fulfillment[4] of the promises, which is also a fulfillment of the Scriptures. Luke's use of the texts is implicit (except for the explicit citation of 2:32), while Matthew's are explicit and formal (except for the implicit allusions of 2:10-11 to Ps 72:10, 11, 15). In both, the time of Christ is historically located by reference to the reign of Herod. But Matthew does not state the duration of the infancy, while Luke symbolically discerns the fulfillment (in miniature) of the seventy weeks, from the first annunciation (1:11-22) to the presentation of Jesus in the Temple (2:22). For both, the infant Christ is indeed the eschatological fulfillment of salvation in the new creation. The rupture in Christ's genealogy, abrupt in Matthew (1:16, 18-20), somewhat softened in Luke (1:33-35), signifies the arrival of this new age. Hereafter, genealogy and posterity are no longer important; what is important is the definitive conjunction achieved in the Son of the Most High (1:32 and 35), Savior and Lord (2:11), God-with-us, (Mt 1:23 and 28:20). Henceforth, the one who "is begotten" according to God is everything. The rest is of little importance. There is implicit evidence of this idea in Matthew, and it is explicit in Luke. For Luke, time as expressed in passing generations is transformed into endless duration (1:33). This renewal of time is manifested in the priority of youth over old age, of birth over death. Physical decline gives way to spiritual renewal, evidenced in the charisms which characterize Simeon and Anna, as well as Elizabeth and Zechariah after the visitation. It is a theme of salvation history, whose source is the arrival of the Messianic Son of God into history for the salvation of all human beings.

New Creation and Eschatology

The signs which renew place and time need to be viewed within the archetypes which inhabit and inspire all symbolism, all poetry, all human interpretation of destiny. According to this basic vision (which is in every human being), the beginning and the end, paradise lost and paradise to come, first birth and birth for the future, are symbolically identified. This dynamic intuition governs all awareness of relationships to the cosmos, to others, and to God. The infancy Gospels must be seen in the context of this profound dynamic of all human thought.

Both infancy Gospels mention generation. They record the birth of the Messiah, his descent from Davidic and Abrahamic origins. They go back further still to the very beginning of the Bible. It is a new creation under the sign of the Spirit (Mt 1:18 and 20; Lk 1:35). As he was present over the primordial waters so that life might be born therefrom (Gn 1:2), so he is present over Mary so that she might conceive the Life which will transform history and the world.

But this new origin is also realized eschatology. The era of generations is transcended, the Scriptures are fulfilled, the messianic era "that has no end" (Lk 1:33) has come. In the eschatological perspective, time intensifies, as the temporal schema of Matthew and the earnest haste of the Lucan characters reveal. For Luke especially, eschatology asserts itself in theophanies that recur under various forms: from 1:35 (the sign of the shekinah) to 2:49, the self-confession of Christ as Son of God, in the house of God. Simeon can indeed see "death" (2:26 and 29), for the end-times have arrived. The Temple of Jerusalem, from which the Ark of the Covenant had disappeared, was replaced by Mary at Nazareth (Lk 1:35; Ex 40:35) and now it contains the Son of God, the Lord (1:35 and 2:11) who is the "Light of the nations and glory of Israel" (2:32), identified with the shekinah. Eschatology is in embryo from the time of Christ's conception and birth.

Shadows and Lights

This symbolism is expressed by contrasts of light and shadows, which correspond to the new relationships of humans and God. The Son of God become Son of Man is situated from his infancy at the convergence of shadow and light, at the confluence of human genealogy and divine filiation. The background is nocturnal. In Luke, it is represented by the night-scene of the shepherds (2:8). In Matthew, we see the wise men following the star (2:2, 9-11), and Joseph, fleeing by night to Egypt (2:14).

The light of the Messiah remains hidden and mysterious—the star of the wise men in Matthew (2:1-13), the day-star illuminating "those who sit in darkness and the shadow of death" in Luke (1:78-79 and 2:32). However, one could ask whether Luke retains this obscure light, or whether he is not already contemplating the Sun of Justice (1:78; cf. Mal 4:2), the glory of God. But the light cannot yet be identified save in the child, lying in poverty, recognized only in the faith and joy of the shepherds (2:15-20). The glory of God awakens the shepherds through the announcement of the angel and envelops them with its radiance, but this light disappears and does not reappear at the crib. Their journey is a night affair and they recognize the Messiah in the sign of his very hiddenness: the manger in which he was laid.

The infant-king of Matthew 2:2 does not radiate with light any more than the infant-Messiah of Luke. The star of the wise men is no longer seen by them when they reach Jerusalem. Though it reappears over the house of the predestined child, inside the house there is no light, except perhaps in the glitter of the gold offered by the wise men.

These contrasts have inspired preaching, poetry, and art. They reveal wonderfully the mystery of the child: light which faith discerns in the shadows.

SIGNS OF HEAVEN

Stars and Angels

It is not by accident that heaven has its role to play in both Gospels. In Matthew (implicitly) it is the heaven of the star (2:2, 9-12); in Luke (explicitly) it is heaven as the dwelling-place of God (2:14)—and of the Christmas angels as well (2:13 and 15), in the only scene where the apocalyptic that underlies Luke 1-2 makes use of the imagery of the ambient culture. The purpose here is to signify the transcendence of "the Lord" who was just born (2:7), and its consequence, the joining of heaven and earth, of God and man. The song of the angels sums up the meaning of Christmas in lyrical form: "Glory to God in the highest and on earth peace among men with whom he is pleased" (2:14), but there is no materializing of heaven. It is the sign of the transcendent God, of whom no description is given, any more than of the angels. The most radical demythologizing is at work here.

What does the sign of the star, common to both evangelists, signify? With or without reference to the prophecy of Balaam (Nm 26:17), no characteristic expression of which is employed, Matthew retains the tradition about stars established in the ancient Near East. The star was the sign of a god and, consequently, of a king, who was always subject to some deification.

> How you are fallen from the heavens,
>   O Day-Star, Son of Dawn!
> How you are cut down to the ground,
>   you who laid the nations low (Is 14:72)!

The episode of the wise men points out the royal, even divine quality of the Messiah (Mt 2:2). The star was also a sign of hope. A Jewish revolutionary (about the year 135) was called Bar Kochba, which means "son of the star." The star, which is evocative of another world, is a sign of God, whose transcendence makes him totally other, though he remains always near.

The richly versatile symbolism of the star extends also to the concept of angels. Matthew makes ample use of this ("the angel of the Lord": 1:20, 24; 2:13 and 19), as does Luke (1:11; 2:9; Gabriel 1:26-38 and the angels of Christmas 2:9-15). Stars and angels have the same function in apocalyptic literature; they are two equivalent ways of expressing God's solidarity with us without compromising his transcendence.[5] To speak of angels or of stars was, at this time, the most obvious way of signifying a divine communication (a profound experience of the believer) with its threefold character of mystery, certitude and mediation, while still safeguarding transcendence. Thus, the angel of Yahweh sometimes seems to be interchangeable in the OT with Yahweh himself.[6] The mention of the angel implies respect for the mystery of God and for the humble character of the signs by which we reach him here below. Thus it was thought (a notion not discredited by mystical experience) that the direct vision of God would result in death.

This is indeed the function of the angel in the infancy Gospels. Matthew and Luke do not insist on their materiality, nor on their visibility. Nothing is indicated other than the relation to God of these beings whose name signifies, etymologically, *one sent.* They are a medium of communication—and God is the communicator.

This cultural background allows for a margin of mystery and of appreciation. To what extent is there a personal appearance of angels? To what extent is this a symbolic device to describe a divine communication? We lack the criteria to answer this with precision. We have seen that several Gospel episodes allow us latitude in this regard (Jn 12:29 and Acts 23:9, where the word "angel" is employed with particular lack of precision). According to Matthew, the angel of the Lord reveals himself in a dream, a method which locates the divine communication in a non-rational context, outside the realm of the strictly miraculous. This nocturnal account, at once mysterious and modest, ought to temper the allergies that certain of our contemporaries have towards the miraculous.

Today, as in earlier days, God can be spoken of only in a relative way. In the vocabulary of an existential and symbolic theology, stars and angels were two equivalent modes of expressing God's presence. To say this is not to relativize God, nor even the means which he employs, but rather to locate human expression in its proper context. (The situation is not all that different today. When a believer says, in more abstract fashion, "God gave me a sign," this is no more than our feeble language groping for a way to describe the ineffable. But this does not exclude the fact that certain people, even today, experience an encounter, visual or otherwise, with spiritual beings whom they identify as angels.) What matters for both evangelists, as for every true believer, is the divine communication conveyed through this finite code (a code which has, nonetheless, its own proper reality). More than our language or even this particular communication itself, it is God who matters, for the believer today as for Matthew and Luke. Language and signs refer to this *term*, which we can attain but never fully comprehend.

The Holy Spirit

Our evangelists have access to a more profound expression of this communication—the Holy Spirit, a divine hypostasis, who spoke through the prophets, and whose character remains unclear because he does not interpose himself, but rather awakens the subject from within to what is best in himself, and nurtures his relationship to Christ and to God.

It is to the Holy Spirit that both evangelists attribute the transcendent act that causes the virgin to bring forth the Messiah-Lord.

In Luke, the role of the Spirit unfolds throughout the infancy Gospel (1:15 and 35 to 2:25-27) with its prophetic consequences (from 1:67 to 2:36). He is the hidden mover, working by way of prophecies (Lk 1:70, 76; cf. Mt 1:22; 2:5, 15, 17, 23) towards the revolutionary novelty of Pentecost (compare Lk 1:35 and Acts 1:8, the Spirit coming upon Mary and upon the infant Church; Lk 1:15, 41, 67 and Acts 2:1-4, references filled with the Holy Spirit).

The intimate activity of God, who does not manipulate human beings but inspires them to what is best in their desires and in their hope—this is what Luke demonstrates with Elizabeth, with John the Baptist, who dances for joy in his mother's womb, with Mary, who sings her Magnificat, with Zechariah, and with Simeon and Anna. The shepherds too are part of this movement.

These earthly and heavenly signs in Matthew 1-2 and Luke 1-2 are in line with an analogously structured world where God, as the one who addresses, raises up for his people, as the ones addressed, the Savior who is salvation.

C. REFERENCE TO GOD

Two Forms of Theocentrism

These contrasting signs are all relative in respect to God. Primary evidence reveals their subordinate, relative character, but at the same time gives them a point of reference which causes their true significance to emerge, while maintaining the nuances proper to each evangelist.

Matthew focuses on God: the Lord brings about all the events. But he is not described. His guidance is effected through signs that preserve his transcendent nature. He is present through the twofold medium, angel and dream, and this presence infallibly guarantees the outcome in the lives it guides.

Luke also thinks of God as one who addresses and who guides events, but in accordance with less apparent prophecies, which are used contemplatively, not as proofs. Here God is not the great master of ceremonies whose word concludes each sequence; rather it is the characters themselves and the evangelist who cite the Scriptures to help discern the meaning of events. The narrative does not unfold from the perspective of the addresser alone but from that of the free, living, communicating characters, who experience fear and anxiety, who can question, react, ponder (1:29), and reflect (1:66; 2:19 and 51). The reader is called to participate in their confidence, their anxiety, their enthusiasm (1:39 and 2:15), and their thanksgiving.

The chief difference between the infancy Gospels lies in the fact that Matthew stylizes references to God who rules all things, while Luke gradually unveils his new presence in the person of the Son who finally declares himself in 2:49. For Matthew Jesus is Son of God (2:15), God-with-us (1:23). Luke's special concern is to demonstrate God's communication through human cooperation. The new creation is already Pentecost. Luke detects its signs at the very beginning of the child Jesus' life, an exemplary model at the threshold of the Gospel.

The selections, then, of the two evangelists are different but convergent. They prefigure, not only the progressive disclosure of Christ's identity through his public life, passion, and Resurrection, but also the life of Christians, called to follow in his footsteps. It is this solidarity with the human condition that ultimately guided Matthew 1-2 and Luke 1-2. Neither reduces God to a mere model. They relate events that are beyond human experience and that Christ makes universal.

The Child Jesus, God with God, Man among Humans

At the point where all these signs intersect, the two evangelists find the response to the question which has guided all of their research: Who was Christ in his infancy? They accept this infancy in the obscurity of its actual occurrence—which implies a certain realism in their portrayal of events, however stylized it might be. They have no need of gimmicks or special effects. They altogether avoid turning Jesus into either a child prodigy or a hero. They refer to him in the ordinary terminology appropriate to all human beings before they begin to reveal an autonomous existence, before they relate any public appearance, speech or action. (Luke and Matthew alike first of all refer to Jesus during his time in the womb as an object, with a grammatical neuter.[7]) But, from the beginning, this mute, passive, neuter entity, without word or autonomous action, is what he will be (the process of deciphering who he always was has begun). Hence the insistence of both Gospels in their accounts of the birth in designating the child by means of two series of titles which at once affirm both his messianic and his transcendent nature, although the borderline between these two categories is not perfectly clear.[8]

The identification of Jesus with God is expressed not only by titles, but by the application to Christ of texts, attributes and symbols which properly pertain to God. This procedure is not peculiar to the infancy

Gospels. It is to be found throughout the entire NT (NTH, 121-123, 231). But it is singularly original and significant in these accounts of his obscure beginning, where no action, no word of Christ (except Lk 2:49) demands it.

This identification with God, which is expressed by means of transcendent titles and symbols, has no hint of polytheism. The strict monotheistic significance is assured in the title "Son of God" (Lk 1:32, 35; 2:49; Mt 2:15), as in the title that Matthew gradually expounds, "God-with-us" (borrowed from Is 7:14 and emphasized at the end of the Gospel, 28:20).

To the question Christ's childhood poses for Christian faith, the infancy Gospels respond by identifying the child Jesus not only with the Messiah but with the Lord himself. It is clear that this child, so like other children, is indeed a man, but the evangelists make the point, in terms veiled but remarkably forceful, that he is also God-with-God, even while being God-with-us.[9]

The symbolic structure of the infancy narratives goes further than the earliest abstract dogmatic expressions—those of Paul and of John. John is a late source, but the ancient Christian hymn "quoted" by Paul in the Epistle to the Philippians (2:6-11), belongs to the earliest layer of Christian expression. The Epistle itself is prior to 60. This text witnesses, with a force that has never been excelled, to the preexistence and divinity of Christ.

Consequently, there is no reason to be surprised that Luke (whose connections with Paul we have already seen) likewise perceives the divine condition of Christ (*morphē Theou*, Phil 2:6) as anterior to the human condition (2:7 and Lk 1:32) in which he radically humbled himself (*ekenōsen*), "taking the form of a servant" (Phil 2:6; Mt 1:16; Lk 2:11-12). This is actually what the crib and Jesus' submission to the Law signify. This is really what the title *pais* signifies: both child and servant, just as Mary his mother twice declares herself "handmaid" (1:38 and 48).

This connection and the particular parallels cited above are certainly open to discussion. But what is clear is that the presence of the Son of God, both in Luke and Matthew, has a dimension of transcendence as well as one of immanence to humanity, and that it inaugurates a new covenant between God and human beings, from the very beginning of Christ's human existence. Both infancy Goseples begin to express the extraordinary character of this gift of God. The mystery is overwhelming but they perceive that God's coming upon earth is not a kind of gnostic emanation, nor a manifestation of polytheism. The infancy of Christ begins to reveal, in a not yet explicit manner, that God is Father (Lk 2:49), Son (Lk 1:32, 35; Mt 2:15), Spirit (Lk 1:35 and *passim*; Mt 1:16 and 18) in the strictest unity and in the most radical community. This is precisely what the NT, as revelation, is attempting to express. The infancy Gospels are a particularly intense moment of this exposition.

We are now ready to work on our response to the question posed by this third section, the question of historicity.

D. WHAT KIND OF HISTORICITY?

The study of historicity, under its twofold aspect—*reference* to the events, *meaning* expressed through a symbolic medium—allows us to specify with respect to historicity, the literary genre which the conclusion of our first part has left undetermined.

The infancy Gospels pertain to history. They were an attempt to establish a precise link between the biblical history of salvation and the work of Christ (extending from his baptism to his Resurrection), whose first consequences Luke relates—the Spirit-filled expansion of the community founded by Christ (Acts 1-28). The infancy Gospels provide the missing link between what is today called the Old Testament—the Bible as announcer of Christ—and the New Testament, the Gospel of Jesus Christ (Mk 1:1) beginning with his baptism and his preaching (Acts 1:22).

Both infancy Gospels preserve the biblical (OT) style, connatural to the Judeo-Christian milieu, attached as it was to "observances" (Lk 1:5-6; 2:21-24) and to the Temple (Lk 1:8-20; 2:21-49; cf. Acts 2:46;3:1-10; 5:21-26, 42). But this is only its supporting structure. The infancy Gospels are not a simple extension of the Bible but a step beyond it. They show the newness of Christ, even from his obscure childhood—a newness still hidden, but discoverable through heavenly and earthly signs.

Matthew expresses this from the outset with his heading "the genesis of Jesus Christ" (1:1 and 18). It is a new beginning, like that of creation, with an analogous reference to the Spirit (Genesis 1-2 and Matthew 1:18-20). Luke 1:35 also expresses the new creation under the sign of the Spirit, but with a clear eschatological orientation. Luke speaks of "Gospel" to denote the Good News of salvation announced to the shepherds (2:10).

Both Gospels respect the character of Jesus' humble, unpretentious beginnings. Their symbolism unfolds against a nocturnal backdrop. What are we to think of the night? What are we to think of Jesus' hidden life? The Gospels themselves have contrived neither anecdotes nor sensationalism. The "history of salvation" takes place in ordinary, day-to-day human existence. Jesus has "come (*genomenon*) from a woman, come (*genomenon*) under the law" (Gal 4:4; cf. Phil 2:6-8). Luke seems to illustrate these two traits in order: he has "come from a woman," Mary (1:26-27); he has "come under the law" (2:21-49). Matthew, for his part, brings out the child Jesus' subordination to the secular law, to the political and murderous dictatorship of King Herod. Luke likewise gives a hint of this in the story of the census. Without exaggerating anything in the facts, both perceive in this situation the irony in which the Messiah, the transcendent king, by the profound humility of his beginnings, makes sport of the powers of this world.

They have perceived in his infancy the fulfillment of the Scriptures, which take their meaning from the fact that the Christ is here; that he exists. What matters to them is his eternal being, which they present from what they know of his humble birth. Their investigations have made them aware that the characters in this important drama did not play their parts unwittingly, but in a free, conscious relationship to God. Thus is shown the obedience of Joseph and of the wise men to providential signs, given in dreams according to Matthew, the lucid and conscious vocation of Mary, according to Luke 1:39 and 2:19; and, by way of conclusion, a laconic oracle proceeding from the human consciousness of the Son of God, already oriented toward his return to the Father.(Lk 2:49)

The infancy Gospels do not present an eloquent or miracle-working child. Even in the Temple he merely questions and responds—and utters one enigmatic word to his bewildered parents (Lk 2:49-50). Both evangelists respect the "night and fog" side of this infancy; they dispel neither. But they discern therein the reality of the Son of God.

The principal sign, Jesus' entry into the human condition, was totally baffling. His human beginning depended on God alone: on the Holy Spirit, the principle of the new creation (cf. Gn 1-2). For both of the evangelists, Jesus was the Christ, the Messiah. Jesus merited this title from the beginning, by the action of the Holy Spirit, to whom Old and New Testament alike attribute the anointing of the Messiah. At this initial stage, the anointing of the Spirit is not prophetic, as it is at the beginning of Jesus' ministry (Lk 4:18 cites Is 61:1: "The Spirit of the Lord is upon me because he has anointed me to preach good news to the poor"). Jesus is not yet announcing the Good News. The infancy Gospels do not present him as prophet, but as king (Lk 1:32-33; Mt 1:16; 2:2; 8:11-12). The Spirit here seems only to signify the royal but spiritualized anointing of the Son of God, whose rule does not correspond to the rituals and powers of this world. The theology of the two evangelists is not expressed by means of some glorious epic (though the private veneration of the wise men in Mt 2:11-12 gives us a hint of this) but by means of the most ample assortment of titles to be found in the NT.[10]

The transcendence of the child is already a worthy object of adoration for Matthew (2:2, 8, 11), and of evangelization for Luke (2:9, 18 and 20). It ushers in the eschatological age, transforms the human condition, indeed, the condition of the universe. Communication with God forms the basis for communication between humans. It is the decisive moment in salvation history, the point of departure for a new covenant which begins in the infancy of Christ. To reduce this theology to a romanticized and dramatized ideology according to some preconceived notions would be to misconstrue the gravity of the realistic and contemplative approach. Doubtless, the evangelists sought out the significant themes, but these did not present themselves ready-made. Patiently working within the real history of Christ as the Judeo-Christian community preserved it "in its heart" (2:19 and 51), they discovered and expressed in admirable fashion, this gift from God.

The historicity of the infancy narratives, as well as their literary genre (pp. 98-107), is really novel. Its originality is the result of data drawn from this obscure and secret period, seen in the light of the major fact against which they measure everything: the reality of the Christ. Because of who he is, he gives a new meaning to Scripture and to the future of mankind. The evangelists came to know Christ in his *kenosis*, in the continuity of the covenant which he came not to destroy but to fulfill. This, according to both Matthew and Luke, is the key to understanding the history of the infant Jesus.

We have often commented on the relative starkness of symbolism in the infancy narratives (e.g., the undescribed star in Matthew, or the manger of a common stable in Luke). Like the literary models, the terms which are used transcend ordinary categories. What is the meaning behind this profound simplicity? It can perhaps best be likened to the theophany of 1 Kings 19:11-12. After the strong wind, the earthquake and the fire "in which Yahweh was not," God manifested his presence in "a voice of imperceptible silence." This is a wonderful expression of "negative" theology, which is misconstrued by most translations. It is not at all the "light breeze" that matters, but the voice that has the sound of silence.[11]

CONCLUSION?

Is it necessary to draw conclusions? Having completed this difficult journey over the threefold terrain of textual, literary, and historical criticism, and having made use along the way of the diverse methods of *Formgeschichte*, identification of composition and sources, semiotics, and so on (each discipline having imposed its own boundaries and to some extent determined its findings), the reader might legitimately wish for such a final summing-up. May we make some kind of conclusive synthesis?

Each discipline can draw serious conclusions only by remaining within the limits of its own methods (as defined by material and objective elements). If one attempts to achieve an overall and definitive view, one runs the risk of slipping away from orderly knowledge with only the illusion of having gained something.

But there is another means of synthesis, though it may not yield a perfect solution to the puzzle. This is a tentative enterprise, and may seem to some to be rather rash. It is not entirely healthy to enclose oneself within a specialization and deny the fundamental questions. The interdisciplinary enterprise is often the only means of resolving practical problems. The great scientific minds have only rarely been able to avoid making some kind of global or systematic synthesis. What is at issue in our search is not so much an adequate resume of the situation as an evaluation of its convergent streams.

Two paths are open in this direction: on the one hand, to grasp the correlations of the various methods (what we shall call evaluation of the convergences), and, on the other, to work out an over-all explanation by going to the root of the narratives, to their basic meaning (or orientation)[1]; how is the marvelous coherence, the ingenious density of the infancy Gospels to be explained (what we shall call the inspiring experience)?

A. EVALUATION OF THE CONVERGENCES

Following the first path (the evaluation of the convergences or correlations), we find that what is really imposing is the congruence of the two infancy Gospels. The diverse and penetrating methods which we have used to study them should have uncovered some flaws. But the flaws and failures which have been pointed out have been the failings of the methodological devices and not of the texts themselves. To the extent that the methodologies have been sound, they have revealed the richness and the density of these Gospels. Textual criticism has confirmed their integrity. Literary analysis has established the unity of authorship: Matthew 1-2 certainly belongs to Matthew and Luke 1-2 to Luke. There has been little success in any attempt to reduce these narratives to prefabricated models or to legendary or mythical processes. The never-ending attempts to do so have yielded only inconsistencies and contradictions. The different methodological approaches have only served to reveal the profound originality of the infancy Gospels, whose task it was to capture the utter novelty of Christ. The "parallel" between John and Jesus (which appears to govern Luke 1-2) turns out to be only the surface framework of what is really a well-constructed contrast which serves to highlight the subordination of the precursor to the Messiah, Son of God. The infancy Gospel of Luke illustrates the saying of the Baptist, "He must increase but I must decrease" (Jn 3:30), and, "After me comes a man who ranks before me, for he was before me" (Jn 1:30). Jesus here comes after John the Baptist (1:31-35 after 1:15-17; 2:1-39 after 1:57-80) but displays his superiority as Son of God (1:32 and 35) by coming to arouse John the Baptist to the action of the Holy Spirit and to messianic joy by his visit.

While it is true that the infancy Gospels utilize all the resources of the OT, it is also true that they go beyond them. Moreover, they "fulfill" them, to borrow a word dear to both evangelists. Likewise, the resources of the earlier literary forms undergo an astounding remodelling, especially in Luke. The annunciation to Mary is a birth narrative, but it is also a vocation narrative. It is apocalyptic, but it remodels the apocalyptic genre by the modesty and the discretion of its style. It is eschatological but in a de-eschatologized fashion. It is theophanic, but in the most radically humble setting: the shekinah in Luke 1:35 is devoid of any extraordinary manifestations, and the divine glory that surrounds the shepherds leads them to the extreme poverty of the crib (Lk 2:12). The meditation refrain (2:19 and 51) combines apocalyptic and sapiential dimensions with the *anamnesis* (memorial) of the faithful witness and the thanksgiving for the *Magnalia Dei*, which Mary began to sing in 1:46-49. Midrash, which was the principal exegetical method at that time, now becomes a *pesher* of a new kind. It is no longer a matter of Scripture shedding light on an event but rather, the Christ-event now explains Scripture, giving it a meaning never before suspected. Knowledge of Jesus becomes more important than the knowledge of the Book. This novelty was too profound to be identified within the narrow framework of *Formgeschichte*, or to be set as the starting point of Luke's theology by the remarkable, but rather too systematic theological approach of Conzelmann.

The attempt has often been made to discard these infancy Gospels arbitrarily as an anomolous block of material not integral to the Gospel message. The science of semiotics, however, reveals the dynamic and profound unity of the texts, their fundamental consistency over-riding the apparent medley of diverse episodes and literary genres. The depth of the text requires us to go beyond the analytic models erected for stories and tales. The infancy Gospels challenge the semiotic method with new dimensions which we are invited to take into account. The "model" is verified here with extraordinary density. The subject is identified with the object (the Savior with salvation) but also with the addresser, since he is designated as God (Great, Holy, Lord) and with the addressees with whom he is united in bodily and spiritual solidarity, from Mary (1:28-38) to Simeon (2:28-32). Working from two entirely different perspectives, the semiotic squares reveal a new and unfathomable message. Their convergences are rooted in an identical tradition and in an identical source of information which is, at one and the same time, historical evidence and spiritual experience.

In Luke, we see the joyous transition from Law to grace, for the proto-typical representatives of the people of God.[2] Matthew, finding his project (to recapitulate the history of salvation in genealogical form, 1:1-17) has been checked, arrives at another vision, where the human process fulfills the gift of God in a totally unexpected way.[3]

The Messiah's royal nature becomes evident in a paradoxical way: not in human glory or triumph, but in the hostility which Herod's dynasty shows him. Everything is programed towards Christ's passion and death. Yet God guides the childhood of Emmanuel, and Herod's dynasty comes to an end. The Messiah, who appears apart from the dynastic process and does not beget anyone, summons all to a salvation which makes negligible vicissitudes of this world.

With both evangelists, the eschatology in which all is fulfilled is humble and without human glory. It appears under the sign of death and trial. Even the mother of Christ, presented in so joyful a manner in Luke 1:28-38, does not escape the trial and the sword which are in store for Christ and for all who believe (Lk 2:35). For both evangelists, the promises made to David and to the prophets are fulfilled in Jesus Christ, but the fulfillment occurs in the lives of Christians called to bear their cross.

B. THE INSPIRING EXPERIENCE

How then did the evangelists manage to combine, in harmony and simplicity, so many cultural traditions and so many novel elements? How did they manage to combine theology and historicity and to achieve clarity and profundity?

The coherence, the density, the quality which make the text itself the arbiter and transcendent judge of disputes over its meaning result from its very inspiration—from the experience which gave rise to it. The remarkable structure of the infancy Gospels is not a clever fabrication. Their structure arises from within, as with a living organism. A living text is always structured from within (in contrast to a product of technical design and construction), because it does not achieve its goal through a fortuitous compiling of elements, but through a vital impulse, an integrating dynamism. An inspired text flows from a source.

This is true in the case of a literary work of genius. It is true in the case of the Gospels, in virtue of a more radical type of inspiration. A semiotician can identify the structure and coherent techniques of a masterpiece. It does not follow that he would be capable of creating it. Any attempt to do so would probably yield an artificial result. Texts worthy of the name are born of a non-rational stimulus, of a profound and creative impression whether of love, beauty, or even of anguish. Once written, a text "functions" in accordance with techniques identifiable by means of semiotic study. But it has in itself the source of its own existence, its organic structure is generated first of all from within, as in the case of a living thing.

Matthew 1-2 and Luke 1-2 were born of an experience of community faith. Neither evangelist would have written if he had not been a believer, nourished by a living tradition, like a plant in well-watered soil, and if the act of writing or of redacting had not been supported by a milieu which at once handed down its traditions and inspired its members with the desire to advance further. An audience (real or potential) is indispensable for the creation of a literary work. What is true at this literary level is much more profoundly true at the level of faith, where the "audience" is the community. This is why, by way of conclusion, we must ask the basic question: From what experience did Matthew 1-2 and Luke 1-2 proceed?

One will discover the answer only to the extent that one shares the experience out of which the text originated: faith, grace, community living. If this is lacking, the exegete encounters only the corpse of a text; he is able to recover, as too often happens, only a lifeless, reduced, ineffective meaning quite foreign to the original creative impulse—just as a musical composition can only be understood and appreciated by one who has a musical sense.

What, then, was the experience that inspired the Gospels of Matthew and Luke? These experiences form the basis for the whole of their Gospels and, in a more special way, their infancy narratives. Both dared to attempt the impossible: to tap new sources with the intention of reaching hidden areas—not the testimonies regarding Jesus' public life which are carefully circumscribed as objects of the *kerygma*, but the obscure reminiscences of the Judeo-Christian circles where there survived family traditions and a response to questions raised regarding the earlier years of Christ's life.

There was no reference in the public life of Jesus to the hidden years of his childhood. Instead of filling these with marvels, as the apocryphal Gospels did, Matthew and Luke went against the cultural expectations of their time and merely presented their hiddenness and humility, while trying to discover in them the very seed of the Gospel. What experience, what intuition guided their choice?

Matthew, Preacher of a Church of Silence

It is difficult to attempt to discern an answer to this question in Matthew 1-2, for his schematic account, stylized to the point of abstraction, provides little to help us grasp the experience that was its inspiration, except that it breathes an air of profound contemplation.

Matthew's experience is the experience of the Lord; we can see better what this means if we look at the whole of his Gospel. It is a community experience: "Where two or three are gathered in my name, there am I in the midst of them," (a saying of Christ reported by Matthew alone, 18:20). He experienced this in the primitive Judeo-Christian communities, the "sheep of Israel" towards whom Christ's public ministry was confined (Mt 10:6). It was a Church of silence because these communities experienced oppression from two sources—Roman paganism and Sadducean Judaism. Matthew's own experience was more specifically that of a teacher, within the context of a purely Jewish tradition, transformed by the Good News of Christ. He was inhibited and wounded, as a special target of the measures taken at the time to silence Christian preachers. He perceived Jerusalem in the light of this threat that came from the official religion, which he ardently desired would open itself to Christ.

What Matthew did by way of presenting the speeches, the public life, and the passion of Christ in the light of the Scriptures, he did in more schematic fashion for the infancy of Christ, under the momentum of his own reflective process. He was able to recognize Emmanuel in his inaugural silence—"God-with-us" from the start (1:23). The very density of his text, its structure, dynamism, and its style all result from the honesty with which he was able to meet what amounted to truly baffling difficulties. This led him very far theologically, as we have seen. What the Son of God does not express in word, he says in the very way he is born, in his life, and in his silence. His silent "genesis" challenges the expectation of the people of that time, just as he does later when he declares, "You have heard that it was said. . . but I say to you. . ." (Mt 5:21-22, 27-28, 31-34). The Scriptures which are cited by way of conclusion to each pericope re-establish continuity in the midst of startling innovations. They serve to clarify what lies ahead.

Matthew 1-2 is the celebration of eschatological "fulfillment" (1:22; 2:15, 17, 23) awaited from the time of Abraham and David (1:1). It would have been more fitting to have Christ emerge from the long chain of human generations, but the genealogy takes a surprising new direction, going beyond expectations to true fulfillment. The heir promised to David is not begotten by Joseph, son of David. The messianic royalty does not take the expected political direction. How keenly Matthew himself experienced this! The reign preached by Christ takes on a divine dimension that was unexpected, through the action of the Holy Spirit upon him. But it is without brilliance. God hides himself. The fulfillment is of a kind foreign to the glories of this world. The persecuted Son of God is a Nazarene by historical accident (1:23). In the obscurity of Galilee, he is marginal to society. But this sets the stage for the emergence of the "great light" (Mt 4:16), a light prefigured by the star from the East.[4]

In Matthew we hear the voice of a Church which no longer expects anything from Jerusalem and views it, from the time of Christ's infancy, as no more than a place of power and threats, working with Herod for destruction. It is curious to note that the narrative program of Matthew 2 is quite similar in its structure to that of Revelation 12: it is polemical, showing the power of darkness intent on slaughtering the new-born child, while God intervenes to save him. This no doubt stems from the the life-experience of the communities from which Matthew and Revelation derived, the one in a Jewish environment and the other in the context of the pagan world. In the case of Matthew, it is the "dark night" experience of a preacher reduced to silence, for the preachers were the outstanding targets of persecution. And Matthew had this charism. He is disillusioned regarding the conversion of Israel—but without bitterness. We do not find here Paul's eschatological hope for his people, but it is possible to surmise a calm prayer for those who persecute. The wise men, foreigners who are the only true worshipers in this scene, prefigure the transfer of salvation to the pagan nations. The kingdom is to be taken away from the people who have rejected it "and given to a nation producing the fruits of it," according to Matthew's harsh doctrine (21:43; cf. 23:13-39).

This negative aspect merely confirms the suffering that the Gospel discloses as also serene and contemplative, because of the belief that God guides everything from the very beginning. Such, according to Matthew 1-2, is the vision of the infancy of Christ. His contemplative perspective and reserve does not allow him to reflect the experience of the witnesses of Christ's infancy. Even Mary, Mother of Jesus (to whom, however, he gives a certain prominence: 1:16, 18, 20; 2:11), remains diaphanous—an object rather than a subject. The only "mirror-character" whose inner struggle and supernatural experience Matthew describes is Joseph, the just man, who accepts a mission whose completion he never sees. (He disappears from the narrative before the public life begins.) We must not, however, give undue prominence to this one feature of the infancy Gospel.

Luke, in the Inspiration of Pentecost

Here the source is more explicitly known: it is the experience of Pentecost, which only Luke recounts (though he was not present). There are several reports of Pentecost experiences in Acts (2:1-12; 4:31; 8:15-17; 10:44-47; 11:15-17; 15:8-9; 19:6). Luke's personal experience is situated within this countinuously renewed context.

According to Eusebius of Caesarea, Luke was a pagan convert in Antioch, the greatest city in the East (along with Alexandria). The Antiochian community (cf. Acts 6:5) was formed from the dispersion of the primitive community. It was here that the Spirit bestowed his most unexpected outpouring, causing the conversion of the pagans without their passing through the Jewish observances. This gave rise to the most serious problem and the greatest crisis of the nascent Church (Acts 11:22-23; 15:1-35). But in its turn it led to the evangelization of the inhabited world in a matter of twenty years' time (Acts 13-28).

The Antiochian community, in which the missionary experience of

Paul and Barnabas began,[5] and with which Luke was associated,[6] was undoubtedly the most charismatic community in the primitive Church. It had no shortage of prophets. In this community the Holy Spirit spoke, filling the Christians with joy (Acts 13:9, 52; cf. 2:4; 4:8; 6:3, 5, 8; 7:55; 11:24 and Lk 1:15, 41, 67 and 2:26). He guided them (Acts 16:6; 20:23; cf. Lk 2:27). They were overflowing with zeal and initiative (like Mary at the visitation, and the shepherds at Christmas). All of this took place in the context of prayer (Acts 13:2). It drew its sustenance from the Bible. But with Luke, Scripture is less a matter of explicit confirmation or proof-text than a light. It is a light produced by meditation, originating, according to Luke, in Mary and in the humble believers who have reflected and pondered for a long time without fully comprehending (cf. Lk 1:66, 2:19, 50-51).

What did this charismatic Christian look for in Christ's infancy? He went right to the heart of the story—with an evident concern to get to know Jesus "from the beginning" (1:2 and 3), from his very origins. He went back further than his "predecessors" (cf. 1:2). He was able to discover in Christ's origins the beginning of eschatology, the first fruits of the Holy Spirit, the earliest flowering of the charisms. This hinge experience is an intermediary stage between the prophets and Pentecost. Luke perceives it in terms of the "small remnant" the prophets were so fond of describing: Elizabeth and Zechariah, Simeon and Anna—all presented under the dominant theme of the Spirit. These four old people symbolize the OT which, as though in the splendor of a setting sun, appears rejuvenated by hope. In the case of Simeon, seeing death is linked to seeing Christ and seeing salvation (2:26 and 30). What he sees in this silent child whom he holds in his arms recalls Moses seeing God, as it were, from behind (Ex 33:23), or Elijah after the earthquake and the storm, perceiving God as "a voice of imperceptible silence." Here the path of "negative theology" is through the lowliness of the Son of God become a child. Simeon and Anna appear as the poor of Yahweh, in the wake of the Christmas shepherds. This people of hope, this "small remnant" of whom the prophets spoke, is focused on the two infants, hidden in the wombs of their charismatic mothers, Mary and Elizabeth. It is in these mothers and these as yet unborn infants that the outpouring of the Spirit and the new future of God-on-earth begins. The pneumatological reading of the infancy according to Luke is not anachronistic. The prophets of the OT enjoyed the experience and the fruits of the Spirit. Luke grasps and expresses this stage of salvation history in its traditional plenitude and radical newness, prefiguring Pentecost.

Unlike Matthew, Luke is not exclusively engrossed in a consideration of Christ. In the infancy Gospel, as in Acts, he follows closely the community which Christ and the Spirit founded. It was his intense concern not to limit the company of Christ to the Twelve. He is the only one of the evangelists to speak of the seventy-two disciples and of their mission (10:1-20). He alone speaks unequivocally of the women disciples (8:1-3).[7]

Luke distinguishes two groups: the women and the family of Christ (Acts 1:14). Where these two meet, only Mary, along with the Twelve, is mentioned by name. Luke also explicitly names her function as the "mother of Jesus" (Acts 1:14). She belongs to the Pentecost community which is "filled with the Holy Spirit" and with its charisms (2:2-4), which "speaks in other tongues" (2:4) to "tell the mighty works of God" (2:11).

The invaluable reference of Acts 1:14 points to the final stage of the ongoing contemplative meditation which Mary fostered "in her heart" from the days of Jesus' early infancy. It is not a finished outline like Matthew's. There are moments in the story of Christ's birth and infancy when Mary is subject to deep disturbance (1:29), reflective questioning (*dielogizeto*, 1:29), fear (1:30), astonishment (2:33), strong emotion (*exeplagēsan*, 2:48), anguish (*odynōmenoi*, 2:48), and even lack of understanding before the unfathomable mystery of the child Jesus and his first prophetic act of independence (2:50). The long process of her meditation is marked by ordeal. It continues even beyond the Resurrection and Pentecost, in company with the apostles, who also did not at first understand. Luke presents the fruit of this reflection in its post-paschal ripening, without embellishments.

His account is devoid of anachronisms, sometimes even to the point of leaving the future enigmatic (2:34-35). Did Luke derive this marvelous view of the infancy directly, by way of Mary, or indirectly, from the community in which he lived? The second solution is by far the more probable.[8] It is from within his community, in a mediated fashion, that he seems to have gathered this legacy of memories, not as anecdotes, but rather assimilated (through comparison and confrontation), matured, processed in the light of Scripture, according to the midrashic mode of meditation.

The affinity in terminology, in themes and in sense, between Luke 1-2 and John 1-2 suggests the influence of the Johannine circle on Luke's account. The Johannine prologue, so strikingly analogous to Luke 1-2, was already in the process of development. John and Mary belonged to "the Pentecost community." They belonged to the theological milieu upon which Luke drew. Luke does not isolate the "mother of Jesus." He does not separate her from the community, or from her people. She is, for him, the "Daughter of Zion." She personifies Israel. She gives thanks in its name. Zechariah and Elizabeth also represent the people of Israel; Simeon and Anna, the "small remnant" of the poor. The shepherds also represent the poor, and they prefigure as well the pastors of the future who are involved in the work of evangelization.

These representatives of the people of God have certain similarities—like the members of any living community. But they also differ in age, in their reactions, in their functions. Each of them is irreplaceable. There is the example of Zechariah, who hesitates and stumbles and must pass through an extended trial before being "filled with the Holy Spirit" (1:67); of Elizabeth, who remains in hiding (1:25) until the time of her pentecost (1:41); of Mary (1:39); and of the shepherds who, under the impulse of the message received, depart in haste (2:16). Thanksgiving is made in various modes. The evangelical diffusion of the Good News is attributed to the shepherds and to Anna, the prophetess, but not to Simeon, whose exclusive function is prophesy, nor to Mary, whose efforts are centered solely on reflection and contemplation.

Mary shares this contemplative role with the neighbors of Zechariah (1:66). But her own contemplation goes much further. It concerns not only John the Baptist, but Jesus as well. It is not simply a questioning (1:66) but an active reflection (1:29) characterized by its confrontation of word-and-event (*symbollousa*, 2:19) and by its scope, expressed by the word *panta* in 2:19 and 51. Mary is the witness *par excellence* in an intimate and integral way—the long-term witness. From the time of the visitation, she perceived God's victory (1:51-53) which she expressed as already won. But she must pass through the trial of incomprehension, and through that extended period of meditation that enables her to grasp in full the utter novelty of Christ.

Mary is not exalted alone; she is part of a community venture which concerns all the people, and especially the poor. Elizabeth outshone her in prophecy (1:41). Undoubtedly, the high point of the narrative is this *calling* of Mary, who enters into dialogue with God regarding the "Son of the Most High," who becomes her son. This is the founding moment, whose dynamic continues in the visitation (and the Magnificat), which harks back to the transfer of the Ark of the Covenant. But after this profound mysterious flash, Luke casts Mary in a role of unassuming, self-effacing believer. After the brightness of the shekinah (1:35), the dark night of faith overshadows her life (2:50). Having completed her exclusive function in giving birth to Christ, Mary seems to retire into the life of one who engages in extended meditation: she leaves the leading roles—announcing revelation, prophesying, spreading the Good News—to others among the poor of Yahweh. As John the Baptist's whole existence was meant to point to Christ, Mary at the Annunciation humbly points to the Messiah-Lord with a discretion that prefigures her position during Jesus' public life. Her existence is wholly relative to Christ and to his future. While Luke is the most laudatory evangelist with respect to the Virgin, he forestalls any form of Marian exaltation that would forget that her glory is rooted in humility and has its ultimate perfection in reference to God alone (1:46-56).

This experience of the first witness of Christ leads, in Luke's view, into Christ's own experience of himself: his first childlike, though not childish, expression of his transcendent self-consciousness (2:49) confirms the predictions of the annunciation and announces the Resurrection.

Concordantia-Discordantium

Matthew and Luke are extremely different in their origins, temper-

Is Mary the Source of Luke 1-2?

A question like this requires a thorough response. The purpose of this note is to summarize the grounds for an affirmative answer, in support of which a number of arguments have surfaced in this book, and also to give a balanced presentation of it.

In the final analysis, Mary is the only possible source of an episode like the annunciation, and the most appropriate source of several others: the visitation, the circumcision of John the Baptist (according to our analysis of 1:56), the birth of Jesus, the presentation and the finding in the Temple.

Luke explicitly refers, in two instances, to memories which "Mary kept in her heart." As we have seen, this is not an exclusively apocalyptic expression. It refers most often to the "wonders of God" in the history of salvation, and Mary makes this explicit in 1:49. "The Lord has done great things (*megala*) for me." This reflection is not a purely material recording, but a dynamic and vibrant preservation "in the heart" (2:19 and 51), accompanied by steady growth in understanding (cf. 2:50), growth which takes place by way of a confrontation *symballousa*: 2:19 (from the same root as "symbol"). In accordance with Jewish tradition, we are dealing here with a midrashic confrontation.

Luke 1-2 appears as the final product of this meditation, woven through with biblical references, going beyond the moments of surprise (1:29; 2:33) and even initial incomprehension (2:50). It is expressed in archaic, Semitic terms and shows signs of etymological allusions to the Hebrew names of the personalities involved (see above pp. 163-165). The frequency of the words "named" and "name" reveals a theology underlying the name of Jesus, in continuity with the theology of the name Yahweh which is of such fundamental importance in the OT (Ex 3:14; cf. 6:2; Lk 1:32, 34; 2:21).

The hypothesis of a literary dramatic fiction does not square with what we know of Luke nor with the statement of intent laid out in his prologue, nor with the overall consistency of his work. It does violence to the text.

Could Luke have known Mary?

The reliable data that are available to help us answer this question are the following:

Mary was born somewhere around the year 20 B.C. This estimate is given on the basis of the marriage age in Israel at the time (around the age of fifteen, and often earlier), and taking account of the fact that our computation of dates is inexact, since Christ was born "in the time of Herod" (Lk 1:5 and Mt 1:1-16), either in 4-5 B.C. according to the established consensus or in 1 B.C. according to other hypotheses (see above page 223).

She was present in Jerusalem at the time of Christ's death (Jn 19:25-27) and at Pentecost (Acts 1:14) in the primitive community of Jerusalem. We know neither the later course of her life nor the date of her death or assumption. It is unlikely that she lived to be very old since she would then have attracted the attention of the earliest Christian writers. Father Bagatti has identified her tomb in Jerusalem on serious archeological bases. It is situated beneath the Basilica where she has been venerated from time immemorial.

According to the three passages of the Acts of the Apostles where Luke speaks as a witness of the events recounted by using the expression *we*, one can date the visits to Jerusalem of this pagan convert of the Antioch community.

1. If we look closely at the "we" passage (Acts 11:27-28), attested only in the Western tradition (*Codex Bezae*), it would seem that Luke went to Jerusalem before 50 A.D. (around the year 48). Mary would then have been a little less than seventy years old—a likely hypothesis. This theory would receive further support if one were to accept the revolutionary thesis of Robinson, according to which Luke's Gospel may have been composed in the early 50s.

2. According to Acts 21:15, Luke accompanied Paul to Jerusalem on the occasion of his meeting with James, the "brother of the Lord" and first bishop of Jerusalem (who could also have been a family source). Would Mary still have been alive? It seems unlikely.

3. If one holds to the commonly accepted dating which places the Gospel of Luke around 80 (a consensus whose bases have turned out to be rather weak), and if one imagines that Luke began to compose his Gospel during those years and not at the time of earlier journeys to Jerusalem, any contact with Mary, who would then have been a centenarian, would seem to be excluded.

Jerusalem, Community of Mary (Acts 1:14)

It seems more likely that Luke gathered together what Mary "pondered in her heart," not directly, but through the agency of the community within which he gives her a fitting place (Acts 1:14). The explicit mention of the two groups (women and family) is an indication of Luke's sources. His ties with these circles explain a remarkable dissonance with both Mark 3:20 and John 7:5, which play down Jesus' family—undoubtedly because of the risk that a kind of family dynasty might develop. This was a concern of the primitive Jerusalem community, whose first two bishops were "brothers of the Lord": James, the distinguished personage and martyr, then Simeon (according to the ancient testimony of Hegesippus, cited by Eusebius, *Ecclesiastical History* 4,22,4: "Everyone preferred him as bishop, since he was a cousin [*anepsios*] of the Lord").

The prominence Luke gives to the women disciples (8:1-3) likewise distinguishes his from the other, less explicit, Gospels (Mt 27:55) and from the conclusion of Mark's Gospel, which seems to discount those women who were first to arrive at the empty tomb (Mk 16:8).

The Community of Jerusalem, the Johannine Milieu

The Judeo-Christian community was the source of Luke 1-2 and of Acts 1-7 (so similar in their archaic and Semitic character). This is confirmed by the close relationship of Luke and John (cf. above pp. 34-38 and A. Feuillet, *Jesus and His Mother*, 1984, pp. 66-78). The undeniable parallel (especially in the case of the prologues Lk 1 and Jn 1) stems from the important position enjoyed by John in the Jerusalem community (where Luke always mentions him first after Peter, a noteworthy trait of Acts 1:13; 3:1, 4, 11; 4:13, 19; 8:19; cf. Gal 2:9) and from his close connection with Mary (Jn 19:25-27; cf. Rv 12).

From the Sources to Luke 1-2

These cross references reveal a connection but they do not allow us to retrace the entire genesis of Luke 1-2. Was he working from written or only oral sources? We cannot settle the matter definitively, given the important role of memory in those days and its decline in the move from oral to written and documentary culture.

As for Luke's part in the final redaction, it is well established (vocabulary, style, etc.; see above pp. 34-38) and analogous to that revealed in his use of Mark: a discreet, elegant and faithful adaptation. He consistently and determinedly respected his source. Most notably, he allowed it to retain its Semitic character. Moreover, if his stylistic characteristics are easily recognizable, literary criticism would nevertheless sound the caution against making him the creator of the text.

In short, there is enough convergent testimony to establish Mary as the source for these chapters, but not enough to allow us to determine in exactly what way she contributed to Luke's Gospel.

aments, charisms, ministries, sources, and particular theologies or perspectives. Yet they addressed the same questions, experienced the same obscurities, the same double paradox of his physical and geographical origins, as problematic to them as it was to other Christians. And with their entirely different sources and lights, they both basically accepted the same general portrait of Christ's childhood story—the darkness and disorientation of poverty, the threats and contradictions.

The common proof of their authentic inspiration is that instead of inventing mythological accounts, they simply accepted the obscurity, the helplessness, and the silence of the child, the fact that his glory was hidden from human eyes. They perceived in Christ's humble, threatened infancy the point of departure for the new creation, and for the total transformation of the anticipated messianic age from a political to a transcendent and divine event. It is this wonderful contrast, of the great gift of God presented in the context of its humble realization that explains the internal coherence of each of the two infancy Gospels, as well as their coherence with the rest of their respective Gospels and with one another: the *concordantia-discordantium.*

The real ground of their interpretation, rooted as it is in the correlative authenticity of their sources and the context of their own experience, is the dawning awareness of transcendence as an interior reality, through the sudden appearance of the Holy Spirit, signaling the beginning of the new creation. Their experiences could only be expressed through a particular symbolic and cultural code, whose many aspects we have investigated, and which has demonstrated its own coherence. It implies a certain amount of relativity, but at the same time it points to an incommunicable experience which is the source and springboard of all the rest. The principal symbolic references do not point to material elements merely. In their rich array of signification, these symbols are transmitted as they were born, in a living tradition which reveals their meaning. Their relativity is only an avenue through which true believers (the poor, according to the Gospel) attain to reality in its twofold aspect, human and divine, which is the Incarnation.

From God's Point of View

Dare we finally refer to the only possible synthetic point of view in this domain—that of God, the inspiring Spirit, who may be perceived working in human lowliness? The two evangelists invite us to this perspective, for it is clearly from God's point of view that they disclose events, each in his own way and employing his own sources of information.

But this final evaluation exceeds the capacities of speech, which is always analytical, because it is of its very nature discursive. This is no longer a matter of analysis or logical expression, but one of contemplation. A spiritual experience is not describable like an object or an item of anatomy. One has access to a spiritual experience only by means of signs and symbols. So it is with the vocation of Mary, at the annunciation, the spiritual and somatic experience of the woman whose son is the Son of God. Her vocation inaugurated a new covenant, for her and for the entire people of God. This is the dawn of the new creation promised by the prophets. The first recorded saying of Jesus expresses its unfathomable meaning: God is his Father, and through the cross and Resurrection he will be reunited with his Father. This is also the path Mary takes, the one to which all Christians are invited.

NOTES

Introduction

[1]Jesus descended from heaven: Jn 3:13; 6:33, 38, 41, 42, 50, 51, 58 (cf. Eph 4:8-10, the eschatological descent after the descent to hell). There is a parallel here with the descent of the Holy Spirit at the baptism: Lk 3:22; Jn 1:32 (cf. Acts 1:8). Here John, for whom all begins with the Incarnation (1:14), joins with Paul: Eph 4:9-10; 1 Thess 4:16 (cf. Acts 14:11, where Paul is taken for a "god descended" from heaven).

[2]Son of David:

Jesus is identified (Mt 12:23; cf. Rom 1:3; 2 Tm 2:8), invoked (Mt 9:27; 15:22; 20:30, 31; Mk 10:47, 48; Lk 18:38, 39), and acclaimed (Mt 21:9, 15; Mk 11:10) under this title.

[3]The tone of superiority which "scientific" exegesis in its stammering stage readily used was employed even by a man as superiorly cultivated as Loisy. He comments thus on the scene of the finding in the Temple: "Your father... My Father: The antithesis seems to us so cold and in such bad taste.... The Gospel could have had a taste different than our own and have found it appropriate, in order to correct the impression that would give the quality of *father* attributed to Joseph, to oppose to this putative father the true Father of Jesus, who is God.... The present anecdote (the finding in the Temple) was first conceived independently of the marvelous account which we have just read" (*L'Evangile selon Luc*, 129-130).

This same tone is found among many exegetes. But we will see that Luke knows what he is doing, and that his writing has a density that cannot be comprehended by a reductionist exegesis.

Part I, Chapter 1: Textual Criticism

[1]Tischendorf, *Novum Testamentum graece*, 8th ed. critica major (Leipzig: Giesecke and Devreent, 1869).

[2]The critical apparatus of Tischendorf (*Novum Testamentum graece*) added two patristic references:

a. Irenaeus of Lyons (d. ca. 202), *Adversus Haereses* 4. 7. 1, *Sources*, v. 100, 456. Manuscripts of equal authority waver between two readings:

—*Elizabeth* said: the Claromantanus (ninth century) and Vocianus manuscripts (1494) as well as the Armenian version.

—*Mary* said: Arundelianus (twelfth century); Latin Vaticanus 187 (ca. 1429); Latin Salmanticensis 202 between 1444 and 1457. The *editio princeps* of Erasmus (1526) adopted the reading Mary but the *Sources* edition retains the reading Elizabeth (p. 456), relying on the Latin manuscripts cited above and on Nicetas (*ibid.*).

On the other hand, in 3. 10. 2 it is to Mary that all the manuscripts of Irenaeus attribute the Magnificat: "Mary exulting proclaimed, prophesying for the Church: *My soul glorifies the Lord. . . .*"

Here there is no variant in favor of Elizabeth (*Sources*, v. 211, 118-119). [Zahn saw in 4. 7. 1 the effect of some accident, while Burkitt attributed to the correction of a scribe the very solid reading "Mary" in 3:10-12.] "Elizabeth" thus appears an aberrant version.

b. Origen (d. 253/4) in the seventh of his *Homilies on Luke* which have come down to us in the translation of St. Jerome, notes that certain manuscripts have Elizabeth: *Invenitur B. Maria sicut in aliquantis exemplaribus reperimus prophetans. Non enim ignoramus quod secundum alios codices et haec verba Elisabeth vaticinetur. Spiritu itaque sancto tunc repleta est Maria, quando coepit in utero habere salvatorem.* But this observation could be the work of Jerome and not of Origen.

The subsequent context shows that Origen does not hesitate over the attribution of the Magnificat to Mary: *Beata Maria magnificat Dominum Jesum: Magnificat autem anima Dominum* (*In Luc Homelie* 7, *GCS* 35, Origen 9, 47).

The critical edition of Westcott and Hort (*The New Testament in the Original Greek*, Cambridge, 1881) gives the same variants. One note: *On Selected Readings*, explains the reading *Elizabeth* as a corruption of the reading *Mary* (p. 52).

In 1893, Loisy was the first to consider the possibility of attributing the Magnificat to Elizabeth ("Les Evangiles synoptiques," *L'enseignement biblique* [1893]: 35-36), a thesis which he defended under the pseudonym of A. F. Jacobe (*RHLR* 2 [1897]: 424 and 432).

About the same time, Völter ("Die Apokalypse des Zacharias im Evangelium des Lukas," *Tijdschrift voor Theologie*, 30 [1896]: 224-229) conjectured that the Magnificat could be borrowed from a pre-Gospel piece of writing, *The Apocalypse of Zachary*, in which it is attributed to Elizabeth.

In 1897, Morin likewise published a hitherto unpublished work of Nicetas, bishop of Remesiana in Dacia ("Deux passages in edits du 'De Psalmodie Bono' de Saint Nicetas [4-5e siècles]," *RevBen* 6, [1897]: 286-288; and "Le 'De Psalmodiae Bono' de l'Eveque Nicetas, Rédaction primitive d'après le ms

Vat. 5729," *RevBen* 14, [1897]: 385-397). Written about 400, this work attributes the Magnificat to Elizabeth. Nicetas says twice that Elizabeth "magnified the Lord with her soul." (Cf. ed. Turner, "Nicetas of Remesiana II, Introduction and Text of 'De Psalmodiae Bono,'" *JTS* 24, [1923-24]: 23 9, 16: *Nec Elisabeth, diu sterelis, edito de repromissione filio Deum de ipsa anima magnificare cessavit*; and 239 19, 11: *Cum Elisabeth Dominum anima nostra magnificat.* Burkitt, "Note on the Biblical Text used by Nicetas," in the edition of Burn, *Nicetas of Remesiana*, cliii-clviii, where he ascribes the Magnificat to Elizabeth; Barns, "The Magnificat of Nicetas of Remesiana and Cyril of Jerusalem," *JTS* 7, [1906]: 449-453, thought that Cyril of Jerusalem also attributed the Magnificat to Elzabeth in his *Catecheses* 17, 6. But one of the editors of the journal refuted this interpretation in the same issue at the end of the article.) This new witness revived the hypothesis. The controversy was at its height between 1900 and 1912 and experienced periodic revivals, but no support was found in any other witness. See the bibliography of the controversy: Laurentin, in *Biblica* 38, 1957, 19-23; and Benko, "The Magnificat: A History of the Controversy," *JBL* 6, (1967): 263-264, who recapitulates the controversy about adopting the Elizabeth thesis.

The endeavor of Davies, "The Ascription of Magnificat to Mary," *JTS* 15, (1964): 307-330 confines itself to explaining how the reading *Mary* could have been able to supplant the reading *Elizabeth*, the latter being supposed the original.

[3]*Exsultat Elizabeth, Johannes intus impulerat: glorificat Dominum Maria, Christus intus instinxerat*, Tertullian *De Anima* 26, PL 2, 694.

[4]Even Loisy, creator of the Elizabeth interpretation, adopts only the reading "And she said" (*L'Evangile selon Saint Luc*, 95), a hypothesis put forward by Durand. In so doing, he invents a reading to which *no* witness attests.

[5]On the possibility of a second *kai eipen*, without a change of speaker, see below, n. 11.

[6]Certain manuscripts would have had the reading "and Mary said to Elizabeth" (*kai eipen Maria Elisabeth*) and one later manuscript may have omitted "Mary."

There are some examples of this process (1:42) where the Syriac Sinaitic and Peshitto versions have added *to Mary*; similarly (1:56) certain manuscripts replace *with her* by *with Elizabeth*. For clarity, some manuscripts could have added *Elizabeth* after *Mary*: *Et ait Maria Elisabeth*; other "copyists could have thought that one of the two words was extra, and preferred Elizabeth for reasons which lure modern critics," concludes Lagrange (*Evangile selon Saint Luc*, 45; cf. *DBS*, 1272).

[7]Antigone, in Sophocles' play (916-918) also mourns being "snatched from life without having known the hymen and its joys... without having nursed any new born babe."

[8]According to Loisy and Harnack, the concluding verse (1:56), "Mary remained with *her*," would refer to Elizabeth, who had just recited the Magnificat (1:46-55). Ladeuze and Brown (*The Birth*, 345) see here a hint that the Magnificat may have been added later, in a context where the final verse, coming after 1:45 would not require a second naming of Elizabeth. This is indeed too faint a hint. It is more natural to suppose that Luke repeated the name of Mary because it was necessary to do so after such a long canticle, just as in 1:34 and 1:39. Why did he not explicitly write "with Elizabeth" (as appears in the Syriac, Sinaitic, and Peshitto versions)? This could be so as not to repeat the name of Elizabeth, which very shortly after (1:57) begins the glorious account of the birth. But Luke does not recoil from repetitions (for the name of Elizabeth: 1:41). This verse has never caused a misunderstanding.

[9]Lagrange, *L'Evangile selon Saint Luc*, 45.

[10]Sahlin, *Der Messias* 66 (where he interpolates the Magnificat 1:46-56 between 64 and 65) and pp. 68-69 (where he interpolates the Benedictus 1:68-79 between 2:38 and 2:39).

[11]It would be strange for Elizabeth to speak two prophecies in a row, the second being in self-praise, with Mary, who is at the center of the scene, saying nothing here, although she has spoken earlier (1:34 and 38).

We will not take up the argument of Gunkel (*Die Lieder*, 46, n. 1) that since Elizabeth has spoken in 1:40-45, according to Semitic usage, it is Mary who speaks in 1:46, for this rule allows of exceptions.

Furthermore, if the discourse of Elizabeth in 1:42-45 continued with verse 46, it would be unnecessary to repeat the formula of 1:42, "She said." However, Lk 4:23-24 (where *eipen* is followed by *de*), 18:1-6 (also *de*), and 21:8-10 (where a *tote* marks a break) repeats "he said" at the beginning of each of the two parts of one discourse. But it will be noted that we are dealing with a teaching of Christ, where the renewed speaking marks a progression. This model would not impose itself in the case of Lk 1:49, if one were to suppose this primitive *kai eipen* reading which no manuscript attests.

It is Burkitt, ("Who Spoke the Magnificat?" *JTS* 7, [1906]: 220-227) who first invoked these texts of Luke to defend the *kai eipen* reading. This article followed "Note on the Biblical Text used by Nicetas" (in Nicetas of Remesiana, ed. A. Burn, cliii-cliv). But Bishop Wordsworth (J. Sarum) had raised some objections ("Additional note on the Ascription of the Magnificat to Elizabeth," clviii). Burn, the editor, who had instigated this debate, while remaining neutral (p. 79, in note), let it be seen that he favored the second position, and formally defended it, in his article on the Magnificat in J. Hastings, *Dictionary of Christ and Gospels*, (New York: Scribner, 1906), 2: 101a-103b, which is an objective argumentation for the traditional thesis. It was in the wake of the publication of this contradictory argument that Burkitt developed his point of view in the article in *JTS*. He draws his argument from the parallel between the visitation and the meeting of Simeon, where the old man speaks twice, while Mary is silent. He argued equally from an etymological allusion to the name of John in the Magnificat. But one would find there a much more evident allusion to the name of Jesus in 1:47 (see the special note, p. 163).

[12]That Elizabeth would praise herself is "completely uncalled for," writes Benoit (*NTS* 3, 1957, 193). That would be in bad taste—something which we are not accustomed to find in Luke, as many exegetes following Lagrange (*L'Evangile selon Saint Luc*, 43) have said in different ways.

[13]The position of the Benedictus in 1:67 is singular. It would seem to fit better in 1:64 where this "benediction" is begun, with the use of the same verb *eulogeō*.

[14]Words common to the Magnificat (1:46-55) and to the prophecy of Elizabeth: *kyrios*: 1:43 and 46; *agalliaō*: 1:44 and 47; *makar-*: 1:45 and 48, the beatitude; *lal-*: 1:45 and 55, the words of the Lord; cf. *pneuma*: 1:44 and 47, but with different meanings.

[15]The expression "to look upon" meaning the favor of God: Ex 2:25; Dt 26:15; Ps 10:14; 13:4; 84:10; 102:20; Is 63:15; Lam 3:50. God also looks upon in *judgment* in Ps 11:4; 33:13; 74:20; Jer 13:20, or in *punishment*: Ex 14:24; Ps 59:5-6; 91:8.

[16]A. Gueuret, "Sur Luc 1:48-55," *Centre protestant*, Supplément d'avril 1977, 1-12. The article is dependent on historical critical arguments, especially those in the article by Durand, found at the end of the typewritten thesis. This is not the place to dwell at length on the topic since Gueuret did not maintain this conclusion, nor some of the arguments, in her additional thesis on Luke 1-2 (*Luc 1-2: Analyse sémiotique*, Paris, 1982).

[17]Zechariah goes to Gabriel. Gabriel, the messenger of the addresser, comes to Mary's home: "The lesser goes to the greater," comments Gueuret.

[18]The singer who speaks of her lowliness or humility (*tapeinōsis*, 1:48) could not be Elizabeth situated *on high* in the "mountains of Judea" (1:39); Mary is situated *below*. Semiotics, properly understood, seems to us to confirm the attribution of the Magnificat to Mary. Gueuret has now recognized that it does not establish the contrary.

[19]Betrothed in Lk 1:27 and 2:5:

The word *emnēsteumenē*, used by Luke in 1:27 as in 2:5, is often translated by "betrothed," but the word only approximately fits the Jewish sense of the word, since marriage was composed of two phases:

—*quiddûshîn* (literally, sanctification) which can be translated as "agreement to marry." This is the Hebrew substratum of Lk 1:27 and 2:5.

—*nishshûîn*, to transfer into the home of the husband, cohabitation.

This is the substratum of the questions underlying Luke, made explicit in Matthew: "Before they had lived together" (1:18); "Do not fear to take home Mary your wife" (1:20); and "And he took [home] his wife" (1:24).

The length of the engagement (or better, the agreement to marry without cohabitation, the agreement being already more a marriage than an engagement) was normally one year. (Lk 1:56 specifies that after the visitation Mary returns "to her home," not to Joseph's home, something which would have been said in the case of cohabitation: Mt 1:25). It seems probable that Luke has avoided this formula, but one should not press that which he does employ. In 1:40 he mentioned "the house of *Zechariah*," in spite of the systematic hiding of the aged priest for the remaining part (Lk 1:24-59).

For the discussion of textual criticism see Lagrange, *Luc*, 70 (he translates it as "betrothed"); Marshall, *Luke*, 1970, 105-106; Brown, *The Birth*, 387 (he translates it as "his betrothed"); Fitzmyer, *Luke 1-9*, 407 ("His fiancée, who was pregnant").

[20]The *Protoevangelium of James*, from the middle of the second century, understood this problem. It creates a "theologoumenal" dialogue on the basis of this word. Joseph says:

"This is my beloved" (*memnēsteumenē moi*).

"She is not your wife?" (gunē) someone asks him.

"I have taken her as my wife and she is not my wife; but she bears a fruit from the Holy Spirit" (*ibid*., 19:1-2).

[21]The interpolation of 1:34 has been very differently perceived by its protagonists.

—1:34-37: Bultmann, *Die Geschichte der synoptischen Tradition*, 6 Auflage, [1964]: 320-322, Weiss (1907), Clemen (1924) who extends the interpolation up to 1:38; Haecker (1906), and others.

—1:34-35: Hillmann, *Die Kindheitsgeschichte Jesu*... 17, (1891): 213-231, the leader. Harnack, "Zu Lk 1:34-35," *ZNW* 2, (1901): 53-57, and others: Loisy, *Les Evangiles Synoptiques* 1, (1907): 294; Usener, "Geburt und Kindheit Christi," *Vorträge und Aufsätze*, Leipzig-Berlin (1914): 180; Holtsmann and more than ten others.

—1:34b: Kattenbusch, *Das Apostolische symbol*, (Leipzig: J. C. Heinrichs, 1900): 621, 666-668, n. 300; Weinel, "Die Auslegung," *ZNW* 2, (1901): 37-40; Merk, *Evangelien*, Berlin (1905): 178-180, and six others including Sahlin, *Der Messias*, 117-136. One will find one of the best inventories of these solutions in Legrand (*L'Annonce à Marie*, 30) and a critical analysis of the arguments in J. de Freitas Ferreira (*Conceiçao*, 103-109).

Chapter 2: Literary Criticism

A. Composition

[1]The formula often expresses the invitation of God to a victorious courage (e.g., Gn 15:1; Is 7:4). This point has been frequently studied.

[2]The name given by the mother:

A woman giving the name is not uncommon in the OT. Out of forty-six cases, the mother gives the name twenty-eight times, and the father eighteen times:

—Eve gives Seth his name (Gn 4:25).

—The daughters of Lot name Moab and Ammon (Gn 19:37).

—Leah names Ruben, Simeon, Judah (Gn 29:32-35).

—The wife of Judah names Onan and Shelah, as she also names her first-born son Er (Gn 38:3-5).

—Hagar names Ishmael, according to the command of the Lord (Gn 16:11).

Similarly:

—Samson (Jgs 13:24),

—Samuel (1 Sm 1:20),

—Jabez and Peresh (1 Chr 4:9 and 7:16).

The logic of the context explains the maternal role for Hagar, who was in flight, or for Ichabod's mother, since his father was dead (1 Sm 4:19-22). But the dating of these texts demands the conclusion that the function of giving the name was exercised most often by the mother in the most ancient strata (J document), while the role was exercised by the father in the more recent strata. In the P document, it is Adam who gives Seth his name (Gn 5:3); Abraham names Ishmael (Gn 15:15, against 16:11) and Isaac (Gn 17:19; 21:3).

It is by way of exception that the father gives the name in two passages from J: Gn 5:28 and Ex 2:22. This could be a trace of the priority of matriarchy over patriarchy (M. Orsatti, *Vergine Perchè Madre di Gesù*, [Rome: BPI, 1981]: 188, thesis given at the Gregorian).

[3]Laurentin, *Structure*, 36, n. 3.

[4]*Pōs* (seven times in Luke, eleven in Matthew, five in Mark, seventeen in John, sixteen in Paul, once in Hebrews, and once in 1 John) is generally found in a context of objection, of discussion, often with a negative sense. These texts have been studied, but from another perspective, by Orsatti, *Vergine Perchè*, 143-149.

[5]The difference seems due less to the nuances between their objections than to the *right to speak*, recognized in Mary, challenged on the part of the priest. The adage in the Pauline correspondence: "That women should keep silence in the churches" (1 Cor 14:34) seems reversed here: "The priest should remain silent in the sanctuary." The last words of the angel to Zechariah find their contrasted parallel in the mouth of Elizabeth (Lk 1:45).

[6]*Kata ti*: "How will I know this?" (Lk 1:18): "By what token. . ." translates Osty; "on the strength of what. . .", Radermakers. The formula seems to imply the request for a sign such as God gave in similar contexts: Gn 15:8, often considered as the source; Gideon's fleece: Jgs 6:36-37; 1 Kgs 20:8-11; Is 7:11.

[7]The refrain of the growth of Jesus (1:40 and 42) as of John the Baptist (1:80) has its counterpart in the refrain of the growth of the Church in Acts 2:41, 47; 4:4; 5:1, 7, 14; 9:31; 11:21-24; 15:5; cf. 12:24; 13:48-49; 19:20.

[8]Brown has the merit of recapitulating and discussing the different approaches proposed by various authors (*The Birth*, 248-249). With reason he opts for a bipartite approach, John-Jesus, but one which would be complicated, at each page, by "confusing factors" due to the use of "material of different provenance" (p. 251). This latter assessment arises from presuppositions of the historical-critical method, which is prone to detecting contradictions or blunders, and to reconstituting, by means of these clues, the original pre-text. What is lacking in this careful synthesis is an understanding of Luke's scheme and of the motivating forces which direct its organization from within. The conclusions of Fitzmyer (*Luke 1-9*, 312), are to be prefered here.

B. Antecedents and Prehistory of the Text

[9]A. Resch, "Das Kindheitsevangelium," *TUU* 10, 5, Leipzig, Hinrich, 1897.

[10]L. Conrady, *Quelle der Kanonischen Kindheitsgeschichte Jesus*, (Göttingen, Vandenhoeck, 1900).

[11]R. Reitzenstein, *Zwei Religionsgeschichteliche Fragen*, (Strasbourg, 1901).

[12]D. Völter, "Die Apokalypse des Zacharias," 224-269; he improved on his hypothesis in *Die Evangelischen Erzählungen von der Geburt und Kindheit Jesus*, (Strasbourg, 1911).

[13]As with Samson (Jgs 13), or with Jesus himself, according to *Protoevangelium of James* (4:1-2).

[14]G. Erdmann, "Die Vorgeschichten des Lukas und Matthaus—Evangeliums und Virgils 4 Ekloge," *Forschungen zur Religion und Litteratur des Alten und Neuen Testaments*, 30 (Göttingen: Vandenhoeck and Ruprecht, 1932).

[15]F. Dornseiff, "Lukas der Schrifsteller," *ZNW* 35, (1936): 129-155.

[16]A. S. Geyser, "The Youth of John the Baptist, A Deduction from the Break in the Parallel Account of the Lukan Infancy Story," *NovTest* 1, (1956): 70-75.

[17]P. Winter, "Proto-source of Luke 1," *NovTest* 1, (1956): 184-199.

[18]Winter, "Magnificat and Benedictus—Maccabaean Psalms?" *Bulletin of the John Rylands Library* 37, (1954): 239-346.

[19]In the article cited in n. 17, "Proto-source," 198, Winter suggests that the expression, "He will be called Holy, Son of God" (Lk 1:35), would be derived from Jgs 13:5: *naziraion estai tō theō*. It would represent an invitation to consecrate the child to God, according to Ex 13:2 (source of 1:35b as of 2:23), as a nazir, that is to say, "a holy one," according to this practice of legalistic holiness. On this point, see the special note on the text "He will be called a Nazarene," below, pp. 277-279.

[20]Resenhoeft, "Die Apostelgeschichte im Wortlaut ihrer beiden Urquellen, Rekonstruktion des Buchleins von der Geburt Johannes des Taufers Lk 1-2," *Europaische Hochschulschriften Reihe* 23, (Frankfurt and Berne: P. Lang, 1974).

[21]Benoit, "L'enfance de Jean-Baptiste selon Luc 1," *NTS* 3, (1956/57): 169-184, criticizes the contrived consensus according to which the Baptist source was often presented "as an established solution which no longer needs to be proven" (p. 169). He thinks that Luke himself composed the accounts concerning John the Precursor, drawing from traditions which do not carry the least trace of a Baptist milieu; and that he composed them beginning with the annunciation, instead of the latter being formed on the basis of an alleged Johannine source.

[22]Brown, *The Birth*, 244-245 and 265-279, is likewise very reticent. Fitzmyer, *Luke 1-9*, 314-315 is more partial to this theory.

[23]Above all it has been argued that the Magnificat and the Benedictus (which are related) depend on a special source: pre-Christian, Maccabaean,

according to Winter, or from a late Christian creation of the communities of "poor ones" according to Brown, (*The Birth*, 346-355).

[24]K. L. Schmidt (*Der Rahmen der Geschichte Jesu*, [Berlin: Trowitzsch, 1919]: 309-314) thought he could discern in Luke 1-2 seven distinct traditions or accounts, joined together by Luke:

—1:8-25, 57-66: the origin of John the Baptist,

—1:26-38: where Mary is spoken of as being from Nazareth,

—1:39-45 and 2:21-40, where she would seem to be an inhabitant of Jerusalem,

—2:6-20: story of the shepherds,

—2:41-49: account which links the Holy Family back to Nazareth,

—finally, two separate canticles: Magnificat (1:46-55) and Benedictus (1:67-79).

[25]C. A. Briggs, *New Light on the Life of Jesus*, (New York: Scribner, 1904): 159-166.

[26]See above, n. 23.

[27]H. Schürmann, "Aufbau, Eigenart, und Geschichtswet von Lukas 1-2," *BibKir* 21, (1966): 101-111. The five accounts would be:

—2:6, developed in 2:1-7,

—2:22-39, another Jewish-Christian account,

—2:8-20, a later composition, likewise Palestinian,

—1:26-38, development by Christians converted from paganism on a Jewish-Christian base: 1:30-33,

—2:41-51, a story stemming from Christians of pagan origin.

[28]H. Sahlin, *Der Messias*. The author reconstructed his proto-Luke according to the following order: 1:5-45, 56, 64, then 46-55 (displaced, since it results in Zechariah singing the Magnificat), 65-66, 80; 2:38, followed by 1:69-79 (likewise displaced, since it is thus the prophetess Anna who sings the Benedictus of Zechariah), 2:2, 39-40. This reconstruction comprises a good many adjustments of details such as the elimination of 1:34b and 1:45 (so that the end of the prophecy of Elizabeth would be followed by these words, "While Mary was staying with her for three months, the time to give birth came for Elizabeth" [1:57]). In 2:11, Christ-Lord becomes, according to the Hebrew substratum, Messiah-Yahweh.

Sahlin eliminates the circumcision of Jesus (2:21) as he does the word purification in 2:22 (and all the disconcerting and significant tensions of this episode; he retains only the presentation); 2:23 is likewise eliminated, as is the finding in the Temple (2:41-52), due to the fact that one does not perceive here the trace of a Hebrew source. In 1:35, Sahlin returns to the substratum which he thinks is, "He will be called a Nazarean" (by analogy with Jgs 13:7 and Mt 2:23): see above, n. 19.

[29]P. Gächter, *Maria im Erdenleben, Neutestamentliche Marienstudie*, (Innsbruck, Tyrolia, 1953, 2nd ed., 1954): 9-77.

[30]We have recapitulated the arguments for a Hebrew source in the article "Traces d'allusions étymologiques en Luc 1-2," 449-456. See below, special note on the text, pp. 163-165.

C. Luke 1-2: Luke and Paul

[31]Kneller, *ZKT* (1910): 394-397; Herklotz, "Zum Zeugnisse Ephräms über Lk 1 und 2," *BibZ* (1910): 387; Merk, *ZKT* (1923): 322-326; Pirot, *DBS* 2, col. 1267.

[32]The controversy is well synthesized by Legrand (*L'Annonce*, 26) and J. de Freitas Ferreira (*Conceiçao*, 109-111).

[33]Machen, *Princeton Theological Review* 19, (1922): 1-38, 212-277, 529-580; 25, (1927): 529-586; and in his book *The Virgin Birth of Christ*, (New York: Harper, 1930); for a more detailed bibliography, see Laurentin, *Structure*, 208.

[34]Conzelmann, *Studien zur Theologie des Lukas, die Mitte der Zeit*, (Tübingen, 1954); and The Theology of St. Luke, (New York: Harper, 1960). A useful bibliography on this stage of the controversy is to be found in J. de Freitas Ferreira, *Conceiçao*, 165-185; and Legrand, *L'Annonce*, 27-29.

[35]Morgenthaler, *Die Lukanische Geschichtsschreibung als Zeugnis: Gestalt und Gehalt der Kunst des Lukas*, (Zürich: Zwingli-Verlag, 1948); "Statistiche Beobachtungen am Wortschatz des NT," *ThZ* 11, (1955): 97-114; *Statistik des neutestamentlichen Wortschatzes*, (Zürich: Stuttgart, Gotthelf-Verlag, 1958).

[36]Morgenthaler, *Statistik*, 52. Macher (cited above, n. 33) had already distinguished "lukanisms" and "septuagintisms," and had shown that the lukanisms were numerous enough to prove that Luke 1-2 has the same authorship as the rest of Luke.

[37]*Conceiçao*, 182-187.

[38]See special note on the text, pp. 35-36. See also: Morgenthaler, *Die Lukanische Geschichtsschreibung*.

[39]An excellent assessment of this point is found in J. de Freitas Ferreira, *Conceiçao*, 177-181, with an inventory of the arguments of Oliver, Tatum, and Minear.

[40]Oliver, "Lucan Birth Stories and the Purpose of Luke-Acts," *NTS* 10, (1963/64): 202-226.

[41]Tatum, "Epoch of Israel: Luke 1-2 and the theological plan of Luke-Acts," *NTS* 13, (1967) 184-195.

[42]Vatican II has moreover emphasized the recurrence of the same terms in Acts 1:8 and Lk 1:35 (*Lumen Gentium*, n. 59 and *Ad Gentes*, n. 4).

[43]Legrand, *L'Annonce*, 29.

[44]In Acts, Luke appears to have been struck by the encounter with the disciples of John: Apollos (Acts 18:26) and others at Ephesus (19:3). He did not wait for this episode in order to evoke the surpassing of John the Baptist by Jesus (Acts 1:5, 22; 10:37; 11:16; 13:24-25).

[45]I gave this a thorough study in *Jesus au Temple*, concentrating especially on 2:40-52; Serra has recently examined 2:1-20 in this context (*Sapienza*, 205-218; 268-277).

[46]See note on Vicent Cernuda, below, Part III, ch. 7, n. 19.

[47]*L'Annonce*, 186-193.

[48]*Ibid.*, 225-228. The analogy with Luke 1-2 concerns the *rhēmata* (Rom 10:8 and 9; Lk 2:19, 51), words in the mouth and in the heart concretized in the person of Jesus Christ (*pesher* of Rom 10:6-7 and the reference by Mary to the word revelatory of Christ in 1:38) and the apocalyptic ambiance which they share. Legrand does not hold to an influence of one text on the other. He is thinking more of two concretizations of Dt 30:14. He notes the differences between the Pauline hearing of Rom 10 and that of Mary.

[49]Contri,"Il 'Magnificat' alla luce dell'inno cristologico di Filippese 2:6-11," *Mar* 40 (1978): 164-168.

[50]It seems unnecessary to compare the empty hands (*kenous*) of the rich (Lk 1:53) and Christ who emptied himself (*ekenōsen*) of his glory (Phil 2:5).

[51]The remission of sins (*aphesishamartiōn*) in Lk 1:28 and Eph 1:7, where Paul does not have *hamartiōn*, which comes in 2:1, but *paraptōmatōn*.

[52]Let us note the occurrence of less significant terms:

—the time (*kairos*: Eph 1:10 and Lk 1:20);

—the word (*logos*: Eph 1:13 and Lk 1:20, 29);

—to bless (Eph 1:3 and Lk 1:28, 45, 64; 2:28 and 34; cf. *eulogia* in Eph 1:3);

—*charitoō* (Lk 1:28 and Eph 1:6 are the only two uses of *charitoō* in the NT. See the discussion of *charitoō* above, pp. 18-19).

[53]Luke retains those characteristics which come to him from a specific source: the concrete coming of the Son of God, and the joy which makes this the inspiration of all the joyful mysteries.

D. The Sources

[54]Le Deaut, "A propos d'une définition du midrash," *Bib* 50, (1969):

395-414; this critique of Wright's book (*The Literary Genre Midrash* [Staten Island, NY: Alba House, 1967]) confirms the path opened by Robert and Bolch, which we followed in *Structure*.

[55]Bloch, "Midrash," *DBS* 3, ed. L. Pirot, A. Robert, H. Cazelles (Letouzey and Ané, 1957): 1263-1281.

[56]Perrot, "Les récits," *RechScRel* 55, (1967): 481-518; a comparison of Luke 1-2 with the *haggadoth*, concerning the characters of the OT, from Noah to Moses and Samuel (bringing out the specificity of Luke as revealed by the absence of certain themes and by the virginal conception).

[57]E. Cardenal, *Chrétiens du Nicaragua: L'Evangile en revolution*, (Paris: Karthala, 1981): 27-30.

[58]These actualizations of Scripture are upheld not only by Legrand, but also by Brown (*The Birth*, 261-262 [Mal 3:1]; 270-271 [Dn 7-9]; 458-459 [Deutero-Isaiah implicitly cited in the Nunc Dimittis]). See also Fitzmyer, (*Luke 1-9*, 316).

[59]Some progress was made in the identification of these texts through an ecumenical effort on the part of Lyonnet, a Catholic, ("Χαίρε κεχαριτωμένη," [1939]: 131-141); Sahlin, a Lutheran (*Der Messias*); Hebert, an Anglican, who contributed the article "The Virgin Mary, Daughter of Sion," *Theology* 53, (1950); 403-410. I took up this line of research in *Structure*, 43-92. It was continued by Max Thurian, *Mary, Mother of the Lord, Figure of the Chruch*, tr. Neville B. Cryer (London: Faith Press, 1963): 18-81.

[60]Notably by Brown and Legrand.

[61]Convergence of God-Savior and Messiah: these two lines of the OT, that which announced the eschatological coming of the Lord himself to his people, and that which made the Messiah and the manner in which the two tended to become joined in the OT itself, were studied in our previous book *Structure* (above all p. 131, n. 3 and 132-133). On the one hand, the transcendent God descends among men and takes root in the midst of them: this is the theology of hypostases. In Prv 8:22-26, eternal Wisdom takes on messianic attributes. In Sir 24:1-29, she exercises priestly functions in the Temple (24:10, cf. 4:11-15; 14:20; 15:10). This is more broadly speaking what Gelin calls "Messianism without the Messiah," the promise of the coming of Yahweh himself in the midst of his people. On the other hand, the Messiah tends to attain to transcendence. The first thrust in this direction is represented by the series of titles which Is 9:6 confers on him. The two currents are joined together in Dn 7, cf. Ps 2:7; 89:27; 110:5-6.

[62]Cazelles, "La mère du Roi-Messie dans l'Ancien Testament," *Maria et Ecclesia* 5, (1959): 39-56, with bibliography p. 51, n. 46; and Laurentin, *Court*

traité sur la Vierge Marie, 165-166.

[63]On the probability of the substratum, see Laurentin, *Structure* 71, n. 3.

[64]Isaiah 7:14 and the virginal conception in the LXX translation:

It is often said that the LXX translation (made in the second century B.C.) made the prediction of Is 7:14 more explicit in using the word *parthenos*, "virgin," where the Hebrew said *'almāh*, "young girl." This is not evident, for the word *parthenos* is understood in a very broad sense in the Hebrew and in the LXX. Thus Dinah is twice called "virgin" (Hebrew: *bethûlāh*, Greek: *parthenos*) in Gn 34:3 after having been violated. The word could simply signify a virgin who *will* bear a child by being married.

According to the Hebrew, it is *the young girl who gives the name* to the child. According to the Greek of the LXX, it is Ahaz who does so; this suppresses one of the best indications of the Hebrew text in the direction of the virginal conception. The LXX thus represents a setback. Luke separates himself from it and agrees with (or returns to) the Hebrew text: it is Mary who gives the name (1:31).

[65]In *Structure* (pp. 71-73), I expressed some hesitancy about this link. But now the coherence of the text and the originality of the parallels (both of words and of meanings) leads me to assert these points of contact. In any case, 1 Sm 7:14 and Is 7-9 belong to the same tradition, and whoever cited them from memory could have superimposed them.

[66]The coming of the Holy Spirit upon Christ is his royal anointing according to Lk 4:18 (in reference to Is 61:1; cf. Acts 4:27; 10:38).

[67]Here is a brief synopsis of these links:

Micah 4	*Luke 2*
The *Lord* (LXX: *kyrios*) will reign on the mountain of Sion. . . forever	cf. 2:11: Christ the *Lord*
And you, tower of the *flock* Migdal eder (cf. Gn 35:32) of the daughter of Sion to you shall return the original sovereignty,	cf. 2:8: Some shepherds were watching their *flock*
the kingship over the house of Israel	cf. 2:4, 11: Jesus was born in the (royal) city of David
. . . Pain has seized you like a woman who gives birth Writhe with pain and cry Daughter of Sion like a woman who gives birth	(Mary is the Daughter of Sion according to Luke 1, in reference to Zep 3, but he suppresses all mention of pain.) cf. 2:7: where Mary gives bith

For now you will go forth	cf. 2:4: He went up
from the city	*from the city*
and you will live in the countryside	cf. 2:8: *agraulountes*
It is there that you will be delivered.	cf. 2:11: Savior-Christ the Lord
It is there that Yahweh will redeem you.	cf. 2:38: The Redemption of Jerusalem

[68]Winter, "The Cultural Background of the Narrative in Luke 1-2," *JewQ* 45, (1955): 238-241; cf. "Some Observations on the Language in the Birth and Infancy Stories of the Third Gospel," *NTS* 1, (1954): 116. Winter judges by various indications that Luke is referring to the Hebrew and not to the LXX, and cites on this point the Targum of pseudo-Jonathan on Gn 35:21.

[69]Micah 4-5 is composed, in chiastic structure, according to the schema ABCCBA: 4:10 and 5:2 are situated at the same level.

a. The eschatological perspective concerning the oppressed nations, 4:1-5; 5:4-8;

b. Parallel oracles about the "remnant", 4:6-7; 5:6-7;

c. Eschatological combat preparing for the Messiah, 4:8-14; 5:1-5.

Micah is one of the messianic prophecies most often cited in the NT: cf. Mt 2:6; Jn 40-42; Lk 2:4-9 and Rev.

[70]The identification of Christ with God had its roots in the OT: the king signified the national god who acted through the dynastic king, his chosen one, his servant, and his son; the psalms recall this (2:7 and 110:3). But Christ accomplished in this area the most radical of revolutions: he who is born poor (Lk 2:7 and 23) and outcast (2:40 and 52) refuses the kingship (Acts 1:6, cf. Jn 6:5) and submits to the powers of this world (Lk 2:1-4) which he secularizes (Lk 20:24-25), and dies condemned by these powers, crucified and abandoned.

[71]Detailed analysis in Laurentin, *Structure*, 57-58.

[72]Mal 3 is one of the keys to the exegesis of the presentation, as we will see later, p. 63.

[73]The evangelists used *eirēnē* to express the greeting *shalôm*: see Lk 10:5, 24:36; Jn 20:19, 21, 26 and the arguments of Lyonnet in *Bib* 20, (1939): 131-141, and of Carmignac, *Pour l'Unite* (February 1973): 11-14. However, *chaire* is used with the ordinary Greek meaning in Mt 26:49 (the kiss of Judas); 2 Jn 3; but never in Luke (see, however, Acts 23:26, *chairein*). In Mt 28:9, the *chairete* of Christ seems to have the resonance of *rejoice* (plural) in the prolongation of the messianic announcements.

The first word of the angel has an emphatic, lyrical, and eschatological value completely different from the typical daily greeting of "good day." The magnitude of the event and the message that follows proceed in the same line. *Chaire* in the sense of "good day" is not used in the biblical annunciations (e.g., Jgs 6:12-14; 13:3). The LXX does not use *chaire* in the sense of "good day" but reserves it for eschatological joy (Jl 2:21, 23; Zep 3:14; Zech 9:9; Lam 1:21). *Shalôm*, however, expresses the everyday greeting equivalent to "good day" (1 Sm 30:21). The parallel with Zep 3:14 might lead us to assume the Hebrew *ranni* (shout with joy), and by the same token Zech 9:9, so often cited by the NT and the Jewish tradition (as Serra has pointed out in an unpublished article): the invitation to joy is greater for Mary than for the Daughter of Sion: she is not only invited to passively receive this joy, but to *cooperate* with its execution (Lk 1:31-38). The theme of joy is striking in Luke 1-2 (cf. p. 61). We could not say that the Greek word *aspasmos* (1:30) indicates an ordinary greeting. The word has a general sense. It reappears twice more in Lk 1:41 and 44 where it takes on a transcendent and lyrical value of the first order; Elizabeth (1:44) saw in it the source of this proto-pentecost, which fills her and her son with the Holy Spirit (Lk 1:41; cf 1:15).

The Fathers of the Church have generally understood it so (in spite of the ordinary sense of *chaire* in the daily life of the Greeks). "He starts with joy, he, the messenger of joy," says, for example, Sophronius of Jerusalem on the Annunciation, 17, PG 87, 3, col 3236. If one tried to translate the *Akathistos* hymn with "good day" or "hello," the platitude, even the ridiculous quality of the translation would become obvious—all the more so for Lk 1:28, its source.

[74]The formula "in the womb" (*en koilia*) or "in the stomach" (*en gastri*) is required with the verb "to have" (Mt 1:18, 23; 4:19; Mk 13:17; Lk 21:23; 1 Thess 5:3; Rev 12:2), but this addition is superfluous and redundant where the word *conceive* (*syllambanō*) is used. It is therefore avoided, except significantly in Lk 1:31 and 2:21. In Is 7:14 (LXX), as in Mt 1, it is the verb "to have" not "to conceive" which is found with *en gastri.*

The contrast of Lk 1:31 (Mary's conception) with 1:24 (Elizabeth's conception) is striking. For the latter, it is enough to say, "After these days, she conceived" (*synelaben*). For Mary the addition of the verb "to give birth to" and the complement, "a son," specifies the meaning more precisely. This wealth of details makes the addition *en gastri* (in your womb), even more superfluous and redundant.

Luke is not content just to say that Mary will conceive (a term which sufficed to indicate the conception of Elizabeth in Lk 1:24 and 36); he adds with apparent redundance "in your womb" (1:31). This is done in order to echo the prophecy of Zephaniah saying to the Daughter of Sion, "The Lord your God is in you," literally "in your inner parts" (*beqirbēk*). It is undoubtedly the reason why Luke uses in 1:31 the Greek word *gastēr* (stomach) and not *koilia* the specific word for womb. The use of *gastēr* was so unique that Luke does not take it up again, once the parallel is established. It is *koilia* that he uses when he takes up the same redundant usage in relating the circumcision when Jesus receives the name "prescribed by the angel before he was conceived in the womb" (*en koilia*).

[75]The presence of God within the Ark:

We find in 1 Kgs 8:10-11 (the transfer of the Ark to the Temple), "And when the priests came out of the holy place, a cloud filled the house of the Lord, so that the priests could not stand to minister because of the cloud; for the glory of the Lord filled the house of the Lord." This text is taken up again in 2 Chr 5:11-14; 6:1. But these two texts insist on the presence *within*, without speaking of the presence *above*. It is therefore Ex 40:35, the basic text, to which Lk 1:35 refers.

[76]"Holy" is the specific name of God all throughout the OT. It seems to define not so much a particular property as the very essence of God. Not only is he Holy, but he is *the* Holy One *par excellence* (Ps 11:9), "the Holy One of Israel," an expression created by Isaiah (Is 5:19, 24). "The only one Holy," because "there is none holy like Yahweh" (1 Sm 2:2); (Laurentin, "Sainteté de Marie et de l' église," 5-6).

"His name is Holy" (Ps 33:21; Am 2:7; cf. Ex 3:14): Yahweh swears by his holiness (Am 4:2). The Hebrew language, which avoids the adjective "divine," accepts as synonyms the names "Yahweh" and "Holy" (substantively), and that this term is solemnly attributed to him, is one of the ways in which the recognition of his identification with God is shown (Lk 4:34; Mk 1:24; Jn 6:69; Acts 2:27; 3:14; 13:35; 1 Pt 1:15; Rev 3:17; 16:5).

We should add that, according to Lv 19:1-2, Dt 7:6 and Is 62:12, the people of God must be holy thanks to the moral and liturgical law, and to a holy and consecrated clergy (Lv 8:12; 23:7-8; Heb 12:10). They are called to share in the holiness of God. Might the neuter participle of Lk 1:35 suggest the new people born with the new Priest in the new Temple?

[77]*Glory* is a technical term signifying the presence of God, no longer only dark (as signified by the cloud), but luminous.

[78]The shekinah held an important place in Jewish theology and became the substitute for the tetragrammaton YHWH (the name of God). But this development is after 135 (A. M. Goldberg, *Untersuchungen über die Vorstellung von der Shekinah in der frühe rabbinische Literatur* [Berlin: W. de

Gruyter, 1968]). We refer to this term here because of the Hebrew substratum for the verb *episkiasei* (*shākan*).

[79]The small literal differences between the Greek of the LXX and the Greek of Luke could be reduced to the level of the Hebrew substratum. Again we find a common theme: holy respect, feeling of unworthiness before the Presence: for David, the *Ark* of the Lord; for Elizabeth, *the mother* of the Lord.

The *Lord* of the Ark: Yahweh is identified with the *Lord* who comes to reside in Mary: Jesus, Son of God.

The difference between the expression "enter my house" and "come to me" (in Greek the same verb *erchomai*, but with the prefix *eis*, 2 Sm 6:9) is reduced by the context wherein Luke has already said that Mary "entered" (*eisēlthen*) into the house of Zechariah.

[80]The charismatic stirring of John the Baptist, "filled with the Holy Spirit even from his mother's womb" as was announced to Zechariah, is described as a dance, like to that of David before the Ark (1:15). This fits in well with the Hebrew substratum *mekarker* in 2 Sm 6:14, 16. In the LXX the word *skirtaō* similarly serves to mean the joyful leaping and dancing which accompany the arrival of the Lord (Mal 3:20, another source of Luke 1-2; also Ps 113:3-4; Wis 17:9: in other words, three of the six uses of this word in the LXX).

[81]Obededom and his household are considered a class of Temple doorkeepers (1 Chr 26:4-8), aids to the Levites (26:15, 19, 21-22).

[82]As for the sword which pierces through Mary's life, Sahlin (*Der Messias*, 272-274), Black (*An Aramaic Approach to the Gospels and Acts* [Oxford: Clarendon Press, 1954]): 115, as well as Winter and Benoit agree that it is an echo of Ez 14:17:

Ezekiel 14:17	*Luke 2:35*
A sword will pierce through the land (Israel)	A sword will pierce through your soul (that of Mary, the daughter of Sion)

This is a further identification of Mary with the Daughter of Sion: the violent contradiction that Christ (identified with God) creates in the people of Israel, pierces the heart of Mary (as Israel personified). We are inclined to maintain it, by virtue of the textual convergences, in conjunction with the reworking of Zep 3 in Lk 1:28-35, and of the material in the Magnificat. Others see the key to Lk 2:35 in Zech 12:9-10 and 13:7, the prophecy of the piercing of the Messiah's side according to Jn 19:37.

[83]Laurentin, *Structure*, 89-90.

[84]The identification of Christ with God could only become clear in the distinciton of the Persons, without altering the unity of God or the priority of the Father. The hypostases of the OT paved the way for it; notably Wisdom (Prv 8:22-26; 6:24) in conjunction with the texts which tended to deify the Messiah (Is 9:5; Dn 7:13) the Son of God (Ps 2:7; 89:27; 110:5-6; cf. Acts 13:33; Heb 1:5 and 5:5).

[85]The prophecy of Simeon to Mary, "This child is set for the fall and rising of many in Israel" (Lk 2:34) seems to echo Is 8:14. Winter showed that Lk 2:35 is nearer to the Hebrew than the LXX translation ("Some Observations on the Language in the Birth and Infancy Stories of the Third Gospel," *NTS* 1, [1954] 118-120). There is a more detailed analysis in Laurentin, *Structure*, 89-90.

> It is Yahweh Sabaoth, him you shall regard as holy: let him be your fear, and let him be your dread. And he will become a sanctuary, and a stone of offense, and a rock of stumbling to both houses of Israel (Is 8:13-14).

Here, it is Yahweh who is both the *building* and the stumbling block. The prophecy of Simeon transfers this image to Jesus.

E. The Dynamic of Luke

[86]In 1956, we dedicated the second chapter of *Structure et théologie de Luc 1-2* to this dynamic. We are now in a position to reinforce the texture of this impetus, which is so essential to an understanding of the meaning and orientation of Luke 1-2.

[87]Cf. 1:48, 76; 2:29-35 where the aorist also takes on a future meaning, asserted in God as present, as if salvation were already accomplished.

[88]If joy does not return explicitly after that, nevertheless it undergirds everything: the wonder of the shepherds on whom the light shone by night, the devotion of Simeon and Anna (the joy is changed into light, 2:32), the amazement of those who hear Jesus and are enraptured before him in the Temple (2:46-47).

[89]The implicit reference of Luke 1-2 to these two prophecies is unanimously admitted today. The significance of this reference, so poignantly alluded to in Mary's meditation (2:19, 51) and which forms part of the underlying structure of Luke 1-2, still needs to be grasped.

Brown himself recognizes the many contacts between Luke 1 and Daniel, particularly in relation to Zechariah, without stopping to explore them in detail (*The Birth*, 270-271). But he concludes: "The theme of the seventy weeks of years, as interpreted by Gabriel in Dan 9: 24-27, serves Luke as the background for the annunciation by Gabriel to Zechariah. . . ." Likewise, the reference to Mal 3:1, (*ibid.*, 261-262, 265-266, 273, 278, 475, the presentation). Fitzmyer, a more radical exegete than Brown on the subject of the virginal conception, also regards these two references guardedly (*Luke 1-9*, 316).

[90]2 Mc 7:27.

[91]With regard to the calendar underlying Luke 1-2, the computation of Luke 1-2 supposes thirty days in each month. Does this mean that the author (Luke or his Judeo-Christian source) followed the Qumran "calendar": four seasons of three months of thirty days each (followed by a sabbatical period) and not that of the lunar months?

Luke 1-2 which mentions *month* three times (1:25, 26, 36) and *days* twenty times attests to a calendar of thirty days. Let us not go so far as to say the "calendar of Qumran" because we do not know what the spread of that old priestly calendar was, i.e., the details of the calendar of Daniel and Henoch upon which the Qumran calendar was based, remain unclear. Was it chosen because the Judeo-Christian circle where the source-tradition of Luke 1-2 was born used such a calendar, or rather, because this religious calendar (of the source text, Daniel) opened the way to this symbolic and fascinating computation? We lack the details to answer these questions.

[92]Serra (*Contributi*, 136-137) explains the defects of the parallelism (the abnormal situation of the third day in Acts 10:40) by comparison with the Jewish literature. The book studies extensively the eight days of Jn 1:19; 2:12 (pp. 90-99), and the expansion of this model in the NT (pp. 99-138) and in the OT (pp. 45-89). He provides a complete analysis of the sequences of days utilized in the NT.

[93]Dn 9:27 and Lk 21:22; cf. Acts 2:16-17. Dn 7:13-14 and Lk 21:27; Mk 13:26. Dn 7:13 and Lk 22:69; cf. 14:60.

[94]On the value of numbers for Luke 1-2 and Luke 7:12, 70, 77 see pp. 121, 347-354.

[95]Lk 2:7 deliberately called Jesus "the first-born" to set into motion (to program, in a way) this presentation in the Temple as the first-born (2:21-23, according to Ex 13:11).

[96]The title *holy* given to Christ in Lk 1:35; 2:23; cf. 4:34; Mk 1:24; Jn 6:69 (Peter's confession); Acts 13:35; 1 Pt 1:15; Rev 3:7; 16:5: The name *Holy* was, *par excellence*, the specific name of God. The *Concordance of Maredsous* emphasizes the use of the word "as a noun," specifying "divine name." That is

the case in varying degrees with the texts cited above. In 1:35 and 2:23, Luke takes the phrase "he shall be called holy" to mean that Jesus receives a divine title. We are on the road to divinization, or better, to the recognition of his identification with God, who alone is Holy.

[97]We should bear in mimd Lagrange's observation that *hagion* can mean consecrated—and as such, *hagion klēthēsetai* could be setting up the following scene where Jesus recognizes his obligation to be "in his Father's house" (Lagrange, *Luc*, 82).

[98]This transfer to Jesus of the sacrifice which should, according to the Law, have been offered for Mary is different from the preceding transfer, which attributed the purification of Mary to a plural subject. But these two transfers are not wholly unrelated.

[99]It would be stretching the intricacies of the text too far to wonder if something here hints at the underlying motive which this sacrifice could have for the nazir (the fortuitous contact with a corpse); death hovers over Lk 2:26 (the death of Simeon) and 34-35, which may be a prophecy referring to the death of Jesus.

[100]The notion of fulfillment is in question here, as in Lk 21:22. On this notion in Matthew 1-2, see Part I, chapter 3, n. 7, below.

[101]The expression "the Law and the prophets" is familiar to Lk 16:16; 24:44 (particularly pertinent for our subject); Acts 13:15; 24:14; 28:23. Cf. Jn 1:45, as well as Mt 5:17; 11:13; 22:40, whereas Mark ignores the Law. This concept *Law and prophets*, structures the presentation (2:22-28); first, the Law (mentioned three times); next is the Spirit (three times named in 2:25-27), and the prophets whom he inspires: Simeon, who pronounces a double prediction (2:29-35) and the prophetess Anna (2:36-38).

[102]On Jesus, "the first-born," according to Lk 2:6 and the importance of this expression in the NT, see pp. 178, 196, and Part III, ch. 8, n. 9, below.

[103]Lagrange, *Luc*, 82.

[104]Cf. Mal 3:3: "He will purify the sons of Levi."

[105]*Hierousalēm*, sacred name; *Hierosolyma*, profane name:

I. de la Potterie ("Les deux noms de Jerusalem dans l'evangile de Luc," *RechScRel* 69, [1981]: 57-60) so characterizes the use of the two forms of the name of the capital. *Hierousalēm* is the sacred name. He refers to the Holy City as the place of the appearance of the Messiah and the advent of salvation. It is the form that is used almost constantly by Luke: sixteen times (out of twenty) in the whole of his Gospel, five times (out of six) in the infancy narrative.

Hierosolyma refers to the profane city that did not recognize the prophets or the Messiah. It is the form consistently used by Matthew: ten times in his Gospel, the sole exception being "Hierousalem killing the prophets" (Mt 23:37); Jesus, rather than manifesting its degradation, refers to the Holy City according to its name of glory. Luke does the same with this word in 13:34. Without a doubt the pleasing repetition of the name is partly the reason.

Luke chose the form *Hierosolyma* in 2:22 to speak of its *purification* (that of the people and the Temple) in reference to the Law of Moses. After the purification it is called *Hierousalēm*.

[106]Lk 24:44; cf. 16:16, 31; 24:27; Jn 1:45; Acts 28:23; Mt 5:17, 7:12; 11:13; 22:40; Rom 3:21-22.

[107]God alone is the source of light, in the sense understood in Lk 2:32. He is light according to the book of Wisdom (which applies the word "light" to the divine essence), and Wisdom is a "reflection of the eternal light," superior to all created light (Wis 7:27, 29). It is in this sense that Christ, already considered as the Rising Sun (Lk 1:78; cf. Mal 3:20; Is 9:1, 42:7) is revealed as "light of the world" throughout the Gospel of John (1:4, 7, 9; 3:19; 8:12; 9:5; 12:46). The meaning here is transcendent. Luke 1-2 at this point is less explicit than John.

[108]The Fathers of the Church who, in other respects, present wavering interpretations of this prophecy, generally agree that it concerns the passion even if, with Origen and those who follow him, they explain Mary's sword as the doubt which the sword of the passion would presumably provoke in her soul (cf. A. de Groot, *Die Schmerzhafte Mutter und Gefährtin des göttlichen Erlösers in der Weisegang Simeon* [Lc 2:35] [Kaldenkirchen: Steyler Verlag, 1956]).

[109]Typical of Luke: after the visitation he finishes his account concerning Mary before relating the birth of John the Baptist, where it is understood from the text that she is present. Likewise he relates the imprisonment of John the Baptist before the baptism of Jesus. In the same way, it appears probable that he is here referring to Mary's presence at the time of the piercing of Christ's side on the Cross, according to the tradition preserved only by Jn 19:25-27 and 34.

[110]We will not dwell on the prophetess Anna (2:36-38) who represents, like Simeon, the people of hope welcoming Christ. We shall return to this in the semiotic section.

[111]It would be fruitless to linger over the roundabout explanation ingeniously proposed by Olivieri, Thibaut, and Bover: Jesus had warned his parents that he was staying in Jerusalem, but they had not understood. We would have to interpret Lk 2:50 with this nuance of the past perfect tense

which reduces the parents' lack of understanding to a simple misunderstanding: "Why were you looking for me? Did you not know [as I had told you at the time of our departure] that I had to remain in my Father's house?" But they had not understood the words he *had* told them (at that time). This interpretation, advanced orally by Olivieri, was published by Thibaut, (*Le sens des paroles du Christ*, Paris, Desclée, 1940). It was taken up again by Bover ("Una nueva interpretación de Lc 2:50," *EB* 10, [1951]: 205-215).

Not only is this nuance of the past perfect too subtle and problematic, this interpretation is moreover excluded by 2:43 where it is stated explicitly that Jesus remained in Jerusalem unknown to his parents (*kai ouk egenosan*).

[112]The age when a young Jew became a son of the Law. But this meaning, dear to Robert Aron (*Jesus of Nazareth: the Hidden Years* [New York, 1962]) and supported by several exegetes is contested by DeJonge ("Sonship Wisdom, Infancy," *NTS* 24, [1978]: 317-354); the age of bar mitzvah is not twelve, but thirteen or fourteen. It matters little, because the bar mitzvah did not exist formally under this name at the time of Christ, and Luke 2 shows nothing to support that particular meaning.

[113]"In my Father's house." This verse has been, in its own way, a puzzle for exegetes. The book *Jésus au Temple* settled the exegetical debate on the translation of Lk 2:49. "About my Father's buisness" had been adopted in the sixteenth century by both Protestants and Catholics. But this translation was unknown until then, with one patristic exception ("Quodvultdeus," *Sermo de symbolo* 5, PL 40, 644 cited in the final documentation of Laurentin, *Jésus au temple,* 218-219). The lexicographic and grammatical analysis, following hundreds of examples taken from biblical Greek and popular Greek (the *koinē* Greek spoken at the time of Christ and in classical times) prove the translation must be: "I must be in my Father's house." This conclusion has been commonly adopted since then. The Jerusalem Bible (French edition, 1956) has revised its translation accordingly (ed. 1973).

[114]But so that Mary might understand (and so that the unwarned reader might understand), the narrative might have explained, though rather clumsily:

> Joseph is only my earthly father. I must obey my heavenly Father. This temple being his house, it is here I must be, and not in the paternal house in Nazareth.

If exegetes have so often dodged this quite evident ambiguity, it is because plays on words have a bad reputation.

[115]The word "must" (*dei*) is more frequent in Luke (eighteen times) than in Matthew (eight times), Mark (six times) or John (ten times). It is more

frequent still in Acts (twenty-four times). It has apocalyptic antecedents (Dn 2:28-29, LXX) and appears quite frequently in Revelation (eight times). It indicates generally what must happen, according to the design of God, the designer. The frequency of the passages where the word "must" focuses on the passion and death, in connection with the three days and the return to the Father in the Resurrection, constitutes a significant index for the understanding of the aim of the finding incident.

[116]The third day characterizes the passion in Luke (9:22; 12:38; 13:32—a text with great symbolic authority—18:33; 24:7, 21-22, 46; Acts 10:40). The expression is used in the same sense (*triduum mortis*) in Mt 12:40; 16:21; 17:23; 20:19; 26:61; 27:40, 63, 64; Mk 8:31; 9:31; 10:34; 14:58; 15:29; and Jn 2:19 and 20, the themes and theology of which have a deep affinity with those of Lk 2:41-49.

The idiom is also attested to in Paul as a fundamental Chistian tradition, 1 Cor 15:4.

Serra (*Sapienza*, 272-276) has made a penetrating analysis on the idea that the third day is "announced by the prophets" in reference to Ex 19:16 (the Covenant), Hos 6:2 (the two days of suffering of the people and the resurrection on the third day), and the targumic re-elaborations of these verses. Luke assigns to Jesus himself the affirmation that the resurrection on the third day was taught in Scripture (Lk 18:31-33; 24:7, 46).

[117]Jesus is laid, asleep, bound in the manger, at his birth, as he would be in the tomb. The words used are, in part, the same; Serra (*Sapienza*, 195-218: "Motivi pascuali in Luca 2:8-20") analyzes the similarities of terms, of structures and of theology: words and signs, etc.

[118]The meditation of Mary has the same implication as the meditation of the apostles after the Transfiguration: "And they pondered over these words, what resurrection from the dead meant" (Serra, *ibid.*, 263).

F. Literary Genre

[119]H. Gressman (*Das Weinachts-Evangelium auf Ursprung und Geschichte untersucht* [Göttingen: Vandenhoeck, 1914]: 19) thinks that Luke's legend embellishes the theme of a royal abandoned child, later found by some shepherds. Bultmann criticized this reconstruction (*Die Geschichte der Synoptische Tradition*, 324).

[120]*Ibid.*, 260.

[121]Gächter, *Maria*, see above p. 47.

[122]Muñoz Inglesias, *Los Evangelios* 5-36.

[123]Cerfaux, "Luc," *DBS* 5, 590-591.

[124]A. G. Wright, "The Literary Genre Midrash," *CBQ* 28, (1966): 456.

[125]Legrand, *L'Annonce*, 20.

[126]See above, pp. 61-62; and cf. Le Déaut and Perrot.

[127]*Theologoumenon*: a theological idea expressed in narrative form. The philosophical origin and the genesis of this idea, which has been systematically abused, have been well treated by J. de Freitas Ferreira, *Conceiçao*.

[128]Kattenbusch, "Die Geburtsgeschichte Jesu als Haggada, der Urchristologie," *ThS* 102, (1930): 454-474. Legrand brought out the remarkable analogies of vocabulary between Rom 1:3-4 and Lk 1:32-35. But he appreciates the complexity of the problem sufficiently not to have classified these verses of Luke as a *theologoumenon* of Rom 1:3-4 (*L'Annonce*, 181-193).

[129]Legrand, *ibid.*, 117-142: we are dealing with a "de-eschatologized. . . de-dramatized. . . " apocalypse, because in Luke "the apocalypse is interiorized" (138-140). "This revelation of the Son of God. . . is an apocalypse. . ., the definitive fulfillment of the promises, the final work of the Spirit, the eschatological act of God. . ., an apocalypse opening up onto history" (214-215).

[130]Lk 2:1-14 (the luminous manifestation of the glory of God) is the only exception to this interiorization of the apocalypse. But Legrand's book does not touch on this episode.

[131]On the comparative study of announcements, biblical and non-biblical, see: J. P. Audet, "L'annonce à Marie," *RevBib* 63, (1956): 346-374; M. Allard, "L'annonce à Marie et les annonces de naissances miraculeuses de l'Ancien Testament," *NRT* 78, (1956): 730-733; Winter, "Proto-source," 184-199, on the birth narrative of Samson according to Pseudo-Philo: Muñoz Iglesias, "Los evangelios," 329-382; Perrot, "Les récits," 481-518; G. Graystone, *Virgin of all Virgins: The Interpretation of Lk 1:34,* (Rome, 1968); B. J. Hubbard, *The Matthean Redaction of a Primitive Apostolic Commissioning: an Exegesis of Mt 28:16-20* (Missoula, MT: Society of Biblical Literature, 1974) tries to define what he calls "commission form": a literary genre of mission sending (starting from the missionary discourse of the first Gospel); Brown, *Mary in the New Testament*, 156-159, with summary tables of the announcements, 156; Legrand, *L'Annonce*, 251, 272, a very elaborate study with several summary tables; K. Stock, "Die Berufung Marias," *Bib* 71, (1980): 467-491, who emphasizes that the annunciation belongs to the literary genre of *calling*. The comparisons between the analogous texts may seem infinitely suggestive, but the final results they yield are very meagre, except that they help us to grasp the originality of Luke 1-2. It is in this direction that scholarly

research has finally made progress, notably with Legrand.

[132]Burrows, *The Gospel of the Infancy*, 1-34, uses 1 Samuel 1-2 as a basis for an examination of the literary genre and the historicity of Luke 1-2. The comparisons deal essentially with the infancy of John the Baptist: the presentation of the parents, the barrenness of the mother, the conception and birth of a son, the refrain concerning growth, the presentation of Samuel in the Temple presents some analogies with that of Jesus in 2:22-25. But these are distant structural analogies which for the most part depend on the nature of things; the origin of a hero passes necessarily through a certain number of key statements: being born, growing up, etc., but the resemblances with Samuel are mostly insignificant, even contrasting. In 1 Samuel, Anna prays, but there is no announcement; for John the Baptist, it is the father (Zechariah) who is in communication with heaven. The only significant analogies are those of the Magnificat with the canticle of Anna. The later canticle moves within the tradition of the earlier one.

[133]Serra, *Contributi*, 169-172.

[134]I examined these structural analogies between Lk 1:35, the baptism and the transfiguration, in *Structure*, 75-78. (In addition, p. 76, the word *glory*, absent from the transfiguration in Matthew and Mark, is found in Lk 9:32.) From the comparison of Lk 1:35 with Rom 1:3, which was made by Legrand and taken up by Brown, we note a witness to this same scheme, which was one of the ways of expressing this new and unheard-of thing, the divinity of Christ.

[135]The Spirit over Moses and the Seventy (Nm 11:25), Othoniel (Jgs 3:10), the offspring of Jesse (11:1), and the Servant (Is 42:1) signified the establishment of God's judgment (Mshpt pqd). *Pāqad* has often been translated "visit" of God in the LXX, but Lk 7:16 uses *episkepsato*: "A great prophet was raised among us and God visited his people." He is the only one to use this image (1:78; 19:44; cf. Acts 15:16).

[136]The different theophanies are indicated in an analogous manner although the key words are utilized in different proportions:

Biblical scenes	Cloud	Power	Spirit	Glory	over	in	Son of God	Holy
Annunciation (Lk 1:35)	+	+	+	+	+	(+)	+	+
Baptism (Lk 3:21-22)	+		+		+		+	
Transfiguration (Lk 9:29-35)	+		+	+	+	+	+	

Biblical scenes	Cloud	Power	Spirit	Glory	over	in	Son of God	Holy
Confession before the High Priest (Lk 22:69-70)	+	+			+		+	
Resurrection (Rom 1:3)		+	+				+	+

The maximum number of meaningful elements come together in the annunciation (seven) and at the transfiguration (six); there are four (variously distributed) in each of the other cases.

[137]Hence the repetitions of the word *eleos* only in the sequence concerning John the Baptist (1:50, 54, 58, 72, and 78) while this word, absent from Luke and John, reappears only once more in the writings of Luke (10:2).

[138]Burrows, *The Gospel*, 1-34. The presentation of Jesus offers scarcely any analogies to that of a Levite (Nm 8:5-22), even though Luke could easily have looked in that direction, given his care in noting the connections of Mary, the mother of Jesus, to the priestly tribe (1:5 and 36).

Burrows (*ibid.*, 18) alleges this comparison, on the ground that the verb *parastēsai* ("to present") has the same meaning as *whqrbt* in Nm 8:10. But this latter verb is never translated by this Greek word in the LXX.

[139]Except for the important work of Dibelius, *Jungfrauen und Krippenkind*, Heidelberg, 1932.

[140]Bultmann, *Die Geschichte*, Göttingen: 4th ed., 1958, 327f.

[141]Dibelius, *Die Formgeschichte des Evangeliums* 4th ed., (Tübingen, Mohn, 1961): Eng. tr. *From Tradition to Gospel* (New York: Scribner, 1965).

[142]The weakness of *Formgeschichte* derives from the following presuppositions which it makes:

a. The Gospels have no organic unity: they are supposed to have been formed like a sort of nebula by the fortuitous conjunction of small, elemental literary fragments of a popular character.

b. The creation of these fragments could not have stemmed from a Jesus-event. It is a functional product of the very community which messianized and divinized Jesus, according to sociological laws bound up with the functions of communities. The Gospel did not result from an event but from the formulation of a kerygma (a preaching) in keeping with psycho-sociological laws. This a priori theory is sustained by a closed system of self-verification, which does nothing to remove the gratuitousness of its initial hypothesis nor to dispel the illusory character of its schematizations.

Still, this method has borne fruit to the extent that it has promoted methodical study of the Gospel pericopes (parables, miracles, etc.) which lend themselves to objective classifications. Systematization and its excesses sometimes have thier fruitfulness, when they stimulate and sustain a coherent method.

[143]This scene has a wisdom dimension. See below, n. 145.

[144]See above, p. 26.

[145]*Jésus au temple*, Chapter 6 "Eclairage de la littérature de sagesse," 123-142. There I study more particularly the points of contact with Sir 24. This point has been raised and extended further by Serra *Sapienza*, 18, 248-258.

[146]Plummer, *A Critical and Exegetical Commentary on the Gospel According to St Luke*, 5th ed., (Edinburgh: T & T Clark, 1922): 30f. and 38f.

[147]Brown, *The Birth*, 358f. and 388f.

[148]On these traces of etymological allusions, see special note below, pp. 163-165.

[149]Brown, *The Birth*, 378; cf. 359 and 388f.

[150]On the titles of Jesus in Luke 1-2, see special note, pp. 109-110.

Chapter 3: Semiotic Study

A. What is Semiotics?

[1]Bibliography on Semiotics:

The basic works are those of A. J. Greimas, *Sémantique structurale recherche de méthode*, (Paris: Larousse, 1966); *Du sens: essais sémiotiques*, (Paris: Editions du Seuil, 1970); and *Sémiotique Dictionnaire de la théorie du langage* in collaboration with J. Courtès, (Paris: Fachette, 1979). For an introduction, see *Analyse sémiotique des textes: Introduction, théorie, pratique*, (Lyons: Presse Universitaires, 1979), written by the Groupe d'Entrevernes which has also edited other works.

On Luke 1-2, see the fascicle "Luc 1-2," *Sémiotique et Bible: Bulletin d' études et d' échanges*, published at Lyons by the CADIR (*Centre pour l'analyse du discours religieux*), 6-25. Rosaz, *Les récits de l'enfance de Saint Luc*, Gueuret, *Luc 1-2*.

[2]The vocabulary of semiotics is coherent, specific, but rather closed. It contains many new words and sometimes detaches ordinary words from their usual meaning. When such vocabularies come into being, the risk arises that those using them will turn into a clique of initiates those who have contracted to understand each other without worrying about being generally understood. Actually, the content of these new terms is less mysterious than it may at first appear.

For example, the *Semiotique Dictionnaire* (see previous note) defines narrative program as follows:

> An elementary syntagma of the surface narrative syntax, consisting of a doing-enouncement governing a state-enouncement, such that the subject of the doing imposes upon the object a semantic investiture under the form of value (297).

In a "tale," all of this can mean something quite simple: "Peter becomes a proprietor (a new state) by building his house." By so doing, he is the subject of the "doing" and this house is the value that turns him into a proprietor.

In other words, the narrative plan is a tissue of actions (doing) which change the state of things or people by giving them (conjunction) or taking away from them (disjunction) some thing (money, properties, knowledge, or power). A narrative program may be the winning of a kingship or, on the contrary, its abdication.

[3]The author as enunciator:

Semiotics recognizes the author insofar as he intervenes in an objectively ascertainable manner. This is the case with Luke in the prologue where he invites the reader to explain his project (1:1-4). This is also the case in Jn 2:9b, interpreting the story of Cana: if the master of the banquet does not know where the wine came from, the servants know. These interventions are called *enunciations*, the author who thus shows his hand, the *enunciator*. The reader is the *percipient*.

These two terms, enunciator/percipient, are formed on the model of addresser (the actant who organizes the program) and addressee(s) (those who benefit from it).

B. Guideposts of Meaning

[4]Aorists with future bearing in the Magnificat were brought to light by J. Dupont, *Le Magnificat comme discours sur Dieu, NRT* 102, (1980): especially 331-334. The author abjures a previous interpretation according to which "the aorists would designate the manner in which God acts habitually and constantly" (p. 333).

[5]The word "week" does not appear. But the story alludes to the seventy weeks in Daniel, as we have seen above.

[6]The word "year" (*etos*) does not appear explicitly in Matthew 1-2. The children "two years and younger," massacred at Bethlehem, are signified by the locution *dietēs*, i.e., *di* + *etēs* derived from *etos* (2:16).

[7]The vocabulary of fulfillment according to Luke 1-2: The terms abound in these two chapters, each with its own value.

Plēroō (twice): the fulfillment of the plan of God (1:20); the fullness of wisdom in Jesus (2:40). This is the verb that Matthew 1-2 uses constantly, as we shall see, for the fulfillment of the Scriptures (1:22; 2:15, 17, 23). This point is rich with meaning.

Pimplēmi expresses the time of liturgical or prophetic fulfillment (Lk 1:23; 2:21-22) or the time of birth (1:57; 2:6). It returns especially in the refrain which regularly marks the fulfillment of the seventy weeks (1:23; 2:1, 21f.). The refrain "when the days were accomplished" loses its specific reference at 1:57 "the time accomplished," at the birth of John the Baptist; but it is still the verb *pimplēmi* which is used in this verse; and it is also used to indicate that John (1:15), Elizabeth (1:41), and Simeon are "filled with the Holy Spirit." The verb *pimplēmi* does not appear again after the fulfillment of the seventy weeks in 2:22; its incidence is thus quite indicative of a code. Afterwards, the idea of fulfillment, so important to Luke, is expressed by other verbs.

Teleō (2:39), the fulfillment of the Law, which balances 2:21-22 (inclusion).

Teleioō (2:43), the completion of the feast days when Jesus performs his first prophetic act.

It is thus astonishing that Brown finds the use of such words to be without significance. To be sure, one must beware of overestimating anything; but the exceptional frequency of these words signifying fulfillment, their occurrence in the form of a stereotyped refrain, the link they have with the fulfillment of the Scriptures—Micah 5 for the birth of Jesus (2:6), Lv 12:4 and 6, along with Daniel and Malachi 3 for his entrance into the Temple (2:22-24)—cannot be reduced to a fortuitous accident. If one neglects these perceptions, the text is hidden in a fog and becomes insignificant.

[8]See above, pp. 64-66.

[9]F. Dattler, *A casa de Zacharias*, in *Riv. Cult. Bibl.* 5, (1968): 112-114, identifies the anonymous town with Bethzacharia (1 Mc 6:32). This mere conjecture does not concern semiotic study.

[10]It makes its mark on the manner of naming cities: the non-mention of Jerusalem in Luke 1; the total non-mention of the neighboring city of Judea where "the house of Zechariah" is located, characterized however as a "high place" (1:39) near Jerusalem; the designation of Bethlehem as the "city of David" (2:4 and 11), when this expression was traditionally a designation for Jerusalem alone (forty times in the OT). See below, p. 174.

[11]In the OT, God is designated one hundred times as the Most High, principally in Sirach (forty-four times), Psalms (twenty times) and Daniel (four times).

[12]No room in the inn (*kataluma*, 2:7) puts Jesus in parallel with the shepherds who dwell not in town, but in the fields: *en tē chōra. . .agraulountes* (2:8).

[13]The verb *aineō* (to praise) is used for the angels of Christmas (2:13), as well as the shepherds (2:20). It occurs nine times in the NT, seven of them in Lucan material.

D. Sequential Division

[14]*Egeneto* has an emphatic value, but it is only a weak indication for division of sequences or sub-sequences. The third *egeneto* of Chapter 1 (1:23) plays a conclusive role which does not indicate a new sequence. The important sequence of the annunciation (1:26) does not begin with an *egeneto*, nor does the conception of John (1:24), nor does his birth (1:57). *Egeneto* reappears only at his circumcision (1:59) and at the birth of Jesus. In the latter narrative, the occurrences of *egeneto* abound and serve diverse functions (2:1, 2, 6, 13), as we shall see later. They disappear at the presentation (supplanted, as at 1:26 and 57, by mentions of time). In the final sequence, *egeneto* occurs twice to signal important moments rather than a beginning or change of sequence. So this criterion requires delicate handling.

[15]P. Bossuyt and J. Radermakers, *Jésus parole de la grâce selon Saint Luc* (Brussels: *Institut d'Etudes Theologiques*, 1981): 1:10-12. But the book's self-imposed conciseness does not allow the authors to indicate the reasons for this division.

[16]Gueuret, *Sur Luc*.

[17]This model also exaggerates the importance of the couples, "dual-subjects," at the beginning of the two annunciations of Luke 1; for these couples are no sooner presented than they are dissociated for different and meaningful reasons. Zechariah receives the announcement alone. Elizabeth disappears at that point (1:8) but reappears just when he finds himself excluded for his lack of faith (1:24). He incurs a humiliating chastisement at the very time when Elizabeth's "shame" is removed. In the announcement to Mary, the exclusion of Joseph is, as we shall see, more radical. The meaning of the story turns upon these changes of subjects (actants) more than upon the changes of action.

This model also exaggerates the importance of the object-possession-child, "child of the first couple," or "child of the second." No desire for a child was indicated in Mary, and the two children are demonstrably destined for the benefit of the people as a whole. They are pulled away from their parents, to the point where John seems, paradoxically, to grow up in the desert (1:80) as if he had not been raised in the family home. As for Jesus, he makes an astonishing break with his parents in 2:41-52.

[18]On these attempts, see Legrand, *L'Annonce*, 33f., and J. de Freitas Ferreira, *Conceiçao*, 137-154; also see above, pp. 28-30.

[19]See above, pp. 15-24, 51-58, 60-88.

[20]We find successively: Zechariah-Elizabeth, dual-subject (1:5-7) then Zechariah, sole subject of the announcement (1:8-23), Elizabeth alone (1:24-25), Mary alone (1:26-38), then together with Elizabeth (1:39-56), Elizabeth alone (1:57-61) and Zechariah appearing as the actant (1:62-79). The characters thus succeed each other in chiastic form, whatever the importance one may wish to attach to a symmetry that can be diagrammed thus:

Mary
1:26-38

Elizabeth 1:24-25 — Elizabeth 1:57-61

Zechariah 1:8-23 — Zechariah 1:62-79

[21]This choice is adopted by the clear-sighted commentary of Fitzmyer (*Luke 1-9*, 313f.).

[22]The most notable dissymmetries or apparent accidents of composition, which resist any reduction of the text due to a "geometric spirit," are the following:

a. While there is a change of time and place between the introduction of John the Baptist's parents (1:5-7) and the announcement to Zechariah *in the Temple* (1:8-23), these minor discontinuities seem to us merely to articulate the first sequence and to mark the contrastive dissymmetry which emerges, step by step, between the two annunciations. Semiotics must pay attention to this contrast, which is so productive of meaning.

b. Another dissymmetry shows the originality (the transcendence) of the annunciation to Mary. The conception of John the Baptist, recounted in 1:24-25, has no equivalent at the end of the annunciation. *We are not told when and how Mary conceived.* The event is *foretold* but not *told*. It will be manifested only through its consequences, i.e., through the visitation, as a dissymmetric counterpart to 1:24-25, i.e., to Elizabeth's conceiving, which concludes the announcement to Zechariah. These two sequences have the theme of thanksgiving in common, but the visitation has plenty of other original functions.

c. One may be surprised that the fourth sequence (1:57-80) joins John the Baptist's birth and circumcision together, while Jesus' circumcision is not attached to his birth (2:1-10) but to the following sequence, the presentation (see below, pp. 191-192). It would be artificial to gloss over this dissymmetry by treating the two circumcisions as parallel scenes, when in fact they are quite uneven, both in length and in function.

d. One should not forget that the last two sections, centered in the Temple (value element) both end with a return to Nazareth (2:39f. and 2:51f.) and with a refrain concerning growth. These elements have often been undervalued or even ignored by the commentaries. The refrains of growth hold a peculiarly paradoxical position, since they posit a new subject, a new duration, and in the case of John the Baptist, a new location (the desert); hence they constitute a sort of new sequence or sub-sequence.

E. Narrative Program for Luke 1-2

[23]The angel of the Lord frequently designates the Lord himself in the Bible. It is an expression which respects and mediates his transcendence, but in a manner which is often ambiguous: are we dealing with an intermediate entity or with a figure of speech? This difficulty appears most notably in the theophanies in Genesis. Mention of the "angel of the Lord" expresses and preserves God's transcendence by way of a mediation.

[24]The praxis of the *nazir* (Nm 6:2-7) required of Samson (Jgs 13:5) extended to his parents as well (13:4, 7, 14). This is not the case here. Later, John the Baptist who "drinks no wine" is contrasted with Jesus whom his adversaries treat as a glutton and drunkard (7:33-34).

[25]The house of Zechariah (*oikon*, Lk 1:23): It will be mentioned again at 1:39; Luke, who is sparing with topographical indications, gives no name to the "town" (1:39) close to Jerusalem. Tradition places it at Ain Karim.

[26]Elizabeth's thanksgiving "he has taken away my reproach," is a repetition of Rachel's words at the birth of Joseph (Gn 30:23). But Rachel's declaration is entirely positive, whereas Elizabeth still hides herself. She will disclose herself through the gift of the Spirit (1:41) and the birth of the child (1:58).

[27]The sixth month (1:26, 36; cf. 1:25) is a marker between two refrains of fulfillment, 1:23 and 2:6 (between which the refrain occurs in a disguised form at 1:57, without use of the word "day"), initiated by the six months of 1:36 and the three months of 1:56.

[28]On this marital situation, see above, chapter 1, n. 21.

[29]The name given by the father, Zechariah (1:13) and by Mary, the mother

(1:31). This is a striking contrast (highlighted by the identical formula, "You shall give him the name").

In the Bible, out of forty-six cases, the name-giving is done by the mother twenty-eight times as against eighteen times by the father. According to an unpublished study by Orsatti (*Luc 1:34*, a thesis submitted at the Gregorianum) it is the mother who gives the name in the most ancient texts (Gn 4:25; 19:37; 29:32-35; Jgs 13:24; 1 Sm 1:20). In later texts, the father does this. In Genesis 4:25, Eve names Seth (J document) while in 5:3 Adam names him (P). There is perhaps an analogous switch between 16:11 and 16:15 in the case of Ishmael, but with more uncertainty as to whether the verses pertain to different documents. This switch may signal transition from a matriarchal culture to a patriarchal one.

This could also be the reason why Emmanuel is given his name by the young maiden in the Hebrew text of Isaiah 7:14, but by Ahaz, the father, according to the LXX translation (third century).

In Luke 1-2 it is indeed Zechariah who is invited to do the name-giving for John the Baptist (1:13). Elizabeth has to try to stand in for him, temporarily, given his muteness (1:60). But he is still the one who fulfills the assignment (1:62). Just so, it is Joseph who is invited to act as father by giving Jesus his name in Mt 1:21.

[30]This same contrast of being and doing is noted in Gueuret's pertinent analysis, "John (1:17) is posited by the addresser with a view to doing, while with Jesus the doing is already achieved: He is described in reference to his being" (*Luc 1-2*, 65).

[31]We can only glimpse this in the light of the first appearances of celibacy at Qumran. Laurentin, *Structure*, 180-188. In this work, see special note below, pp. 417-418.

[32]One should not oppose the two modalities of presence *upon* and *in*, which are correlative (see above, pp. 54-55, the same correlation pertains to Simeon in Lk 2:25-26).

[33]For the import of the term "Son of God" see special note, pp. 145-147.

[34]The verb *kaleō* (to call) appears fourteen times in Luke 1-2: five times for John the Baptist (1:13, 59, 60, 61, 62, cf. 1:36); three times for Jesus (1:31, 32, 35); three more times: twice in 2:21 and once in 2:23; cf. 2:4 for Bethlehem. This verb has a function in the dynamic structuring of the text. See above, p. 68 (confirmed by semiotics). In the same way *onoma* (name) occurs thirteen times in Luke 1-2: four times for John (1:18, 59, 61, 63); twice for Jesus (1:31 and 2:21 which echoes it); once for God (1:49). In Matthew 1-2, *kaleō* occurs only six times and *onoma* three times.

[35]We will return to this below, especially in our treatment of St. Paul (Part III).

[36]The image of the Ark had a great deal of meaning in a period when the Ark of the Covenant had disappeared centuries earlier.

The later prophets placed more value on the Temple than on the Ark (Jer 3:16; cf. 2 Mc 2:4-8). Jer 31:33 foresaw a covenant which, beyond the symbol of the Ark of the Covenant, would be in the hearts: "They shall no more say, 'The ark of the Covenant of the Lord.' It shall not come to mind, or be remembered or missed; it shall not be made again" (3:16).

[37]The positive expression *dynamis* (in 1:35) is confirmed by the double negation, *ouk adynatēsai* (not impossible). The return of the same root *dyna* in 1:35 and 37 is almost untranslatable.

[38]The word *aspasmos* (greeting) occurs twice (a sign of Luke's intended emphasis) in 1:41 and 44, after the initial use of the verb *ēspasato* in 1:40. "To greet" may mean to embrace (2 Cor 13:12), but the word is used especially in the greeting of the Epistles of Paul and therefore of itself has only a general meaning. The salutation of Gabriel to Mary (*aspasmos* 1:29) evidently had nothing bodily about it. This occurrence would seem to present the greeting of Mary as an echo of the celestial greeting with which the narrative began.

It would be going beyond the text to insist on the bodily element of the salutation here. For the visitation, this element is neither excluded nor indicated.

[39]A woman is not normally the subject of the verb "to generate" as is attested to by Matthew 1 (see below, pp. 262-265), except with the case of Lk 1:13, "Your wife will generate for you" where the pronoun refers the generation to the man. The use of the passive (Mt 1:16 and 18; 2:1) is not an exception to the rule, because in this case the subject is hidden and Matthew seems to refer the generation to God as a transcendent Father. In this way the first of the two exceptions in the OT is understood by Bauer's Greek *Dictionary*, Is 66:9. The second is controverted, "Galaad generated Jesse," because Galaad is certainly not the name of the mother, but of the country which could be glorified by this birth. It was customary to use the names of countries for the names of persons (Nm 26:29; cf. 32:1).

The two apparent exceptions of the NT mentioned by Bauer involve the same explanations in a lyrical context (Lk 23:29 and Jn 16:21 cf. 4 Mc 10:2).

[40]For the etymological allusions, see the special note, pp. 163-165.

[41]Should we suppose with Gueuret that "it is not Zechariah who is deaf, it is rather the neighbors who have become mute" (*Luc 1-2*, 88)? They would thus move from the register of opposition (against Elizabeth, interpreter of the

divine prescription) to that of powerless questioning. This nuance may be present, but it seems too subtle. The narrative is now focused on Zechariah who has been excluded for some time. One would rather posit an extreme expression of his punishment, which ceases only at the moment when his authority is reinstated, when he indicates in writing the prescription of the angel.

[42]Concerning the use of the psalms and canticles in the Magnificat, see Plummer, in R. Laurentin, *Court Traité sur la Vierge Marie*, 199; Brown, *The Birth*, 358-359 who indicates some similarities with Qumran.

[43]*Egeirō* (to wake, to raise) is one of the two verbs used for the Resurrection. This usage may not be coincidental.

[44]Gueuret, (*Luc 1-2*, 95, 99) has correctly analysed the "we" which appears only in the last verse of the Magnificat with the possessive expression "our fathers" in 1:55 as in 1:72. It represents, not the neighbors who left the scene in 1:66, but the addressees, that is, the readers of the Gospel.

[45]*Keras* (horn) appears only here and in the book of Revelation (eight times). It is a symbol of power, to be seen as the extension of the *dynamis* which, in Luke, is present in the origin of Jesus in 1:35 and of John the Baptist (*ouk adynatēsei*) in 1:37.

The expression "horn of salvation" is taken from Ps 18:3 (= 2 Sm 22:3) where it is Yahweh who is designated. Fitzmyer (*Luke 1-9*, 383) recognizes this allusion, which seems to be another example of transferral to Jesus of a biblical title for God.

[46]On the star as a divine symbol see below pp. 394-396, 439-440.

[47]For a further development of this idea, see Conzelmann, *The Theology of Luke*, (New York: Harper, 1960).

[48]—*Time*: the "days," still vague in 2:1, are indicated as being "the fulfillment" of the days of the birth of Christ at the beginning of the sequence in 2:7, nine months after the annunciation, a chronological factor important for the seventy weeks which punctuate the infancy Gospel.

—*place*: from "Nazareth in Galilee," where Mary returned in 1:56, to "Bethlehem of Judea" (2:4).

—*actants*: John the Baptist and his parents have disappeared. Joseph, not mentioned since 1:27, reappears in the foreground in the sequence of the census (2:4). Mary, who appears (2:5) will come to the foreground in 2:6.

The division of this sequence is correctly analyzed by Gueuret, *Luc 1-2*, 105-125.

[49]Benoit, "Quirinius," *DBS* 9, (1977), 693-720, with bibliography, col. 717-720. The problem of historicity will be considered later.

[50]St. Jerome commented, "Here we have no midwife (*obstetrix*), nor the use of any assistant woman (*muliercula*). She was herself mother and midwife" (*Adversus Helvidium*, PL 23/192).

Jerome's commentary belongs to a long series of ancient texts. The earliest would seem to be the *Odes of Solomon* (in which Carmignac sees the work of a "member of the Qumran community converted to Christianity," toward the end of the first century in *Qumran Probleme* [Berlin: Akademie-Verlag 1963]: 75-108) which comments, the virgin, become mother with great tenderness. . . , gives birth without pain, so that nothing be done in vain. She did not request a midwife because he made her give birth voluntarily (*Odes of Solomon* 19:6-11).

The same affirmation is found in the *Ascension of Isaiah*, Ignatius of Antioch, and Lactantius.

[51]*Prōtotokon*: Rom 8:29; Col 1:15, 18; Heb 1:6; 11:28; 12:23; Rev 1:5.

[52]Concerning the hour and the date of Christmas, see our special note, pp. 223-224.

[53]Serra, *Sapienza*, 218-221, exhaustively analyzes this reference of the shepherds of Bethlehem to the shepherds of the Church by way of contacts of vocabulary and textual structure.

[54]Rom 10:9; 1 Cor 12:3; Col 2:6 and the ancient Aramaic invocation *marana'tha*. See our special note on pp. 185-187.

[55]The word "sign," which indicates the manger in Lk 2:12, occurs again in the prophecy of Simeon (2:34) to characterize the Messiah, a sign not of humility but of contradiction.

[56]The Messiah will be "Peace" (Mi 1:4). Luke 2:14 seems to round off the allusions to Micah with this significant contact. We have here for the Savior-Christ-Lord (2:11) yet another title, *peace*.

[57]The texts of Qumran have imposed this interpretation.

[58]Concerning Luke 2:19 and 51, see the exhaustive monograph of Serra,*Sapienza*.

[59]The occurrence of the prefix *syn* should be noted in the two verbs of 2:19, *syntēreō* and *symballō*.

[60]Concerning 2:19, Gueuret is correct in contrasting the interiority of Mary's meditation with the evangelizing role of the shepherds and of the prophetess Anna (Serra, cited in n. 58, above, correctly accounts for this). However, we think it is less correct to say "it is rather her 'not-knowing' which is accented" (p. 124), or to compare this meditative position with the "speechlessness of Zechariah" (p. 261). The refrain of "remembering" does not have this negative value. The evangelist, concerned with eyewitnesses

(Lk 1:2) seems to indicate here (as enunciator) that this mature meditation formed the source of the Gospel. Mary exercises her memory in an active way. The term *symballousa* is well chosen to express the process of midrashic meditation. It denotes a normal and long-ranging growth in knowledge: it is to be noted that Jesus is still hidden.

[61]The sequence is divided into four subsequences or segments:

a. The circumcision-presentation in the Temple (Lk 1:21-24) under the sign of the Law (2:22, 23, 24).

b. The coming and the twofold prophecy of Simeon, who is filled with the Holy Spirit at the presentation.

c. The coming of Anna (a new actorial change, characterized by praise and diffusion).

d. The return to Nazareth, followed by the refrain of growth (the twofold element which also closes the further sequence of the finding in the Temple).

[62]Gueuret, *Luc 1-2*, 133: "The addresser is the subject of the doing. . . . The important actor is the Lord, who has the position of a law maker. The movement from the expression 'the law of Moses' (2:22) to the 'law of the Lord' (2:24) causes a movement from the human addresser, typified by Moses, to the Lord, the addresser of new values, the controller of the principal narrative program, who until this time had been operating behind the actorial figures of the angels, the angel Gabriel, or the Holy Spirit."

[63]The word "name" is of considerable biblical importance, used 739 times in the OT and 210 times in the NT, according to the statistics of the Cerf-Brepols *Concordance*. "To call" occurs 469 times in the OT and 199 in the NT. In the LXX *kalein* (to name, to call) fills six and a half columns in the *Concordance*, more than 500 occurrences; *onoma*, more than thirteen columns, more than 1,000 times. See also *onomazein*. In Luke 1-2, *onoma* is used thirteen times and *kaleo* thirteen times (in Matthew, three and six times).

[64]"The first-born" (*prōtotokos*):

This word, used in Lk 2:7, prepares for the presentation, thus expressing its narrative program and insisting already that Jesus had the legal prerogatives (and obligations) of a first-born according to Ex 13:2; Nm 3:12-13; 18:15-16; Dt 21:15-17; cf. Mt 1:25.

It does not imply that there were younger brothers or sisters, C. C. Edgar, "More Tombstones, From Tell el Yahoudie," *Annales du Service des Antiquités de l'Egypte*, 22 (1922): 7-16; H. Lietzman, *ZNW* 22, (1923): 280-286 and J.B. Frey, *La signification du term Prōtotokos d'après une inscription juive*, *Bib* 11, (1930): 378-390; W. Michaelis, *Prōtotokos, Prōtotokeis*, ed. G. Kittel,

TDNT 6, (1968): 871-881 (especially 876-877a). Cf. Peretto, "Recherche sur Mt 1-2" *Scripta Facultatis Marianum* 25, (1970): 33.

Plummer asks why Luke does not here add *monogenēs* (only son) as he does concerning others (7:12; 8:42; 9:38). The reason is that it was not his primary motive to establish monogeneity (as also in 1:57). What was important to him was that Jesus be made humanly dependent on the Law of the first-born in order that 2:23 (where Ex 13:2 is applied to Jesus) might be properly programed.

Certain manuscripts add *monogenēs*, but this seems to be a gloss insufficiently founded in the manuscript tradition (cf. *Odes of Solomon* 18:4, *ōs huion prōtotokon monogenē*; Fitzmyer, *Luke 1-9* 407-408).

[65]The redemption of Jerusalem forms a certain inclusion with the purification of the same human group in 2:22, as we have seen. *Lytrōsis* (three times in the NT) is found in the Benedictus for the redemption of Israel (1:68) and again here (2:38). The third use is Heb 9:12. But *apolytrōsis* is frequent in Paul (seven times) for whom it is a significant title of Christ (1 Cor 1:30).

[66]See p. 206.

[67]"The disappearance and the resurgence of toponyms from the textual surface" were noted by Gueuret (*Luc 1-2*, 294) in reference to Louis Marin *The Semiotics of the Passion Narrative: Topics and Figures* (Pittsburgh, PA: Pickwick Press, 1980): "The neutralization of proper names as such causes them to become other by their becoming common." This neutralization restructures the place "to another level, without spatial relocation, without creating a new world, a new heaven or a new earth." The places become "other, without however ceasing to indicate a specific space." Thus "Jerusalem is named because the hero, Jesus, comes there representing new values."

[68]Fall, rising, contradiction (Lk 2:34-35). Concerning the divergent but not opposing positions of Benoit and Feuillet, see the special note, pp. 202-203.

[69]Gueuret, *Luc 1-2*, 292; cf. 302-303, 359.

[70]Luke is attentive to the extension of the Gospel beyond the masculine. Thus all that was important began with two women, Mary and Elizabeth in 1:28-56.

[71]This figure, 12 x 7, could represent the number of the tribes of Israel (twelve) multiplied by that of the nations (seven), something that might express the completion of the world's expectancy.

According to Burrow, (*The Gospel*, 42), M. P. John ("Luke 2, 36, 37: How Old Was Anna?" *BibT* 26, [1975]: 247), and Bossuyt-Rademakers (*Jésus*, 127), the eighty-four years represent the duration of her widowhood, not her age. By adding to these eighty-four years of widowhood the seven years of marriage, but also (as a guess) fourteen years before this marriage, she would have been 105 years old, like Judith (Jud 16:22-23). If Luke had wanted to indicate this connection, he would have specified the marriage at fourteen years (another multiple of seven). Without this specification the connection lacks a foundation.

[72]The role of diffusion which characterizes Anna relates her to the shepherds at Christmas and to Mary Magdalen at the Resurrection: the role of a forerunner, a dynamic and active role, which the last two evangelists attribute to women. This is one of the many novel and widely unaccepted ways in which the Gospel demonstrates its openness.

[73]Formalization of the presentation according to the aspects of the narrative program (= NP). → = conjunction, ← = disjunction.
NP addresser: Jesus → the human name (2:21) + divine name (2:23);
NP Law: Jesus → Jerusalem (Jesus → Nazareth in 2:39);
NP Spirit: Jesus → Simeon and Anna who recognize him.

This formalization of the simplest elements evidently is not exhaustive. We can further delineate the confluence of the various conjunctions in 2:21-38:
Jesus → human name (2:21) + divine name: Holy (2:23);
Jesus → Jerusalem (2:22), Temple (2:29);
Jesus → the people of hope, Israel figured by Simeon and Anna;
Jesus → Simeon: a somatic conjunction (2:28) and prophetic recognition (2:29-32);
Jesus → Anna, the prophetess who witnesses to the "redemption of Israel" (2:38);
Jesus → the people divided (faithful people ← people falling: contradiction, passion, 2:34-35);
Jesus ← contradictors;
Jesus → piercing of the mother, joined (identified) with the son.

[74]The two final scenes of Luke 1-2 both represent the conjunction of Jesus with the Temple of Jerusalem. But the presentation considers especially the relationship of the Messiah to the people: the purification (2:22), consolation (2:26), and redemption of Israel, the people being typified in Simeon and Anna. The finding in the Temple concentrates on the relationship of Jesus to God his Father, a clarification of what was obscurely sketched in the presentation in 2:23. The witnesses at the Temple are astounded by the intelligence of the child but do not recognize the salvation or the redemption as did Simeon (1:29-32) and Anna (2:38).

[75]The division of the finding is determined principally by the topographical and actantial characters according to a time frame which occurs during the time of the Passover (having a strong symbolic value, the Jewish Passover vis-à-vis the Christian Passover).

a. The parents ascend to Jerusalem and celebrate the feast with Jesus (2:40-41).

b. They return alone, Jesus remaining in Jerusalem without their knowledge (2:43).

c. Not having found him in the caravan, they ascend a second time and find him in the Temple with the teachers. Afterwards the dialogue, which is the center of this scene, expresses the meaning of this event.

d. Jesus goes down to Nazareth with his parents and is obedient to them. There are two ascents, each followed by a descent; the first descent and the second ascent are performed by the parents alone, Jesus remaining in Jerusalem, a symbolic act which is the object of the dialogue in Lk 2:48-49.

[76]The verb *teleioō* (2:43) is not found in Matthew and Mark. Luke uses it only one other time in 13:32, in the mouth of Jesus to signify his passion, "And the third day, I finish my course." Some translate this phrase, "For me it is all over." However, in Luke who uses a large selection of words to indicate achievement, *teleioō* has the sense of a consummation or perfection in the strict sense of the word. Thus it is not in the perspective of catastrophy but of fulfillment that we must understand the word in 13:32. The meaning is more commonplace in 2:43, but we might ask if the recurrence in 13:32 is not an indication that Luke has woven the scene of the finding from words borrowed from the vocabulary of the passion, of which we will give an inventory later.

[77]*Didaskalos* is one of the most frequent titles of Christ in Luke: 3:12; 6:40; 7:40; 8:49; 9:38; 10:25; 11:45; 12:13; 18:18; 19:39; 21:7; 22:11 where "teacher" indicates Christ in a special way. It is often with this respectful title that someone addresses him in the vocative form, *didaskale*.

[78]The symbolism of the *kathezomenon* should be seen in context because Jesus is seated when he teaches (Mt 5:1; Lk 4:20; 5:3) as are his disciples (Acts 13:14; 16:13) according to custom (Mt 23:2), while *kathezomai*, used in 2:46, signifies to be seated (Acts 6:15) the same position is also that of the disciple (Lk 10:39; or Acts 22:3, Paul at the feet of Gamaliel: *para tous podas Gamaliēl pepaideumenos*). Luke's suggestion is expressive, but we should not exaggerate its significance.

[79]The fact that the relatives are outside the circle of the listeners, so strongly observed by Mark (3:31-35), is softened lightly by Luke (8:21) who nevertheless maintains "Your mother and your brothers are standing out-

side." Furthermore, while Mark insists on the circular glance of Jesus on his disciples by the verb *periblepomai* (five times), Luke uses this word only once (6:10). The relatives being outside the circle in the center of which Jesus is seated is not insisted on but only suggested by Lk 2:46.

[80]*Katebē* as opposed to *anabainō* (2:42); the same verb *bainō* with the prefixes signifying respectively up and down; see the above topographical study, pp. 122-123.

[81]The refrain of growth at the end of the presentation (2:40) recalls the parallelism which structured the beginning of Luke 1-2 and yet was not apparent in the scenes of the Temple proper to Jesus. This refrain is used in 2:52. The formula "the child grew" is common to John (1:80) and to Jesus (2:40 and 52). The mode is differentiated: John is strengthened in spirit (formula called for by Lk 1:15); but Jesus is "full of wisdom" (2:40 and 52). *Plēroumenos* signifies plenitude. Wisdom is a favorite word in Luke: seven times against five in Matthew, once in Mark, and none in John. The principal contrast is in the final word, *charis*, which characterizes Jesus in 2:40 and 52.

F. The Model

[82]Unlike that of Matthew 2, see below, Part II, chapter 3, n. 15.

G. Fundamental Structure of Semiotic Square and of Luke 1-2

[83]Luke 1-2 in *Sémiotique et Bible*, (Lyon: CADIR, 1976).

[84]The levels of the CADIR square are arranged in the following categories: level one is the basic deepest level; level two deals with the understanding of the text-event on the level of truth (i.e., truth, appearance, secrecy); level three examines the use of modal values; level four details the relevant apportioning of space; level five explores the family roles in each premise; level six examines the ultimate outcome.

[85]Rosaz, "Les récits."

[86]Gueuret, *Luc 1-2*.

[87]While the Magnificat illustrates the contrast between A (communication) and B (non-domination, the situation of the humble, of the poor, of Mary, the servant), the Benedictus manifests the clear opposition of A (communication) and B (domination, its contrary) which can be summarized in the following table:

	A	B
Cosmic	Life	death
	Light (1:79)	shadows (1:79)

Israelite	Peace (1:79)	war (cf. 1:71, 74)
	Liberation (1:74)	captivity (1:74)
(= social)	Alliance (1:72, 73)	enemy (1:71, 74)
Religious	Salvation (1:69, 71)	sin (1:77)
	Forgiveness (cf. 1:72)	
Somatic	The bowels of mercy (1:78)	hand (of the enemies, 1:71, 74)
Religious	Visit (1:68-78)	hatred (1:71)
	Cultic worship (1:75)	

[88]Grace, unknown in Mark, is found only three times in John (and there only in the prologue, which is dependent on Luke 1-2), but it is found eight times in the Gospel of Luke (three of which are found in Luke 1-2) and seventeen times in Acts. This word, common to Luke and Paul (in whose letters occur three quarters of the uses of this word in the NT) has a structural value in Luke.

This may be attributable to their relationship: was Luke a companion of Paul? The discussions concerning this point are becoming more and more subtle. According to the most detailed analysis, that of S. Berck (*NRT* 103, 1981, 385-400) he would seem to have been only a companion of Paul's travels (not of his apostolate), but certainly his companion at Rome for two years.

Luke poses the contrast between grace (Acts 15:11; see 15:40), the yoke (15:10), and the Law (15:5) in the hinge texts of Acts; the Council of Jerusalem officially endorses the outstripping of the Law by grace (though not without maintaining some observances which witness to the Law).

[89]In this last case, Jesus transcends the Law, custom, the the Temple itself, since his gesture signifies a future beyond the Temple. The phrase "in my Father's house" which accompanies his symbolic gesture at the age of twelve signifies the final return beyond the earth, to his Father who is in heaven (2:13-14).

[90]We could object that the circumcision seems to have taken place (according to the Law) at Bethlehem. But Luke does not name the Law in the first verse of the sequence of the presentation (2:21), and then conceals the place by connecting this verse to the sequence of Jerusalem (see special note, p. 191). The site of the visitation is ambiguous. It has no name but is the place of the transferral from the Law (1:5-25) to the Holy Spirit (1:41 and 67; see

1:15). The residence of the priest, Zechariah, witnesses to the transferral Law-grace; in an intermediary situation between Nazareth, the originating place of grace (the place of the origin of Christ) and Jerusalem, characterized by the Law. Zechariah's residence witnesses the transferral from the Law to the Spirit, which the change of 2:21-24 (Law) to 25-27 (Spirit) manifests so clearly.

[91]The contrast being-appearing comes out clearly in the genealogy of "Jesus, the Son as supposed (= appearing) of Joseph" but who is also manifested Son of God by the voice of the Father at the very threshold of the genealogy (3:22) and by a linear connection to God the creator from whom Adam proceeded as the image of God. This symbolic inclusion emphasizes the fact that Christ had no other (i.e., no human) origin but rather originated from God himself.

Part II, Chapter 1: Textual Criticism

[1]S. E. Legg, *Evangelium secundum Matthaeum, cum apparatu critico novo plenissimo...*, (Oxford: Clarendon Press, 1940): 1-16.

[2]M. J. Lagrange, *Evangile selon St. Matthieu*, 4th ed., (Paris: J. Gabalda, 1927): 6-8; B. M. Metzger, "On the Citation of Variant Readings of Matt. 1:16," *JBL* 77, (1958): 361-363; and "The text of Matthew 1:16," *Studies in NT... Essays in honor of Allen P. Wikgren,* (Leiden: Brill, 1972): 16-24; Brown, *The Birth*, 62-64. P. Bonnard observed already the "interconfessional consensus" on the text received (*L'Evangile selon Saint Matthieu*, 2nd ed. rev. [Paris: Delachaux et Niestlé, 1970]: 17).

Let us add that if we substitute the reading "Joseph begot Jesus" the genealogy becomes incoherent and what follows becomes contradictory.

Chapter 2: Literary Criticism

[1]The translations are very diverse: "Genesis," Jerusalem Bible (correctly, in my view). "Origins," A. Paul, *Matthieu*, who specifies correctly in the text, *Liber de la Genèse*. "Book of the Origin," Lagrange, *L'Evangile selon Saint Matthieu*, 19. "Genealogical Book," Bonnard, *L'Evangile selon Saint Matthieu*, 13. But on p. 15 he says "Book of the genesis," taking the literal sense. "Genealogy of Jesus Christ," Osty, *L'Evangile selon Saint Luc*, 2091, and before him Crampon. "The Birth Record of Jesus Christ," Brown, *The Birth* 57. "Table of the origin of Jesus Christ," liturgical translation. "A Record of the Origin," A. Globe, *Matthew*, 13. "This is how Jesus Christ is the son of

David," P. de Beaumont, (*Les Quatre Evangiles aux hommes d'aujourd'hui*, Tours: Fayard, 1968, p. 1250).

[2]H. C. Waetjen, "The Genealogy as the Key to the Gospel According to Mt," *JBL* 95, (1976): 225-226.

[3]Was Moses the prototype of Christ for Matthew 1-2? Bloch (see bibliography) analyzed in detail the similarities between the infancy of Jesus and the vast Jewish literature on the infancy of Moses. But such analogies are tenuous and could not have played any determining role in Matthew 2. The terminological similarities are mere allusions. They do not have a structural value. The return from Egypt (Mt 2:15) identifies Jesus with the people of Israel, not with Moses.

Chapter 3: Semiotic Analysis

[1]Legrand, "Vidimus stellam," 377-384.

[2]Abraham, whose name is the final word in this ascending genealogy (1:1), becomes the opening word in the descending genealogy: "Abraham begot Isaac" (1:2). He plays the hinge role in this chiastic composition.

[3]The Jews practiced number symbolism (Orsatti, *Un Saggio*, 54-55). The NT continued this practice. Thus the Apocalypse (13:18) plays on the name of Nero, which yields the number 666, a sign of the powerlessness of the fearful beast. We shall return to the role of numerical symbolism when we study the historicity of the genealogies.

[4]Abraham, the first link in the chain, is not connected with any father or any origin—somewhat like Melchizedek in the Letter to the Hebrews (7:3). At the end of the genealogy we find two begottens who do not beget: Joseph and Jesus. This inverted symmetry forms a kind of inclusion.

[5]Jesus begotten (in the passive) in Matthew 1-2.

Mary from whom was begotten (*egennēthen*) Jesus (1:16).

That which is begotten (*gennēthen*) in her (1:20).

Jesus having been begotten (*gennēthentos*) in Bethlehem (2:1).

Matthew continued to use the same word, although he could have used "gave birth" (*tiktō*), as in 1:21, 23 in keeping with Is 7:14 and 25, and as Luke does in 1:31 and 2:6, 7 where he repeats this word to describe Mary's giving birth at Christmas; or *ginomia*, like Paul who avoids the word "beget" in Rom 1:3 and Gal 4:4.

By whom is Jesus begotten? Matthew begins to reveal the true Father of Christ: it is God alone, of whom Christ is the Son (1:23 and, more clearly, 2:15; 3:17; 4:3, 6; 8:29; 11:27; 14:33; 16:16; 17:5; 24:36; 26:63; 27:40, 43, 54; 28:19.

It is noteworthy that the five explicit citations in Matthew 1-2 are all from passages of the Bible in which the word *son* occurs (Mt 2:15 transfers what is said in Hos 11:1 from the people of Israel to *Jesus Messiah*). Perrot has brought out this point in a still unpublished lecture.

[6]The formula "Spouse/Bride of the Holy Spirit" is paradoxically employed by Cosmas, Vestitor, St. Francis of Assisi, St. Bonaventure and St. Maximilian Kolbe (Laurentin, *Revue des Sciences philosophiques et theologiques* 65, 1981, p. 142).

[7]This is in no way pointing to a new fatherhood or a new sonship. The heavenly Father assumes the Son (the only Son) in his human condition. This obviates any form of human parentage. This hidden explanation is implicit, in varying degrees, throughout the NT, especially in the prologue of John. See above, note 5.

[8]Elsewhere the apostle explicitly says "by the will of God," Eph 1:1; 1 Col 1:1; Gal 1:1.

[9]See pp. 403-404. As St. Jerome remarked long ago, "How could Joseph be described as 'just' if he hid the criminal action of his wife?" (*In Matthaeum* 1, PL 26:24).

[10]A. Pelletier, "L'Annonce à Joseph," *RechScRel* 54, (1966): 67-68. Pelletier gives two series of examples:

a. The complete formula *men gar...de* introducing, in succession, an objection, and then the contrary affirmation:

Although (*men gar*) circumcision is useful, if you obey the Law, but, if on the contrary (*de*), you break the Law, your circumcision becomes uncircumcision (Rom 2:25).

For (*men gar*) the judgment following one trespass brought condemnation, but (*de*) the free gift following many trespasses brings justification (Rom 5:16).

For (*men gar*) absent in body, yet (*de*) I am present in spirit, and as if present, I have already pronounced judgment (1 Cor 5:3).

Similarly, 1 Cor 11:7, 2 Cor 9:1-3, in which *de* is lacking, Heb 7:18-19; Acts 13:36-37, and Acts 4:16-17, in which the *de* is replaced by *alla*.

b. The citations of the Gospel:

The initial *men* is omitted giving the formula a more didactic tone:

For (*gar*) many are called, but (*de*) few are chosen (Mt 22:14).

Do not hold me, for (*gar*) I have not yet ascended to the Father; but (*de*) go to my brethren and say to them, I am ascending to my Father and your Father (Jn 20:17; cf. Mt 18:7 with *plēn* in place of *de* and Mt 24:6 with *alla*). The common trait of this dialectic (Mt 1:20-21) is that the central hinge of the reasoning is based upon *gar* followed by *de*, in order to remove an objection flowing from an uncontested fact. Pelletier is prudent in his translation, "Certainly, but, or however it may be, it is no less true." "Although" seems clearer in showing that the objection is removed.

[11]Other references in Laurentin, *Court Traite sur la Vierge Marie*, 176.

[12]On the question: is Mary a daughter of David? see special note, p. 342.

[13]The three stages in Mt 1:18-25 can be formalized:

a. Joseph, conjoined with David by the genealogical chain, is conjoined with Mary by a marriage agreement.

b. He plans a dismissal (disjunction).

c. The angel urges Joseph to take Mary to himself as wife (conjunction: cohabitation without physical union), along with the child.

[14]Acts 24:5; cf. Mt 26:71; Jn 19:19; Acts 6:14.

[15]The polemical program in Matthew 2 (the action of Herod against Christ) is, semiotically, very much like that in Revelation 12. Herod, however, aims only at the child, while in Revelation 12 the dragon pursues the mother as well. In both cases God the addresser brings about the failure of the program (Laurentin, in *E Mar*, 1982, p. 77).

[16]There are some discordances here between the literary composition, which is clearly marked by the citations ending each section, and the semiotic structure. In 2:3, Herod's program takes over from the program of the wise men. But he merges his program with theirs. He receives information from them and gives them information in return (the information supplied by the priests, 2:4-6), but he also continues to make inquiries of them (2:7) and cunningly gains their collaboration (2:8). This establishes a chiastic double program.

[17]*Proskynēsai* means a homage paid to the king in the form of a prostration. The Vulgate correctly translates it "adore." At this time kings were given divine status and, even after the conversion of Constantine, the homage paid to the king was designated in Latin by the term *adoratio*, "adoration." An interpreter would add that this adoration was of the kind known as *dulia* (the type of veneration paid to the angels and saints) and not *latria* (the type of veneration reserved to God).

[18]According to Brown this complete conjunction of wise men-star-king-Messiah helps to define Jesus as the Christ from above. The seeming disorder in the story (about the star) tends to confirm this identification.

[19]According to the LXX in Nm 24:4, 16, Balaam prophesied in a dream (*en hypnō*). For the impact of this prophecy at Qumran cf. below, Part III, chapter 6, n. 11.

[20]Observe how splendidly this citation harmonizes with its context here: the massacre is linked to the tomb of Rachel which tradition located at Bethlehem. The death of the children is conjoined to the death of the mother, to her weeping over this event that was to come, and to her burial place.

[21]The wise men as kings:

In Matthew's narrative itself there are three points that suggest the kingship of the wise men:

a. They are the honored guests of King Herod.

b. They offer royal gifts.

c. Mt. 2:11 makes use of Ps 70:10-11, "The kings of Tarshish," and perhaps Is 49:23, "Kings shall prostrate themselves. . . ."

This adoration (as well as the reaction of Herod who in 2:8 acknowledges that he is a vassal of this new king) shows Jesus to be the king of kings (cf. 2:1-2).

The countless theories regarding the origin of the wise men are clearly outlined by Brown: Parthians or Persians, Babylonians, Arabs from the Syrian desert (*The Birth*, 168). But these suppositions are purely hypothetical.

[22]The spirit and messainic anointing:

The anointing of David and the gift of the Spirit were connected in 1 Sm 16:13, "Samuel anointed him, and the spirit of Yahweh seized upon him." The connection implicit in Is 11:1 and in 42:1, the first Servant song (the word anoint is not expressly used) and explicit in Trito-Isaiah, "The spirit of the Lord is upon me, for Yahweh has given me an anointing" (Is 61:1).

Lk 4:18, which cites Is 61:1, takes over this link between spirit and anointing: "The Spirit of the Lord is upon me, for he has consecrated me by an anointing to bring the good news to the poor" (cf. 1:35 where the spirit comes upon Mary and the holy Son of God).

In Acts 10:38, which says that God has "anointed" Jesus Christ "with the Holy Spirit and with power," we find the same correlation of Spirit and power as in Lk 1:35; cf. also Acts 4:27.

There was a long-standing connection in messianic theology between spirit and anointing. But the anointing was of the prophetic kind, as de la Potterie has persuasively shown in "L'onction du Christ, Etude de theologie biblique," *NRT* 80, (1958): 222-252. Luke refers to this anointing in a royal, rather than a prophetic context (1:32-33). But he relates this anointing to a kingship that is radically different because it is the kingship of the Son of God rather than of an heir of David (this latter theme is relativized and rendered obsolescent by Lk 1:34-35; 2:1-5, 11).

The same conclusion is more hypothetical when ascribed to Mt 1:18 and 20, because the anointing as such is not explicitly stated in his Gospel.

Along the same line, Paul sees Christians as members of Christ possessing the anointing and seal of the Spirit (2 Cor 1:21-22; observe the isotopy of the two images; cf. Eph 1:13 and 4:30): on the anointing of Christians by God himself, cf. Heb 1:9 and 1 Jn 2:20, 27, two texts which are of great spiritual significance. The basic study is still de la Potterie's "L'onction des chrétiens par la foi," *Bib* 40, (1959): 12-69.

Nor should we forget that the very name *Christ* means "anointed," as does *Christian*, one of the first names given to the disciples (Acts 11:26; 26:28). An element of mockery (Christians: "the perfumed ones") may have helped popularize the name, as in the case of *Nazōraios* (Nazarene) for Jesus.

[23]The word kingdom (reign, kingship: *basileia*) appears fifty-four times, and king (*basileus*) eighteen times in Matthew 3-26. The concept of kingdom or reign is central to the Gospel of Matthew.

[24]All in all, this square seemed convincing enough for me to reject other attempts at squares which focused on "divine power and kingly power," "divine lineage and human lineage," once I saw that between generation and kingship there existed the contrariety needed in order to pull these two ideas together in a single semiotic square. I had previously attempted to develop two distinct squares starting with each of these two ideas.

Chapter 4: Matthew and Luke

[1]Which is the earlier infancy Gospel?

We do not know for certain which has priority. There is a broad consensus that the Gospel of Matthew is older than that of Luke, but there is no evidence to prove it. The problem of priority is complicated by the fact that the infancy Gospels depend on very early sources which are more difficult to date than the Gospels as a whole. A comparative study may not therefore assume priority on one side or the other. Such a study would show that neither evangelist knew the other evangelist's infancy narrative.

[2]In Mt 1:20-24; 2:13, 19, the angel of the Lord always appears in dreams; in Lk 1:11; 2:9 he appears to persons in a waking state.

The meaning of the angel is the same in both cases: he serves to signify the presence and action of God while at the same time preserving a sense of the divine transcendence. However, in these oracular scenes, the helpers are different: shepherds in Luke, wise men in Matthew. The helpers are few and far between in Matthew; in Luke they abound: Elizabeth and Zechariah, Simeon and Anna, the shepherds and the listeners at the finding in the

Temple (these contribute to the recognition of the status of Jesus).

[3]Jerusalem, which Luke has before him all through 1:8-23 and then names in 2:22, 25, 28, 41, 43, 46 is named only once by Matthew in his first two chapters (2:3), his non-mention of the name elsewhere is comparable to Luke 1:8-23.

[4]On the prophecy of Balaam at Qumran, cf. Part III, chapter 6, n. 11.

[5]Cf. the section on fulfillment and its two correlated meanings, fulfillment of the history of salvation and fulfillment of the scriptures; this is another point which Matthew 1-2 and Luke 1-2 have in common.

[6]J. Chopineau, "Note sur la généalogie de l'evangile de Matthieu," *Etudes théol. et relig.* 53, (1978): 269-270.

[7]According to Sahlin, *Der Messiah*, 13, and Winter, "The Proto-source," 197-198, both Lk 1:35 and Mt 1:25 refer to Jgs 13:7 where Samson is described as *naziraion* according to the Codex Alexandrinus, and *hagion* according to the Codex Vaticanus. Salin and Winter regarded Lk 1:35 as an erroneous translation of an original Hebrew text, "He shall be called *nazîr*," i.e., consecrated in the sense of an ascetical and legal holiness.

Part III, What Kind of Historicity?

[1]Brown, "Reflections on a Review: A Reply (to J. McHugh)," *Ampleforth Review* (1981): 57f. This is his working hypothesis. He adds by way of conclusion that "symbolism, not history, is the key to mariology," but that this is "not an impoverishment," since symbolism "has as much value as history, but a different kind of value."

[2]C. K. Barrett, "Quomodo historia conscribenta sit," *NTS* 28, (1982): 303-320.

Chapter 1: Luke 1-2

[1]There are those who have insisted, rather single-mindedly, that Luke's prologue emphasizes the "divine aspects" rather than assertions of fact. Marshall, *The Gospel of Luke*, 40, has carefully studied these analyses and concludes as follows: "This thesis is correct in what it affirms, but wrong in what it denies. It is clear. . . that Luke was concerned with the historical reliability of his material." Opposition to gnosticism and docetism may have pushed Luke in the direction of historical concern, he adds.

[2]*Pragmata*, a very general word which may mean deed or affair (Acts 5:4; Rom 16:2; 1 Cor 6:1; 1 Thess 4:6; 2 Tm 1:4), thing (Mt 18:19), reality (Heb

6:18; 10:1; 11:1). In tandem with "fulfilled among us" we render it *events* (cf. Acts 26:26 where the verb *prassō* expresses what has happened—literally, what has been done).

[3]See Part I, chapter II, pp. 33-34; "It is one of the rare points on which critical study reaches a certain consensus," says Legrand (*L'Annonce*, 29, 114). If Luke had wanted his prologue to bear only upon Chapter III, to the exclusion of what precedes it, he would have had the literary skill to postpone the prologue to that point, or phrase it differently.

[4]People have tried to take the refrains of memory as declarations whose meaning is purely apocalyptic. Serra, *Sapienza*, 46-138 and 285-298, showed in an exhaustive way that this refrain has polyvalent meaning, which may indeed include apocalyptic and sapiential nuances, but whose usual reference is to events of salvation history. Mention of anamnesis as a means of transmission is a feature of the Bible as a whole.

[5]See special note, p. 461.

[6]*Akribeia* in the infancy Gospels:

Luke uses the word *akribeia* (rigor, exactitude) in Acts 22:3 and *akribōs* (exactly) in Lk 1:3 and five times in Acts, as against three times in the whole rest of the NT, one of which is in the infancy Gospel in Matthew (2:8). Matthew uses the corresponding verb *akriboō* in 2:7 and 16 (the only two uses of it in the NT).

Akribeia can designate exactness in religious knowledge (Acts 18:25f.; 24:22; 1 Thess 5:2), but primarily it means exactness of facts (Mt 2:7-8, 16; Acts 23:15, 20).

[7]Polybius, 4, 2, 2, cited by Lagrange, *Evangile selon Saint Luc*, cxxix-cxxxi.

[8]Must one say that this *hōs* (about) is only a "literary tic" of Luke's? The word is not more frequent in Luke (twenty-nine times) than in Matthew (thirty-two times), and nineteen times in Mark. The nuance "about" is found seven times in John as in Luke, according to the concordance of the Jerusalem Bible.

[9]According to the categories prevailing in those days, it is clear that one does not descend from a woman but from a man. This is the fundamental reason why the two evangelists relate Jesus to David via the adoptive paternity of Joseph. A connection through the maternal line, however, would have served the purpose of the evangelist well.

In Hebrew and Aramaic, the same root *yld* is used to say both that the woman bears (in the *qal*; positive) and that the father causes her to bear (in the *hiphil*; causative). The *piel* (intensive) indicates the role of the mid-wife, but in another sense. The Hebrew translations of the Gospel render *egennē-*

sen (begot, used thirty-nine times in Mt 1) by *yld* in the *hiphil.* The difference is more marked in Greek between give birth (*tiktō*) and beget (*gennaō*), two different roots.

[10]H. Cazelles, *Naissance de l' église, Secte Juive Rejetée?*, (Paris: Cerf, 1968): 65f., "The Qumran community expected [the Messiah] of Aaron and of Israel to come. . . the advent of the Anointed. . . of Aaron and of Israel" (Community Rule 9:11; cf. Damascus Document 12:23). Cazelles admits that Luke 1-2 alludes to this problem, since the evangelist acknowledges Jesus as Messiah, son of David (1:27, 32; 2:4) but presents Mary as "kinswoman" of Elizabeth (1:36), who is "of the daughters of Aaron" (Lk 1:5), in agreement with the analysis which we developed in *Structure*, 110-116. Luke tends to suggest that Jesus is Messiah of Israel and of Aaron in the line of Malachi 3, but he doesn't press the point.

[11]Osty, *L' Evangile selon Saint Luc* 8-18, has marvelously elucidated the way Luke used Mark, in a personal manner, but with a literal fidelity to what is essential.

[12]On the notion of *theologoumenon*, see the glossary of terms.

Chapter 2: Matthew 1-2

[1]The combination of Mi 5:1 and 2 Sm 5:2 in Lk 2:6 is original and does not correspond exactly either to the Hebrew text or to the Greek of the LXX.

2 Sm 5:2	*Mt. 2:6: the prophecy of Mi 5*
2b: You shall be prince over Israel	For from you shall come a ruler (*hēgoumenos*)
2a: You shall be shepherd of my people Israel.	who will govern (*poimanei*) my people Israel.

[2]Nazarene: In Mt 26:71 the servants of the high priest say of St. Peter, with hostility, "This one was with Jesus the *Nazarene*" cf. Lk 18:37; Jn 18:5, 7; 19:19 (the inscription that stigmatizes "Jesus the Nazarene, King of the Jews"); Acts 24:5 (where Paul is pegged as a leader "of the sect of the Nazarenes").

This title is taken up as a challenge by the apostles, who perform cures in the name of Jesus the Nazarene (Acts 4:10; 22:8; cf. Acts 2:22; 6:14; 26:9). There may have been a certain irony in Christ's words when he appeared to St. Paul, "I am Jesus the Nazarene [always *Nazōraios*, i.e., the name his enemies gave him], whom you are persecuting," (Acts 22:8).

Jesus is called *Nazarēnos* and no longer *Nazōraios*, as in the preceding texts, in Mk 1:24; 10:47; 14:67; 16:6 (Mark's usual form), followed by Luke (at 4:34 and 24:19), who uses *Nazōraios* however in 18:37, even though, here also, he seems to be dependent upon Mark.

Chapter 3: Convergences

A. Luke 1-2 and Matthew 1-2

[1]The classical solution hypothesized that by the time the wise men made their visit (after the presentation in the Temple), the holy family had found lodgings.

Current exegesis finds the manger and the house not incompatible; Lk 2:9 can be translated, "there was no place for them in the residence hall" (i.e., *kataluma*, see above, pp. 180-182). They would thus find themselves relegated to an outbuilding, no doubt the stable, adjacent to the house; hence the crib.

The two solutions are not opposed to each other.

The key study on this is Benoit, "Non erat eis locus in diversorio... Lk 2:7," A. Descamps, *Mélanges B. Rigaux*, (Gembloux: Duculot, 1970): 173-186.

[2]The *Diatessaron* places the wise men (Mt 2:1-12) after the presentation (Lk 2:21-38).

The Arabic version (A. S. Marmadji, ed., *Diatessaron de Tatien*, Beirut, 1935) in which c. 2 = Lk 12:21-38, pp. 18-21 and c. 3 = Mt 2:1-12, pp. 22-24, shows this same order, as does St. Ephrem (*Commentaire de l' évangile concordant ou Diatessaron*, ed. L. Leloir, *Sources Chrétiennes* 121, pp. 73-77).

The attribution of this work to Tatian (attested by Eusebius IV, 296, ed. Bardy, II, 214 and confirmed by many pieces of supporting evidence) seems well established. It seems probable that the bilingual Tatian composed it in Syriac rather than Greek, since a Greek fragment older than 256, discovered in 1933, seems to be a translation, according to the excellent study by C. L. Van Tuyvelde, "Orientales (versiones)" in *DBS* 6, (1960): 855-870; he deals with the original language and the Greek fragment on p. 863.

[3]Uniformity of testimonies is not a good criterion in history; it is rather a suspicious sign of doctored harmonization. What is convincing, instead, is

convergence on a basic fact with a maximum of differences. Xavier Léon-Dufour and other stringent exegetes have admitted this in the case of Matthew 1-2 vis-a-vis Luke 1-2.

B. Agreement with the Rest of the NT

[4]Lk 4:32, 36; cf. Mk 1:22 and 27.

[5]See footnote 1 of the Introduction.

[6]A surprising analogy has been pointed out between Lk 1:44, "The child [John the Baptist] leapt for joy in my womb," and Jn 3:29, "and yet the bridegroom's friend [John the Baptist], who stands there and listens, is glad when he hears the bridegroom's voice. This same joy I feel, and now it is complete. He must increase, and I must decrease."

Some critics have gone so far as to see the visitation scene as a legendary projection of this Johannine text (Klostermann, *Das Lukasevangelium* [Tübingen: J. C. B. Mohr, 1919]: 15f.). For criticism of this view, see Feuillet, *Jesus and His Mother.*

[7]Resch, *Das Kindheitsevangelium*, 241-155; I examined these findings in depth in *Structure*, 135-140.

[8]Jn 1:31 and 33 seem to contradict the data of Luke 1-2. However, in the fourth Gospel, "to not know" whether expressed with *ginoskō* (1:10; 3:10; 8:27, 55; 12:16; 14:7, 9, 17:25) or with *ioda* (1:26; 4:22, 32; 7:27f.; 8:14, 19; 9:30; 10:34; 14:7; 15:21; 21:4) generally concerns knowledge at the level of faith.

The context immediately preceding Jn 1:31 clearly situates John the Baptist's declaration on this level. He says, "There stands among you [hence visible, identifiable, and known as the carpenter of Nazareth] someone *whom you do not know...*" (1:26). In such a case, "know" should be translated as "recognize." This is also the case for John the Baptist, who says that he has *known* Jesus on the basis of the fact that he has "seen the Spirit descend...upon him" (1:32).

On the other hand, Luke does not speak of any meetings between Jesus and John the Baptist except during gestation, after which he has John the Baptist disappear very quickly into the desert, suggesting that he stayed there from childhood onwards (1:80). The picture of the two little cousins playing together belongs to anecedotal iconography, not to the Gospels.

C. Agreement with the Extra-Biblical Data

[9]Benoit, "Quirinius," 693-716, gives the most thorough-going study,

together with the most exhaustive bibliography.

[10]P. Peeters, *Evangiles apocryphes 2. L'Evangile de l'enfance. Rédactions syriaques, arabe, arménienne*, (Paris: Picard, 1914). Aurelio de Santo Sotero, (*Los Evangelios apocrifos*, Edición critica y bilingüe, Madrid, BAC, 1979, 282-372), published the *Arabic Infancy Gospel* and the *History of Joseph the Carpenter*, together with Greek pseudo-Thomas (the basic kernel of the cycle) and then he gives the Armenian and Latin infancy Gospels. We need not tarry over their limitless variations regarding marvels.

Chapter 4: The Genealogies

A. Two Treatments

[1]"A begot B" was a formula in current use. Matthew found it in his biblical sources, 1 Chr 2:10-15, and Ru 4:18-22. But the post-Davidic genealogy of 1 Chr 3:10 progresses differently: "The son of Solomon, Reoboam; his son, Abiah. . . " Matthew has unified the whole, following the pattern of the first.

Luke's more expeditious pattern was also adopted by the fifth book of Esdras.

[2]Adam and God his creator (Lk 3:38).

[3]There are nineteen common links, if one wishes to include their agreement on the role of Mary in connection with the Holy Spirit (Mt 1:18-20 and Lk 1:35). But if Luke does include Mary (on an extraordinary basis, stemming from the novelty of God), he only speaks of her outside of the genealogy, whose norm of male-descent he respects, paradoxically, better than Matthew.

B. Fascinating Septenary Rhythm

[4]Text criticism of the genealogy of Lk 3:23-28:

There are some minor and isolated variants, especially on the number of links:

—seventy-six names according to the Vulgate and two manuscripts: f2 and q,

—seventy-five according to the Syriac-Sinaiticus (Lagrange, *Luc* 121),

—seventy-four according to Codex Alexandrinus,

—seventy-two according to a group of Latin manuscripts, eacdlr (including Jesus and Adam in the count).

On the symbolic uses to which the number seventy-two was put by the Fathers, see below, n. 15.

[5]In the absence of any argument from text criticism, one must respect the

text, but the historicity of Jehoiakim is not in question.

The Holy Spirit (1:18 and 20) should not be counted: A. Paul, *Matthieu* 36, asked this question and decided in the negative. His study has the merit of showing the bonds which Jewish tradition has established between several female ancestors of Christ and the Holy Spirit. But this strand remains tenuous, offering no points of contact with Mt 1:16, 18-20 precise enough to allow one to build a case. If one ought indeed accept the conclusion that Matthew mentions some unusual women in Christ's genealogy in order to prepare the way for the unusual role of Mary, it seems more difficult to go on and say that he chose these women as witnessing to a special relation with the Holy Spirit. Nevertheless, two rabbinic references deserve attention:

—"The Holy Spirit reveals himself and says: Thamar is not a prostitute" R. Yudan, cited by R. Bloch "Juda engendra Pharès et Zara, de Thamar," *Mélanges Robert*, (Paris: Bloud, 1957): 381-389; A. Paul, *Matthieu.*

—"Some have said that the Holy Spirit rested upon Rahab before the Israelites entered the promised land" (H. L. Strack and P. Billerbeck, *Kommentar* I, 21; A. Paul, *Matthieu*, 33).

But these are sparse and vague references in a complex and far-flung tradition.

[6]R. Bloch, "Juda engendra," 381. Cf. Masson, *Jésus*, 180-205 and 504-411. This interpretation is based on the fact that Ruth was a Moabite, a member of a people excluded, according to Dt 23:4, because they are descended from incest, according to Gn 19:30-38; rabbinic tradition does not lack allusions to these sinful entanglements, from which Ruth wanted to free herself through her fidelity (A. Paul, *Matthieu*, 34).

[7]Certain texts interpret the marriage of Ruth, the Moabite, in the light of the case of Thamar, who was also a Moabite (cf. Midrash Bereshith Rabbah on Gn 19:39). According to other texts, Ruth was sterile and had to receive a miracle: "God opened her womb" (A. Paul, *Matthieu*, 33-36). The "irregularity" is in any case less clear in the case of Ruth. She is praised for having repaired the rupture in the royal-messianic line.

[8]Sr. Jeanne d'Arc, "La prostituée aïeule du Christ," *Vie spirituelle* 87, (1952): 471-477; also in *Exchanges* (1955), n. 22, 2-4. A. Paul, *Matthieu*, 35-37; Masson, *Jésus*, 504-511.

[9]*Ibid.*

[10]A. Paul, *Matthieu*, 33f.; J. Masson, *Jésus*, 191-194, 200f.

[11]The propensity for multiples of 7 in the Bible: 70 is used 61 times, but there is *no occurrence* of 69, 71, 76, 78, 79.

If the number 7 is common (384 occurrences), its multiples are not, except 14 (50 uses) and (less commonly) the others: 21 is used seven times, 28 ten times, 35 appears five times, 42 six times, while 43 and 44 are never used; 49 appears twice, 56 once, 63 never; 70 appears sixty-one times, 77 three times, 700 five times, 777 once (Gn 5:31), 7,000 eleven times, 70,000 six times. (These statistics are taken from the *Concordance* published by Cerf-Brepols, whose count is based on the French translation and done by computer. Our figures are for cardinal and ordinal numbers together.)

[12]Contrariwise, Jesus should be counted in the descending order, i.e., as number seventy-seven, as God is in the ascending order.

[13]The law of reversibility of series can be stated this way: Let there be a succession of *n* numbers, beginning with 1, and let it be followed by another equal series of *n* elements; and let the two series be written such that the first goes in increasing order (a), while the second goes in decreasing order (b); it then becomes clear that the multiples of certain numbers (for example, the number 4 in the case illustrated below) are not in the corresponding places in the two series but displaced by one slot. Thus:

a) 1 2 3 *4* 5 6 7 *8* 9 10 11 *12*
b) *12* 11 10 9 *8* 7 6 5 *4* 3 2 1

In order to get the multiples of the number (here 4) into correspondence, one must shift both series one place (which is achieved by making both series start with 0):

a) 0 1 2 3 *4* 5 6 7 *8* 9 10 11 *12*
b) *12* 11 10 9 *8* 7 6 5 *4* 3 2 1 0

Since Hebrew has no zero, the ascending and descending series of Luke and Matthew, respectively, manage to make the multiples of seven coincide in place by assigning *no number* to the first link in either order; this link is thereby set apart, in a kind of position of transcendence. The ancients had a feeling for these rhythms, even though they didn't calculate or reason about them in our modern, analytic manner.

[14]Predilection for the number seven in the NT and in Luke:

It is the most common number in the NT, apart from the first three (1, 2, and 3). Seven is used more often than eight and even more than twelve. The majority of these uses are in Revelation (forty-two times), followed by Luke (fifteen times).

In the infancy Gospel, we find the seven years of Anna's widowhood and her eighty-four years of age, i.e., 7 x 12 (Lk 2:37; cf. the twelve years of Jesus). Though Luke has not retained the logion of Christ that invites us to forgive not just "seven times but seventy times seven," we have seen how he echoes the prophecy of seventy weeks in 1:25-2:22, and he mentions the seventy horsemen in Acts 23:23. Finally, he has listed seventy-seven names in his genealogy (Lk 3:23-38), as we have seen. One should note that this number seventy-seven replaces the "seventy times seven" in certain versions of Mt 18:22; in fact, this reading is so well attested, that the Jerusalem Bible keeps it.

[15]Genealogical numbers and symbolism, according to the Fathers:

The Fathers reckon different numbers in the genealogy, but their purpose is always to arrive at symbolic figures such as these:

—70: Pseudo-Clement, *Homily* 18, 4, PG 2, 408, and Procopius of Gaza, PG 77, 957.

—72: Irenaeus, *Haereses* 3, 33, who sees in that figure the number of peoples accounted for in Genesis; thus, too, Clement of Alexandria, *Stromaties* 1, PG 8, 877; the *Recognitiones* of Clement 2, 42, PG 1, 1269; Epiphanius, *Haereses* 1, 1, 5, PG 41, 134, and *Haereses* 39, PG 41, 673; Augustine, *De civitate Dei* 16, 3, 2: "Septuaginta duas gentes."

—75: Ephorius, reported by Clement of Alexandria, *Stromaties* 1, PG 8, 877, in reference to Gn 46:27.

—77: (attested in the Greek text) is taken up by the Cappadocians and by St. Augustine. The text he was using has only seventy-six names, but he counted God in order to get the full figure.

So the Fathers adopt only figures used by the Bible (70 sixty-one times, 72 four times, 75 twice, 77 thrice), never the ones ignored in the Bible, such as 69, 71, 73, 78. The figures that caught their attention are the ones that have symbolic value.

Brown (*The Birth*, 81) asks whether the seventy generations *from Jesus to Enoch* should be related to the tradition according to which there are seventy generations from the sin of the angels to the Last Judgment. Brown's reference is to Enoch 93:1-10 and 91:12-17. He discounts the symbolism, the numbers for which he has nevertheless kept in place (p. 76, a fact which does credit to his sense of text criticism). One is surprised, therefore, that he dismisses J. E. Bruns' observations on numerical rhythms as imaginary ("Matthew's Genealogy of Jesus," *Bible Today* 15, (1964): 980-985; see n. 73); Masson, *Jesus* 212f., is more radical in rejecting all rhythmic enumeration and all symbolism in Luke.

The best dossier of patristic texts is still that of Lagrange, *Luc*, 120f.

[16]Rhythmic comparison of the two genealogies:

	Mt 1-2	Lk 1-2
God-Abraham	—	21
Abraham-David	14	14
David-Captivity	14	21
Captivity-Jesus	14	21
	42	77

The basis is the binary model: 2 x 7 = 4, derived from biblical sources for the generations from Abraham to David. Matthew sticks to this model which he repeats three times; but Luke, in addition to the number fourteen (Abraham to Daniel), thrice repeats a ternary model, 3 x 3 x 7, or three series of 21.

Symbolism of the number fourteen:

Brown (*The Birth*, 80-81) asks whether the pattern of fourteen might not be half of the lunar month, in agreement with Kaplan "The Generation Schemes," *BibSac* 87, (1930): 465-471. M. D. Johnson (*The Purpose of the Biblical Genealogies*, [Cambridge: University Press, 1969]: 184-208); and L. Sabourin, (*Il Vangelo de Matteo* [Mariano: Edizione "Fede ed. Arte," 1975]) find models, however, in Jewish tradition: the fourteen epochs of world history, the Talmud's speculations on the three sacrifices of Balak and Balaam.

Let us note that the number fourteen is quite common in the Bible, twenty-seven times as a cardinal and twenty-three times as an ordinal number. These are more occurrences than for eleven, or any other number between thirteen and nineteen. If Matthew adhered to this number, it was because this was the number assigned to David.

[17]1 Chr 1:28, 34; 2:1-15; Ru 4:18-28.

[18]Twofold justification of the omissions in the genealogies:

a. On the *erasio nominis* (suppression of certain names), see Orsatti, *Un saggio*, 48; Masson, *Jésus*, 116-124. They base their views on Ex 32:33 and Ps 9:6. Further, among the kings eliminated, the three descendants of Athaliah were the objects of special malediction: 1 Chr 22:7; 24:22; 25:14-16. Most importantly, Athaliah had tried to eliminate all the dynastic heirs.

As far as Jehoiakim (d. 598) is concerned (his being the other name eliminated), we shall make clear further on that he was the enemy of Jeremiah (Jer 22:13-19; 36:9, 16:32; cf. 2 Kgs 23:27; 24:19; 1 Chr 36:8).

b. The principle that "the sons of sons are counted as sons" is attested in Qid 4a, cited by H. L. Strack and P. Billerbeck, *Kommentar*, 31. Orsatti, *Un saggio*, 47.

[19]See the summary of time intervals below, p. 352.

[20]Ezr 7:1-5 (ascending generations) omits six names of priests from the descendants of Aaron.

[21]The number fifty-five appears only twice in the whole Bible: 2 Kgs 21:1 and 2 Chr 33:1, to reckon the wicked reign of Manasseh. It is curious that a good many exegetes have not perceived the genealogy's obvious rhythm and fasten upon the text modern ways of numbering which destroy the symbolism. On this point Fitzmyer (whose commentary is often superior) is less perceptive than Brown: he makes David number forty-three (an insignificant number), Abraham number fifty-seven (an equally unused number), and so on. Brown has at least perceived that one must not count Jesus at the beginning, under penalty of derailing the whole enumeration.

[22]Cainan II (number sixty-four in Lk 3:36) is found in Gn 10:24; 11:12, and 1 Chr 1:18 according to the LXX ms A only. He is omitted from the massoretic texts where Shelah is the son of Arphaxad.

This Cainan II (number sixty-four) must not be confused with his ancestor Cainan I (in Hebrew *Qenan*, number seventy-three in Lk 3:37), attested to in Gn 5:9-16 and 1 Chr 1:2.

[23]Masson, *Jésus*. I should like to take this opportunity to thank him for having revised this chapter. Our perspectives differ but converge on essentials.

[24]On the probable reference to the name of Adam in Mt 1:1, via the initials of the three key names which open the genealogy, Abraham, David, Messiah, see above p. 307.

[25]Omission of four kings by Mt 1:8, 11. Masson (*Jésus*, 25-63) explains the omission of the three links issuing from Athaliah as *erasio nominis*, according to Jewish usage (see above, n. 18).

He explains the omission of Jehoiakim by an accident of manuscript tradition, though he acknowledges the problem of sustaining such a hypothesis in the absence of any support from external criticism. This introduction of a Jehoiakim would disturb the place of Jechoniah (= Jehoiachin in the ordering) and would force him to be counted at the head of the third and last series. That would destroy the symmetry which this first of non-kings (deposed) has with David, the first king and founder, to whom he formed a counterpart. Only with difficulty would one move thus to spoil Matthew's admirable ordering, as the manuscript tradition seems to have conveyed it faithfully to us.

[26]Summarized in 1 Chr 17:1-5.

[27]Was Nathan a priest? He was thus described by a portion of the Greek

manuscripts (see A. Rahlfs' edition of the Septuagint, I:635), and by some Latin manuscripts—for no good reason, most exegetes think. But the TOB keeps the word "priest." However one would resolve this complicated case, this reading could have influenced Luke's choice.

When we read that "the sons of David were priests"—according to 2 Sm 8:18—does this stem from the fact that David, as a king consecrated by anointing, exercised the priestly function of pontiff, at a time when the priestly caste had not yet assumed its later prominence? The priestly function of David is so evident that even 1 Chr 15:26 and 16:1-2, intent upon safeguarding the privileges of the priesthood, did not succeed in totally eliminating this evidence regarding the exercise of priestly functions by David (cf. Laurentin, *Marie, L'Eglise et le sacerdoce*, 183-184.

[28]Was Jechoniah childless? He has been called childless on the basis of the oracles of Jeremiah (22:30): "Childless, a man who shall not succeed in his days, for none of his offspring shall succeed in sitting on the throne of David." The objection is that the text does not seem to be talking about sterility, but about dynastic reign. A later oracle of Jeremiah (33:14-18) tends to correct the previous one.

The hypothesis that Salathiel (Shealtiel) was adopted by Jechoniah has the advantage, no doubt, of explaining how this same person happens to be assigned different fathers according to Matthew and Luke. But there are three problems with this solution:

a. 1 Chr 3:17-24 mentions "sons of Jechoniah." Masson discusses this text (*Jésus*, 261-267).

b. Rabbinic interpretation goes largely in the same direction (Masson, *ibid.*, 258-260).

c. There is a cuneiform text from Nebuchadnezzar, according to which five sons of Jehoiachin shared his captivity. Masson (*Jésus*, 278) conjectures that these may have merely been members of the royal family.

[29]Julius Africanus, who died after 240 and whose text is preserved by Eusebius (*Ecclesiastical History* 1, 7, 3), explains the two fathers of Joseph by the law of levirate marriage: Jacob (his father according to Matthew) and Heli (his father according to Luke) married the same woman, Estaha. When Heli died childless, Jacob married the widow and reckoned his third son, Joseph, to his dead brother. Joseph was thus the legal son of Heli and the biological son of Jacob. St. Augustine adopted this solution in his *Retractationes* (2, 7 and 16). Masson (*Jésus*, 417-511) observes correctly that the levirate law could not obtain between uterine brothers, but he finds a viable solution by identifying Eliud (number 36 in Matthew) with Esli (number 11 in Luke), since the

levirate law governed only in the case of a close male ancestor.

Conjectures have abounded on this difficult point. Some suggest that one and the same Joseph was known under two names, Bar Iacob and Bar Heli; P. Seethaler, "Eine kleine Bemerking zu den Stammbäumen Jesu nach Matthäus und Lukas," *BibZ* 16, (1972): 56-57, says that we are dealing with two different Josephs (homonymy); H. A. Blair wanted to make Matthew's Joseph the father and not the spouse of Mary "Matthew 1:16," in *Stud Evang* 2,*TUU* 87, 149-154.

Just as we must not blame the evangelists, so we must advance no solution but a hypothetical one. Masson is the most coherent, combining the best indications and confirmations (pp. 417-472). He examines the serious research with which the two evangelists composed their genealogies.

[30]Some oddities in Luke 3 that remain unexplained may reflect both the accidents of documentation (which are very frequent) on this matter and the extent of artificiality in the making of genealogies:

—In 3:33, the addition of Admin (number 49), apparently a corruption or doubling of Aminadab.

—The chain of number 0-4 (from Jesus to Levi) is astonishingly similar to the chain of number 28-32, which is also from Jesus to Levi, the latter being in both cases the father of Matthat. Could names from the monarchic period have in fact been supplied for names from the post-monarchic period? The question is raised by Brown (*The Birth*, 92, n. 77).

—There are four Josephs in Luke's genealogy, namely, number 1, 7, 16, 35; and six Matthats (or close derivatives): number 3, 8, 13, 14, 31, 40. It is a name associated with the Maccabaean or Hasmonaean family of the house of Levi, in the second century, according to 1 Mc 2:1; 2:6-48, 69; cf. 11:70; 16:14; and 2 Mc 14:19.

[31]Savior, a title of God, transferred to Jesus: Jdt 9:11; 1 Mc 4:30; Est 8:12n; Ps 7:11; 18:2, 42; 40:18; 70:6; Wis 16:7; Sir 51:1; Is 33:22 (Yahweh our king, our savior); 43:3; 49:26, 63; Jer 14:8; Bar 4:2; Hos 13:4, "no savior apart from thee"; Hb 3:18.

No doubt, God could raise up a "savior" in a lesser and particular sense: Neh 9:26; Jgs 3:9, 15; Is 19:20—all very rare and isolated cases. The significance of the title "Savior" given to Jesus is quite different: in Matthew he is the Messiah and Son of God (Mt 1:21). We have already noted the abstract title of "salvation" given to Christ (see note on the titles of Christ, pp. 109-110).

Cf. also 2 Sm 22:3, horn of salvation, taken up again in Lk 1:69.

Chapter 5: Evaluation of the Sequences

A. The Narratives

[1]J. S. Kennard, "Was Capernaum the Home of Jesus?" *JBL* 65, (1946): 131-141. J. Blinzler, "Die Heimat Jesu," *BibKir* 25, (1970): 14-20, replied to Stegman, who had maintained the same thesis in an inaugural address at the University of Bonn, entitled *Jesus aus Capernaum,* 1969.

[2]This irony is present in the question of Nicodemus: "Can a man reenter his mother's womb?" (Jn 3:4); or the Samaritan woman: "Sir, you have nothing to draw with... where would you get this living water?" (Jn 4:11).

[3]We have noted that in 1:32 in the same order as John's prologue Luke proclaimed Jesus as "Son of the Most High" before calling him "son of David" (1:32b). There is an analogous transfer at the point where Mt 1:23 says that Jesus will receive "the name *Emmanuel,* that is, God-with-us"; one is inclined to think that Matthew would have had good reason to omit this final clause of Is 7:14, since it clashed with the name Jesus, on which his context depended. His perspective seems similar to that of Luke, for whom the divine name of Holy One (Lk 1:32 and 2:23) or Son of God (1:32, 35) eclipses the human name of Jesus (1:31; 2:21).

[4]The historicity of Jesus as son of David:

Brown *The Birth*, 504-508, confirms that the Messiah was expected as a "son of David" (Psalms of Solomon 17:23, dated to the end of the first century B.C.), though he notes that Bar Kochba was taken as the Messiah without being Davidic, while at Qumran people also awaited the coming of a priestly Messiah.

The theory of a *theologoumenon* runs into a major objection (Brown thinks): since the family of Jesus was known in the primitive Church, one could not have invented such a descent with impunity. Yet this title was given early, as early as Rom 1:3 (the epistle itself dates from around 58). Brown's conclusion is that "the historicity is uncertain" but probable: "Joseph belonging to one of the lateral, non-aristocratic branches of the house of David" (*ibid.*, 511). Ignatius of Antioch maintained the Davidic lineage of Mary, on account of the fact that he did not grasp the legal affiliation through Joseph. On this Davidic descent attributed to Mary, see special note, p. 342.

Brown correctly reacts against the theory that Jesus' Davidic descent was just a creation of the community. Still, his acceptance of Davidic descent, probably through Joseph, remains under the cloud of a double uncertainty: on the descent itself (compromised by a historical devaluation of the genealogies); and on the nature of the link with Joseph, (despite the progress made in

The Birth, 517-533 over his earlier work).

The perspective of Matthew and Luke is quite firm on this point, and the way in which they link Jesus to the Davidic line is, as we have seen, full of meaning.

[5]Conformity to custom in Lk 2:41-52 is confirmed by the exegetes: Marshall, *Luke*, 127; and Fitzmyer, *Luke 1-9*, 440f.

According to the Law, Jews were supposed to visit the Jerusalem Temple (the sole sanctuary and place of God's presence) three times a year (Ex 23:14-17; 34:23-24; Dt 16:16; 1 Sm 1:7; 2:19; cf. Josephus, *Vita*, 2). Passover was one of the three feasts to which this obligation was attached, the other two being Pentecost and the Feast of Tabernacles. But for obvious reasons, "custom" (Lk 2:42) limited the journey up to Jeursalem to the Passover feast alone.

[6]G. M. Soares Prabhu, *The Formula*, 293, 297. Following his own method, the author sets store on biblical allusions: to Nm 22:5 and 24:17 (Balaam); perhaps to the cloud that guided the Israelites, according to Ex 13:21 and 33:9; to the foreign kings paying tribute, according to 1 Kgs 10:2; Ps 72:10-15, and Is 60:6.

But from this basis, which we may accept, he goes on to draw conclusions that are merely in line with the typical presuppositions of his historical-critical method (explaining texts in terms of other texts rather than in terms of the event). The event is thus reduced to the legendary form of "capitulation of the pre-Christian world of magic," personified by the "wise men magicians, before Christ, the eschatological King" (*ibid.*, 293). This interpretation goes far beyond the data given in Matthew's text. It depends upon a symbolic interpretation. It is impossible to determine exactly, in the absence of cross-references, what factual kernel Soares Prabhu may have rightly diagnosed.

[7]The description of the massacre is pre-redactional. "The curious precision of two years old and under" suggests "the remembrance of an actual event. . . ." It is "difficult to explain otherwise," observes Soares Prabhu (*ibid.*, 261, 298f.). But the silence of Flavius Josephus seems to him "decisive against its historicity." Can an argument *a silentio* be "decisive"? With R. T. France, we prefer to think the contrary (see below, n. 12).

Finally, he tries to explain the story as a derivation from rabbinic traditions on the birth of Moses (*The Formula*, 298f.). This conjecture exaggerates the slim affinities between the traditions on Moses' birth and the sober, very different account of Matthew. Only systematic presuppositions can turn these traditions into explanations of Matthew. Soares Prabhu furnishes no points of contact that would justify this hypothetical derivation.

[8]R. T. France, "Herod and the Children of Bethlehem," *NovTest*, 21, (1979): 98-120.

[9]Rare and *hapax* words in Mt 2:16:

Two words are found only here in Matthew: *anaireō (aneilen)* and *empaizein* in the sense of "play a trick," which it has here. Four other words are not found elsewhere in the NT: *akriboun* (of which the only other example is in the preceding context, Mt 2:7), *dietēs, katōterō* and *thymousthai.* (Soares Prabhu, *The Formula*, 257-259).

[10]Soares Prabhu, *ibid.*, 298; cf. France, "Herod," 113.

[11]Herod's hands were stained with the blood of his predecessors, Antigonus and Hyrcanus, and also of a number of their partisans, members of the Hasmonaean family and their relations and followers. He eliminated his own children, Alexander and Aristobulus, the sons of Marianne, in the year 7 (Josephus, *Antiquities* 16, 392-394), and Antipater, in the year 4 B.C., shortly before his own death (*Antiquities* 17, 182-196). This action provoked Augustus' celebrated line, "It is better to be Herod's pig than his own son." This play on the words *hus* (pig) and *huios* (son) is recounted by Macrobius (*Saturnalia* 4, 4, 11, ed. Garnier, I: 273).

He executed numerous groups of conspirators, along with their entire families (*Antiquities* 15, 366-369; see also 16, 236). He had a devoted soldier, Tyro, killed, for trying to dissuade him from slaying his own children, as well as three hundred sympathizing officers (*Antiquities* 16, 379-394).

On the eve of his death, he went so far as to assemble all the notables into the hippodrome at Jericho, with the order that they be killed at the hour of his death, so that his funeral might not be marked by an outbreak of joy, but indeed, by tears befitting his memory. He wanted to rule from beyond the grave (*Antiquities* 17, 5-6, 178-181).

[12]The *argumentum a silentio* against historicity:

Isn't the lack of cross-connections with secular history a serious argument against the historicity of the story? France posed this question; here is his answer. "Even the crucifixion of Jesus left no contemporary notices among non-Christians. The few later references that can be considered as independent (Tacitus, *Annals* 15, 44, and F. Josephus, *Antiquities* 18, 3, 53-64) do not stem from the event itself, but from the religious movement which had flourished already. Why, then, should we expect independent confirmation of a minor event. . . among the atrocities of Herod?"

[13]Celsus (mid-second century), cited by Origen in *Against Celsus*, 1, 28, ed. Sources, 132, p. 153: "Jesus, born in secret. . . was obliged by poverty to hire himself out in Egypt; there he acquired the experience of certain magic

powers of which the Egyptians boasted; he returned all puffed up with pride at his powers, and thanks to them, proclaimed himself God."

Regarding the cross-references relative to the flight into Egypt: E. Peretto, *Recherche sur Mt 1-2*, thinks he finds probable traces of a "resistance movement connected with messianism in Bethlehem," which was "smothered in blood." He attempts to clarify the exile of Jesus by reference to the exile of the Master of Justice, according to the Damascus Document (7; 14-15). Bagatti, "La Fuga in Egitto," *Sacra Doctrina* 89, (1979): 131, 141, links this episode (also related in Josephus' history and in the *Dormition Mariae*) to first century sources, but in order to discern in it the common theme of ordeal, rather than to determine historicity.

[14]Perhaps Tannaitic (D. R. Catchpole, "The Trail of Jesus," *Studia post-biblica* (Leiden: Brill 18, 1971): 1-4. France, "Herod", 116.

[15]Sanhedrin 107b; cf. Sota 47a, where the name of Jesus is lacking in certain manuscripts, France, *ibid.*, 116.

[16]One hundred and fifty years of divergent and ephemeral hypotheses should be enough to invite caution. What we are dealing with is a residue of historical research. It is a pity that this too often conceals, for the majority of the public, the considerable and authentic advances of exegesis. The general public suffers a peculiar degree of deception in this matter. It knows nothing of the serious works of Stegeman. But when this exegete (promoted shortly afterward to succeed Bultmann) maintained that Jesus was originally from Capernaum, German newspapers were full of the story. Likewise, French journals a few years ago informed us that Qumran investigation had turned up a Christ before Christ, of whom Jesus was but the shadow; then, that the historical existence of Jesus himself was doubtful, an opinion that made a lasting impression on fifty per cent of the French people, according to a poll taken at the time.

B. Dialogues

[17]In Luke:

—The canticles as monologues: (1:25, 46-56—which can also be taken as belonging to a dialogue with Elizabeth—69-79; 2:14); the double prophecy of Simeon (2:29-35)—the first is a canticle 2:29-32, the second is addressed to Mary, 34-35; the annunciation to the shepherds (Lk 2:10-12), a nocturnal monologue analogous to the dream in Matthew; the evangelizing communication of the shepherds (2:20) and of Anna (2:38); the final reflection of Zechariah's neighbors, "What then will this child be?" may be interpreted as an interior monologue or as a question spread by rumor.

[18]For example, in the opinion of Brown, *The Birth*, 307-309, the scene implies a pre-evangelical tradition regarding divine filiation, but does not tell us anything about a revelation or information received by Mary. It amounts to an explanation fabricated by the author for "the reader."

C. The Canticles

[19]In addition to these we must not forget the shepherds' praise (which extends the angels' praise of God) in 2:20.

[20]M. Trèves, "Le Magnificat et le Benedictus," *Cahiers du cercle Ernest Renan* 27, (1979): 105-110, holds that these hymns reflect the type of hope which 4 Esdras and 2 Baruch express. According to this theory, they would have been composed in the second century, during a Jewish insurrection against the Romans, and would have been adapted at the time of their integration into Luke 1-2. The argument is that they celebrate a political liberation of Israel which neither John the Baptist nor Jesus effected. The motives for such a hypothesis, which cause J. Massynberde Ford to consider them zealot hymns, are understandable (*Zealotism* 18, [1976], 280-292: 1, 51-53, 71, 74).

It is true that the aorists of the Magnificat, in their future oriented significance, are realized during neither the childhood nor the public life of Jesus, hence the temptation to search elsewhere, in a political milieu or in an underground resistance movement to the Roman occupation; but the assurance witnessed to by these aorists is an anticipation founded on trust in God's plan, not on observation of the political situation or on any revolutionary scheme. As soon as a text is detached from its internal context, a thousand hypotheses are possible, none of which get one anywhere; they are conducive to uncertainty by diverting attention from the text to the margin.

[21]Are the Magnificat and the Benedictus post-paschal hymns?

The eighteen words common to both the Benedictus and the sermons of Peter in Acts 3:12, 26 pointed out by F. Gryglewicz, "Die Herkunft der Hymnen des Kindheits evangelium des Lukas," *NTS* 21, (1975): 265-273 (invoked by Brown, *The Birth*, 354 and 363, nn. 50 and 70), amount only to very general terms: Abraham, servant, prophet, power, death, sin, covenant, etc. They are connected in entirely different manners, without thematic analogy (except perhaps for the importance accorded by both to the prophets). This is a matter of eighteen words scattered among several hundred others on both sides (more than 300 in Acts 3:13-26). More specifically, none of the words characteristic of the Resurrection are to be found in the Benedictus. It is rather in Matthew 1-2 that one might find some allusion to that, in the astonishing recurrence of the verb *egeirō* (awaken, 1:24; 2:13, 14, 20, 21) which is also translated as "arise," the most current word used to designate the Resurrection (e.g., Mt 28:6-7).

As for the universalism attributed to the Magnificat, the only element which could be so construed concerns "the powerful deposed from their thrones" (1:52). But this is only a minor aspect, and the prophets of Israel professed a much more explicit universalism.

Brown's principal argument is not lacking in interest: that the aorist of the Magnificat denotes an assurance which would have been unthinkable before the Resurrection, an assurance that God has already deposed the mighty from their thrones, filled the hungry with good things, sent the rich away with empty hands, and so on. This is what makes him attribute the hymns to the Judeo-Christians (*The Birth*, 363). Luke would seem to have placed this post-Resurrectional *parrhēsia* "upon the lips of Mary." But the future significance of the aorist is not an absolute novelty (Ps 46:10, etc).

In fact, the assurance that everything is directed from above was not more materially verified for the Judeo-Christians of the middle of the first century than for Mary in 4 B.C. Why should this assurance have only been born later, rather that with her to whom Luke attributes the canticle? In the absence of argument, are we not called upon by objectivity to adhere to what Luke says, coherent as it is and apparently well-founded?

[22]In addition to these references to the canticle of Hannah, the Magnificat contains reminiscences of numerous other texts, notably the Psalms, which have long been noted by exegetes; Brown, who summarizes them, adds a contact with Qumran (1 QM 14:10-11, *The Birth*, 359).

An echo is found in 4 Ez 9:45, "God has heard the prayer of his handmaid, he had regarded my shame (or humility) and has sent me a son." This canticle may be linked with Jewish prayer of the first century.

[23]While leaning toward the hypothesis of a "very archaic" work of the "believing community" (in conformity with the prestigious theme of the "creative community"), Grelot ("Marie," *DS* 10, [1977]: 416-417) recognizes "nevertheless" the very-similitude of the other hypothesis: "The archaic formulation would be well suited to a composition due to Mary herself, within the framework of the nascent Church, in which Luke shows her assiduous at prayer with the Twelve (Acts 1:14), meditating in her heart upon the events she has lived (cf. Luke 2:19). She could measure the scope of God's promises (1:54-55), now that they had been accomplished in plenitude."

It goes without saying that the canticle was transmitted in the state in which it was assumed by the primitive Judeo-Christian community. But to assert that Mary could not have sung this hymn except in this community and after the Resurrection, that it was totally foreign to her at the time she became the mother of Christ—such an assertion relies on factitious presuppositions, for the archaism of the canticle evades the anachronism which such post-dating would invite.

[24]Nunc Dimittis (2:29-32): If it has been preserved and transmitted as Lk 1:14 would lead us to believe, the transmission cannot be Simeon's doing. But Mary was present at this scene (2:27), in fact, in the foreground (2:34). Thus it is to her memory that we owe the transmission of this canticle and the prophecy of the sword (2:35). This is the inevitable solution, if historicity is not denied a priori and one is not to insist upon making a patchwork of Luke 1-2's superstructure.

Chapter 6: The Wonders

[1]We have given this aspect (which can be called "the extraordinary," or "supernatural") separate treatment, not in function of its exegetical analysis but because of the irrational (and contradictory) reactions of rationalist criticism in regard to it.

[2]Indeed, it has often served to confirm traditions that might have seemed too good to be true. This is the case with the shroud of Turin, to which numerous and rigorous multi-disciplinary tests have furnished authenticating evidence beyond anything even the most naive believers would have dared hope for ten years ago.

A. Miracle, Challenge or Proven Fact?

[3]Gressman, *Das Weinachtsevangelium*, 11.

[4]Our ontogenesis sums up the paleogenesis without abolishing it.

[5]Professor P. Mauriac was the first to use this expression, at the Mariological Congress of Lourdes in 1958. Father Balic, consultor to the Holy Office, came to visit him shortly thereafter urging him to change this expression in the publication of the proceedings of this Congress. Today, however, uneasiness seems to be felt in the other direction. A number of canonization causes have been terminated because of an excess of miracles, while those with no miracles receive a dispensation (as was the case for Father Maxmilian Kolbe). The last apparitions recognized by the Church go back fifty years (Beauraing,

1932, and Banneux, 1933). These raised sharp socio-cultural opposition and the most serious difficulties in Rome itself which deprived Monsignor Heylen, Bishop of Namur, of his normal right to exercise judgment in the matter. Likewise at Lourdes, certified reports of miracles have become rare. There were none for eleven years (1965-1976), then, two miracles were recognized by fortuitous coincidence (1976 and 1978). Only one has been recognized since then.

This recession is due, in part, to the traditional caution of the Church in this risky and ambiguous affair. But, on top of this, there is today a very widespread prejudice.

[6]Philosophical idealism at the roots of historical-critical exegesis. The determining influence of Kant and Hegel has been analyzed by P. Toinet, *Permanence de la foi et exégèse historico-critique* (unpublished memorandum). I discussed this subject at the Catechetical Center of the Diocese of New York, July 16, 1982.

B. Revelations and Communications

[7]The phenomenon is not without precedent. Speaking in tongues, which was a feature of the early Church, seems to have died out over the centuries, in part because it was cataloged as one of the marks of diabolical possession in the Inquisition's list of indictments. Thus, Ignatius Loyola, whose life saw a resurgence of this charism, speaks of it only with great cautiousness (*loquela*, he calls it), and it was only with the recent renaissance of glossolalia that we have been able to understand what he was saying about it.

[8]Few exegetes would now even venture to suggest the validity of the Gloria. Even Daniélou could not risk it. In spite of his apologetical solicitude and his courageous defense of historicity on other points, he suggests that the matter in question is a product of the Christian liturgy (*The Infancy Narratives*, [New York: Herder and Herder]): because it seems fitting to explain everything in terms of the creative community. In this domain the merest analogy is as good as proof.

C. The Star, Angels and Dreams

[9]These media are linked to the receptivity (personal and collective) of the subject. The realm of evaluation here is a very delicate one. Thomas Aquinas quite rightly stressed the relativity of signs that refer to the transcendent "terminus," beyond whom there is no appeal: God in his activity as Savior.

Their relativity does not impede their capacity to point to this divine "terminus."

[10]Interesting observations may be found on this subject, particularly in: Daniélou, *Les Evangiles de l'enfance*, 93-95; Peretto, *Recherche*, 89-96; Perrot, *Les récits*, 79-80; Brown, *The Birth*, 169-176, 195-196. We will return to the symbolism and the cultural code of the stars later in this work, pp. 439-440.

[11]Balaam in Qumran texts:

—4 Q testimonia,

—1 M 11 6 (two allusions of little interest),

—Damascus Document, 7, 18, 20 where reference is assigned to the star and the scepter, the first to the "interpreter of the law," the second to the "prince of all the assembly," that is, the priest of the last days and the messianic heir, the Messiah of Aaron and the Messiah of Israel (cf. Brown, "J. Starcky's Theory of Qumran Messianic Development," 55-56).

—Testament of the Twelve Patriarchs 18, 3; in which Levi speaks similarly of the new priest whom the Lord will raise up in the last days: "His star will rise in the sky as if he were the king." Nevertheless, it is Judah to whom the scepter is applied in Judah 24:5, while Judah 24:1 applies both the star and the scepter to the Messiah who is to issue from Judah. But this interpretation may reflect a later addition.

It is the important position of the prophecy of Balaam at Qumran which motivates Brown to accept it as the common source of Mt 2:2-12 and Lk 1:76. But the comparison is much weaker than some comparisons which Brown himself rejects. Here the parallelism is more in the eye of the exegete than in the text. His argument doubtless demonstrates a probability that the two evangelists of the childhood thought about the prophecy of Balaam, but this probability is in no way a proof.

Regarding the substratum of Lk 1:78 (*anatolē ex hypsuos*, the star arising from on high), see the well-documented note of Fitzmyer (*Luke 1-9*, 387). He translates "the dawn from on high" while "preferring the messianic sense." His translation attempts to retain the ambiguity of the Greek text.

A messianic horoscope was discovered at Qumran, cave 4 II, 1-3. This fragmentary text, provisionally edited by J. Allegro, "An Astrological Cryptic Document from Qumran," *JSS* 2, (1964): 291-294, was studied by Carmignac, *Les horoscopes de Qumran*, 192-217. Here is the essence of it:

1) Red of hair (cf. David in 1 Sm 16:12; 17:42)...

3) Having small stains on his thighs...

4) During his youth he will be like a lion, and like one who has no knowledge until the time of the secret,

5) of. . . three books.
6) At that time, he will acquire prudence and knowledge. . .
8) He will know the secrets of men.
His wisdom will reach all peoples. . .
9) His domination over all living beings will be immense. . .
10) His birth is chosen by God.

This person remains anonymous. But the allusions to David (red-haired, victorious over lions, etc.) and to Solomon (wisdom), the use of Is 11:5, the parallels with the Collection of Blessings (5:20-29), royal homage and universal sovereignty "scarcely permit a doubt that the subject is a future political chief, a prince of the community" charged with "establishing the royalty of his people in perpetuity," as the Collection of Blessings puts it (5:20-21).

M. Delcor, "Recherche sur un horoscope en langue hébraïque provenant de Qumran," *RQ* 5, (1967): 521-542, takes up the study of another horoscope studied by Carmignac in the article cited ("Les horoscopes," 199-206), a critical document with many lacunae.

These texts show the plausibility of the idea of magi interested in signs in the sky concerning the Messiah.

[12]These same observations suggested to Legrand that the star of Matthew had to be interpreted as the manifestation of the glory of God that filled the Ark of the Covenant, or surrounded the shepherds in the night, according to Lk 2:9 ("Vidimus Stellam," 377-384).

[13]The theories that have multiplied since Kepler, about a *supernova* or about a conjunction of Jupiter and Saturn are purely gratuitous and speculative. Comets, especially Halley's comet (11-12 B.C.) which people have sought to identify with the star of Matthew, must be set aside, not only because the date does not square with the data but because comets were seen as a bad omen and would never have been perceived as a supernatural sign of the Messiah. Brown (*The Birth*, 171-174) rightly dismissed these fundamentalist theories as being without exegetical significance.

[14]*Onar* in 1:20; 2:12, 13, 19, 22; and *hypnos* in 1:24.

Chapter 7: The Virginal Conception

[1]See the bibliography.

A. The Problem

[2]X. Pikaza, *Los Origines de Jesus*, 32: "One should not set aside the very

remote possibility that Jesus might be the illegitimate son of Mary. . . . That Jesus should have been illegitimate does not contradict Christian love."

[3]D. Boucher, in *Le Journal de Montréal*, (November 29, 1978): 56: one of numerous articles in a long and lively controversy. We have cited a good many texts in the same vein in our "Bulletins sur la Vierge Marie," *RSPT*, 1970, and subsequent issues.

[4]An interesting index of the distortions involved in reductionist interpretations:

In the estimation of Fitzmyer, "The Virginal Conception of Jesus in the New Testament," *ThS* 34, (1973): 541-575, the evangelists did not consider the virginal conception a reality. Brown excludes this interpretation, while still wondering if the evangelists' affirmation was not the product of a *theologoumenon.*

[5]Brown, *The Birth*, 531.

[6]J. de Freitas Ferreira, *Conceiçao*, has aptly brought out this frequent confusion between exegesis and presuppositions.

B. Exegetical Arguments

[7]See above, literary critique of Luke, pp. 11-12.

[8]Both employ the verb *gennaō* in the passive form and designate Jesus as the begotten one using the neutral participle:

—*to gennēthen* (Mt 1:20: aorist).

—*to gennōmenon* (Lk 1:35: present tense with future value).

[9]Legrand, who clearly perceived this, believed one should conclude from this that Matthew was attributing a male role to Mary. This would suggest a dependence on gnostic thought. The author does not go so far as to defend an inversion of male and female roles, for the gnostic perspective was a sort of transsexuality, with women taking on the qualities of men. The gnostic perspective, however, is completely foreign to Matthew. This comparison and others only serve to reveal what pitfalls our two evangelists managed to avoid. Legrand, "Was the Virgin Mary 'Like a Man' " (*yk gbr*)?, 97-107. The author refers to the ancient Apocrypha:

—*Odes of Solomon* 19, 10a: "She gave birth like a man, at will."

—*Gospel of Philip*, logion 17: "Some have said, 'Mary conceived of the Holy Spirit.' They are in error. What they say, they do not know. When has a woman ever conceived of a woman?" (ed. R. McWilson, 1962, 31). The objection refers to the fact that the name of the Spirit is feminine in Hebrew (*ruah*).

—*Gospel of Thomas*, logia 15, 22 and 114: "Women are not worthy of life," said Peter in an attempt to exclude Mariam. But Jesus said: "I will make her male so that she may also become a living spirit, a male like you; for every woman who shall become male will enter into the kingdom of heaven."

These gnostic speculations are foreign to Matthew and Luke. The author fortunately insists ("Was the Virgin Mary 'Like a Man' ", 106-107) that the matter is not one of inversion but of a transcendence of the duality of the sexes (as in the relations of kinship according to Mt 12:48). See also our discussion above, pp. 341-347.

[10]Theological Contexts:

Matthew and Luke introduce the virginal conception in different manners. Luke does this in a theology of divine filiation, analogous to Paul (Rom 1:3), who does not explicitly refer to the virginal conception. Matthew does not link the fact to divine filiation, which surfaces only later in his Gospel. By contrast, he establishes a link between the virginal conception and the name *Emmanuel* (God-with-us).

Instead of comparing Matthew to Luke on this point, comparisons have been made between Luke 1 and 2, which make no reference to the virginal conception. The birth is reported without reference to Mary's virginity (2:7). Some scholars have emphasized the idea that Mary does not seem to know that Jesus is the Son of God (Lk 2:49-50).

The first objection may be countered by pointing to the unusual designation of Mary as "betrothed" to Joseph (*emnēsteumenē*, that is, accorded in marriage before cohabitation). At the time of the childbirth, when Mary's common life and cohabitation with Joseph required her to participate in the journey to Bethlehem (Mt 1:18-25), the use of this designation recalls the fact that she is not his wife, though some of the variant readings try to smoothe out the difficulty. This point has been studied above; see p. 11. As for the second objection, an objective exegesis of the text makes it clear that Mary's "not understanding" is not in reference to the divine filiation, as we have seen.

[11]Legrand, *L'Annonce*, 255-256.

[12]See pp. 302-308; 442-445.

[13]It is, then, not a simple creation of Celsus, taken from the word *parthenos*. The Christian formula *huios parthenou* has merely guided the choice of the calumniators among names already known.

St. John Damascene (d. 749) curiously took up this name of Panther to make of him an ancestor of Mary: thus, from the line of Nathan, son of David, was born Levi. Levi begot Melchi and Panther. Panther begot Bar Panther for so he was called. Bar Panther begot Joachim. Joachim begot the Holy Mother of God (*De Fide Orthodoxa*, 1. 4, PG 95, col. 115-58; see above p. 343.

[14]We return to de la Potterie's detailed analysis of Jn 6:42 in *La Madre de Jesus*, 26-33. He schematizes the chiastic structure of the text, which presumes the truth to be known beyond objection.

[15]de la Potterie, "La Mère de Jésus," 41-90, clearly demonstrates that the murmurings of Jesus' Jewish adversaries form a counterpart (in a chiastic composition) to the affirmations of Jesus in which he refers to his one heavenly Father by saying that he himself is "of God" (Jn 6:46).

Similarly, in 1:45, Nathaniel's designation, "Jesus, son of Joseph," is answered gradually, in a schema of revelation in which Jesus is defined successively as the Messiah (1:45), the Son of God (1:49), and the Son of Man, in Daniel's transcendent sense: the one upon whom ascend and descend the angels of God (1:51). In this first text there is no confrontation of adversaries, but a triple transcendence of the initial empirical designation.

[16]J. Galot, *Etre né de Dieu (Jn 1:13)*, (Rome: Institut Biblique Pontifical, 1969).

[17]P. Hofrichter, *Nicht aut Blut sondern monogenen aus Gott geboren ...Joh 1:13-14,* (Wurzburg: Echter Verlag, 1978).

[18]de la Potterie, *La Madre de Jesus*, 35-72, 80-92, and "La Mère de Jésus," 59-90. Although the works of Galot, Hofrichter, and de la Potterie have firmly established the reading of Jn 1:13 in the singular, there is still divergence over the meaning. In Hebrew the plural "not of the 'bloods' " most often designates the shedding of blood (to cite only Psalms 5:7; 9:13; 26:9; 51:16; 55:24; 59:3; 106:38; 139:19), while certain usages refer to the subject of sexuality: Ex 4:25-26 (circumcision), Lv 20:18 (menstruation), 12:4, 5, 7 and Ez 16:6, 9 (childbirth).

According to Hofrichter the expression "not of the bloods" would exclude all biological cause of the birth of the Word-made-flesh, the feminine as well as the masculine principle. It was the shocking radicality of this exclusion which caused the change from the singular (he who is born) into the plural (those who are born).

de la Potterie wonders if this might not be a first expression of the virginity *in partu* (miraculous birth accomplished with neither pain nor effusion of blood).

J. Winandy, "Note complémentaire sur la conception virginale dans le Nouveau Testament," *NRT* 104, (1982): 428-431, believes that the plural *haimata* (bloods) refers not to maternal blood but to carnal ancestry in which blood is multiplied through the generations. In support of this interpretation he cites 2 Sm 21:2; Acts 17:26 according to the Western text and the "Treatise of the Sanhedrin," translated by J. Bonsirven, *Textes rabbiniques* (Rome, 1955): 507. Thus, he would translate, "He who was born not of a carnal ancestry."

The most obvious interpretation, in which *ek haimatōn* refers to the conjunction of paternal and maternal blood, is not excluded. The matter is complex. It remains open.

The translation of this verse in the singular has been adopted by the Jerusalem Bible.

[19]A. Vicent Cernuda, "La genesis humana de Jesucristo según S. Pablo," *EB* 36, (1978): 57-77 and 267-289. See in the bibliography the series of articles by Vicent Cernuda, all dedicated to this matter.

[20]A. Vicent Cernuda, article in preparation on Heb 1:6, "When he brought his first-born son into the world," another testimony that the mystery of the Incarnation made its way upstream in the first century culture.

[21]J. de Freitas Ferreira, *Conceiçao*, 109-114. Doesn't this apparent "consensus" explain how Conzelmann got rid of the infancy narratives to establish his theolgy of Luke?—the most obvious error, recognized today by the author himself, in a valuable study (see the bibliography).

[22]Brown, *The Birth*, 526.

[23]Boslooper, *The Virgin Birth* (Philadelphia: Westminster, 1962): 135-167.

[24]*Life of Numa Pompillius*; see also A. Paul, *Matthieu*, 79-81.

[25]See above, pp. 70-75.

[26]Philo, "De Cherubim," 12.15; cf. A. Paul, *Matthieu*, 70-76; Brown, *The Birth*, 524.

[27]"De Cherubim," *Works* (Paris, 1963): 3:39-41; analogous text in "Legum allegoria," *ibid.*, 3:180-181. A more detailed study is to be found in A. Paul, *Matthieu* 70-75; see also pp. 79-88. This method tends to emphasize the analogies more than the contrasts.

[28]Brown, *The Birth*, 523.

[29]Did the theme "without a father or mother" influence the virginal conception of the infancy narratives? This is what H. Cousin holds, invoking the Slavic Enoch ("Une autre exégèse de la conception virginale est-elle possible?" *Lumière et vie* 23, [1974]: 106-111). The late date of this writing appears to exclude it as a source of the infancy narratives.

But the theme (attested for Melchizedek, "with neither father nor mother, nor genealogy," according to Heb 7:3) is very ancient. In the ancient Orient, "The king is called, or calls himself, the son of a god or goddess. This is not simply an image. . . although the personality of Mesopotamian gods [is] not well defined. The believer does not perceive the existence of these gods except through the phenomena which condition his own life (the physical, the political, the psychosomatic, indeed, through personal illumination).... Gudea and Hammurabi are sons of several gods and goddesses. Gudea (c. 2200 B.C.), as well as Assurbanipal (around 660 B.C.), proclaim that God is their father and that they have neither father nor mother, although elsewhere Assurbanipal proclaims himself the son of his predecessor, Essarhadon. Divine parentage is not natural parentage..." (A. Cazelles, *Le Messie de la Bible: christologie de l'Ancien Testament* Paris: Desclée, 1978) 43-44; cf. *Journ cuneiform stud*, 1978, p. 37.

In letter 286 of El Amarna (ed. S. Mercer, *Tell-el Amarna Tabletes*, Toronto: Macmillan Co. of Canada, [1939]: 707, 1.9), Abedi-Iba, the Canaanite king of Jerusalem (1350 B.C.) writes (according to certain translations) to the Pharaoh that he has neither father nor mother. But it should be translated, "Neither my father nor my mother has established me in this place."

These texts are altogether different in their concern and in content from the virginal conception. Divine paternity is linked with human paternity (for these kings as for the Pharaohs). In Luke 1 and Matthew 1, on the other hand, divine filiation excludes a human father, and God does not play the role of human father, but plays a transcendent role. The evolution of the concept can do no more than develop this datum, underlying Luke 1 and Matthew 1, by speaking of the preexistence of the Christ and saying that "he became what he was not, without ceasing to be what he was: the Son of God," from all time, according to a concept of God altogether different from that of neighboring religions. This expression surfaced in Paul. He avoids speaking of the Incarnation, of humanization, and even of the birth of Christ, preferring to say that Jesus "became" man (Rom 1:3; Gal 4:4, cf. Rom 8:3; Phil 2:7; likewise Heb 1:6 and the monographs of Vicent Cernuda).

The trenchant diagnosis of Vanhoye, who challenges all distinction between *gennaō* (excluded by Paul) and *ginnomai* (used by Paul), and attributes the established consensus on this distinction (Legault, Schlier, Grelot, etc.) to an unthinking repetition of Lagrange on their part, seems to us to disregard the complexity of the underlying philological, semantic, and cultural problem ("La Mère du Fils de Dieu selon Ga 4,4," *Mar* 40, [1978]: 237-247).

[30]A seven month gestation period is attributed to Isaac, "I will form him in the womb of her who will bear him, commanding her to return him to me quickly on the seventh month. That is why every woman who gives birth on the seventh month will see her son live, because I have called my glory down upon him" (Pseudo-Philo, *Sources*, 229, pp. 186-187). The same was alleged

of Samuel according to Philo, LAB, 517, in *RechScRel*, 1967, p. 196, but the definitive edition of Philo, LAB, (*Sources* 229, p. 236) does not permit one to retain this case.

According to the *Protoevangelium of James* (5, 2, ed. Strycher, pp. 86-88), Mary was born thus: "On the seventh month, Anna gave birth." But the *Protoevangelium* does not specify the duration of Jesus' gestation.

[31]In his *4th Eclogue* (ca. 40 B.C.), Virgil attributes (v. 61) a ten month gestation period to his hero, who is born from a virgin (v. 6). But there is no question of a virginal conception. The mother is Lady Justice, and his family is purely figurative. The Church Fathers celebrated this poetic prefigurement. But Jerome, the exegete, was not fooled. He saw in this the confused product of ignorance (Epistle 53, PL 27, 544-545). Cf. Lagrange, "Le Prétendu messianisme de Virgile," *RevBib* 31, (1922): 552-572; see also the ample bibliography in Brown's *The Birth*, 564-570.

[32]The polemic of Justin against the Jews in his *Dialogue with Trypho* is a very ancient witness (mid-second century) to this interpretation.

[33]Brown, *The Birth*, 528.

[34]What the later antiphon would express, *cunctas haereses sola interemisti*, was already in effect from the very beginning.

[35]Not only does Luke place the divine filiation before the Davidic filiation (counter to the source text 2 Sm 7:14, and with an altogether different emphasis), but in this context he calls God the Most High (*hypsistos*,) a fairly rare designation in the NT, where it appears only nine times. This designation connotes transcendence and, at the same time, preexistence.

C. Presuppositions for Rejection

[36]The traditional beliefs have lost their psychological supports. That which at one time constituted an attraction has become an object of revulsion. The rejection mechanisms have, in every sense, functioned in a systematic way. They have been stimulated through the influence of the teachers of suspicion and their seductive ideologies, Freud even more than Marx or Nietzsche in this matter.

We have elsewhere (Laurentin, "Conçu de la Vierge," 36-66) studied the path of this disintegration, to which people have often closed their eyes. The magnitude of the crisis will perhaps be revealed by a few concrete examples.

Dr. Pierre Solignac, former "psychiatric physician of the French Mission" and of numerous "religious communities, male as well as female," has written down his experience in a book with a telling title, *Christian Neurosis*, (New

York: Crossroad, 1981). The first cure reported is that of a priest, whose neurosis was terminated by a miracle-solution, which he reports to the attending physician: I have made love to Anne-Marie (a parishioner). The doctor evaluates the spiritual and psychological consequences of this solution. Beaming, full of gusto and confidence, this priest no longer spoke to me of anything but his priestly work. . . . He now continues with enthusiasm to build up this 'house of the Church'." The clandestine situation of this woman, the hypocrisy of this hidden affair, the infidelity of this priest to his commitments to God, to Catholic tradition, and to the ecclesial demands of his ministry, would seem foreign to the first chapter which bears the title "A Beautiful Priest Image." This disclosure aroused no criticism whatever, no reaction within Christian public opinion, which has made a virtue of being open to new perspectives. The rule of desire was silently replacing that of asceticism and of the Cross.

[37]W. E. Phipps, *Was Jesus Married?,* (New York: Harper, 1970) followed by "The Sexuality of Jesus," (1973): CR *RSPT* (1976): p. 479.

Principal novels about the marriage of Jesus: Anthony Burgess, *The Man from Nazareth*, (1976); Barreau, *Les mémoires de Jésus,* (Paris: Editions J. C. Lattès, 1978).

[38]According to a poll taken in the United States of 5,000 Lutherans between sixteen and sixty-five years of age, representing all the synods, 87% accepted the formula "Jesus was conceived by the Holy Spirit, without a human father." Only 6% were against it, and 3% did not respond (results presented by C. Piepkorn, "The Virgin birth controversy — a Lutheran's reaction," *Marian Studies* 24, [1973]: 60-61). According to a more hasty poll, published by J. P. Van Deth in *Unité des chrétiens* 26, (April, 1977): 5, 71.5% of Catholics polled believed in the virgin birth, slightly below the Orthodox (84%), and slightly above the Anglicans (62%) and the Protestants (57.5%).

Since then, it is to be feared that the figures have descended in the direction of the report published by Pélerin-Sofres, according to which only 27% of the French believed in the real presence (cf. Laurentin, "Conçu de la Vierge," 38 and 36-45, on the recession of belief).

[39]X. Pikaza, *Los origines de Jesus*, 32.

D. The Meaning

[40]Already treated in detail in Laurentin, "Sens et historicité," 515-542.

[41]St. Athanasius (295-346), *Lettres festales et pastorales*, ed. according to a Coptic version by L. T. Lefort (Louvain: Durbecq, 1955) taken up by St.

Ambrose, *De Virginibus ad Marcellinam* 1, 47-51, PL 208-210 fully develops the notion that Mary is the model and mirror of virgins.

[42]Laurentin, *Sens et historicité*, 529, wherein are mentioned: Tertullian: "If Christ is born of man, it is clear that it is from a virgin. Otherwise there would be two fathers: God and a man, in which case the mother would not be a virgin" (*Ad Marcionem* 4, 10, 7 CC 2, p. 593); Lactantius: "In order that it might appear, even in his humanity, that Christ is from heaven, he had been created without the intervention of a father, for he had God for a spiritual father; and as his spiritual father is God, without there being a mother, likewise his bodily mother is a virgin without there being a father" (*De Divinis Institutionibus* 4, 27 PL 6, 524); Proclus (beginning of the fifth century): "The same son cannot be born of two fathers" (*Oratio* 1, *In Nativitate*, number 3, PG 65, 713). "The one without mother in heaven is without father on earth" (716; cf. 685: "one and the same [son] is without mother as creator, and without father as creature").

[43]Laurentin, "Sens et historicité," 532-533. See also pp. 533, 538 and the conclusion pp. 539-542.

[44]K. Barth, *Esquisse d'une dogmatique*: 96.

[45]*Ibid.*, 180.

[46]*Ibid.*, 181.

[47]According to the patristic theme adopted by Vatican Council II (*Lumen Gentium*, Chapter 8, no. 53, with reference to the Fathers in n. 1).

[48]"Behold your mother" (Jn 19:25-27).

[49]Regarding Mary, as the source for Lk 1:2, see the special note on p. 461.

[50]This is true even of the most elementary knowledge, sense knowledge. Color perception, which is partly reinterpretation by the brain, is knowledge; it is symbol. The coherence of perception and deciphering makes for objective agreement among various subjects. Even on this level, the correlation of the objective and subjective is indissoluble. All objective knowledge passes through the subjectivity of the subject. It also passes through symbolic intentionality, thanks to which the subject attains the object. This is due to the very nature of knowledge, to the mysterious yet evident manner whereby it reaches the other as other.

Chapter 8: Symbolism

B. The Signs

[1]Cf. above, pp. 121-130, 256-257, Topography.

[2]Cf. above, pp. 120-121, 257, 333-364.

[3]See above, pp. 50-53, 55-56.

[4]Regarding the fulfillment of the history of salvation and the Scriptures which holds an important place in Matthew 1-2 and Luke 1-2, see above, Part I, chapter 3, n. 7.

[5]This analogy is evident in the synonymous parallelism of Job 38:7 and the personification of the stars in Bar 3:34:

Job 38:7	*Bar 3:34*
. . . when the morning stars sang together, and all the sons of God shouted for joy.	the stars shone in their watches, and were glad; he called them, and they said, "Here we are!" They shone with gladness for him who made them.

[6]The angel of the Lord, sometimes used interchangeably with the Lord:

We base this on ancient biblical accounts, in which the angel of Yahweh is not different from Yahweh himself; these names often alternate in the course of one narrative (Gn 16:7; 22:11; Ex 3:2; Jgs 2:1). This cannot be taken as a blanket generalization, however, since, in the alternation of terms which we can discern in these texts, it is important to take into account complex and not entirely clear cultural phenomena.

In the milieu of the Covenant, angels represent powers worshiped locally, which the Yahwist has reduced to being creatures and messengers of Yahweh, bearers of his words (by messages or biblical writings). A parallel phenomenon occurs when the Egyptian "Hymn of the Sun" is taken over by reducing the sun-god to the humble reality of a creature of God (Ps 104:19). This phenomenon (whereby the concept of angels is taken up, refined, corrected, and referred to God) has gone hand in hand with the increasing demand to safeguard the transcendence of God.

C. Reference to God

[7]*To gennēthen* (Mt 1:20); *to gennōmenon* (Lk 1:35); *brephos* (Lk 2:12 and 16); *paidion* (Mt 2:8, 9, 11, 13, 14, 20, 21; Lk 2:17, 27-30); *pais* (Mt 2:16 and Lk 2:43).

[8]On the titles of Jesus in Luke 1-2, see the summary table, p. 109-110.

[9]First-born in Lk 2:7:

The title of *Prōtokos* has, in this instance, a human meaning, intended to set the stage for the oblation of Jesus as a first-born of Mary in 2:23.

The direct article used in 2:7, *the* first-born, emphasizes the significance of the word. The typological and theophanic meanings of 2:23 transfer it to a divine level. This transfer to the transcendent level and the theology of the new creation, which underlies Luke 1-2, calls for a consideration of the fact that this title insinuates that Jesus, Son of God (1:32), before being son of Mary (1:32b) is first-born of all creatures (Col 1:15 and 18) as only Son of God (see also Jn 1:14, 18; 1 Jn 4:9). The sacred nature of the conception of Christ, made concrete by the exclusion of Joseph (1:34-35) tends to suggest that the first-born of Mary is also only son, only begotten. But it is difficult to grasp the significance of suggestions which are not explicit as they are in Paul and John. They are only beneath the surface.

N. B. The term "first-born" was applied to Israel (Ex 4:22; Wis 18:13; Hos 11:1, taken up by Mt 2:15). God begot the people by having them depart from Egypt (Dt 32:6, 18f.), and their journey through the desert was Israel's infancy (Dt 1:31, 32, 10; Hos 11:4-5).

Preexistence?

It is likewise difficult to evaluate to what extent Luke 1-2 already implies the preexistence insinuated by the fact (new with respect to 2 Sm 7:14) that the oracle of Gabriel presents Jesus as "Son of the Most High" (1:32a) before speaking of him as Son of David which, in one sense, is actually more debatable.

We can illustrate from the point of view of dogma the evolving schema according to which the divinity of Jesus, first identified at his Resurrection "must have been progressively transferred back in time: to the transfiguration, then to the baptism, then to the annunciation, and lastly to the eternal birth of the *Word*—according to the Prologue of St. John."

But Benoit previously observed that this schema "has something exact about it" if we see in it "not the gradual creation of a myth, but the dawning awareness of a mystery" ("L'enfance de Jean-Baptist," 192).

The datings which have been presupposed for establishing this schema are in no way "carved in stone." We have examined the archaic nature of the infancy Gospels, and the preexistence of Christ is not a later piece of evidence. Its theoretical form is found to be most developed in Jn 1 (the end of the first century), but it crops up earlier, especially in Paul (Rom 9:5; Col 1:15-18; cf. Ti 2:13) and Heb 1:8 (whose theology seems explainable only if it was written before the destruction of the Temple of Jerusalem). Preexistence is already explicit in the ancient Christian hymn in Phil 2:6-11. The Epistle can be dated around the years 56-57 (Jerusalem Bible) yet the hymn seems to predate it.

This text and several of those cited above are earlier than our Gospels, if one holds for the later dating, (contested by Robinson).

D. What Kind of Historicity?

[10]Cf. pp. 111 and 443-444.

[11]In Hebrew: *qôl demāmāh daggah: qôl*: voice; *demāmāh*: suspension, silence, stillness; *daggah*: subtle, tenuous, imperceptible.

Conclusion?

[1]In French, *sens*, which signifies both orientation or direction, and the inner structure or meaning engendered or inspired by that orientation. Both meanings of the term concern us here.

A. Evaluation of the Convergences

[2]See pp. 434-436.

[3]See pp. 455-456.

B. The Inspiring Experience

[4]The possibility is not excluded that Matthew was an exile who, like the converted priests of Acts 6:7 and Heb 10:32, had to flee the very people whom he addresses in his Gospel. According to certain theories, Matthew is thought to have left his own country in order to find freedom of speech elsewhere in a community of Jews and converted pagans, possibly in Syria. This hypothesis would imply that he had experience, in the nascent church, of an exile analogous to that of the infant Jesus.

Matthew was a man marked by the kinds of persecution described in the Acts of the Apostles (4:1-23; 5:17-40; 8:1-2; 12:1-12). The view he takes of the machinations involved in hunting down the infant Jesus, of the massacre of the Holy Innocents, is that of the Judeo-Christian communities which remained underground in Israel, or even those dispersed throughout the pagan world (Acts 8:4-5).

In Matthew, we are dealing with the contemplative serenity of a Church of silence, sorely tried by a series of repressions that began with the martyrdom of Stephen (Acts 7), who maintained their identity by means of a profound faith. Matthew appropriated this experience. Douglas R. A. Hare (*The*

Theme of Jewish Persecution of Christians in the Gospel According to St. Matthew, [Cambridge: University Press, 1967]) has given a fine analysis of the texts, in which Matthew recalls these persecutions from the tragic perspective of a rejection of Israel and the transfer of salvation to the nations: this is a feature of Matthew's Gospel (21:43; 22:7) which differentiates him from the three other evangelists. This accounts for the value accorded the wise men and the negative view of Jerusalem (Mt 2:3 and elsewhere)—which is expressed by means of a topography (in which the light of Jerusalem is transferred to Galilee).

Hare evaluates the persecutions of the first Christians with the greatest degree of concern to understand the problems besetting Judaism at the time. These persecutions seem, in his view, to have consisted more in expulsions and sporadic outbreaks of violence than in an official program intended to destroy Christianity. This activity was limited to the period of the war with Rome and especially the time of Bar Kokhba. For the evangelists, the persecutions meant that they were reduced to silence.

[5]Acts 11:19-23; 13:1-52.

Acts 11:28, according to D; the "we" passages: 16:10-17; 20:5-15; 21:1-18; 27:1-28:16.

[6]Luke, companion of Paul:

Luke was "by race an Antiochian and a physician by profession, and was a companion of Paul" according to the earliest reliable testimonies (Eusebius of Caesarea, *Ecclesiastical History* 3, 4, 6, Vol. I, p. 197, tr. Kirsopp Lake, Loeb Classical Library). The evangelist presents himself in the most explicit fashion as author, both in the Gospel (Lk 1:1-4) and in Acts (1:1-2); he uses "we" for the most detailed section of Acts: that part in which the peculiarities of his vocabulary and style are the most concentrated (16:10-17; 20:5-15; 21:1-18; 27:1-2; and the much discussed variant of the western text in 11:27-28: "As we were gathered together, one of them, Agabus. . .").

Some critics sought to see in this "we" a literary device (Bovon, "Luc: portrait et project," *Lumière et Vie* 30, [1982]: 17). We consider (with Dupont, *The Salvation of the Gentiles: Essays on the Acts of the Apostles* [New York: Paulist Press, 1979]; cf. p. 112; A. George, "Luc," *Catholicisme* 7, [1975]: 1226-1231; Osty and TOB) that these doubts are not well founded. These passages "present Luke as companion of Paul in a discreet enough manner that his sincerity can be admitted," J. Duplacy indicates (*ibid.*, col. 1232). Luke was very careful to revise his literary sources. It would be odd if he forgot to erase the "we" (which would have been very easy) or to refer it to someone else. It is not surprising that he does not mention the Galatian crisis:

he habitually omits reference to inner Christian conflicts; nor is it surprising that he presents the Law (13:38; 15:5) or the apostolate (13:31) in his own way. He personalizes the influence of Paul where his own gentleness makes up for the latter's harshness.

As for the date of Acts, it is important to be prudent. The hypothesis according to which the redaction of Acts occurred before that of the Gospel seems very unlikely. Given Luke's interest in Jerusalem, it also seems very unlikely (according to Robinson's argument) that he wrote the Gospel and Acts after the year 70, seeing that he makes nowhere any reference to the destruction of the Temple. Considering the importance which he attached to Peter and Paul, it seems equally astonishing that he would not allude to their martyrdom: this would contribute to placing his writings before 64. The prudent critical consensus, which has opted for the latest date possible (around 80 or a little later), might not square with reality.

The present volume need not raise these debates again, but it tends to confirm that Luke was a disciple of Paul (see above, pp. 38-43)—not an imitator of his epistles, but one who reflects his preaching, in a manner consonant with his own temperament, which is not at home with polemics and controversies. His sensibility toward the charismatic gifts of the primitive Church which he makes known to us, and his readiness to pick up and evaluate the anticipations of the Holy Spirit at the very origins of the existence of Christ, seem to confirm from within what is attested by the analysis of his writings by external analysis.

[7]He recognizes their place as being of prime importance—both at the time of Christ's infancy and at his Resurrection. They are the first to go to the empty tomb and the first to tell the Good News to the Twelve, who do not believe them (24:11). They have a choice place in the "upper room" with the Twelve, with the group of 120 disciples (Acts 1:15).

[8]See special note on Mary as the source of Luke 1-2, pp. 461-463.

LEXICON

This book has avoided using technical terms as much as possible and, where they were deemed necessary, has tried to make their meaning clear in context. It may be helpful, nevertheless, especially for readers unfamiliar with the vocabularies of semiotics or exegesis, to have simple definitions of some basic terms.

Semiotic Lexicon

Actant: One who acts in a narrative. An actant may be a person, an animal, a vegetable, or any object (a fire, a river, etc.). Greimas has grouped actants into six categories, according to their functions: addressers, addressees, subjects, objects, helpers, and opponents (see below).

Addressee: Anyone who benefits from the deeds performed by the hero or subject of the narrative; e.g., the people delivered from the devouring dragon.

Addresser: The one who establishes the conditions or defines the value of the narrative's central action; e.g., the father-king who declares that he will give his daughter as bride to the valiant warrior who will slay the dragon and deliver his people.

Atopy, atopical: Without an indication of place (Greek: *topos*).

Code: The collection of rules that govern how groups of terms (topographical, chronological, etc.) are to be used.

Conjunction: Link between subject and object. It is signified by the symbol →. "Mr. Crow held a piece of cheese in his beak," is symbolized thus: crow → cheese, or S → O.

Disjunction: A separation or dissociation; the opposite of conjunction. Disjunction may be somatic, as between Jesus and Mary when Simeon takes Jesus in his arms in Lk 2:28, or topographic, as when Jesus leaves Jerusalem for Nazareth in Lk 2:39 and 51. It is signified by the symbol ←.

Helper: One who aids the hero or subject to complete his performance or exploit.

Immanence: This principle, introduced into linguistics by Saussure, prescribes attending to the internal laws governing textual discourse, without reference to the history or psychology of the author, nor to the readers.

Isotopies: Elements of similitude and analogy which recur in a narrative and manifest semiotic homogeneity. The terms of the Semiotic Square (q.v.) are isotopies.

Mode: That which allows a basic statement to be transformed to other meanings: e.g., I eat, I want to eat (mode of willing), and I am able to eat (mode of power).

Narrative Program: The scheme by which every narrative is interiorly governed. The NP is ordinarily stated by the positing of an act or deed by the hero, which alters another subject's state; e.g., he causes the crowning or abdication of a king. In a well-made story the NP is often announced in the first sentence. "Mr. Crow held a piece of cheese in his beak,"indicates the conjunction of the crow with the cheese, and so the achieving of his program. But the anti-program of the fox hinders the program of the crow. They are parallel and antagonistic programs.

Object: Designates the prize acquired by the subject; a term of great complexity in semiotics.

Occurrence: The repetition of the same word or sign. There is occurrence of the expression, "he will be called holy," in Lk 1:35 and 2:23.

Opponent: One who is antagonistic to the hero or subject and hinders the achievement of his performance.

Performance: The central action accomplished by the hero of a narrative; e.g., to slay the destructive dragon.

Seme: The smallest unit of signification; equivalent to the phoneme in linguistics.

Sememe: A group of semes that produce a meaning. The signification of each seme is modified by the group in which it appears.

Semiotics: The science that studies the forms of signification, in order to try to explain how a text produces its meaning by structural organization of significative elements.

Semiotic Square: The schematization of a concept or semiotic category according to four isotopies. The square is based on the contraries A and B, from which the contradictories A* (non-A) and B* (non-B) are constructed. A and B are contraries; B* and A* are sub-contraries; A and A*, B and B* are contradictories; A and B*, B and A* are correlatives.

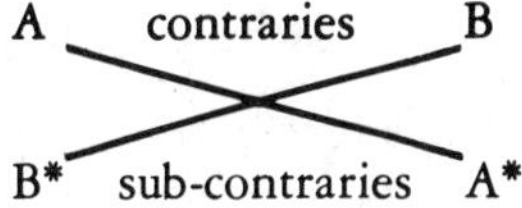

Subject/Hero: The one who accomplishes the Narrative Program; e.g., the one who slays the dragon and receives the reward.

Test: The action or deed accomplished by a subject or hero. There is ordinarily a succession of three tests: qualifying, in which the hero acquires a competence; decisive, in which he accomplishes the deed; and glorifying, in which he is hailed, recognized, rewarded.

Veridiction: Conformity of what is said to the truth; i.e., of *seeming* to *being*. (See the square of veridiction, pp. 115, 237, 300.)

Exegetical Lexicon

Apocalypse: Etymologically, "revelation" (from Greek *apokalypsis*). A literary genre that aims at disclosure of God's plans and purposes by means of symbols.

Dynast: The inheritor of a dynasty (illegitimate sons were offspring of the king but not dynasts).

Eschatological: That which concerns the end of time.

Historicity: A very complex notion, used in this present work to signify the conformity of a narrative to real events. The discernment of historicity means evaluating the correlation between the events and the subject (personal or collective) who expresses it.

Midrash: Exegesis or explication of a Scriptural text, characterized by a confrontation between Scripture and event, with each sharpening the significance and pertinence of the other. It is not properly a literary genre, though instances of it are sometimes wrongly identified as such. The word midrash comes from the Hebrew root *darash*, which signifies a searching out. Judaism distinguished two basic orientations: *haggādāh*, the exegesis of narratives, and *halakah*, finding in Scripture rules of conduct.

Septuagint: The oldest version in Greek of the Old Testament. It is so designated because legend attributes it to seventy-two translators. It was prompted by the extension of the Jewish diaspora into hellenized lands and emerged during the third and early second centuries B.C.

Theologoumenon: Karl Rahner so designates "a doctrine which is not guaranteed by the authority of the magisterium, but commends itself by the manner in which it clarifies other explicit teachings of the Church." In this book the word is referred to in its vulgarized sense, as designating a theological creation in which a narrative is invented to express a theological idea. In this sense, theologoumenon has been used to "explain" all the narratives of the Infancy Gospels. This approach fails to recognize that in the Gospels events and theology are correlative; to eliminate one for the sake of the other would be a ruinous simplification.

Theophany: A manifestation of God (from Greek, *theos*, God, and *phainō*, to appear or manifest).

BIBLIOGRAPHY

Barth, Karl. *Esquisse d'une dogmatique*. Fr. ed., Paris, 1950.

Benoit, Pierre. "L'enfance de Jean-Baptiste selon Luc 1," *NTS* 3, (1957): 169-194.

——— "Non erat eit locus in diversorio...Lc 2:7." A Descamps. *Mélanges B. Rigaux*. Gembloux: Duculot, 1970.

——— "Quirinius," *DBS*, ed. by Henri Cazelles and André Feuillet. Letouzey and Ané, 1979: 693-720 with bibl. col. 717-720.

Black, M. *An Aramaic Approach to the Gospels and Acts*. 2nd ed. Oxford: Clarendon Press, 1954.

Bloch, R. "Juda engendra Phares et Zara, de Thamar (Mt 1,3)." *Mélanges A. Robert*. Paris: Bloud, 1957.

——— "Midrash," *DBS*, ed. L. Pirot, A. Robert, H. Cazelles. Letouzey and Ané, 1957: 3:1263-1281 with bibl. col. 1281.

Bonnard, Pierre. *L'Evangile selon saint Matthieu*. 2nd ed. rev. et augm. Neuchâtel, Delachaux and Niestlé (in France: Delauchaux et Niestlé, Paris), 1970.

Bossuyt, Philippe and Jean Radermaker. *Jésus, parole de la grâce: selon saint Luc*. 2 vols. Brussels: Institut d'Etudes Theologiques, 1981.

Bover, José M. "Noticiano: una nueva interpretacion de Lc 2:50," *EB* 10, (1951): 205-215.

Bovon, François. "Luc: portrait et project," *Lumière et Vie* 30, (1981): 9-18.

Briggs, Charles Augustus. *New Light on the Life of Jesus*. NY: Scribner. 1904.

Brown, Raymond E. *The Birth of the Messiah: a commentary on the infancy narratives in Mt and Lk*. Garden City, NY: Doubleday, 1977.

——— "Reflections on a Review: A Reply (to J. McHugh)," *Ampleforth Review* 2, (1981): 57-60.

——— "J. Starcky's theory of Qumran Messianic development," *CBQ* 28, (1966): 51-57.

——— *Mary in the New Testament: a collaborative assessment by Protestant and Roman Catholic scholars*. Ed. by R. E. Brown. Philadelphia: Fortress Press, 1978.

Bultmann, Rudolf Karl. *The History of the Synoptic Tradition*. Tr. by John Marsh. Oxford: Blackwell, 1963. Originally published as *Die Geschichte der synoptischen Tradition* (Göttingen: Vandenhoeck, 1921).

Burkitt. "Note on the Biblical Text used by Niceta." In *Niceta of Remesiana*, ed. by A. Burn. Cambridge (1905), cliii-clviii.

——— "Who Spoke the *Magnificat?*" *JTS* 7, (1906): 220-227.

Burn, A., ed. *Niceta of Remesiana*, Cambridge, 1905.

Burrows, E. *The Gospel of the Infancy*. London: Burns, 1940.

Carmignac, L. "Les horoscopes de Qumran," *RQ* 5, (1965): 192-217.

——— *Pour l'Unite* 10, (Feb. 1973): 11-14.

Cazelles, Henri. "La mère du Roi-Messie dans l'Ancien Testament," *Maria et Ecclesia* 5, (1959): 39-56.

——— *Le Messie de la Bible: christologie de l'Ancien Testament*. Paris: Desclée, 1978.

——— *Naissance de l'Eglise. Secte Juive Rejetée?* Paris: Editions du Cerf, 1983.

Conrady, Ludwig. *Quelle der Kanonischen Kindheitsgeschichte Jesus*. Göttingen: Vandenhoeck und Ruprecht, 1900.

Contri, Antonio. "Il 'Magnificat' alla Luce dell'inno cristologico di Filippesi 2:6-11," *Mar* 40, (1978): 164-168.

Conzelmann, Hans. *The Theology of St. Luke*. Tr. by Geoffrey Buswell. 1st Fortress Press ed. Philadelphia: Fortress Press, 1982. English edition originally published in New York: Harper and Row, 1961. Originally published as *Die Mitte der Zeit: Studien zur Theologie des Lukas*, (Tübingen: Mohr, 1960).

Daniélou, Jean. *The Infancy Narratives*. Tr. by Rosemary Sheed. New York: Herder and Herder, 1968. Originally published as *Les Evangiles de l'enfance*, (Paris: Editions du Seuil, 1967).

Davies, W. D. *The Setting of the Sermon on the Mount*. Cambridge: University Press, 1964.

de la Potterie, Ignace. "Les deux noms de Jérusalem dans l'evangile de Luc," *RechScRel* 69, (Jan.-Mar. 1981): 57-70.

——— "La Madre de Jesus," (Madrid: Fe Catolica, 1979).

——— "La Mère de Jésus et la conception virginale du Fils de Dieu, étude de théologie johannique," *Mar* 40, (1978): 41-90.

——— "L'onction du Chrétien par la foi," *Bib* 40, (1959): 12-69.

——— "L'onction du Christ, étude de théologie biblique," *NRT* 80, (1958): 222-252.

Delebecque, E. *Etudes grecques sur l'Evangile de Luc*. Paris: Belles Lettres, 1973.

Dibelius, Martin. *From Tradition to Gospel*. New York: Scribner, 1965.

Translated from the revised 2nd ed. of *Die Formgeschichte des Evangeliums* in collaboration with the author by Bertram Lee Wolf.

——— *Jungfrauen und Krippenkind.* Heidelberg, 1932.

Dockx, S. "Luc a-t-il été le compagnon d'apostolat de Paul?" *NRT* 103, (1981): 385-400.

Dupont, Jacques. *The Salvation of the Gentiles: Essays on the Acts of the Apostles.* Tr. by John R. Keating. New York: Paulist Press, 1979. Originally published as *Nouvelles Etudes sur les Actes des Apôtres,* (Paris: Editions du Cerf, 1967).

——— "Le Magnificat comme discours sur Dieu," *NRT* 102, (1980): 321-343.

Durand, A. *L'origine du Magnificat*, in *Revue biblique* 7, (1893): 74-77.

Eusebius of Caesarea. *Histoire ecclésiastique*; texte grec. Translation and annotation by Gustave Bardy. Paris: Editions du Cerf, 1952-60. Tr. of *Historia ecclesiastica.*

Farris, S.C. *On discerning Semitic Sources in Lc 1-2*, in R. T. France and D. Wenham, *Gospel Perspectives.* Sheffield: University, JSOT Press, 2 (1981): according to the 16 criteria of R. A. Martin, *Syntaxical Evidence*, 1974.

Feuillet, André. *Jesus and His Mother: The Role of the Virgin Mary in Salvation History and the Place of Women in the Church.* Still River, MA: St. Bede's Publications, 1984. Originally published as *Jesus et sa mère d'après les récits Lucaniens de l'enfance et d'après Saint Jean,* (Paris: Gabalda, 1974).

Fitzmyer, Joseph A. *The Gospel According to Luke 1-9: Introduction, translation, and notes.* 1st ed. Garden City, New York: Doubleday, 1981.

——— "The Virginal Conception of Jesus in the New Testament," *NTS* 34, (1973): 541-75.

France, Richard T. "Herod and the children of Bethlehem," *NovTest* 21, (1979): 98-120.

Freitas Ferreira, José de. *Conceiçao virginal de Jesus: análise critica de pesquisa liberal protestante, desde a "Declaração de Eisenach" até hoje, sobre o testemunho de Mt 1, 18-25 e Luc 1, 26-38.* Rome: Universitá Gregoriana Editrice, 1980.

Gächter, Paul. *Maria im Erdenleben, Neutestamentliche Marienstudien.* Innsbruck: Tyrolia, 1953. 2nd ed. 1954.

Greimas, Algirdas Julien. *Du sens; essais sémiotiques.* Paris: Editions du Seuil, 1970.

——— *Sémantique structurale, recherche de méthode.* Paris: Larousse, 1966.

Greimas, Algirdas Julien in collaboration with J. Courtès. *Sémiotique Dictionnaire de la théorie du langage.* Paris: Fachette, 1979.

Gressman, Hugo. *Das Weihnachts—Evangelium auf Ursprung und Geschichte untersucht.* Göttingen: Vandenhoeck, 1914.

Groot, A. de. *Die schmerzhafte Mutter und Gefährtin des göttlichen Erlösers in der Weisegang Simeon (Lc 2:35).* Kaldenkirchen: Steyler Verlag, 1956.

Group d'Entrevernes. *Analyse sémiotique des textes: introduction, théorie, pratique.* [L'elaboration et la rédaction de cet ouvrage ont été assurées par Jean-Claude Giroud et Louis Panier.] Lyons: Presses Universitaires de Lyon, 1979. Based on a series of articles published in *Sémiotique et bible* between 1976 and 1978.

Gueuret, Agnes. *Luc 1-2: Analyse sémiotique.* Paris, 1982 (thesis).

——— "Sur Luc 1:48-55," *Centre protestant,* Supplément d'avril (1977): 1-12.

Gundry, R. *Matthew.* Grand Rapids: Eerdmans, 1982.

Gunkel, H. *Die Lieder.* Tübingen, 1921.

Irenaeus of Lyons. *Adversus Haereses.*

Jerome, St. *Adversus Helvidium.*

——— *In Matthaeum.*

Josephus, Flavius. *Jewish Antiquities* II, 9, 6. Loeb Classical Library: 4:265; 17, 13, 339-355; 17, 9-13, 206-355.

——— *Jewish Wars.* 2, III.

——— *The Life.* 2, #9, tr. H. St. J. Thackeray. Loeb Classical Library, Cambridge, 1956: 1:5.

Kattenbusch, Ferdinand. *Das Apostolische symbol: seine entstehung. Sein geschichtlichter sinn, seine ursprüngliche stellung im kultus und in der theologie der kirche; eine beitrag zur symbolik und dogmengeschichte.* Leipzig: J. C. Heinrichs, 1894-1900.

——— "Die Geburtsgeschichte Jesu als Haggada, der Urchristologie," *ThS* 102, (1930): 454-474.

Kingsbury, J. D. *Matthew: Structure, Christology, Kingdom.* Philadelphia: Fortress, 1975.

Klausner, J. *Jésus de Nazareth.* 1933.

Klostermann, Erich. *Das Lukasevangelium.* Tübingen: Mohr, 1919.

Lagrand, James. "How was the Virgin Mary 'like a man': a note on Mt 1:18b and related Syriac Christian texts." *Nov Test* 22, (1980): 97-107.

Lagrange, Marie Joseph. *Evangile selon St Luc.* 6th ed. Paris: J. Gabalda, 1941.

——— *Evangile selon St Matthieu.* 4th ed. Paris: J. Gabalda, 1927.

——— "Le Prétendu Messianisme de Virgile," *RevBib* 31, (1922): 552-572.

Laurentin, René. Conçu de la Vierge Marie...à l'heure des revisions dogmatiques. *Etudes Mariales* 38, (1981): 36-66.

——— *Court traité sur la Vierge Marie.* 5th ed. refondue à la suite du Concile. Paris: P. Lethielleux, 1968.

——— *Jésus au Temple, mystère de Paques et foi de Marie, en Luc 2:48-50.* Paris: J. Gabalda, 1966.

——— *Maria, Ecclesia, sacerdotium.* 2 vols. Paris: Nouvelles Editiones latines, 1953.

——— "Sainteté de Marie et de l'Eglise," *Etudes Mariales* 11, (1953): 5-6.

——— "Sens et historicité de la conception virginale." *Mélanges* Balic (1971): 515-542.

——— *Structure et théologie de Luc I-II.* Paris: J. Gabalda, 1957.

——— "Traces d'allusions étymologiques en Luc 1-2," *Bib* 37, (1956): 435-456.

Le Deaut, R. "A propos d'une definition du midrash," *Bib* 50, (1969): 395-413.

Legrand, Lucien. *L'Annonce à Marie (Lc 1, 26-38): une apocalypse aux originales de l'Evangile.* Lectio Divina, 106. Paris: Editions du Cerf, 1981.

——— "Vidimus Stellam," *Clergy Monthly*, Ranchi 23, (1959), 377-384.

Lyonnet, S. "Χαίρε κεχαριτωμένη," *Bib* 20, (1939): 131-141.

Loisy, Alfred Firmin. *L'Evangile selon Luc.* Paris: 1924.

——— *Les Evangiles synoptiques.* Ceffonds près Montier-en-der, 1907/8. 2 vol. 8.

——— [A. F. Jacobe]. *Rev. hist. Litt. rel.* 2, (1897).

Machen, John Gresham. *The Virgin Birth of Christ.* New York: Harper and Row, 1930.

——— *Princeton Theological Review* 19, (1922): 1-38; 212-77; 529-580; 25, (1927): 529-586.

Marin, Louis. *The Semiotics of the Passion Narrative: Topics and Figures*. Tr. by Alfred M. Johnson, Jr. Pittsburgh, PA: Pickwick Press, 1980.

Marshall, I. Howard. *The Gospel of Luke: A Commentary on the Greek Text*. Grand Rapids: Eerdmans, 1978.

——— *Luke: Historian and Theologian*. Grand Rapids: Zondervan, 1971, c1970.

Masson, Jacques. *Jésus, fils de David, dans les généalogies de saint Matthieu et de saint Luc*. Paris: Téqui, 1982.

McHugh. *The Mother of Jesus in the NT*. London: Darton, Longman & Todd; New York: Doubleday, 1975. French transl. by Cerf, 1977.

Morgenthaler, Robert. *Die Lukanische Geschichtesch reibung als Zeugnis: Gestalt und Gehalt der Kunst des Lukas*. Zürich: Zwingli-Verlag, 1948.

——— "Statistiche Beobachtungen am Wortschatz des NT," *ThZ* 11, (1955): 97-114.

——— *Statistik des neutestamentlichen wortschatzes*. Zürich, Stuttgart: Gotthelf-Verlag, 1958.

Munoz Iglesias, Salvador. "El Evangelio de la Infancia en San Lucas y las infancias de los héroes bíblicos," *EB* 16, (1957): 329-382.

Orsatti, Mauro. *Un saggio di teologia della storia esegesi di Mt 1-17*. Brescia: Paideia, 1980.

——— *Vergine Perchè Madre de Gesu: Spunti di Proposta Esegetica per Lc 1:34b*. Rome: BIP, 1981.

Osty, E. L'Evangile selon saint Luc. Paris: Editions du Cerf, 1953.

Pannenberg, W. *Jesus, God and Man*. Philadelphia: Westminster, 1968.

Paul, Andre. *L'Evangile de l'enfance selon saint Matthieu*. Lire la Bible, 17. Paris: Editions du Cerf, 1968.

Peretto, E. "Recherche sur Mt 1-2," *Scripta Facultatis Marianum* 25, (1970).

Perrot, Charles. "Les récits d'enfance dans la haggada antérieure au IIe siècle de notre ère," *RechScRel* 55, (1967): 481-518.

Philo. *On the Cherubim*, 12-13. Tr. by F. H. Colson and G. H. Whitaker. The Loeb Classical Library, 1950: 33-35.

Pikaza, Xavier. *Los Origenes de Jesus: ensayos de cristologja bíblica*. Salamanca: Ediciones Síquema, 1976.

Plutarch. *Table Talk*. (French ed. *Propos de table*, 8, 1, 2, transl. L. Pautigny, Paris, 1904).

Protoevangelion of James.

Qumran-Probleme; vorträge, hrsg. von Hans Berdtke. Berlin, Akademie-Verlag, 1963. (Symposium held at the Karl Marx University. Leipzig, Oct. 9-14, 1961.)

Ratzinger. *Introduction au christianisme.* Italian ed. Brescia, Queriniana, 1969.

Resch, A. "Das Kindheitsevangelium," *TUU* 10, 5, Leipzig: Hinrich 1897.

Rosaz, M. *Les récits de l'enfance de saint Luc.* Paris: Association de la Roche Colombière, 1977 (typed).

Sahlin, H. *Der Messias.* Uppsala: Almquist, 1945.

Schmid, J. *Das Evangelium nach Matthaus.* Regensburg, 4th ed., 1959. (Italian ed., 1965).

Serra, Aristide M. *Contributi dell'antica letteratura giudaica per l'esegesi di Giovanni 2, 1-12 e 19, 25-27.* Rome: Edizioni Herder, 1977. (Scripta pontificiae theologicae "Marianum" 31; Pontificia facoltà teologica "Marianum" Nova series; 3.) Originally presented as the author's thesis. Pontificium Institutum Biblicum, 1976.

——— *Sapienza e contemplazione di Maria secondo Luca 2:19, 51b.* Rome: Edizioni Marianum, 1982.

Soares Prabhu, George M. *The Formula Quotations in the Infancy Narrative of Matthew: an enquiry into the tradition history of Mt 1-2.* Rome: Biblical Institute Press, 1976.

Spitta, S. *Die chronologischen Notizen und die Hymnen in Lc 1-2* in *Zeit. Neut. Wiss.* 7, 1906.

Stauffer, E. "Die Dauer des Census Augusti" in *TUU* 77, 1960.

Strack, Hermann Leberecht and Paul Billerback. *Kommentar zum Neuen Testament aus Talmud und Midrasch.* 6 vols. Münich: Beck, 1922-61.

Strycker, E., ed. *Protévangile de Jacques.*

Van Iersel, B. "The Finding of Jesus in the Temple (Lk 2:41-51a)" in *NovTest* 4, (1960).

Vicent Cernuda, Antonio. "La génesis humana de Jesucristo según S. Pablo," *EB* 37, (1978): 57-77 and 267-289.

Vogels, H. J. *Zur Textgeschichte von Lk 1, 34ss, ZKT* 43, 1950/51.

Völter, D. "Die Apokalypse des Zacharias im Evangelium des Lukas," *Tijdschrift voor Theologie* 30, (1896): 224-269.

Westcott, Brooke Foss and Fenton John Anthony Hort. *The NT in the Original Greek.* Rev. American ed., with an intro. by Philip Schaff. New York: Harper and Row, 1886.

Winter, Paul. "The cultural background of the narrative in Luke I and II," *JewQ* 45, (1955): 230-242: continued from *JewQ*, N.S. XLV (1954): 159-167.

——— "Magnificat and Benedictus—Maccabaean Psalms?" *Bulletin of the John Rylands Library* 37, (1954): 328-347.

——— "Proto-source of Luke 1," *NovTest* 1, (1956): 184-199.

——— "Some Observations on the Language in the Birth and Infancy Stories of the Third Gospel," *NTS* 1, (1954): 111-121.

Names of Authors

This index includes some of the more important authors mentioned in the text.

Analytical Index